COLORADO
COMMUNITY TREASURES

Maroon Bells near Aspen

by William Faubion

a part of the Morgan & Chase Treasure Series
www.treasurcsof.com

MORGAN & CHASE PUBLISHING INC.

Published by:
Morgan & Chase Publishing, Inc.
531 Parsons Drive, Medford, Oregon 97501
(888) 557-9328
www.treasuresof.com

Printed by:
Taylor Specialty Books - Dallas TX

First edition 2007

ISBN: 1-933989-08-2

THE
TREASURE
SERIES

*I gratefully acknowledge the contributions
of the many people involved in the writing and production of this book.
Their tireless dedication to this endeavour has been inspirational.*
—Damon Neal, *Publisher*

Managing Editors:
David Smigelski and John Gaffey

Senior Story Editor:
Mary Beth Lee

Senior Writer:
Gregory Scott

Proof Editors:
Avery Brown and Robyn Sutherland

Graphic Design:
C.S. Rowan, Jesse Gifford, Tamara Cornett, Jacob Kristof, Michael Frye

Image Coordinators:
Wendy Gay and Donna Lindley

Website:
Casey Faubion, Molly Bermea, Ben Ford

Morgan & Chase Home Team
Cindy Tilley Faubion, Emily Wilkie, Cari Qualls, Anne Boydston, Virginia Arias, Danielle Barkley, Sue Buda,
Shauna O'Callahan, Clarice Rodriguez, Terrie West, Ray Ackerman, Megan Glomb, Heather Allen

Contributing Writers:
Lynda Kusick, Mark Allen Deruiter, Dale Campbell, Trent Bakich, Kerry Brown, Steve Castorino, Scott Woodward, Linn Wright, Dusty Alexander,
Paul Hadella, Mary Knepp, Chris McCrellis-Mitchell, Jennifer Coles, Laura Young, Todd Wels, Jenny Harris, Jennifer Buckner, Heather Allen,
Carol Bevis, Amber Dusk, Alexis McKenna, Maggie McClellen, Mary Sandlin, Nancy McClain, Scott Honeywell, Timothy Smith, Susan Vaughn

Special Recognition to:
Dale Campbell, Carolyn Courian, Jolee Moody, Gene Mitts

To the people of Colorado,
Thank you for your warm welcome.

How to use this book

Colorado Community Treasures is divided by region, city and category. Categories range from accommodations to wineries, with headings such as attractions, bakeries, galleries, home, recreation, restaurants and shopping in between.

In the index, all of these Treasures are listed alphabetically by name as well as by the city where you can visit them.

We have provided contact information for every Treasure in the book. These are places and businesses we have personally visited, and which we encourage you to visit on your travels through Colorado.

We sincerely hope you find this book to be both beautiful and useful.

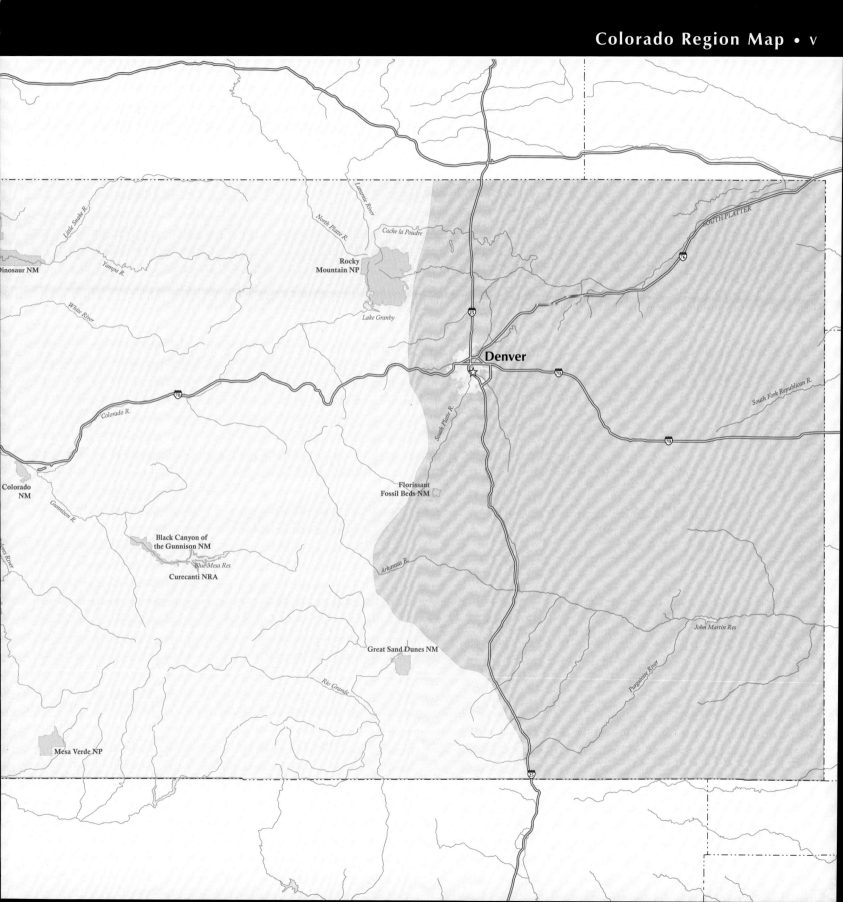

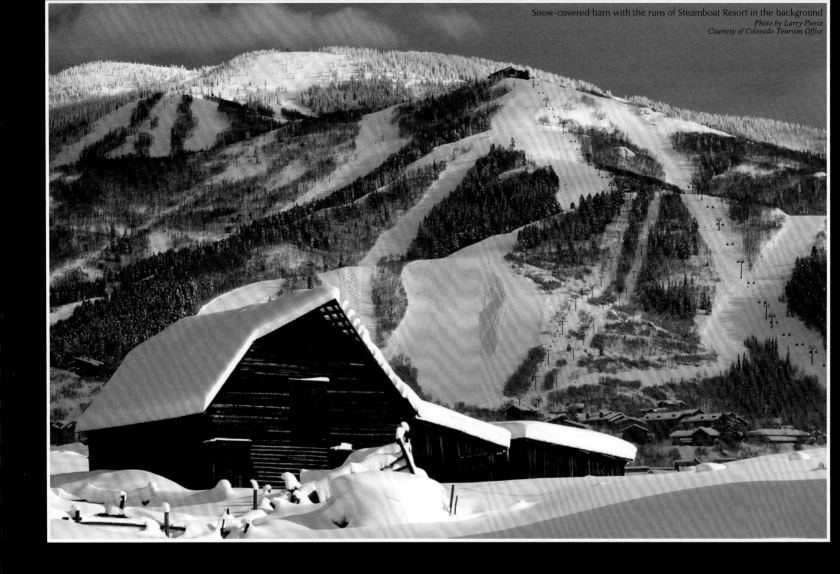

Snow-covered barn with the runs of Steamboat Resort in the background
Photo by Larry Pierce
Courtesy of Colorado Tourism Office

COLORADO FACTS:

Admitted to the Union: 1876, the 38th state

Population (2005): 4,665,177

Largest City: Denver, 557,917

Largest Metro Area: Denver, 2,359,994

Highest Mountain: Mt. Elbert, 14,433 feet

Animal: Rocky Mountain Bighorn Sheep

Bird: Lark Bunting

Fish: Greenback Cutthroat Trout

Flower: Rocky Mountain Columbine

Fossil: Stegosaurus

Gemstone: Aquamarine

Motto: *Nil sine Numine* (Nothing without Providence)

Nicknames: Centennial State; Colorful Colorado

Tree: Blue Spruce

Forward

Welcome to *Community Treasures of Colorado.* This book is a resource that can guide you to some of the best places in the State of Colorado, one of the most beautiful and vibrant places in North America. Colorado is a state of great diversity, from cosmopolitan Denver through the breathtaking, peaceful beauty of Rocky Mountain National Park and the remarkable Native American cliff dwellings at Mesa Verde. This is a state famous for its love of the outdoors, so it's not surprising that in national comparisons, residents stand out for their good health.

The Ute, Shoshoni and Apache Indians inhabited Colorado until the 1700s, when the Apache migrated south and the Arapaho and Cheyenne took their place. Colorado's Front Range entered the United States as part of the Louisiana Purchase. The U.S. annexed the west and south of the state after the Mexican War, and Colorado's Hispanic population is considerable today. In 1859, prospectors discovered gold in what is now Englewood. Settlers arrived in great numbers, and mining towns sprang up all over the Rockies. Many of them are famous ski resorts today, such as Aspen, Telluride and Cripple Creek.

If you love sports, nothing can beat the champagne powder snow you'll enjoy on a Colorado ski trip. Urbanites can relax in Denver's City Park, home of the zoo, or the Garden of the Gods in Colorado Springs. If you are a visitor to Denver, be sure to stop at the State Capitol, the Art Museum and the Botanical Gardens. Shop the 16th Street Mall and Cherry Creek. Root for the Denver Broncos, take in a performance at Red Rock Amphitheatre or attend a film festival in Boulder.

Colorado is home to the nicest, most energetic people you'll ever meet. In preparing this book, we talked to literally thousands of small-business people about their products, their services and their vision. We visited spas, picked up trendy outfits in mountain shops and strolled the galleries in Denver's LoDo. We visited the U.S. Air Force Academy and a Buddhist retreat. We stayed at bed & breakfasts and dined at fine restaurants. We hiked trails near Colorado Springs and celebrated the Cinco de Mayo in Pueblo. You are holding the result of our efforts in your hands. Community Treasures of Colorado is a 647-page compilation of the best places in Colorado to eat, shop, play, explore, learn and relax. We did the legwork. All you have to do now is enjoy.

—John Gaffey

DENVER METRO

DENVER

Denver is the capital of Colorado and the largest city in the state, with a population of more than 550,000 people. The metro area population is more than 2.3 million, and this figure does not include Boulder. Denver's nickname is the Mile High City, because its official elevation, engraved on the 15th step of the state capitol building, is exactly one mile above sea level. General William Larimer, a Kansas land speculator, founded Denver at a time when it and much of Colorado were actually part of Kansas. Larimer named the new town after a Kansas governor. In 1865, Denver became the capital of Colorado Territory, and it grew rapidly by serving local miners. By 1890, Denver was the second largest city west of Omaha, exceeded in size only by San Francisco. Even today it is the largest city within 600 miles, and so it is a natural administration, distribution and communications hub for the entire region between the Midwest and the West Coast. Metro Denver has more federal civilian employees than any other metro area except Washington. The city is a major cultural center, as well. It hosts nationally recognized museums and performance halls and bustles with art galleries, restaurants, bars and clubs. That is one reason it has been repeatedly recognized as America's best city for singles. Denver is one of country's premier sports towns, with major-league teams in every sport. In football, the Denver Broncos draw crowds of nearly 70,000. The Colorado Rockies joined baseball's National League in 1993. The Colorado Avalanche hockey team has won the Stanley Cup twice. Denver is also home to basketball's Denver Nuggets.

Photos by Brian Gadbery
Courtesy of Colorado Tourism Office

Colorado Capitol with early morning snow

Coors Field

Denver's Civic Center Park

PLACES TO GO

- Babi-Yar Park
  Havana Street and Parker Road
- Bible Park
  Yale Avenue at Pontiac Street
- Black American West Museum
  & Heritage Center
  *3091 California Street
  (303) 292-2566*
- Brown Palace Hotel
  321 17th Street
- Cheesman Park
  Franklin Street and 8th Street
- Cherry Creek Shopping Center
  3000 E 3rd Avenue
- Children's Museum
  2121 Children's Museum Drive
- City Park
  York Street and 21st Avenue
- Civic Center Park
  14th Avenue Parkway and Broadway
- Colorado History Museum
  1300 Broadway
- Colorado Sports Hall of Fame Museum
  (and Invesco Field tours)
  (720) 258-3888
- Colorado State Capitol
  200 E Colfax Avenue
- Daniels and Fisher Tower
  1601 Arapahoe Street
- Denver Art Museum
  100 W 14th Avenue Parkway
- Denver Botanic Gardens
  1005 York Street
- Denver Museum of Nature & Science
  2001 Colorado Boulevard
- Denver Public Library
  10 W 14th Avenue Parkway
- Denver Zoo
  2300 Steele Street
- Downtown Aquarium
  700 Water Street
- Hammond's Candies (tour)
  5735 N Washington Street
- Kirkland Museum of Fine & Decorative Art
  1311 Pearl Street

- Sloan's Lake Park
  Sheridan Boulevard and W 17th Avenue

- Stiles African American Heritage Center
  2607 Glenarm Place

- Washington Park
  S Downing Street and E Louisiana Avenue

THINGS TO DO

January
- National Western Stock Show & Rodeo
  www.nationalwestern.com

- Martin Luther King Marade
  (march and parade)
  City Park
  www.denverurbanleague.org

- Indian Market
  www.indianmarket.net

February
- Colorado Garden and Home Show
  (303) 932-8100

March
- St. Patrick's Day Parade
  www.saintpatricksdayparade.com/denver

- Denver March Powwow
  (720) 865-4220

- Starz Global Lens Film Festival
  (303) 534-1339

April
- Doors Open Denver
  www.denvergov.org/doorsopendenver

May
- Cinco de Mayo
  Civic Center Park
  www.newsed.org/cinco

June
- Cherry Blossom Festival
  www.tsdbt.org/cherryblossom

- Juneteenth
  www.denverjuneteenth.org

- Comcast La Piazza dell'Arte
  www.larimerarts.org/la_piazza_dell_arte

- Pridefest
  www.pridefestdenver.org

July
- Cherry Creek Arts Festival
  www.cherryarts.org

Patrons gather at the Denver Performing Arts Complex in downtown Denver

Winter Denver Skyline from City Park

Denver's 16th Street Mall is alive on New Year's Eve with fireworks at 9 PM and Midnight

- Colorado Dragon Boat Festival
  www.coloradodragonboat.org

August
- Grand Prix of Denver
  www.gpdenver.com

September
- A Taste of Colorado
  www.atasteofcolorado.com

- Oktoberfest
  www.oktoberfestdenver.com

- Great American Beer Festival
  www.beertown.org/events/gabf

October
- Denver Mariachi Festival
  www.mariachivasquez.com

November
- Denver International Wine Festival
  www.denverwinefest.com

- Starz Denver International Film Festival
  (303) 534-1339

Castle Marne
Bed & Breakfast

ACCOMMODATIONS:
Best historic bed and breakfast

Castle Marne was a massive undertaking when first constructed in 1889, but the three-story stone structure on Capitol Hill was a mere shell when Jim and Diane Peiker, their daughter, Melissa, and her husband, Louis, fell in love with the structure in 1989. The family proceeded to turn it into one of Denver's leading bed-and-breakfast establishments. Restored to its former opulence, this Denver heirloom is a true getaway, something on the order of spending a holiday with royalty. Each of the nine rooms, some with Jacuzzis and fireplaces, offers pampered luxury. Expect authentic period antiques, family heirlooms and exacting reproductions to wrap you in Victorian romance. Business travelers will appreciate the wireless Internet access, and everyone appreciates the ambience. Weddings (and a fair number of elopements) are so popular here that Castle Marne offers a choice of wedding packages, which include a ceremony performed by one of the castle's owners (licensed by the State of Colorado to officiate marriages), a dozen roses, a wedding cake for two and a room, complete with a sumptuous breakfast. Afternoon teas, Victorian luncheons and six-course candlelit dinners are other choice options at this plush retreat. Your privately prepared dinner must be booked in advance. The Peiker family hails from Denver pioneer stock and actively supports the preservation of Denver's rich and colorful history. Their bed-and-breakfast, on the National Register of Historic Places, is the recipient of numerous awards. For Old World charm and hospitality, plan a visit to Castle Marne.

1572 Race Street, Denver CO
(303) 331-0621
www.castlemarne.com

The Gregory Inn
ACCOMMODATIONS: *A distinctly Western bed and breakfast*

Imagine yourself on a summer evening sitting on a long veranda sipping a cold drink and enjoying the breeze coming from the ceiling fans. The Gregory Inn in Denver brings you these pleasures, along with a view of the city skyline and an expanse of perfectly manicured gardens. The atmosphere here is distinctly Colorado and avoids fussy Victorian décor often associated by many bed-and-breakfasts. Owner Stephen Gregory believes his amenities are what sets him apart from other inns. Each room contains high-end linens, extra pillows, top-notch bath products, a plush bathrobe and a jetted tub. You'll also find a CD player, projection television, ice in the refrigerator and a teddy bear on every bed. Those requiring high-tech accommodations will be well satisfied, since each room has a digital phone, voice mail and a wireless cable Internet connection. A fabulous, full breakfast in the beautifully appointed dining room is a great way to start the day. The Gregory Inn offers special packages for occasions like birthdays, anniversaries and holidays. The popular Romance Package includes a horse-drawn carriage ride, dinner for two, a lovely room and breakfast. The inn is conveniently located near many downtown Denver attractions, including the LoDo restaurant, entertainment and shopping district. For Western charm, superb amenities and the many delights of Denver, treat yourself to a stay at The Gregory Inn.

2500 Arapahoe Street, Denver CO
(303) 295-6570 or (800) 925-6570
www.gregoryinn.com

Inn at Cherry Creek

ACCOMMODATIONS: *Luxurious boutique hotel*

If you can imagine an intimate setting with luxurious comforts in the midst of a posh shopping district, then you must be at Denver's Inn at Cherry Creek. This stunning boutique hotel has 35 guestrooms, each elegantly appointed with granite vanities and furnished terraces, flat screen televisions and complimentary high-speed Internet access. Rooms come with terry cloth bathrobes, work desks and two phones. Some rooms have cozy fireplaces. The hotel is part of the Cherry Creek Shopping District and just steps away from 160 high-end shops, such as Neiman Marcus, Saks Fifth Avenue and Cartier. Pete Weber, owner of the Inn at Cherry Creek since 2004, prides himself on the inn's superior look and services, as well as the options provided for all sorts of private and corporate events of up to 150 people. Hold a private party on the rooftop terrace and its adjoining Garden Room, or celebrate a wedding, family reunion, bar mitzvah or other important personal or corporate event in the comfortable Baumrucker Room. Every space in the inn is thoughtfully designed to put bed-and-breakfast ambience and upscale amenities together. The Weber, the inn's onsite restaurant, seats 26 people. The menu changes weekly, and each carefully prepared meal features seasonal ingredients and artistic presentation. Whether you are traveling for business or pleasure, the Inn at Cherry Creek promises you a quiet and stylish retreat in the heart of an exciting city.

233 Clayton Street, Denver CO
(303) 377-8577
www.innatcherrycreek.com

Photos by Janet Koelling/Creative Dimensions

The Whole Cat (& Dogs too!)

ANIMALS & PETS:
Best place to maintain healthy pets

The best way to maintain a healthy pet is from the inside out. The Whole Cat (& Dogs too!) has everything you will need to keep your pet healthy and ensure they live a long and fulfilling life. Owners Sue Green and Nancy Martin have been friends for years. Both women were working in corporate America when they found themselves in the right place at the right time to turn their love for animals into a career. For almost 10 years, The Whole Cat (& Dogs too!) has been providing holistic health care and natural foods for dogs and cats. The Whole Cat believes in giving alternative medicine to pets, offering chiropractic and acupuncture services to cats and dogs. To help provide the best nutritional products, they will not sell any pet foods that contain by-products, chemicals or preservatives. They sell only food manufactured in the United States due to AFCO control. AFCO is the equivalent of the USDA, but for pet food. They ship their food products all over the country. There is a very personal feel to The Whole Cat. Sue and Nancy make it a point to remember all of their customer's pet's names, if not all of the customer's names, as well. The Whole Cat takes pride in showcasing collars, leashes and other items to highlight your pet's personality that have been designed by local artists. Come to The Whole Cat (& Dogs too!) for all of your pet's nutritional needs.

1540 S Pearl Street, Denver CO
(303) 871-0443

U-Shampooch

ANIMALS & PETS: *Best dog wash*

If an announcement that it's time to wash the dog brings nothing but eye-rolls, moans and excuses, then it's time to load Fido and the family up in the car and head to U-Shampooch. U-Shampooch offers a whole new and convenient way to get your furry loved one all spruced up and looking great. Owner Stephanie Meyer and her two four-footed assistants, Gus, a Newfoundland, and Denali, a white German Shepard, provide a friendly, warm and welcoming place where your pet will be comfortable being bathed and you don't have to worry about carting supplies and cleaning up the post-bath mess. Each of U-Shampooch's four extra large, elevated tub stalls were handcrafted from stainless steel, quality woods and aluminum, and each comes complete with hand dryers, easily used and mild pressure sprayers, and roll out ramps. Everything you need is readily available and included in the price of a wash, such as natural shampoos and conditioners, brushes, ear wipes and aprons. Once bathing is finished you can turn your pal over to the resident groomer, Jennifer, who has more than 10 years experience with all canine breeds and will have your pooch looking runway perfect in no time. U-Shampooch offers a terrific selection of pet supplies and accessories, including fun leash and collar sets, Breeder's Choice pet foods, toys and bedding. U-Shampooch equally welcomes felines and is open varied hours seven days a week. Change your pet's weekly bath time from frantic to fun at U-Shampooch.

7474 E 29th Avenue, Denver CO
(303) 321-5353
www.u-shampooch.net

The Wag Shop
ANIMALS & PETS:
Best unique, quality pet products

You'll receive plenty of wags from your dog at The Wag Shop in Denver. This premier shop was born out of Dave and Deidre Hered's love of animals and their determination to find unique, quality products for their own pets. The Wag Shop prides itself on finding products that have a high value to their customers. To ensure this, they test each product out on their own pets. You'll find everything from vegan leather collars to backpacks and booties, all of which have the style that is sure to give your precocious canine a step up in the dog world. Funky, vintage, seatbelt collars and gourmet treats from Cosmo's Biscuit Bakery make the grade at this cool boutique. Don't forget our feline friends who can enjoy organic catnip and spiffy collars, too. The self-serve dog wash makes the experience of bathing your canine a comfortable one. They provide everything you'll need to wash your pup, from shampoo and conditioner to towels and more. All you need to bring is the dog. The semi-private bathing suites provide elevated tubs to take the backbreaking work out of bathing your dog. Each bay is equipped with stairs for easy access into the tub. Best of all, they clean up the mess. The staff of pet lovers are knowledgeable and on hand to provide grooming tips and guidance throughout the wash process. With what this boutique has to offer, it is truly worth a visit to The Wag Shop.

1222 E 6th Avenue, Denver CO
(303) 282-1894
www.thewagshop.com

Sixth Avenue Pet Source

ANIMALS & PETS:
Cutting edge pet products

The changing field of pet care places more emphasis on pet health and nutrition than ever before. Sixth Avenue Pet Source is on the cutting-edge of this new philosophy, offering quality food, treats and toys for your animals. The premium dog and cat foods contain human-grade ingredients, and descriptions of the food sound like dishes from a fine restaurant. Campfire Trout Feast includes trout, Yukon gold potatoes, carrots, zucchini and Fuji apples. Venison Holiday Stew dishes up red new potatoes, carrots, zucchini, sugar peas and red apples. Dogs love treats like the popular mutton chops and ostrich bones, which go far beyond rawhide. For animals troubled by allergies, treats made with alfalfa, clove and parsley are your best bets. Sixth Avenue devotes a section of the store to cats, with toys, food, catnip and other goodies sure to please the most finicky feline. Owner Rebecca Gershten understands her clients' needs and is always glad to answer questions or help find suitable products. Because of Rebecca's willingness to go the extra mile for her customers, her wide selection of products and frequently updated merchandise, *5280 Magazine* named Sixth Avenue Pet Source the Top Pet Store in 2005. Visit Sixth Avenue Pet Source to pick up nutritious goodies for your pets, and be sure to say hi to resident critters Henry and Walenda while you are there.

810 E 6th Avenue, Denver CO
(303) 733-6410

Quality Paws Natural Pet
ANIMALS & PETS: *Holistic pet nutrition specialists*

Danielle Jarock, owner of Quality Paws Natural Pet, understands that cats and dogs are not just pets, but important members of your family. She knows you want the best for your critters, and she has dedicated her life to improving the lives of animals. At Quality Paws Natural Pet, Danielle and her staff specialize in a holistic approach to pet nutrition and support a raw food diet. Raw food means that meat is fresh and unprocessed without any grains as fillers. Raw meat provides animals with friendly bacteria to strengthen their immune systems. In addition to raw diets, Quality Paws offers a vast selection of dry foods, canned foods and treats that are free from artificial colors, flavors and preservatives. Danielle says the preservatives in most dog foods may cause many dog allergies, behavioral issues, and/or degenerative diseases. In addition to many lines of natural and raw food diets, Quality Paws features nonfood items, such as supplements, grooming products, toys and clothes for your pampered pooch. Danielle also works to improve the lives of animals through her work with the Rocky Mountain Alley Cat Alliance. This group works tirelessly to stop the suffering of feral cats in the Denver area by practicing TNR (Trap-Neuter-Return). In the process, Danielle fosters many tame abandoned cats and kittens until she can place them in loving homes. If the health and well being of your four legged friends is important to you, stop in at Quality Paws Natural Pet.

80 S Pennsylvania Street, Denver CO
(303) 778-PAWS (7297)
www.qualitypaws.com

Remington & Friends

ANIMALS & PETS: *Pet pampering at its best*

Even before Rick DeLuca opened Remington & Friends, he had a reputation in the neighborhood. In competitions with friends to determine who made the best dog treats, the dogs preferred the treats created by DeLuca. Dogs have been known to break free from their yards only to be found at DeLuca's bakery, patiently waiting for those homemade treats. It was a natural progression when he opened a dog-grooming spa named Remington & Friends. The business is named after one of Rick's Irish Setters. Remington is a champion at 11 years old. Canon is three and just entering competition to earn a championship title. Their namesake salon provides treatments that are a cut above the traditional dog and cat grooming center. Nails are ground here rather than cut. Services don't end after a shampoo and haircut. The fur is also conditioned and an optional massage is offered. The crowning glory resides in the all-natural treats that Rick creates in his personal bakery. His bone-shaped birthday cake made of rotisserie chicken breast is a popular invention. Remington & Friends has a fine line of premium foods such as Royal Canin, Wellness, Prairie, Innova and California Natural. Remington and Friends invites you to bring your favorite animal in to be pampered. They know how to do that better than anyone. Your furry friends will love you for it.

278 S Downing Street, Denver CO
(303) 282-8188

Ceramics in the City
ARTS & CRAFTS:
Where art is entertainment

The city of Denver offers just about anything a person could ask for, but in a quaint area of uptown, a mother-and-daughter team, Sharon Scholl and Stephanie Magennis, have managed to make one more contribution. Their offering of Ceramics in the City is a relaxing paint-your-own-pottery studio where art is entertainment. Their studio is interactive with customers in a way few other businesses can hope to be. The process is easy, safe and fun. Customers choose a bisque piece from their massive inventory and design the pottery to their style. With all the tools, idea books, colors and friendly helpful staff, creating a work of art is enjoyable and relaxing. When the masterpiece is complete, it is fired in their kiln and can be retrieved in about a week. There are daily specials for anyone who wants to drop in, and they offer many special events which require reservations. A few of their popular special events include Diva Night, Pajama Party, Wine Tasting and a special Mother's Day Tea. Ceramics in the City is also a great place to hold your own events, such as birthday parties, bridal showers, corporate team building and family reunions. They have something for everyone, so check their website calendar to see what's happening at Ceramics in the City. Then join them for some truly creative fun.

1912 Pearl Street, Denver CO
(303) 200-0461
www.ceramicsinthecity.com

Denver Folklore Center

ARTS & CRAFTS: *Holy shrine of folk music*

To people who know the ins and outs of the American folk music scene of the late 1950s and early 1960s, a visit to the Denver Folklore Center is like a sojourn to a holy shrine. Owner Harry Tuft opened for business in 1962, intending to run a music store that combined instrument sales with teaching, while encouraging a growing community of folk music artists. With no financial backers on the horizon, Harry tossed his $900 worth of savings into his business pot and hoped for a miracle. That miracle is still thriving almost half a century later. In addition to running his store, Harry promotes remarkable musical talent. He once cajoled a local lawyer into co-signing on a $5,000 guarantee he needed to promote a young group known as the Mamas & the Papas. A week before showtime, the group appeared on the cover of *Time* magazine, guaranteeing their success and affirming Harry's instincts for talent. Harry's co-signer later became the governor of Colorado. Harry has befriended many folk music greats over the years, who would stop by for strings and guitar picks and stay to play. He continues to sell new, used and vintage musical instruments and guarantees he will help customers find what they need, even if it means sending them to another store. He also rents instrument and offers music lessons. For a musical venture that's stood the test of time, visit the Denver Folklore Center.

1893 S Pearl Street, Denver CO
(303) 777-4786
www.denverfolklore.com

Kolacny Music

ARTS & CRAFTS: *Best place for musical equipment*

There's this wonderful picture of William J. Kolacny with slick-backed hair and a shy, happy smile. He's wearing an old-fashioned suit, sitting on a stool and playing a saxophone. The smile lets you know he's doing what he loves, and what William Kolacny loved was music. Bill started Kolacny Music in 1930, when Denver was just a bustling, little oil town. Bill's son and grandson, Richard and David, now run the family business along with Richard's wife, Bettie, his daughter, Donna, and David's wife, Debbie. Kolacny Music specializes in the repair and rental of band and orchestra instruments. David offers specialization in harps, repairing, renting and selling that ethereal instrument. The Kolacny family works closely with school music programs and has three trucks that go around the entire state repairing and renting musical equipment. The whole family works in the shop, located in a 75-year-old building with polished wood floors, high ceilings and the warm, folksy feeling of an old Jimmy Stewart movie. The smell of violin polish and strong coffee mingles with the rich sounds of musical instruments receiving tuning and care. Richard and David had the privilege of learning their craft alongside Bill, who worked six days a week until he was 90. If you love music, visit Kolacny Music. You'll meet a family that's made it their business to pass music on to future generations.

1900 Broadway, Denver CO
(303) 722-6081 or (800) 870-3167
www.kolacnymusic.com

Kirkland Museum of Fine & Decorative Art

ATTRACTIONS: *Best collection of 20th-century decorative art*

The first three quarters of the 20th century was an exciting time for decorative art with the emergence of such divergent styles as Arts & Crafts, Art Nouveau, De Stijl, Bauhaus, Art Deco, Modern and Pop Art. Famed Colorado painter Vance Kirkland lived during these times (1904 to 1981) and a Denver museum named in his honor combines the fine and decorative arts of the period in a nationally important collection. Opened in 2003, Kirkland Museum of Fine & Decorative Art displays more than 600 works by 140 Colorado artists and more than 3,300 examples of national and international decorative art. The museum includes Vance Kirkland's historic studio building where he painted from 1932 until his death. Built in 1911 as an art school, the Arts & Crafts-styled studio is the oldest commercial art building in Denver and a National Trust Associate Site. A Vance Kirkland retrospective takes the visitor through the major periods of Kirkland's career, from his early watercolors to the water and oil mixtures and dots of his later years. The collections are presented in six exhibition rooms in salon style. Kirkland paintings are placed alongside other artists' sculpture and decorative arts to provide context to the influences of Kirkland's time. The museum is also the place to turn for a dramatic demonstration of how distinguished modernist Colorado art has been from 1890 to 1980. Due to the fragile nature of the collections, only adults or children 13 to 17 accompanied by adults can visit this lovely space. Be sure to stop by Tuesday through Sunday or by appointment for a journey through 20th-century fine and decorative art.

1311 Pearl Street, Denver CO
(303) 832-8576
www.kirklandmuseum.org

The Energy of Explosions 24 Billion Years B.C.,
Vance Kirkland, 1978, oil and water on linen.

"MAgriTTA" chair
Roberto Matta, 1970, acrylic covering polyurethane foam, fabric covered methacrylate and rubber.

Mizel Museum

ATTRACTIONS:
Museum of Jewish life and culture

Established in 1982, the Mizel Museum uses the arts and educational programs to present the story of the Jewish people and to teach tolerance and acceptance of all peoples. The arts are a key to the identity of the individual and the community, and the museum's programs both express the rich heritage and history of the Jewish people and serve as a springboard for discussions of diversity and appreciation of multiple cultures. Over the years, the Mizel Museum has grown from a small ethnic institution into a nationally recognized, award-winning museum with a wide audience. Topics for exhibitions and educational activities have included lessons of the Holocaust, Jewish life and culture and immigration. Bridges of Understanding, which opened in 1994, changed the face of the museum. From that time on, the museum has broadened its exhibitions and programs to include cultural themes that appeal to all members of our diverse community. About 35,000 people each year attend tours and special events. The museum sponsors summer camps, artist workshops and on-site school programs. In 2007, the Mizel Museum will open a new site at the Civic Center Cultural Complex. The Mizel Museum also offers a compelling tour through Denver's Babi Yar Park, a memorial for victims of the Holocaust. A visit to the Mizel Museum will move you as you discover the impact of Jewish history on world culture. Embrace diversity with a visit to the Mizel Museum.

400 S Kearney Street, Denver CO
(303) 394-9990
www.mizelmuseum.org

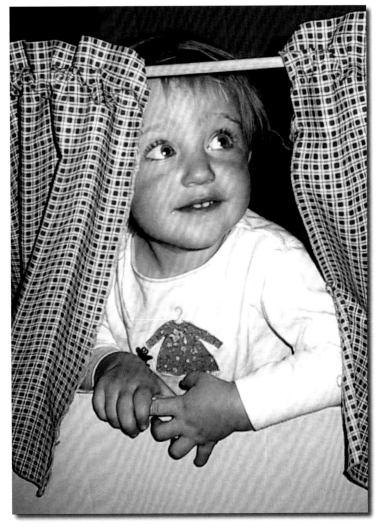

Denver Puppet Theater
ATTRACTIONS: *Best children's theater*

The Denver Puppet Theater is both a theater and a playground for kids and the adults who accompany them. Owner Annie Zook says the best part of doing what she does is watching a sense of awe and wonder descend and transfix a child's imagination. Apparently adult reviewers understand the phenomenon, because the theater has been cited the Best Children's Theater in Colorado by the *Denver Post*, the Best Puppet Store and Best Kid's Birthday Party in Denver by *Westword* and the Top Kid's Outing by *5280 Magazine*. The Puppet Theater stages puppet productions for children three years and older. It also offers a puppet store and a hands-on play area with more than 100 puppets and eight kid-size stages. Puppets include mouth puppets, hand puppets and marionettes from across the world. When weather permits, audience members frequently bring picnics or snacks and enjoy them in the large courtyard before or after puppet shows. The theater offers wonderful children's birthday party plans. Be sure to plan your attendance carefully. The theater is closed on major holidays, during Easter week and throughout the month of September. Visit the Denver Puppet Theater and see why so many media have named it the best place to take kids for parties, playtime and puppet shows.

3156 W 38th Avenue, Denver CO
(303) 458-6446
www.denverpuppettheater.com

Molly Brown Summer House

ATTRACTIONS: *Historic retreat of the Unsinkable Molly Brown*

Margaret Tobin Brown was born the daughter of poor Irish immigrants in 1867. Flamboyant and generous, she became a legend in her own time and was immortalized as the *Unsinkable Molly Brown*. The Molly Brown Summer House was this indomitable woman's celebrated retreat. Visitors hear charming, nostalgic and delightful accounts not only of Molly and J.J., but also of the Fehlmann family who later purchased the property. Molly married James Joseph Brown, multi-millionaire superintendent of the Ibex Mining Company. J. J. Brown purchased land parcels that would eventually grow into a 400-acre country estate, featuring a fishing pond, terraced lawns and stunning flower beds. Molly named the property *Avoca Lodge*, from the Thomas Moore poem *The Meeting of the Waters*. In 1897, the couple built this two-story buttered brick home with a sandstone foundation, window lintels and an attic adorned by eyebrow windows. Handmade finials stand guard on the roof ridge. Over time, the Browns grew apart and separated, selling the property off in pieces. In 1928, The Fehlmann family purchased the house and the remaining 100 acres. Five generations of the family continue to maintain it. Now open to the public as an Event and Cultural Center, this historic home provides personalized tours, an elegant tea room and unique gift shop. The Molly Brown Summer House offers visitors a diverse and fascinating look into Colorado history, culture and growth through a century of change. The Molly Brown Summer House is listed on the National Register of Historic Places. For more information, contact Mary Rose Shearer and Jane Fehlmann Garland. Reservations may be made by telephone.

**2690 S Wadsworth Boulevard, Denver CO
(303) 989-6639 or (800) 971-6639**
www.mollybrownsummerhouse.com

Museo de las Américas

ATTRACTIONS:
Best museum of Latin American art and culture

The Museo de las Américas presents provocative exhibitions of contemporary and ancient arts of the Américas, from Tierra del Fuego to the American Southwest. The museum is one of only a few nationwide that support Latino and Latin American artists through major exhibitions and educating the public about the diversity of these artists and the extent of their cultural influences on our society. The Museo achieves this goal by seeking out contemporary and folk artists and collecting, preserving and interpreting the ancient arts of North and South America. Along with three to four annual exhibitions, the Museo offers tours, workshops and educational presentations throughout the year. It has quickly become a connecting point for the Latino community of Metro Denver and is rapidly gaining a national and international following. The Museo sponsors and participates in many regional celebrations such as Día de los Niños, Cinco de Mayo, El Grito and Día de los Muertos. To encourage community awareness, the Museo often participates in the Cherry Creek Arts Festival, the Capitol Hill People's Fair, and Denver's famous Taste of Colorado. Tax deductible memberships are available for those who wish to support its mission. For more information, please contact visitor services. Museo de las Américas is located in the vibrant Santa Fe Arts District a few blocks from downtown Denver and a quick side-trip off I-25, Denver's central freeway.

861 Santa Fe Drive, Denver CO
(303) 571-4401
www.museo.org

Hooked on Colfax
BAKERIES, COFFEE & TEA: *Best coffee, books and events*

Scott and Malissa Spero opened their Denver coffeehouse in September 2005 with three things foremost in their minds: coffee, books and community. Hooked on Colfax is, as the name implies, located on Colfax Avenue. The Speros get their coffee from a local roaster and their teas from a local supplier. Their retail book area places a heavy emphasis on local authors, and their

downstairs meeting room hosts numerous community-based meetings, book clubs and a weekly movie night. Hooked on Colfax encourages patronage of local artists with an art show every four to six weeks. The show, complete with wine, cheese and live music, is a popular event. The coffeehouse is a new venture that was a natural fit for Malissa, who has worked in coffeehouses for 10 years. The Speros chose a sleek but cozy design for the shop that invites lingering while sipping a latté and becoming part of the community. Next time you want great coffee, interesting events and a good book to read, visit Hooked on Colfax. You'll end up hooked on the community and on the shop.

3215 E Colfax Avenue, Denver CO
(303) 398-2665
www.hookedoncolfax.com

The Tea Box
BAKERIES, COFFEE & TEA: *Best tea stop in town*

Tea can be a passion, a hobby, a career, a comfort or an inspiration. Just ask Regina Chan, owner of The Tea Box in Denver. She has studied the nuances of tea and brings her knowledge to her comfortable, upscale tea salon. The staff at The Tea Box knows how to create a friendly, personal setting that's perfect for a good book or a good conversation. Writers and poets can be found sipping tea and composing stories and poems inside of The Tea Box. In fact, The Tea Box has

been the subject of a poem. When it comes to tea sipping, the choices are vast and distinctive. Similar to wine, connoisseurs shop tea by the year and the vintage. You'll find choice vintages in the whole leaf estate teas at The Tea Box. You can enjoy custom blended green teas, tea slushies and organic chai teas. *Chai* is an Asian word for tea and refers to a black tea blended with herbs, spices and served with milk and sugar. If you are planning to linger at The Tea Box, you may want to pair some food with your specialty tea. The Tea Box features salads with natural dressings and Chinese dumplings, known as dim sum. A visit to The Tea Box is an opportunity to make a friend while developing a discriminating palette for tea.

2353 E 3rd Avenue, Denver CO
(303) 393-7972

Coffee On The Lowell
BAKERIES, COFFEE & TEA:
Premier coffeehouse

Photo by R. Thompson

Today's neighborhoods are incomplete without a coffeehouse, hut or kiosk. The bustling district near Regis University is no different. Owner Elizabeth Luna opened the popular Coffee On The Lowell in 2000 and prides herself on providing personalized service and freshly ground, full of flavor coffee that is a far cry from the wax-cup taste and "take-a-number attitude" that pervades national chains. At Coffee On The Lowell, you can indulge your passion with numerous specialty coffee drinks or choose Italian soda, fresh smoothies or a Cremosa. Elizabeth also offers a wonderful selection of freshly made goodies that will help you jump-start your day. In the morning, savor one of their breakfast burritos or nibble away at a delicious breakfast sandwich made on light and flaky croissants or a tender bagel. At lunchtime, you will find a wonderful selection of popular sandwiches such as the California club or chicken salad. Other not-to-be-missed delights include freshly made cinnamon rolls, muffins, scones and coffee cake. Every treat is a taste temptation. Coffee On The Lowell regularly features live morning music and offers free wireless Internet, with a discount for students. Stop in and visit or have your next event catered by one of Denver's premier coffee stops, Coffee On The Lowell.

4995 Lowell Boulevard, Denver CO
(303) 433-7171

Under the Umbrella Café & Bakery

BAKERIES, COFFEE & TEA:
Congress Park's favorite way to start the day

It's a universal truth that freshly baked treats emit one of the most tantalizing smells on the planet. It's one of the reasons so many people in the Congress Park neighborhood start their day at Under the Umbrella Café & Bakery. Owner Jyll Tuggle took her years of experience in restaurant and bakery management and her passion for baking and opened Under the Umbrella Café in 2005. You'll be off to a great start if you begin your day with one of Jyll's breakfast burritos. Grab a freshly baked cinnamon roll, coffee cake, muffin or scrumptious cookie for a mid-morning snack. Jyll's espresso drinks, to go or to stay, will jump-start your day. To double your satisfaction, return for lunch. Jyll makes conscientious ingredient choices and buys only from quality food suppliers. You'll be nourished and invigorated for the rest of the day with homemade quiche, the soup du jour, hummus served with veggies and warm pita bread, fresh roast beef sandwiches made with pesto or chicken salad garnished with candied pecans, poppy seeds and bits of celery. You can even create your own sandwich from Jyll's fixings. Whatever you decide to eat at Under the Umbrella, know that some truths never change. For the universal appeal of freshly baked treats and more, visit the Under the Umbrella Café & Bakery.

3504 E 12th Avenue, Denver CO
(303) 256-0797

emogène patisserie et cafe

BAKERIES, COFFEE & TEA:
Best patisserie

A treat for your eyes as well as your taste buds, emogène patisserie et cafe offers savory breakfasts and lunches, an espresso bar and outrageous desserts in a comfortable atmosphere. Your first vision upon entering either of emogene's two locations are desserts by pastry chef Deana Lezcano. Deana treats each serving like a tiny masterpiece. The pastries are rich and, as the folks at emogène admit, sinfully delicious. For something a bit more substantial to start the day, try the signature breakfast sandwich, made on brioche with scrambled eggs, Muenster cheese, *frisèe* and *fleur de sel*, a natural French salt. Other must-try treats include the almond *frangipane* sticks and white chocolate and raspberry muffins. Both go perfectly with a steaming hot latte from the espresso bar. For lunch, offerings like the Croque Monsieur sandwich, with black forest ham, béchamel sauce and Gruyère cheese, fill the menu. To complement your meal, emogène serves fine European wines and cordials. The staff at emogène can make your next gathering a hit, with special party menus and chef Deana's specialty cakes. From traditional white wedding cakes to tilting towers of black skulls and crossbones, Deana customizes the cake for the occasion. For decidedly different and sinfully delicious fare, try emogène patisserie et cafe.

2415 E 2nd Avenue, Denver CO
(303) 388-7900
(Cherry Creek North)
433 S Teller Street, Lakewood CO
(303) 325-8888 (Belmar)
www.emogene-cafe.com

Red Elk Bakery

BAKERIES, COFFEE & TEA:
Most inspirational pastry

Red Elk Bakery, a freelance Denver bakery specializing in cheesecakes, expanded to include a storefront in February 2006, when renowned Pastry Chef Robert McCarthy purchased the beloved Paris Bakery. In the world of pastry chefs, Robert McCarthy is a standout performer. After working for the famous Lulu's in San Francisco, he made a name for himself in Denver as pastry chef for Mel's Restaurant and Bar and for Solera. In 2003, his chocolate truffle tart won second place in the prestigious Pastry Masterpiece Competition. You will find an assortment of pastries here that range from American classics like giant cinnamon rolls and pecan rolls to some extraordinary cheesecakes including such favorites as A Shot and a Beer, a melt-in-your-mouth creation featuring Guinness Stout and drizzled with a whiskey-laced fudge sauce. Homemade breads, butter croissants and unusual desserts will make this your first stop for everyday and special occasion baked goods. Robert continues to sell his creations wholesale to restaurants and to ship his products throughout the country. He sells frozen cinnamon rolls in easy-tobake trays, cakes and other desserts by the slice or whole. The name Red Elk was inspired by a symbol on the McCarthy Crest and is destined to become Denver's symbol for inspirational pastry. Stop by for a cup of coffee and a cinnamon roll or take home a specialty cheesecakes, you will become one of the happy customers singing the praises of Red Elk Bakery.

**1268 S Sheridan Boulevard,
Denver CO
(303) 935-9353**
www.redelkbakery.com

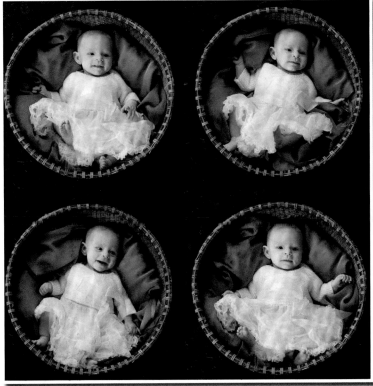

Goodman Photography Inc.

BUSINESS: *Traditional and contemporary portraiture*

Combining the high-tech world of digital cameras and state-of-the-art computer programs with the good old-fashioned warmth of customer service is what you will receive when you have a portrait session at southwest Denver's Goodman Photography, Inc. A relaxing and rewarding experience is provided by owners and photographers Daniel and Leslie Goodman, who jointly create the shots that captivate the heart and preserve your memories. Both are graduates from Brooks Institute of Photography in Santa Barbara, California. Their dedication to their craft is visible in every photograph. Whether they are photographing families, children, pets or high school seniors, the Goodmans offer traditional as well as contemporary and playful portraits. Something out of the ordinary for those celebrating the miracle of life might include a sequence of images beginning in the first month of pregnancy and continuing through the first family portrait. Leslie and Daniel digitally capture each stage of pregnancy, creating a visual DVD journey, set to music, that allows you to recapture the memories. For those who wish to have an artistic nude session, Leslie photographs clients with a sensitive and creative vision providing a positive and uplifting experience, as well as beautiful and creative photographs. Goodman Photography offers the choice of photographs or editioned photo etchings from any of the above sessions. Ensure that your special moments will endure for a lifetime by having your portraits created at Goodman Photography Inc.

(303) 730-8627 *www.dlgp.net www.lesliegoodman.net*

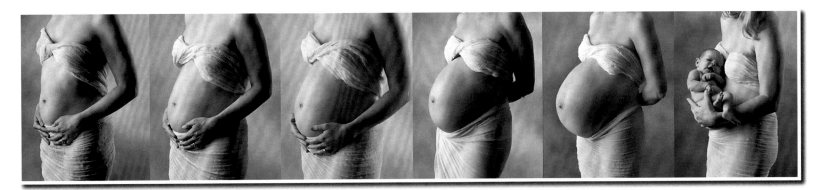

RCS Gallery
BUSINESS: *Specializing in family portraits on location*

RCS Gallery specializes in family portraits on location. RCS was created in 1997 by Randy and Pattie for the purpose of decorating homes with family memories through fine portraiture. They will travel to your home to photograph you in the most comfortable setting possible, and they also have a studio for more intimate portraits, if you prefer. Now they offer fine art watercolor and oil giclèe potraits. They use the computer to paint one brush stroke at a time, which can be seen in the painting above of the precious little girl. Check out their website to view a sample of their portraiture. The most rewarding photographic experience in the Denver area awaits you when you choose RCS Gallery to capture your memories.

4867 S Johnson Street, Denver CO
(303) 948-8292
www.rcsgallery.com

Alliance Française de Denver
BUSINESS: *Best place to learn french*

Whether you always dreamed of learning French or plan to someday travel there, Alliance Française de Denver offers the language and culture tools you will need. Partially funded by the Scientific and Cultural Facilities District, Alliance Française provides a multitude of ways for you to participate in the splendor of French and Francophone cultures. Designed to increase the awareness of and interest in French language and cultures, Alliance Française is a non-profit language and cultural resource center. Established in 1897, the famous Molly Brown hosted some of their first French classes in her home. Currently Alliance Française offers a variety of French language classes, ranging from beginner to expert, for children, teens and adults. If you'd like to learn French with co-workers, you can arrange to have an instructor come to your place of work for French at Your Desk. Private classes like this are available for individuals as well as small groups. Alliance Française stands out among other language schools, because it offers a complete calendar of cultural preforming with social events each month. Film screenings, lectures, concerts, wine tastings, social dinners and theater events give you a chance to use your French and meet others with similar interests. There is also a multimedia library and art gallery housed in their office. Other services such as translation of documents and an online classified section listing anything from apartments for rent in Paris to local companies looking for bilingual employees make Alliance Française the place to go in Colorado for anything French. Why not challenge yourself to learn the French language and experience Francophone cultures by visiting Alliance Française de Denver, your doorway to France.

571 Galapago Street, Denver CO
(303) 831-0304
www.afdenver.org

Décor 'N More

EVENTS: *Best set design*

Since 1992, the Décor 'N More team has been creating an ambience for events that fulfill the visions of their clients. Their staff of designers and artists are skilled at creating innovative custom designs while utilizing their inventory to enhance entryways, perimeters, stage sets, linens and centerpieces. Décor 'N More collaborates with top catering, lighting and entertainment companies to offer complete event production services. For the past 15 years they have served the corporate, social, private and non-profit markets all over the state of Colorado, predominately in the Denver metro area. Team members deliver unparalleled customer service by being involved with the design process from start to finish, including follow up after the event to ensure clients are more than satisfied. Owner Chris Blumke and other members of the design sales team are experienced, professional event planners who understand the quality of product, customer service and attention to detail that is needed to produce a fabulous event. They stay in touch with trends, not only in the event industry, but also in the areas of art, fashion, architecture and interior design. At your next event, let Décor 'N More transform your space in ways that will not only surprise and delight you, but will leave attendees talking about your event for years to come.

4444 Morrison Road, Denver CO
(303) 936-9224
www.decornmoreinc.com

Darkroom 2 Photography

BUSINESS: *Talented staff of photo experts*

Since June 2003, Laura Dombrowski has established a diversified client base for her Denver photography studio, Darkroom 2 Photography. Over the years, Darkroom 2 Photography has been widely used by portrait clients, wedding clients and modeling agencies. Commercial print and advertising agencies have also discovered Laura's studio, located among the eclectic studios, shops and restaurants at Denver's exciting Sherman Corner. Laura's early work earned her a place in Rob Winner's Semester at Sea photography course, offered by the Prestigious Brooks Institute of Photography. The class not only provided her with a technical foundation, but the darkroom assigned to her during the class inspired the name of her business. Laura has taken classes at the renowned Maine Workshops and the Art Institute of Colorado. She's worked as a fashion photographer and was the still photographer for the feature film *American Dream*. Look for Darkroom 2's work on billboards for Jammin 92.5 and on Maverick Sports Television, as well as in the Golden Triangle Art District's first Friday art tours. Laura and her talented staff will capture all the special moments of your wedding day with their photojournalism style. Beyond group photographs, the Darkroom 2 team seeks to quietly document the details of the day. Laura's use of digital photography allows you to receive not only a stunning album of mounted photos, but photos to share online with friends and family. Portfolios of Laura's work can be viewed on her website. When you need a creative and professional photographer, turn to Laura and her staff at Darkroom 2 Photography.

1280 Sherman Street, Suite 202, Denver CO
(720) 366-2011 or (877) 766-2011
www.darkroom2photography.com

Dub Media Recording Studio

BUSINESS: *Best recording studio*

A recording session can be a stressful experience for a band, especially the first time out. The staff members at Dub Media Recording Studio understand this, and are happy to guide a new band through the process. Dub Media is a one-stop recording studio with a highly creative, state-of-the-art environment that is easy-going and artist oriented. Dub Media is retail ready. This means it can record a musical number, prepare the cover graphics, produce the CD, package it and help with marketing and distribution. By lowering the cost of production through computer-based technology and by offering a retail-ready product, Dub Media encourages artists to exercise their creativity and explore their individual sound. All the members of the Dub Media sound team are producers and musicians in their own right. They love music and producing. Their creative

talent can change the direction of the music when appropriate. Studio magic can take something beautiful and make it even better. Each producer and sound engineer is committed to the success of local musicians. The studio actively seeks out new local talent. Dub Media has special duplication packages for DJs. The studio also offers workshops on recording and mixing techniques for producers, musicians and DJs. When you are ready to record your sound, call the experts at Dub Media Recording Studio.

1425 W 13th Avenue, Suite 6, Denver CO
(303) 534-6400
www.dubmedia.net

Mile High Station

EVENTS: *Dynamic historic venue for events*

The Mile High Station is a venue with personality... vibrant, distinctive and definitely unforgettable. Many styles merge inside this historic building to create a dynamic venue, ideal for any important event. Built more than 100 years ago, the Mile High Station was first the Midwest Steel and Ironworks building. The structure has been carefully renovated to preserve much of the original architectural features, including the old-brick exterior walls, I-Beam steel structure and some of the original operational equipment. New features include an elevated mezzanine, kitchen, bar and large outdoor patio on the west side where guests can relax and watch the sunset. The building is full of character, style and personality, yet it can be completely transformed to suit any themed party you can imagine. The venue's versatility makes it intimate enough for small gatherings or spacious enough to hold 1,200 people. Whether you are planning a large corporate event, formal wedding or casual get-together, the Mile High Station is sure to leave people talking long after the party ends.

2027 W Colfax Denver CO
(720) 946-7721
www.milehighstation.com

Fancy to Fantasy Catered Affairs
EVENTS: *Denver's most creative caterer*

Since she was a little girl, Debbie Strom has had a passion for cooking and creating new and innovative dishes. Over the years, her passion was nurtured by entertaining friends and family. A decade ago, a friend asked her to cook for a party she was hosting, and the result was the start of Fancy to Fantasy Catered Affairs. Debbie retains her childhood passion, and prides herself on providing bold and exciting cuisine. She also expresses her creativity in her themed table décor. You might see authentic African curios on a jungle-themed buffet, or a beautiful sandy beach scene for a luau. Whether planning a wedding, a large corporate event or an intimate dinner for two, Fancy to Fantasy will work closely with you to personalize your menu. They can cater any occasion, of any size and do anything but the ordinary. Fancy to Fantasy is a full service catering company with the ability to provide complete event coordination. From locating a venue to booking the entertainment, from table settings to ice carvings, and any other details that may apply, they can handle it all while you relax and enjoy a stress-free event. The friendly staff of Fancy to Fantasy has served delicious food to many of Denver's most influential people, including mayors, CEOs, senators, radio and television celebrities and professional athletes. Debbie and her talented staff love what they do, and it shows. Call Fancy to Fantasy Catered Affairs for your next important event, and make your party the talk of the town.

2706 Larimer Street, Denver CO
(303) 863-1970
www.fancytofantasy.com

SOL . . . Store of Lingerie

FASHION: *Best professional bra fitting*

It is now possible to find a comfortable, great fitting bra. Do your bra straps fall down, does your bra not stay in place, are the cups either too big or too small? These are just some of the reasons women find buying a bra so difficult. This is where SOL, Denver's premier lingerie boutique, comes in. Located in Cherry Creek North, SOL specializes in bra fitting, providing exceptional customer service and teaching women to learn to love their bras. Owners Cindy Johnson and Jeanie Peterson believe that buying a bra can be both fun and educational. Treat yourself to the SOL experience by letting SOL's enthusiastic and knowledgeable staff help you choose comfortable, great-fitting bras to suit your body type and lifestyle. SOL has a full range of styles and sizes to fit every woman. Their top-selling brands are imported from Europe and are chosen for their high quality, fit and design. The result of a professional bra fitting is more than worthwhile. Most women walk out realizing that not only can the right bra change the way their clothes look, it can also change the way they feel. SOL also specializes in sleepwear, bridal lingerie and dress solutions. The beautiful, inviting atmosphere of the store makes it a pleasure to shop for yourself or someone else. A friendly staff and a database that tracks favorite styles and sizes makes gift giving easy and fun. You owe it to yourself to visit SOL.

248 Detroit Street, Denver CO (303) 394-1060
www.sollingerie.com

Sirens on Third
FASHION: *Top lingerie shop*

Sirens on Third is turning heads with its chic lingerie collection. Sirens opened in April 2005 and already *Rocky Mountain News* has named it the top lingerie shop in Denver. With flirty labels like Eberjey, Leigh Bantivoglio and Betsey Johnson, owner Christine Tallarico has gathered some of the finest lingerie and swimwear in town. Customers love the camisole sets and the Scanty and P.J. Salvage pajamas. Sirens on Third also stocks the lingerie that is popular among today's brides. Many of the high-end labels are not available anywhere else in the metro area, but if you do not find exactly what you are looking for, Christine will gladly order what you need. She and the rest of the friendly staff will welcome you and help you feel confident with your selections. Guys, are you looking for something more than flowers for the woman in your life? Sirens on Third has a very feminine feel, but it is also a non-intimidating environment for male gift buyers. Come see the irresistible fashion-forward lingerie at Sirens on Third.

3003 E 3rd Avenue, Suite A2, Denver CO
(303) 322-7500

Trice Jewelers

FASHION: *Largest full-service jewelry store*

With two-time Super Bowl winner Mike Shanahan, head coach of the Denver Broncos, serving as its official spokesperson, Trice Jewelers must be a cut above everyone else. The shop, owned by Ralph and Justin Klomp, has been serving Denver for 50 years and is Denver's largest full-service jewelry store. Trice employs a dozen of the best goldsmiths to design and manufacture gold and platinum jewelry on-site. The shop specializes in creating custom bridal designs and differentiates itself from other stores by custom work, impeccable customer service and reasonable pricing options. It holds an extraordinary selection of bridal and wedding bands that is larger than that of other stores in the U.S. and carries Colorado's largest selection of loose diamonds. Trice is also the place to turn for quality repair of your jewelry. The Trice commitment to excellence has earned it Top Jeweler in Denver status in 2003, 2004 and 2005 and made it the official jewelry store of the Denver Broncos. The store is an honored member of consumer advocate and radio troubleshooter Tom Martino's *Referral List*. The Trice Jewelers facility is huge, but not intimidating, because of the constant efforts of the conscientious and friendly staff. The sheer number of jewelry items available will boggle your mind and amaze even the most experienced shopper. When you want a wide selection and quality options, turn to Trice Jewelers.

2520 S Colorado Boulevard, Denver CO
(303) 759-9661 or (877) TRY-TRICE (879-87423)

Frolik on 32nd
FASHION: *Top of the Town, three years running*

Denver's Highland District is enjoying new vitality as the neighborhood continues to draw a diverse community of entrepreneurs and artists who are turning woebegone Victorian manors and bungalows into upscale restaurants and fabulous boutiques. A jewel among the pearls is Frolik on 32nd, one of Denver's most popular shopping venues for ladies, owned and operated by Jennifer Bonenberger. Frolik on 32nd opened in 2001 after Jennifer realized she wanted to spend more time with her family than what her paramedic-firefighting career allowed. Putting her prior retail history to good use, she designed this stellar boutique, filled to the brim with everything you need for your wardrobe. Touted as a "one stop shop for every gal," Frolik on 32nd offers a wide array of cosmopolitan looks that can take you through the day and into the night, including incredible lingerie by Hanky Panky. Frolik on 32nd carries a great selection of jewelry, belts, bags and gift cards. Jennifer and her outgoing staff are always on hand to assist with your shopping, which makes Frolik on 32nd the ideal place for a fellow to find something special for his favorite gal. This merry shop has been recognized by numerous publications, including *5280 Magazine*, which named it Top of the Town three years running. For the urban look that's right for you, visit the fun and fabulous Frolik on 32nd.

3715 W 32nd Avenue, Denver CO
(303) 458-5575
www.frolikon32nd.com

Sunneshine Couture
FASHION: *Best fashionable casual attire*

If your idea of jeans is embroidered, distressed or anything but ordinary, then you'll want to put together your next casual outfit at Sunneshine Couture in Denver or Boulder, named the best place to buy jeans by *5280 Magazine*. Sunne Meyer describes her shop as a "really cool closet," thanks to youthful merchandise from over 50 makers. The shop specializes in jeans from small, out-of-the-mainstream designers. Jeans for men come from such New Age sources as G-Star, Nudie and Stitch's. Women's lines include Da-Nang, Serfontaine and Miss Sixty. Even an itty-bitty woman will be pleased with the size selection here, and style selection is fabulous. Look for corset tops and skirts, organic clothing lines, and racks inspired by vintage clothing and European fashion. T-shirts for all sizes and attitudes are a mainstay here, including special Hurricane Katrina T-shirts. Sunne donates 100 percent—that's right, 100 percent—of the $30 price tag for these shirts to the American Red Cross Disaster Relief Fund. Sunneshine can also help you put the finishing touches on casual or special occasion outfits with watches from La Mer, necklaces by Katie Price, and wallets and bags by J. Fold. Just before New Year's is a great time to find a party dress here and maybe a pair of brass, gold or wood earrings. For fashionable, casual garb that describes your outlook, come to Sunneshine Couture.

3003 E 3rd Avenue, Suite B, Denver CO
(303) 393-7414
1703 Pearl Street, Boulder CO
(303) 447-8650
www.sunneshine.com

Art of Gold Jewelers
FASHION: *Original jewelry creations*

Beneath an extraordinary amount of talent and an amazing eye for beauty beats the jewelry boutique Art of Gold Jewelers. Art of Gold encompasses fine craftsmanship and knowledge of the industry with two graduate gemologists on staff, as well as Can Van Le, owner, resident jewelry creator and Certified Master Bench Jeweler. Each member of the knowledgeable staff has at least 10 years experience in the business, making this boutique anything but ordinary. With over 38 years experience under Can's belt, the jewelry he produces is tremendous. All jewelry craftsmanship, design and repair are done in-house and with exquisite items for every occasion, including custom wedding sets, earrings, pendants, bracelets, rings and unique gifts. Once you are a client here, you are a client for life. When you purchase one of Art of Gold's gorgeous creations you will receive top-notch service, the finest quality and a special something you just won't find anywhere else.

695 S Colorado Boulevard, Suite 150, Denver CO
(303) 765-4984
www.artofgold.com

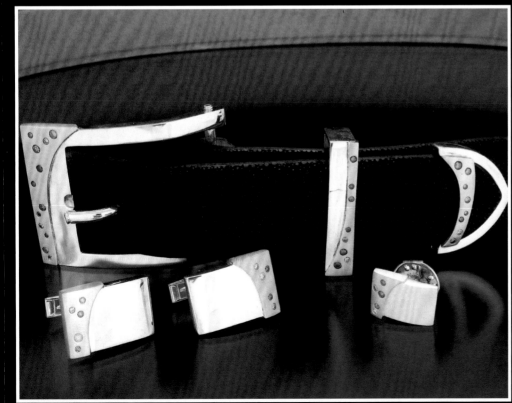

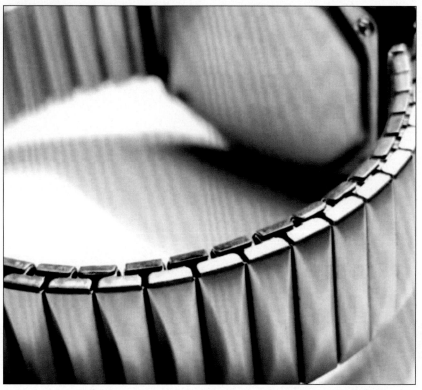

Oster Jewelers
FASHION:
One of North America's leading watch retailers

Oster Jewelers sets out to offer only jewelry and watches with clear artistic value. Owners Melissa and Jeremy Oster opened their own boutique in 2002 after many years in the high-end jewelry business. They were quickly discovered, and have already been recognized as one of North America's leading watch retailers by International Watch Magazine. In 2004 and 2005, Citysearch named Oster the Best Jeweler in Denver. Recently, InSync Magazine recognized Melissa as a Woman of Distinction. The goal at Oster is quality jewelry at every price point. Featured lines include Audemars Piguet, Anonimo and Stefan Hafner. Melissa and Jeremy's knowledge and the quality of their products causes customers from all over the world to seek out the Osters. Jeremy wants customers to choose pieces that speak to them and is happy to educate people about any of the timepieces in the boutique. Uniquely shaped and colored diamonds are an Oster speciality. In custom works, classic items like pearls are sometimes paired with diamonds to create an item that is at the same time avant-garde and timeless. To see one of the finest collections of high-end jewelry in the world, come to Oster Jewelers at Cherry Creek North.

251 Steele Street Denver CO
(303) 572-1111
www.osterjewelers.com

Skye Clothing
FASHION: *Best men's boutique*

If you think that Denver fashion options end at cowboy boots and denim, think again. At Skye Clothing, in the historic LoDo district, fashion aficionados can check out the latest threads from both established and up-and-coming designers of the metro look. Owner Skye Forrest is a former model and actress that wanted to bring contemporary clothing to the Denver area that was unlike anything else currently available. With an inventory that consists of primarily high-end, cutting-edge women and men's clothing, she has succeeded beautifully since her opening in 2004. In the beginning, she teamed up with a buying office in New York City in order to form relationships with popular designers such as Mathew Williamson, Rick Owens and Moschiano. Today, she has the designers lining up to be featured at Skye Clothing. Forrest carries a fabulous array of designer apparel along with accessories and footwear and was recently named by *5280 Magazine's* Top of the Town section as being the Best Men's Boutique. Whether you're searching for quality women's leather garments from the Fani Couture designer Fani Xenophontos or original prints and embroidered apparel from Alice Temperley, no need to head to New York or Los Angeles, you can find it all at Skye Clothing on Blake Street.

1499 Blake Street #1A, Denver CO
(303) 623-0444

Carol Mier Fashion
FASHION:
Best one-of-a-kind clothing

It takes a combination of insight and inner vision to look into an auto repair shop and see a fashion studio for women's clothing. Carol Mier has such vision, which is good news for her discriminating clientele. A designer for 25 years, Carol specializes in one-of-a-kind and limited release clothing of timeless taste and appeal. Her designs come in two distinct forms. The first is a machine washable sueded rayon line that comes in 10 vibrant colors and 25 basic silhouettes. This figure flattering collection can best be described as fluid, elegant and contemporary. Carol's Wearable Art fashion line sports unusual textures, patterns and colors, designed for casual, business and evening wear. Carol chooses her fabrics from the finest outlets throughout the world and offers sizes from petite to plus. She works out of Denver, where the World Modeling Association has named her Colorado Designer of the Year. Her designs are also available in several locations throughout the United States, including Santa Fe, Scottsdale and Chicago. The studio is open Thursday, Friday and Saturday afternoons as well as the evening of the First Friday Art Walk. Carol is available for private consultations throughout the week. For classic women's fashions that are sensitive to a woman's beauty, visit Carol Mier Fashion.

754 Santa Fe Drive, Denver CO
(303) 446-0117
www.carolmierfashion.com

Soul Haus Menswear

FASHION: *One of the 10 Best Bargain Hotspots, 2005*

It's safe to say that Soul Haus Menswear in Denver is nothing like your dad's clothing store. This boutique has stylish selections that shout a distinctive downtown attitude of urban, gritty and cutting edge. Soul Haus specializes in affordable clothing and accessories for an independent and trend driven look. Offering garb from daytime casual to hot night-time club wear, the shelves are also brimming over with watches, cuff links, books and gifts, ensuring there is a little something for

everyone at this Capitol Hill boutique. Soul Haus gives guys the kind of service and choice that is traditionally demanded in women's clothing stores. You'll find new selections each time you visit, great sales and a staff that's proud of its individual service. National clothing brands like BC Ethic and Johnny Max hang on the walls with imported labels from London, Toronto and Istanbul. *Outfront Magazine* has honored this shop as Denver's finest every year since 1999, and *5280 Magazine* named this shop one of the 10 Best Bargain Hotspots in 2005. Visit Soul Haus Menswear for contemporary casual clothing, accessories and gifts that are as stylish, outspoken and unique as you.

226 E 13th Avenue, Denver CO
(303) 830-SOUL (7685)
www.soulhaus.com

Petite Patoot

FASHION: *Best children's clothing boutique*

Petite Patoot is an upscale kids clothing outlet that sells hip clothes at cool prices. Owner Bridget Dornbirer has packed this warehouse store full of endless values. Roughly half of the inventory was purchased new from upscale boutiques. The other half comes from gently used clothing. All of the clothes reflect the highest quality. Bridget has three girls of her own, and she shops for you with a selective mother's eye. She wants only the best for her girls, and she knows that is what you want for yours. These are kids clothes that make a parent smile. They are made of rich buttery fabrics, bold colors, incomparable detail and fantastic patterns by such companies as Baby Lulu, Biscotti, Charlie Rocket, Little Mass, Oilily and Wes & Willy. It is exceptional quality at warehouse pricing. Petite Patoot was named Best Clothing Store for Children and Infants in 2005 by *Colorado Parent Magazine*. *Westword Magazine* liked the little Patoot so much, they featured it in the Best of Denver. Find out what all the fuss is about. Visit Petite Patoot, a unique children's clothing boutique.

1238 S Broadway, Denver CO
(303) 665-8161
www.petitepatoot.com

Belvedere Belgian Chocolate Shop & Wine Tasting Room

FUN FOODS:
Best Belgian-style chocolate

Photo courtesy of belvederesofcherrycreek.com

In 1912, a Belgian, Jean Neuhaus, invented a chocolate shell hard enough to fill with almost any center. Another Belgian invented the chocolate bar in 1921. Belvedere Belgian Chocolate Shop & Wine Tasting Room continues the Belgian chocolate tradition of rich taste, soft textures and delicate, complicated flavors. In addition, the shop gives customers the opportunity to explore world-class, award-winning wines. The fresh, all natural, handcrafted chocolates contain no wax, trans-fats or preservatives. Tastes range from spirited to soothing—from the unusual Fire Flower, a spicy dark chocolate with a hint of cayenne pepper, to the Butter Truffle. Favorite specialties include Rum Delight, a smooth milk chocolate with a creamy rum center. The popular Frogs are similar to the caramel, nut and chocolate Turtles, but are in the shape of a frog. The wines, from Garfield Estates, are equally diverse. European design and Old World tradition blend to create the aromatic Vin de Glace ice wine, the rich, smoky Fumé Blanc, and the multi-award winning Cabernet Franc. Garfield Estates and the Chocolate Shop have both received the Top of the Rocky awards. The Chocolate Shop took first place for Denver's Best Chocolate, and Garfield Estates wines have won many awards in international wine competitions. Belvedere Belgian Chocolate Shop & Wine Tasting Room will treat you to a taste of Europe in Colorado.

231 Milwaukee Street, Denver CO
(303) 771-0758 or (866) 771-0758
www.belvederesofcherrycreek.com

The Daily Scoop Frozen Custard

FUN FOODS:
Richest ice cream in Congress Park

Wayne Evans and Judy Schimer, owners and managers of the Daily Scoop, have a simple philosophy about their gourmet frozen custard. Their focus combines fun and absolute deliciousness, a formula that guarantees smiles on the faces of their loyal customers. Frozen custard is similar to, but not exactly, ice cream. It's the eggs that make the difference. Rumor has it that frozen custard originated as a hot summer carnival treat on Coney Island, New York. Legend continues that an ice cream vendor added eggs to act as an emulsifier to his melting ice cream. Presto! A new premium ice cream with a rich taste and smooth texture took the name *frozen custard*. In 1919, Archie Kohr invented the first frozen custard machine and took it to Coney Island. He sold 18,460 cones on that first weekend. Wayne had his first taste of frozen custard in Milwaukee, and it was love at first lick. He opened the doors of the Daily Scoop in 2003 and has been serving the richest ice cream in the Congress Park neighborhood ever since. Manager Jeff Bailey has been instrumental in creating some of the more exotic flavors, and with over 100 varieties you are sure to have several favorites. Frozen custard cakes, pies, sundaes, shakes, malts, floats and 32 toppings expand the possibilities for a different taste sensation on each return trip. The philosophy is straightforward: For frozen custard made fresh daily, follow the crowds to the Daily Scoop.

3506 E 12th Avenue, Denver CO
(303) 388-3245
www.mydailyscoop.com

Jerry's Nut House
MARKETS: *Best place for nuts*

You certainly don't have to be nuts to go to Jerry's Nut House in Denver. Nuts, popcorn, and candy are what you find here, not crazy antics. The business dates back to 1948 when Jerry Levine and his wife Roie opened a little nut factory to supply the tavern trade. Jerry's Nut House soon grew to become a Denver tradition. The operation was strictly wholesale for many years, but eventually Jerry opened a retail outlet for walk-in customers. To this day, the same family operates the business. Locating suppliers who can provide the highest quality products is a key to its success. Jerry's roasts its own nuts and also prepares popcorn, including cheddar cheese corn and caramel corn. Pretzels and other snacks are also available. The wholesale side supplies grocers, gift shops, bakeries and distributors. Jerry's offers a wide variety of handpacked, decorative tins for its products, and the holiday business is strong. Many corporations buy Jerry's assortments as gifts for their employees or clients. When in Denver, drop by and try some of Jerry's snack products. You will never be satisfied with ordinary nuts or salted snacks again.

2101 Humboldt Street, Denver CO
(303) 861-2262 or (888) 217-0747

Roberta's Chocolates
FUN FOODS: *Best sweet treats*

Discriminating candy connoisseurs in Colorada turn to Roberta's Chocolates for distinctive sweet treats. Since 1995, Roberta Poirier has been tempting her customers with a varied assortment of exquisite chocolates and candies, including customized products to advertise your business or to use as favors for special parties. She has amassed a collection of over 10,000 molds to shape candy into any design. If you can think of it, Roberta's can produce it for you. A heavenly selection of gourmet temptations can be purchased by the piece at the store, where the aroma of chocolate, caramel and nuts wafts through the air to tease away the last of any lingering resistance. Chewy caramels, smooth creams and covered nuts are a delightful way to please family and friends. Roberta's also designs distinctive gifts featuring a variety of Colorado-made delectables including O'Hara's Jams & Jellies, Martha Sue's Cookies and Cottswold Cottage Foods. One taste of Roberta's Mountain Crunch or the delightful mix of flavors in the white chocolate nut patty will fire a craving that can only be satisfied by more of these extraordinary confections. Satisfy your sweet tooth with a visit to Roberta's Chocolates, and you will be hooked for life.

4840 W 29th Avenue, Denver CO
(303) 824-2069

The Open Press Studio and Open Press Gallery

GALLERIES & FINE ART: *Best showcase of fine art printing*

There is a common misconception that a fine art print is merely a reproduction of some original museum work, however a fine art printing is actually a technique in which pigment, dye or ink is applied onto a plate and then ran through a special press. Since the artists' work on the plate, there is no original and the only finished product is the print itself. In 1998, Mark Lunning co-founded Open Press Studio, which is dedicated to the creation and exhibition of this revered art form that has been a medium for many of our most admired artists such as Albrecht Durer and Pablo Picasso. Lunning founded the studio because he understood the need for artists to have proper resources to pursue their chosen craft once they leave school. The 2,000 square foot facility offers artists the space, tools and flexibility needed in order to create innovative, original prints in various mediums while working on their own or with the guidance of a master printer. Open Press Studio is the only fine art printmaking facility of its kind in the nation and much of the artwork produced is shipped nationwide. In conjunction with Open Press Studios, Lunning has also opened the Open Press Gallery as a venue for these stunning art prints. Here you can view incredible art prints hand created by top artists including Ken Elliot, Strasburg and Mark Lunning himself. Explore the world of contemporary fine art prints at Open Press Studio and Open Press Gallery.

Studio: 40 W Bayaud, Denver CO (303) 778-1116
Gallery: 10 E Ellsworth Avenue, Denver CO (303) 778-1116
www.openpressltd.com

McGuinness Studio

GALLERIES & FINE ART:
Best fine art monotypes

Over the last few decades, Denver has become a mecca for those in search of unusual and provocative works of art. Among the leaders of the outstanding galleries and studios that line the streets of this golden city, McGuinness Studio stands out as a shining star. Owner and artist Katharine McGuinness opened the doors to her popular studio in 1998, and it has quickly become a favorite of locals and visitors alike. Her warm and inviting studio space focuses on color. It is laid out in such a way as to welcome the viewer in, while stimulating and encouraging them to relax and browse in a comfortable atmosphere. McGuinness Studio deals primarily with lithography inks to produce an art form that is growing in popularity known as monotype. With monotype, a uniuqe mage is created by the artist using tools such as brushes and brayers to transfer layers of oil-based printmaking ink, often of differing viscosities, onto a zinc or plexiglas plate. The plate is placed onto the bed of a hand-cranked printing press, and a sheet of dampened paper is place over the plate . As the plate moves through the press, the image is transferred to the paper, which produces a one-of-a-kind, viscosity monotype print. Katharine opens the doors of her studio to the public for special events throughout the year, serving wine and small dishes while promoting art and art conversation. Calling for an appointment prior to visiting is encouraged. Experience art like you never have before at McGuinness Studio.

74 W 11th Avenue, Denver CO
(303) 573-5095
www.mcguinnessstudio.com

Hal Gould at The Camera Obscura Gallery

Albert Einstein, 1947 by Philippe Halsman

Camera Obscura Gallery
GALLERIES & FINE ART:
Oldest operating photography gallery

Camera Obscura Gallery in Denver is considered to be the oldest operating photography gallery in the nation. It all began in 1963 when a group of photography enthusiasts joined forces to open the Colorado Photographic Art Center right behind the Denver Art Museum. The non-profit organization managed for 17 years before suspending operations and was taken over by its current owner Hal Gould. Hal renamed it Camera Obscura Gallery and has successfully mounted more than 300 shows during 42 years. Gould's interest in photography began at the age of 12 after winning a camera at a local contest. By 1948, Hal was enrolled at the prestigious Art Institute of Chicago and later became a student at the Ray Vogue School of Commercial Art and Photography. He has completed more than 25,000 assignments and is a member of the Golden Triangle Art Association which celebrates an art walk on the first Friday of each month. During the span of his impressive career, Hal has traveled all seven continents in his pursuit of the craft. Over the intervening years, this popular and provocative gallery has displayed magnificent and highly sought after photographs by some of the finest photographers of our time including Phil Borges, Christopher Burkett and Howard Bond as well as vintage works from such innovators as Edward S. Curtis, Barbara Morgan and Dmitri Baltermants. Gain new perspective and see the world in a whole other light with the inspiring and delightful photographs displayed at Camera Obscura Gallery.

1309 Bannock Street, Denver CO
(303) 623-4059
www.cameraobscuragallery.com

Plus Gallery
GALLERIES & FINE ART:
Best progressive art gallery

Plus Gallery is one of the few respected galleries in Denver that pushes the envelope with its exhibits. Owner Ivar Zeile's background in design and film is the cause. As his focus changed, he became more interested in the concept of merging a design business with a gallery. Consequently, Plus Gallery exhibits art as well as gives featured artists creative authority over their showings. Works exhibited can be in any medium from painting to video to art installation. While selling art is important, Ivar and his wife Karen also want to excite the public by exposing them to new talent.

At Plus Gallery, Rocky Mountain regional and national artists' works are shown such as John Hull, Susan Meyer and John McEnroe. The Zeiles have a passion for helping emerging artists become nationally recognized. Taking a very personal approach to their business, Ivar is a member of the Mayor's Commission on Cultural Affairs. For a chance to view or own some of the best progressive contemporary art around, spend some time at Plus Gallery.

2350 Lawrence Street, Denver CO
(303) 296-0927
www.plusgallery.com

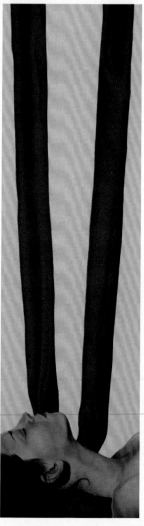

Platte River Art Services
GALLERIES & FINE ART: *Best custom finishing*

Platte River Art Services houses a crew of unparalleled artists. Robert Pietlock opened this business 30 years ago as a natural extension of his fine art business background. The standards Pietlock set for the work and the skill of the people he brought on board soon caused Platte River Art Services to become the primary framing store in the Rocky Mountains. The staff delivers unlimited custom made designs not just to display the art it holds, but to complement and enhance it. The frame never overshadows the work, but is seamlessly integrated, producing an awe-inspiring effect. This shop is trusted by collectors and museums across the nation for the high quality work they do, whether it is a shadowbox project of treasured three-dimensional objects, gilded or ornamental framework, simple, understated design or floating works on wood. The warm camaraderie of the staff is contagious and the business is known in the community for its philanthropic endeavors. Bring in your artwork, Platte River Art Services will return it to you a masterpiece.

350 Santa Fe Drive, Denver CO
(303) 571-1060
www.platteriverartservices.com

Space Gallery
GALLERIES & FINE ART:
Non-representational abstract and contemporary artwork

Explore innovative and provocative art done in a modernistic and boldly contemporary style with a visit to Space Gallery. Located in the heart of Denver's art district on Santa Fe Drive, this must-see gallery offers art aficionados a new and exciting array of non-representational abstract and contemporary artwork. These fabulous works of art are beautifully displayed and have been created by a delightful blend of both local and national, emerging and established artists including Graeme Duncan, Sandra Perlow and John Clark. Owner, creator and curator of Space Gallery, Micheal Burnett was always highly interested in art and his father encouraged him to pursue that interest. He decided to attend Edinburgh College of Art in his native Scotland where he graduated with a Bachelor of Arts Degree and honors in both painting and drawing. Mike opened Space Gallery in 2000 with the original intent of showcasing his own work, however his interest in new media, textures and surface treatments led to the galleries metamorphosis and today Space Gallery pays homage to an emerging art form filled with cutting edge techniques, vivid colors and sophisticated accents. Space Gallery hosts several exhibitions annually and the 4000 square foot gallery makes and ideal venue for private gatherings. The gallery can accommodate groups of up to 300 and both food preparation space and a moveable bar are available. Experience art like never before with a visit to Space Gallery.

765 Santa Fe Drive, Denver CO (720) 904-1088 *www.spacegallery.org*

Sloane Gallery

GALLERIES & FINE ART:
Modern and contemporary Russian masters

The Sloane Gallery, in the Lower Downtown district of Denver, gathers together a stunning body of work by modern and contemporary Russian masters. In 1981, Russian-born Mina Litinsky opened the gallery, which is nationally recognized as one of the country's major dealers in Russian art. The Sloane represents more than 50 artists; some are Russians, some are Russian-Americans, and some hail from former republics of the Soviet Union. A visit to the Artnet website details the Sloane inventory, but only a visit to the gallery can fully capture the power and importance of the work gathered here. The Sloane Gallery shows works in a variety of styles, including surrealist, political, conceptual and abstract. Avante-garde work and the forbidden work of the post-war Sots Art Movement, a Soviet version of Pop-Art started by Komar and Melamid, also finds a home here. Many of the artists represented by the Sloane took strong stands on artistic freedom in the former Soviet Union. Work by Ernst Neizvestny has always been a symbol of resistance, and Mihail Chemiakin's associations landed him in a mental hospital against his will until his 1971 immigration to Paris. Ilya Kabakov, another iconoclast of the period, named as one of the ten best living artists by *ArtNews* in 1999, is likewise featured. The artists represented by the Sloane have international reputations and paintings in the permanent public collections of such prestigious museums as the Guggenheim and Metropolitan in New York, as well as the Centre Georges Pompidou in Paris and the Pushkin in Moscow. Make a visit to the Sloane Gallery part of any trip to the galleries in this resurrected Denver historic district.

1612 17th Street, Denver CO
(303) 595-4230
www.artnet.com/sloane.html

Komar & Melamid "Lenin Hails A Cab" 1993 oil on canvas

Photo by David Menard

Barbara Froula Studio Gallery
GALLERIES & FINE ART: *Best watercolor landscapes*

Denver-based artist Barbara Froula has a decided love of landscapes especially urban landscapes and skillfully renders the light and individuality of places in her watercolor paintings. Says Barbara, "The city is what excites me to paint, the geometric forms of the skyline, the play of light on the detail of an older building, the visual narrative that enfolds as people interact." Barbara started painting as a hobby while working as an architect. Her first show in 1982 in Cherry Creek sold 20 of items the first night and she has pursued art full-time ever since. She celebrates her gallery, in business 14 years, with an Annual Opening on the first Thursday and Friday of each November. Those who appreciate her work look forward to this occasion to visit with the artist. Barbara is well known for her Denver cityscapes and has been commissioned to paint scores of images for Denver organizations as well as individuals. She has traveled widely in Europe and is particularly fond of painting the Tuscany landscape and the city of Prague. In 2004, Barbara and Czech author Václav Cílek published *Prague: Between History and Dreams*, a written tour of Prague that includes 100 Froula paintings. Each Froula painting creates a powerful sense of place. Visit the Barbara Froula Studio Gallery in Denver and experience for yourself the visual imagery that has made her paintings of gardens, landscapes and cities so popular.

186 S Pennsylvania Street, Denver CO
(303) 777-2590 or (888) 360-2590
www.barbarafroula.com

Michael Walter Art & Design
GALLERIES & FINE ART: *Best design studio and gallery*

Michael Walter Art & Design is a Denver area gallery and studio founded by Michael Walter in 2005. The gallery showcases a wide variety of original art including painting, sculpture, photography and printmaking from more than 30 local artists in monthly rotations throughout the year. In addition to the beautiful artwork you will find on the walls each month, Michael Walter Art & Design provides professional art services in a working studio atmosphere, including custom canvases, commissioned art, murals and decorative painting. They also offer custom framing and finishing, repair and restoration, and delivery and installation. The gallery has professional graphic and photography services and consultation available for all visitors. Each of the artists represented at Michael Walter Art & Design offer a specific talent to the art realm and when these efforts are combined together with the wide range of art and design-related services, this exceptional venture provides a full range of options and services for any artistic or design project from beginning to end. A visit to Michael Walter Art & Design is a chance to peruse the best the Denver art scene has to offer and is certain to be a memorable experience. Normal gallery hours are from 11 am to 6 pm Monday through Saturday or by appointment, with evening events throughout the year, including the Art District on Santa Fe First Friday Art Walk on the first Friday of every month.

742 Sante Fe Drive, Denver CO
(303) 825-0606

Fascination St. Fine Art Gallery

GALLERIES & FINE ART:
Best mix of art, wine and memorabilia

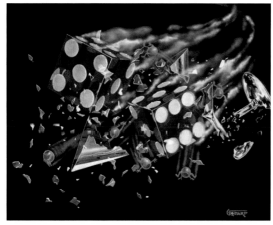

When Aaron and Sandee LaPedis opened the original Fascination St. Fine Art Gallery 15 years ago, their mission was to provide both their Denver and online customers with an exceptional art shopping experience. They've accomplished their mission and opened a second location in Cherry Creek North. By featuring only nationally and internationally acclaimed artists, Fascination St. Fine Art Gallery has been providing outstanding online and offline customer service. Fascination St. Fine Art Gallery's exceptional customer service is comparative only to its selection. They specialize not only in fine art, but in novelties such as original animation cells which are similar to negatives in the animation process. They also carry sports memorabilia including signed helmets, jerseys and photos. Although Aaron and Sandee both have extraordinary backgrounds in the art business, they are known for being laid back. Fascination St. Fine Art Gallery features an on-site wine bar and often holds wine tastings in the gallery. It is not unheard of to be offered a glass of wine while you browse the selections. Their experienced but relaxed style assists in creating Fascination St. Fine Art Gallery's unpretentious atmosphere. This makes it an ideal location whether you are purchasing your first piece or adding to an already extensive fine art collection.

315 Detroit Street, Denver CO
(303) 333-1566 or (866) 293-1566
www.fascinationstart.com
www.animationartwork.com

Masten Fine Framing & Gifts
GALLERIES & FINE ART: *Best place for home accents*

Shopping at Masten Fine Framing & Gifts combines a sense of certainty with the thrill of discovery. You know that you will find the kinds of things that last a lifetime, such as exquisite lamps, art-glass objects and Bulova clocks and watches, as well as ones designed by Frank Lloyd Wright. In addtion, expect a few surprises, as owner Reed Masten's tastes are far-ranging. In ranking Masten number 12 in Denver's Top Style 100, the *Denver Post* recognized Reed's flair for choosing enchanting home accents. "Cowboy pendulums giddyup along one side of his work table," wrote the *Post*, "while blood-red glass vases and spiral-stemmed martini glasses sparkle on the other. This mind-boggling assortment of art objects has one thing in common: all appeal to Masten and his partner." As you peruse Masten's selection of bookends, vases, candles and jewelry, you will understand why local polls have named it Denver's Best Gift Shop and Best Offbeat Store. The shop, established in 1986 as a custom framing shop, still provides thousands of frame choices and specializes in conservation framing and shadow boxes. Over the years, Reed has added home accents and gifts, giving folks more reason to explore his tiny shop on East 17th Avenue near Logan Street. Drop by and see why Denver has fallen in love with Masten Fine Framing & Gifts.

429 E 17th Avenue, Denver CO
(303) 832-6565
www.mastenonline.com

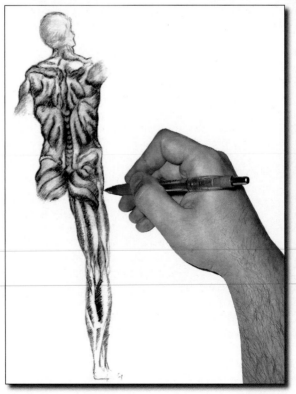

VSA Arts of Colorado
GALLERIES & FINE ART:
Best programs that support artists with disabilities

VSA Arts of Colorado is a glowing example of a gallery with extreme community impact; the kind of enterprise every gallery or art center strives to become. The Access Gallery is operated by Damon McLeese, aided by an incredibly talented minimal staff with exceptional efforts by volunteers, artists and community members. The focus of the organization from the mission statement is to "promote creative power in people with disabilities," and to create an integrated art world that fully encourages and includes artists with disabilities. Access Gallery opened in 1999. In four short years, community response necessitated moving into a space twice the size of the original location. The new location in the midst of the Denver Art District has proved extremely beneficial to the community. Access Gallery continues to expand its services as it grows, fueled by passionate beliefs and creative talents. First Friday art openings attract a large audience; various trainings and children's projects have resulted in the gallery functioning as an art center for the community. The gallery vision continues to focus on cultivating awareness of disability issues as they relate to the arts and education as provided in part by the illustration of the gifts artists with disablilities continue to express through their art. The programs enable deserving artists who have disabilities to build their careers with valuable exposure and representation. The state-of-the-art center hosts four workshops a year to raise awareness of the physical struggles inherent in spaces for people with disabilities as well as to develop solutions for adapting physical spaces and programs to make them accessible and navigable. Access Gallery is a beautiful guiding light shining brightly in downtown Denver.

909 Santa Fe Drive, Denver CO
(303) 777-0797

Metro Frame Works
GALLERIES & FINE ART:
Best custom framing

Gallery artwalks are sweeping the nation replacing movies and bowling while offering viewers a whole new way to savor an evening out with friends. One of the country's hottest artwalks can be found monthly on Tennyson in Denver which is home to numerous original galleries and studios including the innovative and always exciting Metro Frame Works and 44T Artspace. Owners Kevin Paul and Melanie Lunsford opened the doors to their framing shop and art gallery in 1999 and have since created a fascinating space filled with great frames, new art and some very cool dogs. Melanie brings an extensive history of woodworking and furniture making to Metro Frame Works with her years of experience as well as a clever eye for design is reflected in every frame made. They specialize in custom framing and preservation for art collectors, artists, interior designers and average consumers alike. At 44T Artspace, you will find an extensive array of high quality contemporary art that has been masterfully framed, along with the galleries four-footed familiars, a duo of greyhounds and a whippet, who have retired from the racing world and are often on hand to greet patrons. Whether you're looking to frame your latest original, preserve a family heirloom or pick up something new and wonderful to grace the walls of your home, Metro Frame Works and 44T Artspace have what you need. Stop by the corner of Tennyson and 44th Avenue today and discover all that this fabulous gallery and framing center has to offer.

4400 Tennyson Street, Denver CO
(303) 433-1073
www.metroframeworks.com

Studio Lokken
GALLERIES & FINE ART: *Most vibrant illustrations*

If life imitated Lokken Millis' art, it would be splashed in astounding color and full of fun and interesting characters. Preferring the colors of the Caribbean waters, the jewel tones, as opposed to primary colors, the art at her Studio Lokken is bursting with a vibrancy you won't see in just any studio. After studying art at Marysville College in Tennessee, the Art Institute of Dallas and East Texas State University in the early 1980s, she spent six years studying painting with Quang Ho at the Art Student's League. Her post-scholastic career has consisted mainly of painting, contributing drawings to various periodicals and illustrating children's books, such as *Felipe the Flamingo* and *Samson the Hot Tub Bear.* She's had several opportunities to work as an educator with the younger generation, too. In fact, her most memorable teaching experience involves three trips to Haiti, where she taught art to some of the country's rural children. The opportunity warmed her heart and solidified her passion for the hues of the area. It even inspired several pieces you can now view at Studio Lokken, the art studio she's dreamed about for years. Here she likes to show off her wide variety of styles while giving her extrovert side a place to reach out. She even holds life drawing sessions for other local aspiring artists. Take a walk through Studio Lokken next time your in Denver, but don't be surprised if you're getting the itch to pick up a paintbrush when you get home.

4430 Tennyson Street, Denver CO
(303) 908-1140
www.studiolokken.com

Pirate – Contemporary Art
GALLERIES & FINE ART: *Best contemporary art gallery*

Cutting edge contemporary art and a Day of the Dead show each November 2nd have kept patrons alert and interested since Phil Bender, an artist himself, opened the nonprofit cooperative art gallery more than 25 years ago. Pirate-Contemporary Art represents the works of more than 30 local artists, including the humorous mixed media work of Louis Recchia, the distinctive symbols of Steve Alarid and the intriguing use of found art by Craig Robb. Pirate consistently shows the work of up and coming artists who go on to greater fame and fondly refers to these talented individuals as pirates. Recchia, who started showing with Pirate in the early days, experienced the Pirate clout when the Denver Art Museum purchased two of his paintings following Pirate exhibitions. Look for anything the modern imagination can conjure, including paintings, sculptures, drawings, mixed media or computer generated work. Pirate is an important alternative art space and one that has given a home to a mixed bag of artistic adventurers. Maybe that's why the mast from an old sailing ship that used to belong to a seafood restaurant sits near the entrance. It reminds the visitor that everything around us can be recast into art, and that Pirate is the place for such reconsiderations and the artists who create them. Pirate's offbeat character and ever-changing shows make good reasons to visit the gallery, which is open every Friday, Saturday and Sunday.

3655 Navajo Street, Denver CO
(303) 458-6058
www.pirateart.org

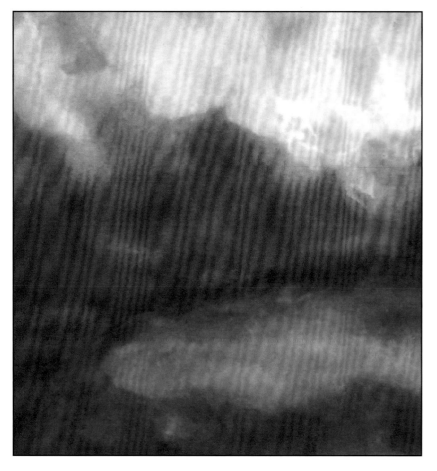

Remmi Fine Art
GALLERIES & FINE ART:
Contemporary mixed media art

Surround yourself with paintings, ceramics, sculpture, and mixed media at Remmi Fine art, featuring contemporary art. Remmi Fine Art offers a fresh perspective on contemporary art. Their open door policy means all are welcome. Novice and seasoned collectors alike will enjoy this gallery which promotes and encourages new ideas in art. Their goal is to offer a broad range of artistic styles. In essence, there is something for everyone at Remmi Fine Art. Artists whose art is highlighted at Remmi Fine Art include emerging and mid-career artists. Not only can you immerse yourself in distinctive fine art at Remmi, you can also receive consultation for the decoration of your personal or commercial space. Art work that adorns your home or office speaks volumes about who you are or what you represent. Remmi's consultants are happy to give advice as to what artistic style could work for your space. Remmi Fine Art is also available to host your own exclusive event. With an elegant backdrop featuring dynamic works of art, your guests will be immersed in a wide variety of artistic styles. Owner Carolyn Naiman and Carlene Frances are both respected in the art community, and for their work at Remmi Fine Art.

776 Santa Fe Drive, Denver CO
(720) 318-6668
www.remmifineart.com

West SouthWest
GALLERIES & FINE ART:
Best Southwest arts and crafts

What is immediately obvious to anyone walking into West SouthWest is the impeccable taste and discriminating eyes of the proprietors. Owners Dudley and Ronda Smith have the eyes for fine Southwest art and love showcasing well known artists and introducing new talent discovered in their many trips between Seattle and Santa Fe. Visitors to the gallery know to check back often to be in on Dudley and Ronda's latest findings, such as colorful serigraphs by John Nieto, Indian jewelry by former senator Ben Nighthorse Campbell and a large selection of Zuni fetishes and Navajo folk art. Located in the Cherry Creek North, Denver's premier art district, West SouthWest caters to clients seeking authentic Pueblo and Mata Ortiz pottery, fine art sculpture and furniture, and special handmade pieces by regional artists. Find contemporary and traditional art, including masks, weavings, baskets and bowls. Dudley is a Denver native who worked for 24 years in local museums cultivating an education in and a passion for Southwest art. He is proud to offer artwork that no other shop carries. Dudley and Ronda invite you to share their passion at West SouthWest.

257 Fillmore Street, Denver CO
(303) 321-4139 or (866) 770-7069
www.westsouthwest.com

Great Western Art Gallery, LLC

GALLERIES & FINE ART: *Best art focused on African-Americans in the Old West*

Hilliard Moore, owner and curator of Great Western Art Gallery, LLC relishes educating people about the role that African-Americans played in the Old West. Have you heard of former slave Aunt Clara Brown, the Angel of the Rockies? How about Barney Ford, runaway slave and Denver hotel pioneer? Fur Trader, James P. Beckwourth, a mulatto who lived with the Blackfeet and Crow Indians and who later discovered Beckwourth Pass through the Sierra Nevada Mountains. The Great Western Art Gallery hosts a versatile genre of both art and artists which caters to a broad spectrum of visitors, tourists and residents alike. They feature award-winning artists with traditional Western wildlife and landscapes, abstract, impressionist and pastel paintings, photography, sculpture, Raku pottery, pencil drawings, designer and Southwestern jewelry, woodturned bowls and natural sculptured mirrors. The gallery represents local and regional artists that are established and emerging artists who tell their stories with their artwork. An in-house custom frame shop completes the gallery's offerings. For an education about the Old West, art inspired by their experiences and an exciting sampling of other artwork, visit the Great Western Art Gallery on the main floor of the Brooks Tower. We are conveniently located steps away from the Denver Performing Arts Complex and the Colorado Convention Center.

1455 Curtis Street, Denver CO 80202 (303) 396-ARTS (2787)

AUM Framing and Gallery
GALLERIES & FINE ART: *Best frame collection in the state*

With a strong emphasis on quality and creativity, AUM Framing & Gallery in Denver covers a wide spectrum within the picture framing world. From simple, clean designs to playfully extravagant, this shop has the ideas, the products, and the expertise to express any sentiment with a frame. Eric Schneider learned the framing trade about 30 years ago from a master craftsman and launched AUM with his wife Linda in 1982. With a staff of seven, AUM boasts over 125 years of cumulative experience. The artistic eyes of four on-site designers assist customers in finding the appropriate design and materials within their budget. This shop carries a frame collection unsurpassed in the state as well as offering diverse glazing and matting options resulting in what seems like infinite possibilities. AUM also undertakes more complex, custom projects for customers as required. In-home or business consultation, pickup, delivery and installation are also available. AUM's small eclectic gallery features the works of several local artists as well as limited edition prints of Seattle artist Dan O'Halloran. Dan's Chinese influenced imagery depicts haunting images that redefine man's relationship with the natural world. Whether you are framing original art or posters, a cherished memento or accent piece, AUM Framing & Gallery's impeccable framing will protect and enhance. They have the selection and know-how to assure you years of lasting pleasure.

2227 E Colfax Avenue, Denver CO
(303) 394-3362

Mudhead Gallery
GALLERIES & FINE ART:
Best Native art gallery

For the serious collector of Native American art, the promise of Santa Clara pottery will lead them on treks to pueblo villages and remote trading posts throughout the Southwest. Fortunately for those aficionados passing through Denver, they can find a fine selection at Mudhead Gallery, conveniently located downtown at the Grand Hyatt Hotel. In addition to museum-quality Santa Clara pieces, the discerning buyer will delight in viewing the pottery that owners Dean and Lois Joseph have gathered from Acoma, San Ildefonso and other pueblos whose names are synonymous with fine craftsmanship. The Mudhead Gallery also carries the colorful jewelry for which the Zuni are known, silver Navajo pieces and a large selection of pawn rings and necklaces. Among the gallery's collection of Navajo weavings are not only exquisite contemporary designs but outstanding vintage rugs from periods that get collectors excited. The Hopi gift for seemingly bringing its pantheon of spirit figures alive in detailed wood carvings is also on display at Mudhead. The gallery takes its name from that clowning character who participates in various Native ceremonies in New Mexico and Arizona. As a subject for art, he has inspired everything from paintings to clay figurines, and you will find superb renderings of him here. Drop by Mudhead Gallery, and you may never have to pursue pottery down a bumpy dirt road again.

555 17th Street, Denver CO
(303) 293-0007
www.mudheadgallery.net

Gifford Ewing Photography

GALLERIES & FINE ART: *Best fine art photography*

Gifford Ewing's black and white photographs capture the purity and natural beauty of a scene, using traditional photographic methods. His work is on display at Gifford Ewing Photography, his Denver gallery, and also graces the permanent collection of the Denver Art Museum. Using a 5-by-7 Deardorff field camera and the zone system for exposure, Gifford has documented the beauty of the Rocky Mountains and the state of Maine. Portfolios focus on such subjects as Yellowstone National Park and the cityscapes of Denver. Gifford's work has been the subject of articles appearing in the Denver Post and Colorado Expression Magazine. His photographic career began with newspaper. In 1972, he moved from Maine to Denver and opened Gifford Ewing Photography, a business that initially served the advertising and architectural communities. His black and white landscape work earned him a reputation as one of the region's finest photographers, and he now devotes himself entirely to his art, which includes his inspired work for Colorado Nature Conservancy. Gifford's photographs are produced in numbered limited editions to increase the value of your purchase. The most economical way to buy a Gifford Ewing print is to purchase one of his boxes of greeting cards. These sets include multiple images of wild buffalo, Western landscapes, Denver or coastal Maine. The complete Ewing Photo Catalog is available on the website. Whether you make an appointment to visit his Denver studio or view his work online, you're sure to be captivated by Gifford Ewing's images.

800 E 19th Avenue, Denver CO
(303) 832-0800 or (888) 989-0800
www.ewingphoto.com

Paulino Gardens

GARDENS, PLANTS & FLOWERS: *Best retail garden center*

In 1915, Pietro Paulino purchased land and farmed it with his son, Mike
Sr. and Amelia, his wife. High-quality produce was sold at the Denargo
Market and grocery stores in Denver. In 1945, after serving two years in
the United States Army, Mike Jr. (Mick) returned to become a partner
in the truck farming business. Soon after, Mick and his wife, Elizabeth,
were married, and they worked on the farm together. In 1958, they began
selling produce to the public on their property. As the business grew,
bedding plants, shrubs and trees were added to the vegetable stand. By
popular demand, greenhouses were built and house plants were added,
as well as gardening accessories. In 1959, Paulino Gardens became a
retail garden center and expanded as funds became available. Today,
Paulino Gardens includes 160,000-square-feet of growing space and
70,000-square-feet of retail greenhouses. They are situated on 23 acres
of property, where every square foot is utilized to the fullest. Paulino
Gardens strives to provide the highest quality merchandise and customer
satisfaction. Enjoy the beauty and wonder of Colorado's largest nursery
and garden center at Paulino Gardens.

6300 N Broadway, Denver CO
www.paulinogardens.com

Cherry Creek Custom Floral
GARDENS, PLANTS & FLOWERS: *Best custom arrangements*

At Cherry Creek Custom Floral in Denver, you can expect to be captivated by the extensive array of extraordinary floral arrangements and gifts. Jae Kim, who is both the owner and head designer at Cherry Creek, has been serving the Denver area since 1992. Her artistic design is inimitable, and she encourages clients to talk with her about their needs so she can customize her creations to suit their occasion. Kim flies flowers in from all over the world. She specializes in a wide array of arrangements, gifts and cards. Among her varied offerings are gift baskets, candles and dish gardens. You can find exquisite Asian designs reflected in flowerpots, artwork, pillows and chests. No job is too big or too small for Kim. She handles corporate affairs, weddings and any other event that requires flowers and creativity. Cherry Creek provides service to many of Denver's premier businesses, including hotels, boutiques, banks and jewelers, but private homes receive the same level of attention that the big businesses receive. Jae Kim enjoys serving up great design, so come in and discover the possibilities at Cherry Creek Custom Floral.

229 Clayton Street, Denver CO
(303) 331-0766 or (800) 316-2851
www.cherrycreekflorist.com

Forever Yours Floral Design
GARDENS, PLANTS & FLOWERS: *Best traditional floral design*

A visit to Forever Yours Floral Design would not be complete without a hello from official greeter Missy, owner Jerry Katrien's cockapoo. The service just gets better from there with assistance from the shop's talented designers and a selection of premium, long-lasting flowers. Jerry was already an expert in the floral industry when he opened the doors to his Denver shop in 1993. He is a graduate of Denver's Academy of Floral Design and a conscientious businessman dedicated to customer satisfaction and to the welfare of the community at large. Forever Yours offers a choice of fresh and exciting floral designs, suitable for everyday occasions, weddings and other celebrations or expressions of sympathy. Live plants and gift baskets are also popular choices. Forever Yours offers free local delivery and can arrange for floral delivery anywhere in the world. The cheerful shop also offers an assortment of silk and dried flowers, balloons, CDs, candy and cards. Forever Yours arrangements are popular with area businesses, and the shop provides weekly delivery of fresh-cut flowers or plants to Denver doctors' offices and hospitals. This popular floral shop can meet your simplest or most complex needs in floral artistry. Recently, Jerry designed a centerpiece to showcase a major story in Colorado Homes and Lifestyles magazine. Next time you need to express a sentiment with flowers, visit Forever Yours Floral Design in Denver's historic old Kaiser Medical Building.

2035 E 18th Avenue, #9, Denver CO
(303) 393-8405 or (800) 898-8405 *www.myfsn.com/foreveryours*

Amore Fiori Flowers & Gifts
GARDENS, PLANTS & FLOWERS:
Best Italian flower market

For some, a trip to Italy is a mere vacation, for others, it is a life-changing experience. When Michelle traveled to Italy, it ignited her longtime desire to do purposeful, creative work with flowers. Returning to Denver after her trip, she was inspired to open Amore Fiori Flowers & Gifts in January of 2003. Michelle's love of floral arranging shows in the details of the European-inspired décor and in the works of art she creates with flowers for events of all kinds. Voted Best New Business in 2004 by *Andiamo*, Denver's Italian community newspaper, the shop is known for its unique flowers and gifts. Michelle modeled her shop after an Italian flower market, with floral gifts in a modern chic style. She presents a personalized hands-on approach to customize gifts to your specifications. Would you like to indulge yourself, a family member or business associate to a floral treat? From spiral twist, hand-tied bouquets for intimate weddings, to wreaths, centerpieces and more, Amore Fiori Flowers & Gifts is your one stop flower shop.

7353 E 29th Avenue, Denver CO
(303) 333-3848
www.amore-fiori.com

Terra Flora
GARDENS, PLANTS & FLOWERS:
Best corporate floral program

Douglas Long, owner of the remarkable Terra Flora in Denver, offers an incredible selection of fresh cut flowers that can be creatively designed into original arrangements for your home or office. This popular, full-service florist offers a spectacular array of roses, tropical flowers and plants and is also an FTD retailer, which assures quality, freshness and shipping services. Terra Flora can provide traditional or contemporary styling, plus a selection of gifts and gift baskets, including numerous items ideal for the corporate environment. Doug and his staff know how to turn your sentiments into heartfelt floral expressions, suitable for such occasions as anniversaries, birthdays and holidays. Terra Flora also makes bereavement displays, thank you bouquets and get-well baskets. Additionally, Terra Flora has a terrific corporate program that allows you to add your corporate logo, business card or promotional material to a floral design prior to delivery, a way to create both exposure and goodwill for your company. Terra Flora can further arrange to deliver an exciting new floral design to your office each week, an ideal solution for high traffic areas like reception desks or waiting rooms. Whether you are planning a gala for 500 or need a romantic bouquet for that special someone, you can find it or have it created just for you at Terra Flora.

5889 E Evans Avenue, Denver CO
(303) 639-6055 or (866) 639-6055
www.terrafloradenver.com

Side Effects Unique Flowers & Gifts
GARDENS, PLANTS & FLOWERS: *Most creative floral arrangements*

For over ten years, the Denver area has been the fortunate home of Tracy Goodman's distinct style and creativity. Side Effects Unique Flowers & Gifts provides custom floral designs for every occasion or event. The friendly, helpful staff at Side Effects can use an extensive variety of cut stems and interesting greenery to create an out-of-the-ordinary bouquet. You can even make your own, if the mood strikes. If you're not sure about what you would like, leave it up to Tracy, head designer and owner, to design your flowers for your special occasion. Her creativity will reward you with memories for life. Side Effects also designs permanent arrangements with silk and dried flowers, as well as gourmet gift baskets. Delivery is available. The store is filled with exceptional gifts, jewelry and home accessories made by Colorado artisans. You will also discover wreaths, wall sconces, cast bronze figurines, potted plants, candles, soaps, lotions and much more. If you are in need of the best flowers in town or the perfect gift, visit Side Effects Unique Flowers & Gifts on South Broadway.

1934 S Broadway, Denver CO
(303) 722-1180 or (800) 756-5635
www.sideeffectsflowers.com

Newberry Brothers Greenhouse & Florist

GARDENS, PLANTS & FLOWERS:
Best wedding florist

In 1947, Weldon Newberry with his brothers bought a greenhouse on Garfield Avenue in Denver and opened the doors to an enterprise that specialized in growing carnations. In the late 1960s, the shop expanded into a retail florist and greenhouse and was dubbed Newberry Brothers Greenhouse and Florists. For decades, the brothers' passion lay in creating magnificent arrangements for weddings. Today this full service florist continues the tradition of fashioning fabulous and always beautiful floral designs for Denver's weddings and most opulent soirées. In 1990, Newberry Brothers Greenhouse and Florists suffered a fire. However, the current owners Paula Newberry Arnold and Elizabeth Newberry turned tragedy into opportunity and upon reopening, the popular florists boasted a whole new and welcoming layout. Now, when patrons enter the shop, they see all of the shop's designers up front creating their floral masterpieces. Newberry Brothers has been the recipient of the *Best Floral Design* award, given by Colorado Expressions Magazine, for the last three years and is considered to be one of Denver's elite florists. When planning your next special event, or when giving the gift of flowers, ensure that your arrangement will be the best by working with Newberry Brothers Greenhouse and Florist, where quality and excellence have been a way of life for more than 50 years.

**201 Garfield Avenue, Denver CO
(303) 322-0443**

Salon Tobie Urban Spa

HEALTH & BEAUTY:
Most innovative treatments

As a fifth generation Denverite with an international education and 23 years in the spa industry, Tobie Rae Snyder understands what her urban customers want from a salon and spa. The staff of licensed professionals at Salon Tobie Urban Spa in Denver offer innovation and customer education in a setting designed to be congenial and community-minded. Expect up-to-date services for all members of the family, which include hair care, skin care, massage therapy, manicures and pedicures, waxing, special occasion 0s and make-up application. The spa also offers Botox and Diamondtome microdermabrasion, which are two of the most popular skin care treatments today. The estheticians provide facials and peels that are designed to meet your unique skin type needs. Salon Tobie offers several lines of professional products that include Bumble and bumble, L'oreal Professional, Dermalogica, YonKa and Pureology. Additionally, one-of-a-kind of pieces of jewelry designed by Tobie are available for sale at the salon. The spa also caters to the growing demand of male services that include brow taming, body waxing, massage therapy and free clean-ups between haircuts. Treat yourself to one of several urban massage treatments including sports massage for easing sore muscles, a hot stone massage to melt away stress, or a classic Swedish massage for tension relief and improved circulation. Tobie's professional staff travels the world for their continuing education and believes that custom prescribing of style and products is necessary to achieve success with each and every client. Tobie and Architect Steve Barsch of Barsch Design designed the three-year-old spa with a focus on the elements of wind, fire, earth, wood and metal. Whether you are visiting, living in, or moving to Denver, visit Salon Tobie Urban Spa where you can expect high standards, education and innovation that all clients deserve. The motto here is "We strive to create service with ease."

200 Quebec Street, 500-115, Denver CO
(303) 577-7777
www.salontobieurbanspa.com

Photos by Amber Proffitt

Renaissance Aveda Spa & Salon

HEALTH & BEAUTY: *Best place to reconnect your mind, body and spirit*

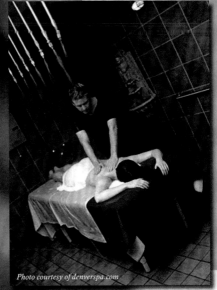

Photo courtesy of denverspa.com

Amidst the hustle and bustle of downtown Denver, Renaissance Aveda Spa & Salon is an oasis of calm. The personal care and attention begins the minute you walk in the door. Located inside Hotel Monaco, Renaissance, the only full-service Aveda spa in downtown Denver, uses and sells plant-based Aveda products to deliver extraordinary skin and body treatments plus total hair care. Hair services include cuts, highlights and updos. Spa services include massages, wraps and facials. In addition, the salon offers waxing, pedicures and manicures. A popular specialty treatment is the Total Body Elixir, which combines hydrotherapy and Ayurvedic massage for an unforgettable experience. The treatment includes seven showerheads aimed at your major chakra points and an application of warm flowers and plants. Owners Sandy Francis and Carrie Perkins are committed to the Aveda concept. Several employees have been with the business since it opened seven years ago, a testament to the positive, healing environment you'll find at Renaissance. Rejuvenate, unwind and reconnect your mind, body and spirit at Renaissance Aveda Spa & Salon.

1717 Champa Street, Denver CO
(303) 308-0524
www.denverspa.com

Roosters
Men's Grooming Center
HEALTH & BEAUTY: *Best men's hair salon*

When it comes to grooming services for men, Jan and Rob Unger can deliver both the look men want in the old-fashioned barbershop atmosphere they enjoy. At Roosters Men's Grooming Center in Denver, Jan and Rob run the business operation while son Adam takes a hands-on role as one of the barbers. "You won't see any of our stylists in lingerie," says Jan, who hires a mix of barbers and cosmetologists so gentlemen can choose services ranging from traditional barber services to modern spa treatments. Haircuts, shaves and massages are popular choices as are manicures, hair coloring and even shoe shines. Roosters is designed to put men at ease while providing all of today's cutting edge, grooming services. It's a popular destination for bridegroom parties prior to weddings. Men will also find quality hair care and shaving products including the American Crew and Nioxin lines. Jan and all her talented stylists are natives of Denver with an understanding of the needs of well-groomed Western gentlemen. Roosters invites gentlemen to enjoy the feel of on old time barbershop without sacrificing today's conveniences.

260 Columbine, Denver CO
(303) 399-5094 *www.roostersmgc.com*

Zen Bath
HEALTH & BEAUTY: *Best tranquility treatments*

Invigorate your senses with a breath of fresh air for your body and mind at Zen Bath. The air just outside is infused with tranquil aromas that gently greet you with a blissful calm. Once you step inside this Asian-inspired center for healing, a member of the skillful team of healing practitioners, whose vitality and synergy is palpable, welcomes you immediately. Zen Bath is nestled in Denver's prosperous Historic Highland Neighborhood. Owner Barbara Lynn Trattle developed the concept of the spa but its true success comes from the guidance and inspiration of her late husband. His spirit and soul are woven into the very fabric of Zen Bath. Like her late husband, Barbara and her staff believe that, "Your mind is not in your body; your body is in your mind." They concentrate on healing and focusing positive energy to instill changes on the inside of a person rather than simply offering cosmetic changes. You can indulge yourself with a variety of services such as a Swedish or Thai massage, Thai Reflexology, or a Prenatal Massage. Christine-Q-Nguyen specializes in acupuncture, the Chinese Herb Clinic, and CranioSacral and Visceral Manipulation Therapy. You'll also find a unique collection of bath accessories to assist with tension relief. Next time you're in Denver, take a break and come to Zen Bath to calm your mind and balance your spirit for this is "The Art of the Bath, and Beyond."

3210 Meade Street, Denver CO
(303) 403-1000

Sattva Spa
HEALTH & BEAUTY:
Best ancient healing treatments

Ayurveda is a wise and ancient body of knowledge for life that incorporates mind, body and spirit. Sattva Spa in Denver is an Ayurvedic Yoga Spa that blends this ancient philosophy into its treatments, fusing them with new modern theories and resulting in an eclectic, healing experience that Owner Keith Loop calls the Transformation Industry. Loop is an Ayurvedic Practitioner who combines his passion for healthy, spiritual living with his career. The goal of the treatments offered at the spa is to change people's life in a positive way. Aided by Healing Coordinator Michelle Colarelli, the spa has established a comprehensive system of healing comprised of many components including diet, yoga, lifestyle counseling, herbal therapies and massage. Personally customized packages help you to attain balance in spiritual and physical as well as the emotional aspects of your experiential life. A luscious variety of treatments are separated into three categories: ancient treatments, elemental energy and massage. The elemental energy treatments offer healing sessions such as the reiki & chakra attunement or reflexology. Ancient body treatments include the detoxifying abhyanga, a body massage using warm herbal medicinal oils, and swedana, a whole-body herbal or eucalyptus steam treatment that comes with a bonus scalp, hand and foot massage. The shirodhara involves a steady stream of warm, herbal-infused oil applied over the third eye and across the forehead. Treatments aimed to detoxify, energize, relax or reduce stress can also be purchased for others in the form of gift certificates. You are encouraged to enhance your life at Sattva Spa.

1045 Acoma Street, Denver CO
(303) 825-8600
www.sattvaspa.com

Ancient Wisdom Medicine
HEALTH & BEAUTY: *Best Medical Qigong clinic*

While many in the Western world know a little about the ancient practice of Acupuncture, knowledge about the related field of Medical Qigong is a somewhat more recent addition to the scene. Traditional Medical Qigong is the form of Chinese Medicine developed over twenty-five centuries ago by ancient physicians and has been referred to as the Fountain of Youth and Secret of Immortality by those who practice its arts. The search for this powerful alternative to standard medical options is a very personal quest for married owners Tanya Mei-Tai Coon and David J. Coon, both of whom experienced extensive problems with physical pain in their own lives before learning about other possible solutions in the oriental healing arts. Tanya is known for her very gentle and effective acupuncture technique. She specializes in a wide range of pain-related issues including digestive problems, weight support, women's concerns, headaches and migraines, and also provides assistance related to emotional issues. David has been practicing Medical Qigong and Martial Arts for over twenty years and uses his background and experience to provide results in a wide-range of medical maladies. Give them a call to find out what they can do to help you and to learn more about the ancient art of healing that has become known as the "Great Grandfather of Acupuncture."

700 E 9th Avenue, Suite 105, Denver CO
(303) 233-3103 *www.ancientwisdommedicine.com*

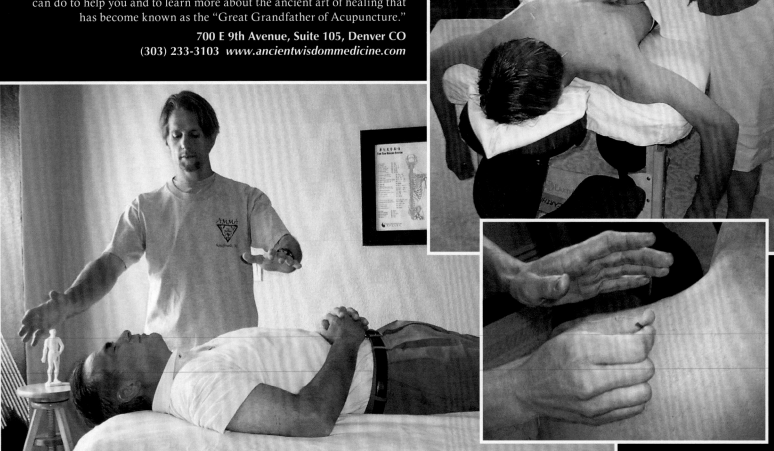

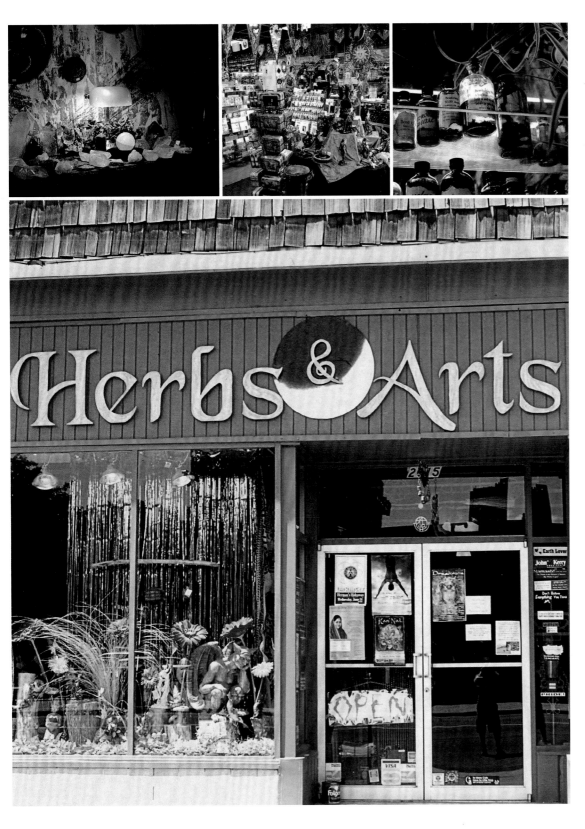

Herbs & Arts, A Metaphysical Shoppe

HEALTH & BEAUTY:
Best metaphysical supply store

The owners of Herbs & Arts on Denver's Colfax Avenue aren't trying to talk anyone into anything, except maybe the connections we all share. Their world view is broad and nature-based. Their products appeal to customers seeking spiritual growth and an ancient and magickal connection with the natural world. Magickal isn't a misspelling; it's the way John Kulsar and Kaewyn Picard (as well as Pagans or Wiccans) spell the term, to differentiate it from garden variety stage magic. On the earthy side of their enterprise is a huge selection of herbs and oils. Look for essential oils that promote physical and emotional wellbeing and hand-blended fragrance oils, good for everything from perfume and massage to blessings and transformation. This tranquil shop also carries incense, candles and tarot cards. It sparkles with crystals, jewelry and statuary and invites you to explore further with numerous books and musical CDs. Kaewyn started as an employee at Herbs & Arts and eventually bought the store with John, who has a degree in counseling and keeps a part-time practice. John and Kaewyn both agree that the shop would not be complete without the added expertise of Store Manager Bo Coyote and Madhbh, their Goddess of mixing. Next time you are looking for connection to the earth or the spirit, visit Herbs and Arts, A Metaphysical Shoppe for a spiritual vibe and the great products that attest to the connections between people.

2015 E Colfax Avenue, Denver CO
(303) 388-2544
www.herbsandarts.net

Shapes Salon & Studio

HEALTH & BEAUTY:
Best classic salon services

Shapes Salon and Studio is dedicated to helping you look and feel your best. This distinguished salon is located just west of downtown on upper 15th Street and has been a part of this up and coming neighborhood for six years. Shapes is a full service salon, offering a range of classic salon services, including color treatments, Great Length hair extensions, permanent waves, skin care and waxing, and nail services. Steve and Richelle Gonzales, owners and Colorado natives, have created a relaxed and comfortable salon ambience where every client is treated to a full-service experience. Richelle has been in the salon industry for 18 years and is dedicated to continuing education in the field for both herself and the salon's stylists and technicians. Richelle is a regional educator for Schwarzkopf color and trains all of the stylists on the latest color techniques. Stylists at Shapes also attend continuing education at Bumble and bumble University and Devachan (home of Deva Concepts for curly hair) in New York City. In addition to its exceptional services, Shapes also carries a terrific selection of products, featuring Bumble & bumble, a full line of Deva products including DevaCurl, DevaCare, and DevaColor, and two skin care lines, Astara and Intaglio. The stylists at Shapes are dedicated to ensuring that their clients enjoy the salon experience each and every time. At Shapes, the stylist's utmost goal is to utilize their continued education as the ultimate compliment to your service, providing you with the best look possible. Enjoy your ultimate salon experience at Shapes Salon & Studio.

2525 15th Street, Denver CO
(303) 964-8077
www.shapessalonandstudio.com

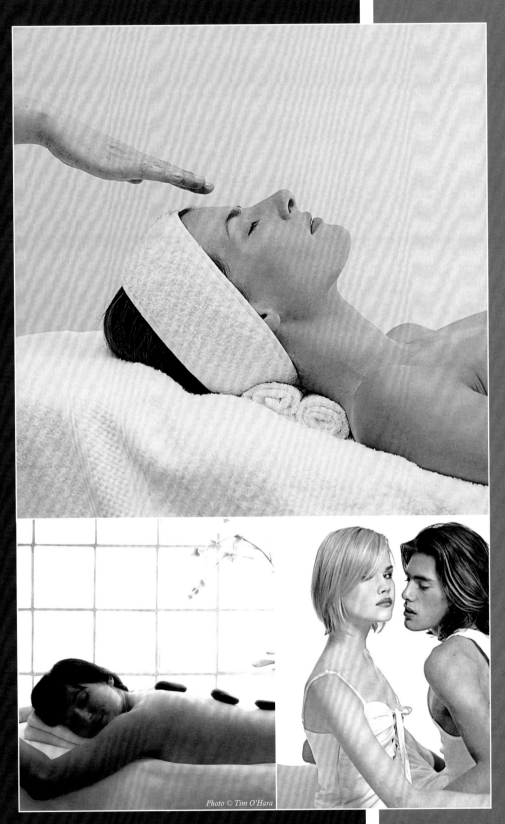

Photo © Tim O'Hara

Zuri Salon and Spa

HEALTH & BEAUTY: *Named a*
Top 30 Cutting Edge Salon by Self *magazine*

As you enter Zuri Salon and Spa in Denver's fashionable Cherry Creek North shopping district, you will notice right away the absence of a reception desk. Instead, the area at the front of the salon has been converted into a Hostess Center. This innovative approach to customer service provides an instant sense of your importance to the salon as you are whisked away by a hostess to begin your day of royal treatment. Zuni caters to your every wish, and that is why it has been named a Top 30 Cutting Edge Salon by *Self* magazine. Owner and master stylist Peter Friedauer began his career in Switzerland, where he developed a commitment to European excellence. Peter's hair designs and drive to be the best have brought national and international attention from such magazines as *Harper's Bizarre*, *Vogue*, *Glamour* and *Mademoiselle*. Zuri treats you to haircutting, styling and color, plus skin treatments, facials and scrubs. Nail care, massage, and wraps are always popular, including everyone's favorite, the Pumpkin Peel Exfoliating Wrap. Zuri's Stay-Spa packages include a blissful day at Zuri Spa, a night at the luxurious Loews Denver Hotel and a sumptuous feast for two at the Tuscany Restaurant. For the ultimate in luxury, consider the Presidential Stay-Spa Package that includes Loews' ultra-luxurious Presidential Suite and a chilled bottle of Cristal Champagne. Make your reservation today and let the pampering begin.

3150 E Third Avenue, Denver CO
(303) 377-3377
www.zurisalonspa.com

Higdon's Hair Studio
HEALTH & BEAUTY: *Best hair artistry salon*

Tracy and her team of stylists at Higdon's Hair Studio want you to enjoy every moment of your hair styling appointment, beginning with the charming atmosphere created by the studio's location in a Victorian home. Tracy attended a beauty school in Boulder, then kept her eye open for a salon of her own where she could provide a warm, comfortable, charming atmosphere and fantastic customer service. The result is Higdon's Hair Studio. Higdon's specializes in color correction, highlights and lowlights to bring out the look you seek. Since their opening two years ago, the professionals at Higdon's have taken the time and energy to build a reputation for consistency, artistry and relaxation that brings customers back time and time again. No wonder the hairdressers and the massage therapists are on a first-name basis with all of their clients. When you leave the salon, you look and feel great. Both men and women enjoy the inspired haircuts and personalized service they receive at Higdon's. The salon's youthful staff has over a decade of experience. If you are ready to be spoiled by your hair salon, visit Higdon's Hair Studio.

2523 16th Street, Denver CO
(303) 455-5208

Blanc the Salon
HEALTH & BEAUTY: *Only salon with an in-house fashion stylist*

The vibe at Blanc the Salon in Denver is trendy, hip and young. Music blasts from speakers around the room, and the environment is electric with creativity. Known as the anti-establishment salon, Blanc delivers looks from chic to trendy for men and women, with the guidance of owner Ty Tomlinson. Ty believes in giving people what they need as opposed to what they want, and by the rave reviews of Blanc clients, Ty is always right. As Ty says, "Constant evolution with your hair leads to constant evolution in your life." Ty graduated in 1999 and began his career by winning Colorado's *Student Hairdresser of the Year* award. He went on to work as the lead colorist and stylist at Raul's Salon in Cherry Creek, where he developed his signature approach to bold, contrasting colors and styles. As his following grew, it became apparent that it was time for Ty to open a salon of his own, so he gathered powerhouse stylists from throughout the Denver area and opened Blanc. Beyond haircuts, color and perms, this full-service salon offers such services as facial waxing and manicures. Make-up application and eyelash extension are also popular. Andrea Tucker, the salon's manager, has a background in apparel and wardrobe design. Her talents complement Ty's perfectly, and Blanc is the only salon in Denver with an in-house fashion stylist. Call today for your appointment at Blanc the Salon, and let Ty and his style team create a new look for you.

1133 Bannock Street, Denver CO
(303) 572-1133

Oxford Club Spa

HEALTH & BEAUTY:
Best fitness salon

Located in the heart of the historic LoDo district in downtown Denver, the Oxford Club has been offering a full range of spa, salon and fitness services to its clientele since opening in 1987. As the first and largest day spa in the city, the Oxford Club has made a name for itself by providing exceptional, leading edge services. All employees go through a rigorous training program to assure that service is top-notch. In addition, staff go out of their way to customize treatments to meet individual requests whenever possible. Services include skin care, massage, signature body treatments, hair care, nail treatments and yoga. For those special occasions, the Oxford club will help you leave an impression with updos and event makeup. The spa can accommodate groups of up to 50 and has six massage rooms, four manicure stations, four pedicure stations and three skin care rooms. In addition to spa treatments, the Oxford Club offers a complimentary fitness center to its spa guests. The variety of services under one roof makes the Oxford Club a convenient place to refresh your look and relax your body and mind, so they invite you to step away from your busy schedule and step into the Oxford Club.

1616 17th Street, Denver CO
(303) 628-5435
www.oxfordclubspa.com

Metafolics

HEALTH & BEAUTY: *Best educational and fun hair salon*

Many of today's high-end salons have gained a reputation for pretentiousness that makes some people feel as if they need to be immaculately groomed and coiffed just to walk through the door. Jason Linkow, owner of Metafolics, is changing all of that. Jason began his career as a simple hairdresser with the dream of one day owning his own business. During his career, he has worked for some well known performers such as Naomi Judd while sharpening his skills for the day that he could make his dream come true. In 2000, his hard work and dedication to the industry paid off and he opened the doors on his own, high-end yet unpretentious, full service salon. Metafolics offers clients all of the same services and exceptional products that one would expect to find at a haute couture salon, but without the attitude. At Metafolics, you can relax and be yourself while being properly pampered and having your hair cut, styled or colored. The exceptional staff at Metafolics can also provide excellent perm treatments and they are happy to offer great customer education on the proper care and treatment of your hair type. Additionally, Metafolics is the site of numerous educational workshops throughout the year, and they are highly active in the community. Return to a time when going to the beauty salon was a fun and thoroughly enjoyable part of your week with a trip to Metafolics on Bannock Street.

1070 Bannock Street, Denver CO
(303) 623-9181

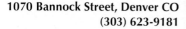

Vitahl Medical Rejuvenation Spa

HEALTH & BEAUTY: *Best skin rejuvenation spa*

Vitahl Medical Rejuvenation Spa passes on the expertise of modern medicine to its clients with a full selection of treatments designed to keep you both beautiful and healthy. This distinctive Denver spa, owned by Dr. Tahl Humes and managed by Molly Haggerty, brings out your vitality with age-defying non-surgical cosmetic procedures. Customized facials include special treatments for men and for people with acne. The spa offers many kinds of massages, including hot stone and reflexology. Clients also benefit from lymphatic drainage, skin peels and waxing services. Vitahl Medical Rejuvenation Spa is the place to turn for laser techniques that remove hair, rejuvenate skin and hide unsightly veins. Microdermabrasion softens and smooths the face, while IPL photo rejuvenation treats pigmented lesions. Staff physicians perform Botox and Restylane injections. They also are available for free consultations regarding your skin care needs. Vitahl Medical Rejuvenation Spa hosts several education events per year, so that clients understand the best methods of treatment for various skin conditions. You can be confident you are choosing healthy, medically safe procedures for your skin at Vitahl: an Urban Sanctuary for Beauty, Health and Wellness. Visit Vitahl Medical Rejuvenation Spa to find a partner for the lifelong care of your skin.

251 Steele Street, Denver CO
(303) 388-7380 *www.vitahl.com*

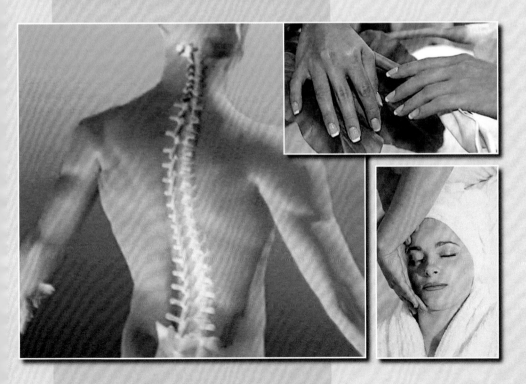

Body Massage Center
HEALTH & BEAUTY:
Best therapeutic massage

When Peggy Irvin dreamed of starting her own business, she envisioned a relaxing place where clients could come for the best in medical massage therapy and a pampering spa experience. In 1986, she opened the Body Massage Center Wellness Spa in Denver. Named Best of Citysearch in 2005, the center has developed a reputation for excellence by bringing highly trained staff together with cutting edge technology. The staff includes eight massage therapists trained in medical massage such as deep tissue, neuromuscular, and Swedish. Peggy's specialty, the six point therapy, relieves chronic neck and back pain. Therapeutic medical massage can offer clients relief from many conditions, including stress, headaches and sciatic pain. The wellness center uses the energetic medical technology of the Quantum Biofeedback to improve your overall health. This high-tech health device provides a personalized evaluation of your body which assists our biofeedback practitioners in finding energetic imbalances and health issues such as viruses, deficiencies, weaknesses, allergies, abnormalities and food sensitivities. It performs a non-invasive body scan and measures how your body reacts to 9,000 different frequencies. While measuring imbalances, it also acts as a therapeutic tool to bring the body's energy back into balance. A certified nutrition specialist is also able to use the biofeedback results to customize a body balancing plan, including detoxification and body typing, that will help bring you back to optimum wellness. In addition to medical therapies, their relaxing spa services include therapeutic manicures and pedicures, facials, paramedical skin care and spa packages. There are special services just for men as well as top quality products for home use. Come in and unwind at Body Massage Center Wellness Spa.

1616 Welton Street, Denver CO
(303) 893-2543
www.bodymassagecenter.com

Shear Productions Salon and Spa
HEALTH & BEAUTY: *Most time-tested and respected salon*

Personalized attention and client pampering are hallmarks of this full-service salon located on the 16th Street Mall in downtown Denver, and a new location in Lakewood. For more than 28 years, Janet Lombardi and her talented staff, all of whom are passionate about delivering quality service, have catered to the comfort, well-being and personal grooming needs of their clients. The Salon offers an extensive array of personal care services for men and women, including expert color, highlights, cuts, perms, hair extensions, makeup, European facials, paraffin manicures and pedicures and waxing. Their new location offers a full-service salon and a complete Spa with massage, reflexology, specialty body wraps and scrubs and exclusive anti-aging treatments for the face and body. Both locations also have an exclusive wedding package for that special day. The wide selection of retail products assures that you can find the perfect product for your hair, nail and skin care needs. Shear Productions have been recognized through local and national media. The many honors awarded to them include publications in fashion magazines, industry editorials and certifications from American Board of Colorists. They were featured in the *Denver Post's* Million Dollar Salon business section, and filmed when they became the Salon for the nationally televised *Ambush Makeover*. Shear Productions has been in business since 1978, and is one of the most time tested and respected salons in metro Denver. Visit Shear Productions Salon and Spa and receive care that goes beyond the expected.

303 16th Street, #150, Denver CO (303) 592-4247
358 S Teller Street, Lakewood CO (303) 934-5700
www.shearproductionssalonandspa.com

Simply Moore
HEALTH & BEAUTY: *Best one-on-one makeup lessons*

Every woman wants to look her best and Michael Moore, owner and creator of Simply Moore, ensures that all clients do. At Simply Moore Makeup Artistry, Michael Moore and his team of artists give women the opportunity to learn how to apply makeup and help them develop the confidence they need to succeed. During a personal one-on-one makeup lesson, the Simply Moore artists help each woman identify her best features and teach her how to accent them with products best suited for the individual. Simply Moore does not just apply the makeup for you, but teaches the skills needed to duplicate the great results at home. They ensure this by applying one side of your face and letting you do the other side. With no loyalty to any product line, you receive recommendations for products to be found in drug stores to department stores. If you have a special event to attend, Simply Moore can do all the work for you, while you sit back, relax and have an artist create the perfect look. The newest addition to Simply Moore is Simply Moore Real Makeup. After nearly 20 years of working in the industry with a variety of clients, including celebrities and designers, Michael found that the missing element in cosmetics was a foundation that matched perfectly to a woman's skin color. He developed a line of all natural, custom blended mineral foundations and concealers. Simply Moore Real Makeup is blended for each person in the Simply Moore Studio so that every woman can have her own formula that matches her skin color, tone and texture. Whether you have a special event coming up or want to update your look, Simply Moore will help you look and feel your best.

3000 E 3rd Avenue, #4, Denver CO
(303) 399-4151
www.simply-moore.com

Salon Posh

HEALTH & BEAUTY:
Best enhancers of natural beauty

Everyone walking out of Salon Posh looks the very best that they can. Salon Posh takes care of hairstyling, makeup, nails and other services. The salon's 12 talented hairstylists take a multi-dimensional approach to hair. They are well-trained and educated in the latest techniques. The four women who own Salon Posh began their careers together in the same salon. They realized that they wanted their own creative freedom and that it was time to take the next step in life. The result is Salon Posh. The salon offers coloring, including highlights. You can get a perm, updo or hair extensions. Salon Posh performs nail treatments and waxing. Gina's Studio, a cosmetics studio within Salon Posh, applies makeup customized to the client and gives lessons in application so that clients can improve their appearance at home. Makeup Artist Gina Comminello says, "Makeup is an accessory, not the main attraction." She knows how to determine an individual cosmetic palette that brings out a woman's natural beauty. Gina's provides eyelash extensions and airbrush makeup, including sunless tanning. Salon Posh specializes in wedding hair and makeup. The salon recommends that brides have a trial run makeover before the wedding. Hair products are the Pureology and Phylologie lines. Gina's Studio has its own g-studio line of cosmetics. Salon Posh has been written up in local and national publications, including the *Denver Post*, the *Rocky Mountain News* and *Allure* magazine. For a personal approach in a comfortable setting, visit Salon Posh.

**300 Fillmore Street, Unit 1A, Denver CO
(303) 333-3750**

Three Cutters on Pearl

HEALTH & BEAUTY:
Named one of the Top Ten Salons by Citysearch

From the moment you walk into Three Cutters on Pearl, a trendy upscale salon, you will know that you are in for a personalized experience. Owner Allisa Cameron created her Aveda Concept salon more than half a decade ago to "put the personal back into personal service." With six stylists and an aesthetician on staff, Three Cutters on Pearl offers a wide variety of services and can accommodate any styling need you might have. Your appointment will begin with a relaxing scalp massage. Then, you will be treated to the work of stylists who know how to create classic cuts and specialize in color correction. They will enhance your look and give you tips on how to maintain your style at home. To make sure your skin is healthy and glowing, Three Cutters offers a full menu of skin care options, too. For those who come by frequently, Three Cutters on Pearl has created the Pure Privilege Program, when the card is full you can redeem it for products and services. Many local brides make Three Cutters a stop on their wedding preparation itinerary, taking advantage of the staff's ability to excel at any style challenge. The next time you want a new look or want to add some panache to your current one, drop by Three Cutters on Pearl.

485 S Pearl Street, Denver CO
(303) 733-0845
www.threecutters.com

Salon E'Vvero
HEALTH & BEAUTY:
Best designer salon

A full-service designer salon, Salon E'Vvero knows how to keep customers happy, with impeccable services and highly-trained stylists who can assist in choosing cuts that flatter the features of individual men, women and children. The salon also offers romantic updos for the formal occasions in your life. Salon E'Vvero attends to your skin with the same royal treatment it gives your hair. An E'Vvero facial starts with an analysis of your skin care needs, followed by appropriate cleansing, exfoliation and gentle steam. Your treatment finishes with a relaxing massage and therapeutic mask. Experienced personnel also offer Botox treatments and permanent makeup. Salon E'Vvero's retail section brims with salon-quality products to use at home, including such lines as L'Oréal Seérie Expert, PureOlogy and Nioxin. Owner Lana Rozendorf wants you to feel comfortable, look fantastic and leave with confidence, and that is just what will happen following a visit to Salon E'Vvero.

5075 Leetsdale Drive, Denver CO
(720) 941-9800

Babooshka

HEALTH & BEAUTY: *Best personalized cuts*

Camila "Cue" Perez enjoys being an active member of her community and working with others to improve their common area. A native of New York, Camila is fusing the gap of community, culture and hair. Camila brings her unique style to Denver where she opened the doors of her hip salon, Babooshka, almost seven years ago. Colorfully decorated, Babooshka is a hair salon and art gallery showcasing a different regional artist every two months. Babooshka offers men's and women's cuts and colors as well as perms, relaxers and waxing. Happy customers rave that the stylist are friendly, creative and talented. With reviews like that, it is easy to see why Redkin hair products names Babooshka one of the cities top hair salons and *Westword* calls it the Best Hair Salon and the Best Multimedia Salon. Babooshka is a place people always feel they belong. So, no matter what your style, visit Babooshka for a personalized cut and style, changing artwork, community and culture.

**3225 E Colfax Avenue, Denver CO
(303) 991-2850**

Glō

HEALTH & BEAUTY: *Best products and services for glowing skin*

Many people will go a long way to find products and services that leave skin glowing with health and beauty. In Denver, Glō brings you this longed-for effect with spa treatments and products you can take home to continue the glow. This specialty retailer carries hard-to-find skin and hair care products, cosmetics and fragrances. Glō General Manager Jennifer Reid and her staff keep their discerning clientele happy with superior services performed in a relaxed and comfortable atmosphere. The body treatments at Glō feature organic and skin-friendly products, like those found in the Coconut Sumatra massage. The Diamond Glō facial combines a hand-applied treatment with a full microdermabrasion for a smooth and youthful complexion. Peels, manicures and pedicures are some of the popular choices here. Customers appreciate the extensive sampling that accompanies browsing through the upscale lines of cosmetics, including Glō's own signature product line. Cosmetics by Glō minerals combine pharmaceutical-grade ingredients with high-pigment minerals and the power of antioxidants. You will find the very latest trends in nail and lip color, so new they change with the seasons. Glō also carries shampoos and gels, candles and home spa products. Finding the right products to bring out your coloring and protect delicate skin can be challenging. Glō takes the frustration out of the process with expert in-depth skin consultations. Put a glow in your complexion with a visit to Glō.

**180 Steele Street, Denver CO
(303) 322-1090** *www.gloskincare.com*

Berenice's

HEALTH & BEAUTY:
Recipient of Top of the Rocky award by Rocky Mountain News

According to the four delightful owners of Berenice's, the Denver area's newest destination salon, this welcoming retreat is dedicated to the spirit, which according to legend, resides in the hair. Legend has it that Egypt's Queen Berenice, wife to King Ptolemy who ruled circa 250 BC, sacrificed her glorious amber tresses and placed them in Aphrodite's temple as she had vowed to do should her husband be victorious in battle. The hair mysteriously vanished only to reappear, according to Ptolemy's astronomer, in the heavens as a group of stars near Leo's tail. You too can feel like a star with the wonderful services awaiting you at Berenice's. This classic salon offers a relaxing setting in which to enjoy a day of pampering from head to toe. Let Berenice's award winning team of professionals ease away your worries and care as they perform soothing conditioning treatments, manicures and pedicures. The salon also offers full hair care services, including all over color treatments, cuts, permanents and hair relaxers, as well as eyebrow care, cosmetics application and waxing. *Rocky Mountain News* gave the salon its 2005 and 2006 Top of the Rocky award, and several of Berenice's staff members serve as guest writers for *5280 Magazine*. The salon further offers a wide range of packages and party specials that are ideal for weddings and other special occasions. Be one with your inner beauty and join your place in the stars with a visit to Berenice's.

**3500 E 12th Avenue, Denver CO
(303) 399-9156**

Statice Salon & Spa
HEALTH & BEAUTY: *Best custom packages*

Statice Salon & Spa promises to help you look and feel fabulous and have a good time in the process. In fact, customers have such a good time they come and hang out even when they are not scheduled for an appointment. Owners Jessica and Jennifer Satterfield create a little bit of heaven for their customers, a warm and personal environment with attentive customer service that entices customers to return many times. And customers do return—for hot rock massages and other body treatments, for hair design and custom facials, for manicures and pedicures. Some take advantage of the 10 percent discount offered on custom packages of three or more services. Some really pamper themselves by purchasing spa packages with names like A Day of Beauty or True Bliss. Additional services include waxing treatments, eye zone wraps, microdermabrasion and cosmetics applications. Six stylists are prepared to fulfill your hair fantasies, whether you need an updo for a special occasion or a wave, color and cut. About 20 wedding parties per year come to Statice to put the finishing touches on their looks. When you are ready to refresh your look and feel your best, visit the specialists at Statice Salon & Spa.

1512 Larimer Street, Suite R-10, Denver CO
(303) 825-2424
www.staticesalonanddayspa.com

One Stop Body Shop
HEALTH & BEAUTY: *Four great services in one simple location*

Head to Denver's One Stop Body Shop for a full spectrum of luxurious spa and personal care treatments that will leave you feeling delightfully relaxed and brimming with renewed vitality. Massage Therapist Amy Geiger opened One Stop in 2005 to indulge weary bodies with four service centers in one location. The centers specialize in massage, skin care, nail care and hair styling. Amy is a 2002 graduate of the Center of Advanced Therapeutics, where she received 600 hours of training in soft tissues and studied medically based massage techniques. At Heavenly Touch, One Stop's massage center, you can experience deep tissue, neuromuscular or Swedish massages as well as hot stone, Reflexology or Raindrop therapy. The African Safari private sauna room adds still another dimension to your care. At One Stop's Sontuosa, Kimberly Harrington gives skin her complete attention with lavish treatments, such as a comprehensive 80-minute facial or a 55-minute acne facial. At Ou La La! Nails, Jenna Fox will help you sit back and enjoy a perfect manicure, pedicure or paraffin dip, or try stylish nail enhancements. Finish your One Stop Body Shop experience at Hair Extraordinaire, where stylist Mark Mawer specializes in inventive haircuts for men, women and children, along with stunning color treatments and highlights. Treat yourself and your body to the ultimate spa experience at One Stop Body Shop, where reservations are appreciated but not required.

2554 S Broadway, Denver CO
(720) 274-1359
www.bodyshopdenver.com

Ageless Art Oriental Medicine

HEALTH & BEAUTY: *Best non-invasive healing techniques*

Three thousand years ago, the goals of ancient Chinese physicians were prevention of disease and support for a long and healthy life, using the Law of Least Action, the least invasive methods that would nudge the body, mind and spirit into self-healing. At Ageless Oriental Medicine in Denver, that is still the goal. Founder Bob Tank Jr. became aware of the art of ancient Chinese medicine after becoming a Tai Chi instructor. He attended the Colorado School of Traditional Chinese Medicine, and in 1999, he opened the doors to his clinic. Bob uses acupuncture, Chinese medicine, herbal remedies and counseling to treat such disorders as back pain, depression, anxiety, allergies and joint pain. Many ailments can be treated using these methods, and results are usually seen within six sessions. Western medicine and Chinese medicine approach disease in fundamentally different ways. Western medicine focuses on external causes for disease, which it then isolates with tests and attempts to cure with drugs or surgery. On the other hand, Chinese medicine takes into account the symptoms, age, lifestyle habits, physical and emotional traits of a person, putting together a picture of the patient as a whole. Next, using traditional Chinese methods, the practitioner formulates a plan to bring the individual to greater whole-body health. At Ageless Art Oriental Medicine, the staff provides medical services that are safe, effective, comfortable and reasonably priced. Call today to set up your appointment.

1060 Bannock Street, Denver CO
(702) 904-0937
www.agelessarts.com

Jon 'Ric International Salon & Day Spa

HEALTH & BEAUTY:

Best state-of-the-art equipment from Amsterdam

Located on the 16th Street Mall, in the heart of Downtown Denver, Jon 'Ric International Salon & Day Spa is an upscale location providing a wide array of services. They offer L'Oréal Serie Expert, which is available only in select salons across the country. Jon 'Ric International can accommodate your requests, whether you're looking for an express lunch service, a full spa day, or a complete makeover. Relax as you experience tranquility, reflect upon your true essence, and renew your vitality. The staff at Jon 'Ric International works to maximize the qualities that comprise the essential you. The spa décor exudes beauty and comfort from the soothing fountains and the gallery of art by regional artists. The talented stylists and therapists offer an impressive list of services, using state-of-the-art equipment from Amsterdam. Every part of your being can be nurtured with a full range of massage and body care treatments, facials, manicures, pedicures, detox treatments, waxing and, of course, the finest hair styling available. The list of massage services reads like a syllabus from a healing arts academy, with offerings that include pre-natal massage, reiki, Swedish and hot stone. All body care treatments are accompanied by an all-over hydromassage using their Thermal M Hydrotone Bed, which combines steam, aromatherapy and Vichy shower functions to detoxify and revive your body. Numerous packages are available, and if you happen to be staying at The Westin Hotel, their spa services can be billed to your room. Book an appointment at Jon 'Ric International Salon & Day Spa for the best care your body has ever received.

1201 16th Street, Suite 216, Denver CO (Tabor Center) (303) 972-1112
www.jonricdenver.com

Jua Salon
HEALTH & BEAUTY:
Best professional color consultations

We could put a bowl over our heads and cut our own hair, then follow the haircut with a home-crafted dye experience, but we would be a mess. We need the experts at Jua Salon to help us look our best. Jua's General Manager Kerri Massey and her Assistant Manager Kristen Quoy have gone to extraordinary measures to create a professional full-service salon. All of Jua's hairstylists, nail technicians and estheticians receive ongoing training in the technical aspects of the business as well as in the latest trends. They can bring extra body to your locks with the most current permanent techniques or perform exotic Japanese thermal straightening. Coloring hair is an art, and Jua's staff specializes in professional color consultations that deliver the look you desire. Kerri and Kristen, along with the owners and stylists, have carefully selected high quality product lines that include Bumble and bumble, Osis, Kerastase, Pureology and Redken. Jua sports the powerful symbol of the lotus for a logo, a plant touted in myth to cause dreamy contentment. From the tranquil shampoo room to the comfortable processing lounge, Jua is certain to bring you contentment by indulging your senses with expert pampering. Give up that bowl cut and the stress of trying to *do* your own hairdo, and visit Jua Salon, where stylists will create a special look just for you.

3030 E 2nd Avenue, Denver CO
(303) 320-4323

Venus Salon & Spa
HEALTH & BEAUTY:
Most laid-back atmosphere and friendly service

Whether you come to Venus Salon & Spa for a stylish cut, pampering spa treatment or relaxing massage, the laid-back atmosphere and friendly service are sure to bring a smile to your face. Owner Jamie Herberts and her professional stylists meet all of your hair care needs. Come in for a quick trim or get a complete style makeover. The salon offers highlights, color retouching and extensions. For those special occasions when you really want to shine, come in for a dramatic updo. Estheticians provide a range of skin care procedures to meet your needs. The PeptiDerm anti-aging facial reduces the appearance of wrinkles without the need for prescription products. Aromatherapy facials offer deep pore cleaning and relaxation, and chemical peels reduce fine lines while encouraging skin to produce collagen at a faster rate. Talented massage therapists offer a choice of Swedish, hot stone and sport massages to ease tension away. If your chakras feel blocked, energy balancing allows them to flow freely, creating a greater sense of overall well-being. Pamper your hands and feet with the French polish manicure and a relaxing pedicure. Call today to make an appointment with one of the upbeat professionals at Venus Salon & Spa in Cherry Creek North.

320 St. Paul Street, Denver CO
(303) 320-3808

Revive Spa

HEALTH & BEAUTY: *Best value for your beauty dollars*

Satisfied customers call Revive Spa a results-oriented urban spa where they can escape the bustle of the city while still being in the middle of it all. Owners Nicole Kerchmar and Jesse Shearman with their professional staff offer a wide range of skin care, massage, body treatments and facial options. The skin care program fuses advanced clinical approaches with holistic healing and a caring touch. Revive also

offers microdermabrasion to rejuvenate the surface of your skin and reduce fine lines or acne scars. Their signature Revive Facial includes a careful analysis of your skin type and personal concerns, and then uses a combination of cleansing and moisturizing with pure ingredients designed to leave your skin replenished and hydrated. Revive has been honored by Citysearch as Best of 2006 for their hair removal and sunless tanning. Waxing, eyelash tinting, makeup application, manicures and pedicures are also available. The body therapies are remedy-focused, which promotes healing while enhancing overall well-being. They also offer body scrubs, wraps, massage and reflexology. The popular hot stone massage uses basalt lava stones to apply deep heat therapy to any massage. Escape to the urban oasis of Revive Spa and experience a serene atmosphere with rejuvenating spa treatments.

500 E 19th Avenue, Denver CO
(303) 284-2550
www.revivespadenver.com

Colorado Athletic Club Downtown

HEALTH & BEAUTY:
Denver's premier fitness club

The full-service amenities and friendly atmosphere at Colorado Athletic Club Downtown will have you looking forward to working out every day. The immaculate fitness club, serving customers since 1978, offers a variety of ways to improve your health in a convenient downtown location that makes it easy to sneak in exercise during a lunch hour or after work. Certified personal trainers can work one-on-one with you to reach your goals, whether they include weight loss, increasing muscle or simply having more energy for daily tasks. With an indoor track, cycling studio, racquetball courts and a full range of strength training equipment, you are sure to discover a regimen that suits you. If you enjoy the camaraderie of working out with others, choose from one of the 70 weekly group exercise classes, ranging from hatha yoga to Super Sculpt. After an invigorating workout, relax your muscles in the sauna or whirlpool, or indulge in a massage by one of the four massage therapists. The club holds several social events for members each month, creating a seamless combination of fun and health. Come to the upscale Colorado Athletic Club Downtown and have a blast working your way to a stronger self.

1630 Welton Street, Denver CO
(303) 607-3306
www.coloradoac.com

The Purple Flower

HEALTH & BEAUTY:
Best therapeutic and hot stone massage

The Purple Flower is a private, client-centered skin care and massage studio. Owner Christy Malles, who provides all services, is a licensed skin care therapist and nationally certified massage therapist. Christy makes it a point to listen to her clients and designs the treatments to meet their individual needs. Her clients are uniformly enthusiastic about her calm spirit and professional approach. Christy's therapeutic and hot stone massages have earned a following and notice from Citysearch, where she was voted one of the best massage therapists in Denver. The Purple Flower was featured in Madison and Mulholland's exclusive Ultimate TV Nominee Gift Bag for the 2006 Emmys. A Purple Flower specialty is eyelash extensions. Only a select number of salons and spas in the area offer this service. Eyelash extensions make mascara unnecessary and are perfect for weddings, proms, the beach and everyday wear. Christy is unusually skillful at waxing and her clients rave about her gentle technique. The Purple Flower also offers face and body treatments that can be fully customized. For skin care, Christy recommends Dermalogica products for their proven results. For truly personal service that will balance your body, mind and spirit, come to The Purple Flower.

1115 Broadway, #205, Denver CO
(303) 300-5244
www.purpleflowerspa.com

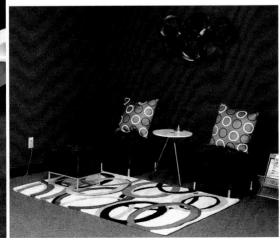

El Salon

HEALTH & BEAUTY: *Best creative-fashion haircuts*

Steven Trujillo takes his job seriously, and perhaps that's why
he's on the cutting edge in the hair industry. Clients who
come in to get their hair done at El Salon receive Steven's
trademark dry cut with blow dry technique. With more than
25 years experience, Steven knows what works, and what
works is looking at hair as a creative fashion expression.
That creative expression begins with the bold interior design
that greets customers here and continues with individualized
services, including expert cuts and styling for men and
women. Changing trends find more men who are willing to
pamper themselves, and El Salon encourages pampering. At
El Salon, multiple stylists, rather than one stylist, contribute
to your look for a team effort that's visible in the final results.
El Salon seeks to make you comfortable during your visit
as well as stylish when you leave. The festive buzz here
contributes to an upbeat and friendly atmosphere. The salon
specializes in wedding and bridal parties, Japanese thermal
straightening, color, cuts and extensions. In addition to hair
care, try the relaxing European facials. Visit El Salon, and
let Steven and his skilled staff work together to bring out the
best in you and your hair.

265 Detroit Street, Denver CO
(303) 399-7175

Salon in the Beauvallon
HEALTH & BEAUTY:
Best styling services

At the Salon in the Beauvallon, stylists believe that the client comes first. The professional staff members listen to your needs, and then give you a cut, color and style to suit your lifestyle. Owner Joyce Werth opened the salon three years ago inside the ultra-hip building, Beauvallon, in the section known by locals as the twin towers. Here, you can choose from a full range of styling options, including highlights, perms and extensions. Wedding services include romantic updos and professional makeup application, to ensure that you look absolutely picture-perfect on your special day. The salon offers only the highest quality professional products, for example the René Furterer Paris line, which can be matched to each user to create healthy hair from the scalp outward. Before heading back out into the world, relax with spa treatments such as the seaweed and mud masks, salt rubs or facials. The salon, always up-to-date on the latest services, offers treatments to improve the look and feel of your skin and increase collagen production. Tanning beds give you a warm glow in just a few short sessions, or you can opt for a sunless spray tan. Manicures and pedicures complete the package, making you look great from head to toe. Come to the Salon in the Beauvallon, for cutting-edge spa and salon treatments and old-fashioned service.

975 Lincoln Street, Suite K, Denver CO
(720) 377-0126

Samadhi Center for Yoga
HEALTH & BEAUTY: *Best yoga instruction*

Samadhi Center for Yoga for the mind, body and soul is anything but a commercialized workout regimen. Owner Anna Freedom was so deeply moved from her first yoga class that she instantly knew opening up a studio was her calling in life. In March of 2002, her dream of sharing the bliss she discovered became a reality. Named after the final stage of yoga meditation, Samadhi is a pressure-free palace of peaceful instruction. The colorful Hindi lanterns and fabrics hanging from the ceiling, breathtaking murals on the walls and open hardwood floor make this an inviting indoor environment to study in. From those who want to learn the foundational elements to those with regular asana practice, there are three levels of classes and dozens of teachers to keep you focused. In addition, Samadhi also offers a Yoga Teacher Training program for those who want to teach others. Samadhi has won awards including Best of Denver from *Westword* in 2003, CitySearch in 2006 and *5280* magazine in 2006. An attached boutique sells books, CDs, video, clothing, artwork and other related materials. The combined aesthetics and attitude have earned Samadhi a Best of Denver award in 2003. Learn to redirect your flow while attaining absolute nirvana at Samadhi Center for Yoga.

639 E 19th Avenue, Denver CO (303) 860-YOGA (9642) *www.samadhiyoga.net*

Grand Salon

HEALTH & BEAUTY:
Best combination of rejuvenation and art

For centuries, the most highly regarded artists have immortalized the visage and bodies of beautiful people. It's no surprise then that Grand Salon specializes in maintaining the work of art that is the human body and showcases art as well. Every two months they showcase another local artist. They host an opening reception on the first Friday of each exhibit. This makes Grand Salon a center for rejuvenation as well as a treat for the senses, providing a platform for photographers, artists working in digital collage, and even mosaicists. Owner Shelly Rewinkle embraces the following philosophy: "With dedication to teamwork, continuing education and self fulfillment we will continue to thrive as individuals and as a business." Using products by American Crew, L'Oreal Professionnel, MOP (Modern Organic Products), Osis, and Phytologie, the Grand's Salon team of talented stylists utilize the most current techniques to keep their clients looking and feeling radiant. Their primary goal is the complete satisfaction of their clientele. Offering comprehensive hair, facial and nail care. Shelly, Jessica, Andrea, Rebecca, Lori and Katie will provide anything from highlights to an elegant updo, or even a brow or lash tint. The building that houses the Grand Salon is secure, so the staff reminds clients to use the call box at either entrance (on Wazee or the South Side of the building) to gain entry. Grand Salon provides excellent customer service to people while doing what they love. If you are looking for satisfaction, visit Grand Salon for the latest styles and trends.

1435 Wazee Street #104, Denver CO
(303) 572-1435
www.grand-salon.com

Salon No Dice

HEALTH & BEAUTY:
Best custom and corrective coloring

If you are looking for an upscale yet affordable salon, look no further than Salon No Dice. The stylists at Salon No Dice take pride in providing quality service in a comfortable, hip environment. Specializing in custom and corrective color, they also provide facial waxing and eyelash tinting. Owner Karen Sterling, a 16-year styling veteran, got her start in Los Angeles, California. After working in Denver for almost a decade, she decided to live her dream and open a salon of her own. Karen was followed to Salon No Dice by an impressive clientele of nearly 300 individuals. Whether it is for a special occasion or you just need a cure for the ever frustrating bad hair day, let the skilled hands at Salon No Dice create a modern vision of you.

515 E Bayaud, Denver CO
(303) 778-1088
www.salonnodice.com

Fiore's Bonnie Brae Aveda Concept Salon

HEALTH & BEAUTY: *Best full-service Aveda concept salon*

For 28 years, Philip Fiore has been serving the Bonnie Brae community while doing his best to make its denizens happier with their appearance at his Fiore's Bonnie Brae Aveda Concept Salon. From designer haircuts and shampooing to full color highlighting and color correction, he's helped transform many a local into a better looking version of themselves. After graduating from barber college in 1977, Philip decided to take over a shop from his mentor. After building his reputation and client list for many years, he's now turned this shop from its humble beginnings into a full-service Aveda Concept Salon, without losing its positive, neighborhood feel. The Aveda line offers high-quality hair, skin and color products from a company that is as concerned about improving your appearance as it is the welfare of the environment. At Fiore, Head Stylists Candace Post and Melissa Garrison and the friendly staff will make you feel at ease, offering free beverages and advice whether you've just popped in for a quick clip or are staying for a full clarifying scalp treatment. The salon also offers makeup services from brow and lash tinting to designer makeup lessons. Come into Fiore's Bonnie Brae Aveda Concept Salon and walk out feeling refreshed, reborn and ready for anything.

743 S University Boulevard, Denver CO
(303) 722-3301 or (303) 722-3330
www.fioresalon.com

The Woodhouse Day Spa
HEALTH & BEAUTY: *Best luxury day spa*

Where can you find a lavish robe and comfortable slippers waiting for you? If you guessed luxury day spa you're right. Since 2004, owners Tina Lovelace and Jeff Sporkin have indulged the residents and visitors of Denver with deluxe pampering at the Woodhouse Day Spa. Tina and Jeff had the idea to start up a spa for ten years. Since Denver lacked a luxury spa, they purchased and transformed the historic Merritt House formerly a bed and breakfast into what is now the Woodhouse Day Spa. This truly is as Tina said, "the destination spa that you don't have to drive to" being that it's located right here in Denver. After slipping into a robe and slippers, guests are greeted with wine, mimosa or champagne. A host of relaxing treatments from massage and facials to purification wraps and Egyptian pedicures are offered. Separate men's and ladies' lounge areas ensure exclusive comfort and seclusion. Regardless of your choice of over 70 specialized treatments, your experience here is paramount. Amenities fit for a king and queen treat guests with posh excellence and extravagance not found anywhere else. Isn't it time you were treated like royalty even for a day? Take time for some well deserved pampering at the Woodhouse Day Spa right here in Denver.

941 East 17th Avenue, Denver CO
(303) 813-8488
www.denver.woodhousespas.com

Red's Antique Galleries

HOME: *Best menagerie of interior and exterior furnishings*

Red's Antique Galleries is a veritable treasure chest for the discriminating shopper. This 22,000-square-foot store is an amazing menagerie of interior and exterior furnishings. Since opening in 1993 in Denver, owners Del and Carole Hurd have often heard customers comment that Red's is so much like a museum that they should charge admission. More than 300 bronze sculptures compliment an eclectic line of furniture, along with an array of cast-aluminum outdoor furniture, statuary, fountains, gazebos and even street lights. Red's customers agree that one visit to Red's is never enough. The *Rocky Mountain News* has named Red's Antique Galleries the top antique store for 2006 to 2007. Del and Carole invite you to come to Red's Antique Galleries in Southeast Denver, where you can browse through the most fascinating collection in town.

5797 E Evans Avenue, Denver CO
(303) 753-9187 or (888) 301-8909
www.redsantiques.com

Djuna

HOME: *Best home furnishings and accessories*

Owners Karen and Jeffrey Moore decided it was time to leave behind the world of contemporary art and now welcome you into their world of eclectic home furnishings at Djuna. Family owned and operated, Djuna has been on Detroit Street for nine years providing patrons with a wide array of furniture and antiques. Djuna also offers home accessories such as candles, books and lighting. Jeffrey's past work as a founder of a contemporary art space in San Antonio and Karen's knowledge of antique Spanish colonial and contemporary art still influence their choices when they acquire pieces to feature at Djuna. Their desire to help make their customers' homes more attractive inspires them to travel to various countries in search of new inventory. In addition to assisting you to make your home more attractive, making women beautiful is part of their mission, too. Their boutique selection of distinctive women's fashions, managed by Natalie Ryder, accomplishes this part of their goal. For that worldly-feel in interiors and women's clothing styles, browse the wonders at Djuna.

221 Detroit Street, Denver CO
(303) 355-3500 or
(888) 88DJUNA (883-5862)
www.djuna.com

Urban Lifestyle

HOME: *Best urban home design*

Steven Whitney noticed the lack of an urban home design store in his native city of Denver. Thinking that necessity being the mother of invention, Urban Lifestyle was born. Open since 2003, Urban Lifestyle is a virtual paradise for anyone in search of modern home furnishings, décor and accessories. Steven pays strict attention to every detail. Urban Lifestyle features details to enhance each aspect of the home such as styles for living room, bedroom, bath or even the kitchen. You will find beautiful commission pieces from renowned architects and industrial designers, as well as an extensive modern lighting and rug collection. With everything from wall art and pillows to a phenomenal aromatherapy section, there is something to appeal to all the senses. Visit Urban Design and let them help you create an ambiance of modern elegance in your home.

1720 Wazee, Denver CO
(303) 572-7900
www.shelterurbanlifestyle.com

Crystalier Cherry Creek

HOME: *Best cut crystal*

Walking into Crystalier Cherry Creek is like entering a kaleidoscope of dancing colors. The high quality crystal giftware sparkles under the light, creating a fairyland of visual sensation. The brilliance of the cuts and contrast of color is breathtaking. As a faithful customer, Barbara Pocrass was so enamored of the store that she bought it from the previous owners in 2005. The Czech Republic is renowned for its beautiful Bohemia glass, and Crystalier brings you Caesar Crystal Bohemiae at the most competitive prices of any showroom in the world. The breathtaking cased crystal, referring to clear glass encased by colored glass, comes in several colors. No dyes or paints, just 24 percent leaded crystal, hand-cut and mouth-blown by highly skilled glass designers, make this line a top collectible. Crystalier glimmers with crystal vases, decanters, bowls, and glassware. They also have a large selection of stained glass lamp shades and miscellaneous gift items. Open seven days a week, it's the perfect destination for a special gift or a fine accent in your home. Visit Crystalier for objects of superior cut and design, fit for royal surroundings.

3000 E 3rd Avenue, # 5, Denver CO
(303) 333-3922

Scandinavian Antiques

HOME: *Best antiques from around the world*

Scandinavian Antiques imports fine antique furniture not only from Scandinavian countries, but from all over the world, as well. Pieces may come from France, Russia, Romania, China or anywhere else imaginable. Buyers travel to Europe six to eight times a year to handpick beguiling items and import them directly to the Denver store. Scandinavian Antiques has an especially broad collection of country pine, original painted pieces and distinctive accent pieces. Look also for both leather and upholstered furniture. All furniture is functional and is restored as needed in Scandinavian Antiques' on-site workshop. This gives the store greater control over the restoration process and makes it easier to meet a client's exact needs. Antiques can be custom fit to specific purposes, such as television pullouts or king-sized beds. A helpful sales staff is ready to show you how you can blend your existing furniture, new furniture and antique pieces together to decorate in your particular interior style. Scandinavian Antiques has also developed projects for a variety of commercial clients, including lodges and hotels. Owner Henrik Follin invites you to come to Scandinavian Antiques and wander among 25,000-square-feet of dramatic and one-of-a-kind antiques that will draw you into the past.

1760 S Broadway Street, Denver CO
(303) 722-2541
scandinavianantiques.com

Medicine Wolf Company

HOME:
Best handcrafted furniture

Jon Weekley, owner of Medicine Wolf Company, can tell you the origin of each piece of wood in his handcrafted furniture, because he harvests it all himself. Jon searches out the best standing dead aspen trees in the Colorado National Forests and hauls them back to his workshop. There, he and his staff hand sand every piece to bring out the natural beauty in the logs. They then craft the logs into heirloom-quality furniture. Medicine Wolf's furniture is as much at home in a rustic cabin as it is in a city loft. The Denver showroom features a large furniture selection, including bedroom sets, living room furniture and bookcases. If you prefer, Medicine Wolf Company will make custom furniture to suit your individual needs. Medicine Wolf uses only those products and techniques that will stand the test of time, such as the mortise and tenon joint, used for centuries to join two pieces of wood. Jon's careful attention to detail makes it clear that he takes pride in each creation that comes from his shop. To purchase your own antique-in-the-making, come to the Medicine Wolf Company, just 10 minutes from downtown Denver.

2645 S Santa Fe Drive, Denver CO
(303) 733-2438
www.medicinewolf.com

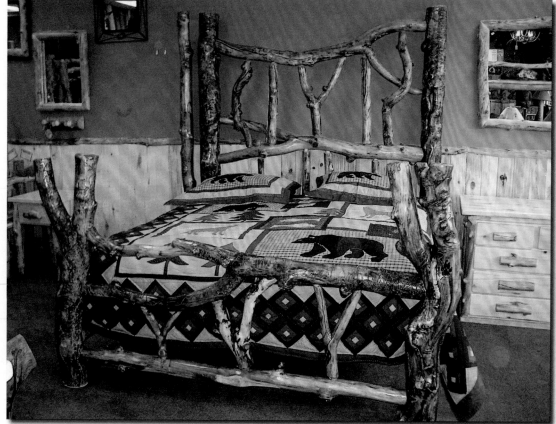

Smart Spaces

HOME:

Best way to organize your space

John MacKenzie and the team at Smart Spaces are experts at making spaces more efficient. With their Murphy and Wall Beds, modular cabinetry options, wide variety of styles and colors, and computer-aided design program, Smart Spaces can show you how to make one room into two rooms. Imagine a home office or a home gym that transforms into a guest room. If your space is limited, Smart Spaces Murphy Beds and Wall Beds can transform one room into two. Smart Spaces carries the largest selection of Murphy and Wall beds in the state. With beds that fold up to reveal a desk, and bookcases that can slide away to reveal a fold-down bed, the options are endless. Once you decide what works best for your needs, Smart Spaces will deliver and install everything. With factory-trained installers, installation usually takes less than a day. They will even follow up with an inspection to make sure everything is working perfectly. When you're ready to make the most out of your space, visit John and the gang at Smart Spaces.

**1295 S Santa Fe Drive, Denver CO
(303) 777-6278 or (877) 557-7223**
www.smartspaces.com

Above the Rim Fine Wines
MARKETS: *Best selection of undiscovered wines*

Above the Rim Fine Wines is an inviting, vibrant gem located in an uptown Denver neighborhood. Don Tubbs and Steve Mohler each had over 20 years of experience with wine when they met. Their goal in opening their shop was to provide stellar service to their clientele. The shop has an ever evolving line-up of over 700 wines from around the world. They focus on undiscovered, superior quality wines at attractive prices and are known for their descriptive write-ups on those wines. Above the Rim's comfortable atmosphere allows patrons to relax and absorb the information Don and Steve can provide about the wines they stock. Their commitment to their customers is reflected in the personal attention they provide and their desire to share their expertise. Unique services offered include party planning, customized tastings on their European style patio, delivery to the area and custom wine of the month clubs.

1936 Pennsylvania Street, Denver CO
(720) 479-9339

Share Colorado
MARKETS: *Best community-minded market*

Have you ever wished for a more cost-effective, community-minded way of buying groceries? Fortunately, there is one, thanks to Share Colorado. This nonprofit grocery cooperative serves Denver's residents with a mantra Dann Aungst, the managing director, calls "good stewards." SHARE is an acronym standing for Self-Help And Resource Exchange. Sponsored by Catholic Charities, non-Catholic volunteers and host sites alike, Share Colorado is a community service providing members of each community access to quality foods at discount prices. With 20 full-time staff members and about 4,000 volunteers, Share Colorado maintains low overhead and substantial savings for each community in which it operates. Dann says, "We are so much more than food." A percentage of each food purchase is utilized by each host site for humanitarian relief in their own local communities. Each food purchaser is not only realizing huge savings in their own household food budget, but also contributing to the feeding of others in their own community. Dann adds, "If we did not have this program, many kids would not be eating fresh vegetables and meat." If you are ready to participate in and benefit from Share Colorado's vision of being good stewards through the simple act of buying groceries, give them a call or pay them a visit.

9360 Federal Boulevard, Denver CO (303) 428-0400 or (800) 933-7427 *www.sharecolorado.com*

St. Kilians Cheese Shop

MARKETS: *Best cheese selection*

Whether your idea of fromage heaven includes a piquant Zamorano, an herbaceous chèvre or a robust cheddar, you can find it all at St. Kilians Cheese Shop. This fabulous shop is owned and operated by Hugh O'Neill and Ionah deFreitas, who opened the store in 2001 after Hugh left the restaurant business so that he could live and work all in one neighborhood. St. Kilians Cheese Shop specializes in European cheeses and raw milk cheeses with over 70 varieties from 10 countries. The shop itself exudes a cozy, European charm and customer service is a focal point for all St. Kilians employees. Here, distinguished cheeses are cut to order from the wheel, a service rarely available at your average grocery or gourmet store. Hugh and Ionah are delighted to help their customers learn more about the textures and tastes of their cheese assortment and equally happy to help you select the ideal cheese to go with a given wine, fruit plate or snack tray. In addition to their extensive array of fine fromage, they stock a terrific assortment of hard-to-find delicacies, such as chutney, salted capers and Old World olive oils. They also offer chorizo, anchovies and, on occasion, delicious homemade soups. Before you pour the wine or light the candles, find your perfect cheese at St. Kilians Cheese Shop, where there's a little taste of paradise waiting in every bite.

3211 Lowell Boulevard, Denver CO (303) 477-0374
www.stkilianscheeseshop.com

Argonaut Wine & Liquor

MARKETS: *Best mix of wine, spirits, tobacco and accessories*

When Owners Hank and Ellen Robinson and Ron Vaughn, of Argonaut Wine and Liquor decided to open their store over 38 years ago, they never dreamed it would become the largest one of its kind in the Denver metropolitan area. Family owned and operated, this treasure is known city-wide for its excellent service, selection and pricing of over 8,000 items including wine, spirits, accessories and tobacco. From the beer geek to the wine connoisseur, Argonaut provides its customers with the professional assistance they deserve and variety of unique products guaranteed to please. Although Argonaut Wine and Liquor has been a celebrated fixture of Denver's downtown community for years, it is has also been awarded the 2005 Reader's Choice title in both *5280* magazine and *The Rocky Mountain News*. A conscientious member of his community, Hank has been actively involved as a board member of the Arapohue House, a drug and alcohol rehabilitation center, plus he's a dynamic participant of both the Denver Lion's Club and Denver Rotary Club. Argonaut even hosts local wine-tasting events whose profits benefit charity. Their online website offers answers to your questions, has weekly specials, reviews and ratings of products and a party planner, as well as drink recipes. Providing efficient on-line ordering and delivery to your door, you will see why Argonaut Wine and Liquor is sure to be your first choice when selecting favorite wines and liquors for your personal enjoyment or as gifts to family, friends and business associates.

718 E Colfax Avenue, Denver CO (303) 831-7788
www.argonautliquor.com

Mondo Vino
MARKETS: *Best hard-to-find wines*

Once the party is planned, the invitations sent and the decorating done, it's time to head to Denver's Mondo Vino for the perfect wine. This highly acclaimed wine and spirits shop offers an extensive selection of fine or hard-to-find wines, beers and spirits from around the world. Owner Duey Kratzer opened Mondo Vino in 1999, and each of his personable staff members are superbly trained and certified sommeliers. Whether you are searching for a tried-and-true favorite or something new and exciting, you are sure to find it at Mondo Vino, where Duey takes pride in stocking the ideal libations to suit every palate and every occasion. The award-winning shop offers wine tasting each Friday and Saturday and a choice of two wine club memberships to satisfy the tastes of its many wine aficionados. Duey and his staff are also happy to help you plan the beverage selections for your next special event and provide delivery within the Denver area. Because Duey believes life is too short to drink bad wine, he offers a liberal return policy. If you open a bottle of wine and find that it doesn't suit, simply recork it and return to Mondo Vino; the staff will attempt to match your palate to a wine that you will enjoy. Find sensational libations, great gifts and terrific service at Mondo Vino, where good taste is sold by the bottle.

3601 W 32nd Avenue, Denver CO (303) 458-3858 *www.mondovino.net*

Corks, The Wine Store

MARKETS:

Best neighborhood wine shop

Picking the right wine has never been easier, less intimidating or more affordable. A great little neighborhood wine shop, Corks is the antithesis of the mega-warehouse and the exact opposite of the stuffy, snobby wine store. Every wine is priced at $15 or less and has been endorsed by professional wine writers from around the world. On any given day, you'll find 250 or more different wines. Selections are always changing—a luxury that comes from having created a proprietary data base of over 70,000 wines. Although the focus is on wine, they are also pleased to offer beer and spirits. Corks's décor is bright and colorful, with wines displayed in simple baskets or bins. Feel free to take a copy of a detailed description, which includes flavors, ratings and food suggestions for every wine. To make choosing even easier, wines are arranged by personality, rather than countries or grapes. Want a light, easy drinking red wine? That's in the sassy section. Something rich and Italian to go with slow-cooked Tuscan lamb and bean stew? Step over to the sensuous cart. In all, nine different personalities, ranging from crisp whites to voluptuous reds, are represented. Corks opened in 2000 and its accolades already include Top of the Rockies, *5280* magazine's Denver's Best Bargains (twice), and *Westword's* Top of the Town. Everyone at Corks knows their stuff, so don't hesitate to ask questions. They also take pride in having enjoyed every bottle they sell—at least twice. No wonder Corks is a destination for both novice and experienced wine lovers.

1620 Platte Street, Denver CO
(303) 477-5799
www.corksonline.com

Divino Wine & Spirits

MARKETS:
Best wine selection by geographic region

If you think wine is just for special occasions, think again. At Divino Wine & Spirits, owner Dave Moore is striving to bring this popular and ancient drink to a younger generation of potential connoisseurs. This contemporary wine seller offers a wide range of wines and liquors from across the globe, majestically arranged in an inviting retail environment. Handcrafted modern racks line the walls and the center corridor, enabling Divino to display bottles by geographic region. At the center of the store, patrons are invited to relax on the sofa while browsing the shop's wine-related reading material or contemplating purchases. All staff members are certified sommeliers with restaurant experience. They are very glad to offer advice on wine and cuisine pairings. The shop has an international selection of more than 750 wines, 60 sparkling wines and 80 dessert wines, along with 450 liquors and 70 beers. As a further treat, Divino offers a special selection of wines for under $10 on a rack near the front of the store, where deals change monthly. Divino Wine & Spirits also houses the largest grappa selection in the state, and every bottle in the shop has been handpicked and tasted to ensure it represents the best of a region or grape varietals. Dave and his staff invite you to come by soon and enjoy the Divino Wine & Spirits experience.

1240 S Broadway, Denver CO
(303) 778-1800
www.divinowine.com

Oliver's Meat & Seafood Market

MARKETS: *Best butcher shop*

Delicious meat and seafood has been the Oliver family's business for more than 80 years at Oliver's Meat & Seafood Market. The Denver butcher shop was opened at its original 6th Street location in 1923 by Ed Oliver. In 1958, current Co-owner Berry Oliver took over the business and in 1988, he was joined by his sons Jim, Rich and Chris. Then, in 2004, Jim's daughter Amanda started working at the store. The store has been at its current location on 6th Avenue since August of 2005, but longtime customers of Oliver's will have no time recognizing the flavor of the delicious dry-aged meats that are hung in-store for up to three weeks, as opposed to the popular quick, wet-aging process so commonly used. This results in a much better-tasting meat. Whether its delicious cuts of steak or sumptuous seafood, you'll find it here, along with a fine selection of Italian meats and cheeses. The Oliver family's decades of experience and the incredible selection of fine meats make Oliver's Meat & Seafood Market a must for the discerning chef.

1718 E 6th Avenue, Denver, CO
(303) 733-4629

Wine Complements

MARKETS: *Best wine accessories*

After almost 20 years of corporate America, it was time for Sheryl Czipott to spread her creative wings. Wine Complements is a fusion of two passions: wine and ambiance. This unique-concept specialty store offers everything wine lovers seek to complement the perfect wine-tasting experience, except the wine. To appeal to all the senses: texture and body are joined by sculptured wine racks, artistic light fixtures and hand-painted bistro tables. The bouquet ranges from soaps (featuring Cabernet Soapignon and Soapignon Blanc) to candles (nutty, fruity, and spice with a hint of vanilla) to gourmet stinky cheeses. As for the discerning palate, you will find Merlot in your vinaigrette, Chardonnay in your Dijon, Cabernet in your Puttanesca, and wait until you see what's in the chocolate sauce. But most importantly, you will find yourself in good company with fellow aficionados and connoisseurs who share a similar flair for taste and passion. Check the website for upcoming, invitation-only special events at Wine Complements including: Chocolate-Tasting, Meet-the-Vintner and Meet-the-Artist.

1620 Platte Street, Suite F, Denver CO (303) 480-WINE (9463)
www.winecomplements.net

Campus Cycles

RECREATION: *Named Top Bike Shop by Rocky Mountain News*

Greg and Mary Seebart and their crew at Campus Cycles love riding bicycles and sharing insights about bicycles, a passion that has been providing pleasure and service to bicycle riders since the Denver shop opened in 1992. The Seebarts started out in the corporate world and the classroom before finding their niche in the bicycle world. Their professional staff takes pride in a store that's large enough to meet all of your cycling needs and small enough to remember your name. Employees at Campus Cycles listen carefully to customers, enjoy their work and stay current on cycling trends and technology. In an effort to cut down on automobile traffic in Denver and provide secure, indoor bicycle parking, Campus Cycles teamed with the nonprofit Transportation Solutions to create an Urban Transportation Center at Cherry Creek North, called the Bike Rack, the first of its kind in Colorado. The Bike Rack provides free bicycle parking, bike repairs, rentals and accessories, including souvenir clothing, energy drinks and snacks. It's also a central place to learn about guided bicycle tours and to pick up maps and bus schedules. It is easy to see why Campus Cycles wins so many accolades. In 2005, *Westword* honored the Bike Rack for its free parking. In 2003, Campus Cycles took the Top of the Rocky award from *Rocky Mountain News* for Top Bike Shop. Greg, Mary and their crew invite you to see what's spinning at Campus Cycles.

2102 S Washington Street, Denver CO (303) 698-2811
www.campuscycles.com
171 Detroit Street, Denver CO (303) 388-1630
www.cherrycreekbikerack.com

Mob Cyclery

RECREATION: *Best professional bicycle fitting*

You don't have to be a professional bicyclist to benefit from a professional bicycle and bicycle fitting. The folks at Mob Cyclery in Denver know this and provide bicyclists with a neighborhood shop that's fit for the pros. The best bicycle fits happen in technically sound fitting rooms manned by expert fit specialists; Mob Cyclery provides this level of fine-tuned care. An adjustable fit cycle, combined with an assessment of your core strength, flexibility and injury history, allows fit specialist George Mullen to assess the most comfortable and efficient ride for each individual. Combining the fit cycle with a CompuTrainer further establishes the perfect balance between comfort and speed. Women cyclists love Mob Cyclery with its woman-specific bicycles, equipment and clothing. Owner Mike Gibson and his staff know bikes and biking concerns. They practice what they preach, speak from practical experience and at least two staff members are former professional champions as well. Mob Cyclery stocks a variety of bicycle styles and equipment lines. Look for bicycles by Javelin, Scott and Redline plus custom built bikes by Primus Mootry. You'll also find Giro helmets and clothing by Louis Garneau and Pearl Izumi. Master basic cycling skills in the store's Endurance Training Center, where the CompuTrainer analyzes your pedal stroke and measures your heart rate. Whether you are a professional cyclist, a weekend enthusiast or an occasional rider, you will want to visit Mob Cyclery and discover the difference great equipment and professional services can make to your bicycle riding experiences.

4272 Tennyson Street, Denver CO (303) 477-4460
www.mobcyclery.com

Tiger Kim's Academy
RECREATION:
Best martial arts facilities

Tiger Kim's Academy focuses on training students in the art of Olympic-style Tae Kwon Do, along with Tang Soo Do or The Way of the Open Hand, the root of Tae Kwon Do. The Academy offers instruction and training in an assortment of traditional Asian martial arts weapons such as the bo staff, sword, kamas and nunchuka. The 12,000-square foot facility houses two training areas and a regulation sized full-contact kickboxing ring. Isolation and free-weight weight training equipment are available, as well as a sauna, steam room and Jacuzzi. Students can test the speed, strength and power behind their punches and kicks by using the computerized Ssaurabi machine located in the academy's main do jang. After spending many years as both student and instructor, Grandmaster Jung Kil "Tiger" Kim founded the academy in 1976 upon arriving in Denver from his native Korea. One of his more famous students was the late Bruce Lee, who personally requested instruction from Kim on the art of Breaking with the Head. Jung Kil's successor, Master Sung Hwan "Tiger Junior" Kim, also a native of Korea, emigrated to the US at age three and began training in Tae Kwon Do at the age of five. Over the years, he has earned numerous state and national championship titles. Come in and learn more about the exciting history of these two men and the ancient art of Tae Kwon Do at Tiger Kim's Academy.

1480 Steele Street, Denver CO
(303) 388-1408
www.tigerkim.com

Tommy's Slalom Shop

RECREATION:
Best snow and water sports gear

Tommy's Slalom Shop keeps a summer attitude year-round with its extensive selection of water sports gear, including boats, wetsuits, water skis and accessories. Owner Tommy Phillips is dedicated to providing his customers with the best equipment available and has also been instrumental in bringing hydrofoils and alternative water sports to the Denver area. Tommy was the promoter for the world's first hydrofoil tournament, held at beautiful Lake Colorado, and for the first-ever wakeboard tournament, in 1986. Additionally, Tommy sold the first commercial wakeboard, now kept on display at the shop. Tommy's is the only Colorado distributor of Malibu boats and carries the largest selection of Hyperlite and HO products in the state. Because personalized customer service is imperative to Tommy and his staff, you can rest assured that the whole family will enjoy shopping for gear and accessories at Tommy's. This shop has it all, from O'Neill wetsuits, wakeboards, kneeboards, tubes to surfboards. Tommy's Slalom Shop further provides instructional classes in wakeboarding and waterskiing and continues to promote wakeboard and waterskiing tournaments at both Lake Colorado, its private lake in Pueblo, and Boulder Reservoir. Experts and rookies alike will be inspired to hit the water in grand style, with all the latest gear, after a visit to Tommy's Slalom Shop. Stop by today and get your summer started.

**3740 North Sheridan Boulevard, Denver CO
(303) 455-3091 or (800) 592-SKIS**
www.gettommys.com

Cherry Creek Dance
RECREATION: *Metro Denver's elite dance studio*

If you've lived in the Denver area for any length of time, you probably already know about Stephanie Prosenjak and her Cherry Creek Dance studio. Stephanie began dancing at the age of three and started teaching at 15. She began dancing professionally at 18 and opened Cherry Creek Dance in 1993 at age 23. She has been the captain of the Denver Broncos cheerleading squad, worked as a Denver Nuggets dancer, danced in Neil Young music videos, and has compiled a resume that is impressive for both its length and diversity. Cherry Creek Dance offers dance instruction for anyone age eighteen months and older in a range of styles including jazz, tap, ballet, hip hop, breakdancing, musical theater and more. For those who take dance seriously, Cherry Creek offers a performing company that gives students ages 6 to 18 the opportunity to perform in venues such as Disneyland, Disneyworld, sports events and stage productions. Cherry Creek Dance is also the home of *7dancers*, a non-profit professional dance company whose mission is to educate the community through the art of dance as well as entertain with many styles of dance. Stephanie, who runs Cherry Creek Dance with her husband, Lee, has racked up numerous awards from regional and national publications and professional associations, giving validation to her dream of bolstering the Denver arts community. If you want to learn to dance visit Cherry Creek Dance, a studio that has contributed in large measure to Denver's reputation as one of the best cities in America.

3000 E 3rd Avenue, Suite 19, Denver CO
(303) 399-8087
www.cherrycreekdance.com

Brothers BBQ

RESTAURANTS & CAFÉS:

Best signature barbecue sauces

First Nick and Chris O'Sullivan fell in love with American barbecue styles, then the English-born brothers set out to recreate the best from those styles at Brothers BBQ in Denver. Nick developed a love of barbecue during a career as a race car driver that took him to the States, and Chris developed a similar taste from travels around this country. The duo quit their careers and set out to become experts in preparing barbecue true to the distinct styles of the South and Texas. They apprenticed with barbecue masters they admired and experimented heavily on friends and family in their spare time. Seven years ago, they started their first Brothers BBQ in a converted garage and now own seven restaurants and manage more than 70 employees. A visit to Brothers is your opportunity to try award winning ribs, beef brisket, pulled pork or chicken along with a cold beer. Brothers BBQ uses one of two signature sauces on its meats—a vinegar-based sauce and a sweet sauce. The restaurant provides individual servings, family packs and catering services. The brothers' efforts to become connoisseurs in the world of barbecue, introducing Denver to the best of the authentic flavors they've sampled, has won them recognition from numerous local publications and three consecutive championships at Denver's Blues 'n' Buns BBQ Contest. For barbecue flavor that will make any Southerner homesick, come to Brothers BBQ.

616 Washington Street, Denver CO
(720) 570-4227
www.brothers-bbq.com

La Fogata
RESTAURANTS & CAFÉS:
Real Mexican, Real Good, Real Fresh

Voted Best Mexican Food in Denver by *Road Food* magazine, La Fogata prides itself on real Mexican cuisine. With two Denver locations, La Fogata is the place to go for fresh Mexican fare with origins in north central Mexico. Guests can start their evening with one of the restaurant's delicious appetizers, such as the shrimp quesadillas or the Mexican sausage with cheese and tortillas. Main courses include the taquitos al carbon with diced rib eye steak, served with grilled onions, lettuce, tomatoes, cilantro and guacamole. Enjoy scrumptious cinnamon sopapillas or flan for dessert. Wines, beers and a choice of tequilas make sure you can quench your thirst in a fashion that pleases you. Margaritas are a La Fogata specialty. Consider the signature margarita, made with La Fogata's special blend of margarita mix, Cazadoras tequila and Grand Marnier. The Quincy Avenue location offers a large patio for parties up to 60 people. Let La Fogata cater your next special event with a choice of menu offerings, which include vegetarian dishes. For an authentic Mexican dining experience in Denver, visit La Fogata.

8090 E Quincy Avenue, Denver CO
(720) 974-7315
5670 E Evans Avenue, Denver CO
(303) 753-9458
www.la-fogata.com

Mickey's Top Sirloin
RESTAURANTS & CAFÉS: *Best steaks*

Three generations of Mickey Broncucia's family have made their living at 70th and Broadway, but it's Mickey's Top Sirloin that has become a beloved Denver institution. Micky's Top Sirloin has been bringing back customers again and again to sample hand-cut choice meats, Italian and Mexican fare, all served up with his special brand of good humor and the help of his grandchildren, including granddaughter and manager Stacy Hamilton. Mickey's grandfather grew vegetables and his father started a grocery store that Mickey turned into an Italian restaurant in the early 1960s. A few years later, after a buddy taught Mickey how to prepare green chile, he added Mexican food to the menu. In 1966, after learning to cut meat, he added steaks, and from then on, he had Denver eating out of his hand. In 2003 and 2006, Mickey's earned a Best of Denver award from Westword magazine. In 2005, Mickey's moved to a new building just across the parking lot from the original location, a good sign that the family intends to continue the tradition. "I give away my labor," says Mickey who offers steak at a "price you can't get anywhere else." When Mickey loves something, it becomes part of his restaurant which accounts for the menu, family photos and a bocce ball court outside the back door. The Italian bowling game allows Mickey to get together regularly with old friends and, in a way, so does the restaurant. Slip into your blue jeans and discover Mickey's Top Sirloin soon.

6950 N Broadway, Denver CO
(303) 426-5881

Brix—
A Neighborhood Bistro
RESTAURANTS & CAFÉS: *Best festive dining*

Named after the Brix scale used to measure the sugar concentration of wine, Denver's Brix Bistro is a hip spot to relax after a long day. Friends meet here to enjoy great wine and relax over a meal. Owners Chuck Cattaneo and Charles Masters are proud to call their establishment the Anti-Bistro, thanks to its easygoing charm and lack of all pretension. The cuisine here is comfort food with a twist. Simple foods take on new presentations in such dishes as Moroccan chicken, grilled achiote pork loin and blackened salmon. An extensive selection of drinks adds to the fun, including more than 60 beer and wine choices and rare liquors from small distilleries around the globe. Happy hour is a two-hour nightly occurrence, with specials on drinks and appetizers. Wednesday through Saturday nights, the place gets hopping as popular DJs spin an eclectic mix of jazz, funk and reggae. A visit the Anti-Bistro is an opportunity for fine dining without fine dining stuffiness. Chuck and Charles invite you to visit Brix for good food, good wine and good chat.

3000 E 3rd Avenue, Denver CO
(303) 333-3355
www.eatatbrix.com

Bacchus Wine Bar
RESTAURANTS & CAFÉS:
Best wine bar

Bacchus Wine Bar, named for the Roman god of wine, has a sign on the door that reads: "Take your shoes off. This is not an uptight place." So, make yourself comfortable and prepare for the rare treat of exceptional wines and delicious, inventive cuisine. Bacchus features boutique wines from small wineries where production is limited and quality is extraordinarily high. The wine bar's international collection includes over 100 red, white and dessert wines by the bottle and 30 wines by the glass. Each wine has been hand picked by owners Scott Branning and Bret Baccei, with the assistance of their sous chef, Nathan Nelson. To complement the wine, Bacchus offers home-cooked American specialties, like wild sockeye salmon fish and chips, duck carpaccio and a Po-Boy sandwich made with fried green tomatoes. Be sure to leave room for one of the heavenly desserts. This special place is perfect for either a business meeting or a romantic dinner for two. *5280* magazine has named it one of the top ten new restaurants in Denver. Visit Bacchus Wine Bar for an evening of relaxation with great food and wine. As always, shoes are optional.

2817 E 3rd Avenue, Denver CO
(303) 321-0705

Kate's at 35th Avenue

RESTAURANTS & CAFÉS:
Best elegant dining

When you want to get away from chain-restaurant food in the Denver area, Kate's at 35th Avenue offers a superior dining experience ensconced in a cozy Victorian house. Kate's at 35th Avenue features a comfortable, yet elegant atmosphere that makes you feel right at home. The staff is always warm and inviting and a visit to Lynn Smith's century-old restored mansion is always a nourishing experience for both body and soul. Opened in 1983, it was named for Lynn's daughter Kate. The family still lives upstairs with the downstairs serving as the restaurant along with the new Event Center expansion. The menu is changed daily and you will find it written on the board at the entrance as you come in, so be certain to pay attention to your dining options. If possible, grab a seat downstairs, where large windows flood the room with sunlight and exquisite art pieces decorate the walls. During the warmer times of year, head for the patio which also offers a grand dining experience in the great outdoors. Meals are made to order and lovingly prepared, so plan for a leisurely dining experience that is worth every second. This old Victorian serves sumptuous meals, a feeling of country charm and the occasional dose of mystery during its Friday night interactive murder mysteries. For a truly charming atmosphere conducive to "fine eating, entertainment and enlightenment" come by Kate's and take part in a special culinary event.

3435 Albion, Denver CO
(303) 333-4816

The Handle Bar and Grill

RESTAURANTS & CAFÉS:
Best theme restaurant

The Handle Bar and Grill puts a whole new spin on a theme restaurant. Owner Mike Miller is a bicycle enthusiast who has turned his passion into a destination spot where you can savor great food surrounded by cycling memorabilia and paraphernalia. Menu items are all named for bicycle goods and cycling greats. Trophies, photographs and bike parts are displayed throughout the restaurant. The fare is American with a Caribbean twist. Among the outstanding sandwiches is the Biemme BLT, singled out as the best in Denver by *5280* magazine. The Singletrack club sandwich is also superb, as is their additive-free beef burger. You'll also want to try their nontraditional chicken, veggie or buffalo burger in one of 11 different styles. Salads such as the Schwinn Southwest are entirely organic. The soups and many other items are homemade. The Handle Bar and Grill has a full bar with numerous beers on tap and six televisions for your viewing enjoyment. The restaurant is completely at home in the fascinating Denver neighborhood of Washington Park. Crowds fill the restaurant during the year's highlight, the Tour de France. Pedal into the Handle Bar and Grill, where the food and the bicycle theme offer inspiration.

305 S Downing Street, Denver CO
(303) 778-6761
www.handlebarandgrill.com

Photos by Tanya L. Haynes/ProComm

Sabor Latino Restaurant
RESTAURANTS & CAFÉS: *Best Latin American dishes*

Sabor Latino is known for consistently outstanding cuisine. Owners Dan and Marie Jimenez along with Marie's brother Robert Luevano moved from its tiny quarters on West 32nd to the present storefront location on the corner of 35th and Tennyson. These three Denver natives offer treasured Latin recipes with roots in Peru, Columbia, Chile and Mexico. Among the many fine selections on the menu are steak chimichurri, empanadas, ceviche and Columbian tamales. Sabor's award-winning paella is served only on Friday and Saturday nights. This beloved entree is prepared with a mix of saffron rice, chicken, orange roughy, shrimp, mussels, scallops, Spanish sausage and ribs. Denver's best selection of South American wines complements the dazzling fare. An assortment of tequilas is deservedly popular. The restaurant enjoys a far-reaching reputation and was named one of the top 50 restaurants in the nation by *Hispanic Magazine* for several years in a row. Everything about Sabor Latino is designed to increase customer pleasure, from the food to the festive Spanish theme. Exposed brick walls, comfortable seating and soft lighting invite relaxation. A Latin staff looks after your needs in this casual dining establishment with fine dining overtones. When you want a relaxed meal and outstanding Mexican and South American food, visit Sabor Latino.

4340 W 35th Avenue, Denver CO
(303) 455-8664
www.saborlatinorestaurant.com

Il Vicino
RESTAURANTS & CAFÉS: *Best Italian trattoria*

Veteran restaurateurs Richard Post, Greg Atkin and Tom White pooled their talents to create the contemporary Italian Trattoria, Il Vicino. Il Vicino, a name that means *the neighbor* in Italian, seeks to be a neighborhood restaurant and has made itself at home in eight neighborhoods in Colorado, Kansas and New Mexico. Casually upscale, Il Vicino is a fun place for dates or a night out with friends or family. It specializes in authentic wood-fired thin-crust Italian pizza. One popular choice is Bianca, a white pizza with capocollo ham, portobello mushrooms, caramelized onions, goat cheese, mozzarella, Gorgonzola, fresh tomatoes and rosemary. Panini-style sandwiches, calzones, baked lasagna, soups and entrée-size salads round out the menu. Beverage choices here are diverse and exciting, with award-winning microbrew ales from Il Vicino's own Santa Fe brewery, plus wines from Italy and California, espresso drinks and Italian water. Naven Ram manages Il Vicino in Denver and invites everyone to come in and enjoy the large open dining room with its 25-foot ceilings or patio dining in season. Add to this the friendly service and first-rate pizza, and you can see why anyone would gladly welcome Il Vicino to their neighborhood.

550 Broadway, Denver CO
(303) 861-0860
www.ilvicino.com

M & D's Café
RESTAURANTS & CAFÉS: *Best ribs*

M & D's Café in Denver is the kind of rib establishment that transplanted Texans rave about. Naturally, the place belongs to folks from Texas, Mack and Daisy Shead. For a true Southern taste, you can start with fried okra or the battered, deep-fried green tomatoes. Homemade lemonade or iced tea in mason jars will cool you off between courses. The most popular entrée is the ribs, smoked with hickory and mesquite wood and served with M & D's special barbecue sauce in any of three heat levels. You get two sides from a list of 10 options. You can pick a garden salad, but for down-home tradition you might try the yams, baked beans or the mac and cheese. Other barbecue options are beef brisket, homemade hot links and chicken. Combo plates satisfy the indecisive diner. Some people consider the fish to be M & D's real secret. Catfish is the favorite, rolled in cornmeal and deep-fried. Red Snapper and whiting are also mighty fine. A kid's menu contains smaller portions of barbecue or fish. Several of M & D's desserts are famous, including the peach cobbler, banana pudding and sweet potato pie. The pecan pie tastes of real pecans and is mellowed with Kahlua. From appetizers to desserts, everything is made from scratch. The restaurant was completely renovated in 2003 and is shiny and new. Come taste the many reasons magazines have repeatedly graced M & D's Café with best barbecue awards.

2000 E 28th Avenue, Denver CO
(303) 296-1760

Blake Street Tavern
RESTAURANTS & CAFÉS: *Best sports bar*

Photos by James Nally

The Blake Street Tavern is a real sports fan's sports bar in the Ballpark Neighborhood in Downtown Denver. Located just two blocks from Coors Field, this classy, upscale establishment is serving it up in style. Owners Chris Fuselier and Rich Salturelli opened Blake Street Tavern in 2003. In three years, the Tavern has become a prominent fixture garnering rave reviews from *Citysearch.com*, *AOL Cityguide* and *5280* magazine for Best Sports Bar, Best Bar Menu and Best Beer Choice in Denver. The friendly staff of this Cheers-type bar makes it a point to know repeat customers by name. The Tavern offers 20 beers on tap, featuring imports, domestics and all of the award-winning ales from Flying Dog Brewery, which is located right next door. Classic pub fare includes burgers, prime rib, nachos and buffalo wings. On the lighter side, you can order the Blackened Salmon Caesar Salad or Thai Ahi Tuna Salad. There's even a menu for the kids. For spectacular sports viewing, the Tavern has 15 high-definition, flat screen plasma monitors and carries all of the major DirecTV sports viewing packages. The Tavern expanded last year and added a private lounge, banquet room and 22-foot shuffle board table. To top things off, if you're going to a game at Coors Field, you can use your ticket stub for a free Flying Dog Beer. Blake Street Tavern hits a home run for the ultimate tavern experience.

2401 Blake Street, Denver CO
(303) 675-0505

Paris Wine Bar
RESTAURANTS & CAFÉS: *Best themed wine tasting events*

Paris Wine Bar is not a typical bar. It is a comforting and relaxing place to enjoy a nice glass or bottle of wine while you socialize until the wee hours. Faye and Jeff Maguire owned the bookstore that used to be in this building and the café right next door. After 18 years, they decided it was time for the bookstore to mature into something that would compliment the café. Faye's idea came from fond memories of a place where she and Jeff spent their wedding reception. Paris Wine Bar features a selection of wines from all over the world as well as small mom and pop wineries. There are 40-50 varieties of wines by the glass or bottle. Every third Monday of the month Paris Wine Bar hosts a wine tasting event. This is a themed event based on the type of wine that is featured, the geography of where the wine is from, whatever major holiday is in that month, and any other fun criteria. The main goal is to create an atmosphere where wine is not so intimidating. Novice wine drinkers are sometimes intimidated by the lingo used at wine tasting events. Paris Wine Bar has a down to earth yet knowledgeable approach that even beginners can appreciate and understand. Come to Paris Wine Bar and enjoy a relaxing evening while tasting affordable wines in an eclectic atmosphere.

1549 Platte Street, Denver CO
(303) 217-5805
www.pariswinebar.com

Photos by Clinton T. Sander

Steve's Snappin' Dogs
RESTAURANTS & CAFÉS: *Best hot dogs*

Denver has fallen hard for the juicy New Jersey hot dog classic at Steve's Snappin' Dogs. Snappin' Dogs serves Thumann's brand frankfurters, the ones with that distinguishable juicy snap and smoky flavor when you first bite into the natural casing with its delicious beef and pork filling. Steve Ballas, owner of Steve's Snappin' Dogs, wanted to introduce the people of Denver to the taste he grew up with, so he trucks the real deal in from Jersey, and the folks in Denver are glad he does. He and his wife, Linda, used to do deli, and now they do dogs, complete with a choice of memorable toppings. In 1998, their corporate deli and grill in downtown Denver won a Westword award for Best Sandwiches in Denver. Westword has noticed them once again with the 2006 award for Best New Store on Colfax. In May 2006, AOL City Guide did a search of best hot dogs across America, and Steve's Snappin' Dogs was again recognized when they came in at #11 for an honorable mention. Steve and Linda first began selling the dogs from a 20-foot truck at farmers' markets and special events. Finally, public demand dictated the need for a permanent location, and the couple moved their operation into a renovated gas station in February 2006. The menu at Steve's is loaded with family favorites and some unusual items, like deep fried green beans, fresh squeezed lemonade and limeade, or a frozen banana on a stick. This new, family-friendly enterprise also serves up a hearty breakfast. Discover the snap in a tasty New Jersey dog at Steve's Snappin' Dogs.

3525 E Colfax Avenue, Denver CO
(303) 333-SNAP (7627)
www.stevessnappindogs.com

Papou's Pizzeria & Italian Eatery
RESTAURANTS & CAFES: *Best Greek-style pizza*

Papou is Greek for grandfather, and Papou's Pizzeria & Italian Eatery is a favorite lunch and dinner place for the whole family. Papou's serves Connecticut-style pizza, also called New England or Greek pizza. What really sets this pizza apart is the way it's cooked: pan-baked in a brick oven. With a buttery, airy, crispy crust, Papou's pizza strikes the perfect balance between the thin-crust New Yorker and the deep-dish Chicago pie. The Denver press has lauded this pizza, including the *Rocky Mountain News, w* and *Westword*. Yet amazingly, pizza is only a small part of the menu. Papou's has a wide variety of salads, grinders (subs) and Italian dinners. You can have Greek as well as Italian specialties. Try the gyro sandwich or the Real Greek Salad with stuffed grape leaves, feta cheese and homemade Greek dressing, a secret family recipe. For dessert, you can enjoy New York cheesecake, baklava or homemade chocolate chip cookies. The Papou's story started in 1969 when Jimmy Loukopoulos opened a pizzeria in Plainville, Connecticut. His son, Luke, grew up in the business. After Luke earned his MBA at Denver University, he realized that pizza was in his blood. The result is Papou's, where the staff makes everything in-house. For a warm atmosphere and passionate cooking, come to Papou's Pizzeria & Italian Eatery the next chance you get.

5075 Leetsdale Drive, Denver CO
(303) 388-3211
www.papouspizza.com

Zaidy's Deli Downtown
RESTAURANTS & CAFÉS: *Best kosher deli*

Zaidy's Deli Downtown is a traditionally styled kosher-deli where every savory and delicious dish is made from scratch the old-fashioned way using fresh, quality ingredients. This popular eatery first opened in the mid-1980s under the ownership of Gerard Rudofsky who was later joined in 1992 by his son Jason. Together, this fabulous father and son team serve up a diverse array of terrific dishes that will have your taste buds taking notice. Here you will find all of your traditional favorites such as potato latkes, matzoh ball soup and kugels along with a few contemporary and tantalizing treats such as their famous Ruben Sandwich made with potato pancakes or the Matzo Brei with applesauce, grilled salami and onions. Zaidy's Deli Downtown also serves up breakfasts daily until 4:00 pm and include such possibilities as Challah French Toast or Lox with eggs and onions as well as an extensive selection of perfectly prepared omelettes such as the Hot Pepper Cheese or the Greek omelettes with kalamata olives. If that isn't enough to get your tummy rumbling then come in and check out their truly phenomenal homemade desserts from the Keylime cheesecake or rice pudding to the Sour cream coffee cake or any one of their numerous pie varieties. On your next visit to Denver, slip past the fast food places and chain restaurants into one of the Zaidy's Deli locations and indulge in something that will really hit the spot.

1512 Larimer Street, Denver CO (303) 893-3600
121 Adams Street, Denver CO (303) 333-5336
www.zaidysdeli.com

Daphne's Deli
RESTAURANTS & CAFES:
Best bagel dishes

A visit to Daphne's Deli can include the irresistable aroma of chai latte or, perhaps, the taste of a delicious sandwich accompanied by a fresh salad of baby greens, cranberry, and pine nuts. One look at the menu at Daphne's Deli, and it's easy to see why owner Denise Anderson gave up 15 years in the corporate world for a better quality of life as a delicatessen owner. She dreamed of starting her own business and saw a need for an extraordinary sandwich shop in the neighborhood. Denise started as a coffee shop owner, so the legacy of that business lives on at Daphne's Deli in their offerings of Silver Canyon espresso and coffee. When you prefer something a little chillier, their frozen blended coffees are sure to please. A succulent selection of bagels adds to the coffee to make for a pleasing breakfast stop. Enjoy a bagel with enticing, original toppings such as hummus and tomato. For a real treat, take a bite out of the hearty Denver bagel with green and red pepper, onion and your option of ham or bacon. The sumptuous quality continues with a sandwich menu that can't be beat. The Daphne features turkey and avocado with Cajun sauce. Daphne's offers a classic Reuben sandwich as well as a ham and Gouda; capicola, ham, salami, provolone and olive spread, and several meatless sandwiches for the vegetarian or simply health-conscious. Daphne's gets ingredients from local vendors, contributing to the community feel. Stop by Daphne's Deli and try any number of tasty treats for yourself.

393 Corona Street, Denver CO
(303) 733-1212

Miss Talulah's

SHOPPING: *Best source for whimsical gifts*

Robin Lohre is the mastermind behind two of Denver's most unusual treasures, Talulah Jones and Miss Talulah's. Both offer exquisite, whimsical gifts and personal treasures. The shops specialize in items that are sure to become dear keepsakes. The award-winning Miss Talulah's has the added attraction of Fred, a customer-greeting dog who is well-loved by Denver locals. The shop is also known for playing host to festive, mini sidewalk sales. Both shops support the arts by providing visiting artist shows and carrying an inventory of jewelry made by local artists. The eclectic merchandise includes enchanting children's toys and handcrafted handbags. Talulah Jones is also a source for classic children's books. Romantic merchandise such as velvet flowers and handmade slippers make beautiful presents for a special friend. In addition, a selection of personally crafted chandeliers is one of their specialties. These two fabulous shops are unlike any other and must be seen to be appreciated. Make a special trip to Talulah Jones and Miss Talulah's the next time you are in Denver.

Talulah Jones: 1122 East 17th Avenue, Denver CO (303) 832-1230
Miss Talulah's: 7477 East 29th Place, Denver CO (303) 293-8436
www.talulahonline.com

Colorado Scientific Co

SHOPPING: *Best science education store*

Colorado Scientific Company is a fantastic resource for both students and professionals who are in search of specialized equipment, tools and chemicals. In addition to the scientific community, this versatile and diverse company also caters to those who work within the art world. Colorado Scientific was founded by a chemist in 1953 during the uranium boom and has evolved into today's large assemblage of products to help customers find viable solutions to everyday issues that arise in the scientific, educational and art communities alike. They offer a potpourri of science products which range from microscopes and telescopes to chemicals and formulas for metal artists. They also have instruments for use in environmental and weather monitoring as well as in food production, plus an array of great gifts such as beginners' kits for budding scientists. Colorado Scientific works with the general public along with the educational and professional community and welcomes individuals who need specific scientific equipment, whether they are using it to study the world around them or bring that world to stunning life through an amalgamation of art and science. Find the products you need, in quantities large or small, to complete the projects dearest to you with a visit to Colorado Scientific Company. Colorado Scientific also offers products and services via its active website.

95 Lincoln Street, Denver CO
(303) 777-3777
www.sciencecompany.com

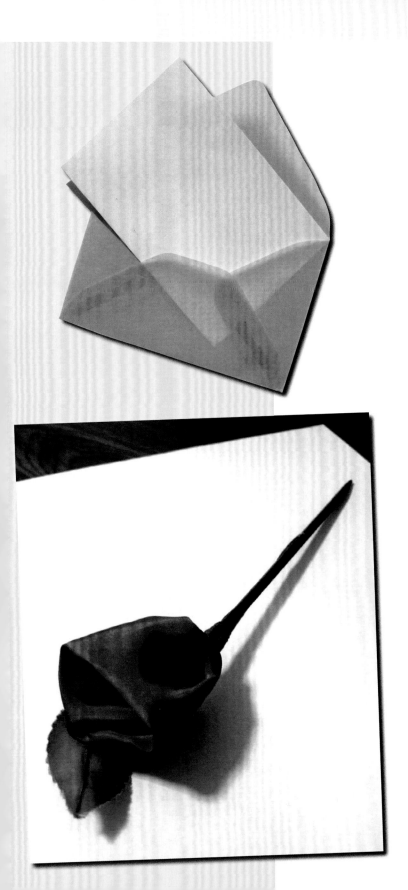

Merci for stationery & fine things

SHOPPING: *Best choice in Denver for life's finer things*

At Merci for stationery & fine things, you will find chic stationery and other luxury wares. Most of the items that this boutique carries can be personalized, engraved or monogrammed. In addition to stationery for personal or social correspondence, items that can be customized to your needs include wedding or baby announcements, invitations and holiday cards. Merci for stationery & fine things is an exclusive distributor of the Pineider line of fine stationery from Italy. Beyond paper, They can customize photo albums, cosmetic cases, linens and other fine goods. What sets Merci for stationery & fine things apart is its high-end designs and hands-on approach. Owners Gillette and Susan personally attend to all customers. Their shop is contemporary and fun, but it is also welcoming and cozy. Gillette and Susan both come from the world of interior design. Both have worked as dress consultants; Gillette with wedding gowns and Susan with debutante dresses. Both have turned their passion for the finer things in life into Merci for stationery & fine things. Friends for more than 25 years, they began meeting every month to compare notes about their favorite stationery, always with the thought that they might open a store one day. That day has arrived, and you can now benefit from their success. Consult Merci for stationery & fine things.

2620 E Louisiana Avenue, Denver CO
(303) 282-9900

El Cid's Tobacco Boutique

SHOPPING: *Best rare and unusual tobacco flavors*

Father and son team Ron and Jack Rogers understand the intricacies of tobacco blends the way some people understand fine wines. They carry over 100 of the world's premium cigar brands and make 80 to 90 of their own pipe tobacco blends at El Cid's Tobacco Boutique in Denver. Tobacco enthusiasts can sample rare and unusual tobacco flavors from the world's exotic tobacco growing locales such as Africa, Brazil, Nicaragua, Honduras, Mexico and the Dominican Republic. In 2003, Westword magazine cited the shop as the best place in Denver to buy real Cuban cigars. El Cid's carries the Pinar cigar, a pre-embargo Cuban cigar rolled from tobacco leaves imported from Cuba prior to 1962. Fifty years of aging creates a mellow smoke unmatched in the greater Denver Metropolitan area. Ron and Jack have been selling tobacco for ten years and moved to their present location six years ago. In that time, they have treated their customers not only to the world's best tobacco, but also to a little fun and a chance to learn something about tobacco such as how to roll a cigar. "We enjoy working with our people and work hard at giving them a rewarding smoking experience," says Ron. To personalize your experience and get the most enjoyment from your tobacco products, seek out the experts at El Cid's Tobacco Boutique.

4401 Zenobia Street, Denver CO
(303) 477-2864

Freakys

SHOPPING:
Best source for strange gifts and body art services

When it has to be fun—and maybe a little bit freaky— customers turn to Freakys. Owners Ken Church and Jim Sampson have spent 13 years specializing in products and services that exist purely and completely for the fun of it. The fun starts with a visit to one of Freakys' seven locations: four in Denver, two in Colorado Springs and one in Boulder. Gifts, tobacco products, tattoos and body piercing are their specialties, but you will also find posters, knives and swords alongside incense, hookahs and skateboards. Whether you wear a suit or a T-shirt, chances are Freakys offers something you've been wanting. The tattoo salon caters to many stars and employs some of the best tattoo artists in the industry. You'll find a huge selection of body art and body jewelry plus clothing, lotions and any number of products that are fun and sexy. Nostalgia from the 1960s and 1970s joins newer products to make the store attractive to a diverse clientele. Whether you're looking for a Bruce Lee poster, a fine cigar or a drop dead, gorgeous tattoo, Freakys is the store you need. The Freakys staff promises you will have fun during your visit.

2 Broadway, Denver CO
(303) 329-0420
www.freakys.com

Ro Sham Beaux

SHOPPING:
Best cards and gifts for all occasions

Ro Sham Beaux is one of the world's premier card and gift stores. George and Beth Stephens firmly believe in communication as the healing element for the world. Cards sent and gifts given are the expression of love in action. Our selection will inspire giving in fresh, wonderful ways.

500 16th Street #124, Denver CO
303-595-5526
www.roshambeaux.com

The Watermark
SHOPPING: *Best party boutique*

Carmen Mix has always appreciated fine stationery, cards, and invitations. This interest, combined with an entrepreneurial spirit, resulted in the birth of The Watermark in September of 2003. The Watermark specializes in clever papers for clever people. The selection includes the expected paper products as well as monogrammed soaps, funky gifts, and personalized printing. The store is large enough to find anything you need but still intimate enough to provide exceptional customer service. It is a small boutique with a personal neighborhood feel. It is the perfect place to stop by and pick up a quick gift or personalize an invitation. Notable gifts and specialty items make it easy to spoil your friends and family as well as to plan that special landmark life event. The Watermark is an excellent choice to supply all of your needs for the birthdays in your life. Whatever the occasion may be, from wedding to party to corporate event, when you want it to be special, you know where to go. Visit The Watermark and let the experts show you how it's done.

200 Quebec Street, Building 500-103, Denver CO
(303) 577-0058
www.cleverpapers.com

Bill's Sports Collectibles
SHOPPING:
Best source for sports memorabilia

Bill Vizas has always been a sports fan. As a child, he collected sports cards of all kinds, and, as he grew older, he expanded his collecting into other types of sports memorabilia. Bill opened Bill's Sports Collectibles in 1981. His vision was to provide a fun place for the sports fan. From 500-square-feet in 1981, Bill's has grown to more than 5,000-square-feet today. Bill's carries over one million sports cards along with a huge selection of memorabilia. From autographed jerseys and photographs to bobbing-head dolls and old programs, guides, books, pins and posters, if you're interested in sports memorabilia, Bill's Sports Collectibles is the place to visit. Stop by Bill's Sports Collectibles for a nostalgic tour of sports history, and to find a treasure for your own collection.

2335 S Broadway, Denver CO
(303) 733-4878
www.billssportscollectibles.com

Phoebe's Past & Presents
SHOPPING: *Fun, funky and fabulous*

There's something decidedly fun about a store that houses pet treats, jewelry, baby gifts, lotions, and great cards all under one roof. "Fun, funky, and fabulous" was the tone owner Amy Oviatt had in mind for Phoebe's Past & Presents in downtown Denver, an eclectic gift boutique named after Amy's yellow lab Phoebe. Amy's natural design sense and the lessons she learned in her mother's bridal boutique when she was a child have allowed her to create a shop with a wonderful, homey atmosphere. "I want people to see how they can apply the designs from the store in their own homes," says Amy. The delights at Phoebe's include bestsellers such as baby t-shirts and magnetic picture frames plus a surprising variety of new and old treasures. A Paris-inspired nook features vintage women's hats, boas, and pastel china, while outdoorsmen are bound to appreciate throw pillows and picture frames with sporting themes. Another area is filled with offbeat baby gifts, another with 1950s glassware, and still another, called Phoebe's Corner, with locally-made pet treats like Catnip Tea Energy Drink and Good Dog Breath Mints from Mouthfuls, Inc. Stationery and shiny baubles are everywhere. Amy is a strong supporter of Colorado manufacturers and a discerning buyer. She opened Phoebe's in 2004 as a place where anyone can feel comfortable and find an appropriate gift. Come on in and enjoy the splendid variety at this new and vibrant addition to Denver's downtown shopping scene. Phoebe and Amy look forward to your visit.

1535 Platte Street, Denver CO
(303) 458-5544

National Speaker & Sound

SHOPPING:
Setting the standard for audio quality

For more than two decades, National Speaker and Sound has set the standard for audio quality in the Denver area. An independently owned store in a business dominated by national chains, owner Michael Martinez's operation has maintained its edge by offering exceptional personal service along with top-of-the-line products. Whether you're looking for a high-end guitar or a professional audio sound system, National Speaker is the first place to go, when you want that perfect piece of equipment. For those who have a little less to spend, National Speaker and Sound offers used units and will even occasionally trade equipment with customers. The brightest stars of the Denver music scene look to National Speaker, so you can be certain that this business offers the best products and great service. If you're an audiophile who wants to enjoy a vast array of the finest offerings in the field of sound technology, come by and spend some time playing with the equipment at National Speaker and Sound. You are sure to enjoy your visit.

1559 S Broadway, Denver CO
(303) 777-6400 or (800) 748-2213
www.nationalspeaker.com

T-Trove Asian Décor

SHOPPING: *Denver's Asian treasure-trove*

T-Trove Asian Décor is an oasis of calm, containing over 3,000 decorative and useful items from China, Japan and Korea. When you enter, you smell the sweet scent of incense and hear the sound of trickling water from the indoor fountains. Elliot, a canine concierge, will greet you with dignity. The store carries distinctive items in many price ranges. Chopsticks, as well as candles, tea accessories, and jewelry make elegant and moderately priced gifts, along with a wide selection of vases and much of the wall art. More valuable items include bronze vases, large leather-covered boxes and jade carvings. T-Trove offers dinnerware, statuettes, pillows and an endless supply of home accessories. T-Trove also stocks quality East Asian furniture in modern and traditional styles, or the staff can assist you with custom furniture orders. *Westword*'s Best of Denver 2006 named T-Trove the best store for Asian treasures. Owners of T-Trove share a passion for art. Years ago, they brought art and embroidery back from China to the United States for their own use. The overwhelming response they received from those purchases prompted them to open T-Trove, and their success led to the opening of a larger store in 2005. For an escape from the ordinary, visit T-Trove Asian Décor.

189 S Broadway, Denver CO
(303) 722-0949
www.t-trove.com

Photos by ByChanceProductions.com

Healing Glow Candle Studio

SHOPPING: *Best handcrafted candles*

Jeff Schitter always loved candles and began crafting his own in college upon discovering how overpriced they could be. During his years of making candles as a hobby, Jeff learned how to create candles of unusually high quality for a reasonable price. After starting his business in 2002 in Austin, Texas, he had to leave the state because of the hot summer. He began traveling the country displaying his work at art fairs, craft shows and music festivals. He then settled in Denver, a good environment for candles, and opened Healing Glow Candle Studio. Located at the corner of 32nd Avenue and Perry Street in NW Denver's Highlands Neighborhood, his business has boomed since opening in November 2003. At Healing Glow, you can view hundreds of unique, scented candles in more than a dozen shapes and multiple sizes. There are over 40 scents to choose from including Nag Champa, pomegranate and green tea, and many have multiple wicks. As a result of Jeff's candle-making talents, each candle burns down to the very bottom and lasts an exceptionally long time. For example, one of the taller ones, a four inch diameter by 12-inch tall pillar will burn for over 400 hours. All of the candles are heavily scented, but with their extended life, the scent is released subtly. Customers can also design their own candles either at the store or on the website. If you love candles, you owe it to yourself to visit Healing Glow Candle Studio.

3939 W 32nd Avenue, Denver CO
(303) 477-3972
www.healingglow.com

max & me

SHOPPING: *Best fashion for women and children*

Max & Me is a clever boutique brimming with women's and infants apparel. Don't miss the individual state glasses, dish towels and pillows by Cat Studio. One of the newest additions to the supremely cool Highlands neighborhood, Max & Me is a clever combination of funky fashion basics and oh-so-precious baby gifts, making this boutique one of a kind. Named after the owner's adorable nephew Max (who sweetly models the delightful baby garb), Max & Me appeals to urban moms, hip trend-setters and gift-givers alike. Shoppers will find stylish clothing from such designers as Tag Demin, OMGirl, XCVI Wearables and the Denver-based phenomenon, Ollie Sang. Once you collect a pile of must-haves for yourself, find delicious treats for the moms in your life. Squeal over Little Chums gift sets, hilariously charming onsies by Urban Smalls and other gifts for wee ones. Please call Max & Me for store hours.

3867 Tennyson Street, Denver CO
(303) 455-9663

Tibetan Sisters Art

SHOPPING: *Best art of the Himalayas*

In 1980, at the age of 18, Palden Yangsto Hester, a Tibetan refugee, started selling objects from her beloved homeland on the side of the road in Pokhara, Nepal. In 2004, she opened Tibetan

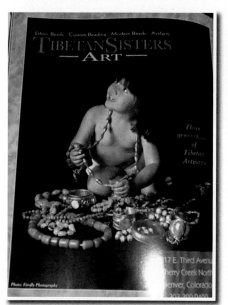

Sisters Art, where she shares the beauty and art of the Himalayas along with her broad smile and a banner that bellows, Save Tibet. Walk into Tibetan Sisters Art to explore objects from Buddhist Tibet, Nepal and India. Browse through fierce tiger handwoven rugs, statues from Nepal and hand painted antique cabinets. Look for silver jewelry from Bali and complicated Tibetan thangka paintings with silk borders. Feel the inspiration radiating from prayer wheels, prayer flags, Buddha statues and traveling altars. Tibetan Sisters Art is one of the 320 independently owned businesses at the posh Cherry Creek North. Hester carries rare, semi-precious stones from all over the world and lovely jewelry, including handcrafted strings of natural coral, amber and turquoise, hung with etched silver pendants. The store received *Westword*'s 2006 Best of Denver award for Best Tibetan Treasures. For items of rare beauty and significance, visit Tibetan Sisters Art.

2817 E 3rd Avenue, Denver CO
(303) 320-9400

Red Carpet Baby!

SHOPPING: *Best interactive toys*

A child's first five years of life have the most influence on their future. Interactive and creative play in youth helps foster an adult who will be more active and engaged. At Red Carpet Baby!, you can find plenty of unique items to help develop your child' mind and motor skills. Owner Emelia Metzger was teaching pre-school when the idea for this original store came to her. At first, she considered creating educational play spaces for people's homes, but changed her focus and began selling wooden toys out of her garage. The business and inventory grew until she had enough to open her first store. In April of 2002, she moved and expanded again, setting up her concept store at its current location. There are still plenty of wooden toys for the five-and-under crowd, but now Red Carpet Baby! also carries miniature cookware and baking sets, colorful mobiles, tables and chairs and lots of gift ideas for baby showers. Many products come from local designers and American toy companies, but there are specialty items from as far away as Germany and Poland. The emphasis of the entire store is quality and beauty. Each piece has also been carefully selected to cover every stage of your little one's advancement. Metzger is a Montessori certified Early Childhood Educator, and Red Carpet Baby! is filled with everything the scholastically minded parent could want. Give your child a head start with something head smart from Red Carpet Baby!

1511 S Pearl Street, Denver CO
(303) 698-BABY (2229)
www.redcarpetbaby.com

Talulah Jones
SHOPPING: *Best source for whimsical gifts*

Robin Lohre is the mastermind behind two of Denver's most unusual treasures, Talulah Jones and Miss Talulah's. Both offer exquisite, whimsical gifts and personal treasures. The shops specialize in items that are sure to become dear keepsakes. The award-winning Miss Talulah's has the added attraction of Fred, a customer-greeting dog who is well-loved by Denver locals. The shop is also known for playing host to festive mini sidewalk sales. Both shops support the arts by providing visiting artist shows and carrying an inventory of jewelry made by local artists. The eclectic merchandise includes unique children's toys and handcrafted handbags. Talulah Jones is also a source for classic children's books. Romantic merchandise such as velvet flowers and handmade slippers make beautiful presents for a special friend. In addition, a selection of personally crafted chandeliers is one of their specialties. These two fabulous shops are unlike any other and must be seen to be appreciated. Make a special trip to Talulah Jones and Miss Talulah's the next time you are in Denver.

Talulah Jones: 1122 East 17th Avenue, Denver CO (303) 832-1230
Miss Talulah's: 7477 East 29th Place, Denver CO (303) 293-8436
www.talulahonline.com

L & L Coins & Stamps
SHOPPING: *Best appraisals and advice*

What do you do when you're cleaning out that old steamer trunk in the attic and find some coins your grandfather brought back from Italy after World War II? How about that old necklace your great-grandmother used to wear with the strange-colored stones? If you want to know their monetary value, other than the emotional one attached to such items, bring them into L & L Coins and Stamps for an accurate appraisal. Owner Roger Loecher has been buying and selling coins, guns, stamps and other antiques for nearly 30 years. It's safe to say, he's got an eye for what's out there. Gold scrap and gold bars get the same respect here, and antique watches are given the same attention to detail as heirloom diamonds. Whether it's advice on how to handle a collection of rare stamps or the best way to manage a portfolio of coins, Roger has sage advice worth hearing. He can also perform appraisals for private parties, estates and F.D.I.C. matters. Nothing is too big or too small, so bring your questions to the man with the answers at L & L Coins and Stamps.

5500 W 44th Avenue, Denver CO
(303) 422-8500

Decade

SHOPPING:
Best gift boutique

When Kristin Tait and Dylan Moore opened Decade in 1998, they had no retail experience, but they had a vision and saw a need in the neighborhood. The couple, originally from Boulder, saw Decade as a way to spend more time together and exercise their joint passions for business and design. The store sells vintage furniture and gift items as well as clothing for men and women. Merchandise moves quickly, giving shoppers a constantly changing array of affordable gifts for babies and adults, bath products, candles, and jewelry. Providing eclectic product selections at good prices is the aim of the owners. As active members of the community, Kristen and Dylan also donate gift baskets for fund-raising and charity events. A visit to Decade usually includes a greeting from Stella the Fella, an adopted cat who is free to roam the store and has proven a favorite with customers. Whether you are looking for a special gift or something unusual to dress you or your home, you will want to visit Decade often to see what's new.

56 S Broadway, Denver CO
(303) 733-2288

Real Baby

SHOPPING:
Best baby gifts and supplies

Eda J. Le Shan said, "A new baby is like the beginning of all things - wonder, hope, a dream of possibilities." As any parent knows, babies are also the beginning of a virtual avalanche of necessities. From the basics such as strollers and blankets to the toys and books that delight and educate, Real Baby has you covered. Real Baby calls itself, "a store for life with baby." Real Baby has everything you need to pamper your little one and take care of your new addition in style. Since opening in March of 2003, Real Baby has been recognized with several awards. They were voted Best Place for Hip Moms to Buy Maternity Clothes in 2004 by Westword magazine as well as Best Baby Store on City Search. Colorado Parents magazine gave them the Best New Clothing Store for Children and Infants award in 2005. Owners John and Hilary Horan opened Real Baby in order to spend more time together as a family. This warmth and passion for family is reflected throughout the business. From the whimsical to the essential, their inventory is a joy to browse. They even have a selection of décor for nurseries that wouldn't look out of place in a Museum of Modern Art gift catalog. Their store is filled with items that are joyfully functional with a distinctive flair. Whether you are shopping for a mom or dad to be or becoming one yourself, visit Real Baby and discover all they have to offer. Their registry will be extremely helpful in selecting the perfect item for baby as well as their useful online shopping website.

3616 West 32nd Avenue, Denver CO
(303) 477-2229
www.realbabyinc.com

Honey Bear Fruit Basket Company

SHOPPING: *Best gift baskets*

Honey Bear Fruit Basket Company wants to be a part of your gift giving experience by offering suggestions in the spirit of generosity and good taste. In the business since 1995, the company buys only premium quality fruit from local and national sources. Long-time employee Sandy Frank purchased the business in 2006 and moved it to its present location in North Denver. Sandy and her staff take great care in selecting the finest gourmet foods to match the quality of their fresh fruit selections. They offer luscious chocolates, locally made fruit jams and honeys, fine cheeses, savory nuts, many varieties of gourmet cookies and more. Each basket is packed and decorated by hand, wrapped in cellophane, and topped with a hand-tied bow. The finishing touch is a personalized gift tag and instructional card. Honey Bear offers a discounted corporate sales program and is able to handle any size order while still creating distinct baskets. Customers can place phone orders and expect dependable delivery services locally and to anywhere in the country. If you would like to include a bottle of wine in your basket, you can drop the wine off at the shop. Sympathy and get-well baskets, housewarming baskets, Colorado-themed baskets, tins and boxes—you name it, and Honey Bear can address your need. Check out the website or call for a free brochure to see what Honey Bear Fruit Basket Company has in store for you.

6321 Washington Street, Unit N, Denver CO
(303) 297-3390 or (888) 330-BEAR (2327)
www.honeybearbaskets.com

Photos by Jesse Dawson

Pandora Jewelry

SHOPPING: *Best jewelry boutique*

If you ask any stylish lass in Denver, she will tell you that Pandora Jewelry is the city's definitive destination for finding the perfect piece of jewelry for your best gal pal, along with a little trinket to take home for yourself, as well. While the shop is renowned for its rows and rows of jewelry-filled showcases, this boutique is also breathtakingly crammed from floor to ceiling with paper lanterns, boxed notes, imported soaps and candles, crafting supplies, porcelain dishware and lovely bound journals. Seek out the turn-of-the-century inspired La Vie Parisienne collection from Catherine Popesco, peruse the carved Lucite rose pendants of Lucky Loo Loo, and don't leave until you own one of Megan Kelley's hand-painted cigar box purses, exclusive to Pandora Jewelry. Dedicated staff willingly assist bewildered gift-searchers with insightful ideas and creative suggestions from a unique stock of goodies like Scrabble tile pendants, handcrafted cards and birthstone rings. The hodgepodge continues with an eclectic corner of goofy, must-have items like bacon band-aids, pretty, pink velvet covered Buddha banks and pirate lunchboxes. Regulars know that the diverse selection of gifts at this 13-year-old staple changes seasonally, but one thing remains constant: Pandora Jewelry is a delightful jewelry and gift sanctuary where everything seems to just sparkle.

220 E 13th Avenue, Denver CO
(303) 832-7073
www.pandorajewelrydenver.com

Composition

SHOPPING: *A modern store committed to good design*

Why go through life with just the basics when you can add the visual excitement of great design to the simple tools of daily living? That's where Composition and owner Jennifer Roberts come in. Composition sells items that are both practical and suffused with visually entertaining color and form. Her modern store carries surprising selections that are out of the ordinary and show a strong commitment to good design. Composition carries gadgets, laptop bags, wallets, shoes, binders and books that are sure to attract visually oriented, creative professionals who appreciate the value of design in their lives. Look for an eclectic mix of items as diverse as playful jewelry and housewares, all designed to add color and style to the modern lifestyle without sacrificing function. Jennifer's Border Collie Abby endorses the colorful dog leashes and feeding bowls. The award winning Composition website is a masterful mix of artistry and usefulness with hundreds of products catalogued to provide a satisfying and nearly effortless shopping experience. Jennifer opened Composition three years ago. It marries her lifelong interest in design with her desire for community involvement. She's worked with Rocky Mountain College of Art and Design to involve students in designing useful lines for her store. Her passion and artistry, along with a great eye for extraordinary wares, capture the imagination of all who experience Composition. Stop by the store, and put some Composition in your life.

1499 Blake Street, Denver CO
(303) 894-0025
www.shopcomposition.com

Ella Bleu

SHOPPING: *Best women's boutique*

Ella Bleu is a fabulous, feminine and chic boutique for women that is sympathetic towards men too. Owners Kim and Thierry Inghilterra are former fashion models with an eye for style and design. Ella Bleu perfectly mirrors Kim's perspective on style—classic and timeless, as well as French chic. Here you will find an extensive bath and body section, jeans, dresses, lingerie and accessories, all at affordable prices. With designers such as BCBG, Cosabella and Tracy Reese, the clothing you purchase will always be in vogue and last a lifetime. Ella Bleu is not a slave to trends. Kim purchases in small batches so you won't see anyone else with the same outfit. In addition, Ella Bleu holds a guy's night, strictly for men to shop in a fun, relaxed atmosphere. Ella Bleu provides lingerie models and beer, an enticing combination that smooths the uncertainties of buying lingerie for the special woman in their male clientele's life. Ella Bleu has accessories to compliment the home as well as individual styles. Chandeliers light the boutique casting a brilliant sparkle on the jewelry. Decorative ceramic vases, housewares and antique furniture are all beautifully displayed and functional for any home. Come to Ella Bleu to discover your hidden style.

200 Quebec Street Building 500 #109, Denver CO
(720) 859-3111
www.ellableuboutique.com

Balistreri Vineyards
WINERIES: *Best full-bodied red wines*

Balistreri Vineyards is a unique Denver treasure. Known predominantly for their full-bodied red wines, they also offer a few interesting white wines along with delicious dessert wines and a Port. Balistreri Vineyards is a family operation. Winemaker John Balistreri has been making wine for more than three decades, combing traditional winemaking methods with modern technology. His wines are handcrafted, one barrel at a time, with grapes that are fermented on their own yeast, unaltered by sulfites and aged in American Oak. All Balistreri wines are hand-dipped and sealed in white wax. The Balistreri's have a small vineyard of merlot and cabernet sauvignon near their winery, and they purchase the majority of their grapes from growers on the Western Slope of Colorado. The Balistreri Winery offers tasting & tours year round, wine gift baskets and a wine club. They host numerous wine tasting events throughout the year. For a special taste of what the Colorado wine industry has to offer, indulge yourself with a glass of Balistreri Wine. They are located just 10 minutes north of downtown Denver.

1946 East 66th Ave., Denver, CO 80229
303/287-5156
www.balistreriwine.com

Spero Winery
WINERIES: *Best white wines*

For the Spero Family, fine wine making is a generations-old tradition that has culminated in the creation of a fabulous urban winery, conveniently located in the popular city of Denver. Clyde and June Spero have a two-and-one-half acre vineyard that was planted in 1996 in Denver, where Cabernet Sauvignon and Merlot are grown. The family owned and operated Spero Winery uses grapes from its own vineyard. However, due to limited growing space, they also import grapes from Colorado's Western Slope and from Lodi, California, where some of the grapes come from a vineyard owned by June's cousin. Spero Winery has a fabulous selection of wines, each aged in oak barrels for two years before bottling, including vintages such as Muscat, Chardonnay and Sangiovese, along with Zinfandel and their own Colorado Cabernet Sauvignon. They additionally make a wonderful Merlot and a delightful Cabernet Franc, as well as two fabulous fruity dessert wines made from plums and cherries. Spero Winery hosts a wine tasting each Saturday, which includes a tour of the winery, and they are also happy to arrange for a private tasting with advance reservations. The Spero's further offer a wonderful assortment of gift baskets filled with great wines and favored Italian treats. Enjoy fine wine, good friends and time-honored traditions at Spero Winery.

**3316 W 64th Avenue, Denver CO
(720) 519-1506**

ARVADA

Arvada got its start in 1850 with the first gold discovery in Colorado, along the banks of Clear Creek. Prospectors found more gold in 1858, but yields were never great. Farming the fertile soil near Clear Creek was a better bet, and by 1870 Arvada had a thriving crop exchange. At one time, it was known as the celery capital of the world. Since then, the city has become a major player in the Denver Metro Area, with more than 100,000 residents. While in the area, visit the Arvada Center for the Arts and Humanities, which features a museum, two art galleries, performing arts theaters and classrooms. Each summer, the center's small outdoor concerts are a big draw.

PLACES TO GO

- Arvada Blunn Reservoir
  18001 W 64th Parkway

- Arvada Center for the Arts and Humanities
  6901 Wadsworth Boulevard
  (303) 431-3080

- Lake Arbor Community Park
  6400 Pomona

- Van Bibber Park
  58th Avenue and Ward Road

THINGS TO DO

January
- Colorado Cowboy Poetry Gathering
  Arvada Center (720) 898-7200

February
- Arvada Performing Arts Festival
  Arvada West High School

June
- Gold Strike Days
  (303) 420-6100

- Arvada Celebrates Its Trails
  (720) 898-7405 or (303) 289-0867

September
- Arvada Harvest Festival
  www.arvadaharvestfestival.com

Clear Creek and Clear Creek Canyon in fresh snow
Photo by Eric Wunrow
Courtesy of Colorado Tourism Office

West Bros. Inc.

ANIMALS & PETS: *Best handmade custom saddles and tack*

Step back in time to a simpler way of life where honesty, loyalty and hard work were the measure of a man or woman. Step back in time to West Bros. Inc., where the Old West is alive and well. This horse, livestock, tack and feed store is now headed by brothers Scott and Steve West, who with a friendly tip of the hat, a smile and a handshake, reassure you that you are in the presence of the cowboys who wear the tall, white hats. Located on the western edge of Arvada, Steve and Scott display their beautifully handmade custom saddles and tack, high quality cowboy gear for the ranch and rodeo, a complete line of livestock feed, and the finest horses available for sale. According to Scott, "You might say we are bartenders of the horse world." West Bros. Inc. is a third generation business dating back to Scott and Steve's great-grandparents, who arrived in Colorado in 1873. Today these brothers view their business as a natural offshoot of their rodeo days where they spent their younger years producing rodeos, as well as livestock. Steve freely admits, "We've always been cowboys. We shoot straight with everybody, giving them a good product at a fair price. And the best part is the advice is free." Whether you are a serious rancher, horse breeder, cowboy, cowgirl or weekend horse aficionado, you must visit West Bros. Inc., your one-stop shop for horses and gear.

7040 Indiana Street, Arvada CO
(303) 403-0288

The Healthy Hound
Natural Pet Supply & Wash

ANIMALS & PETS: *Best selection of natural pet supplies*

The Healthy Hound Natural Pet Supply & Wash offers pet owners a healthy and holistic approach to pet care. Owned by president and Top Hound Shari, this inventive new shop opened in 2005 offering its patrons an extensive selection of pet supplies designed to help pets lead happier, healthier lives. Located one block south of the Westwoods golf course, The Healthy Hound's specialized cat and dog foods are all prepared using whole, natural foods and without added fillers that can be harmful to your pets digestion, like corn, soy or wheat. These highly palatable and nutritious animal entrées are made using ingredients such as millet, potato and blueberries or pears, along with alternative meats such as venison and duck. The Healthy Hound provides a convenient and clean pet wash, featuring oversized tubs that are ideal for large dogs. You can either wash Sparky yourself or, for an additional fee, have one of the friendly and pet knowledgeable staff members do it for you. Ask about the amazing honey washes. The best part is that either way you don't have to take care of the cleanup afterward and all necessary items are supplied for you. The Healthy Hound is dedicated to the overall well being of your pet and offers canine massage by a Certified Canine Masseur. Shari is also certified in Reiki, an ancient healing art. Both massage and Reiki are ideal for dogs with emotional issues, dogs recovering from surgery or dogs with physical challenges. Treat your pets to the very best at The Healthy Hound Natural Pet Supply & Wash.

16255 W 64th Avenue, Suite 2, Arvada CO
(303) 432-7373
www.healthyhoundpetsupply.com

Joyco MultiMedia
BUSINESS: *Best video, multimedia, music and theatre productions*

Whatever your production needs, from a polished corporate video, making a fundraising video that tugs at your heart, or even a concert event involving 25,000 people, Joyco Multimedia in Arvada is ready to tackle your project. Owners Bob and Joy Coffin and their production team combine years of experience with exemplary customer service and state-of-the-art equipment. Bob has 40 years experience in video, multimedia, music and theatre productions. Since opening in 1987, Joyco Multimedia has become a leader in production services, including live and post-production and DVD/CD work. Discovering what you want and knowing how to make it happen is what Joyco MultiMedia will help you figure out. The team at Joyco will listen carefully to your desires, then craft a product that accomplishes your goals. They can script, shoot, edit, narrate and publish your project from beginning to end and turn your vision into a reality. Your project, large or small, will receive the same level of professional attention you deserve. Joyco MultiMedia not only has the skills and topnotch equipment for expert production work, but also a staff who puts their passion and creativity into each and every project, assuring that their clients will return to them for all their production needs. When you need production services, turn to Joyco MultiMedia, where your desires will become reality.

8795 Ralston Road, Suite 113, Arvada CO
(303) 421-0093
www.joycomultimedia.com

Crystaline Photography & Multimedia
BUSINESS: *Best wedding photography*

Crystaline Photography & Multimedia is finely tuned to the services and artistry that every wedding couple hopes to find from a photographer. Owned by husband and wife team Michael and Jamie Striplin, Crystaline also does portraits and commercial work, but the business focuses on wedding packages. After the photographs are taken, Crystaline will provide you with a bound proof book of all the images from your special day. From the proofs, you can select photos for a custom-made coffee table photo album that captures the day's excitement. Clients often say that there are so many great images in the proof book that it is hard to narrow down the choices of pictures for the album. Crystaline can also produce a recording of your event on DVD. Your disc will include digital linear editing, complete with music, titles, transitions and a personalized DVD menu. Michael and Jamie are masters at putting their subjects at ease, which allows them to create genuine, candid portraits. Because all of their work is by appointment, they are very easy to contact by phone. They will travel anywhere within 100 miles of Denver at no extra charge. Let Crystaline Photography & Multimedia create a photojournalistic record of your wedding or other special event while you relax and enjoy yourself.

Arvada CO
(303) 432-2954
www.crystalinephoto.com

Randall's Photography

BUSINESS: *Best portraits for families and individuals*

Randall's Photography offers stunning and highly personalized portraits for families and individuals that will become treasured memories for generations to come. Randall's Photography is housed in the historic 1910 White Church located at 7400 Indiana Street in Arvada. The church, complete with a few pews and pulpits, offers a wonderful, inviting and open space for indoor backdrops. The church sits on a one-acre lot that has been outfitted with portrait gardens that are lined with waterways, ponds and wildflower fields, along with vintage car bodies, a tractor and a myriad of other delightful props. Photographers and owners Randall and Cheryl Miller and their staff have been in the business for more than 20 years. They are truly dedicated to creating the best portraits possible. To this end, Randall feels it's important to spend time getting to know his subjects so that he can gain a feel for their true personalities and allow them show through in the finished product. Randall's Photography focuses a lot on full family, children's and senior portraits and additionally specializes in capturing handicapped children. In conjunction with portraits, Randall's Photography also does automobile photography, and some commercial work worldwide, including work in Australia, Hawaii, Mexico, Venice, Greece and London. The studio can further assist you with archiving and restoration work. Ensure that your memories are captured by the best with photographs by Randall's Photography, where they combine professionalism, technology and originality to create beautiful memories that will last forever.

7400 Indiana Street, Arvada CO
(303) 425-6077
www.randallsphoto.com

Colorado Pine Gift Basket Company & Gift Shop

BUSINESS:
Best Colorado-themed gifts

Delight your friends, relatives and business associates with a unique "All Colorado" gift from Colorado Pine Gift Basket Company & Gift Shop. Owner Carol Kinder has owned her shop for more than 15 years and is proud to offer her distinctive approach to gift giving. She loves living in the state of Colorado, and is proud to support the diverse and talented Colorado artisans and businesses that create some of the best tasting food and handcrafted products in the country. You can choose from hundreds of food and gift items to create your own custom handcrafted gift basket. Pre-made baskets are also available. The one-of-a-kind baskets come in many different packages, such as cowboy hat, old-fashioned gold pan, Colorado pottery or an all-wood crate. Items are branded with Colorado to add to their authenticity. These are the types of gifts that make a lasting impression. The only problem you'll encounter is trying to decide what to put into your basket, because you'll want a little of everything. Don't worry, though, because help is readily available. Colorado Pine Gift Basket Company is open year round and offers local delivery or UPS nationwide, so check them out next time you need a gift.

9660 Ralston Road, Arvada CO
(303) 422-4271
www.coloradopine.com

Small Gatherings
EVENTS: *Best event planning*

If you need to plan a small to large gathering from seven to 700 guests, Small Gatherings is the only place you need to call. Owner Gregg Wolfe has operated this full service business since 1996. A variety of events take place through Small Gatherings, including meetings, parties, receptions and memorial services. Small Gatherings has helped customers host anniversaries, baptisms, baby showers, retirement parties and photo shoots. With several venues available in downtown Denver and suburban areas, this treasure can house your guests in a park, church or hall that is the perfect size for your next event. The optional amenities Small Gatherings provides consist of catering, DJ's, limousine service, pastors, photographers, videographers, bartenders, wait staff, audio-visual equipment and decorating services. Small Gatherings' rental rates are kept low by keeping spaces filled with a wide variety of events and activities. Patrons of various cultures return to use Small Gatherings, because they are invited to include their own cultural food and details for any event. A recent addition to Gregg's business is the Art Gallery Café, which highlights the best of the Denver area's multicultural community through art, music, dance, literature and storytelling. You are encouraged to call Gregg at Small Gatherings for your next event to ensure it will run without a hitch or glitch.

9110 Ralston Road, Arvada CO
(303) 456-7188 *www.smallgatherings.com*

Das Meyer Fine Pastry Chalet

EVENTS: *Best wedding cakes*

A German chalet-style building, an accommodating family to put you at ease, and a talented pastry chef are the tried-and-true ingredients the Meyer family combines at the popular Das Meyer Fine Pastry Chalet in Arvada. Das Meyer specializes in European pastries, wedding cakes and tortes with a widespread reputation for excellence. Last year, the family sold more than 1,300 wedding cakes in 11 months, then relaxed a little south of the border in the 12th month. Dennis Meyer and son Zachary handle the baking and cake decorating while daughters Hillary and Rachael and their mother Elaine run the pastry shop. The Meyer family opened Das Meyer in 1990 and stole Arvada's heart with their confections. They also manage an events center and haunted house located on the property. Dennis is a master chef, recently inducted into the Colorado Chefs Hall of Fame. He has been recognized as a certified master baker by the National Retail Bakers Association and as a certified executive pastry chef by the American Culinary Federation. He is also a proud father, who brought his children up in the family business. He hails from old German stock, but is proud to merge European pastries with American confections. (Although you won't find any donuts here, because Dennis burned out on donuts early in his career.) Son Zachary is head cake designer and decorator, but any family member might be found creating a design. Beyond their abilities in the kitchen, the Meyers offer an easy hospitality that immediately puts all visitors in a great frame of mind for enjoying Das Meyer Fine Pastry Chalet and its delectable offerings.

13251 West 64th Avenue, Arvada CO
(303) 425-5616

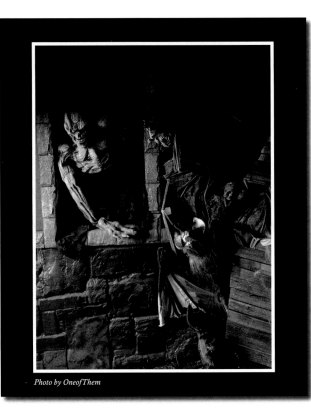

Photo by OneofThem

Field of Corpses

EVENTS: *Best haunted house*

Field of Corpses ventures where no other haunted house attraction dares to go. It's the biggest and scariest haunted house in Colorado and ranked 13th in the nation. This winner of Haunted Denver's People's Choice award in 2003 and 2004 is the brainchild of Zachary Meyer, with encouragement from the close-knit Meyer family who also run a bakery and events center on their five-acre Morningside Manor property in Arvada. When not perfecting his haunted house, Zachary designs and decorates cakes for the family business. The mystery that inspired Field of Corpses revolves around a discovery made by Torrence White and his family in their field in the fall of 1801 and the subsequent disappearances that ensued. The visitor who dares cross this threshold enters 38 to 42 separate horror-packed rooms featuring catacombs, a root cellar, electrocution chamber and sprawling cemetery. "Our aim is to scare the fluids out of you!" says Zachary. He has accomplished that goal beyond even his vivid imagination. Each year, Zachary recruits a staff of 45 volunteers from local high schools to man the haunted house during the month of October. The students and their parents sign contracts committing to the volunteer arrangement. In exchange, the students earn school credit and funds for their sponsoring organizations, which include bands, dances, forensics and boosters. Come to Field of Corpses, Colorado's first house of horror and a place where nightmares are born.

13251 W 64th Avenue, Arvada CO
(303) 423-FEAR (3327)
www.fieldofcorpses.com

Morningside Manor

EVENTS: *Best event center*

Special events deserve special surroundings, which accounts for the popularity of the family-owned and operated Morningside Manor in Arvada. At the heart of the events center is an original 1885 Arvada homestead. The facility has grown to encompass 5,500 square feet of indoor space plus immaculately cultivated grounds. Elaine and Dennis Meyer and their children own and manage three businesses on the five-acre property: Morningside Manor events center, Das Meyer Pastry Chalet and a haunted house called the Field of Corpses. Daughter Hillary manages the event center along with her duties as hostess and decorator at Das Meyer. Morningside manor boasts a country Victorian ambiance that gives it an understated feeling of warmth and domesticity in keeping with the Meyer family spirit. A park-like setting with a lush expanse of lawn, two gazebos and mature landscaping provides the perfect light filtration for photographing weddings, ceremonies and parties. The Manor can accommodate large and small parties with indoor seating capacity for 130 and a formal dining area that doubles as a dance pavilion with hardwood floors and a full window view of the gardens. Weddings can be arranged for indoor or outdoor seating with access to private rooms for the bride and bridegroom. Whether you are planning a business meeting or an anniversary, wedding or graduation celebration, Morningside Manor and the Meyer family will assure that your event is everything you hoped it would be.

13251 W 64th Avenue, Arvada CO
(303) 420-4500

Purple Avocado Catering
EVENTS: *Best catering*

For your next party, business meeting or special event, exceed all of your catering needs with the specialty creations from Purple Avocado. President Adam Thodey has been in the catering business since 1999. He prides himself on customer service as well as the providing maximum satisfaction to his clients. Purple Avocado Catering features a vast array of menu options made with only the freshest ingredients to create a gourmet cuisine selection. From Vanilla Bean-Pecan French Toast for breakfast to Mahi Mahi with Mango-Habanero salsa for dinner, the Purple Avocado Catering service will make your next event a success, and minimize your stress! Purple Avocado Catering allows for flexibility to accommodate each customer's plans, and works to create delightful displays while pleasing with exquisite tastes. With a basic menu to use as a jumping off point, they can also create luscious appetizers, entrees and desserts for your special event. With a mobile kitchen, selections are prepared on-site ensuring a fresh feast for your guests. Purple Avocado Catering also offers choices for specialized diets including vegetarian, vegan and lactose intolerant. For late nights and early mornings, Purple Avocado Catering also offers 24 hour service. Meat and cheese trays can also be supplied to events requiring just a few munchies and lite bites. For your next event, Purple Avocado Catering is able to provide everything you need to make you next event a success.

11651 W 64th Avenue, Suite A6, Arvada CO
(303) 725-9050
www.purpleavocado.com

Toni's
FASHION: *Best corset selection*

Until recently, corsets have been regaled to the annals of history as quaint and curious contraptions that were designed for the enhancement of beauty, but known to be unbearably discomforting. Over the last few decades, a resurgence of this foundation classic has made its way to boardrooms, catwalks and bedrooms across the nation. Toni's offers a wide selection of hand made corsets in a multitude of styles that are designed to enhance your figure, make you appear slimmer or offer additional support and improve posture. Unlike corsets of old, today's sexy, sultry and delightful models are made for comfort as well as appeal and have given a whole new generation of women confidence in their sensuality. Contemporary styles have taken the corset, a long held mainstay for bridal gowns, to a whole new level by offering stunning pieces that are as ideal for outerwear as they are for underwear. Owner Toni Mares offers not only an excellent array of quality corsets from top designers such as Axfords and Vollers, they also offer education on waist training, a method of combining exercise, proper nutrition and corseting to train your waist to the size and shape that suits your physique. Toni's offers a full spectrum of sizes, textiles and colors available in a multitude of styles including transgender, Victorian, gothic and bridal. Add a new dimension of allure to your wardrobe with a selection of corsets from Toni's.

7588 Harlan St Arvada, CO
(303) 215-5113

D & K Jewelry
FASHION: *Best jewelry in Arvada*

A visit to D & K Jewelers will fire your imagination and make you feel like you have found old friends. David and Kim Purdy own and operate the quaint shop in the Arvada Connection Shopping Center. They specialize in custom pieces created by David. Everything about D & K Jewelry involves respect for each customer's individuality. Kim will remember your name; David will remember your jewelry; and both owners will take the time to find you the piece that meets your needs. "We try to carry items not found everywhere else," says Kim. Shoppers can expect to find gold and silver necklaces, bracelets, earrings and pins from small and big companies, representing a wide price range. Look for big names such as Chase-Durer, Jaguar and Citizen and an unusual line of tungsten carbide watches. David apprenticed under an Old World German jeweler in Colorado Springs and has over 30 years experience as a gemologist. He is adept at rebuilding and repairing jewelry as well as building and designing individual pieces. The Purdys met at a jewelry store, married and opened D & K Jewelry together. Bring your heirlooms to D & K Jewelers where the coffee, candy and peanut brittle are always ready, and the owners take a personal interest in your satisfaction.

5220 Wadsworth Boulevard, Suite U, Arvada CO
(303) 421-4194
www.dkjewelers.com

Let's Frame It
GALLERIES & FINE ART:
Best custom framing

Let's Frame It is on the cutting edge of custom picture framing. Located 20 minutes from downtown Denver, Let's frame It offers a very large selection of sizes, mats and colors. Customers can place the item they want framed on a flat surface, experiment with different frame pieces and then be able to get a sense of the finished product from the mirrors over head. Owner, Jeni Jankowski manages a large staff that prides itself on the caring attention given to customers needing extra time. You will be pleased to learn all work is done in house. Typically, items can be framed in 4 to 5 days. Sports memorabilia stores enlist the services of Let's Frame It for various mountings such as the very popular framed sports jerseys.

What better gift for a friend or relative than a beautiful picture and a gift certificate to Let's Frame It. Jeni extends a warm invitation for you to visit Let's Frame It to see for yourself the number of ways she can dress up a picture.

6410 Ward Road, Arvada
(303) 423-1658

Tranquility Salon & Day Spa

HEALTH & BEAUTY:
Most innovative salon and day spa

Tranquility Salon & Day Spa brings relaxation and rejuvenation to a whole new level. Owner Bonny Wohlcke has been in the beauty industry for 35 years. A renowned educator, Bonny has lectured nationally with Nioxin Research Laboratory on the subject of hair loss and restoration. She has also helped with perm techniques, and has taught hairstylists a better understanding of perm chemistry. In 2001, she opened Tranquility Salon & Day Spa in Arvada. Her hairstylists are on the cutting edge and can help you with fine hair and hair loss problems. With VLP technology, they can remove hair, take years off with the photo light rejuvenation system and minimize spider veins on the face and legs. They are a full-service salon with expert stylists performing foils, tints, perming and hair cutting techniques with the latest fashion in styling. Tranquility offers a full menu of facial treatments, including European, paraffin, multi-vitamin and acne treatments. Bonny's estheticians will even design a chemical peel or microdermabrasion treatment specifically for your skin type. She also has permanent make-up artists on staff who specialize in eyeliner, eyebrow design, and lip design, and can also help with corrective services. Manicures, pedicures and reflexology are available, along with an assortment of massages, including Swedish, hot stone, prenatal, Reiki and couples massage. You can get a cranial sacral massage to ease those worry lines, get rubbed down in a salt glow or body treatment, or be transported by aromatherapy. No matter what you choose, your body will thank you. When it's time for serenity and renewal, Tranquility Salon & Day Spa is the place to go.

7841 Wadsworth Boulevard, Arvada CO
(303) 432-9SPA (9772)
www.tranquilitysalonanddayspainc.com

Apple II Day Spa & Salon
HEALTH & BEAUTY: *One of Colorado's largest spa/salons*

If you are searching for your own little slice of heaven here on earth, the family-owned and operated Apple II Day Spa & Salon in Arvada may be just what you are seeking. Co-owned by mother-and-son team Janice and Christopher Apple, Apple II was originally begun by Janice in 1985 as Apple Blossom Beauty in a 700-square-foot building in Olde Towne Arvada. With the addition of Christopher, it has evolved into one of Colorado's largest and most comprehensive spa/salons, covering 5,000 square feet and with a staff of more than 25 people. Apple II does just about everything and, according to Christopher, "We do it well." In an age of automation, Apple II remains a customer service oriented business. Nearly every phone call is answered by a member of the Apple family, often by co-managers and Apple sisters-in-law Kristine Apple or Niamh Fitzpatrick. The beauty and spa business is a people business, so the staff pays close attention to all the details of every customer's experience every time they visit the spa. Apple II's always immaculately clean facility includes three steam areas, a dry sauna, 27 jet hydrotherapy tubs and men's and women's shower and locker facilities. The Apples believe that they can only be as good as the people who represent them and they have been fortunate to retain many long time staff members, including the best group of hair designers in Colorado. Apple II Day Spa and Salon also offers a full retail area with more than 30 lines of professional beauty products. Visit often and be well pampered at Apple II.

7279 W 52nd Avenue, Arvada CO
(303) 431-6346 *www.apple2dayspa.com*

Yacht Club Salon

HEALTH & BEAUTY: *Expert salon services*

The Yacht Club Salon creates more than business relationships; its customers become extended family. Owner Heidi Marks Casler, director Brooklyn Motta and the staff will see to your comfort with a warm and relaxed environment while treating you to quality hair, nail and skin care at reasonable prices. Hair design services include cuts, styling, coloring, permanent waves, extensions and straightening. For weddings and special occasions, the stylists here can create just the look you seek. They have many suggestions for pre-wedding services that can include the entire wedding party. The salon features the finest in professional product lines and specializes in Dermalogica and Sanitas skin care and Glō™ Minerals cosmetics. Expert manicures and pedicures will keep you primped from head to toe. The Yacht Club Salon also includes massage among its relaxing services. The salon is proud of its apprenticeship program, which accepts only promising students with raw talent and friendly personalities. In addition to professional salon services, Heidi and her team actively give back to the community through their annual fundraisers and donations to Locks of Love, an organization that creates hairpieces for children who have lost their hair due to medical procedures. For great looks, high standards and a warm welcome, visit the Yacht Club Salon.

6790 Sheridan Boulevard, Arvada CO
(303) 427-2567

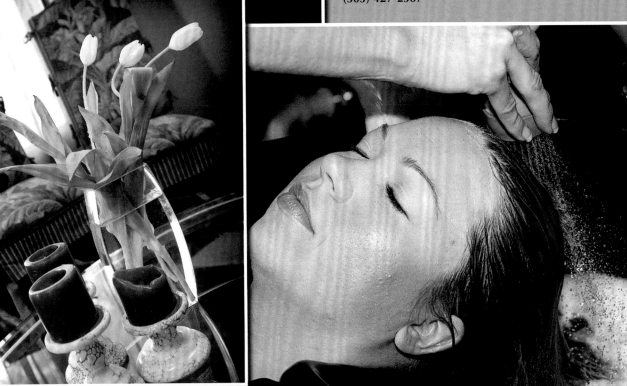

Photos courtesy of Spirited Images Photography

Green Mountain Yoga
HEALTH & BEAUTY: *Best yoga courses*

Green Mountain Yoga, which opened its doors in April of 2005, offers a full spectrum of yoga courses from beginning through expert levels. This fabulous new center provides a warm, welcoming and stress-relieving atmosphere that is the ideal backdrop for this ancient practice. Owner and founder Mindy Arbuckle has created a wonderful and enriching place where anyone, or any body, can come to learn and practice the art of yoga, which provides stress relief, flexibility, strength and relaxation, among other benefits, such as improved balance. Green Mountain Yoga focuses primarily on a variety of hatha yoga styles, which are "flowing classes that focus on balancing the body, mind and spirit," according to Mindy. Green Mountain also offers kundalini classes based on the science of the body and the technique of yoga. Green Mountain Yoga also offers teachings designed to heal the body through the use of yoga therapy, and further teaches how to keep one's body, heart and mind in natural alignment, which can enable yoga practitioners to lead longer, healthier and ailment-free lives. Green Mountain Yoga offers chakra balancing and specially designed classes for children who wish to pursue yoga, as well as instruction for those who wish to learn yoga in order to lose weight and tone their muscles. The center has a yoga store where you can find chakra necklaces, local artwork and gear. Experience better health, relaxation and peace of mind at Green Mountain Yoga in Arvada.

8566 Five Parks Drive, Arvada CO
(303) 421-4131
www.greenmtnyoga.com

Curves For Women
HEALTH & BEAUTY: *Best weight loss center*

A treasure catering to women in Arvada is the local Curves For Women fitness center owned by dynamic duo Virginia Nigg and Teresa McCubbin. In business since January of 2000, these sisters show no signs of sibling rivalry, as their joint goal is to help women live healthier lives by providing them with a 30-minute total workout in a comfortable environment, complete with weight-loss guidance. Virginia adds that this "makes health and fitness an achievable goal". For those with health concerns, including diabetes, heart disease or cancer, curves gives safe low-impact workouts. Curves For Women even earned its place in the *Guinness Book of World Records* as the World's Largest Fitness Center Franchise. Besides its prestigious name, Curves For Women of Arvada, one of 8,000-plus locations worldwide, provides members with weight loss and fitness instruction in one center, an idea unique to the fitness industry. Curves was designed to belong to a town like Arvada, providing a community-oriented atmosphere, where members see family and friends alike during workouts. Using hydraulic resistance machines and aerobic recovery stations, members exercise in a circuit system. Each 30-minute workout includes cardiovascular, strength training and stretching with the motivation of music and guidance of a qualified instructor. With no required contracts to sign and a low monthly fee, becoming a member of Virginia and Teresa's Curves For Women is as simple as it was to voice last year's intended New Year's resolution of "I'm going to exercise this year."

6480 Ward Road, Arvada CO (303) 467-2776 *www.curves.com*

Dance Boulevard
RECREATION: *Best dance studio*

As owner and artistic director of Dance Boulevard in Arvada, Amie Bergondo seeks to create a dance environment filled with joy, commitment, energy and the true love of dance. With this philosophy, Amie opened Dance Boulevard in 1995. Amie has extensive professional training as a dancer and choreographer and worked for Manhattan Dance Project while she studied under director Bill Hotaling. Currently, she employs six additional teachers and has a student enrollment of 300. Dance Boulevard teachers provide instruction in a full complement of dance styles for all ages, including jazz, ballet and tap. The studio specializes in Broadway-style dancing for children up to age 18. Amie's students make up the largest contingent in the Arvada Harvest Festival Parade, dancing the entire two-mile parade route. She is the choreographer for Faith Christian Academy's special program that is performed each year at the Oberon Arts Festival. Dance Boulevard is also in demand for Sweet 16 parties where everyone at the party learns a dance technique. Movements and costumes are always age appropriate. "We try to make dance fun for students," says Amie. Her students have appeared in music videos for Sony Music Entertainment and were the first dance group from Colorado to perform in Roses, Spain, at the St. John's Day Festival. Whatever your age or dance interest, Amie invites you to come be a part of the excitement at Dance Boulevard.

12351 W 64th Avenue, Arvada CO
(303) 421-8462

HomeScapes
HOME: *Best home décor*

If you've grown weary of doppelganger lampshades and carbon-copy knick-knacks then it's time for you to discover the surprisingly exciting and oft-changing array of fabulous home décor items that awaits you at HomeScapes in Arvada. Owner Brenda Bott opened this chic décor boutique in 1994 and offers an astounding array of incredible pieces for your home that range from gorgeous artificial floral arrangements to must-have pine furniture. HomeScapes is the ideal place for husbands to scout out gifts for upcoming events because it's hard to go wrong with anything you find. At HomeScapes, they also have one-of-a-kind pieces of decorative art and accessories along with window treatments, rugs, lamps and baskets. However the excitement doesn't stop there, they also have an incredible selection of gift items including candles, cards, Brighton jewelry and accessories. HomeScapes is undoubtedly well known for their selection exceptional customer service and are equally touted as one of areas most popular destination stores. Long time customers often bring in out-of-town guests so that they can also enjoy this exquisite shopping experience. Brenda is constantly changing and updating inventory so that each visit is a new adventure. Whether you are in search of the perfect hostess gift or just need a splash of something new for the living room, head to HomeScapes where every visit brings forth new discoveries.

12650 W 64th Avenue, Arvada CO
(303) 421-2600
www.HomeScapesDesigns.com

Colorado Coins Cards & Comics

SHOPPING: *Best comics and collectibles*

Colorado Coins Cards & Comics in Arvada is a treasure trove for the collector. This meticulously clean, service-oriented store engages kids and adults with its many unusual collectibles, including Star Wars action figures, rare coins, sports cards and comics. The shop, owned by the Wray family, stocks over 200,000 comics from inexpensive 10-cent titles to high priced, hard-to-find X-Men issues. Look for new releases every Wednesday. Every comic copy comes complete with a bag and a board to preserve its original condition. Collectors who need additional organizational and preservation supplies for their collections will find an extensive selection of useful items,

including boxes, rigid plastic holders and frames. The Wrays believe in excellent customer service and employ coin, sports card and comic book experts to answer customer questions. If you can't find it in the store, just ask, and the Wrays will make an effort to locate the item you seek. One of the perks of shopping at Colorado Coins Cards & Comics is a subscription service to useful publications for collectors. Visit Colorado Coins Cards & Comics, it's just 15 minutes from the Denver metro area and provides a world of entertainment to anyone who enjoys three of the country's favorite collecting pastimes.

**6695 Wadsworth Boulevard, #A-B, Arvada CO
(303) 425-0924**

Lollipop's Doll Shoppe

SHOPPING: *Best doll shop*

Linda Nowak has been taking a discerning look at dolls for more than 25 years and has owned several doll stores. In 2004, she partnered with Terry Shannon to open Lollipop's Doll Shoppe in Arvada. The shop carries everything from modern Barbie dolls to 1920s collectibles. Look for angel dolls, celebrity dolls, Madame Alexander dolls and several lines of imported dolls including Zwergnase dolls from Germany. Stuffed animals of the very best quality, including the famed Steiff brand German teddy bears, also occupy this house-turned-shop, renovated by Linda and Terry. Lollipop's is most well known for its newborn nursery and adoptions center, featuring newborn-sized baby dolls. If a child selects a baby doll on a Saturday, Linda prepares

an official adoption, complete with a little paperwork and a check-up, where Linda dons nurse's scrubs. A photo of the new parent and child completes the adoption, much to the delight of everyone present. Lollipop's is just as attractive to grown-up doll lovers as to children, and Linda knows many serious doll collectors. Linda is the buyer for the shop and can acquire special dolls not in the inventory for her customers. She also stocks doll clothes and books about dolls. Whether you are a big or little, Lollipop's Doll Shoppe is sure to delight you and bring out your instinct to protect and adopt these well-crafted treasures.

**6905 Webster Street, Arvada CO
(303) 463-550**

Marcia's Costumes
SHOPPING: *Best costumes*

Arvada is home to one of the most imaginative businesses in the region, the renowned Marcia's Costumes. All types of costumes are available at Marcia's including theatrical, professional clowns and live action role-playing attire. The enterprise caters to school parties, plays and theme parties as well as a multitude of festive events. Entertainers and clowns consider Marcia's Costumes the headquarters for business. The shop provides theatrical makeup and face paints as well as an unmatched expert knowledge of all aspects of the business from Marcia and the whole staff of employees. The shop is also stocked with an excellent supply of wigs for rental or purchase. Chemotherapy patients are welcomed and will find the professional service invaluable. Marcia's Costumes accommodates many costume weddings, providing theme costumes for the entire wedding party. They feature a convenient Internet shopping experience with the option to pay on-line and expedient shipping. Take your time browsing through Marcia's Costumes, there is a lot to see. It's a great way to spend an afternoon. Plan early for Halloween or seasonal events. Make your next party a theme party and let Marcia's Costumes dress you for a day.

5368 N Sheridan Boulevard, Arvada CO
(303) 288-8330
www.marciascostumes.com

AURORA

Aurora is Colorado's third largest city, with a population of about 300,000. Founded in 1891, the town adopted the name Aurora in 1907. In 2004, *Sports Illustrated* honored Aurora as its 50th Anniversary Sportstown for Colorado because of its exemplary support for sports. A large number of professional athletes hail from the city. Aurora supports seven municipal golf courses. Among Aurora's many festivals is the unique PumpkinFest, where ingenious gourd-launching devices hurl pumpkins hundreds of feet into the air.

PLACES TO GO

- Aurora History Museum
  15051 E Alameda Parkway (303) 739-6666

- Aurora Reservoir
  5800 S Powhaton Road (303) 690-1286

- Cherry Creek State Park
  4201 S Parker Road (303) 699-3860

- Expo Park
  10955 E Exposition Avenue

- Morrison Nature Center at Star K Ranch
  16002 E Smith Road (303) 739-2428

THINGS TO DO

May
- Java Fest
  Fletcher Plaza
  www.auroragov.org/JavaFest

June
- Fiesta Aurora
  www.auroragov.org/Fiesta_Aurora

- Aurora Asian Film Festival
  Aurora Fox Arts Center (303) 326-8695

July
- Kidspree
  www.auroragov.org/KidSpree

September
- Aurora's Festival International
  www.aurorabusiness.org/Festival_International.cfm

October
- PumpkinFest
  www.auroragov.org/PumpkinFest

Houses in the Stapleton redevelopment in Aurora

Back on the Rack Beadery
ARTS & CRAFTS: *Best bead shop*

Back on the Rack Beadery is a treasure trove of sparkling goods waiting to be strung together by your own two hands. Owners Diane and Rick Ott are professional jewelry designers who have poured their passion into offerings for the jewelry hobbyist or professional designer. Trays of beads and semiprecious stones lay in glittering piles. Rows of beads in every shape and color beckon from their racks. Back on the Rack stocks over 100 stones, including Swarovski crystals. Look for Czech glass and Bali beads, plus carved wood and bone. The one thing you won't find is plastic. The shop's certified instructors give classes and workshops for people aged 10 and older. They teach

techniques of wire wrapping, working with precious metals and molding clay. Students create pendants, necklaces and earrings using newfound skills in jewelry design and construction. Back on the Rack Beadery offers a fun venue for your next birthday party or special occasion. Whether you are inspired by sterling and gold filled beads or fresh water pearls, a visit to Back on the Rack Beadery will offer the products you need to create something precious for yourself or a loved one.

4325 S Buckley Road, Aurora CO
(720) 870-4820
www.backontherackbeadery.com

Colpar Hobbies
ARTS & CRAFTS: *Best hobby shop*

When thoughts turn to spare time activities, hobbyists turn to Colpar Hobbies in Aurora. Colpar Hobbies and Owner Richard Wolf have been serving the Denver area since 1969, so there's not much about hobbies he and his staff don't know. The Aurora shop opened in 2002 and is best known for its radio controlled cars and planes. The hottest items in today's hobby world are radio-controlled helicopters, a specialty at the store's Lakewood location. Other favorites include radio-

controlled sailboats. Look also for popular slot cars and train sets. If you are looking for a gift or specialized items, you'll find the kind of knowledgeable help you need at Colpar Hobbies, where most of the employees are avid hobbyists. From rocket kits to jigsaw puzzles, the variety at Colpar is astounding. Science lovers will want to take a good look at the chemistry sets, microscopes and telescopes. A staggering selection of model tanks and planes fill the military model section. You'll also find sci-fi and car models, making Colpar's model selection the largest in the Denver area. As the store's motto proudly announces, "Your spare time is our business." Colpar Hobbies takes that business seriously and gives Denver superior selection and service, including repairs on many of its products. Next time you have time on your hands, visit the spare time experts at Colpar Hobbies.

804 S Havana Street, Aurora CO
(303) 341-1554 or (800) 876-0414

Daniel's of Paris
BAKERIES, COFFEES & TEA:
Best bakery in Aurora

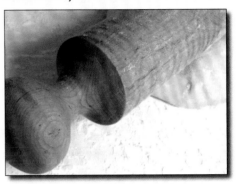

Daniel's of Paris has been a leading Colorado bakery for 23 years, and its small staff takes extreme pride in its work. The people at Daniel's strive to ensure that only the finest cakes, pastries and breads are presented to their customers. Daniel's specializes in wedding cakes and can customize the cake of your dreams. The shop uses treasured recipes of generations of famous European chefs. All cakes begin with a French *genoise*. Slightly dry, the light texture and delicate flavor of *genoise* are enhanced by simple syrup. When assembled with frosting, the result is a dessert that is elegant enough for any occasion. Daniel's also offers pastries, cookies and quiche. The award-winning cinnamon rolls have a wonderful sliver of baked almond cream in the center. You can stop by the shop and enjoy these fresh-baked products with a cup of coffee. If you do, staff members greet you with a friendly smile. Daniel's makes every effort to give customers what they want, when they want it. While it is always best to book wedding orders well in advance, Daniel's does its best to take last-minute orders that most other bakeries would decline. The shop has been voted Aurora's best bakery four years in a row and has also been repeatedly cited for best cookies. Owner and baker Jim Pasquariello invites you to enjoy the great baking traditions of France and Europe by visiting Daniel's of Paris. *Merci beaucoup* for your continued patronage.

12253 E Iliff Avenue, Aurora CO
(303) 751-6084

Denver Lincoln Limousine Inc

BUSINESS: *Best limousine rental service*

When your special occasion calls for luxurious transportation, charter your Chauffeured vehicle from Denver Lincoln Limousine, Inc. Operating under Colorado Public Utilities Commission LL-139 issued 1988, president A. C. Poppenberg, III, has more than 20 years in the industry. Classroom training for all chauffeurs offered by Executive Chauffeuring School and *Limousine & Chauffeured Transportation Magazine* results in highly trained chauffeurs who have earned the trust and confidence of such notables as the Denver Broncos' owner and family, his coaching staff, the NFL Commissioner, United States Secretary of Commerce, Donor Alliance Coordinators, Specialists, and Transplant Surgeons. You'll be buying unmatched safety with style and comfort. Their all-black fleet of Lincolns includes 85" and 120" DaBryan stretched Town Cars, as well as the L series Town Cars that come from the factory with an additional six inches of rear passenger leg room. Winter driving is no problem, with a fleet of 4x4 Navigators making a short trip to Vail and Aspen effortless, regardless of weather. This fleet of vehicles is the largest new fleet to meet or exceed all Federal Motor Vehicle Safety Standards (FMVSS). Other safety features include real time internet GPS tracking and DriveCam video protection. Denver Lincoln offers parents peace of mind when their children charter any vehicle with a Strictly Alcohol Free Event (S.A.F.E.) agreement, signed by children/students and parent. Their discounted wedding packages are also very popular. On March 05, 1999, Denver Lincoln Limousine, Inc. became the first Denver area company to qualify for national certification* in safety and service quality. At Denver Lincoln Limousine, it's what you don't see that makes a difference. See them on their website, or give them a call.

3760 Wheeling Street, #6, Aurora CO (303) 741-5466 or (888) 741-LIMO (5466) *www.741limo.com*

Before

After

Leading Lady Photography
BUSINESS: *Best women's photography*

Since 1985, Leading Lady has been Colorado's first and finest women's photography studio. For women by women, Leading Lady is nationally known for its flattering, sensual photos. Women of all ages are transformed into extraordinary beauties under the expertise of owner Shirlee Robinson and her staff. Shirlee has been a featured guest on many televisions and radio talk shows, is a national speaker at photography seminars, and is rated one of the top women's photographers in the world. More than just a fabulous experience; Leading Lady has been called "The Masters of Makeover." Patricia Rivera, longtime stylist and make-up artist, works her magic to fine tune an already great look or create a fabulous new one. Ladies love the soft, glamorous look they achieve in the comfortable, safe environment. The studio is a cross between a full-service salon and a classy hotel suite. Leading Lady's clients come from all over the country to create a special birthday or anniversary gift. Of course, Christmas and Valentine's Day always book up early. Some women even do a shoot as a weight loss reward or for a great photo for *match.com*. Artistic mother-to-be photography is very much in demand, as are 12-month custom calendars. Giving someone a sexy photograph is as much fun for the giver as the receiver, and is a terrific ego boost. Call or visit Leading Lady Photography's website for a magical, unique experience and romantic photos guaranteed to keep the home fires burning.

12380 E Bates Circle, Aurora CO
(303) 337-9393 *www.leadingladyphoto.com*

Sir Chocolate, LLC
EVENTS: *Best chocolate fountains*

Sir Chocolate can help you relive childhood fantasies of a house made entirely of sweets, or help you place a large chocolate waterfall at your next party. Owners Doug and Linda Whittaker began this delicious business in 2003 and bring elegant presentations of melted chocolate cascading down three or four-tiered fondue fountains to any special event. Choose from milk, dark or white fondue, or offer your guests all three. If you're having a themed party, Sir Chocolate can color the chocolate to match your décor. Graduation parties with school colors flowing through the fountain or red, white and blue Independence Day fountains are sure to be the talk of the night. For true chocolate aficionados, the fountains already decadent chocolate flavor can be enhanced with such rich overtones as mint, butterscotch or amaretto. Choose from a wide assortment of goodies to dip in the melted chocolate. Strawberries and chocolate are always a winning combination, but equally delicious are fresh pineapple, mini cream puffs and brownies. With gift baskets and gourmet fondue jars from Sir Chocolate, you can have a spur-of-the-moment fondue party whenever the mood strikes. Call Sir Chocolate to bring stunning chocolate fountains to your next get together. Sir Chocolate also offers franchise opportunities for chocolate lovers looking to start their own business.

13900 E Florida Avenue, Aurora CO (303) 671-7150 *www.SirChocolate.com*

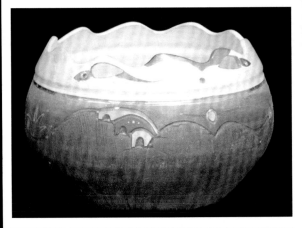

Sunrise Art Works
GALLERIES & FINE ART: *Best pottery*

Primitive pottery of ancient civilizations brought the mystery of symbols sculpted into classic vase forms into the 20th century. Such are the creations of Walt Weinberg. Walt is a Colorado native who graduated from the University of Colorado in 1968 with a BA in Spanish. Shortly after graduating, Walt became interested in pottery and apprenticed for a Boulder potter. In 1971, Walt opened the Santa Fe Pottery studio in Denver, which became the retail showcase for several ceramic artists and painters. In 1998, Walt moved to his current location on Florence Street in Aurora where he established Sunrise Art Works. Sunrise Art Works houses a variety of working artist's studios and galleries. Walt's pieces are decorated with a variety of glazes, iron oxide washes, carvings, sculpting and the unique use of gold and lusters that give the artwork a distinctive look. Walt Weinberg began his career in pottery over 35 years ago, incorporating his knowledge of languages and his innate ability in sculpture which is a powerful combination. Hearkening back to the petroglyphs, hieroglyphs and woven basketry of our forbears are Weinberg's very personal symbols etched into the earthly colors and matte finishes that are then thrust into the present with the sophistication of 24 karat gold and luster glazes. His functional sculpture reflects spirited ancient forms of contemporary beauty.

1556 Florence Street, Aurora CO
(303) 361-9282

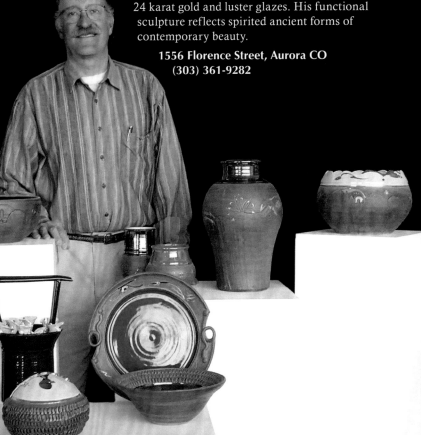

Emmet Fine Furniture

HOME: *Most creative furniture*

Emmett Malone, the name behind Emmett Fine Furniture, is one of those do-it-yourselfers who turned a project into a career. Needing a footboard and headboard for his bed, he decided to forego the trip to a furniture store and try to build them himself. Not only did he enjoy the experience, but he realized he had a real talent for working with wood. Today, he shares his skills and love of woodworking with the public by creating unique pieces for his Aurora-based store. It's not just the shapes of his chairs, tables, cabinets and desks that make them so different, Emmett loves to mix his woods, making for fantastic and artistic lines and grains. He deftly melds American hardwoods like cherry, maple and walnut, with exotics, such as mahogany, bloodwood, wenge and zebra. In all, he uses 18 individual types of wood to work his magic. For Emmett, each project is a spiritual experience. For the consumer, this means heavenly curves and color combinations. Whether you're looking for a radical rocking chair, sophisticated stereo cabinet or vivacious vanity, Emmett's fashionable furniture is as practical as it is photogenic. Discover a conversation piece you can really use with a visit to Emmett Fine Furniture.

755 Lola Street, Aurora CO (303) 520-9217
www.emmettfinefurniture.com

Carmine Lonardo's Meat Market— Gourmet Italian Deli

MARKETS: *Best gourmet deli*

Imagine producing more than 1,500 pounds of sausage a day. That is just one of the many ways Carmine Lonardo's Meat Market has been serving local restaurants and the community for more than 25 years. This is a family-run business started by Carmine, Sr. and his wife, Lois, in 1979. Their original store is located in Lakewood. The Aurora location opened in 1993. Carmine and Lois, with their four children, Tony, Louise, Carmine, Jr. and Maria, incorporate Old World values and work ethic to deliver authentic Italian fare. Carmine, Jr. runs the Aurora store while his other siblings help out at the Lakewood location. This is Old World Italiano at its best, combining the finest of hormone-free meats, gourmet Italian foods, cheeses, bakery items, balsamic vinegars and fine oils. Lonardo's is famous for their homemade Italian sausages. There's also Parma prosciutto ham, Genoa salami, capocolla, provolone and more. Lonardo's deli menu features sandwiches, like slowly smoked barbequed beef brisket, Italian meatball, hot pastrami and calzones. The deli allows you to sit in, carry out or call ahead for delivery. Need a break from cooking? Carmine Lonardo's can help with such prepared items as Lasagna, baked ziti and eggplant Parmesan. Visit Lonardo's the first chance you get. They will make you feel like family.

158380 Smokey Hill Road, Aurora CO
(303) 699-4532
7585 W Florida Avenue, Lakewood CO
(303) 985-3555

Sir Loin Meat Shoppe

MARKETS: *Aurora's best deli-style market*

The neighborhood butcher shop is perhaps the most revered memory of America's halcyon days. The Sir Loin Meat Shoppe in Aurora incorporates the best of those old time shops, but they go a few steps further with a selection of exotic meats and gourmet products their bygone brethren did not even imagine existed. At Sir Loin Meat Shop you will find all the favorite cuts of high quality beef, pork lamb and chicken. You will also find Rocky Mountain elk, venison, alligator, buffalo, ostrich, quail, wild boar, frog legs and more. Sir Loin can provide game processing and knife sharpening. The shop features live lobster and fresh fish, along with a mouth watering assortment of sauces, spices, soups, homemade sausages and brats. They carry nearly 2,000 items in all. Sir Loin is the only retail outlet to carry Piedmontese beef, an all natural beef raised in Montana, that is incredibly tender and more lean with less fat and cholesterol than other types of beef. New to Sir Loin is a line of Kosher meat and grocery items. Types of meat include chicken, turkey and Piedmontese Kosher beef. Sir Loin has a friendly and knowledgeable staff that includes Johnson and Wales Culinary students. Sir Loin Meat Shoppe started 35 years ago and has been named the best deli in Aurora. The Pissare family bought the shop in 1999, and while continuing the tradition of excellence, they have added their stamp with new offerings and enthusiasm for gourmet enjoyment. Whether you're stocking your freezer, or just want to stop in for one of their gourmet sandwiches, which use only the finest Boars Head deli meat, be sure to visit Sir Loin Meat Shoppe in person or online.

1910 S Havana Street, Aurora CO
(303) 751-0707
http://sirloinshop.stores.yahoo.net

La Cueva Restaurante
RESTAURANTS & CAFÉS: *Best Mexican food*

When Norma and Nabor Nuñez opened La Cueva Restaurante in Aurora in 1974, seating was limited to a few booths, a counter with 13 stools and a unisex bathroom. In 1987, the Nuñez family bought the building next door, knocked out part of a wall to expand the dining area and hired their daughter, Molly, who is a designer, to update the décor. Today La Cueva seats 80 to 100 patrons, and the cheerful dining room sports turquoise banquettes and bright neon. The food, however, has not been updated. Their son Alfonso still rises at five in the morning to begin preparing the same family recipes his father grew up on in Guanajuato, Mexico. Everything is made fresh from scratch, and the attentive, professionally-trained staff makes sure everything arrives at your table piping hot. La Cueva's menu includes traditional tamales, enchiladas, and chile rellenos, as well as house specialties and fresh homemade tortillas and salsa. Try the innocent-looking but fiery green chile, said by some to be legal lip remover, but definitely worth it. La Cueva features daily lunch specials Monday through Saturday and weekend dinner specials. *Westword* honored La Cueva for Best Chips and Salsa in 1992, *5280 Magazine* honored them for the Best Margarita in 2001, and La Cueva was voted the Best of *Citysearch* for 2006/2007. La Cueva also gets a thumbs up from AAA, *Mobile Travel Guide*, *Zagat's* online survey, and the *Denver Post*. Find out why people line up outside the door for the authentic Mexican food and colorful setting at La Cueva Restaurante.

9742 E Colfax Avenue, Aurora CO
(303) 367-1422
www.lacueva.net

Señor Miguel's
RESTAURANTS & CAFÉS: *Hottest chile in Aurora*

Are you looking for that hole-in-the-wall where the locals find authentic, inexpensive food? Come to Señor Miguel's, a cozy New Mexican restaurant which boasts the Hottest Chile in Town. The restaurant is small, with seating for just 30, but large in flavor with portions sized to fit even the healthiest appetites. Señor Miguel's is a favorite of the Gabby Gourmet, a local food reviewer and radio personality. All dinner entrées, from flautas to tamales, are less than $10. When you order a burrito, you can choose a handheld version or one smothered in green chile sauce. Señor Miguel's provides home deliveries for the nights when your day went too long to plan dinner. Orders of chiles, menudo and salsa are available by the pint or quart. If you are getting on the road early, try a selection from the Eye Openers menu of assorted breakfast burritos, which Señor Miguel's serves weekday mornings beginning at 6:30 am. You can choose chile the way you like it, from mild green chile to a full-flavored hot version or something in between. Whether you enjoy fire on your tongue or something milder, visit Señor Miguel's for food that speaks directly to your taste buds.

14583 E Alameda Avenue, Aurora CO
(303) 360-7784
www.senormiguelsnewmexicanrestaurant.com

Fatburger

RESTAURANTS & CAFÉS: *Best burger in Aurora*

Food franchises sometimes get a bad rap, but there is a reason some concepts spread like wildfire: Because they're good. In 1952 Lovie Yancy came up with one of those concepts worthy of fame. She created big, fat juicy burgers that could only be named one thing: Fatburger. Half a century later, Lovie's burgers are as fat and juicy as ever and being served all over the country, including four restaurants in Colorado. The burger menu is huge, with a list of condiments that allow you to customize your burger any way you want. Their buns are baked fresh, onion rings are cut daily, and the restaurants themselves are fun places, filled with ever-blasting jukeboxes cranking out classic soul, rock'n'roll, R&B and hip hop. Besides beef burgers, you can fill up on turkey burgers, chili dogs, grilled chicken sandwiches, real milk shakes with hand-scooped ice cream and a lot more. It's no wonder Fatburger has received the Best Burger award by local newspaper readers.

14221 E Cedar Avenue, Aurora CO
8255 S Chester Street, Centennial CO
9344 Dorchester Street, Highlands Ranch CO
7465 N Academy Boulevard, Colorado Springs CO
(303) 740-6069 *www.fatburger.com*

Jim 'N Nick's Bar-B-Q
RESTAURANTS & CAFÉS: *Best barbecue*

A good idea is bound to get out and about, just like Jim 'N Nick's Bar-B-Q restaurant, an inspiration born in the American South that is now available in Aurora. Its origins spring from the belief that great barbecue and outstanding Southern food are the best ambassadors for Southern culture, and that Southern hospitality is high art. At Jim 'N Nick's, barbecue is more than meat and sauce. It's a get-together of the highest order, a shared experience of hickory and fire, of past and present, where passionate people share memorable experiences. The meat that feeds the passion is smoked over hickory wood and finished on a true brick pit. The process takes 14 hours, but the food can be on your table five minutes after you order it. Consider smoked pork hot links, classic spare ribs or pulled pork. Baked potatoes here come piled with smoked bacon, butter, sour cream and cheddar cheese. Chili, stews and salads are also popular, along with such munchies as hand-breaded onion rings and their signature cheese biscuits. Jim 'N Nick's is at once upscale and downscale, a place for quick takeout or a relaxed dining experience. To get the same great Jim 'N Nick's flavors that folks in Alabama, Georgia and Florida have known for some time, local owner Todd Koone invites you to Jim 'N Nick's Bar-B-Q.

24153 E Prospect Avenue, Aurora CO
(720) 274-5300
www.jimnnicks.com

Angelo's CDs & More
SHOPPING: *Best music and movie store*

When people in the Denver metro area go shopping for music and movies, they inevitably visit Angelo's CDs & More, one of the reasons this store keeps opening new locations. The first shop opened in Aurora in 1990, followed by a Littleton location in 1991, a Thornton location in 1997 and a Wheat Ridge store in 2005. Chances are you will find what you are seeking in Angelo's inventory of more than 20,000 refurbished CDs, 6,000 DVDs and 40,000 new CDs. You can find hip-hop, heavy metal or a hard-to-find movie here, and you can trade or cash in on your own personal stock of CDs and DVDs. Regular Angelo's shoppers earn free CDs and DVDs as their purchases mount. In 15 years of operation, Angelo's has given away more than 22,000 CDs and DVDs to loyal customers. Angelo's shoppers benefit from the customer service, fine merchandise and fun atmosphere here. The Angelo's website will keep you up-to-date on special events and area performances by popular bands. Owner Angelo Coiro loves music and knows how to make people happy, both his customers and employees. His store has been voted best used CD store in the Denver area and best hip-hop store in the Rocky Mountain region. When you want music or movies, come to Angelo's CDs & More, where compact discs have been a way of life since the early days when they first revolutionized the music industry.

16711 E Iliff Avenue, Aurora CO
(303) 337-1399
www.angeloscds.com

Snuggle Bugs
SHOPPING: *Best baby boutique*

For the best dressed babies, mothers shop at Snuggle Bugs. Like the original Parker store, Snuggle Bugs in Aurora is a baby boutique, specializing in gifts and clothing you won't find at large retailers. Lesleigh Potter stocks the shop with everything from handmade furniture, with custom choices of style, design and color, to diaper bags and bedding. She carries birth announcements and invitations for showers and birthdays, and monogramming services are available for that special touch. Specialty products abound, and high-end baby clothing, christening gowns and plush animals from Gund bring parents and gift seekers the quality and choices they crave. You'll even find books on caring for a baby. Snuggle Bugs provides everything you need for a fully outfitted nursery. Look for dressers, lamps and cribs, along with accessories and special frames for those first endearing photographs. When you register for baby gifts on the Snuggle Bugs website, your friends and family know right where to turn when contemplating a baby shower gift. Gift certificates are available. For the best dressed baby in the neighborhood and a nursery that's the envy of all new moms on the block, shop at Snuggle Bugs.

6240 S Main Street, Suite 103, Aurora CO
(303) 805-4446
www.snuggle-bugs.com

Dry Dock Brewing Co.
WINERIES & BREWERIES:
The Beer Barons of Aurora

The first microbrewery in Aurora started out as a hobby for Kevin DeLange and Kevin Kellogg. The two Kevins own Dry Dock Brewing Co., a business that celebrated its first year with a Gold Medal at the 2006 World Beer Cup for its HMS Victory Extra Special Bitter (ESB). The award signifies the ESB is a world-class beer that accurately represents its particular style of brew. When you reach this level of expertise in competition with 540 breweries from 56 countries, you are worth the consideration of beer connoisseurs everywhere. Kevin DeLange began as a home brewer, then bought the Brew Hut to sell supplies to home brewers. When the space next door became available, DeLange teamed with Kellogg to start Dry Dock. These two owners are enthusiastic about beer and willingly share their recipes with their home brewing customers, who can enjoy a brew while shopping for supplies. The microbrewery is open to the public afternoons and evenings Tuesday through Saturday, when you can sample five stock beers, three seasonals and an occasional experimental batch. The stock offerings include Dry Dock's now famous Extra Special Bitter, an India Pale Ale, a foreign-style stout, a light Scottish ale and a vanilla porter. Known as the Beer Barons of Aurora, the two Kevins share their expertise in a monthly column in the *Aurora Daily Sun*. They invite beer aficionados and the mildly curious to sample their microbrews at Dry Dock Brewing Co.

15110 E Hampden Avenue, Aurora CO
(303) 400-5606
www.drydockbrewing.com

EDGEWATER

Much of Metro Denver consists of large suburban municipalities. In contrast, Edgewater is a small suburb of one square mile and a little more than 5,000 people. In Edgewater, a single citizen can have an impact. This friendly community has a colorful past. It is literally across the street from Denver's Sloan Lake Park. In 1861, Thomas Sloan activated an underground spring while digging a well to irrigate his farmland. The well flooded 200 acres overnight. People rode horse back from Denver to see Sloan's Lake. Sloan switched from farming to cutting winter ice, which he packed in sawdust stored in sheds. The community west of the lake became known as Edgewater. The Manhattan Beach amusement park was built on the north side of the lake in 1891, and included a zoo, roller coaster and skating rink. Bands played, hot air balloons carried passengers aloft and a lady was shot from a cannon. The early 20th century was a time of saloons and gambling, and people moved to Edgewater to escape the reach of the Denver police. Ladies of the evening clustered along Emerald Street (now 25th Avenue). Fires, accidents and Prohibition closed the amusement park, the houses and the saloons. Still, grape-growing became suddenly popular during Prohibition.

THINGS TO DO

August
• Edgewater Days
  (303) 232-4201

A Girl and Her Ribbon
SHOPPING: *Best Victorian-themed gifts*

Queen Victoria's reign, Britain's first modern monarchy, symbolized morality and family values and gave rise to elegant fashions. At A Girl and Her Ribbon, the Victorian age comes to life in an attractive selection of dolls, gifts, jewelry, and a wide assortment of greeting cards. Owner Lupe Gallegos opened this specialty shop in 2003 in an effort to bring a little civility and distinction to the avenue. Located at 25th Avenue and Sheridan, A Girl and Her Ribbon is just 15 minutes from downtown Denver. True-to-life Victorian dolls stand two feet tall and wear authentic period dresses. Step into the past where life was fit and proper and women dressed in feminine, romantic styles, donning ruffles and lace. Lupe invites you to journey back to the era of elegance at A Girl and Her Ribbon.

5217 W 25th Avenue, Edgewater CO
(303) 462-1158

ENGLEWOOD

Englewood was the site of one of the gold discoveries that touched off the Pikes Peak or Bust gold rush of 1859. Settlers soon turned to agriculture. At the end of the 19th century, the area developed a saucy reputation because of saloons and gambling houses erected outside the reach of Denver law. In 1903, a group of pioneer ladies led a successful effort to clean up the town by incorporating it as a city. In 1905, a young Swedish doctor founded a tuberculosis sanatorium, and thereafter Englewood gained a reputation for hospital care. Today, Swedish Medical Center has a Level 1 trauma center designation and Craig Hospital is rated as one of the top 10 rehabilitation hospitals in the United States. CityCenter Englewood, built on the site of the old Cinderella City shopping center, is a national model for mixed-use transit-oriented development. Englewood Station, a light rail and bus transit hub, is an integral part of the development. The station, part of metro Denver's developing rapid transit system, is open for business.

PLACES TO GO

- Belleview Park and Children's Farm
  5001 S Inca Drive

- Museum of Outdoor Arts
  1000 Englewood Parkway, Suite 2-230
  (303) 806-0444

- Pirate's Cove Aquatic Center
  1225 W Belleview Avenue
  (303) 762-COVE (2683)

- Recreation Center
  1155 W Oxford Avenue
  (303) 762-2680

THINGS TO DO

March
- Englewood Arts National Juried Art Show
  (303) 781-0035

August
- Englewood Fun Fest
  Belleview Park
  (303) 798-6927

Rocky Mountain Beadtrader

ARTS & CRAFTS: *Largest bead selection*

A word of warning: the fine (and tiny) art of beading can become an addiction. If you happen to be one of those fortunate enough to be afflicted by this decorative habit, then the Rocky Mountain Beadtrader is a place you don't want to miss. Cindy Imbraguglio and Jay Phillips are passionate about beads and beading. Cindy has more than 30 years experience in jewelry and beading. She designs and creates her own beads, so starting the Rocky Mountain Beadtrader was a labor of love. The Beadtrader now carries the largest assortment of beads in the state. The store has beads of every kind, shape, size and material, from semiprecious beads to pearl and metal beads. Cindy and Jay

even import gorgeous, hard-to-find beads from exotic places like Africa. The Beadtrader features Colorado bead artisans who work in both glass and porcelain. Cindy and Jay offer classes for beginning to advanced beaders and carry all the supplies and equipment you need to get started. Their class times are flexible, and no class is ever more than six students, because they want to be sure to give each person individualized attention. They'll even work with a student one-on-one. Cindy and Jay want to introduce people to this intricately delicate pastime and provide them with the kind of customer care that is certain to get them hooked. Once you are hooked, let Rocky Mountain Beadtrader be your bead shop.

2750 S Broadway, Englewood CO
(303) 781-2657

Diversions Needlepoint

ARTS & CRAFTS: *Best needlepoint supplies*

With more than 200 kinds of thread and 9,000 different needlepoint canvases, Diversions Needlepoint can keep you in stitches for a long time. Established in 1970, Diversions continues to supply the materials needed for this specialized form of embroidery, which lends itself to wall art, upholstery, pillows, holiday décor, purses and decorative boxes. The knowledgeable staff adds many personal touches to their products and services and will help you find what you need to create successful pieces at your level of experience. Needleworkers appreciate the variety of thread

choices at Diversions, including silks, cottons, wools and synthetics, as well as the large selection of hand-painted needlepoint canvases, which provide an easy to follow visual guide. Stitch and thread guides are available with a select group of canvases to add ease and accuracy to the projects. For threads, supplies, and great ideas that will captivate beginning and advanced needleworkers, make a trip to Diversions Needlepoint.

1610 E Girard Place, Suite G,
Englewood CO
(303) 761-7766
www.diversions-needlepoint.com

Passionate Palette

ARTS & CRAFTS:
Best cooking classes

If you have always wanted to be a chef, but career and family responsibilities have forced you to put your dream on hold, fear not. The Passionate Palette in Englewood is a cooking school for the home chef. Founded by the culinary partnership of Ben Davis and Jenifer Suydam, the Passionate Palette offers hands-on cooking classes in a fun and comfortable setting where you can learn the finer points of the culinary arts. Ben and Jenifer offer classes for families and teens, single folks and couples. Ben was formally trained at the California Culinary Academy in San Francisco and boasts an impressive resume. Jenifer was an experienced restaurateur who served in several management positions at fine-dining establishments. Together they have created a culinary cottage industry that brings people together and allows both beginners and advanced cooks to sharpen their skills. Ben and Jenifer want you to feel comfortable and at home at the Passionate Palette, whether you are planning a corporate team building event, a client thank you class, a 50th birthday party or are just joining a scheduled class. They are sure that you will have a memorable evening. As they like to say, "Why settle for dinner when you can have an experience." Take them up on their offer by dropping into the Passionate Palette and develop your inner chef.

9623 E County Line Road, Englewood CO
(303) 754-0005
www.passionatepalette.com

Tint Crafters on Broadway
BUSINESS: *Best window tinting services*

Tinted windows are sleek, ecological and protective. A car with tinted windows looks distinguished; tinted windows keep sunlight from fading fabrics as well as providing passengers relief from the heat. At Tint Crafters, owner Lee Knight along with David and Vicki, her installers, pride themselves on giving the best service to their customers. In business for 15 years, Lee is a car nut who strives to provide superior care for automobiles. With this goal in mind, Tint Crafters offers the Clear Bra, a technology used on vehicles during Desert Storm to protect the front end from corrosion. Are you interested in having custom graphics applied to your car? Tint Crafters can do it. Additionally, Tint Crafters can provide window tinting to your business or residence, giving the home or office the same protection from the sun as a car and cutting down on air conditioning use. Clients with medical conditions that require minimal sun exposure find such a service indispensable. For a distinguished look to your car, nothing works better than the creative customization Tint Crafters can deliver.

48305 Broadway, Englewood CO
(303) 761-8330

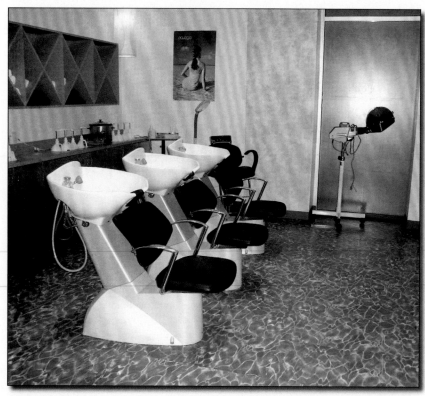

Salon Trendz
HEALTH & BEAUTY: *Best salon in Englewood*

A visit to Salon Trendz in the fashionable Englewood City Center is a refreshing way to improve your look and your outlook. Owner Lisa Phelps and a team of stylists, aestheticians, nail technicians and massage therapists run a modern salon with old-fashioned customer service values. Salon Trendz is, as its name implies, a place that keeps abreast of innovative new styles. Stylists receive ongoing education and put their knowledge to use providing everything from cuts and color to braiding, updos, waxing, and eyelash and eyebrow tinting. Add to your overall refreshment with such spa services as a sugar scrub facial or one of several specialty massages, including the hot stone, deep tissue or chair massage. Salon Trendz specializes in providing makeup and hair services for wedding parties. The salon also hosts glamour parties for girls between the ages of 10 and 16, giving them a fun experience in proper makeup application. You can buy your favorite haircare products here, including those by such well known companies as Redken, American Crew and Aquage. When your hair and the rest of you is ready for some well deserved professional attention, let the experts at Salon Trendz show you what cutting-edge styles and services can do for you.

901 W Englewood Parkway, Suite 100, Englewood CO
(303) 783-2889
www.salon-trendz.com

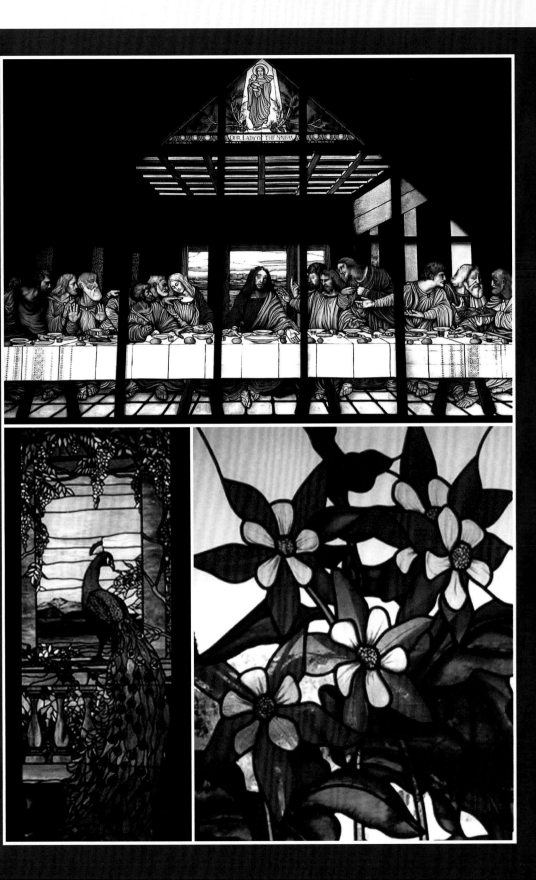

Watkins Stained Glass Studio

HOME:
Best stained glass windows

You could say that stained glass artistry is in the blood of Phillip Watkins, Jr., owner of Watkins Stained Glass Studio. For eight generations, members of the Watkins family have dedicated their lives to creating stained glass, a tradition that goes back to England in the mid 1700s. Phil's great grandfather came to Denver in 1868, bringing his tools and glass in a covered wagon, and continued the tradition here. Four generations of Watkins men have created beautiful stained glass windows that adorn churches, buildings and homes throughout the state and the Rocky Mountain region. Phil began helping out at the studio at age five and made his first church windows, by himself, at the age of 12. Many of the techniques that he uses today are the same ones that his grandfather and great grandfather used a century ago. He does all steps by hand and each piece is a custom project. Whether it is a huge cathedral window or a small sidelight for a modest home, Phil approaches each commission with the same careful attention to detail and precision. Large projects like the Last Supper, made for Our Lady of the Snow Catholic Church in Granby, can take a year or more to create. Also helping out at the studio are Joan Chandler, his wife Jane and his daughters. There is also a gift shop in the front of the studio with fine glass gifts, the most popular are the fused glass necklaces made by Jane and Kitt. For a close-up look at a centuries-old craft in a museum setting, visit Watkins Stained Glass Studio.

3821 S Broadway, Englewood CO
(303) 798-1515
www.WatkinsStainedGlass.com

Wagner's
HOME: *Best dining furniture*

The dining furniture you purchase for casual dining is probably going to see plenty of use, whether you're eating breakfast with the family or enjoying a summer barbecue on the patio with friends. Wagner's in Englewood specializes in casual dining with styles that appeal to many tastes. You'll find everything from kitchen tables and chairs reminiscent of the 1950s to elegant metal and wood tables, many with super-comfortable upholstered rolling chairs. Gary Oxman's establishment brims with dining options, including options in fabrics and finishes. Wagner's can also help you extend the entertainment options at your home with finely crafted bar and stool setups by quality manufacturers like Walton and Masterwork. Recreational tables can transform a family room and bring friends and family together. Wagner's stocks such choices as pool and air hockey tables, along with card tables and foosball tables. The patio furniture is stunning with cast aluminum, wicker and wood choices that add enduring beauty and practicality to your deck or porch. Patio season is also the time to find extraordinary specials at Wagner's that exceed even the usual great prices. With three floors of furniture, Wagner's aims to meet and exceed your demands for quality, style and choice. You are certain to find styles you appreciate here right along with professional assistance to answer your questions and help you with customization options. Find out just how stylish casual dining furniture can be with a visit to Wagner's.

3400 S Broadway, Englewood CO
(303) 789-4206
www.wagnersfurniture.com

On Target Computer Arena
RECREATION: *Best on-line game parlor*

On Target Computer Arena is a gateway to the World Wide Web and all of its vast possibilities. Customers can log on to one of the 32 computers in the local area network at On Target and play games with people from all over the world. The excitement over Internet gaming has swept the nation as more and more people find out about online role-playing games, such as World of Warcraft, Counterstrike and Halo. In these virtual worlds, gamers develop characters, go on various missions and interact with other people playing at the same time. On Target is a convenient place to drop in to check your email or surf the Web, too. For true computer aficionados, On Target even offers birthday parties. The hourly rates for Internet access are very reasonable, and you will begin earning discounts after you have used On Target's service for 25 hours. You can purchase a membership and receive even lower rates. The staff at On Target understands that sometimes players just have to get through one more level before leaving the game, so they stay open late into the night. The Internet offers something for everyone, and you can access it all at On Target Computer Arena.

3461 S Broadway, Englewood CO
(303)783-4714
www.ontargetarena.com

United Martial Arts Center
RECREATION: *Best martial arts center*

Imagine knowing you could defend yourself against an assailant if the situation ever arose. The instructors at United Martial Arts Center in Englewood hope you never are attacked. Still, the rewards for learning self-defense go far beyond being able to fight effectively. Even if you never have to use your skills on the street, you will develop confidence while increasing your fitness, energy and mental focus. Classes at the United Martial Arts Center use Tae Kwon Do as a basis for blended instruction, which includes Brazilian Jiu Jitsu, Muay Thai kickboxing and Hapkido. "It isn't just punching and kicking," says Theresa Doster, director of the center. The tenets of Tae Kwon Do, she points out, stress integrity, self-control and perseverance. The life skills that students learn, in other words, are just as important as the street skills. Through the center's Little Ninjas classes, children as young as four learn martial arts techniques that help develop balance and coordination and encourage team work. Adults need no previous experience to take a class. The center offers beginning, intermediate and advanced instruction for both women and men. For self-defense and a better sense of self, enroll today at the United Martial Arts Center.

1610 E Girard Place, Englewood CO (303) 783-9632 *www.umac.us*

Pan Asia Bistro
RESTAURANTS & CAFÉS:
Best Southeast Asian cuisine

The Pan Asia Bistro offers a sensational variety of Southeast Asian menu items influenced by Thai, Chinese, Vietnamese and Mongolian cuisine. As you enter you'll appreciate the circular iron staircase and beautiful floors that grace this contemporary Englewood building. The arrangement of tables in the dining room facilitates comfortable conversation, while the lighting, flowers and table settings all set the mood for fine dining. Upstairs, an exclusive private dining room, complete with its own bar and lounge, is an excellent location for private family gatherings or corporate functions. Start with any of the delicious appetizers, including potstickers, wontons, egg rolls or lettuce chicken wraps. Sushi rolls include numerous raw and cooked temptations, and favorite soups include egg drop, hot and sour, miso and wonton. Your hardest task here will be making a selection from the assorted entrées. The Malaysia chicken curry consists of chicken, sweet onions, carrots and lemongrass simmered in yellow curry and presented in a coconut shell. Other tempting options include noodle bowls, Kung Pao Triple Delight, General Tao's Chicken and lo mein with beef, shrimp or chicken. Cap off your feast with one of the restaurant's American desserts, such as cheesecake, chocolate mousse, ice cream or a raspberry chocolate pyramid. For attention to detail in service, food and surroundings, visit Pan Asia Bistro.

10520 El Diente Court, Englewood CO
(303) 708-9088

The Bridal Library

SHOPPING:
Best resource for planning a wedding

Planning a wedding can be one of the most stressful events in your life. An excellent way to reduce the tension is to rely on The Bridal Library for all your planning needs. At The Bridal Library, you have access to hundreds of wedding locations and professionals for your wedding. There is always a certified bridal consultant on hand to answer your questions via e-mail or phone. Use of The Bridal Library is free. They offer additional consulting and coordination services if you need them. The Bridal Library's business model is similar to that of an old-fashioned travel agency, with the fees paid by the vendors of the services you book. Services arranged by The Bridal Library can include finding the perfect location, caterer or florist. They can also assist you with finding the highest quality photographers and entertainers. They also produce small bridal shows and other events monthly. Visit The Bridal Library to find out how they can help you.

**3384 S Broadway, Unit B, Englewood CO
(303) 593-2091**

Rocky Mountain Clocks

SHOPPING: *Best clock shop*

Clock lovers will want to make special note of this treasure. Rocky Mountain Clocks in Englewood is Colorado's largest clock shop, featuring hundreds of clocks, from antiques to modern timepieces. Owner Pat Downey's shop is a mecca for clock collectors. He can fix any clock that doesn't work. If the parts you need can't be found, he'll make it himself. No matter what kind of clock you want, this is the place to start. Anitque clocks are Pat's first love, and he usually has at least 200 of them on hand; Everything from the most casual of kitchen clocks to pocket watches and the grandest of longcase clocks. He carries Kieninger clocks, Hermle clocks, Howard Miller clocks and other famous names. If your clock needs repairs, Rocky Mountain Clock company will pick it up and deliver it if necessary. If you buy a grandfather clock from Rocky Mountain Clocks, they'll deliver it, set it up and cover it with a full warranty. When it comes to clocks, there really isn't any need to go anyplace else. Visit Rocky Mountain Clocks and you'll see what we mean.

2739 S Broadway, Englewood CO
(303) 789-1573
www.rockymountainclocks.com

Colorado Wildflowers
Photo by Tom Stillo
Courtesy of Colorado Tourism Office

GLENDALE

Glendale, with a population of less than 5,000, is entirely surrounded by Denver. Glendale's fire department is merged with that of Denver through an agreement between the two municipalities. This is a high-density community, with nearly 100 percent of the population in multi-family housing. Still, it is the kind of community where it's easy to get to know your neighbor. Residents value the city's urban village feeling. Cherry Creek Trail is popular with walkers, bicyclists and skateboarders. During regular business hours, Glendale's population increases by about 12,000 as employees flock to more than 300 businesses. The Colorado Department of Public Health and Environment is in Glendale, as are several insurance businesses and non-profit organizations. Shopping is ample and many restaurants, both locally owned and national chains, offer everything from drive-thru service to fine dining. Glendale's new 3,000-seat rugby stadium opened in 2007.

PLACES TO GO

• Four Mile Historic Park
  715 S Forest Street
  (303) 399-1859

THINGS TO DO

July
• Glendale Fireworks
  Creekside Park
  (303) 759-1513

Cherry Creek bike path
Photo by Brian Gadbery
Courtesy of Colorado Tourism Office

For the Love of Dog

ANIMALS & PETS:
Best doggie day care

Leaving a dog home alone for the day can breed boredom, unhappiness and destructive behavior. Dana Hood at For the Love of Dog in Glendale offers a doggy day care and spa to keep your beloved best friend happy and healthy in your absence. Dogs are never caged; they receive love and attention, safe play areas, clean surroundings, healthy snacks and constant supervision. Dana, a member of the Association of Pet Dog Trainers, is passionate about working with dogs and offers basic training for all of her charges, with help from operations manager Robb Horen and floor supervisor Punkin, Dana's Pomeranian. Your dog builds positive social behavior and confidence in your absence and at the end of the day when you are ready to relax, your happy and tired pet will be ready to join you. For the Love of Dog also offers grooming services for that stinky pooch, or you can use the professional grooming equipment yourself and let the staff clean up the mess. The *Denver Daily News* called For the Love of Dog "the best doggie day care on the planet," Glendale Chamber of Commerce named it Small Business of the Year in 2004, and they won the 5280 Top of the Town 2006 Editor's Choice award. A retail shop on the premises offers natural foods, fun toys and dogwear. The Bark-n-Ride dog limo service can even transport your pet to and from daycare. Let the experts at For the Love of Dog provide your beloved dog a home away from home.

4751 E Virginia Avenue, Glendale CO
(303) 355-6700
www.fortheloveofdog.com

Arvilla Skin Care and Spa

HEALTH & BEAUTY:
Most exceptional treatments

Clients love the welcoming spirit and professionalism of the staff at Arvilla Skin Care and Spa. *Citysearch* gives this spa its highest ratings. Owners Tawnya and Jackie Hutchinson, mother and daughter, lead the team of beauty and wellness professionals in a spa that brings together exceptional treatments in a quaint, Old World atmosphere. Four massage therapists and four aestheticians provide treatment programs that yield impeccable results and complete relaxation. Arvilla customizes both skin care and massages to customer needs. The shop offers a wide range of facials, from a quick pick-me-up to a full treatment that will leave you sparkling like a diamond. Microdermabrasion can diminish scars, discoloration and wrinkles. Arvilla has a treatment for almost every part of you, from a soak and massage for feet, called the Foot Haven, to the Crowning, which involves massaging aromatic and revitalizing oils into your scalp. Swedish, deep tissue and hot stone massages are available. Arvilla also offers special massages for new or expectant moms. The Traveling Chair massage can come to your place of business. Clients remark on Arvilla's pain-free waxing. Arvilla's uses all-natural skin care products, such as the organic Arcona and Eminence lines. The shop hosts bridal, teen and birthday parties and sends birthday cards to all clients as a personal touch. Arvilla supports many charities, including animal rescue services and the Avon Walk against breast cancer. Come to Arvilla Skin Care and Spa to discover why customers love this spa.

**4340 E Kentucky Avenue,
Suite 147, Glendale CO
(303) 758-5145**
www.arvillaskincare.com

Horseback riding in Colorado

GREENWOOD VILLAGE

By 1950, the area now called Greenwood Village was a happy little community of farmers and suburbanites with a few creative types thrown in. These people viewed the inexorable advance of urbanization with some trepidation. When Englewood sought to condemn some local land to build a reservoir, distressed residents petitioned to form a town. The measure passed narrowly and the new town organized a community fair to pay its legal expenses. Today, Greenwood Village retains its open feel with more than 300 acres of parks and 100 acres of undeveloped open space. The village also houses the Denver Technological Center, the home of many technology-oriented companies. Commuters into the Tech Center raise Greenwood Village's daytime population from around 13,000 to more than 70,000 people. Greenwood Village has two stations on the metro area's light rail rapid transit system, at Arapahoe and Orchard Roads. The *Rocky Mountain News* claims that Westlands Park has the best children's playground in the metro area.

PLACES TO GO

- Curtis Arts & Humanities Center
  2349 E Orchard Road

- Westlands Park
  5701 Quebec Street

THINGS TO DO

June
- Greenwood Village Goose Chase
  www.goosechase.org

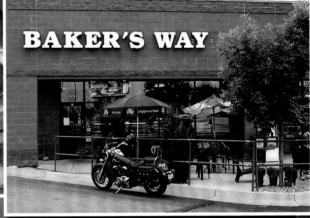

Baker's Way

BAKERIES, COFFEE & TEA:
Best breads and muffins

You can smell the baking bread from the parking lot,
even before pushing open the door to Baker's Way in
Greenwood Village. Once inside it's a game of hurry
up and wait as bread lovers shuffle to the register, each
customer ordering favorites, such as braided challa, San
Francisco sourdough or garlic parmesan. Baker's Way
bustles with regulars who know the menu by heart and
newcomers who are perplexed by the bounty of bread,
pastry and sandwich choices. The 13-year-old bakery is
tucked in a strip mall just off Arapahoe road, but feels
like a small town shop where neighbors gather and gab,
trading stories, news and histories. When it's finally your
turn, you might choose a loaf of dark raisin walnut and
the turkey panini with sharp cheddar and fresh basil from
the menu board. When the sandwich arrives stuffed with
goods, you can savor each bite from a sunny corner table.

8181 E Arapahoe Road, Greenwood Village CO
(303) 770-1966
www.bakersway.com

Paula's

FASHION:
Best social occasion gowns

All eyes are on the bride as she glides down the aisle, but this day is not hers alone. The mother of the bride wants to look as special as her daughter, and that's where Paula Mitchell comes in. Paula is the creative source behind Paula's, a social occasion boutique in the Cherry Hills Marketplace in Greenwood Village. Paula's is the place where mothers and grandmothers of the bride and groom go to find the gowns to match the significance of the day. It's the place for prom dresses and social occasion gowns, from cocktail party attire to outfits for rehearsal dinners and corporate to-dos. Paula's sells one-of-a-kind dresses, while offering specialized tailoring, alterations and consultations in a bright, friendly and accessible shop. You'll be served by a staff of long-time employees and be greeted by Buffy, the resident Pomeranian. The next time you need a gown that will allow you to look as you have always dreamed of looking, visit Paula's.

**2500-A E Orchard Road,
Greenwood Village CO**
(303) 689-9593

The Palms Tanning Resort
HEALTH & BEAUTY: *Best tanning facility*

The Denver Broncos cheerleaders are seen by millions of people while performing during the football season. They depend on The Palms Tanning Resort, the official tanning resort for not only the Broncos cheerleaders, but also the cheerleaders of the Denver Nuggets, the Colorado Rapids and the Colorado Crush. You don't have to be a cheerleader to have the desire for a great tan. Anyone can avail themselves of The Palms Tanning Resort's stellar services, and at a reasonable price. The Palms utilizes top-of-the-line equipment, changing bulbs frequently and cultivating a friendly atmosphere. The Palms is the first tanning resort of its kind. The number one tanning salon in North America, they pride themselves on their service and attention to detail. In the few short years they have been open, they have already received prestigious national and local accolades from the indoor tanning industry, including recognition from the *Denver Business Journal* as a successful upstart tanning resort that is taking on the best of the established tanning salons in the area. The Palms has several different types of equipment to meet your tanning needs, with affordable tanning sessions depending on the time and type of equipment you select. With two locations to serve you, visit The Palms Tanning Resort to maintain your year round healthy vibrant glow.

8577 E Arapahoe Road, Suite A, Greenwood Village CO   (720) 488-6890
9325 Dorchester Street, Suite 128, Highlands Ranch CO   (303) 346-1154
www.ThePalmsTanningResort.com

Chicago Mike's Deli

RESTAURANTS & CAFÉS: *Best pizza in Greenwood Village*

Chicago Mike's Deli brings good old-style Chicago to Greenwood Village. Owners Barry Fiore and Steve Schnarr have been in the restaurant business since 1984. Many sports fans will remember Fiore's, Barry's original restaurant/sports bar in Littleton. Barry had thought he was ready to retire. He closed the doors to Fiore's in 2002. Truth be told, he really missed his business. He teamed with Steve and pulled all the memorabilia out of the closets and went back to work. Barry and Steve love to feed people and they love to feed people what they enjoy most of all, good old Chicago food. They've got a true Chicago pizza recipe that's more than 80 years old and is second to none in Colorado. How about some homemade sausage and meatballs served with roasted sweet peppers and/or hot Giardiniera peppers on Italian bread? Barry and Steve feature a world-class Stromboli, Maxwell Street-style Vienna Polish sausage, and a Reuben to die for. When you're looking for a bite of old Chicago out west, head on over to Chicago Mike's Deli and say hello to Barry and Steve . . . MANGIA! MANGIA!

9614 E Arapahoe Road, Greenwood Village CO (303) 925-1334

3 Margaritas
RESTAURANTS & CAFÉS:
Best Mexican food

For the past seven years Erik Sorenson Nieto and Gladimiro Roja Aguilera of 3 Margaritas have been serving up spicy and satisfying Mexican food at their Greenwood Village classic. The flavorful touches of homemade tortillas, a full bar flowing with freshly blended margaritas and Sundays filled with live mariachi music keep hungry visitors returning to this appealing dining room. Diners enjoy lunch and dinner daily specials from comfortable booths arranged in rooms with high ceilings and arched doorways. For new taste sensations try the seafood chimichanga or tacos al carbon. The restaurant features generous happy hour specials on some drinks and appetizers in the early evening, late night and midday on Saturdays and Sundays. 3 Margaritas offers takeout, outside seating with mountain views and a large children's menu. Fresh and healthful choices include burritos, enchiladas and salads with your choice of chicken, beef or seafood. House specialties, complete with rice, beans, tortillas, guacamole and salsa, can be ordered in full or half portions. The *sopa de albondigas* (meatball soup) is a meal in itself. It's made of minted pork meatballs and vegetables and served with tortillas and onions. A private dining room serves parties up to 50 people. Bring the whole family to 3 Margaritas, and take home warm memories of dining satisfaction.

**6864 S Clinton Street,
Greenwood Village CO**
(303) 925-1667

Stanley Pappas Cigars

SHOPPING: *It's not just a cigar; It's an experience*

Stanley Pappas Cigars in Greenwood Village provides much more than a great cigar; it offers a rich experience in cigar smoking. Family-operated for 14 years, the shop treats the visitor to the comfortably masculine atmosphere of an actual railroad dining car from 1888. Sitting at your intimate table for two, you are surrounded by the dark comforts of hardwood cabinetry and leather furniture. Hanging from the arched ceiling of the dining car is a row of elegant crystal chandeliers. Cabinets with glass doors house over 400 styles of fine cigars. Stanley Pappas cigars are made from a three-tobacco blend, grown in the Dominican Republic from Cuban and Dominican seed. Consider the full-bodied flavor of the Classic Corona, hand rolled in a spicy Sumatran wrapper. If your taste runs to mild, savor the aged tobaccos in the Epiphany cigar with its Connecticut wrapper. In the Athena, master rollers use a double wrapper of Dominican and Connecticut tobaccos along with a refreshing Pappas tobacco blend. The chocolate flavored smoke of the Alexandra is pure heaven. Since Stanley Pappas Cigars supplies hotels, restaurants and casinos, you may find a Stanley Pappas cigar anywhere in the United States, Europe, Australia or South Africa. You can order some cigars by the bundle instead of by the box, making it easy to fill your home humidor. Join worldly adults enjoying such pleasures as the Victoria or the Nemphi along with their espresso at Stanley Pappas Cigars.

9656 E Arapahoe Road, Greenwood Village CO
(866) 229-9356
www.stanleypappasfinecigars.com

Bouldering in Colorado

HIGHLANDS RANCH

Highlands Ranch is one of the country's most successful master-planned communities. Where the metro area meets the Western wilds, Highlands Ranch is home to more than 80,000 people. In a few years, Highlands Ranch will be fully developed with up to 90,000 people and commuter light rail into Denver. Among the most architecturally unique structures in Colorado is the historic Highlands Ranch Mansion, which gave its name to the community. The mansion features 14 bedrooms, five fireplaces, a great room, a ballroom and a private courtyard. The property is still a working ranch.

PLACES TO GO

- Falcon Park
  9555 Fallbrooke Drive

- Highlands Heritage Regional Park
  9651 S Quebec Street

- Northridge Park
  8800 S Broadway

- Red Tail Park
  2674 Pemberly Avenue

- Redstone Park
  3280 Redstone Park Circle

THINGS TO DO

May
- Taste of Highlands Ranch
  (303) 471-8888

July
- 4th of July Celebration
  (303) 471-8888

August
- Arts Festival and Wine Tasting
  (303) 471-8888

- Colorado Scottish Festival & Rocky Mountain Highland Games
  www.scottishgames.org

September
- Highlands Ranch Days
  (303) 471-8888

- Oktoberfest
  (303) 471-8828

Jacobs Eyecare Center

HEALTH & BEAUTY: *Best eye care*

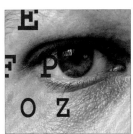

Most of us dislike going to the doctor, whether it's the family doctor, dentist or eye doctor. That's why you may be surprised to find that the folks in Highland Ranch actually look forward to going to their eye doctor, because a very special clinic is in their midst. Jacobs Eyecare Center is well known for taking good care of their patients. Every patient receives outstanding personal assistance from start to finish. Dr. Lawrence Jacobs and his excellent team of opticians have passion for not only the eyes, but for their patients as well, and many are known on a first name basis. Family and child focused, Jacobs Eyecare Center provides eye care for the entire family in an exceptionally comfortable environment. Along with providing personalized vision exams with state-of-the-art diagnostic equipment, patients are educated about eye health and learn about ergonomics and other techniques so they can take preventative measures to protect their eye health. Patients are invited and encouraged to attend informational events and seminars featuring the latest in eyecare treatments, such as laser surgery, so they can be better informed of techniques available for particular conditions. With all this personalized service and genuine care, it's easy to see why Jacobs Eyecare Center was voted Best of the Best by the *Littleton Independent* for best eye care provider from 2001 to 2003 and again in 2005. Make an appointment to view the selection of more than 1,500 eyeglass frames at Jacobs Eyecare Center.

2000 County Line Road Suite B, Highlands Ranch CO
(303) 794-2020
www.eyecarecenterhr.com

LAKEWOOD

With a population of more than 140,000, Lakewood is one of the two largest suburbs of Denver. Lakewood has one of the best views of the Rocky Mountain foothills. Lakewood's new Belmar downtown area, finished in 2007, sports narrow streets and small pedestrian-friendly blocks with a million square feet of shops, restaurants and services. The development includes 1,300 new townhouses and lofts, and 700,000 square feet of office space. Parks and plazas give people places to relax and enjoy festivals and markets. Belmar offers galleries and studios to artists. The new downtown is kitty-corner from the Lakewood Heritage Center in Belmar Park, which includes 10 historic structures and 30,000 artifacts, plus a popular outdoor amphitheater. With more than 80 parks, Lakewood is tops for outdoor activities. Bear Creek Lake Park is the city's most popular playground. Filled with a large fishing lake, paved and dirt biking and hiking trails, picnic areas and a summer water-skiing concession, this 2,600-acre park has something for everyone. For mountain lovers, the steep terrain at Green Mountain Open Space Park offers a great workout and scenic mountain views. The city maintains two public golf courses.

PLACES TO GO

- Bear Creek Greenbelt
  2900 S Estes Street (The Stone House)

- Bear Creek Lake Park
  15600 W Morrison Road, Morrison

- Dinosaur Ridge
  16831 W Alameda Parkway, Morrison

- Lakewood Heritage Center in Belmar Park
  801 S Yarrow Street

THINGS TO DO

August
- Lakewood Art Fest
  (303) 987-7850

October
- Lakewood Cider Days
  (303) 987-7850

Premier Fish & Reef

ANIMALS & PETS:

Healthiest fish in Lakewood

Aquarium buffs will take to Premier Fish & Reef the way fish take to water. With its large inventory of common and exotic fresh and saltwater fish plus aquarium supplies, the Lakewood store has everything a beginning or advanced aquarium owner needs. Owners Jack W. Calabrese and Will Lindquist put a high priority on fish health by placing all tanks on separate filters and quarantining new fish until they determine the fish can join the store's current stock. Premier wants you to find what you seek, and the friendly employees will gladly order a fish for you, if they do not stock the variety you seek. Jack and Will appreciate return business and reward their regular customers with special discounts. If you want to enjoy the beauty of your tanks without the upkeep, Premier offers traveling aquarium maintenance for both fresh and saltwater tanks in homes and businesses. If you prefer to take care of your own fish, the staff at Premier, with a combined 50 years of experience, can answer any question you might have about maintaining a healthy environment for your fish. For an aquarium shopping experience guaranteed to go swimmingly, come in to Premier Fish & Reef.

3255 S Wadsworth Boulevard, #D,
Lakewood CO
(303) 716-5700
www.premierfishreef.com

FISH & REEF

Rockley Music Center
ARTS & CRAFTS:
Best pianos, guitars and band instruments

Since 1946, Rockley Music Center has been a fixture on West Colfax in Lakewood. Originally opening as a musical instrument and appliance store, Mel Rockley and his wife Mildred would have loved seeing the store their family created 60 years later. Three generations of musicians, educators and savvy entrepreneurs have witnessed changes in the field of music and grown with it. Each generation has created a new store to embrace the musical trend of the day. Melvin's grandson and current owner Tobin and his wife Liane now operate a full-line destination music store. Customers can select from a sizable inventory of pianos, guitars and band instruments. Rockley Music Center is the pulse of Lakewood's musical community. The center provides a quarterly newsletter on its website. Perhaps you are thinking about your children's musical future or maybe renewing a passion of your own? You're invited to stop by, tickle the keys and let the beautiful instruments inspire you.

8555 W Colfax Avenue, Lakewood CO
(303) 233-4444
www.rockleymusic.com

Colorado Camera Company
ARTS & CRAFTS: *Best imaging center*

Colorado Camera Company is a full-service imaging center and one of only two professional photo labs left in the Denver Metropolitan area. The company is known for extraordinary quality. Beyond traditional film services, Colorado Camera Company specializes in photographic digital output in addition to high quality Giclée printing for reproducing fine photos and artwork. Keith, Dave and Carlene Shrum run the family business, started in 1957. They feature an unusual lineup of cameras and work to match customers with the right camera purchase. In addition, they have the expertise required to advise novice or professional customers on any new or used camera in their inventory. The Shrums also offer an intensive class at their store on the use of the newest digital camera equipment. You can earn college credit from Red Rocks Community College and become a better photographer with this five-night, 15-hour class. If you can think of a photo-related service, chances are you can find that service at Colorado Camera. They recently instituted a free online finishing service that allows their customers to email images for printing and have those images expertly printed, then shipped or picked up at the store. Whatever your interest in photography, a visit to Colorado Camera Company is bound to be satisfying.

2480 Kipling Street, Lakewood CO
(303) 233-4788 or (866) COLOCAM (265-6226)
www.coloradocamera.com

Showers of Flowers Yarn Shop

ART & CRAFTS:

Largest yarn shop in Colorado

Showers of Flowers Yarn Shop is an inspirational answer to prayer. Owner Sharon Sturm, an accomplished seamstress, taught herself to make intricate flowers out of yarn while recovering from a broken leg. As a result, she now has more than 100 patented flower designs, providing kits to her customers as a way to pass down the art and leave a beautiful, long-lasting legacy in flowers that do not wilt or wear out. Sturm has provided floral yarn bouquets for celebrities and political figures, but more importantly she met her best friend and business partner, Jackie Briggs, through the enterprise. The shop is a wonderland that features more than 14,000 square feet of every conceivable supply designed to help you create your own yarn art. Besides being the largest yarn shop in the state, Showers of Flowers Yarn Shop is stocked with kits, notions, books and a multitude of supplies. Sharon also teaches her own distinctive signature art of crocheted bouquets in classes. Beginners enjoy the Monday night Knit Happens classes, and the more experienced crafters flock to Socks in the City on Tuesday nights. Enjoy the virtual tour on the Showers of Flowers website, but come in person to experience the upbeat atmosphere and creative charge in the air. The heartfelt prayer that Sharon Sturm uttered was to find a gift to share with others. You are invited to be a part of the blessing that is Showers of Flowers Yarn Shop.

6900 W Colfax Avenue, Lakewood CO
(303) 233-2525 or (800) 825-2569
www.showersofflowers.com

Great Harvest Bread Company
BAKERIES, COFFEE & TEA: *Best fresh-baked bread*

The Great Harvest Bread Company offers the ingredients for freedom, fun and livelihood and uses them to make a recipe of success for their business owners. Russ and LaNae Steinhaus are the owners of the Lakewood Great Harvest Bread Company. They provide a perfect example of the ideals behind this innovative company. This is the community's whole grain headquarters where they mill their own wheat and use no preservatives. Hand-kneaded and baked from scratch, the bread is possibly the tastiest whole grain food ever concocted. As it comes from the oven, slices of bread are offered to every customer who walks in the door. Homemade cookies, sweet rolls, biscotti, and pancake mixes are only a few of the additional delights to be found. Whole wheat dog biscuits make an appreciated gift for your four-legged friends and the two-legged variety enjoys four-inch signature sandwiches either straight from the menu or custom-ordered by the customer. Gourmet soup mixes make great healing comfort foods and jams and jellies put a sweet topping on any meal. It is because owner Russ Steinhaus can hand out bread in a festive, music-filled shop smelling of heavenly fresh-baked bread that he chose this lifestyle and this business. Come enjoy the aroma and savor the bread at The Great Harvest Bread Company, conveniently located 15 minutes from downtown Denver at the southwest corner of Kipling and Jewell.

11068 W Jewell Avenue, Lakewood CO
(303) 716-0905
www.knead2bake.com
www.greatharvest.com

Sweet Traditions
BAKERIES, COFFEE & TEA: *Best wedding cakes*

Sweet Traditions is the home of experts in the difficult art of creating wedding cakes that not only look amazing, but taste fantastic. Freshly baked cakes and topiaries of chocolate covered strawberries spark the imagination and tempt the palate. The chefs thrive on challenges and variety, such as baking every tier a different flavor or creating a custom-shaped sculptured cake. They offer an incredible variety of flavors and designs, including fresh flowers and fruits as well as some look-alike blossoms artfully fashioned from airbrushed gumpaste. There is a line of unusual and traditional cheesecakes with imaginative flavors such as margarita, banana split and a delightful caramel pecan. Sweet Traditions provides delivery and set-up anywhere in the Denver-Boulder-Brighten area. The brain-child of Jamie Kelldorf, the bakery caters especially to brides-to-be, meeting one-on-one with them to design the perfect accompaniment to their special day. Colors, themes, flavors and designs are carefully planned and crafted based on the consultations with each customer. The result is an artistic rendering that will reflect the customer's wishes down to the last careful detail. Sweet Traditions will also provide catering for your special event. Make an appointment to visit Sweet Traditions and add some magic to your special day.

3265 S Wadsworth # J, Lakewood CO
(303) 929-0901 or (303) 697-7612
www.sweet-traditions.net

Atlanta Bread Company

BAKERIES, COFFEE & TEA:
Best bakery and café experience

If customers know a good thing when they try it, then the Atlanta Bread Company is a very good thing. ABC started in 1993, and in 10 years, 160 of these bakery-café franchises had sprung up around the nation. The two-eateries-in-one concept, combined with an easygoing ambience, makes the Atlanta Bread Company an irresistible choice for everything from gourmet coffees and baked goods to signature soups and sandwiches. Two enterprising couples possess joint ownership in the Aurora and Lakewood branches of ABC. Before joining the Atlanta Bread Company team, Bob Lawrance was a manufacturing executive, and Joy Lawrance taught school, while Rob Rudloff served as an Air Force captain, and Krista Rudloff was an astronomer. The four restaurateurs find their mixed backgrounds surprisingly useful in operating ABC. Both locations offer wireless Internet access and comfortable settings for friends to gather for smoothies or such coffee extravaganzas as cafechillo. On the café side of the house, expect a shifting array of soups, including the Loaf of Soup, a sourdough bread bowl filled with soup. Sandwiches, like Bella Basil chicken, come on ABC bread with innovative fillings. The bakery offers take-out, but also invites lingering with gourmet coffee and a scone. Nothing goes to waste at Atlanta Bread Company, where the sun never rises twice on the bread, because any baked goods not sold at the end of the day go to local charities. For a bakery and café experience, where caring people serve quality products, come to the Atlanta Bread Company.

14262 E Cedar Avenue, Aurora CO
(303) 341-6200
7740 W Alameda Avenue, Lakewood, CO
(303) 991-4400
www.atlantabreaddenver.com

Village Roasters

BAKERIES, COFFEE & TEA: *Best gourmet coffee, tea and pastries*

An ideal cup of coffee can be likened to a beautifully orchestrated symphony, a harmonious blending of aromas and flavors that swirl together to awaken the senses. For more than a quarter century, the Village Roaster has been orchestrating a symphony of superior coffee beans that have been perfectly roasted in-house to optimize the subtle nuances of this delicious and popular brew. The Village Roaster, a community

favorite, was founded by Mary Ellen and Gary Mencimer in 1979 and is now owned and operated by Mary Ellen's sister and brother-in-law, Kathleen and Jim Curtis. They have maintained the roaster's original mission of providing top-notch customer service and high quality products at fair and reasonable prices. Village Roaster carries 17 types of coffees that are used to create 35 individual blends and flavors. Additionally, they offer 27 different bulk teas as well as numerous packaged teas and more than 150 bulk herbs and spices. Because they do all of the processing and packaging on-site, Village Rooster customers save by purchasing from them rather than at a grocery store. The shop offers a choice selection of tea and coffee accessories along with candies and gourmet treats. In 2000, Village Roaster expanded and opened a second location at the Lakewood City Commons, where they serve fine pastries in addition to their gourmet coffee and teas. Add harmony and flavor to your day with a visit to Village Roasters.

9255 W Alameda Avenue, Lakewood CO (303) 238-8718 or (800) 237-3822
7978 W Alameda Avenue, Lakewood City Commons, Lakewood CO (303) 445-9325
www.villageroaster.com

Food Concepts Inc.

BUSINESS:
Best packaged soups, stews and chilis

For meals that taste like they just came from the range, the professionals turn to Food Concepts in Lakewood. Owner Susan Smith and chef Michael Datino oversee the preparation, cooking, packaging and shipping of soups, stews and chilies that have been carefully prepared from the best ingredients. The food is prepared in state-of-the-art, cook-chill equipment that permits a longer refrigerated shelf life than would otherwise be possible. Food Concepts' quick chilling methods involve cooking to the peak of doneness, packaging at above-pasteurization temperature, then quickly chilling to 40 degrees Fahrenheit and storing at 29 to 32 degrees Fahrenheit. They are experts in preparing signature menu items to your specifications, and can develop a chef's specialty dish into a product that can be manufactured in large quantities, thus assuring consistency of product with no recipe loss. Food Concepts is an acidified food manufacturer, inspected by the FDA, which permits them to bottle signature sauces that can create an additional profit center for you. Michael is a longtime chef with 30 years of experience in the food industry. Susan has 45 years experience in the food industry, and is a Food Scientist and Registered Dietician. Bring your chef's recipes to a broader clientele, or improve the food offerings at your business, with help from the experts at Food Concepts Inc.

2545 Kipling Street, Lakewood CO
(303) 202-9982
www.foodconceptsinc.com

Portraits by Piare Mohan
BUSINESS: *Best portrait photographer*

Award-winning photographer Piare Mohan has been helping people in Lakewood to create permanent reminders of the big events in their lives since 1981 at Portraits by Piare Mohan. Mohan has been recognized by Ms. Photogenic USA, Inc. as its Photographer of the Year for his ability to capture the spirit of his subjects on film. He has won numerous other awards as well. Mohan specializes in high school and wedding portraits, but is available for all kinds of photography. Customers have the option of the lights and glamour of an indoor studio photo shoot or the natural beauty of the three outdoor settings offered by Mohan. Mohan's hours arc by appointment only, so you'll have to call ahead for a sitting time. He's available for evening and weekend shoots as well. Mohan also offers a variety of specials, including a Buddy Special for those who bring a friend along. With more than two decades of critically lauded experience, Portraits by Piare Mohan is focused on creating the best pictures possible for you to treasure the memory of your special event.

1830 S Wadsworth, Lakewood CO
(303) 988-2534
www.piaremohan.com

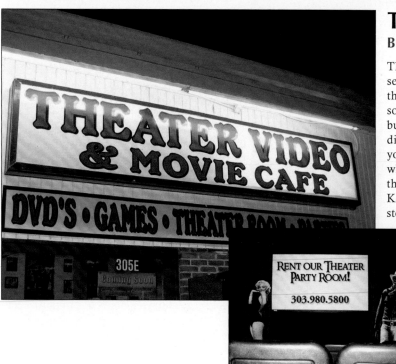

Theater Video
BUSINESS: *Best movie rental store*

Theater Video is not your run-of-the-mill video rental store. Theater Video serves up movies with the hand of a connoisseur. One marvelous amenity is the private theater with stadium seating for 12, great acoustics and surround sound. Rent the theater for private events and it comes complete with hot buttered popcorn, candy and soda pop, just like a regular movie theater. The difference is that this theater only shows your favorite movies because it's your party and you get to choose. If you prefer to do your movie watching while lounging in your favorite recliner at home, you can sign up for one of the no-brainer unlimited monthly movie packages. Owners Brian Torres and Ken Cornell hire staff that know and love movies. With over 9000 DVDs in stock along with a broad selection of games, the chances are excellent that they have what you're looking for. Theater Video also specializes in finding any movie that's available on DVD and will place a special order for you. A free movie rental as a gift on your birthday and the ability to call ahead and reserve your movie choices are customer service extras that make Theater Video patrons feel truly appreciated. Stop by Theater Video and browse the offerings or just hang out in their Movie Café and enjoy a hot or cold beverage in a relaxing atmosphere where a movie is always playing.

305 S Kipling Boulevard, Lakewood CO
(303) 980-5800
www.denverdvd.com

A Chapel in the Village
EVENTS: *Best wedding chapel*

Celebrate your day of magic at the romantic and intimate setting created by A Chapel in the Village, where all of your wedding daydreams can come true. Elegantly remodeled, this quaint chapel features a beautiful rose garden. It is family owned and operated by TLC Wedding Services, which was founded by Corla Reeves and her daughter Terri Jaussi. Terri is a Certified American Sign Language Interpreter and provides translation services for the deaf. She is also the chapel's ceremony coordinator. Granddaughter Lauren Cron serves as a ceremony coordinator and the chapel's floral designer. Terri's husband Robert is the chapel's officiant, providing non-denominational wedding ceremonies. A Chapel in the Village was created to provide the community with a beautiful and affordable location for celebrating your most special moments. The family encourages you to share your traditions and ideas so that your wedding ceremony reflects your personal preferences. Optional on-site services include photography, floral arrangements, invitations and live or pre-recorded music enhanced by an amazing sound system. The chapel is also available for infant blessings, memorial services and other ceremonies. TLC Wedding Services invites you to commemorate your wedding day surrounded by quiet charm and serenity at A Chapel in the Village.

1360 Garrison Street, Lakewood CO
(303) 237-6888
www.chapel-village.com

d' Anelli Bridals

FASHION:
Best bridal and formal dress shop

All things are possible at d' Anelli Bridal's. This magnificent bridal and formal dress shop carries over 500 sample wedding gowns from over 50 top designers to ensure that you can find the perfect dress that you have been dreaming of. Additionally, they have a full selection of bridesmaids, flower girl and mother-of-the-bride dresses in an amazing range of styles and colors. Fortunately, the inventory at d' Anelli's doesn't end there; they further carry a terrific array of tuxedos, special occasion dresses and accessories. Each member of Anelli's personable staff is a fully trained bridal and tuxedo consultant who is happy to assist you on everything from browsing for last minute accoutrements to helping you design your entire wedding ensemble. Additionally, the shop has an expert staff of professional seamstresses who specialize in bridal apparel and are able to tailor your chosen garments into a perfect fit. Owner Sandi Schreirogel has more that twenty years of experience in the bridal apparel industry and is dedicated, along with her staff, to providing a personalized and stress free environment in which to shop for that most special of special days. They understand how important each decision can be and strive help you make sure that each item is just what you wanted so that you can enjoy wedding that you have thought of since you were a child. Let your happy wedding memories begin right away with a visit to d' Anelli Bridals.

7301 W Alameda Avenue, Lakewood CO
(303) 980-1400
www.coloradobridal.com

Purvis Jewelers

FASHION: *Best family-owned jewelers*

For more than 30 years, Purvis Jewelers has been earning a reputation of excellence by offering patrons premium customer service and quality custom-made pieces of fine jewelry. This distinguished family-operated shop is owned by Pam and John W. Purvis III, Certified Gemologist Appraiser. Purvis Jewelers has an American Gem Society Accredited Gem Lab where you can receive in-house appraisals. John Purvis has received numerous awards and accolades for his incredible jewelry designs including the highly prestigious DeBeers Diamonds of Today award, Beyond Nature, as well as the Jewelers of America National award. At Purvis Jewelers, you can have your outdated pieces exquisitely redesigned, as if by magic, into new and fabulous creations that will go on to become treasured by future generations. They focus primarily on 18-karat gold and platinum designs and carry an extensive selection of both colored gemstones and fine diamonds, all of which are competitively priced. Purvis Jewelers also provides their patrons with repair, cleaning and inspection services done on-site as well as offering an exceptional diamond up-grade program for diamonds purchased at Purvis Jewelers. Allow the Purvis family to put their extensive experience at your disposal with a visit to Purvis Jewelers.

9190 W Colfax Avenue, Lakewood CO
(303) 233-2798 *www.purvisjewelers.com*

Sweets From Heaven
FUN FOODS:
Lakewood's candy experts

At Sweets From Heaven in the Colorado Mills Mall, candy is more than a treat; it's an essential. Owners Darren and Jennifer Adelgren take candy seriously, stocking everything from imported sweets to fudge that they make themselves. They know that the more candy they have in their shop, the wider will be the smiles on the faces of everyone who comes through the door. That's why they carry just about every kind of gum and candy bar you can imagine. They keep 350 bins filled to the brim with candy of all kinds, including sugar-free and diabetic choices. You'll find over 20 varieties of M&M's alone. What's your favorite color? If you're planning a party, Sweets From Heaven is the place to load up on all reds, all oranges or any other color in the rainbow. The longer you stay in Lakewood, the more you'll enjoy Sweets From Heaven, because this is a customer-friendly shop that rewards your loyalty with freebies after you have filled your punch card. Stop by Sweets From Heaven, staffed by experts in the business of being sweet to their customers.

**14500 W Colfax Avenue, Suite 322,
Lakewood CO
(303) 590-1800**

Magill's World of Ice Cream
FUN FOODS: *Best ice cream in Lakewood*

Magill's World of Ice Cream started in New York City in 1976. It moved to Lakewood in 1981 and recently celebrated its 25th anniversary in Colorado. Owner Tom Kinney makes all of Magill's ice cream in-house using ingredients carefully obtained from all parts of the United States and even the world. The ice cream contains 14 percent butter fat for extra richness. Magill's offers 76 flavors, some of which are made on request. Bulk ice cream to go is also available. Popular flavors include black raspberry and double dark chocolate fudge crunch. The sugar-free butter pecan ice cream is so outstanding, you won't miss the sugar one bit. Magill's also makes novelty cakes and shakes, banana splits and malts. The shop has drawn the attention of the Rocky Mountain News and the Denver Post. If you would like to time-travel to an old-fashioned soda fountain, a visit to Magill's is just what you need. Magill's World of Ice Cream is open long hours for seven days a week.

8016 W Jewell Avenue, Lakewood CO
(303) 986-9968
www.magillsicecream.com

The Artful Framer
GALLERIES & FINE ART: *Expert framing services*

For more than 18 years, The Artful Framer has been beautifully framing the art, treasures and memories of Lakewood denizens. The Artful Framer himself, Michael Dutton, is an extremely talented local artist who has received awards for both his oils and watercolors. He took first place in the Applewood Community Fair Art Competition, receiving an award from the Evergreen Artist Association. Michael is an avid photographer who specializes in scenes of nature such as the vast Colorado Mountains and other lovely aspects of the great outdoors as he sees them. The walls of The Artful Framer are lined with some of Michael's wonderful paintings and photographs that are available for sale. Mike studied framing at R&D Framing School and is an active member of the Professional Picture Framers Association, where he serves on the board of the Mountain State Chapter. Michael masterfully blends all of his skills and experiences to create stunning, beautifully matched frames for your treasured pieces of art. He takes significant pride in his innate ability to color-coordinate and is always able to choose the ideal frame for your special piece. The Artful Framer offers all types of custom framing including hand-cut and custom-design mats, limited editions, original art, custom museum framing and posters. So take that Picasso from the attic and your grandchild's latest masterpiece and head for The Artful Framer, where you can crown your art with expert framing that will remain a treasure for ever.

2600 Willow Lane, Lakewood CO
(303) 235-0411

The American Picture Framer

GALLERIES & FINE ART: *Over 25 years of experience*

Turn your keepsakes into treasures that will last a lifetime with custom framing by Jeanette Crabb, owner and proprietor of the American Picture Framer. Jeanette brings more than 25 years of experience to every project she takes on, and is dedicated to serving art collectors nationwide. After establishing her retail store in 1982, she relocated five years later to a home-based business in 1987. Art galleries and art consultants have remained loyal customers throughout the years. Other clients include private collectors and notable artists of the Colorado Pastel Society, and the Colorado Watercolor Society. Jeanette provides a stress-free and thoroughly enjoyable atmosphere for her framing business. Clients are greeted by her two white German Shepherds named Noble and Nikko; then they are invited into her most welcoming home office. During a consultation, Jeanette will assist you in choosing the ideal picture frame for your special project. She works with you according to your specific needs, while introducing you to an array of proper techniques that will work best for mounting your piece. With hundreds of frame samples, and linen, suede or paper mats to choose from, you will find her expertise in design complimentary to your satisfaction. Whether you are mounting expensive art or preserving your child's priceless first drawing, let The American Picture Framer make your piece picture perfect. Home and office consultations are available. Contact Jeanette at the phone number below.

Lakewood CO (303) 238-6884

Bella Fiori

GARDENS, PLANTS & FLOWERS: *Best floral arrangements*

If you're searching for distinctive floral arrangements full of imagination and creativity, look no further than Bella Fiori in Lakewood. This spectacular floral design shop offers many services, but specializes in weddings, galas and themed events. Owner and designer Alicia Schwede opened Bella Fiori in 2003 as an outlet for her love of flowers, which she gained as a young child working alongside her grandmother in the rose garden. In addition to running her shop, Alicia is the chairwoman of the Denver Art Museum's Flower Council. She has studied with America's most honored floral designer, Phil Rulloda, and has been the recipient of many floral honors, including the 2005 People's Choice award for best table design from Entertaining Colorado Style. In 2006, she made Manchester's Who's Who list. Bella Fiori has been named in numerous publications, including Confetti magazine. In 2005, Elegant Bride cited Alicia as a top floral designer for weddings. Bella Fiori utilizes exquisite flora from across the globe, including items rarely seen in today's commercial designs. Alicia's signature design style is English Garden, a romantic style that allows her to use wonderful natural material, like berries, twigs, fruits and vegetables. When a special event requires floral design of unsurpassed polish and attention to detail, call on Alicia and her talented staff. Visits to Bella Fiori are by appointment only.

7711 W 6th Avenue, Lakewood CO
(303) 233-5566
www.bellafiori-events.com

Silk Petals
GARDENS, PLANTS & FLOWERS:
Best silk flowers

Silk Petals offers a spectacular array of permanent floral arrangements and customized gift baskets that are ideal for all occasions. Owner Leslie McCarthy opened her specialized home-based business in 2003 and, in just three short years, established herself as one of the Lakewood area's premier floral and gift basket resources. Silk Petals specializes in designing original floral arrangements out of quality materials constructed to last and look sensational for a lifetime. Additionally, Leslie creates themed gift baskets filled with appropriate goodies for the receiver, such as kitchen baskets stuffed with gourmet treats or baby shower baskets laden with darling toys and accessories. Silk Petals also offers baskets and florals specially created as thank you gifts, holiday gifts and wedding party gifts. One of Leslie's thoughtful get-well baskets is certain to put a smile on anyone's face. Leslie works closely with customers to exactly meet their requirements and accommodates busy schedules by providing evening and weekend consultations when necessary. When it comes to weddings and other gala events, Leslie takes pride in her attention to detail, which includes the placement of floral arrangements at the event site to ensure that no harm comes to them. Make an appointment with Leslie for delightful gift baskets, old-fashioned service and flowers that look so real they even fools the bees.

(303) 995-1947
www.silkpetalsbasketsandfloral.com

Tan the Moon

HEALTH & BEAUTY:
Best indoor tanning

Tan the Moon indoor tanning salon
provides a safe, secure means to
acclimate skin to outdoor environments.
Controlling the amount of ultraviolet
light you receive prevents sunburns,
one of the leading causes of premature
aging and skin damage. Various tanning
beds utilize different combinations of
ultraviolet alpha and beta waves, and it is
these different mixtures that determine
how much time is needed in each type of
bed to give your skin that healthy, golden
glow. Skin products have come a long
way in recent years as well. Tan the Moon
offers a selection of moisturizing lotions
that keep skin supple and youthful.
Moisturized skin tans better. The
informed staff can advise you on lengths
of time needed to tan without burning
and help you devise a plan for graduated
increases. The staff also monitors your
progress to keep you and the skin you
live in safe and healthy. A plethora of
information is available on-site. If you
have ever considered indoor tanning
before, pay them a visit. Take a tour of
the facilities and see why so many people
have decided to rely on Tan the Moon to
develop and maintain their healthy glow.

150 S Union Boulevard, Lakewood CO
(303) 969-9488
www.smarttan.com

Weight Mastery Clinic
HEALTH & BEAUTY: *Best weight loss clinic*

Are you trying to loose weight, kick the smoking habit, gain confidence in speaking in public or increase your prosperity and abundance? Harriet Storrs has mastered a set of tools that can help you reach your goals. She is a psychotherapist, counselor and Certified Clinical Hypnotherapist and owner of the Weight Mastery Clinic in Lakewood. Harriet uses such techniques as hypnotherapy, Neuro Linguistic Programming (NLP) and Eye Movement Desensitization Reprocessing to accelerate change and promote lasting wellness in your life. The Weight Mastery Clinic also performs the Emotional Freedom technique to alter pain, phobias, grief, depression, obsessive compulsive behavior and numerous other feelings and emotions. Harriet has been in the weight loss field for over 25 years and has maintained a personal 100 pound weight loss herself. Her program uses private counseling sessions and techniques to examine and heal past experiences and get to the core issues. Clients choose food and exercise plans to fit their individual lifestyles and reinforce their choices with personalized audio tapes that include their personal affirmations. Harriet also offers weight loss and body image hypnosis and subliminal CD's. Harriet provides Aqua-Chi Detoxification treatment to all her clients to assist in loosing weight, and improving other physical conditions like arthritis, gout, allergies or fluid retention. Take charge and transform your life at Weight Mastery Clinic.

1360 S Wadsworth Boulevard, Suite 104, Lakewood CO
(303) 526-0489
www.weightmasteryclinic.com

Fitness Evolution
HEALTH & BEAUTY: *Best fitness club*

What was your New Years Resolution this year? Was it, like so many other people, to make this the year you finally lose weight and get fit? Then let the professionals at Fitness Evolution help you make this the year you reach your fitness goals. At Fitness Evolution in Lakewood, professional personal fitness coaches provide a structured, supportive environment where you can make your health a priority and aim at feeling and looking your best. Your workout is a private, one-on-one session with a certified trainer. All trainers have at least a four-year degree in fitness, and some have advanced degrees. The instructors pride themselves on creating personalized exercise programs for each individual, thereby maximizing every moment you spend moving toward your goals. Nutritional instruction and massage therapy are also available. Fitness Evolution has been a local favorite since owner Brian Miller opened the business in 1996. Clients are encouraged to schedule workouts from one to three times a week for optimum results. Fitness Evolution opens early in the morning and closes late at night on weekdays and is open by appointment only on weekends. No membership is required at Fitness Evolution, so stop by and start working on the body you've always dreamed of.

12790 W Alameda Parkway, Lakewood CO
(303) 238-5015

Accent Art Glass
HOME: *Best stained glass in Lakewood*

With its reverence for the time-honored stained-glass art and its knowledge of up-to-date restoration techniques, Accent Art Glass is the ideal place for those in search of new art or looking to repair a damaged piece. Accent Art Glass in Lakewood offers a full range of stained-glass services. The company stocks a wide variety of art pieces in many sizes and shapes. If you're looking for an original piece, designed to your specifications, the staff at Accent Art Glass will help you make your vision a reality. The company uses the latest in repair technology, which allows for the retention of more of the original stained glass. When your project is done, they'll even install it for you. Accent Art Glass works closely with decorators, architects and homeowners to make sure all special requirements are met. Accent Art Glass has a rainbow of solutions for those with stained glass needs.

11590 W Colfax Avenue, Lakewood, CO
(303) 275-8986
www.accentartglass.com

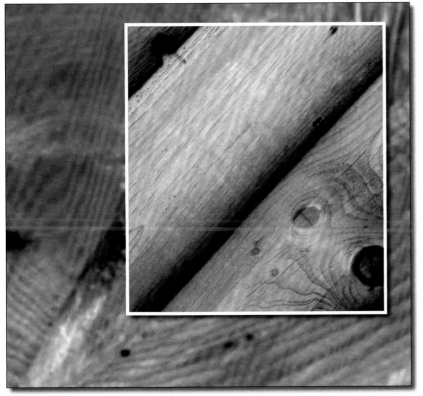

Lakewood Furniture
HOME: *Best log furniture in Lakewood*

Log furniture adds a beautiful, unique touch to any room of your home. Lakewood furniture has the largest selection of rustic, Western ranch and cabin furniture in the West. Mile Blount has been providing custom log furniture at low prices since 1999. With the factory on premises and two master wood carvers on site, they can create a special piece of furniture or a whole room full just to your liking. Lakewood is a complete dealer in unfinished furniture which uses aspen, pine, alder and juniper. The knotty look of the wood makes each piece one of a kind. Unfinished pieces allow the natural beauty of the wood to shine through. The smooth texture of each piece begs to be touched. Custom bed frames can be made in any size, including a miniature version for your pet. Armoires, coffee tables and desks can be created to enhance the look of any room. Furniture is available in many styles, including Old World, Mexican, cowboy and even customized. Pieces can be created with antlers and other accessories to customize the design. For a truly authentic look, they feature a complete line of pieces made from barn wood. Lakewood Furniture was named Best of Denver by Westword newspaper. Shipping is available worldwide. Lakewood takes pieces on trade and will do refinishing and upholstery work. Visit Lakewood Furniture and take home a custom piece of log furniture.

8425 W Colfax Avenue, Lakewood CO
(303) 233-5811

Gourmet Meat & Sausage Shop
MARKETS: *Best gourmet meat and sausage*

There are many advantages to buying meat at a meat shop instead of a grocery store. One advantage is that the meat is cut in-house; another is that the meat is aged for five weeks, resulting in extremely tender meat. It doesn't get more delicious than that. The staff at Gourmet Meat & Sausage Shop, owned by Larry Davis, makes eight different types of tasty sausages in-house and provides Lakewood with the finest beef, pork and poultry on the planet. From buffalo to elk, the shop features the highest quality meats available. Fresh Redbird poultry makes any day a holiday. Iowa Gold pork means the meat is natural as well as healthy and tender. The pork and poultry are natural, hormone-free, high-quality premium meats, individually hand cut to-order for the customers. Gourmet Meat & Sausage Shop also provides top-of-the-line specialty frozen foods for quick dinner menus and several kinds of jerky for healthy snacks. If buying in bulk is your need, beef sides, hind and front quarters or bundle orders are available. The meat is fresher, tastier, and the prices are better for the quality you get compared to supermarkets. Convenient hours make it easy to swing by and pick up a variety of packages. Tell the staff what you want, they will know how to serve your needs at Gourmet Meat & Sausage Shop.

9168 W Jewell Avenue, Lakewood CO
(303) 985-0126

Tom's Seafood

MARKETS: *Best fresh seafood selection*

It's a long way to an ocean from Lakewood, but you wouldn't know it from inside Tom's Seafood, where fresh fish abounds. Owner Thomas Butler casts a wide net over Alaskan, Hawaiian, East Coast and Florida suppliers to fly fresh catches to his shop three to five times each week. He also maintains the largest fresh seafood selection in the Denver area. Not only are Tom's fish far fresher than those in any local supermarket, but customers look forward to hearing an entertaining fish tale or two from this 30-year veteran of the fish business. If you enjoy fish but don't have a clue how to prepare it, you've come to the right place. Tom can tell you how to prepare and season your selection and what side dishes best complement it. Surf 'n turf lovers can be sure the quality of their beef matches the quality of their lobster, because Tom carries certified Angus beef, dry-aged for tenderness and flavor. The big one didn't get away at Tom's, where the crab legs are extraordinarily large, making it much easier to separate that delicious meat from the shell. Tom's fish are so fresh that your guests will be expecting to hear your big fish tale. To prepare a gourmet fish dinner, you need a gourmet fish store such as Tom's Seafood to fulfill that need.

767 S Xenon Court, Lakewood CO
(303) 969-9334

Mile High School of Dance

RECREATION:
Best family-oriented dance school

Showing children they can improve is a critical objective at Mile High School of Dance. Owner Trixie Johnson brings 40 years of experience and a methodology proven to create dancers for a lifetime. She manages an exceptionally talented staff of dancers with extensive teaching credits. At Mile High School of Dance, instructors must first posses a genuine love of children. Four brand-new family-oriented studios offer a variety of disciplines from ballet to pilates. It's possible for adults to be studying tap in one studio while children learn pirouettes in another. Recitals display student progress year round while developing performance skills and self-confidence. Class sizes are limited to 12, guaranteeing students the maximum one-on-one time with instructors. An assistant is provided for classes under age six. Best of all, a separate administrative staff allows teachers to focus on their craft. When you think of a passion to share with your family, consider Mile High School of Dance.

7985 W 16th Avenue, Lakewood CO
(303) 237-4132 or (303) 237-4147
www.milehighdance.com

Academy of the Performing Arts
RECREATION: *Best dance studio for all skill levels*

Academy of the Performing Arts is a dance studio of professionals dedicated to teaching grace, creativity, dancing skills and love of the arts. From age two to pre-professional dancing, all skill levels are encompassed within this building, providing the building blocks for dreams to come true. Owners Caren Diebold and Deborah Christopher and their entire staff are well-qualified to teach and they know how to make it fun. Caren teaches belly-dancing, and Deborah draws on her training with the Bolshoi Ballet to teach ballet and pilates. Husband David Christopher, also a professional dancer, instructs the boys. The studio also offers classes in authentic Tango from Argentina, taught by teachers from Argentina. David Escoe is the hip-hop teacher and a former member of Medea Sirkas. Jazz Teacher Jenni Sue Briggs studied extensively in Los Angeles, California, and covers jazz, lyrical and tap. Ballet classes are kept small for maximum benefit to the members. Performances are offered twice a year, giving all students the opportunity to shine in front of an audience. Early dance training offers lifelong benefits in posture, flexibility and creativity that can carry through into all other areas of life. Academy of the Performing Arts provides the gift of dance, fosters a love of the arts, and generates an inner grace and beauty of the soul that is beyond price. Call to register your child for a free trial class at Academy of the Performing Arts.

12792 W Alameda Parkway, Unit C, Lakewood CO
(303) 716-5707
www.academyoftheperformingarts.biz

Action RC Aircraft Center
RECREATION: *Best model aircraft*

Back in 1903 when the Wright Brothers ushered in the era of powered flight on the shores of Kitty Hawk, they could have never imagined what their creation would one day become. However, owner Glen Magree and the friendly staff of experienced modelers at Action RC Aircraft Center in Lakewood understand why the fascination with flying devices continues into the Twenty-first Century. They understand the RC aircraft hobby inside and out. At RC Aircraft Center, they take the time to go out and fly the various devices that they sell allowing them to educate their customers on the details of each product they offer. Their stock includes a wide range of all types of RC model aircraft, electronics and accessories from airplanes, gliders, helicopters to small autogyros. They stock all the major hobby brands and carry more than 250 airplane kits in their extensive stock. Glen has won numerous awards for his RC airplane exploits and enjoys seeing younger kids of the video game generation learn to fly these remarkable mini-aircraft. A large selection of more than 200 propeller sizes and more than 80 types and sizes of fuel tanks have given RC Aircraft Center the reputation as the RC aircraft place that has everything. When you visit RC Aircraft Center, make sure you take the time to try out your own flying skills on the RealFlight RC computer simulator available to customers in the expansive showroom.

1477 Carr Street, Lakewood CO
(303) 233-6275

The Board Room
RECREATION: *Best board shop*

At the tender age of five, Vince Sander of Lookout Mountain received a Christmas gift that changed his life. He received his very first snowboard, an all-wood model from Burton Backhill Snowboards. More than twenty years later, Vince has not only enjoyed a long career in snowboarding, but he has also become the owner and operator of The Board Room, Colorado's premier snow and skate boarding equipment and supply shop. Located in Lakewood, this 2,100-square-foot shop is filled to the brim with everything you need to hit the slopes in grand style. Vince carries a wide variety of superior quality boards from companies such as Salomon, NeverSummer and Nidecker. Additionally, he offers a wide selection of gear designed to keep you safe and comfortable, such as bindings from TechNine and K2, and goggles from Anon. The shop also offers men's and women's gloves, jackets and pants from Burton and 686, as well as packs from Dakine. Vince first decided to open The Board Room in 1985 after becoming interested in the business and retail side of his sport. His dream came to fruition in 1987 and he has been going strong ever since. If you want the best in skate or snow boards, along with the all the right equipment to keep you riding in style, then come check out The Board Room.

12810 W Alameda Parkway, Lakewood CO
(303) 986-4883
www.boardroomco.com

Slammers Baseball & Softball Sports Complex

RECREATION:
Best baseball and softball complex

If a ballplayer's dream is 365 days of hitting and pitching and playing the game of baseball in a land where the sun shines every day, then Slammers Baseball & Softball Sports Complex is that dream come true. Slammers is a state-of-the-art indoor training facility, where players of all ages can come to work on their skills, whatever their level may be. Slammers has a professional staff with over 75 years of combined major league experience, which is why baseball and softball teams from all over the state come here to train every year. The complex holds special clinics and camps for every level, from little leaguers to high school teams and men's leagues. You'll find a strength and conditioning center, five coin operated batting cages, 14 indoor tunnels for pitching and hitting practice, plus a pro shop that carries only top-of-the-line, name brand equipment for all your playing needs. Slammers also hosts a series of baseball tournaments and a high school development program for young players aiming at professional careers. Even better, what Slammers does for baseball and softball, it now does for golfing as well. Colorado's newest premier golfing facility, Slammers Golf, offers personal instruction from top-ranked PGA golfers that is guaranteed to lower your handicap. Their methodology, combined with an advanced system of analysis, gives the committed golfer the tools to dramatically improve the entire golfing experience. Whatever the size of the ball you're playing with, come let Slammers help you find your own personal field of dreams.

1878 S Wadsworth Boulevard, Lakewood CO
(303) 988-7426
www.slammersbaseball.com

White Fence Farm
RESTAURANTS & CAFÉS:
Best family dining and entertainment

White Fence Farm has perfected the art of wholesome family dining since it first began bringing families together at its Lakewood facility in 1973. However, the friendly staff isn't content only with serving their guests plates piled high with fried chicken and mounds of creamy mashed potatoes. They want to make sure you have a great time before and after you eat, too. Fun is guaranteed inside the Americana Barn, where amusement games and a pig-chute slide are the main attractions. Outside, a treehouse, playground and petting zoo are the sites for plenty of smiles and laugher. When it's time to eat, you will appreciate that all dinners are served with a generous variety of side dishes, including corn fritters and pickled beets. Although the fried chicken is legendary, the steak, pork chops and shrimp dinners are not to be overlooked. Pies, parfaits and hot-fudge sundaes top the list of delicious desserts. After such a filling meal, a stroll around the grounds might be in order. You can admire the pretty birds at the aviary and feed the ducks along the Waterside Walk, a national landscape award winner. You can even tour the farm in an old-fashioned horse-drawn carriage. In short, sitting down to a family meal is just part of the White Fence Farm experience. Relaxation and amusement are in store, as well, so bring the whole gang to White Fence Farm.

**6263 W Jewell Avenue, Lakewood CO
(303) 935-5945**
www.whitefencefarm.com

Talking Books Plus
SHOPPING: *Largest selection of audio books*

If you love to read but just don't have the time to cozy up to the latest best sellers or your favorite classics, then it's time for Talking Books Plus, home to Colorado's largest selection of books on tape or compact disk. Talking Books Plus has more than 15,000 audio books in stock including such genres as biographies, comedy and fantasy along with romance, true crime and historical fiction. Talking Books Plus offers all of their newest, and hottest, audio books at 25 percent off of the retail price and offers used audio books at a 50-percent discount ensuring that you never again have to pay full price for a book on tape or compact disk. Additionally, Talking Books Plus offers numerous rental packages that are ideal for everyone from the occasional listener to the audio book addict. For additional convenience, Talking Books Plus offers online rental and purchasing options for frequent listeners. Audio books are ideal for those who travel extensively or for those whose vision is failing, making traditional reading difficult as well as those who are just to busy to sit down and enjoy a good book. Talking Books Plus also offers a full selection of children's' books which are ideal for beginning readers or for those struggling with dyslexia, as studies have shown that children who can dually hear and see the information learn faster and generally go on to become better readers. Rediscover the joy of great books at Talking Books Plus.

3355 S Wadsworth Boulevard-H101, Lakewood CO
(303) 969-8848
www.comehearbooks.com

International Collectable Exchange
SHOPPING: *Largest selection of colored gemstones*

For the largest selection of colored gemstones in Colorado, look no further than the International Collectable Exchange. Owners Ron and Cheryl Pingenot not only have more than 50 years of experience in cutting stones, but they also specialize in one-of-a-kind collectibles, diamonds, consultations, antiques, watches and appraisals. The focus of International Collectable Exchange is exposing a stone in its most beautiful state. Gems are cut to show off the ideal clarity and brilliance as possible. Importing diamonds and gems from around the world, Ron and Cheryl have an expert and unbiased opinion in helping you understand the value of your jewelry and investment. International Collectable Exchange also handles mineral specimens and fossils, antique glass and porcelain. This is

not only the place to admire, but if interested purchase pieces of the highest value available on the market today, being confident its quality. International Collectable Exchange is also home to the American Institute of Gemological Research, educating consumers on many of the facets of the jewelry industry. Questions on insurance, documentation, technology, resale and liquidation, A.I.G.R., is your resource for any information you need in regards to diamonds and gems. For a well informed jeweler and gem cutter, come to International Collectable Exchange, not only will you find the highest quality products, but also people you can trust, ensuring you made the smartest investment possible.

8008 W Jewell Avenue, Lakewood CO
(303) 988-5801

Full Moon Books, Coffees & Events
SHOPPING: *Best book store*

Besides baseball, the great American pastime might have to include books, coffee and live entertainment. Full Moon Books, Coffees & Events serves up a hearty helping of each. For seven years, Owner Cathy Washburn has been soothing the psyche with her eclectic wares at Full Moon. Having owned a store in Silverthorne for 18 years, her experience has taught her that in order to survive a store must diversify. At Full Moon, customers are delightfully inspired with new and used books, an intriguing selection of clothing and gifts, or by the psychic readings and Reiki energy work which are offered throughout the week. Full Moon hosts a metaphysical fair once a month as well as weekly yoga and other assorted classes. Perhaps, the most compelling feature at Full Moon is the spontaneity. Creative energy permeates the air as performance artists take the stage in an adjacent room. The event center is available to rent for workshops, weddings, parties or any other host of entertaining events. Cathy and her staff invite you to enjoy an afternoon relaxing with a good read or joe sipping and toe tapping when you visit Full Moon Books, Coffees & Events, on the corner of Garrison and West 6th Avenue in the Meadowlark Center.

9106 W 6th Avenue, Lakewood CO
(303) 233-MOON (6666)
www.fullmoonbooks.com

DVD Stop
SHOPPING:
Low prices on DVDs, games and CDs

The DVD Stop is an innovative business owned by Morgan and Cary Troyer. If you are looking for a DVD, this should be your first stop. Fair cash trade-in values are given for games and movies. Special orders are welcomed as well. The upbeat, lively store has fantastic prices on used DVDs, games, video games and CDs. They also carry T-shirts, posters, accessories and storage cases for the products they stock. They can repair scratched DVDs and CDs, making them as good as new. This Better Business Bureau member offers perks such as every 16th DVD for free and special coupon deals. DVD Stop also stocks rentals, and a selection of entire seasons of television shows, including 24, Deadwood and CSI. They are 10 minutes from downtown Denver, located near 6th Avenue and Wadsworth. The brightly inviting interior of DVD Stop beckons you to stop in and see what's available for your viewing pleasure.

98 Wadsworth Boulevard, #120, Lakewood CO
(303) 238-7722

Mesa Imports
SHOPPING: *Best import store*

Good import stores fire the imagination with exotic treasures from distant places. Mesa Imports is just such a store. Carol Steers owns this Lakewood shop in Westland Plaza. Carol enjoys traveling and adds a new country to her buying trips each year. Customers drive a long way to see the merchandise at Mesa Imports. Clothing and gifts are imported from places such as Bali, Kenya and China. Goods from Mexico, Russia and Brazil are on hand, as well. Striking, colorful hand-woven garments from Guatemala made up Carol's first stock in 1975, and they are on display today. Ethnic jewelry and natural fiber clothing are the largest part of the inventory, but there is much else to find in the massive collection of merchandise. Check out the clip earrings, wind chimes and wind socks. One of the most intimate representations of a region is the local folk art, and Mesa Imports makes this art available to the public. The shop offers a large selection of imported greeting cards. At Mesa Imports, you can be graced by other cultures in a way not possible in most chain stores. Enjoy a shopping experience that is like world travel without the jet lag. Mesa Imports offers you the treasures of the world. All you need to do is open your bag and receive them.

1545 Quail Street, Suite 9, Lakewood CO
(303) 232 5846

LITTLETON

In the 1860s, as the fledgling metropolis of Denver began to grow, the need arose for irrigation ditches. Among the engineers hired to build this system was a young man, Richard Little, of New Hampshire. Surveying an area south of Denver, Little fell in love with the site of present-day Littleton. He filed a home stake and brought his asthmatic wife, Angeline, from the East. The dry climate all but cured her condition. When the Denver and Rio Grande Railroad reached the area in 1871, settlement began at a rapid pace. In 1902, Littleton became the seat of the newly defined Arapahoe County.

PLACES TO GO

- Chatfield State Park
  11500 N Roxborough Park Road

- Depot Art Center and Gallery
  2069 W Powers Avenue

- Littleton Historical Museum
  6028 S Gallup Street

- Roxborough State Park
  4751 Roxborough Drive

- South Platte Park
  7301 S Platte River Parkway

THINGS TO DO

July
- Colorado Irish Festival
  www.coloradoirishfestival.org

August
- Western Welcome Week
  www.westernwelcomeweek.com

- Rocky Mountain Balloon Festival
  www.rockymountainballoonfestival.com

October
- Harvest Festival & Pumpkin Sale
  (303) 795-3950

The Pedigree Shop
ANIMALS & PETS: *Best pet store in Littleton*

The Pedigree Shop is the ultimate pet store. Originally known as Pet City, they have been in Littleton since 1971. The name was changed in 2000 when owner Lori Senecal moved the store to the Park Meadows Mall. Anything you need for your four-legged friend is here, including your four-legged friend. The Pedigree Shop usually has about 35 breeds of dogs and cats in the store to choose from. Find Siamese, Burmese and Bengal kittens. They carry puppies in all shapes and sizes, and feature some rare breeds, such as Skye Terriers. All puppies come with a health warranty, and are current on their shots. You'll even receive a free pet vet exam. When you take that new puppy or kitten home you'll be happy to know you don't have to make any more stops. The Pedigree Shop can help you out with beds, collars, leashes, bowls, and a huge assortment of toys. They keep some of the best food on hand, such as Royal Canin, to make sure you and your new pet get the most out of every day. You'll find small mammals here, too, including guinea pigs, chinchillas, gerbils and hamsters. Backed with 35 years of pet industry knowledge, The Pedigree Shop is the one-stop shop for all your pet's needs.

**8505 Park Meadows Center Drive, Suite 2020, Littleton CO
(720) 875-0181**

The Poodle Shop
ANIMALS & PETS: *Best pet grooming in Littleton*

The Poodle Shop in Littleton offers quality dog grooming by appointment only. Owner Rachel Diller is an expert in dog behavior and has worked with dog toy manufacturers and numerous boarding kennels. She has worked in the industry for 13 years and is careful to ensure that pets leave with a great haircut and are happy to return. Dog breeders refer much of The Poodle Shop's clientele. The breeders know that the staff here can correctly groom to the standard. The Poodle Shop staff is well versed in grooming both rare and common breeds and will treat animal clients with respect and care. Canine and feline services are all inclusive. They ensure that every pet gets a warm bubble bath, massage, ear cleaning, pawdicure, gland expression, hand drying and full style. The Poodle Shop is an independent distributor for Oxyfresh, a company based in Coeur d'Alene, Idaho that sells health related products for people and pets. Pet products include

antioxidant pet wafers to give your pet more energy and reduce pain from injuries and arthritis. There is an entire line of pet dental products which can also be used in addition to your pet's grooming visit. Treat your dog to stress-free grooming and good health at The Poodle Shop.

**1500 W Littleton Boulevard, #118,
Littleton CO
(303) 730-3200**

Music Go Round

ARTS & CRAFTS:
Best used musical instruments

Music Go Round buys, sells and trades quality musical instruments and equipment. The greatest share of the store's business is in new and used guitars and drums, but it also buys and sells keyboards, as well as band and orchestra instruments. Scott Nason's shop in Littleton also buys, sells and trades pro-sound and recording equipment, MIDI equipment, lighting and DJ gear. The shop is always looking for inventory, which means it buys used instruments for more than other stores. Technicians carefully recondition all used instruments. Students can also get lessons at Music Go Round. The store's instructors teach drums, guitar, violin, brass, woodwinds, piano and other instruments to hundreds of students every week. Music Go Round has a P.A. system it rents out to bands nightly for gigs. It doesn't rent out other gear because you can almost always own an instrument for less than it costs to rent it—especially when you can sell the instrument back to the store. Music Go Round has a special buy-back guarantee for band or orchestra instruments that can save parents a lot of money. Under this plan, buying never costs more than the cost of renting, and if you sell the instrument back, the store promises to pay at least half of the purchase price even if the student keeps the instrument for several years. Whether you are a family on a budget or a musician looking for the best deal in town, Music Go Round is the answer.

**8055 W Bowles Avenue, Suite 2S,
Littleton CO
(303) 932-8277**
www.musicgoround.com

Highlands Ranch Automotive
AUTO: *Best auto repair*

Highlands Ranch Automotive in Littleton offers no bells, no whistles and no freebies, just some of the best automotive repair and preventive maintenance services available anywhere from ASE-certified master technicians. Owner Kevin Mangone has 23 years experience in the business, opening Highlands Ranch Automotive in 2000. He specializes in repairing domestic and import cars as well as providing preventive maintenance services on newer models. His clean, well-organized shop features five lifts and five service bays. He offers the convenience of after-hours vehicle drop off and a shuttle to get you where you need to go while your vehicle receives service. Mangone not only has a great reputation for quality work, he actively supports his community and is the proud sponsor of the state champion Thunder Ridge High School girl's basketball team. Highlands Ranch Automotive is a welcome alternative to big chain automotive garages. Make it your first choice in automotive repair and maintenance. At Highlands Ranch Automotive, you'll get great personalized service from Kevin and his technicians.

3672 W Norwood Drive, Littleton CO
(303) 791-7750

Cassoulet Entrees
BUSINESS: *Best cooking innovation*

Cassoulet Entrees offers exciting new concepts in family dining for the residents of Littleton. Developed by a team consisting of three sisters plus one friend, this fabulous and creative culinary service center was founded with a mission based upon providing the community with affordable and time-saving meals that are both nutritious and high in quality. Founders Laura Leovic, Melissa McKay, Leslie Young and Elizabeth McVay are all professional career women who each developed a cosmopolitan passion and flair for entertaining that centered on the exploration of culinary delights. Cassoulet Entrees provides the community with many wonderful epicurean programs and events including culinary and wine education that encourage social interaction within the diverse factions of the community. Another fabulous aspect of Cassoulet is their Contemporary Alternative Meals Program, or CAMP, which designs meals with your family in mind. At CAMP you are provided with a gourmet kitchen and quality recipe ingredients where either you or your personal chef can prepare multiple meals to take home and freeze to later serve at your convenience. This unique opportunity gives you the freedom to choose the meals that will fit your individual or family's needs. The personal chefs at Cassoulet can create wonderful meals for special events and holidays throughout the year and have them ready to go so that you can spend you time focused on friends and family. Visit Cassoulet Entrees to let them help you save time and money while still enjoying the finer things in life.

10125 W San Juan Way, Littleton CO
(303) 979-COOK (2665)
www.cassouletentrees.com

Mountain View Photo, LLC

BUSINESS: *Best wedding photographers*

Tim and Jennifer Mosholder, owners of Mountain View Photo, take pride in their client's most memorable moments. It is through the passion, personal commitment, and unwavering dedication that Mountain View Photo offers high quality and reasonably priced photography services. They specialize in photo journalistic and traditional-style weddings throughout the year, and high school senior portraits during the spring and summer. Other services include traditional portraits, sporting events and photo restoration services. Mountain View Photo offers secure online proofing for all events at no additional cost to their clients. Every photograph is displayed online in color, black and white, and sepia, and each is available for purchase by a click of a button. If you are looking for high quality and reasonably priced photographic services, visit Mountain View Photo.

1360 W Littleton Boulevard, Littleton CO (720) 253-5276
www.mountainviewphoto.com

Jared's Nursery and Garden Center
GARDENS, PLANTS & FLOWERS: *Best garden center*

Successful gardening depends on connection with the land, and the knowledge of which plants will thrive in which conditions. Jared's Nursery and Garden Center in Littleton is a place with deep connections to the community and a place of knowledge on every aspect of gardening. Jared's was founded in 1979 by Jared Bauman, a very special man who built his business by connecting with the people he served. Jared passed away in 2004, but his family has carried on the tradition, offering the finest selection of plants and garden supplies in the South Jeffco area, along with the knowledge and expertise to help gardeners maximize their success. Juanita Bauman, along with her sons Loren and Aaron, provide everything a gardener could need for their lawn and garden. From a large selection of trees and shrubs to bedding plants, seed, fertilizer and statuary, Jared's offers variety at very affordable prices. If you're having any sort of problems in your garden, the employees can help diagnose and solve them. Jared's Nursery and Garden Center is open year-round and selection changes regularly, so you'll want to visit often. They sell pumpkins in the fall and Christmas trees in the winter. Visit their website for informative articles about gardening, and to learn about specials.

10500 W Bowles Avenue, Littleton CO
(303) 979-6022
www.jaredsgarden.com

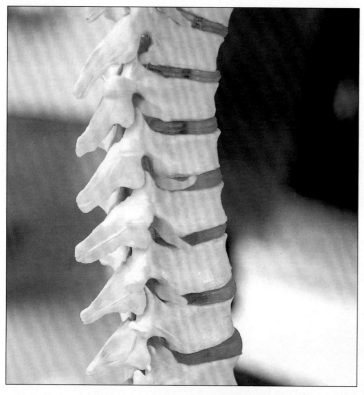

Van Wyk Chiropractic Center
HEALTH & BEAUTY: *Best family chiropractic center*

Littleton is home to the Van Wyk Family Chiropractic Center, which has a steady stream of regular local patients that are grateful for that fact. It is no accident that the doctors at Van Wyk Family Chiropractic Center all have the same last name. The grandfather, father and son team are about to be joined by another son, making this a family affair with over 50 years of collective experience in the chiropractic profession. Dr. Chris Van Wyk was the first one to work in Littleton, but he was soon joined by his father, Dr. Paul Van Wyk. Together, they opened the Van Wyk Family Chiropractic Center in 1979. Dr. Chris welcomed his son, Dr. Trevor Van Wyk to the practice in 2000. Dr. Trevor's brother Andy will join the practice in 2006. The center is equipped with a Pro-Adjuster, an FDA approved instrument utilizing a sophisticated technology. The treatment works to reduce or remove nerve pressure by adjusting the spine, which reduces or eliminates health problems. Beneficial side effects from this treatment include reductions in stress, deeper sleep and increased energy. Flexibility is also often increased. Van Wyk Family Chiropractic Center was recognized by the Colorado Community News as the *Best Chiropractic Practice* in Littleton. The center provides health care classes and serves all ages. Most clients using the center for maintenance require only one or two visits a month. Check in and let them improve the quality of your life at Van Wyk Family Chiropractic Center.

7321 S Broadway, Littleton CO
(303) 794-8754
www.vanwykchiropractic.com

Avalon Salon and Day Spa
HEALTH & BEAUTY: *Best day spa in Littleton*

Everybody needs a place to go where they can relax, be themselves and revive their body and soul. For the residents of Littleton, that place is Avalon Salon and Day Spa. This paradisal hideaway is a safe haven where you can escape the every day stresses and demands of life. Director Kathy Romero and her staff have created a peaceful environment where you will be cared for by a team of highly trained and dedicated professionals who strive to help you look and feel your very best. Avalon is an Aveda Lifestyle Salon and Spa, and they are committed to providing a refuge where clients can find the balance between body and spirit. Avalon offers their patrons a wide selection of care for the entire body. From their fabulous hair stylings to their great pedicures, Avalon can primp and pamper you from head to toe. The spa has a full range of luxurious massages available including the Hydrotherm massage and the popular Aveda massage. Avalon further offers a full spectrum of decadent body treatments such as the Aveda Aqua Polish and the Caribbean Therapy Treatment. If you've been searching for the perfect something for that special someone, give them an Avalon gift certificate; it will be the ideal present for any member of the family. You are invited to experience the very best in lifestyle spas at Avalon Salon and Day Spa.

7301 S Santa Fe Drive, Suite 350, Littleton CO
(303) 730-9399
www.avalonsalon-spa.com

Von Ya's Salon

HEALTH & BEAUTY:
Best salon in Littleton

Racheal Blackburn opened Von Ya's Salon three years ago to get back to her small town roots. In these days of super salons, Racheal wanted to offer a quaint, comfortable and intimate alternative. Von Ya's is a full-service salon for men and women. The name Von Ya's combines the name of an Iowa City salon named Ya Ya's with a North Carolina salon called Von Kekel. Several factors distinguish Racheal's salon besides its name. Besides being the youngest entrepreneur on Main Street in Littleton, Racheal uses and sells only Aveda products, while all of her stylists receive training by Aveda trainers on a continual basis. Racheal chose to become an Aveda Concept Salon because Aveda products contain fewer chemicals than other lines, and Aveda promotes recycling. She and her staff realize the importance of keeping up with the beauty industry and of fully serving their clients in ways that make the exchange worthwhile for both parties. Racheal takes pride in knowing the salon clients and making sure they enjoy their experience in every way, beginning with a scalp massage before every cut. The experienced stylists offer highlights, full color, retexturizing, manicures, pedicures and facial waxing. Racheal and the Von Ya's staff are dedicated to the image industry and to your experience at their salon. They invite you to stop by and get to know Von Ya's Salon.

2850 W Main Street, Littleton CO
(303) 797-0393
www.vonyas.com

Reflections Day Spa
HEALTH & BEAUTY:
Premier skin care specialist in Littleton

Reflections Day Spa provides its clients with a custom approach to skin care, massage and body treatments. Owner Tracy Christensen understands that each person's needs are different, and caters to individual preferences at the full-service spa she opened in 2005. Let one of the skin care professionals evaluate your unique needs. The signature Vitamin C facial delivers immediate results, bringing a healthy glow back to your skin, and the Advanced Eye Soother reduces the appearance of puffiness and dark circles around the eyes. The sugar rub exfoliates your skin and uses essence oils and vitamins to leave skin silky smooth. Themed Escape Packages set the stage for a romantic evening for two or a girls' night out. Nine and Unwind includes nine holes of golf at a local course followed by a relaxing massage. Visit Reflections Day Spa in downtown Littleton for a relaxing spa experience that is as individual as you are.

2629 W Main Street, Littleton CO
(303) 738-0222

BodyBlast Pilates
HEALTH & BEAUTY: *Best Pilates studio*

Founded in 1996, BodyBlast Pilates is now owned and operated by Geri Young, Karen Kerin and Laura Adams. They bring to their studio nearly 60 years of combined experience in the fitness industry. BodyBlast's certified trainers offer a variety of classes in Pilates-based movement, core and strength training, and personal training. Small classes, hands-on instruction and a comfortable, supportive atmosphere make this studio a welcome alternative to large, impersonal health clubs. BodyBlast Pilates adheres to the philosophy and methods developed over a period of six decades by Joseph Pilates. By strengthening the core muscles of the abdomen and lower back, Pilates results in increased energy and stamina as well as improved breathing and overall balance. Pilates programs include reformer classes, mat classes, Pilates on the Ball with Weights, strength training, the universal classes and private training. The BodyBlast Pilates studio also offers therapeutic massage, which promotes increased circulation, easier movement in your body's joints and a strengthened immune system. For individual attention, alignment, balance, core and more, visit BodyBlast Pilates.

6905 Broadway, #55, Littleton CO
(303) 738-8481
www.bodyblast.info

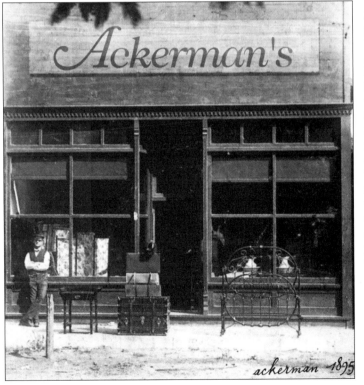

Ackerman & Sons Furniture Workshop
HOME: *Best furniture restoration*

Ackerman & Sons Furniture Workshop was established in Minnesota in 1895 by Jim Ackerman's great, great grandfather. Jim brought the business to Colorado in the 1970s and continues the tradition of knowledgeable service and quality workmanship into the fourth generation. Ackerman's has achieved a national reputation for quality and integrity in furniture restoration, repair, refinishing and reupholstering. Whether you have a priceless antique or an inexpensive family keepsake, Ackerman's gives each piece the greatest possible care and attention. Ackerman's skilled craft workers are trained to exacting standards. They provide full-service repairs, complete refinishing and touch-ups. They offer restoration of old hand-applied finishes and French polishing. The upholstery department has one of the broadest selections of fabrics anywhere. Its design-oriented staff can help you select just the right fabrics when you want to redo your sofa or chairs. In addition to the full-service shop in Littleton, Ackerman's also provides in-home services for minor repairs and touch-ups. Its staff is fully trained to inspect and estimate moving damage and insurance claims when a problem arises. Jim and his staff are proud of their personalized, knowledgeable service and quality workmanship. They are always willing to answer questions about furniture, whether it is new, antique or found at a garage sale. Call on Ackerman & Sons for the repair and restoration of your furniture.

2400 W Belleview Avenue, Littleton CO
(303) 798-3220
www.ackermans.com

Photo courtesy decorandyou.com

Decor & You

HOME: *Best interior decorating*

Decor & You provides full-service interior decorating and beautiful client-focused plans to residential and commercial clients throughout the United States. Give local owner Donna Buckalew a call. Your personal service begins with a phone consultation followed by a visit to your home or office. Don't spend your valuable time in endless searching and shopping—Donna brings everything to you. She can create an exciting new look for existing furniture and color schemes, or she will create a visual presentation with custom fabrics tailored to your exact specifications. All services come without a design fee, which is easy on your decorating budget. No project is too small. Do you need pillow and artwork accents, or accessories to finish a room? Do you need an entire room makeover, with a new area rug or carpet, furniture, lighting, window coverings and more? Donna can manage any project for you at a price you can afford. Donna also provides real estate enhancements, recommended by local realtors. She helps sellers increase the appeal of homes being placed on the market, and she helps buyers negotiate for improvements prior to purchase. Why stress over where to get started on your decorating plan and risk making costly mistakes? At Decor & You, their vision is to change the way people achieve comfort, style and preserve value in their homes and businesses. Let Donna and her professional staff at Decor & You manage the details for you.

(303) 840-9938
www.decorandyou.com

Game-Set-Match

RECREATION: *Best selection of tennis equipment*

Love is more than just a tennis score at Game-Set-Match. It's also how owner Adam Burbry feels about the game, and his stores, located in Littleton and Denver, reflect his love of the game. Players will find everything they need here for a great experience on the courts. Look for a huge variety of tennis racquets, balls and shoes from your favorite makers. You'll find the major brands you've come to rely on here, such as Wilson, Fila, Nike and Reebok. Customers will also find court equipment, including ball machines. Put some extra bounce into your game with a restrung racket. Game-Set-Match will have your racket back to you within 24 hours. The store is also an official sponsor of the United States Tennis Association and the Colorado Tennis Association. For those unable to make it to either location, the store can ship to anywhere in the world. Come to Game-Set-Match for tennis equipment that will keep you in the game

8375 S Willow Street, #208, Littleton CO
(303) 790-1991
333 S Colorado Boulevard, Denver CO
(303) 394-1991
www.gamesetmatchinc.com

Littleton Dance Academy

RECREATION: *Best ballet academy*

The professional staff at the Littleton Dance Academy understands that children learn best in a nurturing environment and offers a disciplined classical ballet program while honoring individual strengths and weaknesses. Performance is an integral part of youth training here, and the academy offers its own youth ballet company. A well-balanced dance program takes into account many aspects of dance, and Littleton supplements its ballet training with conditioning classes, stretch routines and injury prevention workshops. Students also have opportunities to learn tap, hip-hop and jazz. They study the history of dance, take music and acting workshops, and learn about proper nutrition. All teachers here have a background as professional dancers who understand the value of being a diversified dancer. Co-director Bobbie Jaramillo joined the Louisville Civic Ballet at age nine and went on to become a prima ballerina. She's also performed extensively in theater and has been on national tours, sharing the stage with such legends as Betty Grable, Ginger Rogers and Dorothy Lamour. She also appeared on Broadway in *Hello, Dolly!* with Ethel Merman. Her daughter and fellow co-director, Alison, has danced professionally for fifteen years with such companies as the Dayton Ballet, Oregon Ballet Theatre, David Taylor Dance Theatre and the Boulder Ballet. She has performed leading roles in both classical and contemporary works. The academy features three studios complete with sprung wood floors to prevent injury. For exceptional professional dance training in a non-competitive environment, come to Littleton Dance Academy.

5239 S Rio Grande Street, Littleton CO
(303) 794-6694
www.littletondanceacademy.com

The Agency Bike & Board

RECREATION: *Best place for bicycles and snowboards*

If you ride, you want to buy your bikes and boards from people who ride. If you ride in the Southwestern Denver area, you want to buy your bikes and boards from The Agency. Especially known for their suspension expertise, The Agency is a full service bicycle and snowboard shop staffed by a group of riders that go the distance to get the best performance out of your ride. Whether you're into free-ride, all-mountain, BMX, road, or another riding discipline; they can fill your bike or parts needs with brands like Kona, Haro, Eastern, Masi, Maxxis, Marzocchi, Dangerboy and WTB. When it comes to boards, The Agency carries K2, Nitro, Flow, Unity and Morrow. Owner Lance Tueller, a United Bicycle Institute Certified Technician, has been snowboarding for more than 20 years and on two wheels for even longer. If you'd rather do your own wrenching, The Agency offers bicycle repair classes through Park Tools. The next time you need equipment, service, or friendly advice about your bike or board, visit The Agency. But don't visit on Sundays or Mondays, because they're out riding.

5935 S Zang Street, Unit 11, Littleton CO
(303) 703-6800
www.agencybikeboard.com

Adventures in Dance

RECREATION: *Best dance studio*

Holly Collins, owner of Adventures in Dance, knows that dancing with confidence can open up a whole new world to children and adults, which is why she concentrates on social ballroom dancing in classes taught at her school. Children ages seven to 12 who have a desire to one day look like the dancers in *Dancing With the Stars* will find the moves they seek in Mad Hot Ballroom Basics. Couples can become expert at such dances as West Coast Swing or burn up the dance floor with spicy Latin dances such as salsa, cha cha or the mambo. Do you dream of dancing a graceful waltz at your wedding or taking on a vigorous foxtrot, tango or quickstep? Holly can help with all

this and more. She teaches the steps and provides plenty of opportunities for practice, including senior center mixers, weekly dance parties, along with one Saturday night DJ dance and one Saturday night live music dance event each month. Serious dancers can take part in out of state competitions, while partners concentrate on synchronizing their moves and families find something all members can enjoy together. Perhaps you simply want to be comfortable in a nightclub or other social dance setting. Whatever your motivation, from exercise to performance, Holly has the moves for you. Don't be shy; find your groove at Adventures in Dance.

1500 W Littleton Boulevard, #123, Littleton CO
(720) 276-0562
www.adventuresindance.com

Arapahoe Coin & Stamp

SHOPPING: *Best shop for collectors*

Rod Haenni, owner of Arapahoe Coin & Stamp in Littleton, has developed a reputation for his large stock of coins and stamps, which come from the United States and around the world. He carries rare and exotic items as well as more common offerings, which provides a range of opportunities for novice and professional collectors alike. In addition to offering individual coins and stamps for sale, Arapahoe Coin & Stamp buys complete collections. The store specializes in filling wish lists for customers in search of one or two specific coins or stamps to complete their own unfinished collections. If collectors are seeking something not available in his store, Rod will search it out and order it for them. Arapahoe Coin & Stamp also offers a full range of collectors'

tools and accessories. Stamp collectors will find protective Showgard mounts. They will also find stamp hinges, tongs, mint sheet files and safe vinyl pages by Vario to help them properly maintain their collections. Serious collectors will appreciate the store's Scott catalogues and Brookman price list. Coin collectors will find the storage containers they require, including foldovers, coin tubes, coin albums and hard plastic cases. If you collect coins or stamps, Arapahoe Coin & Stamp speaks your language.

1295 W Littleton Boulevard, Littleton CO
(303) 797-0466
www.arapahoecoin-stamp.com

Gars and Grapes
WINERIES:
Best wine and cigar shop

A fine cigar and a good glass of wine go together like bees and honey and at Gars and Grapes (Avanti Winery) in Littleton you can find both at one convenient and welcoming location. Owner Jim Griffin opened the innovative shop in 1998 after having worked in the existing cigar shop for just six months. He started Avanti Winery, named after one of his canine companions, a yellow lab named Avanti, in 2001. Jim uses primarily Colorado grown grapes to produce his exquisite vintages, which include Port, Syrah, Chardonnay and Cabernet Sauvignon as well as Viognier, Merlot and Zinfandel. At Gars and Grapes, you'll find 25 of Colorado's finest vintages, all in one place. In addition to Jim's exquisite wines, you'll also find many varieties from the state's other popular wineries including Breckenridge, Mt. Spirit Winery and Two Rivers. The shop's three canine mascots, Avanti, Gracie and Niko, are always on hand to ensure that only the highest-quality wines are being sold and that you receive nothing but the finest service possible. The cigar shop itself boasts a beautifully crafted walk-in humidor that is constantly temperature controlled at an ideal 70 degrees Fahrenheit and holds a plethora of your favorite cigar selections such as Opus X by Fuente, Davidoff and Monte Cristo. Gars and Grapes further offers its patrons a choice selection of cigar accessories that will help to ensure that your smoking experience is always a pleasurable one. Gars and Grapes (Avanti Winery) offers wine tasting every Thursday through Sunday and offers wine for purchase on Sundays as well. Experience Colorado's finest wines and some of the world's best cigars at Gars and Grapes (Avanti Winery).

**9046 W Bowles Avenue, Littleton CO
(303) 904-7650**

NORTHGLENN

Nine miles north of downtown Denver, Northglenn is a growing planned community which saw its first residential development in 1959. Northglenn is an ideal pull-off spot during any road trip. Those who stay longer may enjoy Northglenn's 550-acre park system. The Webster Lake and E. B. Rains, Jr. Memorial Park received America's Crown Community Award by *American City and County Magazine* for its rehabilitation and re-design. The updated park is one of the town's most popular spots and includes three acres of improved trails, a sensory playground and a place to rent paddleboats. Croke Reservoir in Hugh Danahy Park is another top spot for nature lovers. Visitors can fish, stroll around the lake or observe waterfowl and wildlife from the under the shade of giant cottonwoods.

PLACES TO GO

- E.B. Rains, Jr. Memorial Park
  11701 Community Center Drive

- Hugh Danahy Park
  10709 Huron Street

- Karl's Farm Dairy
  12265 Race Street
  (303) 452-1619

THINGS TO DO

February
- Mid-Winter Bluegrass Festival
  Northglenn Ramada Inn
  www.seamanevents.com/midwinter

September
- All about Art Festival
  Marketplace at Northglenn
  (303) 450-8909

Scales 'N Tails
ANIMALS & PETS:
Best variety of exotic reptiles

Many people have discovered the satisfaction of owning a reptile, and the number of local enthusiasts is growing, thanks to the enthusiasm of Jim Whitt and his three Scales 'N Tails reptile pet shops. Jim's appreciation for reptiles started with a boyhood spent in the high desert around Las Vegas, Nevada. His commitment to animals and his dream of owning a business culminated with the opening of the Northglenn Scales 'N Tails ten years ago. At Scales 'N Tails, customers can choose from a large variety of reptile and amphibian pets, including ball pythons, bearded dragons, caiman alligators and chameleons. "It's all about the animals. I want to provide each of our customers with the best animals and products available," says Jim. Scales 'N Tails sells complete terrarium set-ups that include all the necessities, such as an enclosure, heaters, full spectrum lights, substrates and nearly every type of reptile and amphibian food imaginable. The Scales 'N Tails staff has the expertise to ensure that your reptile lives a long, full and happy life. Scales 'N Tails dedication to reptiles extends into the neighboring communities where employees teach school children about keeping reptiles as pets and work to improve animal treatment. In 2004 and 2006, Scales 'N Tails won the *Pet Product News'* prestigious Retailer of the Year award in the Specialty Pet Shop category. With three shops in the Denver Metropolitan area and two more on the horizon, the chain is growing quickly. For an out of this world experience that will take you back to the days dinosaurs roamed the earth, visit Scales 'N Tails and bring home a new friend.

1470 W 104th Street, Northglenn CO
(303) 450-6169
3928 S Broadway, Englewood CO
(303) 761-5087
2099 Wadsworth Boulevard, Lakewood CO
(303) 462-0039
www.scalesntails.com

Karl's Farm Dairy Country Market

MARKETS: *Best country market*

Northglenn is home to Karl's Farm Dairy Country Market, a family owned farm with cows, horses, donkeys, llamas, goats, sheep, two ducks and an ever changing number of rabbits. But the real treasure on this multi-generational farm is the country market. It is the best place to come for farm-fresh milk in traditional glass bottles and farm-raised, all-natural beef, elk, buffalo and free-range chickens. You will find specialty products such as organic and gluten-free groceries, bakery-fresh breads, smokers and grills, pellets and propane, plus a variety of fun and flavorful sauces and hand-blended rubs. With your first visit to the farm, you will understand why some say that the folks at Karl's Farm Dairy Country Market have found the long-lost way of life. They make the functional fun, and they sell products that make a difference in your life. If that isn't enough, there are horse-drawn buggies and classic cars to view in the store, and animals to pet out by the yellow barn. With so much to do here, make it a family outing by visiting Karl's Farm Dairy Country Market today.

1741 E 120th, Northglenn CO
(303) 452-4909
www.karlsfarmdairy.com

EARLY 1900'S MILK WAGON

HOME DELIVERY (303) 452-1619

OLD FASHIONED SER...

BUFFALO & ELK MEAT Available Here

Derby Bicycle Center

RECREATION: *Best bicycle shop in Northglenn*

Whether you're tired of the prices at the gas pump or you want to lose a few pounds by pedaling your way around the Rocky Mountain region, Derby Bicycle Center has plenty of two-wheel solutions. Although it looks somewhat like a fun, family-style restaurant on the outside, inside are people who are serious about bikes. They are so serious, in fact, that they have a Body Scanning CRM system to provide you with complete ergonomic and demographic data to ensure you get the best bike for your body. With their 12-month, Ride Now, Pay Later policy, you can finance your new wheels, and you can get a warranty plan to keep them in peak condition. Derby is the number one Giant bicycle provider in the Rocky Mountain region. After 30 years of selling the myriad of other brands available, owner Bill Riley has found that Giant offers the highest quality products with the best customer satisfaction approach. In addition, Derby is proud to sell a fine selection of Haro, Diamondback, Redline, DK and Electra models that meet their high standards. Derby carries fitness bikes, too, along with parts, clothing, helmets, accessories, books and magazines. If it has to do with human-powered, multi-wheeled transportation, Derby has it and can fix it in their full-service repair shop. Get the most out of your riding experience with a visit to Derby Bicycle Center.

410 E 104th Avenue, Northglenn CO
(303) 288-4100 or (866) 566-7898
www.derbybicyclecenter.com

SHERIDAN

Sheridan was named for Philip Sheridan, a Union general in the Civil War. The name is appropriate because the town grew up around Fort Logan, an army post established in 1887. General Sheridan himself picked the location of the fort. Bars, hotels and stores mushroomed to serve the soldiers and their families. The Southern Pacific and the Denver Rio Grande both had spur lines directly to the fort. After World War II, the army declared Fort Logan surplus. The closure did not slow Sheridan's development, however. Located immediately next to Denver, Sheridan's 20th-century growth was inevitable. The great flood of 1965, which destroyed much of the city, including City Hall and the fire station, interrupted progress for a time, but citizens pulled together to recover.

PLACES TO GO

• Sheridan Community Park
3325 W Oxford Avenue

THINGS TO DO

September
• Sheridan Celebrates
*http://ci.sheridan.co.us/celebrates/
celebrates.htm*

Orange Skye Body and Beauty Bar

HEALTH & BEAUTY: *An elegant experience in casual surroundings*

Orange Skye Body and Beauty Bar promises you relaxation and renewal with body and beauty treatments for women and men of all ages. This charming, hidden Sheridan retreat inspires customers to assume a slower pace, leave daily stressors behind and spend time taking care of themselves. Orange Skye features a full range of rejuvenating services for women, including body wraps and scrubs, European facials, colored acrylic nails and sunless airbrush tanning. Orange Skye Body and Beauty Bar also provides custom makeup blending with its own line of mineral cosmetics that provide a natural 20 Sun Protection Factor (SPF). Additional services include body sculpting and an infrared sauna and ionic foot spa that both assist with detoxifying the body and weight loss. Orange Skye Body and Beauty Bar also offers a terrific selection of services for men, such as massages, sunless airbrush tanning, sport pedicures and a variety of waxing services. Owner Linda Dillon and her professional staff specialize in fabulous spa parties customized to appeal to bridal parties, birthday parties, groups of friends, business groups or others looking for a special day. Treat yourself to a day in paradise with a visit to Orange Skye Body and Beauty Bar and be sure to look for additional Orange Skye Body and Beauty Bar locations across the country.

2049 W Hamilton Place, Sheridan CO
(303) 781-8323
www.orangeskye.com

THORNTON

Modern-day Thornton was composed solely of farmland until 1953, when Sam Hoffman purchased a lot off Washington Street about seven miles north of Denver. The town he laid out was the first, fully planned community in Adams County and the first to offer full municipal services from a single tax levy, including recreation services and free trash pickup. Thornton was named after Dan Thornton, the governor of Colorado at the time. By the end of 1955, Thornton had 5,500 residents in more than 1,200 homes. Thornton was incorporated as a city in 1956 and has more than 100,000 inhabitants today. The North Metro rail corridor, a proposed commuter rail line to Denver's Union Station, will pass through Thornton. Construction is scheduled to begin in 2011.

PLACES TO GO

- Hyland Hills Water World
  1800 W 89th Avenue, Federal Heights
  (303) 427-SURF (7873)

- Margaret Carpenter Recreation Center
  11151 Colorado Boulevard
  (303) 255-7800

THINGS TO DO

May
- Thorntonfest
  www.cityofthornton.net/rec/
  Thorntonfest.asp

September
- Harvest Fest
  Community Park
  (720) 977-5906

December
- Winterfest
  www.cityofthornton.net/rec/WinterFest.asp

Stormclouds over Thronton
Photo by nine-worlds

Wild Birds Unlimited

ANIMALS & PETS: *Best wild bird resource*

You don't have to have a copy of *The National Audobon's Field Guide to North American Birds* or a pair of expensive binoculars to appreciate the wonderful assortment of winged creatures that share our air space. At Wild Birds Unlimited's two locations, you'll discover the products and proper techniques for bringing our fine feathered friends into your backyard for intimate, up close and personal viewing. The entire staff is made up of certified backyard bird-feeding specialists who can give you the best advice on what habitat or particular regionally formulated seed blend is right for where you live. Besides a diverse collection of birdhouses, you'll find heated birdbaths and heaters to attract rare birds even in the coldest weather, and specially designed feeders to keep out pcsky squirrels or other birds that take away from your intended targets. They take their desire to bring people and nature closer together so serious, they've even established their own conservation fund, Pathways to Nature. If you're getting no live action at home, check out their website for live bird feeder web cam views and more information on how to be a more successful bird feeder. Bring some new life into your world with help from Wild Birds Unlimited.

1281 E 120th Avenue, Unit H, Thornton CO (303) 255-9001
7677 W 88th Avenue, Arvada CO (303) 467-2644
stores.wbu.com/northmetro

Something Borrowed Bridal & Prom

FASHION: *Best women's formal wear rentals*

Something Borrowed Bridal & Prom gives women the unprecedented convenience of renting formal wear, an option usually only available to men. Sal and Kelli Licata's innovative shop serves a large population with its convenient location at 104th and I-25 in Thornton. Customers have the option of renting or purchasing designer quality formal clothing for a fraction of the retail prices. Alternations are performed at the store. Whether you are dressing up for a wedding, prom, holiday, cruise or other special occasion, renting allows a woman to wear a fabulous gown without preserving, storing or ever wearing it again. Renting at Something Borrowed is not settling for second best. Instead, it's an intelligent solution to having beautiful clothing for that one-time occasion and saving something equivalent to a house payment. Bridesmaids are particularly grateful to Something Borrowed for giving them a lovely product that will not spend years collecting dust in the far reaches of a closet. This two-year-old business has captured the minds and imaginations of Colorado women by offering stunning variety, big savings, convenience and a helpful staff. A full-service bridal boutique serves customers six days a week. The name for the Licatas' shop was inspired by the time-honored formula for a bride's wedding day apparel: Something old, something new, something borrowed, something blue. Visit Something Borrowed Bridal & Prom, a store with the variety and quality women demand and the convenience men have been experiencing for years.

10351 Grant Street, Unit # 2, Thornton CO
(303) 254-5440
www.somethingborrowedbridal.com

WESTMINSTER

Before the opening of the Denver-Boulder Turnpike in 1952, Westminster was a quite community best known for its apple and cherry orchards. Today, Westminster is a growing suburban community with hundreds of recreational activities. *Money Magazine* listed Westminster as one of the country's 25 Best Places to Live. To learn more about the history of the area, visit the Bowles House Museum. You can also drive by the Pillar of Fire building, a majestic neo-Romanesque edifice dating from 1892 that now houses the Belleview schools of the Pillar of Fire Church. Another striking structure is City Hall, where you can climb 181 steps to the top of the bell tower for a fabulous view of the entire metro area and the Rocky Mountains. You can also tour the sculpture garden and other gardens located around the building. One of the outstanding amenities by Westminster is the trail and open space system. The Big Dry Creek trail is one of the jewels of the system, extending about 10 miles from the eastern boundary of the city to the magnificent Standley Lake Regional Park.

PLACES TO GO

- Bowles House Museum
  3924 W 72nd Avenue (303) 426-1858

- Butterfly Pavilion
  6252 W 104th Avenue (303) 469-5441

- City Hall
  4800 W 92nd Avenue (303) 430-2400

- Standley Lake Regional Park
  100th Avenue and Simms Street

- Westminster City Park
  10455 Sheridan Boulevard

THINGS TO DO

June
- Open House on the Hill
  Pillar of Fire building (303) 427-5459

August
- Westminster Faire
  www.ci.westminster.co.us/res/rec/faire

Treasured Dolls & Collectibles
SHOPPING: *Best doll shop in Westminster*

When Nancy Whynot and her mom, Elizabeth, opened Treasured Dolls & Collectibles in 2005, they had more than special gifts and dolls in mind. They wanted to know their customers by name and provide them with a fun place to shop. Today, you can sip on free coffee and bottled water while perusing a grand collection of vinyl, silicone and porcelain dolls, from limited editions for the collector to just the right baby doll gift for your youngster. You'll find dolls from two inches to 36 inches high, priced from $2 to $1,000. Doll clothing also abounds, including such knit goods as baby bonnets, booties, sweaters and blankets to add irresistible charm to your favorite baby doll. If you are searching for a special sort of doll, Nancy and Elizabeth will try to find it for you. Antique dolls, figurines and fragrance candles join stuffed animals, including collectible teddy bears, and greeting cards to make gift giving a snap. Unusual gift options here include post office box coin banks, made from actual vintage post boxes. Children will be delighted with the dolls but also with the free gumballs and candy that comes out of a machine when your child taps the button. To buy an heirloom gift for the little girl in your life or a collectible for yourself, visit Treasured Dolls & Collectibles.

10138 N Wadsworth Parkway, #900, Westminster CO
(303) 469-3459

Supper Solutions
BUSINESS: *Best meal assembly kitchens*

Today's lifestyles leave little time for all the shopping, cooking and cleanup that goes into preparing healthy, filling, delicious meals for yourself or your family. Enter Supper Solutions, a growing chain of meal assembly kitchens with 18 Colorado locations to-date. Sandy Gargac and Leanne Deister operate this creative business, designed to honor your time, your money, your taste buds and your health. Singles, couples and families throughout Colorado praise the Supper Solutions approach. Customers pre-select supper choices online, then attend two-hour sessions to assemble 12 appropriately-sized dinners in two hours or less. Your preparation station is equipped with the necessary recipes, ingredients, utensils and food storage containers to get the job done. Help is available, and Supper Solutions cleans up. If even that level of support is too stressful, simply read the Supper Solutions monthly menu and order your meals prepared and ready to pick up. The meals are low in preservatives and varied to include meat, fish and poultry options. You can also choose spicy or vegetarian meals. Supper Solutions honors your preferences and special dietary concerns. Choose natural Coleman beef, hormone and steroid-free Red Bird chicken or meals particularly designed to be non-fat, low fat, low carbohydrate, low sodium or non-dairy. Evening meals can once again be something to look forward to with help from Supper Solutions. Take the edge off the coming month's mealtime demands with an appointment at Supper Solutions. They will be ready and eager to meet or exceed your expectations.

8471 Turnpike Drive, Westminster CO
(720) 849-9979
www.suppersolutionsinc.com

The Wave Car Care Center
AUTO: *Best car wash in Westminster*

Welcome to car washing of the future. The Wave Car Care Center uses a state-of-the-art touchless wash system. This means that no brushes or rubber strips ever touch your car. The only thing to touch your vehicle is pure water and soap. The Wave has been bringing you a better way to wash your car since 1988, and Wayne and Angela Palinckx have been the owners for the last four years. Wayne started at The Wave when he was in high school and has worked in all positions in the company. Wayne and all his employees firmly believe in their product and it shows in the smiles, helpfulness and efficiency that can be found here. Another unique quality of this car care center is that your car is pushed through on a conveyer belt, not pulled through like other car wash places. This has been proven to eliminate the possibility of front end alignment problems that can occur from pull through car washes. The Wave Car Care Center is a complete one stop shop. In the service shop they can change your oil, flush your radiator and transmission and do a complete tune up on your car. Don't forget to gas up before leaving. *5280 Magazine* awarded The Wave Best Detail Shop in the Metro Area. With credentials like these, there is no excuse to go anywhere else.

9195 Wadsworth Parkway, Westminster CO
(303) 431-4900
www.thewavecarcare.com

Simply Homemade Dinners
ARTS & CRAFTS: *Best meals for busy people*

Carol Swearman, the owner of Simply Homemade Dinners, believes that with a few hours of time you can capture the essence of the slow cooking experience. When you come to Simply Homemade Dinners, you make your menu selection, schedule a session, assemble meals to last from two to four weeks and take them home. Available ingredients include fresh herbs, vegetables and sauces. Carol's low fat Alfredo sauce boasts only 300 calories per serving, reflecting her belief that healthier foods make better meals. For your entrées, consider the artichoke and spinach calzones, Mediterranean couscous or pork chops with cinnamon apples. Simpler fare includes the Thai noodle bowl or tortellini soup. If you want something exotic or dramatic, try the tandoori chicken or herb crusted lamb loin chops. Simply Homemade Dinners is ready to help you celebrate special days, too, with selections like the Guinness Irish stew for St. Patrick's Day. Carol's goal is to help people with all kinds of needs develop a healthy meal plan with individually packaged, portion controlled, delicious meals that are ready to serve after 15 or 20 minutes in the oven. She also offers culinary classes on such useful topics as wine pairing, knife usage and how to start kids out right in the kitchen. Her six-week success program helps people with weight loss goals. For fresh meals that taste slow-cooked without taking all day to make, come to Simply Homemade Dinners.

12037 Pecos Street, Westminster CO
(303) 346-6374)
www.simplyhomemadedinners.com

Cartridge World
BUSINESS: *Best recycled print supplies*

Cartridge World is an exemplary example of a globally aware business with a conscience. A successful history in Australia and Great Britain prompted company developers to expand into North America. By 2004, business was exploding and shows no signs of slowing. Incredibly, one new store is opened each day, on average. All of this means good things for the environment in a technology-driven world. It is no secret that the imaging industry is not focused on environmental issues. Some components in the plastics used to make products take over one thousand years to decompose. Cartridge World addresses the issue head-on, re-manufacturing cartridges to reduce waste and to tackle the paradigm of the disposable society. The Westminster store is owned by Vernon Cox. Under his leadership, the store maintains the principles at the core of the Cartridge World mission. In addition to recycled cartridges, the shop supplies products and services such as specialty papers, fax rolls and refurbished laser printers. Stop by and see how many of your imaging needs can be filled by Cartridge World. You'll be supporting an environmentally sound business endeavor and receive excellent products and service in the process.

5088 W 92nd Avenue, Westminster CO
(303) 428-4013
www.cartridgeworldusa.com

Lombardi's Roman Garden

EVENTS: *Best party center with Italian cuisine*

When a big event is on the horizon, Lombardi's Roman Garden knows the most important part of the event is the food. Toss away your worries and trust your next big party to Joe and Dolores Lombardi. Lombardi's Roman Garden is a full-service catering and reception center. This all-inclusive catering company, opened in 1993, is available to provide on-site catering for small gatherings and meetings. Additionally, they have a fabulous convention hall, which is centrally located at the corners of Federal Boulevard and West 72nd Avenue in Westminster. The hall can accommodate up to 500 guests and is home to a large dance floor and band stand, making it ideal for hosting weddings, quinceañeras, anniversary parties and all of the other special or important gatherings in your life. Lombardi's Roman Garden offers a traditional and contemporary mix of your favorite Italian dishes, as well as a full-service bar for any event. Let Joe and Dolores ease the stresses of event planning by hosting your next celebration at Lombardi's Roman Garden, where superlative cuisine and exceptional service will combine to make fond memories for you and your special guests.

**3006 W 72nd Avenue, Westminster CO
(303) 412-9485**

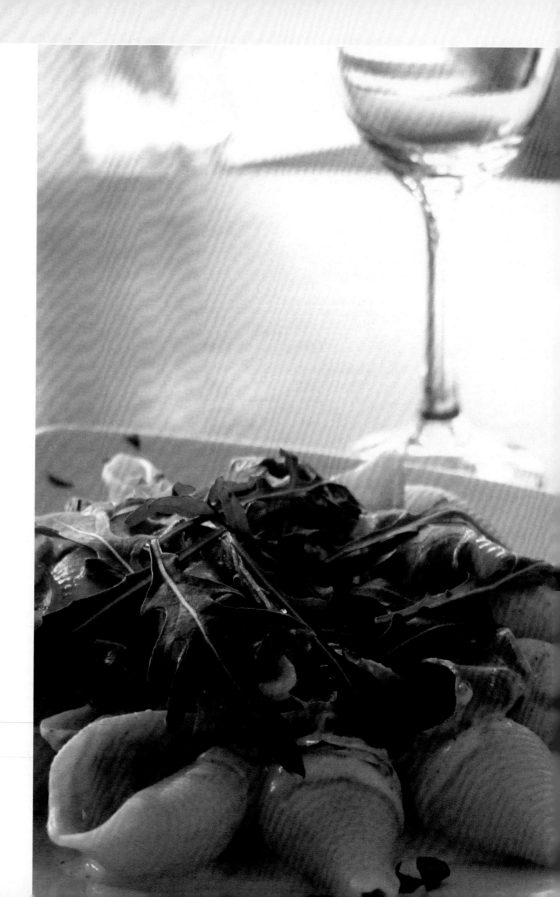

The Event Center at Church Ranch
EVENTS: *Best outdoor event venue*

The Event Center at Church Ranch is a spacious, beautifully landscaped location with rustic charm. An attractive setting that is distinctively Colorado, the 7,000-square-foot building has the look and feel of a log cabin, complete with pine log walls and open wood framing. The Center features 30-foot ceilings and an open floor plan, with the main room comfortably seating more than 450 guests. The outdoor venue at The Event Center at Church Ranch features two acres of winding pathways through attractive landscaping, magnificent waterfalls and ornate fountains. Archways and pillars nestled amongst the trees, shrubs, and flowerbeds create a picturesque setting for wedding ceremonies. A 3,500 square foot patio is available for outdoor receptions and dancing so your guests can enjoy the beautiful Colorado weather while experiencing a scenic atmosphere. The Event Center at Church Ranch is perfect for weddings, rehearsals, and receptions, company parties and picnics, quinceañeras, graduation parties, anniversary celebrations, concerts, dances, and any other event you can imagine. Call or visit today and the Event Center Staff will be happy to help you plan an event for any special occasion.

10200 Olde Wadsworth Boulevard, Westminster CO
(303) 404-3777
www.theeventcenteratchurchranch.com

All About You Laser Clinic

HEALTH & BEAUTY: *Best laser clinic in Westminster*

Have you been looking for a one-stop shop with services including laser hair removal, skin rejuvenation, dermal art, a full-service salon and a gym with a personal trainer? Amazingly, all this is located in one professional yet friendly place. For over 25 years, Tammy Johnson has been owner and certified laser specialist of All About You Laser Clinic. Her passion is to help people feel better about themselves. She says, "Not all of us are genetically gifted. For those of us who are less gifted, All About You Laser Clinic offers hope." Originally designed as a one-stop shop for serious body builders, specializing in competition, nutrition and personal training, Tammy has branched out to include laser services and a hair salon. From microdermabrasion and chemical peels to laser hair reduction, your body can be refined and revitalized by a visit to All About You Laser Clinic. Using state-of-the-art equipment and techniques like LightSheer for permanent hair reduction and DiamondTome for skin rejuvenation and resurfacing, Tammy offers clients modern effective treatments. Bodybuilders can benefit immensely from Tammy's expertise, personal gym and training, to gain an edge in their sport and become their personal best. Tammy is a concerned professional whose primary focus is on the health and well-being of all her clients. To visit this chic business, call Tammy today and schedule a treatment that will enhance your body's inherent beauty.

8951 Harlan Street, Westminster CO
(720) 540-3022
www.allaboutyoulaserclinic.com

Capabilities

HEALTH & BEAUTY: *Best home-healthcare products in Westminster*

Whether temporary or permanent, illness or injury affects us all, and the odds increase with age. Products and furnishings designed to extend independent living despite disability can be hard to find, especially in one place. That's why Pamela Pressel and Kathryn Arbour opened Capabilities in September of 2005. This Westminster shop lets customers test a wide range of products for home health care and independent living before buying. The store offers choice and style, plus access to additional resources and information. Displays include typical rooms of a home outfitted with products that afford greater accessibility, from adjustable kitchen cabinets and beds to the smallest of tools to assist with dressing, writing and eating. People with conditions resulting in low vision can also find assistance here. Capabilities provides a comfortable shopping experience in a spacious, interactive showroom filled with traditional and state-of-the-art products that increase mobility and home safety. Pamela and Kathryn have also stocked Capabilities with an array of lotions, teas and fitness products designed for comfort and health. If you know someone who could use help in the quest to live independently, tell them about Capabilities. It's a store with a mission that also provides a pleasurable shopping experience.

6805 W 88th Avenue, Westminster CO
(720) 214-0339
www.capabilitiesinc.net

Pilates Central
HEALTH & BEAUTY: *Best Pilates studio in Westminster*

Pilates is not just a trend, it is a lifestyle. At Pilates Central, the goal is to take the mystique out of Pilates. Owner Holly Cameron has her Master's Degree in exercise physiology. She has been involved in athletic training and instruction since 1980. Holly saw a need in the area for a quality, friendly Pilates studio. In June 2005, Pilates Central was born. Pilates is a form of exercise developed by Joseph Pilates. The focus is on quality of movement instead of quantity. It is designed to lengthen your muscles and create flexibility. It is a non-impact, full body strength and flexibility program based on control, concentration, precision, flow, breathing and centering. At Pilates Central, Holly creates a friendly, welcoming atmosphere for everyone. Each Pilates program is designed to meet the individual needs and personal fitness goals of the client. It also removes the insecurity of working out. The feeling you get when you walk into Pilates Central is one of relaxation and calm. Classes typically last an hour ,and all classes can be scheduled online. No matter what your age, profession or level of physical fitness, at Pilates Central you will feel better and move better.

**11859 Pecos Street, Westminster CO
(303) 410-1600**
www.pilatescentral.us

Wally's Quality Meats & Delicatessen

MARKETS: *Best meat market*

It takes fantastic customer service, the highest quality and terrific choices for a meat store to compete with the big supermarkets. The customers of Wally's Quality Meats & Delicatessen in Westminster rely on all these attributes when they visit this family-owned shop for premier quality beef and pork custom cuts including crown roasts, bone end pork roasts and rib steaks. Owner Jayson Smith says, "Our people appreciate the higher quality, fresh cuts of choice and prime meats, all naturally tenderized and aged." Jayson, a business graduate from Northern Colorado University, purchased the store to carry on a family tradition of providing personalized service on a first name basis. His daughter Kaylee created the business card logo. Her artwork hangs alongside photos of family and friends, reminders of the neighborhood nature of this specialty meat store. Jayson's traditional glass case displays an array of sausage, franks, choice cuts of meat and jerky. "Our jerky has been to the top of Mt. Everest twice," says Jayson. People who appreciate quality cuts of meat also appreciate great equipment for preparing that meat. Wally's comes through with hardwood pellets plus quality smokers, grills and accessories by Traeger. Be sure to stop at Wally's Quality Meats and Delicatessen to treat your family to the finest meats in the industry.

11187 N Sheridan Boulevard, Suite 8, Westminster CO
(303) 439-8024

Amici's
RESTAURANTS & CAFÉS: *Best Italian restaurant*

Amici's has been bringing the pleasures of the Italian table to Westminster for more than 20 years. Tony and Diana Domenico founded Amici's in December 1985 using authentic recipes that were passed down from one generation to the next. Today, Owners Bart Greff and Chris Dupuis continue to maintain the traditions that earned the restaurant its reputation. In 2004 and 2005, they proudly received the Primo Award of Excellence for Best Italian Restaurant. Amici's genuine family atmosphere, combined with superb food, service and hospitality, provides an unparalleled dining experience. "We share the food we love to make," says Bart. Amici's offers a wide variety of traditional Italian favorites, such as minestrone soup, pizza and pasta with handmade sauces. Fresh appetizers are favorites here along with house specialties like stuffed pepper and spaghetti. You'll also find some tempting seafood and veal selections. Amici's offers catering services, suitable for all your special occasions, including baby showers, graduations, wedding receptions, anniversaries or business parties. This community-driven restaurant sponsors a school night as a fund-raising opportunity for local schools. Amici's donates 20 percent of the night's proceeds to the sponsored school. When you are looking for traditional Italian cuisine served with zest and joy, visit Amici's for a dining experience that will keep you coming back for more.

7727 W 92nd Avenue, Westminister CO
(303) 422-7333

The Exchange Tavern
RESTAURANTS & CAFÉS: *Best Irish-themed pub*

Bradburn Village is an upscale, urban retail and office center in Westminster. Here you will find a great selection of small shops and eateries such as The Exchange Tavern, artfully arranged around a series of offices. The Exchange Tavern offers a beautifully appointed interior, highlighted by rich and dark decorative wood paneling, high ceilings and wood floors along with a huge crescent-shaped stone bar with a 20-foot long, mirrored and under-lit back-bar liquor display area. Additional features of The Exchange Tavern, which has always been non-smoking, include patio seating, flat screen televisions and a cheery fireplace. This one-of-a-kind family-owned and operated business is designed with just one thing in mind: to bring out the best in people, employees and customers alike. This goal is paired with a genuine Irish theme. Owners Gary and Teddi work in tandem with their daughter, son and extended family to provide a welcoming, friendly and approachable atmosphere where a new patron never feels like a stranger. The Exchange Tavern provides a hearty and delicious menu that is the perfect complement to their delightful array of upscale drafts, which they keep chilled all the way to the taps. Popular favorites include Buffalo wings and succulent center cut steaks, along with their flavorful two-handed sandwiches—including a classic Wimpy and Reuben–and savory soups. Discover a place where you can connect with your neighbors while enjoying Old World hospitality, fabulous food and terrific drafts and drinks, and discover why this is the place to "Lift your spirits...," at The Exchange Tavern in Bradburn Village.

11940 Bradburn Boulevard, Westminster CO
(303) 469-0404
www.exchangetavern.com

WHEAT RIDGE

In 1859 a small group of farmers, some who came to Colorado in search of gold and silver, began a rural village at Wheat Ridge, where they found good soils and plentiful water. The community's most significant historical structure is the James H. Baugh homestead, the house of a settler who followed the mining rush to Colorado and founded a farm. Until World War II, the Wheat Ridge community was a major supplier of fresh produce to Denver. During the 1940s and 1950s, carnation production was a major industry, and Wheat Ridge became for a time the largest carnation producer in the world. Today, several carnation greenhouses remain, and each year thousands of people join the city in celebrating its heritage at the Carnation Festival. Wheat Ridge features five retail centers and more than 20 parks. Antique-hounds will enjoy 44th Avenue, home to antique shops, consignment stores and a co-op antique mall. Family-run restaurants, with menus ranging from South American to authentic Italian, are scattered throughout the town. The Gold Line of the metro area's light rail system will pass through Wheat Ridge. Construction is expected to begin in 2012.

PLACES TO GO

- James H. Baugh Homestead
  11361 W 44th Avenue

- Crown Hill Park
  W 26th Avenue and Garland Street

- Wheat Ridge Historic Park & Museum
  4610 Robb Street
  (303) 421-9111

THINGS TO DO

August
- Carnation Festival
  www.wheatridgecarnationfestival.org

The Cat Spa Kennel
ANIMALS & PETS: *Best boarding for cats*

Cats are a special part of their owner's lives. In spite of their independence and even though your cat is considered part of your family, there are times when your pet needs boarding. For 46 years, the Cat Spa Kennel has provided that safe room and board. The kennel has enough housing to accommodate over 100 feline companions, whether it's just for one day or an extended stay. Owned by Robert Christianson, Cat Spa Kennel will provide pick-up and delivery of your pets if requested. The facility is carefully constructed to make your pet's stay a mini-vacation for them. Cats can enjoy outdoor runs and the exercise trapezes in each suite. The indoor/outdoor suites are spacious for maximum stretching room. Services include a wet and dry feeding twice a day, and superior sanitation and care are provided at all times. For a small, extra fee, you can also have them groomed and bathed during their stay. The Cat Spa Kennel is conveniently located only 15 minutes from downtown Denver. You'll be able to rest easy, secure in the knowledge that experienced, caring professionals Donna and Heather are watching over your beloved friend. When you can't take your cat with you, bring him or her to The Cat Spa Kennel where they board cats with family care.

12410 W 44th Avenue, Wheat Ridge CO
(303) 422-7300

American Piano Schools
ARTS & CRAFTS: *Best piano school*

In the late 1980s, there was a growing interest for baby boomers to learn or re-learn how to play the piano. Jim McRay wrote a book titled *Accelerated Adult Piano* for his piano students in Colorado, and in 1989 American Piano Schools was established to meet the growing interest in learning to play music. The concept of American Piano Schools was to become a cooperative with independent owners collectively running their own private facilities. Richard and Patrice Turner began their involvement in 1994 when they opened an American Piano Schools in the city of Wheat Ridge. Richard and Patrice have enjoyed long and varied music and musically inspired careers. In 2005, Patrice went back to professional performing and college music studies, while Richard continued to own and manage the Wheat Ridge American Piano Schools with the help of dedicated professional music instructors. The popular facility offers private instruction and classes to students of all ages and skill levels for piano, guitar, drums, voice and other instruments. The

school offers preschool music training and helps amateur and professional performers polish their skills. Recording and performance opportunities are available as well. Students and teachers have performed at a variety of venues, including fairs, festivals, events, clubs and cabaret establishments throughout Colorado. You are invited to enrich your life and the lives of those you love with the gift of music at American Piano Schools, home of fast, fun and affordable music lessons. Music truly is a gift that lasts a lifetime.

Wheat Ridge CO
(303) 232-7313 or (303) 421-2243

Your Paper Garden
ARTS & CRAFTS:
Cutest shop in Wheat Ridge

Your Paper Garden, a scrapbooking store in the heart of Wheat Ridge, is one of the cutest little shops around. Owner Lisza Nazarenus has filled Your Paper Garden with everything you need for scrapbooks, cards and invitations. Her inventory will inspire you with new ideas for your projects. You'll find a wide variety of art supplies, including paper and stationery. The shop stocks ribbon, stickers and rubber stamps. Attractive wooden stamps come from My Sentiments Exactly. Local school and activity items help you preserve your precious memories in a fun way. Your Paper Garden can also prepare smart-looking gift baskets. The shop sponsors scrap nights where regulars enjoy their favorite hobby, scrapping. Your Paper Garden offers classes, and ever-popular teachers Jen, Robin and Dawn ensure that both new and experienced enthusiasts have a good time. Class topics include holiday cards, gift making, and scrapping and cropping techniques. Classes fill up quickly. You can also schedule a special birthday party craft class or similar celebration. Let your favorite pastime soar with a visit to Your Paper Garden.

5840 W 38th Avenue, Wheat Ridge CO
(303) 425-0459

Steve Casey's Recreational Sales
AUTO: *Best recreational vehicle dealership*

The staff at Steve Casey's Recreational Sales in Wheat Ridge knows all about fun and sells the vehicles that put you on the road with roaming spirit in gear. You'll find new and used motorhomes, travel trailers and fifth wheel trailers at Casey's, along with truck campers and sport utility trailers, known as toy haulers. Look for high end diesel motorhomes from Travel Supreme and fifth wheelers from Mobile Suites. Casey's carries all the national brands you trust including Winnebago Itasca, National RV, Roadtrek, Weekend Warrior and Keystone. Steve Casey's has consistently won Dealer of the Year awards from many top manufacturers. Steve Casement is president of Steve Casey's Recreational Sales; he has been offering top product lines and top service for the ultimate RV experience since 1989 and carries a large selection of RV accessories. When it comes time for repairs, Casey's is prepared with a three-acre service and parts department that features indoor space for up to 18 rigs. To make your travels in the United States worry-free, Casey's provides a ReDex priority service card with the purchase of an RV, good at over 90 RV service centers across the country. Stop by Steve Casey's Recreational Sales soon and discover the many vehicles designed to put more fun and luxury into your free time.

4120 Youngfield Avenue, Wheat Ridge CO
(303) 422-2001 or (800) 309-2085 (Sales)
(303) 216-2003 (Service)
www.stevecaseys.com

Vincenza's Italian Bakery and Deli
BAKERIES, COFFEE & TEA: *Best Italian bakery*

Vincenza'a Italian Bakery and Deli, on West 44th Avenue, began as a small bakery that specialized in offering a made-daily selection of wonderful breads, tasty cookies and éclairs along with scrumptious creampuffs. Over the years, Vincenza'a Italian Bakery and Deli grew and changed however, owner Greg Allan still provides his patrons with a delightful selection of delicious, freshly baked treats and breads. Additionally, Vincenza's also now offers a savory selection of gourmet Italian dishes that are all perfectly prepared to order and filled with flavor. Sit back and enjoy traditional entrees such as the tender clams served with linguine and white sauce or the delectable Veal Marsala. Other popular favorites include their house garlic bread, mussels with marinara and the incomparable Mare Munde, a house specialty consisting of prime lobster, veal, shrimp and calamari served in a spicy and piquant sauce. This is also the ideal place to go for a great pizza as they were named as having the Best Authentic Pizza in Denver by *5280 Magazine*. Vincenza's further offers a spectacular array of fine desserts and pastries including raspberry tiramisu, cannoli and Italian wedding cookies. The warm and welcoming atmosphere and friendly service at Vincenza's serve as ideal backdrops to their truly fabulous cuisine making this the perfect place to experience a leisurely meal on your own or with family and friends. Stop into Vincenza's Italian Bakery and Deli today and treat yourself to a true taste of Italy.

8000 W 44th Avenue, Wheat Ridge CO
(303) 420-8400

Feltner Photography
BUSINESS: *Best portraiture*

Time passes by so quickly… You see it in the sparkle of your baby's smile. You feel it as your child prepares to take the next step in life. You share it in special moments with loved ones. Life is filled with beauty. All these fond memories are captured in the thoughts of our mind. Soon they become faint in our mind as they fade away over the passage of time. Yet, these precious moments are captured as family heirlooms in a professional portrait and will stand the test-of-time for all to share. We, at Feltner Photography, know how important family is, because we have been a family owned and operated professional portrait studio since 1969. Michael & Nancy Bray and staff are now photographing the families of the high school seniors that were photographed ten years ago. What a legacy of memories we have! Now using the latest in digital photography, we have 2 specialized indoor camera rooms and more than 60 different posing areas in our onsite outdoor posing park. We specialize in infant photography with our "Watch-Me-Grow" program (complete with 3, 6, 9 and 12 month sessions); Children's Designer Theme Sets; indoor, outdoor and on-location high school senior portraits as well as family portraiture. Feltner Photography, Your Family Portrait Studio!

4330 Harlan Street, Wheat Ridge CO
(303) 420-3505
www.feltnerphoto.com

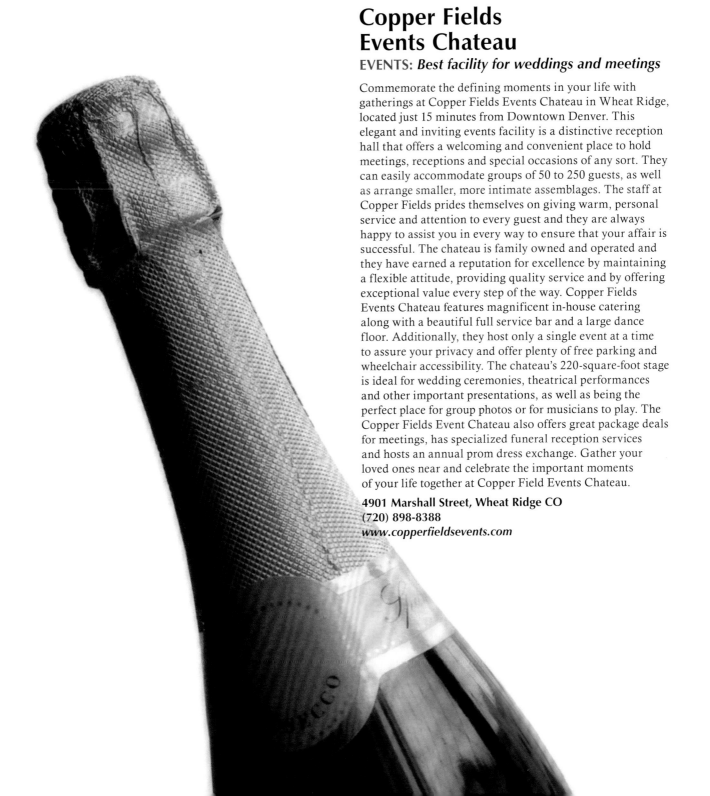

Copper Fields Events Chateau

EVENTS: *Best facility for weddings and meetings*

Commemorate the defining moments in your life with gatherings at Copper Fields Events Chateau in Wheat Ridge, located just 15 minutes from Downtown Denver. This elegant and inviting events facility is a distinctive reception hall that offers a welcoming and convenient place to hold meetings, receptions and special occasions of any sort. They can easily accommodate groups of 50 to 250 guests, as well as arrange smaller, more intimate assemblages. The staff at Copper Fields prides themselves on giving warm, personal service and attention to every guest and they are always happy to assist you in every way to ensure that your affair is successful. The chateau is family owned and operated and they have earned a reputation for excellence by maintaining a flexible attitude, providing quality service and by offering exceptional value every step of the way. Copper Fields Events Chateau features magnificent in-house catering along with a beautiful full service bar and a large dance floor. Additionally, they host only a single event at a time to assure your privacy and offer plenty of free parking and wheelchair accessibility. The chateau's 220-square-foot stage is ideal for wedding ceremonies, theatrical performances and other important presentations, as well as being the perfect place for group photos or for musicians to play. The Copper Fields Event Chateau also offers great package deals for meetings, has specialized funeral reception services and hosts an annual prom dress exchange. Gather your loved ones near and celebrate the important moments of your life together at Copper Field Events Chateau.

4901 Marshall Street, Wheat Ridge CO
(720) 898-8388
www.copperfieldsevents.com

Swiss Flower and Gift Cottage

GARDENS, PLANTS & FLOWERS:
Best flower arrangements and gifts

When looking for an exceptional gift or a stunning flower arrangement, Swiss Flower and Gift Cottage, a professional flower shop for more than 35 years, is the place that has it all. Carrying on the family tradition is second nature to Proprietress/Designer Heidi Haas Sheard. Heidi brings her original talent and experience to this shop which specializes in unique floral creations, gift baskets and European designs beyond your expectation. Browse through delightful rooms which showcase unusual home décor, furniture, garden accents, jewelry and other fine niche items. Whatever you're searching for, from contemporary to rustic, the perfect treasure awaits you at every turn. From wedding celebrations to corporate functions, professionally trained design staff at Swiss Flower and Gift Cottage assures your selection will be impressive as well as memorable. You can select whatever your heart desires from custom silks to gourmet gift baskets to seasonal décor. Swiss Flower and Gift Cottage has expanded its unique space to include Swiss SereniTea, a High Tea menu with petite sandwiches, scones, seasonal fruit cups and irresistible desserts. For a spot of tea, amazing catered food and excellent company, call in advance to create a social gathering or holiday staff luncheon everyone in your group will enjoy. The next time you're visiting the Wheat Ridge area, make a stop here to find out why Heidi and her dedicated staff are an area favorite. Swiss Flower and Gift Cottage will give you the quality and personal service you expect and deserve.

9840 West 44th Avenue, Wheat Ridge CO
(303) 424-7421
www.swissflowerandgift.com

Mr. Harold's
HEALTH & BEAUTY:
Best custom hair replacement

Harold Wilborn and Bernie Swartz were roommates back in 1944. Then, in the 1950s, in the Wichita area and in the surrounding five states, Harold Wilborn became known as Mr. Harold. His reputation was molded out of a grassroots knowledge of hair and hair styling and confirmed when he was awarded first place for his original creation for the Heart of America Hair Styling Competition. That "baby beige blonde look," modeled by former Governor Hall's wife who looked to Mr. Harold as her personal hair stylist, made every major newspaper in the USA. His creation of the geometric part, that has now been seen countless times on television, prompted him to trademark his name, "Mr. Harold's." By the way, Mr. Harold's former roommate Bernie was best known as international movie star Tony Curtis. Mr. Harold's philosophy is simple and direct: "Celebrate Your Life with Great Hair." Mr. Harold's has most recently spent over 12 years working with the Necessity Hair Foundation researching the use of hair replacements and prostheses for people with a genetic or other medical hair need. The research has opened the door for many clients who have had hair restoration funded through their medical insurance. A treating physician's prescription is all that is needed for submission to the client's insurance provider. Many physicians will provide this prescription for hair prosthesis due to a medical condition, either thinness or a complete loss of hair. No longer is hair replacement considered just a cosmetic process. Mr. Harold's knows how to handle these claims. Give him a call for more information.

Inside Colorado (303) 232-7676
Outside Colorado (800) 326-2221
www.mrharolds.com

Healthtouch Massage

HEALTH & BEAUTY: *Best massage therapy and rehabilitation*

Paula Cates has the ability to feel the individual fibers of the body's muscles to focus in on the areas that will benefit most from massage. With a thorough knowledge of muscular anatomy and her advanced neuromuscular certification, Paula is able to provide superior care to her clientele. In addition to providing the exquisitely relaxing service that any massage therapist can give, she has an integral part of her practice focus on soft tissue injury rehabilitation. Her attitude with regard to such cases is to treat and stabilize the injuries so that she renders herself obsolete by assisting the body's process of returning itself to a well state. At the same time she prides herself on having many repeat customers who understand that regular massage therapy is an essential part of their deeper healing and well-being. Paula is available to see clients at Healthtouch Massage by appointment only. Visit Healthtouch Massage to receive the benefits of Paula's innate healing touch.

6650 W 4th Avenue, Wheat Ridge CO
(303) 249-3279

Lampshade Gallery

HOME: *Best lamp repair and custom lamps*

This is not your typical gallery. Lampshade Gallery is unique and special because you will find lampshades, lampshades and more lampshades. There are only a handful of shade shops left in the entire country, one of which is this quality business that has been built through the years by Joe and Rebecca Balog. They have the best creative talent working for them. Lynda Ferris enjoys helping you select the perfect shade and finial. A finial is the decorative piece that holds your shade on the lamp. When you visit, remember to bring your lamp with you. There is absolutely no substitute. Lynda can make a lamp look better than it ever did with a new shade. Perhaps something different will be very appealing. The shades and finials range from simple to elegant and they can make a plain lamp become a beautiful work of art that complements any room. The quaint shop offers silks, rawhides, strings, papers and other fabric shades in many shapes and sizes. An important service of the shop is lamp repair and making custom lamps from your items. Lamps can be made from vases, crystal and other treasured pieces. Whether you need lamp repair or a beautiful new lampshade, remember to always take your lamp with you to Lampshade Gallery.

4575 Wadsworth Boulevard, Wheat Ridge CO
(303)420-2010

Gold's Corner Grocery
MARKETS: *Best grocery store*

Shopping at Gold's Corner Grocery in Wheat Ridge is like getting in a time machine and returning to the slower pace and specialized services of another time. Owners Joann and Bob Gold opened the store in 1988, after moving from Leadville where they also owned a grocery store. They cater to their customers with extremely fresh USDA choice meats that are tastier than the meats found at major grocery stores. They also invite customers to request special products. Gold's has a bakery and a deli where sandwiches are made-to-order and all salads are fresh daily. Bob goes directly to local farms for the freshest seasonal produce and also stocks some relatively obscure merchandise, including Scandinavian lutefisk and herring. Customers appreciate the excellent assortment of greeting cards. Many members of the Gold family work in the store alongside hardworking and helpful employees, who will take your groceries to your car, procure products from high shelves as well as delivering groceries to the homes of several elderly customers. For first-class products, old-fashioned service and values, easygoing friendliness and competitive prices, visit Gold's Corner Grocery. You may begin to look forward to grocery shopping once again.

10021 W 26th Street, Wheat Ridge CO (303) 232-8849

Wally's Quality Meats & Deli
MARKETS: *Best cut-to-order meats*

Wally's Quality Meats & Deli in Wheat Ridge is not only a specialty meat market but a family-owned, old-fashioned butcher shop. Wally's offers the highest quality meat, poultry and seafood products available in Colorado. From beautifully trimmed, fine aged steaks to the exceptional bacon

and hams from their smokehouse and homemade sausages, a stop at Wally's will guarantee a fine evening meal or the best in entertaining. Wally's specializes in the finest cut-to-order meats, from tender prime rib to homemade beef jerky. Personalized service is the trademark at Wally's, where every customer's individual needs can be accommodated. Wally's also offers a vast array of specialty items such as side dishes, grilling sauces and rubs for all kinds of meats. Wally's also offers a wide range of all-natural products including beef, lamb, pork and poultry. You are invited to discover the sensational flavors to satisfy your craving at Wally's Quality Meats & Deli.

12755 W 32nd Avenue, Wheat Ridge CO (303) 232-5660

Vinnola's Italian Market

MARKETS: *Best Italian deli, market and bakery*

Vinnola's Italian Market in Wheat Ridge has been called the crown jewel of Italian markets. Its atmosphere is like an East Coast deli of many years past, marked by friendly laughter and enthusiastic yelling. With a deli, market and bakery all under one roof, come prepared for a complete culinary experience, to enjoy on the premises or take home. After pizza, panini or an Italian sausage sandwich with cheese and peppers, you can indulge in spumoni ice cream, a mini éclair or a chocolate cannoli. Vinnola's offers a variety of imported meats and cheeses, but also prepares much of its tempting food in-house. Cookies, pastries and fresh breads come straight from Vinnola's bakery. The business is owned by Joe and J'Laine Pergola, and daughter Gina helps out as well. For those without the time or skill to cook for themselves, the Pergolas offer a unique service. Bring your own dish, and they will fill it with any of several mouthwatering made-to-order meals. Vinnola's also provides catering and custom cakes for any occasion. This authentic Italian market has been praised as the best market and deli of its kind by many local publications, including the Rocky Mountain News, Westword and Andiamo! (a Colorado Italian newspaper). When you come to Vinnola's Italian Market, Deli and Bakery, bring a hearty appetite and a sweet tooth!

7750 W 38th Avenue, Wheat Ridge CO (303) 421-3955
www.vinnolas.com

Murphy Repertory Company

RECREATION:

Best dance company in Wheat Ridge

Lena Line wants her dance students to develop positive self images while using their bodies, minds and spirits for dance expression. As director of Murphy Repertory Company in Wheat Ridge, she fulfills this goal by creating a learning environment that is optimistic, challenging and fun for all ages from toddlers to seniors. Lena has performed and taught in various cities such as New York, Japan and Colorado. She holds a bachelor's degree in performing arts from Colorado State University and has the know-how to prepare a student for a professional dancing career. Modern dance is her specialty, but you'll find a full repertoire of dance classes at Murphy Repertory Company including ballet, cardio kickboxing, swing, jazz and hip-hop. There's even a stomp class just for boys and a movement class for very young children. "Passion for performance, coupled with the desire to inspire, is what makes my students and this company a success", says Lena. Whether you are headed for a career in dance or simply want help choreographing a first dance by the bride and groom at the wedding reception, step into Murphy Repertory Company for all your dancing needs.

8035 W 44th Avenue, Suite 100, Wheat Ridge CO
(303) 463-5363

Lavender & Lace
SHOPPING: *Best gift shop*

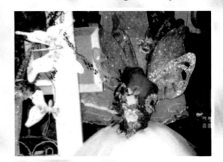

At Lavender & Lace, you will find an ever-changing inventory of gifts for all occasions. Owner Janie Olsen prides herself in providing excellent customer service to each guest in her store. Formerly called A Tisket A Tasket, Lavender & Lace continues to provide items that enhance the enjoyment of any lifestyle. One visit to Lavender & Lace will confirm why this high-end gift store has so many repeat customers. From the moment you walk into the shop, the scent of McCall candles invites you to experience tranquility. The shop carries rustic gift choices along with elegant Demdaco figurines, stationery and the exquisite line of Sweet Romance Victorian jewelry. Look also for garden décor and custom gift baskets. Janie and her staff are more than willing to design a one-of-a-kind gift basket for Valentine's Day, Father's Day, a housewarming or any occasion that calls for something special. Lavender & Lace features products made exclusively in Colorado, such as Prairie Thyme Raspberry Jalapeño Ambrosia. An interesting line of European soups also draws the attention of numerous customers. Stop at Lavender & Lace to discover a gift for yourself or to bring joy and excitement to someone else.

**4185 Wadsworth Boulevard,
Wheat Ridge CO**
(303) 425-5988

FRONT RANGE

BAILEY

Bailey is one of the largest communities in Platte Canyon, east of Kenosha Pass in the valley of the North Fork of the South Platte River. The community consists of several small businesses, and most homes are located in mountainside divisions atop Crow Hill or throughout the river basin. In 2006, the Coney Island Hot Dog Stand, a landmark building shaped like a giant hot dog, moved to Bailey from its previous home in the Aspen Park neighborhood of Conifer. McGraw Memorial Park in Bailey features self-guided tours of historic structures, including William Bailey's 1864 log cabin and a one-room schoolhouse that dates from 1899. Bailey sits just inside the Lost Creek Wilderness Area in the Pike National Forest. The logging roads and pack trails that crisscross the area's hilly terrain are a great for day hikes, backpacking trips and mountain biking. Anglers can find first-rate fly-fishing in local streams. A herd of about 200 bighorn sheep live in the mountains around Bailey.

PLACES TO GO

• McGraw Memorial Park
  43 County Roa 68

Kenosha Pass
Photo by Tom Pratt

SongBird Flowers

GARDENS, PLANTS & FLOWERS:
Best floral arrangements

When Nancy Anderson's mom told her she belonged in the flower business, Nancy took her seriously. In 2003, Nancy opened Songbird Flowers in Bailey, where she continues the affinity for flowers her mom noticed. Nancy has always been a naturalist, enjoying walks in the mountains, where she often gathered bouquets of wildflowers for friends and family. The bouquets she creates at Songbird thrill customers with their fresh approach to floral decoration and earned Nancy the 2006 Best Florist designation from the local newspaper, *The People Have Spoken*. Nancy's specialty is her Mountain Hand-Tied Bouquet, similar to the bouquets she collected on her walks. She regularly creates arrangements for weddings, parties, funerals and holidays. She is equally skilled at creating something special when the occasion for the flowers is as simple and delightful as just because. Nancy also carries silk flowers for those in need of a carefree ambience, and she makes European style plant baskets, which group several small potted plants together. For the cooks in your life, Nancy makes herb kitchen wreaths. This decorative and useful gift features 14 culinary herbs that are ready for use right from the wreath. The wreaths are long lasting reminders of your thoughtfulness as well as tempting additions to your own kitchen. Songbird Flowers can deliver its bouquets and wreaths from the greater Bailey area all the way to Denver. Think of Nancy as Your Neighborhood Mountain Florist, and call Songbird Flowers for floral arrangements as spirited as a bird's song.

Bailey CO
(303) 816-0065 or (800) 964-1059
www.songbirdflowers.com

Bailey Massage & Fitness

HEALTH & BEAUTY: *Best massage and fitness facility*

Sam and Diane Moy of Bailey Massage & Fitness have a combined experience of over 22 years helping people fight stress, overcome pain, and live healthier lives. Sam is a Fitness Trainer/Therapist with experiences offering a wide range of services. Diane is a Massage Therapist, specializing in neuromuscular therapy, craniosacral techniques and hot stone massage. Together, they can help you, whether your goal is to lose a few pounds, excel in athletics, help regulate blood pressure and cholesterol, or rehabilitate from injuries or disease. Sam works successfully with many athletes and people suffering from back pain, neck pain, auto accidents, disease, joint replacements and other distresses to the body. Sam and Diane's mission is to treat the root cause of the problems which would help eliminate the symptoms. Most of all, they are committed to getting results. Bailey Massage & Fitness carries various lines of health care products, weight loss programs and conducts health seminars. For personalized services that help you *get fit and feel great*, try Bailey Massage & Fitness.

40 Pine Tree Circle, Bailey CO (303) 816-1945

This N That Gifts

SHOPPING: *Best locally made gifts*

The spirit of Colorado is both rugged and beautiful, and the items filling This N That Gifts reflect those qualities. Artwork from local artists lines the walls of the shop and ranges from delicate feathers to large carved wooden pieces. The store carries Hanson's Wood N Stuff, a line of wooden gifts made in Bailey. Some pieces, like the handcrafted leather dream catchers and friendship feathers, reflect Native American culture. Traditionally, dream catchers were believed to filter a person's dreams and let only the good ones through. The feather is a symbol of friendship, a perfect present to someone who has shown kindness. These items are thoughtful ways to tell someone you care. Locally made products at This N That include Nature's Gift candles, with fragrances like Sweet Wilderness and Woodberry, and Colorado Skin Care products, made to keep your skin supple in Colorado's harsh climate. Those with adventurous taste buds will want to pick up a bottle of Colorado Gourmet hot sauce. It is made in Denver and comes in various levels of spiciness to suit your taste. For a taste of Colorado, stop by This N That Gifts, at the top of Crow Hill.

**1 Delwood Drive, #6E (Top of Crow Hill), Bailey CO
(303) 838-1401**

BERTHOUD

Berthoud sprang into being as a railroad stop; the community was named for Edward Berthoud, railroad surveyor and engineer. In the early 1880s, however, the Colorado Central Railroad recognized that Berthoud's location on the river bottom caused its steam-powered locomotives to labor excessively when climbing out of the valley. At their urging, during the frigid winter of 1883 to 1884, the buildings of the tiny burg were loaded on skids and pulled by teams of draft animals to the town's present-day location on the bluff one mile north of the river. Today's Berthoud, the Garden Spot of Colorado, is a small town surrounded largely by farmland. In much of this Norman Rockwell town, trees overarch the city streets. The town's Main Street organization sponsors a farmers' market every Thursday through the summer.

PLACES TO GO

- Fickel Park
  620 Mountain Avenue

- Little Thompson Valley Pioneer Museum
  228 Mountain Avenue (970) 532-2147

- Town Park and Berthoud Pool
  200 7th Street

THINGS TO DO

June
- Berthoud Day
  (970) 532-4200

September
- Fall Festival
  Fickel Park (970) 532-4200

December
- Holidays in Berthoud
  (970) 532-4200

Nightwinds Tack Shop
ANIMALS & PETS: *Best tack shop in Berthoud*

Ann Materasso, owner of Nightwinds Tack Shop, likes to say her store is full of everything you need for horses except the hay. With one look inside this 3,500-square-foot shop filled with Western and English-style tack, show clothing and saddles, you will surely agree. Ann is a long-time horse lover whose quest to find affordable saddles and tack for herself and her daughters led her to opening her own shop more than 25 years ago. Ann's in-depth knowledge of various breeds and show equipment has earned her respect among horse trainers and owners. Both new and used saddles line the aisles, with something for every budget. Nightwinds is Colorado's exclusive dealer for Albion and German-made MasSimo saddles and offers a three-day test ride for any saddle, as well as a saddle-fitting service. Nightwinds carries a full line of horse care products, grooming tools and veterinarian supplies, and your equipment will stay in tip-top shape with their tack and saddle repair services and clipper blade sharpening. The hats, boots and horse-related gifts are sure to please any rider on your gift list. Stop by Nightwinds Tack Shop in downtown Berthoud for all of your equestrian needs.

357A Mountain Avenue, Berthoud CO
(970) 532-2463 or (888) 617-3651
www.nightwindstack.com

Mountain Prairie Quilts
ARTS & CRAFTS: *Best source for quilting supplies in Berthoud*

Growing up in Missouri, Dana Richardson remembers many hours her mother and grandmother spent quilting beautiful items for the family. They passed their love of quilting on to Dana, who later enjoyed quilting with a group of friends. When the opportunity to have her own shop arose, Dana jumped at the chance, opening Mountain Prairie Quilts in 2000. The store specializes in variety with an extensive fabric selection that includes flannels, Oriental designs and florals by specialty designers. Customers enjoy the friendliness of the store's employees and the welcoming atmosphere. Dana frequently receives compliments on the neatness and arrangement of the shop. You can always find what you are looking for, whether it's a quilting magazine or a fabric reproduction from the 1930s. If you would like to hone your quilting skills, the store offers several classes for various skill levels that range in length from a day to nine months. Several clubs meet at the store on a regular basis, or you can drop in on Mondays for an open sewing time. Each June, Mountain Prairie Quilts sponsors the Berthoud Outdoor Quilt Show, a true community event displaying the works of many talented, area quilters. Come share in Dana's love of quilting and find everything for your next project at Mountain Prairie Quilts.

516 Mountain Avenue, Berthoud CO
(970) 532-3386
www.mountainprairiequilts.com

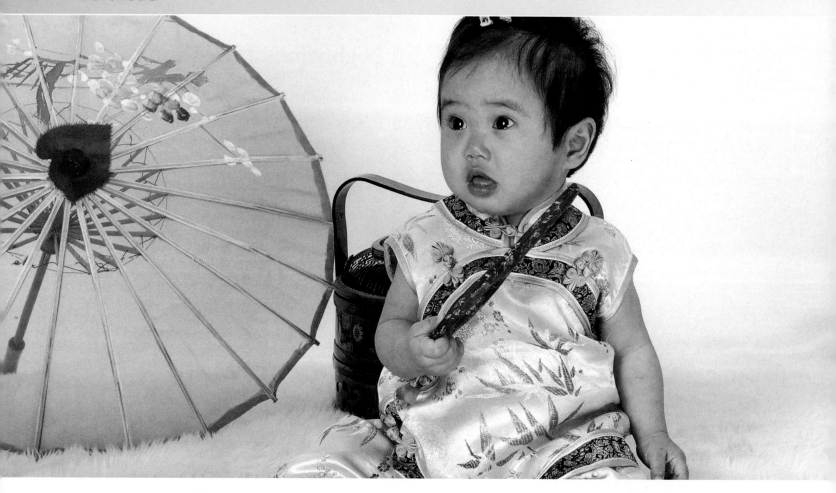

A.A.C. Adoption & Family Network
BUSINESS: *Best support for adoptive parents*

With a family of 26 children, 24 of them adopted, Larry Bebo knows firsthand the joy adoption can bring. He believes a family is made up of people who love each other, regardless of their bloodlines. In 1994, Larry and his wife, Jackie, teamed up with experienced adoption worker Kim Matsunaga to found the A.A.C. Adoption & Family Network, so that more families could experience the joy of adoption. A.A.C specializes primarily in adoptions of children born in China and Korea and has processed more than 1,400 adoptions. The agency is able to keep wait times to a minimum and offers support for parents throughout the process. There are ongoing support groups and kid-friendly outings that continue after the families grow, encouraging family bonds and new friendships. Each of the employees at A.A.C. holds a personal connection to adoption, being adoptive children or parents themselves, so each understands the need for excellent personal service and compassion during the adoption process. For their outstanding work promoting adoption and foster parenting, Kim and Larry both received the congressional Angel of Adoption award. If you would like to open your heart to one child or many, contact A.A.C. Adoption & Family Network.

735 E Highway 56, Berthoud CO (970) 532-3576 *www.aacadoption.com*

"Apple Turnover"
by Diane D. Mason

D.D. Mason Sculpture

GALLERIES & FINE ART:
Best bronze animal sculptures

Sculptor Diane Mason brings her love and knowledge of animals to each creation at D.D. Mason Sculpture in Berthoud. Diane, who studied ethology in college, has a special expertise in animal behavior, which is one reason her bronze pieces were featured in 2003 on the cover of the *Journal of the American Veterinary Medical Association.* She also was listed as an Artist to Watch by *Southwest Art* magazine in 2005 and displays her work at the Master's Gallery in Loveland and at numerous shows throughout the country. In 2003, Diane's work earned the prestigious Leonard J. Meiselman Memorial Award from the Society of Animal Artists. Her lifelike bronze sculptures, produced at her home, portray animals caught doing what animals do. Her fondness for her subject matter, whether a squirrel, a beloved bird or a barnyard pig, is evident in the gentle humor and careful detailing she employs to capture animal personalities. To see Diane's work, contact her by phone or through her website, where she provides photographs of her sculptures and a list of upcoming shows.

**5451 Sedona Hill Drive, Berthoud CO
(970) 532-1489**
www.ddmason.com

L&M Enterprises
GARDENS, PLANTS & FLOWERS: *Best garden and landscape company*

L&M Enterprises has been beautifying the Colorado landscape for 30 years. You can come into their garden center for a packet of seeds, or hire them for site development and master plans. They are a complete design, furnish and install company that runs one of northern Colorado's most inspiring garden centers. They feature a wide variety of imports, including pottery, statuary and furniture, and carry a large line of pond plants and supplies. They stock more than 150 varieties of trees, plus orchids, Jackson & Perkins roses, gooseberries, blueberries and a host of other plants. You name it, it's here. These are passionate folks with a global perspective. They exhibit that viewpoint at the Garden Center, and can incorporate it into your residential or commercial project. The Associated Landscape Contractors of Colorado awarded L&M the Excellence in Landscape Grand Award for outstanding achievement in improving our environment. L&M also won a Contractor of the Year award from Army Corp of Engineers for their downstream channel improvements on the South Platte River. L&M is a diverse company that wins big awards for big projects, yet is a family-owned company that is personal enough to help you pick out roses and plan your garden. They will even remove your snow. Whether you need a pond on your property or a packet of seeds to plant, visit L&M Garden Center.

735 E Colorado Highway 56, Berthoud CO
(970) 532-3706 (Corporate) or (970) 532-3232 (Garden Center)

Berthoud Athletic Club

HEALTH & BEAUTY: *Best fitness club in Berthoud*

The Berthoud Athletic Club encourages its members to discover their own strengths and let go of any preconceived ideas about appearance. The club's motto, Aspire to Have a Healthy Body, Not a Perfect Body, refers to that lifelong focus on health and overall well-being. Owner Caroline Creager, a trained physical therapist, who is very well respected in the fitness field and has authored seven books on fitness and methodology, brings her expertise to the gym. The club's small, personable atmosphere welcomes people to get fit, regardless of current fitness level or age. The gym offers equipment to support resistance training, circuit training and ball aerobics as well as many classes, including yoga, Pilates and spinning. An indoor climbing wall, karate classes and a jump rope program keep exercise fresh and fun. Experienced personal trainers can assist you in assessing your current fitness status and setting goals, whether that includes weight loss, sport training or building strength. In the children's programs, kids can choose from a variety of activities to instill a love of fitness at an early age. Come to the Berthoud Athletic Club and make the commitment to improving your health.

247 Mountain Avenue, Berthoud CO
(970) 532-2582

Renaze Salon & Day Spa
HEALTH & BEAUTY:
Best salon in Berthoud

As a busy accountant, Dorothy King enjoyed escaping to a spa to relax, so when she opened Renaze Salon & Day Spa in 1997, she knew exactly what other time-crunched people would need to unwind. Dorothy says that the spa is "a pampering retreat for people on the go." You're sure to notice this a few short moments after you enter and begin to relax and breathe more slowly. Start your spa experience with a Radiant Skin Facial, designed to bring out your glow. Indulge in a therapeutic massage to ease away your tension, and follow that up with a full-body purifying wrap. A manicure and pedicure complete an afternoon of pampering. To achieve even more dramatic results, inquire about lymph drainage, craniosacral therapy and electrolysis. Hair care services include cuts and styles, as well as coloring, permanents and extensions. The salon offers a full line of professional body care products, so you can be whisked away to a state of relaxation at a moment's notice. Readers of *New Beauty* magazine voted Renaze one of the top beauty destinations in all of Colorado. Call Renaze Salon & Day Spa for an appointment, because you deserve to take some time out of your hectic schedule for a day of relaxation.

509 7th Street, Berthoud CO
(970) 532-1066

Bennett's Tackle
RECREATION: *Best tackle shop in Berthoud*

Fishing is as much about freedom as it is about catching fish, and without a doubt, Bennett's Tackle in Berthoud is staffed by free spirits. It's a little bit weird, but that's the way they like it. Bennett's Tackle is what a tackle shop should be; it's run by guys who fish, and it shows. Fishing isn't fishing without fishing stories, and Bennett's is the place to hear all the banter. You can learn a lot here, because owner Bob Todd is as knowledgeable about fishing as they come. Bennett's Tackle is where you want to go for anything that will help you catch fish, from rods and reels to maps, tackle and advice. They build and repair rods, and they have the low-down on every good fishing hole in the area. They won't try to sell you gadgets; Bob knows that knowledge and common sense are the real keys to catching fish, not the amount of stuff you have in your tackle box. Bennett's sponsors a number of events through the year, from fishing derbies to an annual garlic growing contest. They

hold a yearly redneck bike/fishing derby, and a group of beekeepers meets at the shop weekly. Bennett's works closely with conservation organizations, including the Division of Wildlife and Trout Unlimited, because they believe in preserving and passing the lifestyle along. If you are a fisherman, commune with the kindred spirits at Bennett's Tackle. From equipment, to repair to great stories, they've got everything you're going to need.

121 Bunyan Avenue, Berthoud CO
(970) 532-2213

Grandpa's Café
RESTAURANTS & CAFÉS: *Best family dining establishment in Berthoud*

When Kathy Frakes responded to a help-wanted ad for a cook in the local newspaper, she had no idea it would someday lead to owning one of Berthoud's most popular eateries, Grandpa's Café. Kathy, a Colorado native, returned to Berthoud after moving away. When she came home, she began as a cook at Grandpa's Café, which has been a local favorite since it opened in the late 1970s. Nearly 10 years later, Kathy purchased the restaurant and turned it into a true family establishment. Several members of Kathy's family, including her mother, son and daughter, work in various capacities at the café. Grandpa's serves breakfast, lunch and dinner. Be sure to check

the board for the daily specials, but the green chile is always a winner, and the restaurant is known for its juicy, six-inch high hamburgers. The homemade pies and cinnamon rolls satisfy your sweet tooth, and the malts and shakes deliver classic good taste. Kathy and her employees keep in touch with community events and enjoy sponsoring local sports teams. For old-fashioned goodness from Kathy's family to yours, come to Grandpa's Café.

239 Welch Avenue, Berthoud CO
(970) 532-2254

Abeyta's Main Street Bar & Grill
RESTAURANT & CAFÉS: *Best haunted dining in Berthoud*

Owners Paul and Jan Abeyta know a few things about the old building that houses Abeyta's Main Street Bar & Grill, such as that it was originally an Odd Fellows lodge. One thing they don't know is how the ghosts got here. Folks claim to see three of them from time to time: a lady in a black dress and two men. No doubt they long for a taste of the steaks, burgers and Mexican food that have made Abeyta's so popular for many years. Paul, Jan and their staff make all the food themselves. About the only complaint they ever hear from customers is that the portions are too big. Paul is a musician who actually gigged here at the tender age of 13. Now he owns the place and keeps his musical skills

sharp by performing for his guests now and then. Live music is a regular feature on Friday nights and, yes, there is a dance floor. Sundays feature a Denver Broncos potluck that combines football and great food for a party all football fans will enjoy. Paul and Jan are proud that theirs is a completely self-sustaining business with no corporate ties. Get well-fed and entertained at Abeyta's Main Street Bar & Grill, and perhaps even leave with a ghost story.

**335 Mountain Avenue, Berthoud CO
(970) 532-6213**

Blue Moon Creations
SHOPPING: *Best stained glass studio in Berthoud*

Owner Cindy Nevins says that first-time customers almost invariably fall in love with Blue Moon Creations. She describes her Berthoud store as "a blend of flea market and art gallery," and her own love for the store is downright infectious. Blue Moon carries antiques, collectibles and furniture along with handcrafted arts and crafts. Cindy welcomes consignments. Blue Moon specializes in glass artwork by local artists and carries a collection of stained glass, blown glass and fused glass pieces. Cut glass is also displayed. A stained glass studio offers glass and supplies for the glass artist, custom creations for the glass admirer and classes for anyone interested in learning to work with glass. A collection of ready-made stained glass windows just might hold the finishing touch you've been waiting to add to a room in your home. Blue Moon Creations inspires other areas of artistic endeavor, too, with classes in watercolor, drawing and oil painting. A gift center offers original jewelry, artwork and decorator accents along with a charming set of greeting cards and Donald Duck collectibles. Like many of the objects in the store, the jewelry is crafted by local artists and includes hanging crystals, fused glass pieces and semi-precious stones. Let Cindy's eclectic tastes stimulate your imagination and fire your curiosity with a visit to Blue Moon Creations.

**212 Mountain Avenue, Berthoud CO
(970) 532-0303** *www.bluemooninberthoud.com*

PLACES TO GO

- Boulder History Museum
  1206 Euclid Avenue (303) 449-3464

- Boulder Museum of Contemporary Art
  1750 13th Street (303) 443-2122

- Boulder Reservoir
  5565 N 51st Street (303) 441-3461

- Celestial Seasonings Tea (tour)
  4600 Sleepytime Drive (303) 581-1202

- Chautauqua Park
  900 Baseline Road

- CU Art Museum
  318 UCB (303) 492-8300

- CU Museum of Natural History
  1035 Broadway Street (303) 492-6892

- The Dairy Center for the Arts
  2590 Walnut Street (303) 440-7826

- Fiske Planetarium & Sommer Bausch
  Observatory
  408 UCB (303) 492-5001

- Flagstaff Nature Center
  Flagstaff Summit Road (303) 441-3440

- Leanin' Tree Museum & Sculpture Garden
  of Western Art
  6055 Longbow Drive (303) 530-1442

- National Center for Atmospheric Research
  (tours)
  1850 Table Mesa Drive (303) 497-1174

BOULDER

Boulder is in Boulder Valley where the Rocky Mountains meet the Great Plains. Just west of the city are imposing slabs of tilted sedimentary stone. Known as The Flatirons, they are a traditional symbol of Boulder. The city is the home of the University of Colorado's main campus (CU-Boulder), the National Center for Atmospheric Research and a half-dozen other major research institutions. After UCB, Boulder's largest employers are IBM and Ball Aerospace. A greenbelt of city trails and open spaces surrounds the city, which also has miles of bike paths and unusually frequent bus service for a community of its size. Beginning in 2014, commuter rail will travel between Longmont, Boulder and Denver, with stops in major communities along the way. Year-round art and cultural activities include a twice-weekly Farmer's Market in the summertime, the annual Bolder Boulder, Shakespeare Festival and the Boulder International Film Festival. Boulder has landed on many magazine lists in categories such as Best Place to Live and Most Bicycle-Friendly Community. With its distinctive Tuscan architecture, the CU campus may be one of the most beautiful in the country.

Flowers on the Pearl Street Mall in Boulder Colorado
Photo by Eric Wunrow
Courtesy of Colorado Tourism Office

THINGS TO DO

January
- Mahlerfest
  www.mahlerfest.org

- Boulder Bach Festival
  First Presbyterian Church (303) 776-9666

February
- Boulder International Film Festival
  Boulder Theater (303) 449-2283

March
- Boulder Revel
  Dairy Center for the Arts (720) 406-1215

April
- Conference on World Affairs
  www.colorado.edu/cwa

- Boulder Adventure Film Festival
  Boulder Theater (303) 818-6402

May
- Kinetics (human-powered device race)
  (303) 631-2973

- Bolder Boulder (footrace)
  and Boulder Creek Fest
  www.bolderboulder.com

June
- International Dance Festival
  Pearl Street Mall (303) 499-3001

July
- Downtown Boulder Art Fair
  Pearl Street Mall 303-449-3774

July-August
- Colorado Shakespeare Festival
  CU campus www.coloradoshakes.org

August
- Boulder International Fringe Festival
  www.boulderfringe.com

- Boulder Asian Festival
  Pearl Street Mall (303) 499-0108

September
- Hometown Fair
  *Boulder Public Library Lawn
  (303) 652-4942*

September-October
- Toofy Film Fest
  www.tooty.com

- Downtown Boulder Fall Festival
  (303) 449-3774

December
- Lights of December Parade
  Downtown (303) 449-3774

Gunbarrel Veterinary Clinic
ANIMALS & PETS:
Your pets are our priority

Pets bring unbounded joy to our lives, They share in our triumphs and sorrows by acting as both stoic heroes and loving members of the family. Ensure that your pets have the attention and care they deserve by taking them to Gunbarrel Veterinary Clinic. Gunbarrel Veterinary was established in 1969 in a charming, remodeled farmhouse. Doctor Louis Brad purchased the clinic in 1992 and established a reputation for excellence throughout Boulder County with his caring and skillful treatment of animals. By 2001, Gunbarrel Veterinary had outgrown its vintage facility, and Doctor Brad began making plans for a new building on the five-acre property. The updated 10,000-square-foot facility opened in July 2004 and is a delightfully spacious and efficient building that offers maximum comfort for animal patients and caregivers. Gunbarrel Veterinary Clinic is dedicated to small animal care, including routine checkups, medical and surgical care. The clinic offers emergency services, dental procedures, geriatric pet care and animal acupuncture. The clinic offers two surgical approaches to treat injury to the cranial cruciate ligament, a common orthopedic problem found in dogs. The facility boasts 50 dog runs, a doggie day care and a separate kitty condo that gives your feline a cozy and secure place to stay. Allow Doctor Brad and his friendly, professional staff to manage your pet's well-being with care and kenneling from Gunbarrel Veterinary Clinic.

4636 N 55th Street, Boulder CO
(303) 530-2500
www.gunbarrelvet.com

Colorado Canines & Felines too!
ANIMALS & PETS: *Best animal supply store in Boulder*

Colorado Canines & Felines too!, Boulder's first all-natural pet product store, reflects owner Alex Teller's lifelong love of animals. A former pet sitter, dog walker and trainer, Alex opened Colorado Canines in 1999 to act on her belief that animals have specific nutritional needs just as people do. Major, her German Shepherd, was her first employee. The store has expanded twice since then and now includes a dog wash and café. Colorado Canines has also branched out into organizing adventure trips for people and their dogs. Still, the focus of this growing business remains on providing the products and information you need to help pets eat right, fight disease and stay active. Store employees receive special training designed to educate customers about

the foods sold at Colorado Canines, which contain no by-products or chemicals. The store also hosts classes on such topics as raw diet and flower essences for pets. With so many ardent animal lovers gathered under one roof, Colorado Canines is a great a place to socialize too. In fact, Alex Teller met her husband at the store. Their three dogs took part in the wedding. Make your pet's day, and visit Colorado Canines & Felines too!

1738 Pearl Street, Suite 120, Boulder CO
(303) 449-5069
www.coloradocanines.com

H.B. Woodsongs
ARTS & CRAFTS: *Best place to buy musical instruments in Boulder*

H.B. Woodsongs is a friendly, relaxed shop where customers enjoy buying and renting musical instruments with help from experienced musicians. Dana Flitcraft and her staff love music and their enthusiasm is getting noticed. For two years in a row, Woodsongs has been voted the best place to buy musical instruments in the *Boulder Daily Camera's* Best of Boulder contest. Once known as Folk Arts Music, established in 1970, the shop has outgrown one name and three locations. It has also expanded its offerings to include electric as well as acoustic guitars and continues to feature an assortment of brand-name band instruments and folk instruments including banjos, mandolins, autoharps and dulcimers. Woodsongs' customers can depend on knowledgeable salespeople for the

information they need to select, maintain and play an instrument. There is a fine selection of new and used instruments priced to suit every budget and an option to apply rental fees towards the purchase of student instruments. All the needed accessories and care products along with printed music, videos and recordings are also available. The store is home to Woodsongs Lutherie, specialists in stringed instrument restoration and repair, and Woodsongs Studios, which offers instruction by teachers of critical acclaim on the guitar, banjo, mandolin, violin, cello and dulcimer. The staff at H.B.Woodsongs invites music lovers everywhere to come by and discover why Boulder loves this music shop.

2920 Pearl Street, Boulder CO
(303) 449-0516
www.hbwoodsongs.com

The Drum Shop

ARTS & CRAFTS: *Best source for ethnic percussion instruments*

Indulge your passion for drumming at The Drum Shop, where owner Billy Hoke offers a diverse selection of ethnic percussion instruments ranging from traditional and custom made drum kits to Indian tablas, African djembes, Middle Eastern doumbeks and Native American drums. This popular destination shop features Tribes Custom Drums, which are made by drummers for drummers at prices that won't break the bank, and which are created by a company where everyone involved, from the builders to the accountant, are drummers. The Drum Shop is a favorite of players and sound men alike. Resident instructors are available to teach people of all ages and skill levels the necessary techniques needed to become drummers. Children especially love to drum and Billy is delighted with how much enjoyment he gains from teaching kids about drums. Boulder is home to a vast drumming community, as well as numerous world-class musicians. The Drum Shop is dedicated to facilitating the love of music within that community. Learn new skills, make new friends and find the custom drums you've been dreaming of at The Drum Shop.

2065 30th Street, Boulder CO
(303) 402-0122

Taylor Moving
BUSINESS:
Best moving company

Whether they are moving people out of their homes or moving companies across town, Boulder's homegrown moving company says business is thriving. Personal attention and experienced, friendly movers were cited again and again as the basis for success by this company. Glen and Leah Taylor, who started Taylor Moving out of their home over 11 years ago, say customers are attracted to the personalized service their local company provides. Glen says many people feel good about using local companies over national chains, which has proven excellent for business. All the movers at Taylor Moving have at least three years of experience and many have been with Taylor Moving much longer. Taylor Moving does work with Whole Foods, Boulder History Museum and the Academy Retirement Community, and they are members of the BBB and Tom Martino's Exclusive Referral List. All of their trucks are outfitted with professional moving pads and equipment and no extra charge. They have professional packing services available and a complete selection of boxes and packing supplies for the do-it-yourselfers. They have secure storage in their warehouse and offer customized long distance moves with direct, express service to your new home with guaranteed pick up and delivery dates and a guaranteed price. You will receive the same quality move every day of the year. Call today to speak to Glen, Leah or the two office dogs, Scout and George, or check out the whole crew on the web.

4949 N Broadway #110,
Boulder CO
(303) 443-5885
www.taylormove.com

Honest • Experienced • Reliable
TAYLOR MOVING
LLC

Taylor-ed To Your Needs
303-443-5885

Shamane's Bake Shoppe
BAKERIES, COFFEE & TEA:
Best baked goods from scratch

Pastry Chef Shamane Simons brings a world of culinary experience to Shamane's Bake Shoppe, her café and bakery. While she has deep experience in many cuisines, Shamane now focuses her talents on elegant and delicious wedding and special occasion cakes, pastries and desserts. Everything is made from scratch using the finest ingredients. The pastry menu includes a wide variety of petits fours, cookies, cakes, tortes, various mousses and fruit pies. Shamane frequently caters private events for up to 50 people. She works with each client individually and tailors her offerings to help create a truly memorable event. When you stop by the café, you can enjoy any of her homemade croissants, quiches, breakfast burritos or pastries. Shamane is a graduate of the Scottsdale Culinary Institute and has continued her formal training ever since. In France, she worked as the chef of an exclusive hot air balloon excursion company, preparing five-course dinners while floating over Italy, the Czech Republic, France and the Swiss Alps. Upon her return to the United States, she became a pastry chef and bakery manager for both the Brasserie Ten Ten and the Mediterranean restaurant in Boulder. She opened Shamane's Bake Shoppe in 2004. For exquisite treats from a world-class chef, visit Shamane's Bake Shoppe.

2825 Wilderness Place, Sweet 800, Boulder CO
(303) 41-SWEET (417-9338)
www.shamanesbakeshoppe.com

Redstone Catering
EVENTS: *Best caterer in Boulder*

When you plan an event, you want seasoned caterers you can rely on. Redstone Catering was named Best Caterer by the *Daily Camera* in its annual *Best of Boulder* issue. Owners Dan and Mary Dietrich have 25 years of experience in the culinary industry. Redstone continues to serve up the same recipes for success and service that have satisfied customers for 14 years. The experienced staff brings superb cuisine, flawless presentation and outstanding service to every event, whether small or large, a corporate affair or casual family reunion.

Committed to working intimately with every client to assure a stunningly successful event, they provide recommendations for decorators, florists, photographers and musicians. Clients may peruse an extensive menu of options and make changes as they see fit. Redstone believes in tailoring their approach to meet your needs. They'll prepare their delicacies in your home, at an event site, or make it in advance and bring it to you. Whatever is needed, they're prepared.

Hire Redstone Catering for your next function. You'll be able to relax knowing your special event is being handled by pros.

Boulder CO
(303) 443-1201
www.RedstoneCatering.com

Starr's Clothing Co.

FASHION:
Best clothing store in Boulder

The story of Starr's Clothing Co. began in the early 1900s, when Polish immigrant Ben Wigotow undertook the difficult three-week journey to America with only $10 to his name. He worked long hours six days a week in a variety of jobs in New York City, then made his way West on the advice of a doctor. After falling in love with Boulder, he founded Starr's Clothing Co. in 1914. Today, owner Steve Wigotow and his wife Karey are the fourth generation to run the family business. In the early days, Starr's carried classic men's wear, but it has evolved along with Boulder and now carries outdoor clothing and men's and women's casual wear. The store's specialty is jeans for any occasion, from work to weekend, and it has a huge selection. With over 140 different women's styles and 50 men's styles, the denim experts at Starr can find the perfect fit for your body. Lines from Free Purple, Christopher Blue, Carhart and many other high-quality denim brands make it easy for Starr's to put everyone in quality jeans. For a bit of Boulder history and the perfect pair of jeans, visit Starr's Clothing Co.

1630 Pearl Street, Boulder CO
(303) 442-3056

Edible Arrangements
FUN FOODS: *Best edible bouquets*

A veteran gift giver, Betsy Sherman knows a good gift when she gets one, so when a friend gave her an edible bouquet as a gift, she kept the tag to investigate the company. In 2004, she purchased an Edible Arrangements franchise. Betsy is one of more than 600 such franchise owners in the United States and abroad. She loves running Edible Arrangements, which involves picking top quality fruit and cutting it into a variety of shapes to create attractive edible bouquets, guaranteed fresh and tailored for any occasion. Mylar balloons, gourmet chocolate dips and keepsake containers complement the innovative and delectable bouquets. The fresh fruit designs come in an array of styles and sizes, so you can please one special person or everyone who attends your next office party. When you need a unique gift for the chocolate lover in your life, choose chocolate dipped strawberries or chocolate covered apple slices wrapped in elegant gold boxes. Among the delicious and health-conscious designs is the Delicious Fruit Design with Dipped Daisies, a symmetrical arrangement of chocolate-dipped pineapple daisies, strawberries, grapes, cantaloupe and honeydew that comes in several sizes. Betsy takes the same care in choosing and arranging the fruit as any professional floral designer takes in arranging flowers. When you want to give a novel gift that's as practical as it is beautiful, contact Betsy at Edible Arrangements.

4800 Baseline Road (Meadows Shopping Center), Suite C-111, Boulder CO
(303) 499-9222
www.ediblearrangements.com

The Growcery Store
GARDENS, PLANTS & FLOWERS: *Best hydroponics supplier*

Imagine a garden where you can grow food year-round regardless of your climate or soil with a method called hydroponics. Erich Bielek and Gibran Khal opened the Growcery Store two years ago with the desire to make hydroponics a mainstream method of individual food production. Beginners and experts will find the products and information they need to pursue this efficient method of food production, capable of making 100-square-feet of greenhouse space equivalent in production to a ten-acre farm. Creating a controlled environment that can break climate barriers requires some specialized equipment such as grow lights, pumps, nutrients, air purifiers and plant propagation supplies. The Growcery Store is fully stocked with the supplies you need and the expertise to bring you results. Erich and Gibran have a passion for growing and a strong desire to share information. They teach their customers how to make hydroponics a cost effective alternative to buying fruits and vegetables at a grocery store. They also understand how controlling the growing environment can produce more nutritious produce. Whether you want

to start a rewarding hobby or grow food for sustenance, the Growcery Store is ready to serve you. Hydroponics is a soilless method of plant production widely used in such countries as Japan and Scotland. It is a practical way to produce high quality fruits and vegetables in limited space. Visit the Growcery Store for the equipment you will need to produce the garden of your dreams.

1501 Lee Hill Road, #17, Boulder CO
(303) 449-0771
www.thegrowcerystore.com

Photo courtesy of thegrowcerystore.com

Art of the Flower
GARDENS, PLANTS & FLOWERS: *Best fresh floral arrangements in Boulder*

Select fresh floral arrangements for your next event or as a special gift at Art of the Flower, where owner Tim Weckerly and his dedicated staff take a creative approach to floral design with European styling and blooms from around the globe. Look for this special shop in the University Hill district adjacent to the University of Colorado—Boulder's answer to San Francisco's Haight-Ashbury. Art of the Flower is a full-service florist that offers a distinctive array of fresh-cut florals and living plants, along with design services for special occasions, including weddings or sorority functions. Tim is passionate about his business and his customers. He and his talented designers, Kate and Marie, take pride in listening to their clients' needs and fulfilling their floral dreams. The shop can deliver throughout the Boulder area for a small charge, with

free delivery to the hospital or the campus. Many of Art of the Flower's repeat customers make a point of stopping by just to smell the flowers and to say hello to Tim and his official greeters, Mougli and Willie, a pair of charming cocker spaniels who take their hospitality duties very seriously and are always happy to accept a bone or a treat from generous visitors. Whether you're searching for the classic simplicity of a single rosebud or the flair of a stylish and contemporary arrangement, you're sure to find florals for your taste and budget at Art of The Flower, where Mother Nature and creative inspiration come together.

1140 13th Street, Boulder CO
(303) 447-2260
www.artoftheflower.com

Boulder Quest Center
HEALTH & BEAUTY: *Best martial arts and meditation programs*

Do you seek to act effectively in all areas of life? You can explore your potential at the Boulder Quest Center through the ground-breaking martial art of To-Shin Do or by Blue Lotus Assembly mind-science meditation. Quest Kickboxing and Quest Yoga are great workouts to complement your training. You can take any of these programs individually or in combination. To-Shin Do, a modern approach based on Japanese traditions, fosters a sense of self-confidence and security through carefully tested techniques for grappling, throwing and striking. The mind science program begins with training in Calm Focus and then moves on to observing, understanding and directing life itself. Quest Kickboxing, which includes calisthenics, shadow-boxing and aerobic punches and kicks to a heavy bag, promotes cardiovascular health and increases bone density. Four to six-year-old children can join the Mighty Dragons to develop motor skills and mental focus in an environment that is exciting and playful, but safe and non-competitive. Mighty Dragons teaches leaping, ducking, rolling and dodging skills and a simplified form of To-Shin Do. Owner Mary A. Casey II and her husband Kevin study under Stephen K. Hayes, a Black Belt Hall of Fame member and Buddhist priest who founded To-Shin Do and Blue Lotus Assembly. Mary and Kevin are delighted to pass these skills on to you, the student, at the Boulder Quest Center.

1200 Yarmouth Avenue, Boulder CO
(303) 440-3647
www.boulderquest.com

Mountain's Edge Fitness Center

HEALTH & BEAUTY:
Best individualized fitness programs in Boulder

Jason McQueen and Scott Carew, owners of Mountain's Edge Fitness Center, are hands-on entrepreneurs who, as part of their contribution to their community, have created a masterpiece of a fitness center. Their center is known for a friendly atmosphere that makes it a comfortable place to work out. Mountain's Edge has one of the largest weight rooms in Boulder, so any time you stop by you can be certain that you will get the workout you desire. Fitness Director Shannon Derby helps develop individualized programs for customers, puts emphasis on the use of personal trainers and has established a variety of classes, including cycling techniques, muscle training and kickboxing. Mountain's Edge is also a great place to take a step class, learn about interval training or try out a discipline like pilates or yoga. Because Mountain's Edge is locally owned, you can easily contact an owner if you have customer service needs, and you can be sure that the staff will always know your name. With bonuses like ample parking and day care, Mountain's Edge will quickly become a part of your daily routine. Men, women and even kids can find activities to please. Drop by Mountain's Edge Fitness Center and see how Jason, Scott, and their respected staff can help you improve your fitness level.

693K S Broadway Street, Boulder CO
(303) 494-5000
www.mountainsedge.net

Peak Form Physical Therapy

HEALTH & BEAUTY: *Best physical therapy clinic in Boulder*

Peak Form is a physical therapy clinic that specializes in the rehabilitation of a variety of orthopedic conditions, including, but not limited to, sports medicine, post-surgical, repetitive stress injuries, work-related injuries and motor vehicle accidents. The clinic has a special interest in sports medicine. In fact, many of the staff members are current and past athletes. Clinic Director and Physical Therapist Jeanette Hrubes competed in the 1987 Pan American Games as a member of the Canadian National Gymnastics Team. She was a contender for the 1988 Canadian Olympic Team, but was

sidelined by a serious back injury. Kerry Barnholt, lead Physical Therapist, has been an active member in the local Boulder cycling community, racing professionally for the Subaru Gary Fisher mountain bike team. What sets Peak Form Physical Therapy apart from other clinics is the individualized attention in a one-on-one setting, to assure high patient satisfaction. Peak Form is strategically located immediately next to Mountain's Edge Fitness Center, a 15,000-square-foot athletic facility. To help recovering patients as they regain independence, the patients receive a free, one month membership to the fitness center upon discharge. Patients can use the membership to continue their individualized exercise regimes. If you need physical therapy, Peak Form Physical Therapy can help you regain and maintain a healthy and active lifestyle.

693 E South Broadway, Boulder CO
(303) 402-9283
www.peakformpt.com

Enchanted Ink, LLC

HEALTH & BEAUTY: *Best body art studio in Boulder*

The practices of tattooing and body piercing have been revered through time and been practiced by every known civilization. Today, tattooing and piercing are once again highly popular forms of personal expression. At Enchanted Ink, LLC in Boulder, you can safely express yourself under the watchful eyes of registered nurses and owners, Tara and Gwynn "Wolf" Wolfstar. Combined, the duo had more than 30 years of nursing experience before they decided to leave it behind and open Enchanted Ink in 1998. Not surprisingly, the first thing that visitors notice is the clean, fresh scented and welcoming atmosphere of this family-owned business. Visitors also cannot help but take note of the fabulous artwork and the Wolfstars' dedication to their craft. At Enchanted Ink, the motto is, Do No Harm. Not only will you receive highly personalized and exceptional service, you will also receive education about how to care for your tattoo or piercing. While Enchanted

Ink offers a wide selection of standard tattoo stencils, they are best known for their ability to pull creative, original ideas from their customers' thoughts and turn them into one-of-a-kind tattoos that are true expressions of individual personalities. At Enchanted Ink, the owners know that the decision to tattoo or pierce your body is highly personal and deeply spiritual. They therefore strive to create an atmosphere where you will feel supported, comfortable and encouraged. Express yourself with your body as the ultimate canvas at Enchanted Ink, LLC.

1200 Pearl Street, Suite 35, Boulder CO
(303) 440-6611
www.enchanted-ink.com

Photo by Tara Gray-Wolfstar

NatureMed

HEALTH & BEAUTY:

Best naturopathic family medicine clinic

Naturopathic medicine is the miracle bridge between alternative medicine and allopathic, conventional western practices. Naturopathic Doctors Stephen and Kelly Parcell provide a multitude of professional services at NatureMed, aimed at addressing health care issues while remaining grounded in a holistic philosophy foundation. The result is a comprehensive clinic offering the best of all worlds. Naturopathic physicians are trained in medical science and conventional diagnostics. In addition to the basic medical training, naturopathic studies go above and beyond the normal medical education in order to incorporate clinical nutrition, plant medicine, homeopathy, hydrotherapy, naturopathic physiotherapy, natural childbirth, classical Chinese medicine, pharmacology and minor surgery. NatureMed is a naturopathic family medicine clinic with an evidence-based approach to health. Under their expert direction, the body's natural healing powers are maximized, giving patients greater control over their own health in a positive environment. The biggest benefit associated with naturopathic medicine is that it treats the causes of illness, not just the symptoms. The natural conclusion is that long-term solutions are achieved in this manner and the evidence supports this theory. NatureMed succeeds where other methods have failed. Whenever there is an imbalance, health concerns often ensue. Let NatureMed help you restore your own personal balance.

1440 28th Street, Suite 4, Boulder CO
(303) 884-7557
www.naturemedclinic.com

Susan Melching
Skin Care Professionals

HEALTH & BEAUTY: *Best scientific skin care clinic*

Somewhere between the pampering of a spa and the medical treatment of a doctor is the approach that Susan Melching and her team take to skin care. Susan points out that when you come to Susan Melching Skin Care Professionals, you are coming to a clinic that seeks a whole-body approach to your needs and that commits to long-term results rather than treatments that make you feel good for the day. Clients receive a comprehensive assessment that looks at all facets of skin care, from nutrition and physical health to lifestyle, genetics and hormones. Susan is an internationally trained esthetician and permanent makeup artist, well known for her pioneering work with microdermabrasion. One of her clinic's most popular treatments, the age-management peel, combines microdermabrasion with the power of vitamin C, active peptides, salicylic, lactic and citric acids to restore the skin's health, vitality and youthful appearance. In addition to skin care for women, Susan Melching Skin Care Professionals offers skin management just for teens and facial treatments especially for men. For results-oriented skin care in a warm, welcoming environment, consider Susan Melching Skin Care Professionals.

2449 Pine Street, Boulder CO
(303) 442-7921 or (877) 238-7361
www.susanmelching.com

RallySport Health and Fitness Club

HEALTH & BEAUTY: *Best health and wellness programs in Boulder*

Get more out of your workout at RallySport Health and Fitness Club, where fitness isn't a hobby, it's a way of life. This unique fitness and health center gives new meaning to the concept of full service by offering a diverse curriculum of health and wellness programs such as yoga, step and strength training classes, along with body sculpting, meditation and *Tai Chi*. RallySport boasts nationally certified personal trainers and a full staff of fitness-minded individuals who are dedicated to giving you the time, information and tools needed to create a balance between mind and body. Members of RallySport receive as much hands-on training and acknowledgement from trainers and staff members as they need, which leads to a more fulfilling workout experience and ultimately long-term success with their wellness program. The club is proud to be a place where friendships are created and offers a wide range of social activities for all ages, along with comprehensive childcare programs. They schedule a variety of exciting outings throughout the year, including horseback rides, snowshoe excursions, and both mountain and road biking tours. The club offers a Masters swimming program, has an Elite youth swim team, and teaches swimming lessons for children ages six months and up. After your workout you can enjoy a healthy meal or snack at the Club Café, get a massage or relax in one of the club's steam rooms, saunas or hot tubs. Make your lifestyle a fit one at RallySport Health and Fitness Club.

2727 29ᵗʰ Street, Boulder CO
(303) 449-4800
www.rallysportboulder.com

Bolder Pilates

HEALTH & BEAUTY: *Best personalized Pilates instruction in Boulder*

Donna Rosen, the owner of Bolder Pilates in Boulder, knows firsthand the benefits of taking part in a healthy exercise regimen. She endured chronic back pain for many years before discovering Pilates. After a year of Pilates training, she found that her back, and, indeed, her entire body, was the strongest and healthiest it had been in years. Donna's experiences with pain and recovery give her an added edge in understanding her clients. She possesses the knowledge and the equipment to turn every session at Bolder Pilates into productive time spent furthering personal rehabilitation. Her many clients can attest to the benefit of time spent at Bolder Pilates, and Donna's background and experience means that she approaches each situation with understanding and compassion. "I truly love Pilates," Donna says. "I believe in the method 100 percent after rehabilitating my own body into health and strength after suffering through 15 years of chronic pain." In addition to her training as a certified Pilates instructor, Donna has studied anatomy and physiology, allowing her to tailor treatments to the individual needs of her clients. Working out of a fully equipped home studio, Donna and one other certified instructor offer personalized Pilates instruction designed to reflect your personal goals and individual needs. If you or someone you know is struggling with chronic pain, set up an appointment and see why Bolder Pilates has become a fixture in the lives of many area residents who want to return to a state of health and wellness.

2215 20th Street, Boulder CO
(303) 544-5930
www.bolderpilates.biz

Heat Wave Stove & Spa
HOME: *Best hearth and spa suppliers*

Heat Wave Stove & Spa in Boulder can teach you everything you want to know about hearths and spas for your remodeling or building project. Owners Greg Balmer and Ty Miller combine superior knowledge with excellent customer service to educate their customers about the products that are the best for their lifestyles as well as best for conserving energy. Greg, Ty and their entire staff use the stoves they sell in the store in their own homes, so they can share their personal experiences with you. The store carries fireplaces, fireplace inserts and freestanding stoves in many different brands, including Regency and Kozy Heat. All of the Regency products allow you to customize your stove with a mantel and your choice of accessories. The National Fireplace Institute, an independent nonprofit organization that promotes safety and education for the hearth industry, has certified all installers of Heat Wave Stove and Spa in the areas of wood, gas and pellet installations. Heat Wave represents the Beachcomber line of therapy spas, offering many sizes and different configurations so that your spa will be a perfect fit for you. Beachcomer spas are durable and functional and carry an unconditional guarantee. Greg and Ty work hard to make sure that you have a good experience when you shop at Heat Wave. They want you to be truly happy with the appliances you choose for your home. Whether you want to relax by the fire or soak in a hot tub under the stars, visit the experts at Heat Wave Stove & Spa to get just what you need.

2840 28th Street, Boulder CO
(303) 442-7980
www.heatwavestoveandspa.com

Tibet Carpet and Home
HOME: *Best source for Ralo Tibetan carpets*

Tibet Carpet and Home is one of the oldest Tibetan-owned manufacturers and distributors of the exclusive Ralo brand of Tibetan carpets in the U.S. Its provenance has earned the highest level of custom satisfaction and trust. Tibet Carpet and Home maintains a large stock of Ralo carpets in both contemporary and traditional designs. In addition, Tibet Carpet can weave rugs up to 22 feet by 32 feet. The hallmarks of a true Ralo Tibetan carpet are the unique, organic vegetal dyes with their iridescent saturated palettes, and pure high-lanolin, stain-resistant Tibeten wool that is carded and spun by hand. Ralo carpets adorn several five-star hotel suites and luxurious homes throughout the country. In addition to carpets, the Tibet Carpet and Home showroom displays an array of outstanding Tibetan handicrafts, jewelry, antiques, furniture and curios. Visit this unique business to view exotic treasures from Tibet, The Roof of the World.

1644 Walnut Street, Boulder CO
(303) 541 9233
www.tibetcarpet.com

Boulder Mountain Furniture
HOME: *Best place for functional furniture in Boulder*

A couch by day and a bed by night, the futon has been a staple of dorms, guest rooms and living rooms since the early 1970s. Boulder Mountain Furniture breathes new life into the foldable futon and its cousin the platform bed with creations that are as comfortable and stylish as they are convenient. Owners Cary and Katrina Schram purchased the floundering furniture store space in 2002 and have since turned it into an outstanding resource for functional furniture for the home. This service-driven shop offers more than 40 different futon frames, ranging in size from twin to queen, along with more than 20 pad styles that are made for easy handling, relaxed sitting and dreamy sleeping. The Schrams offer 1,300 different decorator fabrics, so that you can choose the futon cover that fits your taste and style. Boulder Mountain Furniture also carries memory foam, a natural, organic mattress material that lasts longer, is good for the environment and has proven beneficial to allergy sufferers. In conjunction with its broad range of fabulous futons and platform beds, Boulder Mountain Furniture provides an excellent selection of accessories, including pillows, mattress toppers and dressers. Come to Boulder Mountain Furniture, where functional furniture is also comfortable and stylish furniture of superior quality, backed by owners who promise excellent service.

2125 Pearl Street, Boulder CO *(303) 938-9800 www.coloradofutons.com*

Danceophile
RECREATION: *Best ballroom and folk dance studio in Boulder*

Photo courtesy of Back Country Tours

Discover the pleasures of dancing at Danceophile Ballroom and Folk Dance Studio, where programs appeal to participants and spectators alike. Professional dance instructor and choreographer Tom Masterson has been sharing his enthusiasm for ballroom dance and the folk dances of many cultures since opening his studio in 1987. Tom directs Postoley Dance Ensemble, which specializes in the dance of Ukraine and Poland. He presents workshops in Ukrainian and Polish dance for recreational and performance groups across the country and around the world. Through Danceophile, Tom teaches ballroom, swing, salsa, country-western and traditional ethnic dances. Over the years, Tom has received numerous charming thank you cards and public acclaim, including the 1998 Pace Setter of the Year Award from the *Boulder Daily Camera*. More importantly, he has touched thousands of lives by bringing to Boulder the world of ethnic dance and the cultures it celebrates. Tom, who holds a doctorate in physics, began dancing in 1972 and started the challenging job of teaching dance one year later while living in Eastern Europe. A native of Canada, he has traveled, climbed, and danced in many countries around the globe. As an avid mountaineer, Masterson is acclimated to challenge. He scaled Mount Everest in 2004, and is the founder and owner of Back Country Tours, which offers guided expeditions to Nepal and other exotic locales. He also loves running ultra-marathons in the mountains. Explore all that Tom Masterson and dance can do for you at Danceophile.

250 31st Street, Boulder CO
(303) 499-6363
www.postoley.org
www.danceophile.com

Rocky Mountain Anglers
RECREATION: *Best angling outfitters in Boulder*

Whether you are an experienced fly fisher or a curious beginner, you'll find all the gear you'll need just a block from the University of Colorado. Rocky Mountain Anglers carries the broadest selection of flyfishing rods and reels, flies, tackle, maps and books. A *Colorado Daily* award winner for Boulder's Best Fishing 2004 and 2005, Rocky Mountain Anglers is owned by Robin Black, who offers the advice, "Fly fishing can be as simple or as complicated as you make it." The customer service and advice given at Rocky Mountain Anglers is unbeatable. General Manager Rob Kolanda counsels new or developing fishers by offering his perspective. "There's a riddle to this sport, an etymology behind each story," he says. "You can take a lifetime just solving the riddle. That's the fun of it." Specializing in guided day trips as well as destination adventures,

Rocky Mountain Anglers' staff are experienced professionals not salesmen. Friendly and outgoing, they regularly invite customers along to their favorite fishing holes. A supporter of local fly fishing clubs at such places as Fairview High School, Naropa University and University of Colorado, this business is community-minded. If you're in the mood for some flyfishing fun, visit Rocky Mountain Anglers for some keen advice and goods to help you catch dinner tonight.

1904 Arapahoe Avenue, Boulder CO
(303) 447-2400
www.rockymtanglers.com

Neptune Mountaineering
RECREATION: *Best climbing and skiing equipment*

Enter a world of rugged adventure at Neptune Mountaineering, where founder Gary Neptune has created an irresistible equipment selection for climbers, skiers and backpackers of all skill levels. Gary is a lifelong climbing enthusiast who has scaled some of the planet's most daunting peaks, including Everest. In 1967 and 1968, Gary worked in Antarctica for Al Wade, who had accompanied Admiral Byrd in the 1930s. While in Antarctica, Gary made the first ascent of Mount Andrus in West Antarctica's Executive Committee Range. When Neptune Mountaineering opened in 1973, the shop primarily repaired climbing and ski boots. Today, the Neptune name is known to climbing and skiing enthusiasts across the globe, who search out the shop for products and equipment sold and tested by people who know the sports and can offer great advice about many of the world's most exciting climbing and skiing adventures. Neptune Mountaineering's Ski Museum

houses the most extensive collection of climbing and skiing artifacts in the nation. The displays include an impressive selection of climbing and skiing equipment, dating from the mid 1800s to the last half of the 20th century, a span than encompasses significant achievements in mountain and polar exploration. A hightlight of the collection are the remnants of Dudley Wolfe's 1939 K2 high camp. Let loose the adventurer in you with a visit to Neptune Mountaineering.

633 S Broadway, Unit A, Boulder CO
(303) 499-8866
www.neptunemountaineering.com

Boulder Bikesmith
RECREATION: *Best bike supply and repair in Boulder*

One of the best ways to enjoy all of the adventures that the popular community of Boulder has to offer is on a bicycle from Boulder Bikesmith. This ingenious company is owned and operated by master biker, designer and head mechanic Jon Stabile who purchased the existing company in 2001. Jon left behind a high-pressure job in the software industry in order to build his own business. He began by working as a mechanic at Boulder Bikesmith, a rent-a-bike company established in 1992, which he eventually took over from the previous owner. Jon has remained true to the company's origins by keeping the rental business going, and he has added a retail section offering a variety of popular bikes such as Giant and Haro. Boulder Bikesmith carries for rent or sale a variety of bicycles, including city bikes, cruisers, kids' bikes, and recumbent or mountain bikes with full suspension. Boulder Bikesmith can also help you with repair and maintenance issues, including everything from a tune up to a major overhaul. Jon freely admits, however, that his passion lies in the creation of custom bikes such as his Indian motorcycle replica, complete with soft tan saddle, fire engine red paint and gold trim. With the emphasis on service instead of the bottom line, you are sure to get exactly what you need at Boulder Bikesmith in the Arapahoe Village Shopping Center, located just minutes from the bike trail.

2432 Arapahoe Avenue, Boulder CO
(303) 443-1132
www.boulderbikesmith.com

Boulder Running Company

RECREATION: *Best running gear supplier*

Boulder has established itself as a hotbed of endurance sports, especially running. For the last decade, this image has been enhanced by the Boulder Running Company, a store largely responsible for raising the bar of specialty running stores throughout the country. By using its free, video gait analysis in conjunction wiht the talents of its professional staff, the store has proven that the right shoe can make the difference. Johnny Halberstadt and Mark Plaatjes, South African émigrés and running legends, are majority owners of the award-winning Boulder Running Company. Johnny and Mark add incredible character to the store. Johnny, the 1973 NCAA 10000-meter champion (the year that Pre won the 5000), moved to the United States and established himself as one of the leading innovators in footwear technology with patents such as the divided heel. With Johnny's help, Mark, a South African black athlete in the late-1980s, was able to secure a scholarship and eventually gain asylum in the United States. He proudly won the 1993 World Championship Marathon for the U.S. and is now a world-famous physical therapist. Both spend time in the store and are easily approachable. Boulder hosts the annual Bolder Boulder, fourth largest 10k in the U.S. With almost 45,000 runners participating each Memorial Day, the store is constantly assisting runners and solving problems. For those who stroll at a more leisurely pace, the Boulder Running Company is proud to display its new footwear and clothing selections, including Birkenstock, Keen and Prana. Stop in and see them for yourself.

2775 Pearl Street, Boulder CO
(303) RUN-WALK (786-9255)
www.boulderrunningcompany.com

Gateway Park Fun Center
RECREATION: *Best family fun center*

Gateway Park Fun Center in Boulder brings out the kid in everyone with 15 acres of recreational opportunities. Four local dads put Gateway Park on the map in 1997. Michael Johan, David Vorzimer, Dan Wolfson and Les Ronick, members of the local slow-pitch softball team The Daddy O's, saw an opportunity to breathe life into an outdated amusement park, while contributing to healthy play in their community. Among the varied play possibilities in this park-like setting are two 18-hole miniature golf courses complete with streams and waterfalls, a driving range, nine batting cages and the only human maze on the Front Range. The state's longest go-kart track puts participants in refurbished racecars, while a state-of-the-art in-line hockey arena features a smooth-as-glass concrete surface for optimal skate and puck movement. Children under six enjoy a supervised go-kart track, crawl-through play stations and a choo-choo train. An indoor pavilion favors sports-related video arcade games, like skee ball and air hockey. The food here is as fun as the games with all your favorite carnival fare, including pizza, ice cream, shakes, malts, hot dogs, burgers, burritos, lemonade and sodas. Two child-friendly party rooms and a private big-top tent make Gateway a superior place to hold a birthday party or a company picnic. The corporate party area features a sand volleyball court, horseshoe pits and barbecue facilities for up to 500 people. Next time you and your family are itching for a good time, visit Gateway Park Fun Center.

4800 N 28th Street, Boulder CO
(303) 442-4386
www.gatewayfunpark.com

Karliquin's Game Knight
RECREATION: *Boulder's game expert*

Karliquin's Game Knight is the only game store
in Boulder with in-store gaming. Karliquin's has
all of your favorite games, including Hordes,
Dungeons and Dragons, and Warmachine.
Owner Karl Schwols is the game expert in
Boulder. When he meets a new customer, he
asks detailed questions about the customer's
interests. He can then recommend just the right
kind of game. In addition to role-playing and
collectible games, Karliquin's stocks traditional
games, including board, card and parlor games.
With such a mix of games, the store attracts
game players of many ages and interests. Role-
playing game players love to visit Karliquin's
because the battlefields or other environments
are already set up. They need only jump in and
start playing. New players arrive constantly,
and the weekends are very busy. Karliquin's is
a great place for fellowship. The store is open
six days a week and closed on Tuesday. Get in
on the action at Karliquin's Game Knight.

3330 Arapahoe Avenue, Boulder CO
(303) 545-1745
www.karliquin.com

Proto's Pizzeria Napoletana

RESTAURANTS & CAFÉS:
Best Neopolitan-style pizza

What do you do if you crave Neopolitan-style pizza and can't find it anywhere? If you are Pam Proto, you find a partner like Rayme Rosello and start Proto's Pizzeria Napoletana. Evidently, there are plenty of folks who share the partner's pizza cravings; business boomed from the start, and it is showing no sign of slowing. The dough is handmade and the pizzas are cooked in brick ovens imported from Italy. Entrées are complemented by salads, desserts and a full bar. Proto's stresses a warm, friendly atmosphere, and the staff is trained to remember customers and their preferences. Restaurant critics and media sources have found plenty to rave about. *5280* magazine declares Proto's an Editor's Pick and proud purveyors of the area's best cannoli. *Rocky Mountain News* declares that Proto's makes the best pizza in Colorado, and *Bon Appétit* magazine named Proto's a top neighborhood restaurant. A special wine tasting event takes place once a month. The night varies for each location—there are Proto's in Longmont, Lafayette, Denver and Boise, Idaho—so customers willing to travel can experience them all. For authentic Italian pizza with toppings for every taste, visit Proto's Pizzeria Napoletana, and plan on having loads of fun with your meal.

4670 Broadway, Boulder CO
(720) 565-1050
2401 15th Street, Denver CO
(720) 855-9400
489 N Highway 287, LaFayette CO
(303) 661-3030
600 S Airport Road, Longmont CO
(303) 485-5000
www.protospizza.com

Photos by Heather Curtis

Café Blue American Grill

RESTAURANT & CAFÉS:
Best American cuisine

From the outside, it would be easy to mistake Café Blue American Grill in Gunbarrel for a no frills, no thrills place to eat. But try the seafood here or one of the satisfying Café Blue specialties, and you'll know you've wandered in to an American classic. The goals of owners Kevin and Leslie Middleton are deceivingly simple: provide quality food at a reasonable price in a fun environment. Kevin is the chef, and Leslie, a graduate of the Cooking School of the Rockies, is a wine and dessert expert. Their menu has engaging offerings for every taste. You'll find soups, salads, burgers and sandwiches. The stacked enchiladas, corn tortillas covered with vegetarian green chili and layered with refried beans, cheese and onions, are a customer favorite. You can customize this enchilada dish with the addition of chicken, prime rib or vegetables. The Cincinnati Chile is another crowd pleaser, served on thin spaghetti with a choice of toppings. Leslie's wine list offers global selection at reasonable prices. Her wine philosophy has a down-to-earth American charm; she would rather sell the wines than dust them off. For meals representative of American diversity from experts in food and wine, come to Café Blue American Grill.

5280 Spine Road, Boulder CO
(303) 530-4345

Redfish Fishhouse & Brewery
RESTAURANTS & CAFÉS: *Best seafood and microbrewed beers*

Since 1996, Redfish Fishhouse & Brewery has been a Boulder destination for seafood, microbrew beers and live entertainment. You'll also encounter Rodrigo, the bar manager, who has been mixing dynamite cocktails and answering any and all questions since the Redfish opening. Ask him to recommend something from the menu, and he will tell you that anything Executive Chef Seth Witherspoon creates is wonderful, but, in particular, "the ahi tuna is fantastic, the sea bass is fabulous, and the Idaho red trout is a definite winner." For Cajun flair, try the jambalaya or crawfish gumbo. If you aren't in the mood for seafood, the smoked duck egg rolls or the beer cheese soup made with house Pilsner will intrigue and delight. Rodrigo's choice at the tap would be the smoked porter or the stout, both medal winners at the Great American Beer Festival in Denver. In all, Redfish brewmasters make 14 different styles of beer. You will always find nine on tap. Ask Rodrigo if there will be music tonight at Redfish, and he'll tell you, "If it's Wednesday, it's reggae. If it's Friday or Saturday, it's dance floor, rock, blues or salsa. And don't forget Sunday Jazz Brunch." Owner Steve Shenk and Rodrigo invite you to come to Redfish Fishhouse and Brewery when you are in Boulder.

2027 13th Street, Boulder CO (303) 440-5858 *www.redfishbrewhouse.com*

Ziji
SHOPPING: *Best Tibetan gifts*

Ziji is a Tibetan word that conveys a blend of elegance, splendor and confidence. The store itself radiates all these qualities, along with a relaxed and welcoming ambience. Housed in the Boulder Shambhala Center, Ziji offers a vibrant sampling of Tibetan Buddhist literature and practice supplies, along with stunning home accents and wearable art from all over Asia. The shelves are stocked with books and CDs on yoga, Buddhism and other aspects of Asian culture. Beautifully crafted tables, which are also for sale, display statues and sacred ritual implements. Prayer flags greet you at the door, while wall hangings encircle the space. Presented in rich array are functional creations designed specifically to uplift your home, such as intriquing jewelry, vases, tea sets and lamps. If you're looking for an unusual gift, you won't find a better selection than at Ziji. There are even eye-catching cards to accompany your present. If you can't drop by the store, owner Amy Kida invites you to browse Ziji's extensive online catalog. After you do, you'll certainly want to bookmark it for return visits.

1345 Spruce Street, Boulder CO
(303) 661-0034 or (800) 565-8470
www.ziji.com

BookCliff Vineyards

WINERIES: *Best sustainably grown wines in Boulder*

More than 100 years ago, wine makers discovered that the warm days, cool nights and low humidity of the western slope of the Rockies provided a perfect environment for growing grapes. Engineers John Garlich and wife, Ulla Merz, owners of BookCliff Vineyards, joined the renaissance of wine making in Colorado because of their desire to make award-winning wines and help rebuild the industry in this area. John and Ulla became wine lovers in the late 1970s. John made his first Zinfandel in 1981, followed in 1995 by the purchase of their first 10 acres in Palisade. Their federally licensed winery, which is still in the basement of their home in Boulder, began production in 1999. Their wines, made exclusively from sustainably grown grapes, are winning awards in many venues around the country. According to John, "Growing our own grapes allows for consistency in flavor and lets us control the use of pesticides." They have used pesticides only once in six years. All of their wines are made from 100-percent Colorado grown grapes. Their Viognier wines are closer in flavor to French wines than to those from California. You can sample BookCliff wines in their wine-tasting room next to the Pearl Street Mall in downtown Boulder, at farmers markets in Boulder, Vail and Denver, and at several area wine festivals. The BookCliff Vineyards wine-tasting room serves its award-winning wines with fine cheeses, smoked cured ham, gourmet chocolates and European cakes and pastries.

15th Street, Boulder CO (tasting room and wine bar)
(303) 449-WINE (9463)
www.bookcliffvineyards.com

Augustina's Winery

WINERIES: *Best affordable wines in Boulder*

If you're in search of a wine-tasting experience that doesn't involve dilettantes, stuffed shirts, or conversations that revolve around dead poets or the weather, head to Augustina's Winery. Owner and operator Marianne "Gussie" Walter received the license for her one-woman winery in 1997, making Augustina's Winery the first in Boulder and one of the first in Colorado's Front Range. Gussie has a slightly different philosophy when it comes to wine drinking and is, in her own words, "dedicated to making wine that goes with backpacking adventures, raucous poker parties, family barbecues, good mystery novels and gingersnaps." Each of her masterfully made wines is created from Colorado-grown grapes and labeled with Gussie's distinctive Art Deco labels. The majority of her distinguished wines are in the $9 to $14 range, sold primarily at farmers' markets and fairs. Augustina's Winery produces numerous vintages, including WineChick White, a delightful blend of Riesling and Viognier, and Bottoms Up White, a light and fruity blend of Colorado grown Chardonnay and French hybrid grapes. Other popular favorites include the WineChick Cherry, made from Colorado grown Montmorency cherries, WineChick Blues, a stunning Merlot flavored with blueberries and oak, and the robust Boulder Backpacking Wine, a Cabernet Franc infused with dark berry flavors and a distinctively smoky, earthy taste. Augustina's Winery is open Saturday afternoons, but call ahead before visiting. Enjoy wines that compliment your lifestyle at Augustina's Winery.

4715 North Broadway, Unit B-3, Boulder CO
(303) 545-2047
www.winechick.biz

BRIGHTON

Brighton is located just 20 miles northeast of downtown Denver on the edge of the eastern Colorado plains. Incorporated in 1887, the city became the Adams County seat in 1904. Today, the town has grown to almost 30,000 people. Every year, Brighton hosts the Adams County Fair, where an infamous tomato-throwing contest paints contestants and parts of the town red. Brighton's own day-use facility, Barr Lake State Park, is home to the Rocky Mountain Bird Observatory. With over 300 different bird species, Barr Lake is a birder's paradise. You'll that find some of the best views are from the lakeside gazebo.

PLACES TO GO

- Adams County Regional Park and Museum
  9601 Henderson Road
  (303) 659-7103

- Barr Lake State Park
  13401 Picadilly Road
  (303) 659-6005

- Benedict Park
  1855 Southern Street
  (303) 655-2204

- Brighton Park
  555 N 11th Avenue
  (303) 655-2204

THINGS TO DO

August
- Adams County Fair
  Fairgrounds
  www.adamscountyfair.com

October
- Murray Maize Maze
  www.murraymaze.com
  (303) 289-4264

Barr Lake
Photo by lostinfog

Brighton Feed and Saddlery
ANIMALS & PETS: *Best selection of quality saddles in Brighton*

Brighton Feed and Saddlery has remained a strong and committed business for more than 60 years, thanks to forward thinking owners and a commitment to the local community. Clyde Peterson, a rodeo man, started the business in 1943, with emphasis on livestock, dairy feed and poultry. Today, Brighton Feed and Saddlery, just 20 minutes north of the Denver International Airport, is a force in the saddle industry for horse owners across America and as far away as Italy, France and Sweden. Current owners Roger and Verna Allgeier purchased the operation in 1973, with the intention of building a fine tack and saddle shop. As the area around them filled with small horse ranches, the Allgeiers met the needs of their customer base with quality leather goods, feed and personalized service. Working closely with their customers, Roger and Verna realized that saddles needed to change to fit today's more athletic horses. In 1989, he and Verna joined forces with custom saddle maker Brad McClellan of Vernal, Utah to begin production of the McCall saddle. Brighton Feed and Saddlery currently displays more than 350 saddles on any given day, and that number swells to over 700 during their Annual Saddle Sale in July, which coincides with the first weekend of the Cheyenne Frontier Days. The store is well stocked with good used gear, as well as gift items and instructional videos for those looking to improve their horsemanship. Whether you are a suburban cowboy, make your living on horseback or simply have an interest in Western heritage, stop by Brighton Feed and Saddlery. You will be greeted by people who know the equine industry and are eager to serve you.

370 N Main Street, Brighton CO
(303) 659-0721 or (800) 237-0721

Black Forest Bakery Ltd.
BAKERIES, COFFEE & TEA: *Best European-style baked goods*

True to its name, The Black Forest Bakery has a distinctly European style. It's a place where once-upon-a-time happens everyday, a place where a dash of fantasy and a pinch of imagination ensure a delightful experience. At Black Forest, owner and Chef Marjorie Mitchell have created an atmosphere that conjures up childhood fantasies to go with exquisite baked goods and light lunch offerings. Margie, who studied under the culinary arts program at Denver's Johnson & Wales University, is a stickler for fresh, natural ingredients and preparation from scratch. She uses no mixes and no preservatives in her exquisite confections. For breakfast, the bakery uses Margie's own dough recipe to create hot caramel sticky buns and enormous artisan cinnamon rolls with melt-in-your-mouth appeal. Lunch includes sandwiches served on the bakery's freshly-made bread. The classic turkey cranberry panini on foccacia bread and the lemon caper chicken panini are extremely popular, as are the signature soups. Dessert selections include chocolate confections, pies and pastries. You can complement your selection with made-to-order espressos and other coffee drinks. The bakery also offers box lunches and breakfast trays, which are sure to wake up any business meeting. Step into a fairy tale at Black Forest Bakery.

117-A N Main Street, Brighton CO
(303) 659-6060

Photos by Patrick McCutchan

Petals & Pearls
GARDENS, PLANTS & FLOWERS:
Best flower arrangements in Brighton

The overriding reason for the success of the Petals & Pearls flower shop in Brighton is owner Connie Doehring's dedication to a daily dose of extraordinary results. Connie does not measure success by money or fame, but by marrying her personal goals for artistry to the needs of her community. When the Red Hat Society needed flowers for a high tea, Connie knew how to provide flower arrangements that would suit the sensibilities of an organization of women devoted to greeting middle age with verve and humor while sporting red hats and purple dresses. She's equally at home with cut flower and silk arrangements for any occasion that one can think of; showers, weddings, and seasonal or specialty themes are only a few. Beyond the innovative and highly individualized arrangements that have attracted so much interest, Connie stocks gifts and home décor items. Whether you are sending your sentiments with flowers or filling a banquet hall with guests, come to Petals & Pearls for timely service and striking results.

995 E Bridge Street, Brighton CO
(303) 659-1164
www.petalsonpearlstreet.com

Whiteside's Boots, Western and Work Wear
FASHION: *Best selection of footwear in Brighton*

Customers walking into one of the two Whiteside's Boots, Western and Work Wear stores can expect a straightforward approach to quality footwear. These are stores that offer honest value for your hard-earned wages, according to sibling owners Steve and John Whiteside, who started the business in 1985. "We serve the working man, the salt of the earth. Our gear is of the highest quality, with the greatest selection, at a fair price," says Steve. The Whitesides operate their stores like those they prefer to shop in. Employees here personally greet all their customers and thank them for stopping by. It's friendly service and individual attention that make the sale Whiteside's, not hard-sell tactics. The extensive selection of footwear includes everything from dressy Western-

style Tony Lamas to steel-toed, lace-up work boots by Chippewa and Wolverine. The Durango line ranges from fancy and casual cowboy boots to motorcycle boots and ladies' Western styles. You can keep it simple with deer, bull and calf hide or step out in exotic ostrich, crocodile or rattlesnake hide. Double H brand can satisfy a host of practical footwear needs, from dressy and working-style Western boots, to lace-up packers and hardworking Wellingtons. For a no-nonsense store that respects your time, your money and your footwear needs, come to Whiteside's Boots.

855 Bridge Street, Brighton CO
(303) 637-9774
202 19th Street, Loveland CO
(970) 669-7808
www.whitesidesboots.com

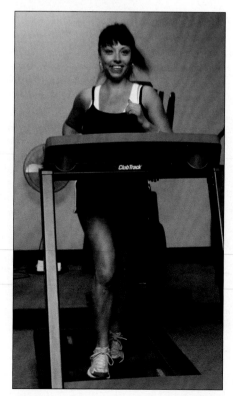

The Body Firm
HEALTH & BEAUTY: *Best fitness center*

Whether you are a serious sports competitor or a stay-at-home mom who wants to keep in shape, the Body Firm's two locations have you in mind. Owners Mark and Paula Hough want you to meet your fitness goals in a friendly workout environment that will put you at ease and afford opportunities for light socializing while you lose weight, sculpt your body, and build strength and endurance. "Our people come in all shapes and sizes. There is something here for everyone," says Paula. New members receive a free orientation and can join group classes or take advantage of access to a personal trainer. Classes include yoga, kickboxing and step aerobics. The Body Firm's gym offers outstanding amenities in an atmosphere that inspires confidence. Helpful, skilled professionals and top-of-the-line equipment are a formula for success at this community-minded fitness center. For a serious workout among friendly faces, give the Body Firm a try.

1292 E Bridge Street, Brighton CO
(303) 655-8382
721 E Platte Avenue, Fort Morgan CO
(970) 542-0180

Palizzi Farm
MARKETS: *Best local produce in Brighton*

What does Ronald Reagan, the 40th president of the United States, have in common with husband and wife Carl and Margaret Palizzi and their son Carlie, deceased owners of the Palizzi Farm in Brighton, Colorado? The answer is they have all been immortalized by designer and sculptor George Lundeen for their respective historical roles. The Palizzis performed on a smaller stage, but the contributions of their farm were exceedingly important to the development of their region. The Palizzi sculpture, entitled Autumn Harvest, stands at the corner of Brighton's 4th Avenue and Bromley Lane. The Palizzi Farm remains an important part of the local fabric and is still owned by the Palizzi family. Carl and Margaret's daughter Gloria owns and operates the farm with her daughter Deborah. The mother and daughter team is known for their fresh produce, which includes peaches, green beans and okra. The black-eyed peas, brussels sprouts and chili peppers are standouts, as are the artichokes and pumpkins. The Palizzis make their own fresh salsa and relish, using their own garlic, peppers and tomatoes. They also make and sell salad dressings, ciders and cherry juice. For customers interested in canning what they buy, Gloria and Deborah are glad to offer advice on proper procedures. Celebrate outstanding produce and the Brighton family that devotes themselves to its production with a visit to Palizzi Farm.

15380 Bromley Lane, Brighton CO
(303) 659-1970

BROOMFIELD

Incorporated in 1961, Broomfield grew through annexations, many of which crossed county lines into three adjacent counties, Adams, Jefferson and Weld. In the 1990s, city leaders began to push for the creation of a separate county to avoid the inefficiencies of dealing with four separate court districts, four different county seats and four separate county sales tax bases. Broomfield reasoned that it could provide services more responsively under its own county government, and sought an amendment to the state constitution to that effect. The amendment passed in 1998, and in 2001, Broomfield County became the 64th county of Colorado. Broomfield has an extensive trail system; a spectacular trail connects Stearns Lake and Josh's Pond on the west side of town. Broomfield's largest employer is IBM. FlatIron Crossing is a large shopping and entertainment center, anchored by Nordstrom, Macy's and Dillard's. The Northwest Rail corridor, a proposed commuter rail line from Denver's Union Station to Longmont via Boulder, will pass through Broomfield. Construction is to begin in 2011.

PLACES TO GO

• The Bay Aquatic Park
  250 Lamar Street (303) 464-5520

• Brandywine Parks
  124th Avenue and Lowell Boulevard

• Broomfield County Commons Park
  13th Avenue and Sheridan Boulevard

• Community Park
  2nd Avenue and Main Street

• Conoco Inline Hockey Rink
  128th Avenue and Lowell Boulevard

• Midway Parks
  Midway Boulevard and Laurel Street

THINGS TO DO

September
• Broomfield Days
  Midway Park (303) 464-5530

Broomfield
Photo by raveller

Hilltop Inn Guest House & Suites
ACCOMMODATIONS: *Best suites in Broomfield*

What is a guest house? It is larger than a bed-and-breakfast, yet small enough to provide a personal touch absent from large hotels. Accommodations at the Hilltop Inn Guest House & Suites are limited to 12 mini-suites and four luxury suites, so experienced owners John and Maureen Odde can provide the ultimate in hospitality. The Inn's loyal regulars swear by the warm service and look forward to coming back. The Hilltop Inn has a country feel, but it is also in the middle of everything. You can see mountains in one direction, and the Denver skyline in another. In season, the outdoor lounge is a delight. Local art embellishes the public spaces. Every suite has premium bedding, high-speed Internet, a cozy gas fireplace, a refrigerator and microwave. Amenities such as the guest laundry, in-room snacks and a full breakfast are free. The Wildflowers Tea Room, a recent addition, is as intimate and exceptional as the inn. The tea room specializes in high tea and luncheon tea, but it is also a full-service restaurant with a gourmet chef. The Hilltop Inn easily accommodates groups of up to 100. The Conference Room and the Board Room have all the audiovisual equipment needed for productive meetings. Guests have celebrated their weddings here as well. The Hilltop Inn has romance packages for couples and getaway specials for anyone. Come enjoy the Hilltop Inn Guest House & Suites, where a French cottage atmosphere combines with modern Colorado flair.

9009 Jeffco Airport Avenue, Broomfield CO
(303) 469-3900 or (800) 233-5633
www.guest-house.com

Willow Run
ANIMALS & PETS:
Best feed store in Broomfield

When Steve Porter purchased Willow Run in 1988, it had been known as "that place on the hill" for ten years, the place where animals are invited and their well-being is the predominant concern. The evolution from traditional feed store to a haven of superior products extends from agriculture, to pets, and from wild birds to human needs and wants. Natural, holistic, kosher, organic, raw and functional food and treats are deemed the pinnacle for quality life for your pets. The supplements, both human and animal, are chosen for their pre-eminence and reputation in their respective fields. The extensive line of high calibar wild bird seed, feeders and houses are the essence of Willow Run's commitment to do it right. Some of the gift lines include pottery from Texas and porcelains from St Petersburg, Russia that have been in production since 1744. Willow Run also stocks candles from two of the oldest candle companies in America and Lithuanian candle houses that were originally developed as a silent protest against communism. Willow Run is honored to sponsor the Colorado Bureau of Investigation Arson dog and have hosted Working Dogs Day to express gratitude to these dedicated animals. This freestanding country store is comfortable and friendly—a place straight from your memories—and offers welcome relief from the boring sameness that pervades malls across America.

5700 W 120th Ave, Broomfield CO
(303) 466-5971
www.willowrunfeed.com

Hilltop Inn Guest House & Suites
BAKERIES, COFFEE & TEA: *Best suites in Broomfield*

What is a guest house? It is larger than a bed-and-breakfast, yet small enough to provide a personal touch absent from large hotels. Accommodations at the Hilltop Inn Guest House & Suites are limited to 12 mini-suites and four luxury suites, so experienced owners John and Maureen Odde can provide the ultimate in hospitality. The Inn's loyal regulars swear by the warm service and look forward to coming back. The Hilltop Inn has a country feel, but it is also in the middle of everything. You can see mountains in one direction, and the Denver skyline in another. In season, the outdoor lounge is a delight. Local art embellishes the public spaces. Every suite has premium bedding, high-speed Internet, a cozy gas fireplace, a refrigerator and microwave. Amenities such as the guest laundry, in-room snacks and a full breakfast are free. The Wildflowers Tea Room, a recent addition, is as intimate and exceptional as the inn. The tea room specializes in high tea and luncheon tea, but it is also a full-service restaurant with a gourmet chef. The Hilltop Inn easily accommodates groups of up to 100. The Conference Room and the Board Room have all the audiovisual equipment needed for productive meetings. Guests have celebrated their weddings here as well. The Hilltop Inn has romance packages for couples and getaway specials for anyone. Come enjoy the Hilltop Inn Guest House & Suites, where a French cottage atmosphere combines with modern Colorado flair.

9009 Jeffco Airport Avenue, Broomfield CO
(303) 469-3900 or (800) 233-5633
www.guest-house.com

Saucey's Catering, Wedding & Event Services

EVENTS:
Best gourmet catering and cakes

Saucey's Catering takes the worry out of planning a wedding or other special event. Since 2000, owners Vanessa and Chris have been adding to the success of wedding receptions, business conferences and other special events with their enticing menus. They are graduates of the Art Institute of Colorado, renowned for its culinary training. Vanessa and Chris have earned a reputation for professionalism and exemplary customer service that begins from the moment they answer the phone. They'll treat you with a level of attention that will make you feel like you are their only customer. With Saucey's Catering, Wedding & Event Services, you can expect quality, experience and creativity at a price you can afford. From fire department banquets to graduation parties and baby showers, you can count on Saucey's to keep your taste and budget in mind while designing a menu. Sugar Flowers Cakes & Bakery, Vanessa and Chris make specialty cakes using only the highest quality ingredients. Cakes come in several great flavors your guests will love with artful designs that suit the occasion. Saucey's Catering, Wedding & Event Services provides menu packages or customized planning that ranges from a Mexican style buffet to an Italian sit-down dinner including the cake. The success of your event is important to Vanessa, Chris and the entire staff of Saucey's Catering, Wedding & Event Services.

Saucey's Catering:
1995 W Midway Boulevard, Suite A,
Broomfield CO (303) 920-5027
www.sauceyscatering.com
Sugar Flowers Cakes & Bakery:
(303) 457-0918
www.sugarflowerscakes.com

Summit Chiropractic Care Center

HEALTH & BEAUTY:
Best chiropractic clinic

Summit Chiropractic Care Center focuses on helping people get well without the use of drugs or surgery. Dr. Bradley L. Richardson, D.C. has been offering chiropractic care in Broomfield for nine years. His patients know him as a compassionate and caring doctor who is there when they need him. He believes in educating his patients about the health results that can be achieved with proper alignment of the spinal column. At Summit Chiropractic Care Center, Dr. Richardson teaches that all bodily functions trace their beginnings to the spinal column and brain. He occasionally encounters skepticism from patients, until they experience treatment for themselves. To determine an appropriate treatment process, Dr. Richardson begins with medical evaluation and diagnostic testing, including on-site x-rays. His adjustment methods vary depending on individual problems and include a traditional/ diversified method and a more moderate activator method. The Summit staff includes a licensed physical therapist and two massage therapists. Five therapy beds feature traction, roller, water-jet and heat therapies. Dr. Richardson is a certified acupuncturist and adds this ancient skill to a modern set of chiropractic tools, including the latest DRX900 spinal decompression system for patients with disc problems. Still another component of care at Summit is nutrition counseling and a full line of reputable name-brand dietary supplements. Dr. Richardson believes that comprehensive chiropractic care is appropriate for a broad range of health concerns. Visit Summit Chiropractic Care Center to investigate state-of-the-art alternatives to drugs or surgery.

56 Garden Center, Broomfield CO
(303) 466-3232
www.summitchiropractic.com

Athletic Advantage

HEALTH & BEAUTY: *Best specialized athletic training facility*

For athletes of all ages and activity levels, a specialized training facility located in Broomfield is the perfect tool with which to gain a competitive edge. Athletic Advantage is the exclusive tool athletes use to enhance their physical and mental abilities, achieving their personal bests. A certified strength and conditioning specialist with a BA from the University of Wyoming in kinesiology and exercise science, owner Jason Moen is skilled in his trade, and possesses qualities of responsibility and leadership. After three years as a strength coach, Jason opened Athletic Advantage in 2004. The 10,000-square-foot facility includes a spacious weight room with bodybuilding equipment and a full range of free weights. Half of the facility consists of a dedicated Astroturf area for stretching, free movement and running. One-on-one as well as group training classes are available, with exercise routines that are never routine. Focusing on the development of younger athletes, Jason organizes and hosts football camps, baseball clinics, kickboxing and other sporting events. In addition to muscular development, coordination and strength, Athletic Advantage teaches personal responsibility, leadership and ethics. Jason encourages each athlete to take ownership of his or her own body and life direction. Any athlete in search of skill sets that are readily transferable to real world applications in high school, college and professional athletics needs to give Jason a call at Athletic Advantage, so they can achieve their maximum potential.

7180 West 117th Unit B, Broomfield CO
(303) 466-3172
www.athleticadvantages.com

Photos © Scott Dressel-Martin/Dressel-Martin Mediaworks Inc.

Golden Bear Bikes

RECREATION:

Best bike selection in Broomfield

John Di Palma, owner of Golden Bear Bikes, says, "Life is an experience," and he thinks few things rival the experience of viewing what life has to offer while astride a bicycle seat. He bought Golden Bear in 2005 and describes it as a "big little store." The big parts include a 9,500-square-foot showroom, a service and repair center plus storage for the 8,000 items in inventory. The little part of the equation lies in personal attention to each customer, which includes plenty of after-sale support. Golden Bear also houses a fit center and group cycle fitness room. At the fit center, staff measures an individual's dimensions and strength, then feeds pertinent data into a computer to help a customer find the right bicycle. From November through March, customers can attend group training sessions on stationary bikes in classes taught by a certified instructor. At Golden Bear, you'll find brands such as Trek, Haro and LeMond. Gary Fisher, Cannondale and Klein bicycles are also available. The store stocks numerous bikes specifically designed for women, children, racing and freestyle riding. Golden Bear provides customers with free adjustments for the life of the bike as well as two free tune-ups in the first two years. John points out that the cost of a bike from Golden Bear will be comparable to any purchased in a big-box shop and their service is unsurpassed. For two wheels fit just for you, visit Golden Bear Bikes.

290 Nickel Street, Suite 100, Broomfield CO
(303) 469-7273
www.goldenbearbikes.com

Runway Grill
RESTAURANTS & CAFÉS:
Best dining on the airstrip

For an unequalled, panoramic view of the majestic, snow-capped Rockies, a seat on a Colorado airport runway shouldn't be missed, if that seat is in the Runway Grill at the Jefferson County airport. Just minutes from Denver and Boulder, the restaurant welcomes guests with a comfortable setting, open-air deck and affordable menu of traditional American foods. The Grill offers pork medallions and rich, juicy, made-to-order rib eye steaks that practically melt in your mouth. The Red Baron Reuben sandwich and homemade pecan pie are customer favorites. Sun-dried tomato fettuccine, with or without chicken, tops the pasta list. Stuffed chile rellenos, homemade soups and daily specials round out the menu. Showing a flair for the flavors of the Southwest, the Grill's homemade, non-traditional Dark Cherry and Charred Apricot salsas are delicious. The traditional red salsa, served daily, won first place in the Boulder County Fair Chef's Competition in 1999, and the People's Choice award in 2000. The salsas have also taken home blue ribbons in regional food and cooking competitions. Listeners of Warren Byrne's Restaurant Show, a popular radio review of local eateries, have frequently praised the Runway Grill. Owners Dwight and Daya Colborn invite you to enjoy their delicious, award-winning food and great service, while basking in the full beauty of Colorado at the Runway Grill.

11705 Airport Way, Broomfield CO
(720) 887-1004
www.therunwaygrill.com

Iron Mountain Winery
WINERIES: *Best custom tailored wines*

Iron Mountain Winery, a custom winery and wine bar, puts a new spin on role reversal. Owners Bryan and Karen Oldham bring the vineyard to the winery instead of locating the winery near the vineyard. By importing grape musts, unfermented juices, from around the world and completing the transformation into wine at Iron Mountain, the winery can produce any wine, from Italian Chianti to Australian Chardonnay, right here in Colorado. This method of winemaking enables Iron Mountain to tailor wines to individuals who may prefer a slightly sweeter wine, for instance, or one with more oak. The winery can also create signature house wines for retail establishments like restaurants and casinos. Iron Mountain's wine bar offers a gourmet cheese and dessert menu, guaranteed to weaken anyone's willpower. Italian, French, Spanish and American cheese plates, served with artisan breads or crackers and delectable bite-size tidbits, complement wines from the same areas. Tantalizing desserts, such as cheesecake and Phillip's Chocolate Decadence, are the icing on the cake. You can order a glass or a bottle of wine to enjoy inside or on the patio. Iron Mountain Winery can host special events, from weddings to retirement parties, and can even create unique wines with personalized wine labels to commemorate special occasions. Now with a second location in the new Northfield at Stapleton shopping center. Come to Iron Mountain Winery for an international wine experience.

1 W Flatiron Circle, Suite 336, Broomfield CO
(303) 464-9463
8316 E 49th Avenue, Suite 1610 (Northfield at
Stapleton), Denver CO
www.ironmountainwinery.com

PLACES TO GO

- Castle Rock Historical Museum
  420 Elbert Street
  (303) 814-3164

- Castlewood Canyon State Park
  2989 S State Highway 83, Franktown

- Daniels Park (buffalo preserve)
  Daniels Park Road

- Fairgrounds Regional Park
  500 Fairgrounds Drive

- Rock Park
  1710 Front Street

THINGS TO DO

May
- Rotary Duck Derby and StreetFest
  Plum Creek
  (720) 218-9992

June
- Elephant Rock Bike Tour
  Fairgrounds
  www.elephantrockride.com

June-July
- Colorado Renaissance Festival
  Larkspur
  www.coloradorenaissance.com

July
- Winefest
  The Grange in the Meadows
  www.castlerockwinefest.com

August
- Douglas County Fair
  Fairgrounds
  (720) 733-6900

- The International
  Castle Pines Golf Club
  www.golfintl.com

September
- Artfest
  Wilcox Square
  (303) 688-4597

October
- Oktoberfest
  Wilcox Square
  (303) 688-3128

CASTLE ROCK

Rocky buttes and stunning views of the Rocky Mountains surround Castle Rock, incorporated in 1881. Named for the prominent rock formation that overlooks the community, Castle Rock features several planned developments tied together by its historic downtown. Castle Rock gained its first significant population when the newly defined Douglas County picked it as the county seat. The town soon became a center for mining rhyolite rock and an important station for north-south railroad traffic. It has grown from about 4,000 people in 1980 to more than 35,000 in 2005, but it retains its small-town character and distinct sense of community. In its 2005 report on the best places to live, *Money* magazine ranked Castle Rock number one in job growth. Castle Rock has about three-and-a-half times as many jobs today as it did in 1990. Castle Rock's outlet mall, with a hundred-plus name-brand stores, is a major draw.

Castle Rock
Photo by Alexia Bautista

Gannon Grooming

ANIMALS & PETS: *Best pet grooming in Castle Rock*

If you feel like you can't stay ahead of the hair your pet is shedding, give a thought to turning the problem over to the professionals at Gannon Grooming in Franktown. Jennifer Gannon runs her kennel-free grooming business in a spacious, comfortable, home-like setting without yapping critters in the background. It's a place where your pet won't suffer from separation anxiety, because you can bring along your other dogs to keep one another company. Jennifer uses the patented FURminator Shed-Less treatment that not only gets rid of more hair than traditional shampoo-and-brush treatments, it cuts down on the amount of future shedding by making your pet's skin and coat healthier. Because Jennifer only uses premium-quality grooming products, one of the many shampoos she offers can help reduce rashes, hotspots and other skin problems. Jennifer works by appointment, so if you work unusual hours or have a hectic schedule, it's likely that she can accommodate you. Don't live with excessive pet hair and dander anymore. Call Jennifer at Gannon Grooming and let her perform. Your pet will thank you for it.

4647 N State Highway 83, Franktown CO
(303) 805-0409

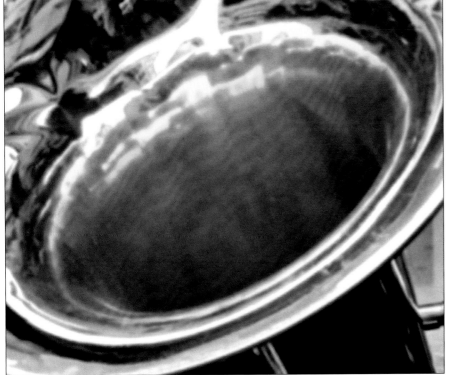

Castle Rock Music

ARTS & CRAFTS:
Best selection of musical instruments in Castle Rock

If you dream of making music, Castle Rock Music can help. Owners Jason Bower and Joshua Price bring years of performing and teaching music to their enterprise, offering just the right level of expertise to patrons who hear jazz riffs, Latin percussion or Big Band swing in their heads. Browse through the wide assortment of instruments, and decide whether a saxophone or a trombone, an electric guitar or drums is most likely to liberate your inner musician. Castle Rock Music promises competitive prices on instruments and takes pride in providing the right guidance for your musical journey. Offering a full range of lessons featuring many musical instruments and styles, Castle Rock's team of professional musicians can assist beginners and virtuosos alike. Explore music theory or songwriting, or try your hand at jazz trumpet, blues or classical guitar. For a life filled with music, visit Castle Rock Music, because whatever instrument or style calls to you, the folks at Castle Rock Music can help you select your instrument and find your tune, then teach you how to play it.

429 Wilcox Street, Castle Rock CO
(303) 688-0300
www.castlerockmusic.com

Castle Creek Bakery
BAKERIES, COFFEE & TEA: *Best European bakery and café*

In Europe, where the culture of the bakery café was born, a cappuccino and pastry are more than a perfunctory snack—they're an experience. The Castle Creek Bakery in Castle Rock is proud to uphold that tradition. With its exceptional array of gourmet delights, enviable location and atmosphere, this is a café to escape to and to linger in. Owner and manager Eva Rinehart always knew she wanted to open a bakery and created a menu that reflects her European heritage. Along with the usual homemade bagels, muffins and scones, you'll find strudels, fruit tarts and Sachertorte, a traditional Viennese cake. The full coffee bar offers hard-to-find Thai iced tea. On weekends, you can enjoy omelets or Eggs Benedict in the café's special Breakfast Room. The Castle Creek Bakery opened two years ago in the Village at Castle Pines, an elite outdoor shopping center with the feeling of a European village. Footpaths and flower beds connect the businesses in the village, making for a picturesque people-watching scene from the café's outdoor patio or windows. The café itself connects to Wrinkles Newsstand, where you can find choice reading matter to go with your coffee. Whether it's a simple pleasure you're after or something out of the ordinary, come to the Castle Creek Bakery and rediscover the bakery café experience.

**858 Happy Canyon Road, Suite 110, Castle Rock CO
(303) 660-1109**

Annie's At The Courtyard
FASHION: *Best women's apparel in Castle Rock*

Annie's At The Courtyard offers ladies a welcoming and relaxing atmosphere reminiscent of early-American couture houses, where elegant women of the day would gather to view the latest European styles. This charming shop belongs to Kathryn Gunderson and her husband Mark. Mark lends a male perspective to this decidedly feminine shop, making it the ideal place for gentlemen to pick up gifts and apparel for special ladies in their lives. Annie's At The Courtyard offers many exclusive clothing lines not duplicated anywhere else in the Denver metro area. Kathryn's inherent good taste assures selections worth your time and attention. Whether you're looking for casual daywear or sensational eveningwear, Kathryn and her charming associates can help you find the right ensemble for every occasion. Annie's At The Courtyard carefully tracks which outfits customers have purchased for which occasions around the area to ensure duplicate dresses are not worn to the same event. Kathryn and her staff also act as personal shoppers by keeping track of customers' tastes and favored designers and then apprising them of new arrivals. Annie's had the distinction of selling Miss Colorado the dress she wore for the Miss Colorado pageant in 2005. Enjoy exceptional, personalized service while finding superior apparel for every occasion in life with a visit to Annie's At The Courtyard.

**333B Perry Street, Castle Rock CO
(303) 688-3371**

Olde Towne Creamery
FUN FOODS: *Castle Rock's award-winning ice cream shop*

What's the best accessory on a warm spring day? An ice cream cone, of course. The best ice cream in Colorado can be found at Olde Town Creamery. Owner Pat Horn loves to tempt the citizens of Castle Rock and the surrounding area with hand-crafted ice cream. "I missed the simple pleasure of an old fashioned ice cream parlor we adults remember gong to as a child," says Pat. As a result, Olde Town Creamery was opened. It offers old-fashioned ice cream delights like homemade ice cream, milk shakes, malts, and hand-brewed root beer floats. You'll also marvel over their cakes and pies made from scratch, their caramel and fudge, gelatos, frappes and all-natural, fruit smoothies. The Creamery also offers an assortment of premium-quality chocolates from companies around the globe, names like Belvedere, Callebaut, Guittard, and Schokinag. For lunch, Pat offers fresh, inventive, homemade soups like Pumpkin Curry, Broccoli Bisque, Chicken Tortilla, Carrot Ginger and more. Quiches are on the menu, and lunches come with an organic salad and locally-baked, flat bread. Everything is made with the freshest ingredients and an eye for quality. Specialty items for business events, birthday parties, weddings and baby showers, as well as centerpieces and gift baskets are all the rage at this trendy little café and bistro of fashionable panache. This is one place where you can have your cake and eat it too. Visit the Olde Towne Creamery for a special treat that will take you back to the time of your grandmother and provide memories for your children that will last a lifetime.

350 Perry Street, Suite A, Castle Rock CO
(303) 688-1301
www.belvederechocolates.com

Petra Petite
FASHION: *Best children's clothing*

Find whimsical gifts and the latest in fashions for little ones inside the charming children's boutique Petra Petite. Owner Liza Boyd took over the cheerful bright blue and yellow store in September 2006. The shop carries clothing for children of all sizes, ranging from tiny preemie outfits to boys size seven and girls size 16. Shilav, a line of clothing made in Israel, offers the comforts children need and the adorable detailing parents love. Frilly ballet outfits created by a local designer are sure to please diminutive dancers, and hair bows by Caitie Q Creations complete the outfit. Robeez and Bobux soft leather-soled shoes allow comfort and flexibility for growing feet and stay on even during crawling and climbing. The boutique also carries a variety of special gifts for any occasion, from silver baby items to Webkinz, a line of plush animals that come with a secret code allowing kids to adopt the critters online. Visit Petra Petite to outfit the children in your life with everything they need.

313 3rd Street, Castle Rock CO
(303) 663-5565

The Art Collector

GALLERIES & FINE ART: *Best gallery and frame shop in Castle Rock*

When you are in Castle Rock looking for original art, a print or a frame for your artwork, go to the gallery recommended by the locals. In 2001 and 2003, Castle Rock residents voted the Art Collector the number one art gallery in town. The gallery carries oils, watercolors, photography and other work by artists with national and regional reputations. It also subscribes to the Virtual Gallery, which gives customers looking for prints the opportunity to search 46,000 images by title, artist name or subject matter. The Art Collector also operates as a picture framing business, using mouldings by industry leader Larson-Juhls. Frame choices run from gold and silver to rustic barn wood. Rich woods, burls and inlays assure stunning results for your fine art or memorabilia. Owner Jon Dirks and his wife, Janis, enjoy getting to know each customer on a first name basis. They bring personalized service and artistic expertise to their enterprise. Jon is an accomplished artist who began painting at the age of nine and has won numerous awards in the past 25 years. He has participated in more than 100 shows and produced more than 1,000 works of art. His main medium is oil, but he also works in acrylics, pen and ink and markers. His pieces often depict Colorado landscapes and weather. Recently, he began painting large-scale murals. For striking art and first-rate framing from people who understand art, visit the Art Collector in the little yellow house on Wilcox.

706 Wilcox Street, Castle Rock CO
(303) 688-4476
www.theartcollectorgallery.com

The Cat's Meow Flowers and Gifts

GARDENS, PLANTS & FLOWERS:
Best floral arrangements and accessories in Castle Rock

Put a spring in your step and jazz up your next special event or special occasion with elegant floral arrangements and accessories from The Cat's Meow Flowers and Gifts. Linda Bicknell opened her shop in 1996 and treats Douglas County to her talents each summer with The Cat's Meow float entry in the Douglas County Fair Parade. Linda's full-service floral shop has the design and flower choices to help you with all your floral needs, whether they be whimsical, solemn or formal. The shop rents and sells formal wear for men and boys, supplied by Jim's Formal Wear, a well-established company founded in 1964 by Jim Davis. The shop rounds out its offerings with balloons, plush animals and candles, as well as cards, candies and collectibles. For Linda and her friendly staff, no job is too big or too small. You can browse the shop and relax with a complimentary beverage while the exceptional team at The Cat's Meow creates gorgeous floral arrangements or custom corporate gifts on your behalf. Delivery is available throughout the Denver metro area, and The Cat's Meow works closely with major floral wire services around the world, allowing you to send floral arrangements anywhere your loved ones may be. You can make a statement at your next occasion, or send a thank you, birthday or holiday bouquet that will be fondly remembered, when you call on Linda Bicknell and her staff at The Cat's Meow Flowers and Gifts.

15 S Wilcox, Castle Rock CO
(688) 688-6350 or (800) 929-6369
www.catsmeowflowers.com

Inner Connections Yoga & Whole Life Center
HEALTH & BEAUTY: *Best yoga and lifestyle coaching center*

Operating in two locations, Inner Connections Yoga & Whole Life Center is much more than a yoga studio. Owners John and Jeanne Adams have built a personal wellness Mecca, combining yoga practice with bodywork therapies, fitness training, counseling and life coaching. Inner Connections Yoga & Whole Life Center offers a generous array of classes, making it easy to find the right fit for your skill level and focus. You will stretch, strengthen and add mobility to every joint, stimulate every system and add health to every organ of the body. You will learn how to breathe and relax, teaching your mind and body to let go of stress. John and Jeanne enjoy watching their students learn better ways of taking care of themselves physically, mentally and spiritually. Reserve your Saturday for the family yoga class, where your whole clan is invited to practice together. The morning and evening class schedule at Inner Connections Yoga & Whole Life Center makes space for yoga in the busiest of lives, while the serious yogi can take part in popular mountain retreats. A 10-week, nationally-recognized yoga instructor training program brings students from all over the region. The massage therapists were voted Best of the Best in Douglas County. Visit Inner Connections Yoga & Whole Life Center and renew your commitment to a healthy lifestyle.

821-A Park Street, Castle Rock CO (303) 688-8598
19563 E Main Street, Parker CO (303) 840-1881
www.InnerConnectionsYoga.com

Advanced Physical & Sports Therapy

HEALTH & BEAUTY: *Best physical therapy clinic*

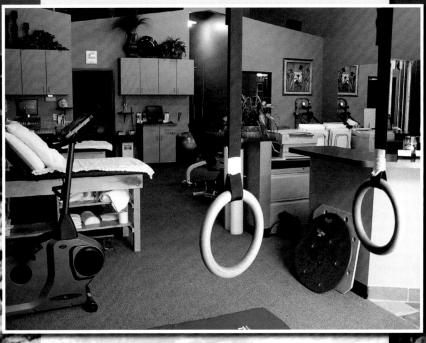

For sports injuries and rehabilitation, Advanced Physical & Sports Therapy offers a hands-on approach to recovery. Douglas T. Heckenkamp, physical therapist and owner, is a former gymnast and coach who worked with the 1984 and 1988 U.S. Olympic Gymnastics teams. He and therapist Sara Tibby want to make sure that all your needs are met. Whether you come in on your own or are referred by a physician, your first visit will be 60 minutes and will include manual therapy and deep tissue massage to work on problem areas. Once the abnormality is discovered, continuous work with the same therapist concentrates on a solution. The goal is always to restore pain-free movement by working joints, muscles and tendons. Doug and Sara also offer free 15-minute evaluations for injuries or pain. If you have been told that nothing can be done for your current pain situation, give the physical therapists at Advanced Physical & Sports Therapy a call. They will do their best to take the pain away and help you live a more active and productive life.

880 Happy Canyon Road, Suite 145, Castle Rock CO
(720) 733-3655

Innerspace

HOME: *Castle Rock's window fashion experts*

The team at Innerspace Shade & Drapery in Castle Rock knows that windows are portals to the world. Owners Kathy and Gene Collins and their talented design team offer Hunter Douglas Window Fashions and promise professional, personalized attention to help you convey your personal style. Whether you're draping a window in a breakfast nook or a banquet hall, Innerspace offers the consultation and design services you'll need for satisfying results. If you want your bedroom to bask in morning light but subdue harsh afternoon sun, designers can recommend blinds, shutters and drapes with appropriate qualities. Browse the showroom for shades that conserve energy and delight the eye. Discovering colors, styles and fabrics to highlight your space and frame your view is only part of the window picture. Innerspace design consultants will visit your home free of charge to help you choose the right product. Once you've decided on the perfect treatment, Innerspace sends experienced certified installers to do the job right and make sure you're completely satisfied with the effect. The company also offers repair services. Visit Innerspace and let the staff help you match your windows to the world.

117 Wilcox Street, Castle Rock CO
(303) 688-4549
http://innerspace.hdwfg.com

Brittany Hill Ltd.

HOME: *Best furniture company in Castle Rock*

Brittany Hill Ltd is an established furniture company reflecting comfort, class and quality. This charming custom furniture and home accessory showroom specializes in handcrafted reproductions of fine, antique English, French and country furniture, utilizing distressed, hand painted and crackled finishes. The craftsmen of Brittany Hill Ltd are third-generation artists whose hand carvings and handcrafted furniture have adorned some of this country's most exquisite resorts and estates. You're able to select from showroom ensembles or work with their friendly staff to produce that unique piece you have always wanted. The diversity of this custom furniture company provides homeowners the ability to create a look and feel that exudes comfort, class, and quality. At Brittany Hill Ltd, the possibilities are endless. Every piece of furniture is handcrafted and finished to perfection. No matter where you cast your eyes, they fall on something exquisite, something delightful and something unique. You'll find the most elegant accessories from glorious floral arrangements to original oil paintings, crystal vases, beautiful pillows, candelabras, exquisite lighting and some country Asian antiques. Brittany Hill Ltd can take a client's vision and turn it into reality. New and exciting items are arriving daily in the showroom, or you can order that special handcrafted piece just for you. We encourage you to visit the showroom in Downtown Historic Castle Rock.

360 Perry Street, Castle Rock CO (303) 688-0319 *http://brittanyhillltd.com*

Vinos del Mundo

MARKETS: *Best wine boutique*

Photo courtesy of vinosdelmundo.biz

"Where there is wine, there is celebration," says Susan Gomez, owner of Vinos del Mundo in Castle Rock. She calls her business a wine boutique, meaning that it offers more atmosphere than an ordinary wine shop. Guests find it an inviting place for wine tasting parties. The wines featured at Vinos del Mundo come mostly from small vineyards. "The small vineyards have a lot more character and charm," Susan claims. Here is your chance to purchase wines not widely available, such as those bottled under the Carl Lawrence label. Founded by Susan's childhood friend, Michael Trujillo, Carl Lawrence wines are from California and are sold only to fine restaurants and boutiques, such as Vinos del Mundo. Susan's previous career in the travel industry put her in touch with many fabulous wines, experience that she draws on in selecting what she carries in her boutique. While personal favorites get priority when it comes to stocking Vinos del Mundo, Susan listens to her in-house wine specialist, John Meredith, the former wine columnist for the *Denver Post* and the current editor and publisher of a subscription-only newsletter on wine and food. Encounter a selection of hard-to-find wines at Vinos del Mundo, where every day is a celebration.

872 Happy Canyon Road, #110, Castle Rock CO
(303) 663-9463
www.vinosdelmundo.biz

Fake Skateboards & Snowboards
RECREATION:
Castle Rock's first and only core snow and skate shop

Fake Skateboards & Snowboards declares its independence proudly when it says that it is Castle Rock's first and only core snow and skate shop. The word *core* refers to skate shops that are actually owned and operated by skaters. Often, when something becomes very popular, it gets taken over by large corporations, which edge out small businesses. John Magee, owner of Fake, is determined to fight the giants by offering customers a real alternative to chain stores. He calls his shop Fake as a commentary on life in the big box era. With an inventory that includes around 100 different brands of boards, shoes and accessories, Fake has the product to back up its feisty attitude. You will find popular brands here as well as core brands with limited distribution. Always, Fake emphasizes treating customers as individuals, finding the products that are right for them, and not trying to steer them towards something just to make a killer sale. If you are looking for a skate and snow shop where individuality is definitely encouraged, try Fake Skateboards & Snowboards.

821-B N Park Street, Castle Rock CO
(720) 733-2840
www.fakeskateboards.com

River & Stream Company
RECREATION: *Best fly fishing store in Castle Rock*

River & Stream Company offers 2,500 square feet of specialty flyfishing equipment, apparel, books and gifts, along with expert advice and service. As the only flyfishing store in Douglas County, owner Stan Pomeroy recognizes the importance of keeping his community fully equipped. Stan has been outfitting fly fishers for the past seven years. Originally, River & Stream was located at Southglenn Mall in Centennial. Newly located in The Village at Castle Pines, River & Stream Company equips fishers just four miles south of Sedalia for quick access to trophy trout waters on the South Platte. Get fully outfitted with Sage, Ross, Lamson and Scientific Anglers before you head out. You will find all the major brands like Patagonia, Columbia, Rio and even Crocs. River & Stream is proud to offer the highest quality equipment to the most discerning flyfisher. Once outfitted, River & Stream can help you find that perfect pool with The Flyfisher Guide Service. Fly fishing is their passion, a key necessity of life for these folks. Their fly-fishing guides are experts on the local waters, and can accommodate both private and public access, leading you on the ultimate fly-fishing journey. In addition, River & Stream offers once in a lifetime adventures to Alaska, or can assist you with other exotic fishing destinations. Drop on by or give them a call with any questions you may have. Then get on the water with help from River & Stream Company.

858 Happy Canyon Road Suite 100, Castle Rock CO
(303) 794-7864

Rocky Mountain Krav Maga

RECREATION:
Best self defense center in Castle Rock

John Hallett, owner of Rocky Mountain Krav Maga, knows how frustrating it can be to learn self defense techniques, especially when the method demands the mastering of specialized positions and techniques. Krav Maga isn't like that. Due to its emphasis on simple, instinctive movements, Krav Maga is becoming an increasingly popular self defense and fitness choice for people of all ages. At the Rocky Mountain training center, John conducts sessions for children, teens and adults, focusing on practical defenses against real attacks. Other classes stressing the fitness aspects of the Krav Maga system offer complete head-to-toe, 60-minute workouts with kicks and punches. The Israeli military developed Krav Maga, which means contact combat in Hebrew. It now serves as the official self defense and fighting system of the Israeli Defense Forces. Many law enforcement agencies throughout the United States require it for their officers because it is practical, not technical. The fact that its two most famous practitioners are Jennifer Lopez and Angelina Jolie proves that Krav Maga is suitable for women. For self defense and fitness without technical barriers, try Rocky Mountain Krav Maga.

119 Wilcox Street, Castle Rock CO
(303) 681-2622
www.rmkravmaga.com

Castle Rock Bicycle Company

RECREATION:

Best bike shop in Castle Rock

Hit Colorado's grand slopes and rugged trails in safety and style with bikes, rental skis and boards as well as accessories from Castle Rock Bicycle Company (CRBC). Owners Mark and K.C. Neel opened this full-service shop in 2001 featuring a complete line of name-brand bicycles from Trek, Scott, Rocky Mountain, Diamondback and Electra. CRBC's trained, professional staff will take the time to find the bike and bike gear that best fits your cycling habits and style. They are dedicated to provide the highest level of service for the life of your bicycle, including free, lifetime brake and derailleur adjustments. The company also offers a generous lay-away option and a trade-up program that allows you to trade in your child's outgrown bike for discounts on a new model. In 2003, the shop launched a full-service ski and snowboard rental operation featuring Salomon and Elan products. Already, CRBC is known throughout the region for its expert ski and snowboard tuning and repair services. With services like these, you can bypass the crowded ski slope shops and get right to the powder. CRBC's team is actively involved in the community and the shop donates bikes and accessories to local charities throughout the year. *Douglas County News Press* readers give an enthusiastic thumbs-up to this business, naming it Best Bike Shop in the Castle Rock area for six years running. Find the equipment you need to enjoy the outdoors at Castle Rock Bicycle Company.

420 3rd Street, Castle Rock CO
(303) 688-1722
www.castlerockbikes.com

Izzy's

RESTAURANTS & CAFÉS: *Best International food*

Go to Izzy's in Castle Rock, and you won't have to travel far and wide for a national and international food fest. Owner Regina Izydorek's menu will provide you with tempting choices from many regions of the world. Wisconsin roasted chicken and Wisconsin beer cheese soup might start your national tour. Try Izzy's tender St.Louis pork ribs that have been cooked for as long as nine hours. The restaurant's famous Midwestern pork tenderloin sandwich might strike your fancy. You'll wonder if you're still in Castle Rock when you choose Regina's lobster bisque soup, and you'll definitely believe that you've landed in coastal heaven when you experience Izzy's Friday night fish fry with all the fixings. For your international stop you'll want to savor the Italian smothered sausage or meatball bomber sandwich. Down-home desserts include frozen custard, apple crisp and peach cobbler. Just think, you can accomplish this food expedition without the hassle of complicated travel arrangements. All you have to do is place your order, settle back and relax on Izzy's covered patio. Bon voyage and happy eating.

215 N Wilcox Street, Castle Rock CO (303) 663-4677

Skadoodles

SHOPPING: *Best gift shop and baked goods emporium*

You'll find so many fun things at Skadoodles, a gift shop and baked goods emporium in downtown Castle Rock, we thought that a shopper's guide to some of the most popular items would come in handy. For starters, there's the recycled furniture that co-owner Pam Morgan paints and makes into funky masterpieces. Her business partner, Kim Beaver, gets into the act with her own line of cooking sauces, including the bestselling teriyaki and spicy peanut sauces. Pam and Kim say that the Magic Slice cutting board sells like crazy and that the line of inspirational framed pieces called Pressed Petals is a crowd pleaser as well. Among the fresh-baked snacks served in this shop, located in an old carriage house, the cookies and scones usually sell out. They are best enjoyed with a cup of coffee from Kaladi Brothers, a local coffee maker, or with a cup of chai from Third Street Chai of Boulder. Our guide only scratches the surface. No doubt you'll find something that is irresistible, whether a piece of pottery or a carved rooster, perhaps. If you are looking for an eclectic place to shop and eat, try Skadoodles.

521 Wilcox Street (facing 6th St, behind Augustine Grill Restautant), Castle Rock CO
(303) 660-9993

Camino Real of Castle Rock

SHOPPING: *Best variety of vibrant Mexican imports*

Camino Real of Castle Rock is referred to as the house that's gone to pot, and it's true. There are about 2,500 giant urns, patio chimneys, planters and other colorful objects from Mexico displayed outside the Perry Street house. Lucius Romero and Lupita Real, who opened the store in 2005, have literally brought Mexico to Castle Rock. Camino Real is the newest in a chain of import stores owned by the Real family, which includes stores in Pueblo and Alamosa. Lupita grew up helping out in her father Jesus Real's store in Taos, New Mexico. While the outside of the store is full of pots, the inside displays a huge variety of vibrant Mexican imports, including mirrors, blankets, teapots, rain sticks, margarita glasses, dishware and serapes. Tiles, pounded copper and colorful ceramic Talavera sinks offer many creative decorating ideas. The store's enormous assortment of crosses features designs for the wall and crosses to wear as jewelry. In a departure from their Mexican imports, Lucius and Lupita carry genuine Native American rugs and jewelry, Southwestern furniture and handblown glassware. Opals from Australia will be sure to attract your attention. Come on over to Camino Real of Castle Rock; it's easy to find. Look for the pots – lots and lots of pots.

207 N Perry, Castle Rock CO
(303) 663-1877

Horse farm between Decker and Castle Rock
Photo by David

CENTENNIAL

Centennial is Colorado's newest city, organized only in 2001. Residents, who previously had little use for municipal government, were stirred into action when a neighboring city sought to annex Centennial commercial districts to add to its tax base. The measure to create Centennial passed by a thumping 77 percent of the vote. The new city is committed to limited government and does not even have a city hall—it rents space in an office building. With about 100,000 residents, Centennial may be the largest new city in the United States. Centennial Airport is one of the largest general aviation (private plane) airports in the country. The names of the town and airport come from Colorado's nickname, the Centennial State. Colorado joined the Union in the centennial year of 1876. Centennial commuters can now make use of metro Denver's light rail system, which has opened several stations along the I-25 corridor.

PLACES TO GO

- DeKoevend Park
  6301 S University Boulevard

- Goodson Recreation Center
  6315 S University Boulevard
  (303) 798-2476

- Holly Park and Pool
  6651 S Krameria Way
  (303) 770-0333

- South Suburban Ice Arena
  6580 S Vine Street
  (303) 798-7881

Ace Grooming By Sara
ANIMALS & PETS:
Best pet grooming services

When you bring your pet to Ace Grooming by Sara, your pet receives personalized grooming services from the owner, Sara. Sara loves dogs and cats and has plenty of experience with over 20 years in the dog grooming and veterinary businesses. Centennial locals know Sara from the years she worked as an owner of a franchise self-serve dog wash business and many loyal customers have followed her to her own independent business. Most of her customers live within a five-mile radius of Ace Grooming so they have easy access to Sara's personalized attention to their pets. She knows what fits each dog best and how often each animal needs to be groomed. She is also glad to educate customers on the care and grooming of their pets and she stocks a line of quality pet foods and supplies. Sara's parents and several employees help run the business, but all the grooming is done by Sara. Let your pet experience the difference quality pet grooming can make with Ace Grooming by Sara.

7475 E Arapahoe Road #18, Centennial CO
(303) 850-7266

A Photo Opportunity
BUSINESS: *Best photographers in Centennial*

A Photo Opportunity captures the special moments in life with their vibrant wedding, portrait and corporate photography. By specializing in on-location photo shoots, husband and wife photographers Jason and Suzanne Wille can create relaxed subjects and achieve a more candid look. Jason, Suzanne and their assistants are always ready to catch the glow of the bride or the proud smile of a father as he walks his daughter down the isle. They also offer business photography. The creativity and emotions revealed in Jason and Suzanne's photojournalistic pictures set these shots apart from more traditional posed portraits. The energy in the pictures is one of the reasons these photographers have been featured in *Modern Bride Colorado* for the past two years. As members of Wedding & Portrait Photographers International, Jason and Suzanne keep current on the latest technology and receive ongoing education to provide customers with top-quality images. The couple only uses digital photography, which allows them to take more images at an event and lets them be creative in the design and creation of digitally enhanced albums and images. These images are simply unique for exciting and energetic portraits you will enjoy for years to come. Let Jason and Suzanne at A Photo Opportunity capture your important event.

(303) 617-0025 *www.aphotoop.com*

Paper Wares
EVENTS: *Best party goods*

For over 25 years, Paper Wares has been providing the Denver Metro Area with the very best party goods, invitations and gifts for all occasions. Whether you are planning a small get-together or a fabulous wedding, their party planning experts will help you select everything you'll need from balloons and decorations to the essentials such as napkins, plates, table covers and cups. If you want to make your own invitations Paper Wares has a giant selection of card stock to choose from or, if you like, they can print them for you. Need gifts? Between the candles, house wares, baby gifts, over-the-hill gag gifts and unique cards, they've got it all. Paper Wares also has over 50 books of wedding invitations to choose from, covering the widest range of styles. They carry accessories to complete your wedding, including flutes, unity candles, ring pillows and guest books. There's something for everyone at Paper Wares and they invite you come in and see why they are Denver's premier invitation, party goods and gift boutique.

7475 E Arapahoe Road, Centennial CO
(303) 850-0520
www.paperwares.net

Photos courtesy of Party Crashers Photography

Celestial Bride
FASHION: *Best conservative bridal shop*

Sisters Shirlene Simcox and Nancy Shotts are convinced that there is still a desire in our tell-all, show-all world for modesty. Bucking the trend for revealing clothing, which has even infiltrated the world of formal wear, they present Celestial Bride, a boutique for ladies who wish to leave something to the imagination. "We are the only bridal shop in Colorado that has bridal gowns with sleeves," says Shirlene. Covering up does not mean sacrificing one's femininity. Whether you are dressing for a wedding or a prom, Celestial Bride offers gowns and dresses which, though conservative by today's standards, remain modern and sophisticated. Casa Blanca, Venus, and Allure are just a few of the top designers represented. They also carry private label gowns that can't be bought elsewhere. An incentive for shopping at Celestial Bride is its generous discount policy. If you buy a dress here, you receive a discount on everything else that you purchase, which may include an engagement ring or wedding band. Savings could amount to hundreds of dollars. Don't fret that the fashion pendulum isn't swinging your way. You are not alone. If modest is the way that you feel, drop by Celestial Bride and meet Shirlene and Nancy, your allies in fashion.

8262 S University Boulevard, Suite 135, Centennial CO
(720) 529-2000
www.celestialbride.net

Nan's Acupunture Clinic

HEALTH & BEAUTY:
Best acupuncture clinic

Zhizhong Nan, M.D. is the third generation in his family to practice acupuncture and Chinese medicine. He began his training in acupuncture by studying with his uncle. After graduating from medical school in China, he moved to Colorado in 1992. Nan opened Nan's Acupuncture Clinic in 1997. Acupuncture is the practice of inserting very fine needles into the skin to stimulate specific points on the body. This stimulation balances the movement of qi or life force energy within the body to restore health. According to Nan, acupuncture works on 95 percent of the population. In many cases, it changes people's lives as well as relieving physical symptoms. The success of Nan's treatments has resulted in a booming business based on the referrals of current patients. He has treated several professional and Olympic athletes, including members of the Denver Broncos and Colorado Rapids teams. Nan has also done clinical research work with Kaiser Permanente on pain control. To find out what acupuncture can do for you, contact Nan's Acupuncture Clinic.

7700 E Arapahoe Road #275, Centennial CO
(302) 761-6123

Yoga & You

HEALTH & BEAUTY: *Best yoga instruction in Centennial*

Literally, yoga means *to unite*. In this harried and busy world, it is essential to reconnect and to unite the body and spirit. Yoga & You offers a variety of yoga classes to suit your needs and enable you to reconnect. Yoga & You offers a gentle form of yoga, called the Day-Star method, which applies effort and rest equally. In this type of yoga, emphasis is placed on experiencing the poses slowly, without pain and with mindful breathing. They also offer Power yoga, which emphasizes breathing to connect the body and mind. Developed by Baron Baptiste, Power yoga is a flowing practice that heals, detoxifies and exhilarates the body, mind and spirit. To maximize the efficacy and authenticity of their Power yoga classes, the classes are done in a room kept at eighty degrees. Yoga & You maintains a Monday through Saturday schedule of classes, including the styles mentioned above for adults and Day-Star for kids ages nine to twelve and a Day-Star based yoga called Stressbusters. Yoga & You also offers Jin Shin Jyutsu, a Japanese acupressure system, to maintain balance of energies within the body. Yoga & You invites you to find who you are, here and now.

8170 S University Boulevard # 230, Centennial CO
(720) 488-3638 *www.relaxwithyoga.com*

Scottish Stained Glass

HOME: *Best stained glass design in Centennial*

Stained and leaded glass applications were once reserved for upper end homes, churches and commercial buildings until Scottish Stained Glass came to town. Martin Faith's innovative company opens the leaded glass market to a wider range of customers without reducing quality or design possibilities. In the last decade, the company has grown rapidly to 40 employees with installations of 100 to 200 windows a week as Colorado homeowners discover the possibilities for adding privacy, beauty and glare control to the many windows so popular in modern home design. Designers customize each window to the size, shape and design needs of the client. Sixteen artisans work full-time simply making the windows, while other employees specialize in design or installation. With a database of over 10,000 designs, over 1,000 bevel shapes, hundreds of glass colors and textures and in-home consultation services, Scottish Stained Glass stands in a class by itself. Stained and leaded glass creations from Scottish Stained Glass adorn churches, commercial buildings, mansions and homes throughout Colorado. Entryways, odd-shaped windows and bathroom windows are particularly popular targets for leaded glass designs as Colorado's homeowners seek to let light into their homes while controlling heat, glare and privacy. Faith learned his craft in his native Scotland; his reputation for service, artistry and quality bring the very best glass experts to his door, assuring that your next leaded glass window will be everything you hoped it could be from Scottish Stained Glass.

Denver Metro Area: (303) 766-3811
Northern Colorado: (970) 613-0377
Southern Colorado: (719) 380-9193
www.scottishstainedglass.com

Centerstage Starz Theatre and Dance Studio

RECREATION:
Best dance studio and performance academy

Centerstage Starz Theatre and Dance Studio does exactly what their name implies: they produce a generation of centerstage stars. Centerstage Starz is a dance and theatrical training studio that operates out of a state-of-the-art 12,000-square-foot facility in Centennial. It is run by local dance and performance legend Taami M. Bash, and her 15 world class professional choreographers and teachers. Centerstage Starz is a multi-disciplinary academy that is as successful as it is versatile. The academy offers classes in jazz, ballet, lyrical, hip hop, break dance, tap, voice, theater and ballroom. They also sponsor both a competitive touring dance company and a performing theater company which has produced professional artists in both the theater and dance industry. They are home to an elite group of hip hop dancers, ages 5 to 13, known as the Denver Nuggets Lil' Bustas Hip Hop Crew who perform at Nuggets games. They are home to the Colorado Rapids cheerleaders. They sponsor professional dance and cheerleader preparatory workshops, and are involved in too many community events to list. If you are looking for a dance studio and academy that will help you reach your dreams of dancing or performing, Centerstage Starz Theatre and Dance Studio could not be more highly recommended.

8150 S University Boulevard, Unit 120, Centennial CO
(303) 713-0355
www.centerstagestarz.com

Champion Gymnastics

RECREATION:
Best gymnastics training center

Champion Gymnastics is a five-star training center in Centennial with a 30,000-square-foot facility featuring some of the best equipment in the country. When you want your daughter or son to learn how to use their body to its fullest capacity, this is the place to go. Tilly Coupe established Champion Gymnastics in 1993. She and her staff teach both competitive and non-competitive gymnastics, cheerleading, trampoline and dance. Classes reach every skill level from beginner to advanced. There is a Mom & Me program, where moms bring kids between the ages of 15 months and three years to receive basic locomotor and tumbling guidance. They work with Children's Hospital to provide a fun and supportive environment where physically challenged youth can learn at their own pace. Champion Gymnastics also trains future Olympians. They have the expertise and equipment to offer the elite training required for international Olympic competition. You can attend a summer camp or have a birthday party here. Tilly keeps more than 25 instructors on staff. The facility includes three 1,600-square-foot competition floors, including an AAI Stratum Floor, a 50-foot tumbling track, two in-ground trampolines, 12 balance beams, 11 uneven bar stations, an AAI vault table, strap bar, and a rod floor. Safety is paramount here. They have foam-filled pits to cushion falls, and boast that they've had no serious injuries since Tilly opened the doors. If you're looking for the best place to bounce, dance, cheer and learn gymnastics, visit Champion Gymnastics.

8237 S Holly Street, Centennial CO
(303) 843-0711
www.championgymnastic.com

Wingin' It
RESTAURANTS & CAFÉS: *Best hot wings in Centennial*

In 1983, pop star Robert Palmer told us, "Some feel the heat and decide that they can't go on." Nearly 20 years later, Derrol Morehead decided that he couldn't go on without sharing his love of hot wings. Laid off after 15 years in corporate America and with no previous restaurant experience, he and his wife opened Wingin' It. As you can imagine, the menu featured his beloved hot wings. Today, the menu features all sorts of fun foods including funnel cake, cream cheese poppers, beer-battered fries and deep-fried Twinkies or candy bars. More than 20 handmade wing sauces are made from scratch and range from milder fare like honey mustard to the appropriately named Fire. The food isn't the only thing that makes Wingin' It an enjoyable experience. The playful décor features wall paintings depicting the local sports scenes, a collectibles case filled with memorabilia and an arcade for gamers. Despite their initial inexperience, the Moorhead's have since created a loyal following of regulars with just the right mix of easy meal choices and beverages to handle the fast pace of the lunch crowd to the more demanding family dinner set. Catering is available and wing orders range from six to 250. For your next meal, don't wing it yourself, let Wingin' It show you how it's done.

8200 S Quebec Street, Centennial CO (720) 207-2435 *www.winginit.biz*

Places to Go

- Bear Creek Cañon Park
  501 Bear Creek Road

- Cave of the Winds
  U.S. Highway 24, Manitou Springs

- Cheyenne Mountain State Park
  410 JL Ranch Heights

- Colorado Springs Pioneers Museum
  215 S Tejon Street

- Eleven Mile and
  Spinney Mountain State Parks
  4229 County Road 92, Lake George

- Fine Arts Center Modern
  Plaza of the Rockies, 121 S Tejon Street

- Florissant Fossil Beds National Monument
  Teller County 1, Florissant

- Garden of the Gods Park
  1805 N 30th Street

- Manitou Cliff Dwellings
  U.S. Highway 24, Manitou Springs

- Memorial Park
  1605 E Pikes Peak Avenue

- Miramont Castle
  9 Capitol Hill Avenue, Manitou Springs

- Monument Valley Park
  170 W Cache La Poudre Street

- Mueller State Park
  State Route 67, Divide

- North Cheyenne Cañon Park
  2120 S Cheyenne Cañon Road

- North Slope Recreation Area
  Pike's Peak Highway, Cascade

- Palmer Park
  3650 Maizeland Road

- Pike's Peak Cog Railway
  515 Ruxton Avenue, Manitou Springs

- Seven Falls
  2850 S Cheyenne Canyon Road

- U.S. Air Force Academy Visitor Center
  Tours: (719) 333-2025

- U.S. Olympics Training Center Visitor Center
  1 Olympic Plaza Tours: (719) 632-5551

- Western Museum of Mining & Industry
  1025 N Gate Road

Garden of the Gods
Photo by J.C. Leacock
Courtesy of Colorado Tourism Office

COLORADO SPRINGS

With about 375,000 residents inside the city limits, Colorado Springs is the second most populous municipality in Colorado. In 2006, *Money* magazine ranked Colorado Springs the best place to live in the big city category. The city is the seat of El Paso County and is located near the base of one of the most famous American mountains, Pikes Peak. You can ascend the peak using the Pike's Peak Cog Railway. Though Colorado Springs is a major metropolis today, General William Palmer originally established it as a posh resort community. In 1893, English professor Katharine Lee Bates wrote "America the Beautiful" in Palmer's Antlers Hotel after a visit to the top of Pikes Peak. The town's economy received a major boost when prospectors made a major gold strike in nearby Cripple Creek. Today, tourism remains important. The city boasts many high-tech businesses. A large number of religious organizations and churches make their headquarters in Colorado Springs. The most famous institution in town, however, has to be the United States Air Force Academy. Colorado Springs is also home to Fort Carson and a large number of other important national defense sites. The North American Aerospace Defense Command, or NORAD, is just outside of town in Cheyenne Mountain, south of Pikes Peak. Colorado Springs contains one of the nation's most fabulous city parks, Garden of the Gods, famous for its stunning red rock formations.

Things to Do

February
- Manitou Springs Carnivale and Parade
  Memorial Park, Manitou Springs
  (719) 685-5089

March
- St. Patrick's Day Parade and Race
  Old Colorado City (719) 635-8803

- Wine Festival
  Fine Arts Festival (719) 634-5581

May
- Cinco de Mayo
  Memorial Park (719) 520-2416

- Hummingbird Festival
  Starsmore Discovery Center
  www.tfocc.org/hummingbirdfestival.html

- Territory Days
  Old Colorado City (719) 475-0955

- SpringAbouts/Celebration of the Arts
  Manitou Springs (719) 685-9655

June
- Springs Spree
  Downtown www.springspree.com

- Colorado Wine Festival
  Soda Springs Park, Manitou Springs
  (719) 685-5089

July
- Patriotic Celebration Concert
  Memorial Park (719) 385-CITY (2489)

- Teddy Bear Days
  Cheyenne Mountain Zoo (719) 633-9925

- Pridefest
  Acacia Park www.ppglcc.org/pridefest

- Colorado Festival of World Theater
  www.cfwt.org

September
- Colorado Balloon Classic
  Memorial Park www.balloonclassic.com

- Colorado Folk Art Festival
  Rock Ledge Ranch (719) 578-6986

- Commonwheel Arts & Crafts Festival
  Manitou Springs
  www.commonwheel.com/festival

December
- *Holiday Evenings at Rock Ledge Ranch*
  (719) 385-5256

The BRO^DMOOR
ACCOMMODATIONS: *Best resort*

At the base of Cheyenne Mountain, wealthy entrepreneur Spencer Penrose purchased 440 acres of land with a vision to build an imaginative, multi-faceted resort. The Broadmoor is the result of Penrose's dream. The raised "A" in the name was purposeful, to make the name unique. In every respect, the grand resort fulfils the quest for excellence and continues to add to its own legacy. The comprehensive training of employees in the European tradition of service has resulted a steay, reliable staff that translates to exceptional customer service. The opulence and luxury of the original establishment have endured and increased over time. Everything at The Broadmoor is world-class. A luxurious amenity spa looks as magical as it feels. Pools and Jacuzzis, whirlpools and water slides provide exercise and entertainment. There are also glorious offerings of food at the poolside cafe. Golf and tennis pro shops, a golf clubhouse, exercise room and an aerobics studio ensure convenient opportunities for developing your skills in these areas. There are now three championship golf courses at The Broadmoor. They can also arrange for outdoor adventures such as horseback riding, rafting and rides on Pike's Peak Cog Railway. The meeting rooms are top-notch facilities that feature state of the art tools to enhance any presentation. The rooms vary in style, but every room is pure luxury. Dignitaries, politicians and celebrities all enjoy The Broadmoor's hospitality, cuisine and lodgings. The one drawback to your stay at The Broadmoor is that eventually you must leave!

One Lake Avenue, Colorado Springs CO (719) 634-7711 or (800) 634-7711
www.broadmoor.com

Candlewood Suites

ACCOMMODATIONS: *Best suites*

Candlewood Suites provides everything you need for a memorable stay in the Colorado Springs area. Since 2002, owner Jannie Richardson and General Manager Suki Ko have provided guests with friendly and attentive service, including recommendations for local activities. From your suite with its view of dramatic Pikes Peak, you're less than 10 minutes from downtown's shopping and dining options. Even a business traveler will want to find some time to explore such attractions as Garden of the Gods, Seven Falls and Cheyenne Mountain Zoo. Suites at Candlewood include a fully equipped kitchen, free high-speed Internet access and a guest laundry. You can keep your workout schedule too, thanks to complementary guest passes to nearby Bally's or the YMCA. Business travelers appreciate the meeting room and board room options here as well as spacious workstations. Free videos, a CD library and outdoor gas grills offer many choices for good times. For a comfortable home away from home in one of nature's most beautiful playgrounds, come to Candlewood Suites.

6450 N Academy Boulevard, Colorado Springs CO
(719) 590-1111
www.candlewoodsuites.com

Arctic Spas of Colorado Springs

HOME:
Best spas for the Colorado climate

Residents of Colorado should know how important it is to purchase a spa that is energy efficient and engineered for the state's harsh climate. If you didn't know this, it's time to visit Arctic Spas of Colorado Springs and talk to the experts. Owners Carol and Dave Hennekens provide their customers with spas that use a heat lock system. This allows the motors to run at 65 percent efficiency with 35 percent of the energy given off as heat, so the hot tubs use a low amount of electricity. The frame, shell and plumbing are also impressive. The cover alone can support the weight of 12 people. The shell is one of the most durable in the industry and is made from a composite material that is stronger than steel by weight and carries a lifetime structural warranty. Plumbing is made from very durable hose, and the filter system is 50 times finer than that of competitor products. Choose custom jets according to your needs, whether you are looking to relax muscles, relieve tension or take pressure off your joints. Technicians can even install the jets where you need them most. Options include aromatherapy, lighting and Aquatremor sound system with sound wave therapy, an amplifier and MP3 hookup. Your hot tub can be set up on gravel or any level surface; a concrete pad is not required, making your spa truly portable. Arctic also sells gazebos, Guild billiard tables and hot tub chemicals. For an investment in heat therapy, comfort and durability meant to last a lifetime, visit Arctic Spas of Colorado Springs.

**6480 N Academy Boulevard,
Colorado Springs CO
(719) 264-0112**
www.arctic-cos.com

Hot Tub Heaven
HOME: *Best place to buy a hot tub*

When you're in the market for a hot tub, it's often not enough that a store carries the best brands. At Hot Tub Heaven, conveniently located in the Colorado Springs area, you'll find a business that sells superior products and stands behind all the products it sells. Family owned and operated since 1978, Hot Tub Heaven services all brands of spas, swimming pools and saunas, whether residential or commercial. Sharon Vernon and her late husband, Sam, started the business. They instilled in their children, Sam Jr. and Steve, the importance of attention to detail and lasting relationships with customers. Sharon and her sons are keeping people in hot water by providing a great selection, affordable prices and old-fashioned customer service. Hot Tub Heaven takes pride in carrying a large selection of Caldera Spas, chemicals and water maintenance products. Caldera is one of the most trusted names in the industry. Experienced technicians are always on hand to answer your questions. When you're in the market for a spa, come to the Vernon family at Hot Tub Heaven, where they keep people in hot water.

4039 Tutt Boulevard, Colorado Springs CO
(719) 528-8011 *www.hottubheaven.com*

EATON

Eaton, located just north of Greeley, is an affluent, suburban community with a mix of old, appealing single-family dwellings and large, elegant newer homes. Eaton is named after Benjamin Harrison Eaton who served as governor of Colorado in the 1880s. Eaton helped found the town in 1892 and was responsible for the beginning of crop irrigation in the area. Today, Eaton is experiencing considerable growth with the opening of new subdivisions. From 2000 to 2005, the population increased almost 40 percent to about 3,800 residents, with more to come.

Places to Go

- Antique Washing Machine Museum
  (by appointment only)
  35901 Weld County Road 31
  (970) 454-1856

- City Park
  Park Avenue and 3rd Street

Things to Do

July
- Eaton Days
  City Park
  (970) 454-3426

DJ Flowers

GARDENS, PLANTS & FLOWERS: *Best flower shop in Eaton*

The saga of DJ's Flowers is a love story with settings ranging from the Far East to the mountains of Colorado. It started in Thailand, the place they call the Land of Smiles, when a native girl fell in love with an American fighter pilot. They married and moved together to the great American West. Not long after, although D.J. Washburn could barely speak English, she told her husband she intended to start her own business and enrolled in floral design school. The money to start the business came from the 80 floral orders she landed during her work breaks on a Valentine's Day weekend while working as a cashier. She states her formula for success simply: "Work hard and trust people." That interest in working with others is obvious. DJ still sells flowers to some of her original customers and recently opened an addition to her business. Her experience as a member of the Eaton Chamber of Commerce convinced her Eaton needed a place for people to gather, so she opened an ice cream shop with a fireplace and chairs arranged to maximize conversation. Locals gather to play cards, discuss books and host parties. DJ's is still the place to buy flowers for your valentine throughout the year, and now it's the sort of place a person could meet a valentine as well.

110 Oak Avenue, Eaton CO
(970) 454-3178

Ultimate Salon Spa

HEALTH & BEAUTY: *One of the 10 best things about living in Eaton*

Treat yourself to a day of total relaxation while enhancing your own natural beauty with a visit to the Ultimate Salon Spa, a full service salon that offers European flair without the European pricing. This wonderful spa is considered to be one of the 10 best things about living in Eaton, according to a community poll. It is centrally located between Fort Collins and Denver, which makes it an ideal destination for day-trippers. Over the years, Ultimate Salon Spa has earned a reputation for providing excellent service in a warm and hospitable environment. Many of Owner Shirley Lindsay's regular customers compare the

place to Dolly Parton's salon in the film Steel Magnolias, due to the inviting ambience and friendly staff. The spa team includes manager Christina and massage therapist Jaye, as well as a quartet of talented cosmetologists and two tanning technicians. Ultimate Salon Spa offers a full range of traditional services for both men and women, including facial and body waxing, eye brow tinting and European-style facials. The spa features a variety of hair-care services, including permanent waves, coloration, cuts and styling. Soothe achy muscles while letting your worries drift away with one of the spa's rejuvenating massages, such as a Swedish or Prenatal massage or the Neuromuscular Therapy massage, which is often used to improve range of motion. Discover a place where you will always be welcomed upon arrival and completely renewed upon departure with a visit to the Ultimate Salon Spa.

121 1st Street, Eaton CO
(970) 454-1455

ERIE

The original plat for Erie was filed in 1871, following establishment of the Briggs Mine, the first commercial coal mine in Weld County. Until that time, horse-drawn wagons delivered surface coal to customers. It was also in 1871 that the Union Pacific Railroad extended a spur westward from Brighton to Erie. Soon coal from Erie mines was being shipped by rail to markets in Denver and as far east as Kansas City. Today, downtown Erie is the home of eclectic businesses and wonderful eateries. Discover for yourself why Erie is becoming a restaurant destination for folks who love to eat great food. Between 2000 and 2005, Erie's population almost doubled, to more than 12,000 residents. The town's Comprehensive Plan calls for an ultimate population of about 38,000.

Places to Go

- Coal Creek Park
  Kattel Street and Cheeseman Street

Things to Do

May
- Erie Town Fair
  Downtown
  (303) 828-3440

September
- Biscuit Day
  Downtown
  (303) 828-5250

October
- Oktoberfest
  Downtown
  (303) 828-5320

December

- Light up on Briggs
  Briggs Street
  (303) 828-3440

Anderson Farms
ATTRACTIONS:
Best hayrides and tours

If a down home gathering is your idea of paradise or if you're looking for a back to basics field trip that will delight the whole family, then head to Anderson Farms in Erie. This charming and delightful farm has been in operation since 1958 and is under the ownership of Peggy Shupe and Jim Anderson. Families, organizations and school groups can gather and celebrate in the joy that comes with spending a day out-of-doors while getting acquainted with farm animals. The farm sponsors numerous field trips and special events such has their highly popular Terror in the Corn, which runs throughout the month of October and offers a finely set stage with a corn maize full of thrilling chills and horrifying haunts. In the spring and summer months, you can learn about the importance of seeds with Anderson Farms Planting Big Smiles field trip or discover more about the care and feeding of the animals that make the farm their home on the Maizing Animals trip. The tour features a whole host of goats, donkeys, bunnies and other barnyard favorites. In addition to the field trips, corn maizes, hayrides and animal antics, Anderson Farms is a creative place to hold your next reunion, wedding, birthday party or other special event. Their party barn can seat 196 and Old West Barbecue catering is available on-site. With guaranteed fresh air and stunning views, you're invited to visit Anderson Farms when you want to get back to basics.

6728 WCR 3 1/4, Erie CO
(303) 702-1844
www.andersonfarms.com

EVANS

Evans was named for John Evans, a territorial governor. The town is immediately adjacent to Greeley—no farmland separates the cities. In 2004, Evans received the Gold Medal for Excellence in Park and Recreation Management, the Oscar of parks and recreation. City Park features a playground, pavilion, horseshoe pits, softball arena and lots of shade for picnics. Riverside Park contains a seven-acre fishing lake with more than two miles of scenic trails, ball fields and open lands. Seven other parks complete the picture. The population of Evans grew 73 percent from 2000 to 2005 to a total of more than 16,000 residents.

Places to Go

- City Park
  39th Street and Golden Street

- Evans Historical Museum
  3720 Golden Street
  (970) 506-2721

- Riverside Park
  42nd Street and Golden Street

Things to Do

September
- Evans Fest
  (970) 330-4204

K&K Laser Creations

BUSINESS: *Best laser engraving in Evans*

For several years, Kip McLeland worked in the computer field and enjoyed spending his time off the clock as a hobby woodworker. Then, while visiting a trade show, he saw how he could combine his computer expertise with his love of woodworking in the laser engraving business. In 1999, Kip started K&K Laser Creations. The store's staff soon expanded to include his adult children. Kip's four young grandkids also enjoy spending time at the family business. K&K Laser Creations uses a computer-controlled laser, which allows for greater precision and finer detail than traditional engraving methods, to create custom engraving for trophies, plaques and gifts. Whether you would like to honor a Little League team with trophies recognizing their team spirit or create a special plaque for the employee of the month, Kip and his team will produce a piece to suit your needs at a very competitive price. The company also provides custom embroidery services, and can give your staff a polished look with matching shirts embroidered with the company logo. Come to K&K Laser Creations for custom engraving to commemorate each special occasion.

3951 Carson Avenue, Evans CO
(970) 330-2244

Schwartz's Krautburger Kitchens

RESTAURANTS & CAFÉS: *Best (and only) Krautburgers in Evans*

The specialty at Schwartz's Krautburger Kitchen is, naturally, the Krautburger. For many years, Dave Schwartz worked long, hard hours farming sugar beets, corn and alfalfa. He looked forward to coming home from the fields each evening, where his wife's delicious sweets such as German coffee cake or grebble, a German donut, would be waiting. After Dave quit farming and worked as a milkman and later a delivery driver, he and his wife Margaret still knew that her home cooking and baked goods could draw a crowd, so 18 years ago they opened a take-out bake shop in the town of Evans. Schwartz's was an instant hit with customers and Dave earned more in the first two years at the Krautburger Kitchen than his entire time as a farmer. The Krautburger is homemade bread stuffed with cabbage, hamburger, onions and spices. More daring folks order their krautburgers with jalapenos and cheese for a bit of a kick. For dessert, or a snack, make sure to try the grebble or coffee cake. At Schwartz's, everything is made from scratch. The Schwartz family knows how hard the local farmers work to produce the best crops, so they buy ingredients locally wherever possible. Customers say the Krautburger is a delicious alterative to fast food. Schwartz's also delivers to the hungry employees of several local businesses. After Margaret passed away, Dave decided to keep the Kitchen going, and at age 77 he still enjoys going to work every day. Stop by, say hi to Dave and pick up some delicious German food from Schwartz's Krautburger Kitchen.

820 39th Street, Evans CO
(970) 330-0509
www.krautburger.com

Places to Go

- Alderfer/Three Sisters Park
  Buffalo Park Road (County Highway 89)

- Elk Meadow Open Space Park
  Evergreen Parkway

- Evergreen Lakehouse
  29614 Upper Bear Creek Road

- Evergreen Recreation Center
  5300 S Olive Road

- Hiwan Homestead Museum
  and Heritage Grove
  4208 S Timbervale Drive

- Humphrey Memorial Park/Museum
  620 S Soda Creek Road

Things to Do

April
- Mountain Area Earth Day Fair
  (303) 674-8610

May
- Evergreen Academy Country Fair
  (303) 670-8957

June
- Evergreen Rodeo
  www.evergreenrodeo.com

- Animal Protective League Paw-Fest
  (303) 674-4550

July
- Evergreen Arts Council Summerfest
  (303) 674-4625

- Evergreen Jazz Festival
  (303) 697-5467

August
- Mountain Heritage Festival
  (303) 674-6262

- Fine Art Festival
  (303) 674-4625

September
- Big Chili Cook-Off Music and Arts Festival
  www.bigchili.org

- Bavarian Night
  (303) 674-5429

- Hot Air Balloon Night Glow and Launch
  (303) 674-0182

December
- Bergen Village Holiday Festival
  (720) 940-6611

EVERGREEN

Evergreen is a prime location for Denver-area residents who want a home in the mountains. Downtown Evergreen is 7,014 feet above sea level and the altitude reaches 9,000 feet elsewhere in town. The community encompasses more than 100 square miles of heavily forested hills. Average lot sizes run from one-half to five acres. Forestry was Evergreen's first industry in the late 19th century. By the 1920s and 1930s, the town was a vacation community for visitors from Denver. The wealthy and famous streamed to resorts such as Troutdale in the Pines, the Greystone Guest Ranch and the Brookforest Inn. By the 1950s, roads improved to the point where people could live in Evergreen and work in Denver. Growth was inevitable. Depending on how you define its boundaries, the unincorporated town now has from 9,000 to 23,000 residents. Visitors continue to flock to the area for recreation and cultural activities.

Evergreen Lake ice skaters
Photo by Brian Gadbery
Courtesy of Colorado Tourism Office

Bear Creek Cabins

ACCOMMODATIONS:
Best cabin resort in Evergreen

Imagine the soothing sound of Bear Creek mere feet from you doorstep, washing all your worries away while you relax at the renovated Bear Creek Cabins in Evergreen. Bear Creek is a fly-fishing stream and home to plenty of healthy native brown and rainbow trout, which guests enjoy catching and releasing back into the wild. The four, duplex, log cabins enjoy a lovely setting in a spruce and pine forest with scenic rock formations and nearby opportunities for outdoor fun in every season. The Davidson family built the resort in 1947 as a summer getaway. In 1996, Bruce and Jayne Hungate left their careers to purchase and restore this historic mountain resort, a project which involved interior and exterior refurbishing. Each one-room cabin has its own bath, a fireplace and a kitchen area, complete with major appliances, dishes and cookware. Private picnic tables and grills located right outside each door invite summer cookouts. Larger groups may want to ask the Hungates about their two-bedroom mountain house rental. Bear Creek Cabins makes a restful retreat or a great jumping off spot for nearby recreation. A full-service Orvis shop with a fly fishing school is just minutes away, and nearby Evergreen Lake offers paddleboats and canoes in summer and ice fishing and skating in winter. Snowshoeing and cross-country skiing are popular winter pursuits, with downhill skiing 45 to 90 minutes away. Dining and shopping are nearby. Members of Trout Unlimited, owners Bruce and Jayne Hungate practice a catch-and-release policy; you can literally fly-fish 30 feet from your front porch. Whether you are simply passing through, or Bear Creek is your destination, you are sure to enjoy your stay in one of these splendid log cabins. Take in the scenery, and release your cares to the breezes at Bear Creek Cabins.

**27400 Highway 74,
Evergreen CO
(303) 674-3442**
www.bearcreekcabinsco.com

Beaver Brook Pet Center
ANIMALS & PETS: *Best pet care in Evergreen*

Whenever you're looking for someone to take care of your best non-human friend, be it cat, dog, bird or reptile, look no further than Beaver Brook Pet Center in Evergreen. Veterinarian David Manobla and his staff offer everything from traditional veterinary care and small animal operations to the latest techniques in laser surgery. With 30 indoor and outdoor kennels, they can even provide a temporary home for your animal companion, if you need to leave town for a time. Practicing nontraditional techniques, such as homeopathy and acupuncture, has kept David's practice on the cutting edge of developments in treating animal medical concerns. The professionals at Beaver Brook Pet Center have a strong commitment to the community and to the welfare of all furry, feathered or scaly patients left in their charge. They can even make house calls For pet care you can trust, check out Beaver Brook Pet Center and the many services and options they offer to help your beloved animal friends live long and healthy lives.

77 Elmgreen Lane, Evergreen CO (303) 670-0838
www.beaverbrookpc.myvetonline.com

M & M Music
ARTS & CRAFTS: *Best place to rent or buy musical equipment*

M & M Music carries just about everything an experienced or budding musician needs, from picks and reeds to sheet music and strings. Mike and Marie Coleman opened the first M & M Music store in 1996 and soon followed with a second store. The full-service music stores offer rental and purchase of some of the best brands of musical and band instruments on the market, with names like Crafter, Garrison, Ovation and Spencer. Find Phonic mixers, Mega amps, Sonor drums and Casio or Suzuki keyboards. You can rent DJ and karaoke equipment and find staff willing to help you plan special events or weddings. Both the Evergreen and Pine stores offer music lessons on a variety of instruments and repairs on most equipment. The Colemans attribute their success to a family orientation, a focus on community service and customer care that extends to treating customers like part of their family. *The National Register's* 2004 Who's Who in Executives & Professionals recognized Mike for success in his field. The Congressional Youth Leadership Council cited the Colemans for outstanding service as educational advisors to national scholars in the National Young Leaders Conference. Mike and Marie invite you to visit M & M Music and join their musical family.

3743 N Evergreen Parkway, Evergreen CO
(303) 674-7725
67318 Highway 285, Unit 7, Pine CO
(303) 838-6238
www.mandmmusic.net

Crossroads School of Music
ARTS & CRAFTS: *Best approach to music education*

After teaching guitar for several years in a local music store and seeing students parade in and out every half hour, John Wyburn thought that there had to be a better, more personal approach to music education. At his Crossroads School of Music, John encourages young guitarists to make the music they are learning their own. Of course, John teaches the basics, while stressing the importance of honest practice. For those ready to take the next step, he offers the incentive of the Student Recording Program. Designed to encourage the developing guitarist to closely study a song of his or her choosing, this program enables the student to work through the various guitar parts of the song. The goal is to record the song onto a CD. For those students interested in the actual hands-on process of recording, the school's Home Recording Workshops provide the necessary training to operate a home recording studio. Students test what they have learned by recording fellow students participating in the Student Recording Program. For fun-filled instruction that puts concepts into practice, sign up at Crossroads School of Music.

6949 Highway 73, Evergreen CO
(303) 810-1828
http://CrossroadsSchoolofMusic.home.att.net

The Bagelry
BAKERIES, COFFEE & TEA: *Best bagels in Evergreen*

The Bagelry in Evergreen serves espresso from an Italian espresso machine, good food and really big bagels. The bagels are made the East Coast way, boiled and then baked fresh every day. These handmade bagels are head-and-shoulders above the competition. The Bagelry also specializes in a wicked tuna sandwich and the Bergen Peak, a lox, cream cheese, tomatoes, sprouts and onion extravaganza. With the bagels, outstanding coffee and free, wireless internet connections, The Bagelry has become a community hub. Everyone comes to The Bagelry, from the skiers and boarders to the bikers and hikers. The many televisions feature cable access and the bagels are considered to have an attitude. They are low fat, no cholesterol, low sodium healthy treasures served with your choice of an assortment of flavorful whipped cream cheeses to spread on your own piece of paradise. The menu also features a fruit tray, assorted breakfast tray of bagels, cream cheeses, muffins, pastries and cinnamon rolls and a veggie tray. Awesome coffee beverages, fruit smoothies and a caramel apple cider will make it hard to pick a favorite and will bring you back often to try something new. You are invited to take part in all the activity at The Bagelry or call and have them cater your next event.

1242 Bergen Parkway, Evergreen CO
(303) 674-1413
www.thebagelry.net

Java Groove
BAKERIES, COFFEE & TEA: *Best coffee*

The first thing you notice when you enter Java Groove is a comfortable atmosphere, enhanced by soft jazz playing in the background. Quickly, your senses are bombarded with a mixture of aromas that your brain interprets to mean you have died and gone to coffee heaven. Java Groove offers a superb, locally roasted line of coffee, but this enticing shop doesn't limit itself to coffee in its various incarnations. Beyond coffee, you'll find meals ranging from handy and tasty breakfast options, like bagels, crêpes and waffles, to sandwiches and salads. The Groove's most popular dessert option, the Java Love, gets the nod of approval from coffee connoisseurs thanks to the irresistible combination of coffee, cinnamon, hazelnut and crème brûlée. A visit to Java Groove is an opportunity to turn one of Colorado's most important daily rituals into moments of pure pleasure. Imbibe one of the specialty coffees while you enjoy visits with friends, or bring your computer along. Then take a moment to answer the question: How much groove do you need in your day? Get what you need at Evergreen's own Java Groove. Your daily routine will be richer for it.

28136 Highway 74, Evergreen CO
(303) 674-4494
www.javagroove.com

A Ticket to Ride

BUSINESS: *Best travel agency*

Paula Keyser started travel consulting in 1986. She joined A Ticket to Ride in 1987 and purchased the agency in partnership with Barbara Britton that same year. Barbara had traveled extensively and was a great mentor. Barbara retired at the end of 1994, leaving Paula with an acquired wealth of knowledge about the travel industry. In their years together, plus the years that followed, Paula has had the opportunity to travel to many places around the globe. She has been applying her extensive knowledge to travel situations for 20 years and is ready to help you plan your next vacation. Paula can arrange for all your transportation needs, advise you regarding places to stay and provide you with her valuable insights about issues you might not otherwise know. For instance, you might think Tahiti is just what you need to chase away those winter blues, but it would be better to go in the summer or fall to avoid the January heat and rain. In addition to having access to Paula's thorough knowledge of many destinations, A Ticket to Ride can arrange five-star or other levels of accommodations with the assurance that your travel requests will have been fully researched. Paula has a customer-comes-first attitude which is reflected by the agency's impeccable record with the Denver Better Business Bureau. A large percentage of the agency's clientele are returning customers or referrals. Paula has guided clients through family vacations, then students off to college and eventually honeymoons. Whether you imagine yourself sitting by the pool or climbing up a mountain, Paula can get you there. The next time you catch yourself dreaming about relaxing on a sun drenched island, call A Ticket to Ride and make your dreams come true.

(303) 987-9343 or (800) 383-7659

www.atickettoride.vacation.com

Juna Clothing
FASHION: *Best handmade clothing from around the world*

Through her poetry and fiction, award-winning author Linda Hogan has been a voice for people who often go unheard. Now, Linda is working to improve people's lives through Juna Clothing, her boutique. The store specializes in fair-trade clothing and gifts from around the globe, especially third-world countries stricken with poverty. The people who produce these items are guaranteed good working conditions and fair prices for their work, which includes beautiful hand-dyed and hand crafted silks, silver jewelry and colorful dresses. Some of the socially-aware brands showcased at Juna are A People United, Global Village and Sacred Threads. The store carries items from countries such as Tibet, Haiti, Guatemala, Peru, Vietnam and Indonesia, and also supports local artisans, women's collectives and farmers. The care taken with each individually made piece is clearly visible in the intricate Native American silver and beadwork and traditional Eskimo jewelry. Native American spa products include soaps and lotions made with natural plant ingredients. Richly colored hand-woven skirts and blouses fill the racks. You are sure to receive compliments when wearing the signed clothing made by women in India. Offerings from People Tree include a line of items handmade in Bangladesh and an extensive selection of Haitian goods. For beautiful handmade clothing and gifts that promote the emancipation of artisans around the world, shop at Juna Clothing in the Bergen Village.

**1260 Bergen Parkway, Evergreen CO
(303) 674-0166**

Daniel Diamonds
FASHION: *Best diamond jewelers*

The radiance of diamonds can only be outmatched by the smile of the woman who receives them. When searching for fine diamonds and stunning custom jewelry, go no further than Daniel Diamonds. Owners Danny and Karen Alkayam offer their patrons a spectacular array of masterfully cut diamonds that come from the family diamond factories in Netanya, Israel. Because of these origins, the Alkayams have a personal and trusting relationship with the men who cut these coveted gems . Their care and passion for their work shines through in the cut, clarity and quality of the diamonds that are represented at Daniel Diamonds. Danny and Karen are proud to sell these magnificent and precious stones from craftsmen who strive to create a gem-quality diamond out of a mined rough. This popular jeweler has two locations, their original one at the Lowry Town Center in Denver and a second in Evergreen, which opened 1994. The Alkayams bring more than 40 years of experience to their enterprise, making them the ideal assistants for helping you to choose the exact color and cut of your perfect diamond. Karen, a gifted jewelry designer, can utilize gold, platinum or sterling silver to create a stunning custom piece that will become a treasured heirloom for future generations. Add radiance to each day with the marvelous diamonds and jewelry that awaits you at Daniel Diamonds.

1193 Bergen Parkway, Evergreen CO   (303) 674-6673

What a Girl Wants

FASHION:
Best apparel for any occasion

What a Girl Wants, a boutique in Evergreen, will take you from the bedroom to an active lifestyle. This versatile shop has a wide range of intimate apparel, lingerie, sleepwear, yoga and active-wear for any occasion in a girl's life. You'll find practical and sexy sleepwear along with an assortment of candles, which could help set the mood for a romantic evening. If you are planning a honeymoon or a romantic getaway, come by What a Girl Wants for fun lingerie in a wide range of sizes and prices, as well as oils and lotions by Kama Sutra and other products from their pleasure chest. One of the store's specialties is a line of pajamas by Wicking J, made particularly for menopausal and pregnant women, cancer survivors and chemotherapy patients suffering from night sweats. This line is specially designed to keep you dry and help you sleep through the night. They also offer sleepwear, robes and slippers by Frankie & Johnny, P.J. Salvage and Mary Green, just to name a few, that will have you looking forward to a day's end. What a Girl Wants also offers makeup, lingerie parties, and a space for bachelorette parties and bridal showers. There are many unique items that would make a wonderful gift for that special girl. For the active girl, this store carries The Balance Collections by Marika, and yoga-wear by Spiritual Fitness and other designer brands. Owner Shelley Petrilli works between this boutique and her salon, Genesis for Hair, which offers full-service hair artistry. For a day of pampering, get a new do at Genesis and then pick up something silky or comfy at What a Girl Wants. Beware: these products have been known to add spark to a love life.

1254 Bergen Parkway (Bergen Village), Suite D, Evergreen CO
(303) 670-0991 (What A Girl Wants)
(303) 674-0199 (Genesis for Hair)

Ladidoodles
FASHION: *Most captivating beadwork in Evergreen*

Kris Hilker brings a long, artistic heritage to her one-of-a-kind jewelry creations at Ladidoodles in Evergreen. Kris's late father, former pilot and renowned Denver/Boulder artist Rich Hilker, raised her in a creative environment that blended art with fun. As a result, the inherent beauty of the brilliantly colored gemstones she uses is displayed to the best possible advantage. The name of Kris's shop derives from the Indian word Ladi, which means good luck. The doodles part of the name reflects the light-hearted attitude she brings to her work. Hilker does her homework on the value and lore of the stones she uses, and all of her work is stunning and built to last. Beads are strung on steel wrapped in nylon, with a clasp designed to pop open if too much pressure is applied. This saves the strand from breaking and renders it nearly child-proof. Kris's glowing work is priced to own. She encourages customers to share in the planning of custom jewelry that can be kept for a lifetime and passed down as a personal piece of family history. The mesmerizing, wearable art of Kris Hilker exudes the magic that can only come from a passionate artist. Visit Ladidoodles and see her creations for yourself.

6945 Highway 73, Evergreen CO
(303) 670-6573
www.ladidoodles.com

Evergreen Fine Art
GALLERIES & FINE ART: *Best framing gallery in Evergreen*

The art is constantly rotating at Virginia Haley-Runne's Evergreen Fine Art gallery, which means customers get plenty of opportunities to see fresh and exciting selections. The gallery, founded in 1993, features paintings, sculpture, limited edition prints, jewelry and gifts. Beyond fine art, the gallery also offers custom framing services with our in-house master framer. Evergreen Fine Art features only nationally known artists, ensuring that your purchase has long-lasting value. The gallery hosts several special events throughout the year, such as ladies days, jewelry trunk shows, artist openings and more. Evergreen Fine Art, just 30 minutes from downtown Denver, is the largest art gallery in the state. The responsibilities of running a large operation mean that Virginia employs a 12-person staff dedicated to meeting the needs of customers. The gallery recently expanded its jewelry offerings due to customer requests. In addition, Evergreen Fine Art takes an active interest in the community. Each autumn, the gallery designs and presents the Evergreen Angel, a sterling silver angel pendant to benefit hospice programs around the country. Evergreen Fine Art is also home to the John Runne Studio. Original acrylics on canvas, Runne's affable characters have found their way to limited edition lithographs and entertaining books. You can find something for everyone in this world-class gallery, where a creative and friendly staff can answer questions about the artists and where you can be assured of excellent service. Stop by and enjoy the variety at Evergreen Fine Art.

3042 Evergreen Parkway, Evergreen CO
(303) 670-1867 or (800) 452-9453
www.evergreenfineart.com

The Evergreen Gallery

GALLERIES & FINE ART:

Best selection of art from Colorado artists

Evergreen is a picturesque Colorado city that has proudly grown through community service rather than city government. In keeping with this strong sense of local community, Meryl Sabeff, an award-winning potter, opened The Evergreen Gallery, in 1987, to display renowned Colorado artists' works and to introduce outstanding new Colorado talent. As the oldest existing gallery in the Evergreen community, the focus still remains on being a mixed-media gallery representing pottery, limited edition prints, batik and woodwork that shares the space with paintings, jewelry and blown-glass. All of the art is sold on consignment to support local artists inspired by Colorado's colors and textures. The Gallery offers a bridal registry, making it easy to give an original gift. In 2003, The Evergreen Gallery was selected as a nominee for Niche magazine's Top 100 Retailers of American Craft Awards. The galleries were chosen for this honor by more than 18,000 professional craft artists throughout the United States and Canada. This award recognizes businesses that have treated artists with courtesy and respect, and mentored emerging artists, as well as promoting their crafts and operating in a professional manner. In 2004, they were named one of the five Best Art Galleries by *Mountain Living Magazine*, Best of the High Country award. Sabeff also owns the attached restaurant next door, SoHo Evergreen, fulfilling a vision of providing fine dining and fine art to the residents and visitors of Evergreen. Come for dinner and cocktails or just to enjoy the art. For the full experience, linger for both and take home a piece of Evergreen.

28195 Hwy 74, P.O. Box 431, Evergreen CO
(303) 674-4871
www.theevergreengallery.com

Moon Doggie Gardens
GARDENS, PLANTS & FLOWERS: *Best florists*

At Moon Doggie Gardens in Evergreen, your floral arrangement is not created until you order it. Owner and designer Susan Smith, one of the few certified floral designers in the area, will ask you a series of questions about the gift recipient to ensure that she gets the order just right. Her goal is to elicit a wow from anyone who sees the arrangement. Susan starts with the freshest flowers possible, which means she orders her stems from local markets only after you place your order. If you are looking for innovative wedding day designs exhibiting arches, candelabras and other props, Moon Doggie Gardens can oblige. This 16-year-old company also provides customized gift baskets, an assortment of gift items and preassembled bouquets for holidays when flowers fly off the shelves. Susan and Business Partner Dewey Herod will work with you to get your flowers where you need them when you need them. They can arrange both local and national delivery. They ask that you call ahead to arrange for pick up orders or viewing gift selections. The shop provides a gift giving reminder service, so you won't be caught short for an important occasion in the future. Moon Doggie can even decorate your home inside and out, so you're ready for that big holiday gathering. Let Moon Doggie Gardens be your personal shopper, and make the special occasions in life worthy of wows.

(303) 674-0227 or (866) 804-8033
www.moondoggiegardens.com

Whispering Pines Day Spa
HEALTH & BEAUTY: *Best custom-tailored spa therapies*

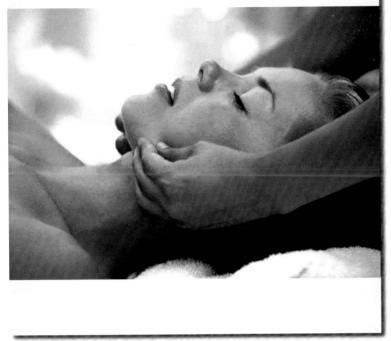

When it comes to spa services, one method does not fit everyone. That's why the owners of Whispering Pines Day Spa customize their therapies especially for you. Owners Marla Haley, Colette Kinkopf and Lisa Wormer opened Whispering Pines in 2002. They and their staff create a restful atmosphere and excel at determining the right spa treatments for each individual client. The sports massage targets aching muscles, while the Swedish massage stimulates circulation. Perhaps you need an invigorating hot stone massage or one that targets stress relief, detoxification or spinal problems. A steam shower is available to enhance your level of relaxation before and after massages. Additional services include manicures, pedicures, waxing, body wraps and several types of facials, including the Better-than-Botox facial, a rejuvenating treatment that is particularly useful to people living in Colorado's dry climate. The spa's gift boutique features pampering body products, home spa items, pajamas, books and unusual jewelry. Whispering Pines is a fantastic location for a bridal shower, baby shower or special birthday. You can cater the party yourself or let Whispering Pines make all arrangements. Gift certificates are also available and can be ordered by phone and delivered to your e-mail for instant downloading. All this and more awaits you at Whispering Pines. Plan a retreat for your body and soul at Whispering Pines Day Spa, just half an hour from downtown Denver.

32156 Castle Court, Suite 209, Evergreen CO
(303) 674-SPA3 (7723) *www.whisperingpinesspa.com*

Nick's Pro Fitness
HEALTH & BEAUTY: *Best workout center*

Nick's Pro Fitness in Evergreen is a workout center that offers an entirely new approach to life. A first visit to Nick's Pro Fitness begins with an interview by owner Nick Kapande, who seeks to determine the full spectrum of your fitness interests and personal goals. Nick can then help you develop conditioning regimens along with the necessary accountability for you to be successful in your workout pursuits. One of the reasons that Nick is so impressive is that he directs by demonstration; he believes that participants are much more likely to follow someone who leads by example. The results of his programs are impressive, indeed. His clients can attest to improved conditioning, weight loss and other traditional body refinements. Nick's programs are designed for those who are prepared to fully commit themselves to becoming the best they can be. With that level of physical, mental and emotional commitment, Nick knows you will succeed. He holds a fourth-degree black belt in Tae Kwon Do and is sought after as a personal coach, martial artist and motivational speaker. This inspirational teacher is devoted to your success and looks for students ready to try discipline, focus and a lot of hard work to create change. Stop by for a trial class and see what Nick's Pro Fitness can do for you.

2788 Meadow Drive, Units D and E, Evergreen CO
(303) 679-6267
www.nicksprofitness.com

Healthy Glows
HEALTH & BEAUTY: *Best tanning salon*

Owner Cindy Rolofson calls her Healthy Glows business in Evergreen a 20-minute vacation spot. Customers can drop in for a session in one of the four tanning units and leave looking like they just got back from the Caribbean. They can enhance that sunny feeling with a smoothie, perhaps something exotic like the Elk Meadow Mango, with its creamy mango and pineapple taste of the tropics. Cindy combines tanning and refreshments in a number of creative packages. The Jamaica Break includes 15 minutes in a tanning bed, a lotion shot and a regular smoothie, while the Maui Wowi offers a 12-minute Turbo Ultra Bed session with a high-pressure facial, a lotion shot and a large smoothie. Many customers come by for the smoothies only, or for coffee, latte or chai tea. You can purchase oxygen by the minute at the oxygen bar. Healthy Glows promotes tanning as a safe way of providing the skin with Vitamin D. Dermatologists often recommend the treatment for acne and dermatitis. You'll find clean, maintained beds and a facility certified by the Smart Tan Association. For a vacation during your lunch break, go to Healthy Glows.

32156 Evergreen Court, Suite 104, Evergreen CO
(303) 679-1385

Pangaea Handmade Carpets
HOME: *Best handmade carpets from around the world*

T. Robinson, owner of Pangaea Handmade Carpets, was 12 years old when his grandfather gave him his first nomadic rug. That marked the beginning of his magic carpet collection. Twenty-five years later, Robinson founded his rug specialty shop in Evergreen. To fill his shop, he began traveling the world in search of beautiful and unique rugs. He has achieved success in his business because of his laid-back personality and his business acumen. When locating rugs and exotic carpets, Robinson determines what people will like by listening to his own instincts and to customer requests. "When I decided to make a life change and wanted to focus on all my interests, experiences and travels, I established Pangaea," says Robinson. "My customers want their homes to look and feel warm and unique, so I help them achieve that goal with an exclusive collection of styles, sizes and prices." Pangaea provides fair prices on a large selection of imported rugs from all over the world, including Turkey, Tibet, Iran and Pakistan. These hand knotted beauties will easily outlast machine made rugs by as much as 50 years, all the time delivering their artistic splendor to your home. Treat your floors to a work of art at Pangaea Handmade Carpets.

27965 Meadow Drive, Evergreen CO (inside Mountain Home)
(303) 679-4447
www.pangaeacarpets.com

The Village Gourmet

HOME: *Best kitchen and pantry supply*

It's gratifying to know when your patronage supports local business. Buying products of Colorado acts as a home grown guarantee that residents and visitors find irresistible. The Village Gourmet, located 30 minutes from downtown Denver, offers a unique assortment of locally manufactured gourmet foods, mountain kitchenware and gifts for the home. Owners Lori and Timothy Ward opened their business over 20 years ago in the Market Place at Bergen Park. They've built a considerable clientele that are dedicated to utilizing their home keeping and body care products. Among the kitchenware items shoppers will be amazed at the seemingly limitless selection of kitchen gadgetry or other favorites such as the many gourmet foods from all over the United States. Name brands like Stonewall kitchens and Henckel's cutlery have distinguished The Village Gourmet as a high quality establishment. Laurie and Timothy invite you to stop by The Village Gourmet for gift shopping or a gadget or two for yourself.

1193 Bergen Parkway, Evergreen CO (303) 670-0717

Mountain Hearth & Patio
HOME: *Best fireplace and stove selection*

The friendly professionals at Mountain Hearth & Patio, a division of Mountain Man Fireplace and Chimney, Inc, are dedicated to improving the warmth, comfort and beauty of your home. Their extensive lineup of high-quality fireplaces, stoves and hearth accessories is certain to meet your needs and their focus on customer satisfaction will exceed your expectations. What really sets Mountain Hearth & Patio apart, however, is their impressive list of industry credentials and their ability to expertly install and service everything they sell. They've got it all: sweeps certified by the Chimney Safety Institute of America, installers certified by the National Fireplace Institute and even a F.I.R.E. Service Certified Fireplace Inspector. And if that wasn't enough, they're also now qualified to design and install an outdoor room on your deck or in your backyard. Whether it's a gas burning firepit, a complex grilling island or even a snazzy water fountain, Mountain Hearth & Patio has the quality and selection you need and want. Nita and Jake Johnson invite you to visit them for all of your hearth and patio needs—you'll be glad you did.

7001 Highway 73, Evergreen CO
303.670.0658
www.mtnhp.com

Mountain Home

HOME: *Best handcrafted furnishings and decorative art*

Evergreen is one of those distinctive areas in the United States that attracts a population of highly educated, well-traveled, interesting and independent people. Mountain Home has created an offering of furniture, antiques, rugs, art and decorative accents and placed them in the remodeled barn that was once a part of the historic Hiwan Homestead. This combination is one of the most unique settings to be found in the Rocky Mountain West. It allows furnishings and decorative art to be seen in a building that synthesizes the concept of a mountain home. The wood and vaulted ceilings of the barn reflect the handcrafted character of the pieces displayed in the store. Customers of Mountain Home are able to see the items they are interested in as they might be placed in a home. The friendly sales staff adds to the value of shopping at Mountain Home by assisting with interior design ideas, experience and knowledge. Kay, Ted, Charlie, Gwen, Birgit, Laurie and Kim invite you to share this wonderful, old building and its exciting contents.

27965 Meadow Drive, Evergreen CO (303)-674-3345 or (303) 674-3346

Rustic Point

HOME: *Best mountain home furnishings*

Rustic Point is Evergreen's source for quintessential, mountain home furnishings. The log furniture and leather upholstery at Rustic Point set a distinctive tone in your home or cabin and speak to the Rocky Mountain way of life enjoyed here. Rustic Point builds heirloom quality pieces for any room in your house, using northern white cedar and juniper wood. Bunk beds, living room pieces or a knotty cedar billiards table are some of the possibilities and owners Dave and Sara MacBean and their friendly staff will happily show you more ways to add rustic charm to your dwelling. Master craftsmen build each piece by hand, sculpting aromatic cedar into functional designs with the look of the west and the features sought by modern homeowners, such as dovetail drawers and concealed hinges. The store's craftsmen can build to your specifications or design for timeless pieces that will be passed down to the next generation. In addition to high quality, hand made furniture, Rustic Point offers a full range of unique mountain accessories and gifts to compliment any home. Rustic Point can help turn your home into a true mountain getaway.

27945 Meadow Drive, Evergreen CO
(303) 225-4660
www.rusticpoint.com

Monica M. Durante Interiors

HOME: *Evergreen's expert in home transformation*

Whether you are building a new house from the ground up, need a kitchen remodeled, or have one room that just needs a little updating, let Monica M. Durante Interiors make your home fabulous. Monica, whose love of design began when she was a young child remodeling her dollhouse, works with customers on any budget to beautify their living quarters. If you have bland spaces where nothing seems quite right, but the furnishings remain in good condition, call for Monica's signature one-day room makeover. Using items the homeowner already has, Monica redesigns and rearranges to give the area an entirely new look. Check out her website for before and after pictures of the transformations. For people preparing to put their homes on the market, Monica offers real estate enhancement, in which she makes changes that allow a house to stand out from the competition, resulting in a quicker sale at a better price. When transitioning to a new place, explore your decorating options in a consultation or personal shopping appointment and make your next abode reflect your personality. The fresh and inviting designs recently earned Monica's business feature stories in *Mountain Living* and *Boulder County Home & Garden* magazines. Though she is a busy woman, Monica makes time for community service work, including volunteering as the design coordinator for Blue Spruce Habitat for Humanity. Call Monica M. Durante Interiors to let your house shine.

Evergreen CO
(303) 670-6731
www.monicadurante.com

Paragon Sports
RECREATION: *Best sporting supplies*

Jennifer and Casey Boone started Paragon Sports in 1985 to express their love of mountain sports. The store carries a full line of equipment for skiing, snowboarding, soccer and swimming. It also specializes in outdoor clothing and shoes. Paragon has repeatedly been named Business of the Year by the Evergreen Chamber of Commerce and the best place to buy sporting goods by local publications. Service is key to Paragon's success. Casey and Jennifer speak glowingly of their staff, including Becky Cooke, a marketing and advertising specialist, and Colleen Gottlieb, buyer and floor manager. Staff members in turn believe the Boones foster a family atmosphere. Paragon's employees are well versed in the characteristics of the products they sell and can describe the advantages of a particular line of skis or of merino wool clothing. Paragon stocks only the highest quality products. If a manufacturer does not maintain quality, Paragon will stop selling its goods. Paragon also rents skis and other equipment and has an annex shop for heavily discounted off-season merchandise. Evergreen, west of Denver, has many community-oriented businesses, and Paragon Sports is second to none in community spirit. In addition to giving to many local charities, the store sponsors an annual fund-raiser for the local high schools that includes a fashion show. Casey Boone was formerly a backcountry guide and is one of the most avalanche-savvy people in the region. He makes gripping educational presentations on avalanches. Visit Paragon Sports for the best in sporting goods!

2962 Evergreen Parkway, Evergreen CO
(303) 670-0092

The Blue Quill Angler
RECREATION: *Best angling outfitter*

"Gone fishing," reads the sign hanging in the closed shop window of The Blue Quill Angler whenever the proprietors are off rejuvenating. Located 25 minutes west of Denver, The Blue Quill Angler has been voted Outfitter of the Year by Orvis two years in a row. They feature world-class fly fishing gear in the store as well as online. Their guide service is endorsed by Orvis and accesses many of the best public and private waters in Colorado. Scheduled guide trips serve from three to fifty anglers at a time, all from different walks of life. The highly-skilled staff guides hundreds of full day as well as half day fishing experiences year-round. The Blue Quill Angler School of Fly Fishing offers a variety of courses for different interests and proficiency levels. Check the website for staff biographies, product lines and course descriptions. Since 1988, the Rocky Mountain fly fishing experts from The Blue Quill Angler have been providing group instruction for team building events. If you are planning professional development for your company or simply need some individual rest and relaxation, hang up your gone fishing sign and visit The Blue Quill Angler.

1532 Bergen Parkway, Evergreen CO
(303) 674-4700 or (800) 435-5353
www.bluequillangler.com

Tin Star Café and Donut Haus

RESTAURANTS & CAFÉS: *Most creative café and caterer in Evergreen*

Tin Star Café and Donut Haus in Evergreen appeals to just about everybody, thanks to owner Andrew Shutt's culinary talents and taste for variety. As the chef at Tin Star, Andrew keeps the food interesting from 5:30 am to 5:30 pm, seven days a week, with such startling delights as the asparagus pita. Pork lovers can get their fill with the Pig Pile, and beef lovers will rejoice over the Tasty Cow. Tin Star might be the only business of its kind in the world, specializing in both BBQ and homemade donuts. You will fall in love with the homemade apple fritter, a local favorite. Andrew is also a caterer who puts his talents to work at occasions both large and small throughout the foothills. He is also a concessionaire for Evergreen Lake Presents, a summer concert series that features bands every other Wednesday from June through September. Andrew would be a good choice for your next shindig in the hills. Give Andrew a call to discuss your needs, or better yet, stop by and try the creative selections at the Tin Star Café and Donut Haus.

28025 Highway 74, Evergreen CO
(303) 674-STAR (7827) (Catering)
(303) 679-1155 (Store)

Cactus Jack's Saloon & Grill

RESTAURANTS & CAFÉS: *Evergreen's best for live music*

Cactus Jack's Saloon & Grill offers customers great food and good times every day of the year, serving up classic pub fare in a laid-back atmosphere. Owner Gary Mitchell bought the bar and grill in 2001 from his good friend Allen Major, who opened it in 1996. At Cactus Jack's Saloon & Grill you can snack on jalapeño poppers, onion rings or chicken wings, or dig into a juicy burger for something more substantial. You can make the burger into your own masterpiece with a host of toppings, including bacon, mushrooms and pepper jack cheese. The accompanying fries are hand cut in-house and tossed in Cactus Jack's secret spices. Wash your meal down with an ice-cold beer on tap, poured by one of the people named best bartender by *Citysearch*. The creek-side deck, open year-round, is home to a music series that runs Saturday and Sunday afternoons throughout the summer. Relax in the fresh air while rock, bluegrass and cover bands jam. Friday and Saturday nights, head indoors for the live shows with no cover charge. Two pool tables where tournaments regularly occur, a pinball machine and a jukebox add to the fun of an evening at CJ's. Come to Cactus Jack's Saloon & Grill, which promises Good Times, Great Food and the Best in Live Music.

4651 Highway 73, Evergreen CO
(303) 674-1564
www.cactusjacksaloon.com

Fabulous Foothill Flurries

SHOPPING:
Best whimsical gift store

Imagine yourself completely surrounded by thousands of moose, bears and other woodland creatures. Visit Foothill Flurries in the charming town of Evergreen and you might just find one to take home with you. This darling store is packed to the brim with the most original and whimsical mountain furnishings and décor, which will surely find a place in your home and your heart. Lesley Fried, who runs the store, says, "It is extremely rare that someone comes in here and doesn't find something, if not many things, that they like." No matter who you are shopping for, this fine selection of affordable gifts makes it easy. They have rustic tabletop photo holders, Banky's for the little one (a snuggly little blanket with a critter head on one corner and a little critter bottom on the other), and day clocks. Foothill Flurries carries Colorado's largest selection of Bearfoots and Mountain Moose by Big Sky Carvers. If you are looking for decorations perfect for a mountain home, this is your place. The assortment of natural garlands, gold and silver plated, authentic aspen leaves made in Colorado, and ornaments of all varieties will keep your guests impressed. They also feature a full array of candies, such as huckleberry-filled chocolate cordials, Elk Droppings chocolate candies and cute woodland bowls to hold it all. Not only does Foothill Flurries have some of the greatest mountain merchandise around, but their selection of carved bears, moose and bunnies are made by a local craftsman. They carry candles by Evergreen Candleworks, which are made with a refillable soy-based wax and are affectionately referred to as their spa candles. Find a complete line of Colorado Dallas wrought iron lighting fixtures, bath accessories and wall hangings in a variety of different designs and made in nearby Jefferson. So when you find yourself in an avalanche of lighting, furnishings, and bears... oh my, you've found your way to Foothill Flurries. The wondrous wildlife and friendly folks at Foothill Flurries are located between Safeway and the Post Office on the Evergreen Parkway frontage road.

3783 Evergreen Parkway, Evergreen CO
(303) 670-1550 or (888) 506-6292
www.foothillflurries.com

Creekside Cellars

WINERIES: *Best winery*

Located downtown in the charming mountain community of Evergreen, Creekside Cellars is a family owned business that started as a hobby for its owner, Bill Donahue. Bill developed his interest in wine in high school while dating his wife-to-be. Her grandfather was a winemaker and, according to Mrs. Donahue, wine was always served with Sunday dinner. This led to Bill's appreciation for the relationship wine shared with food in his wife's Italian family. The Creekside website explores this relationship with helpful information on appropriate pairings. Wine selections are numerous and include such favorites as Moscato Bianco, Moscato Arancio and Cabernet Franc Reserve. All wines are subject to availability and sold exclusively at the winery. Creekside Cellars offers tours, tastings and classes, suitable for novices and connoisseurs. Creekside also offers a full delicatessen with an outdoor deck overlooking Bear Creek. Taste a variety of wines and pair them with such delicacies as the antipasto platter, cheese board, the homemade soup of the day or any one of the large Italian sandwiches. The deck offers opportunities for viewing deer, elk and ducks. Creekside Cellars provides a special place to celebrate intimate dinners or private parties with family and friends along with catering services. The weekly acoustic guitar and vocal performances of Rick Schiedman are also popular. Bill invites you to visit Creekside Cellars when you are looking for good wine and good food among good people.

28036 Highway 74, Evergreen CO
(303) 674-5460
www.creeksidecellars.net

FIRESTONE

Firestone is a comprehensively planned community with more than 35 parks, 12 miles of trails and other recreational facilities. A key component of the park and recreation system is the Firestone Trail, which is more than 12 miles long and provides connections to area parks, the regional St. Vrain Legacy Trail and the Colorado Front Range Trail system. In 2005, Firestone's population exceeded 5,750 people. That is three times the town's population in 2000. The town is busily developing parks and other infrastructure to meet the needs of its new residents. Firestone cooperates with Frederick and Dacono, adjacent towns, on many issues. Both towns are experiencing growth similar to Firestone's. The three towns, known collectively as Carbon Valley, were founded a century ago as coal-mining communities.

Places to Go

- Firestone Central Park
  Sable Avenue and Colorado Boulevard

- Milavec Park
  Colorado Boulevard and Grant Avenue, Frederick

- St. Vrain State Park
  3525 State Highway 119
  (303) 678-9402

Things to Do

July
- Fourth at Firestone
  (303) 833-3291

St. Vrain River
Photo by Jordan Klein

Cho Cho's
RESTAURANTS & CAFÉS:
Best authentic Mexican food

Do you rate eating good food as one of your passions? Do you love big portions of authentic Mexican food? If so, you are a perfect candidate for regular attendance at Cho Cho's Mexican Restaurant and Cantina. Danny and Melody Martinez made a family dream into reality for Danny's parents, Joe and Agnes Martinez, who always wanted to own a Mexican restaurant. Today, the entire Martinez family is involved in bringing the best of their family traditions to their customers. Danny and Melody enjoy presenting their customers with treasured recipes that are over 50 years old. Cho Cho's is the nickname for their empanadas, which are a homemade tortilla dough stuffed with a variety of ingredient's, then deep fried to a golden brown. A deluxe Cho Cho is smothered with green chile and topped with lettuce, cheese and tomato. Breakfast selections include breakfast burritos, Huevos Rancheros and a Firestone special. Dinners include combination plates, Warrior tacos and chile rellenos. tamales, burritos, flautas, chimichangas, enchiladas, tacos and tostadas are other authentic and delicious options. Repeat customers show their faces many times a week as they indulge in the restaurant's signature green chile. Beyond coffee, tea and soda, look for margaritas and a variety of domestic and Mexican beers. Dine in or drive thru, either way you are guaranteed that your passion for a big authentic Mexican meal will be a fulfilling experience.

11078 Cimarron Street, Firestone CO
(303) 776-4277
http://chochosrestaurant.biz

Sassafrass

SHOPPING: *Showcasing Colorado's foremost women artisans*

Does a visit to an eclectic collection of elegant primitive merchandise sound intriguing? If so, the magical collaboration of creative friends at Sassafrass is for you. Owner Amy Schmidt envisioned Sassafrass after several years of producing and merchandising her own artwork. She met other artists along the way and discovered that together they could augment and complement each other's work. Eight women run the store, but the treasures found in Sassafrass come from as many as 20 of Colorado's foremost women artisans. Hand painted furniture, custom stained glass, hand thrown pottery and original oil paintings offer tantalizing options for home decoration. Gift possibilities include vintage and hand stitched pillows, linens, hand stamped cards, beaded jewelry and clay doodles. Interior and exterior metal art, custom silk floral designs, lamps, rugs, hand sewn dolls and vintage antiques and artifacts all contribute to the eclectic mix. The shop also carries such fine collectibles as Sid Dickens decorative tiles and Vaillancourt chalkware Santas. Trendy clothing, belts and purses will inspire a new look. Merchandise changes with the seasons and the inspirations of the artists. Committed to excellence, the women at Sassafrass are excited to share their enthusiasm with their clientele family. Browse frequently at Sassafrass, where nothing is run-of-the-mill, and there is always something new and intriguing to engage your senses.

11078 Cimarron Street, Firestone Co
(303) 776-4277

Photos by Jim Oberlander

FORT COLLINS

Money magazine believes that Fort Collins is the number-one best place to live in the entire country. It follows that it's a great place to visit, too. The army founded Fort Collins as a post in 1864. The town has Franklin Avery to thank for the wide streets he established when he surveyed it in 1873. Old Town Fort Collins is filled with shops that feature nature goods, antiques, candy and much else. Almost a hundred restaurants can satisfy any craving. You may notice that Old Town strongly resembles Disneyland's Main Street, U.S.A. Actually, Disneyland modeled its street after downtown Fort Collins. On weekends you can ride a restored trolley from downtown to City Park. Situated on the Cache la Poudre River, with more than 125,000 residents, Fort Collins is the largest city and the seat of Larimer County and is home to Colorado State University. The large college-age demographic helps support a thriving local music scene. Lincoln Center is home to the Fort Collins Symphony Orchestra and regularly attracts national tours. The city boasts a number of well-regarded microbreweries as well as an Anheuser-Busch plant.

Places to Go

- Budweiser Brewery (tours)
  2351 Busch Drive

- City Park Pool
  1599 City Park Drive

- City Park Railway (miniature)
  1599 City Park Drive

- Colorado State University Arboretum
  630 W Lake Street

- Discovery Science Center
  703 E Prospect Road

- Edora Park
  1420 E Stuart Street

- Environmental Leaning Center
  3745 E Prospect Road

- Fort Collins Museum
  200 Mathews Street

- Fort Collins Museum of Contemporary Art
  201 S College Avenue

Edora Skatepark, Fort Collins
Photo by Gregor Younger

One of the many creatures on display in the Swetsville Zoo
Photo by Sean Mason

- Fort Fun
  1513 E Mulberry Street
- Fossil Creek Park
  5821 S Lemay Avenue
- Gateway Mountain Park
  5216 Poudre Canyon Highway
- Horsetooth Mountain Park
  County Road 38E
- Lee Martinez Park
  600 N Sherwood Street
- Lory State Park
  708 Lodgepole Drive, Bellvue
- Rocky Mountain Raptor Center
  Environmental Drive
- Rolland Moore Park
  2201 S Shields Street
- Swetsville Zoo (metal sculpture)
  4801 E Harmony Road

Things to Do

March
- St. Patrick's Day Parade
  (970) 484-6500

June
- Old Town Car Show
  (970) 484-6500
- Colorado Brewfest
  (970) 484-6500

July
- Independence Day Celebration
  fcgov.com/july4th

August
- NewWestFest
  (970) 484-6500

September
- Native American Music Festival
  www.counciltree.org
- Northern Colorado Greek Festival
  (970) 667-5778

October
- Sundance Bluegrass Festival
  (970) 224-6026

December
- Carolfest
  (970) 484-6500
- FirstNight Fort Collins
  (970) 484-6500

Sheldon House Bed & Breakfast
ACCOMMODATIONS: *Best bed and breakfast*

The place you stay should be as memorable as the trip itself, contend Maryann and Jack Blackerby, owners of the charming, two-story Sheldon House Bed & Breakfast. The B&B, a Fort Collins historical landmark, was built at the turn of the 20th century for Charles Sheldon, a Fort Collins banker, and his family. An example of the Foursquare style of architecture, the Sheldon House features four distinctively decorated rooms, each with a private bath and wireless Internet access. Its location puts guests within walking distance to Colorado State University and downtown shopping, dining and nightlife. The innkeepers see their current career as a natural extension of what they have done their entire working lives. Maryann spent 37 years as a nurse and Jack continues his position as a part-time physical therapist. They always wanted to own a bed-and-breakfast, and since taking over the Sheldon House in 2000, they have enjoyed welcoming people from all over the world. Part of the pampering here includes a sumptuous breakfast with generous portions of fresh fruit, juices, homemade baked goods and coffees to accompany the special daily breakfast entrée. Jack and Maryann treasure the opportunity to share stories with guests about their home and family, Fort Collins, or traveling. Guests can certainly look forward to a memorable stay at the historic Sheldon House Bed & Breakfast.

616 W Mulberry Street, Fort Collins CO
(970) 221-1917 or (877) 221-1918
www.thesheldonhouse.com

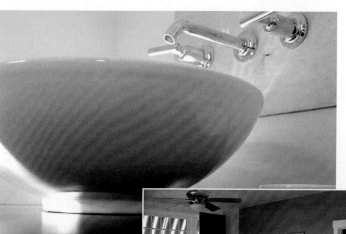

The Armstrong Hotel
ACCOMMODATIONS: *Best rooms and suites*

The Armstrong Hotel opened in 1923 and is the only historic hotel still operating in downtown Fort Collins. After years of decline, the classic hotel had been vacant for three years before Steve and Missy Levinger purchased it in November 2002. Amazingly, in June 2004, only nine months after the Levingers began their award-winning restoration, the hotel reopened. The 34,000-square-foot boutique hotel features 37 nostalgic and distinctive rooms and suites that offer comfort and elegance without being pretentious. The retro modern décor reflects both the hotel's heritage and the vitality of its lively downtown setting. The Levingers' painstaking restoration received the Governor's Award for downtown excellence, a State Honor Award from Colorado Preservation Inc., and a Certificate of Excellence from the Fort Collins Historical Society. The bedding for each room includes a pillow-top mattress, 100 percent cotton sheets and a snuggly down comforter and pillows to ensure a good night's rest. Some rooms feature wet bars and kitchenettes, and every room offers complimentary high-speed Internet access with a wireless option, along with spacious workstations and standard cable television. Guests can borrow a complimentary cruiser bicycle to explore the shopping, dining and entertainment in bustling Old Town. Whether you're traveling for business or pleasure, come to the historic Armstrong Hotel for ambience, comfort and an accommodating staff.

259 S College Avenue, Fort Collins CO
(970) 484-3883 or (866) 384-3883
www.thearmstronghotel.com

Rover's Ranch

We know you don't want to, we know you don't like it, but sometimes you have to leave your pet behind when you travel. For those times when we absolutely must leave our loved ones behind, it's good to know there are people like Serene Flesch out there. Serene, owner of Rover's Ranch in Fort Collins, brings 16 years of pet care experience and a lifetime of love to soothing the anxiety of human/animal separation. Whether canine or feline, your partner will smile when you come home, because they will have been well-fed, well-handled and allowed to play. Serene, who spent six years as the primary caregiver for a humane society chapter before opening Rover's Ranch, doesn't flinch at special dietary or medical needs, and she doesn't discriminate against breeds. She brings the same personalized care in a facility that boasts three play yards for large dogs and another for small dogs. She offers grooming services, and both long-term pet vacations and short-term doggy day care. There's nothing nicer than picking up a happy, freshly groomed pet when you come home. Call Serene at Rover's Ranch next time you need a reliable, caring place to entrust your friend.

4837 Terry Lake Road, Fort Collins CO (970) 493-5970

The Tea Table

BAKERIES, COFFEE & TEA:
Best on-line tea source

Tea, with its exotic flavors and time-honored rituals, has long been enjoyed by numerous cultures across the globe. But what many people are learning is that tea can also be a healthful addition to any diet. The Tea Table, a tea-oriented Internet business based in Colorado, is owned and operated by Lori Bricker, a registered dietitian who focuses her studies on the healthful benefits of tea. The Tea Table offers more than 150 varieties of loose tea that can be purchased by the ounce or in bulk, along with a fabulous selection of tea accoutrements, such as teapots and cups by Bee House, whimsical infusers and a delightful assortment of spoons, sugar tongs and strainers. The Tea Table additionally stocks a terrific collection of books dedicated to both the art of tea and the importance of proper manners. You can give the gift of tea with Lori's wonderful gift sets, which are artfully arranged and filled with an assortment of teas and goodies that are sure to please. For those interested in trying a variety of teas, The Tea Table offers a Tea of the Month club that lets you select a Tea Plan of interest, such as the Oolong or Chai Plan. Lori will ship new and flavorful selections from your plan to you monthly. Learn more about the healthful properties of tea and have your favorite selections shipped right to your door with a visit to The Tea Table, your online source for exceptional tea.

PO Box 8154, Fort Collins CO
(970) 221-5520 or (866) 551-5520
www.theteatable.com

OpenStage Theatre & Company

ATTRACTIONS: *Best theater company in Fort Collins*

Somebody should write a play about OpenStage Theatre & Company in Fort Collins. It is a tale of dreams and perseverance, of decades of births and deaths, of reversals and triumphs; a story that has run longer than any of the original players could ever have imagined, with an ending yet to be written. OpenStage Theatre & Company began on a shoestring in 1973 when Denise Burson Freestone and her husband Bruce Freestone decided to launch their own theater company. Thirty-four years later, the company is home to over 150 artists, 700 season ticket-holders and two off-shoot projects, Rabbit Hole Radio Theatre and *openstage etc*. The name of the company came partly from the fact that their first productions were staged outdoors, but mostly from the open-minded philosophy of the company's founders and artists when it comes to the projects they tackle. OpenStage, which moved into the Lincoln Center in 1978, has been honored numerous times through the years, including a Governor's Award for Excellence in the Arts. The town of Fort Collins is something of a phenomenon when it comes to theater and the arts, boasting more aspiring and successful companies than a town its size could ever expect. OpenStage Theatre & Company, one of Fort Collins' artistic pioneers, deserves a lot of the credit for the vibrancy of the local arts scene. The next time you are in Fort Collins, be sure to call or visit the OpenStage website to learn about their ongoing projects. OpenStage Theatre & Company is a big part of the reason Fort Collins is such a wonderful place to visit or live in.

417 W Magnolia Street, Fort Collins CO
(970) 484-5237 or (970) 221-6730 (box office)
www.openstage.com

Sunflour Bakery

BAKERIES, COFFEE & TEA: *Fort Collins' most popular bakery*

Tempting aromas waft across the Square Shopping Center luring visitors away from their shopping and straight to the Sunflour Bakery. Once inside, they can satisfy cravings they didn't even know they had with an array of decadent delights. Sunflour Bakery is owned and operated by two talented couples, Eryn and Dave Rogers and Sarah and Clay Lant. Opened in 2000, the bakery is a source for such freshly baked treats as brownies, cookies and cheesecakes, as well as their elegantly crafted, custom wedding cakes. They have recently started serving breakfast and lunch, along with

a full line of desserts. In the morning you can choose from fluffy three-egg omelettes, perfectly prepared eggs Benedict or French toast made from handmade Texas toast or banana bread. The lunch menu features equally tempting options, including a variety of sandwiches, burgers and pasta dishes. Since opening, Sunflour Bakery has doubled its business each year. Clay and Dave each had more than 20 years of experience in the restaurant field prior to opening the bakery, and their expertise resonates in every aspect of the business. In addition to offering personalized customer service, the quartet supports local sustainability by using fresh ingredients purchased from area farmers and local businesses. Indulge your desire for delicious treats and gourmet goodies at the Sunflour Bakery.

3500 S College Avenue, Suite 14, Fort Collins CO
(970) 226-1836
www.thesunflourbakery.com

Portraits By Betsy
BUSINESS: *Best portraits*

Anybody with a camera can capture an image, but it takes an artist like Betsy Strafach to go deeper and capture the essence beneath the image. Betsy, the creative genius behind Portraits By Betsy in Fort Collins, is an award-winning artist who is known as an expert in capturing the lives of families, especially babies, on film. A photographer for 20 years, she is passionate in her belief that families should take the opportunity to record the irretrievable moments of their journey together, because life is a series of stages that do not repeat. A baby is two weeks old only once. A child turns five only once. Every moment in life, though we may not always appreciate it, occurs just once. Betsy is a master at helping families record these moments for posterity. She is one of the few Colorado photographers to donate her services to Now I Lay Me Down To Sleep. This is an inspirational program in which families facing the loss of a terminally ill infant are given the opportunity to photograph their child as an aid in the family's healing. At a family's request, the program sends photographers like Betsy to a hospital or hospice to shoot a sensitive portrait session. Parents are provided with an archival DVD or CD containing portraits of their cherished baby at no cost. Don't let another precious moment slip away. Call Betsy Stafach and let her work her photographic magic for you.

(970) 225-9220
www.portraitsbybetsy.com

The Cottonwood Club

EVENTS: *Best banquet and events center in Fort Collins*

Ensure that your next special occasion, be it a wedding, reunion or corporate function, is a complete success by hosting it at the Cottonwood Club, where nothing is ever compromised or left to chance. The Cottonwood Club is one of northern Colorado's largest and most inclusive banquet and event centers, as well as being one of the area's favored off-site catering companies. Kerry E. and Michael Schroeder, life and business partners, opened the Cottonwood Club in 1996 and have since earned a reputation for excellence in service and hospitality. The Schroeder's strive to make each visitor feel like honored guests who are being welcomed in to enjoy a once-in-a-lifetime gala that is highlighted by outstanding cuisine, gracious service and the elegant ambience and romance of the French countryside. The event center offers more than 10,000 square feet of space, which includes several rooms that can comfortably accommodate 10 to 50 people for meetings or corporate events, and up to 225 for banquets and weddings. The Cottonwood Club has a full conference package available that includes a Continental breakfast, beverage service and luncheon, as well as necessary audiovisual equipment. The event center's full time chefs are experts who use finely honed skills to prepare exquisite wedding cakes and pastries, along with delicious hors d'oeuvres, entrées and side dishes that will leave you satiated and smiling. Create joyous memories that will last a lifetime at the Cottonwood Club.

6813 S College Avenue, Fort Collins CO
(970) 226-3463
www.cottonwoodclub.com

All Occasions Catering/Nita Crisps
EVENTS: *Best caterers in Fort Collins*

It would be very difficult to categorize Paul and Nenita Pellegrino, except to say they are in love with food, their community and each other. The owners of All Occasions Catering, Paul and Nenita are also the makers of Nita Crisp crackers, a flattened bread cracker sold extensively through natural foods stores and specialty markets across the country. Paul comes from a rich and colorful food background. His grandfather and father sang as they peddled vegetables from the back of a horse-drawn cart in New Jersey in the 1920s. Paul's father owned a restaurant in New Jersey called Ralph's that was a local institution. Carrying on the family tradition, Paul became a chef at large resorts in the Cayman Islands, Virgin Islands and elsewhere. Today he and Nenita run one of Colorado's best-loved catering companies, All Occasions Catering. They are the caterer of choice in Fort Collins, with a Who's Who list of clients, ranging from The Beach Boys and Willie Nelson to Ray Charles and the Fort Collins Chamber of Commerce. They can handle any kind of event, no matter how large, from weddings to major corporate and show business events. Paul and Nenita are known for their generosity, giving back to the community in numerous ways. They consider the Nita Crisps business to be a community endeavor, using disabled people to package and label their products. The next time you need a caterer who can provide excellence and personality, call Paul and Nenita at All Occasions Catering.

446 S Link Lane, Fort Collins CO
(970) 224-5643
www.all-occasions-catering.com
http://nitacrisp.com

Simply Chocolate
FUN FOODS: *Best chocolate in Fort Collins*

As a native of Belgium, Martine Deboodt, owner of Simply Chocolate, knows all about chocolate. She has turned that knowledge and her passion, into a thriving business in just three short years. Martine, who moved to the United States in 1999, became the face of Simply Chocolate in 2002 and has since earned a reputation for having some of the best chocolate in the state. Martine says that many of her faithful customers claim that hers is the best chocolate they have ever tasted, which is due to the fact that she uses only the freshest products and finest European chocolates from Ghent and Brussels. Simply Chocolate offers more than 60 different kinds of sumptuous truffles, as well as a distinctive selection of American candies and fine ice cream. Martine also offers a delightful array of gift baskets that have been lovingly designed and filled with decadent treats and crave-satisfying chocolates. Simply Chocolate can provide custom-wrapped chocolates and candies which are ideal for corporate or special events, such as weddings, class reunions and charitable affairs. Martine's ultimate goal is to provide exceptional chocolate and bring a touch of Europe to Fort Collins. Indulge yourself in a taste of heaven at Simply Chocolate, where every bite is chocolate perfection.

238 E Harmony Road, Ste D10, Fort Collins CO
(970) 226-8770

Eileen's Colossal Cookies
FUN FOODS: *Best cookies in Fort Collins*

There is nothing quite as tasty as a freshly baked cookie. Warm and chewy from the oven and bursting with a sweet mix of flavors, they are redolent of afternoon snacks and lazy summer days. Savor those flavors you remember or crave at Eileen's Colossal Cookies, a phenomenon that started in Colorado and has since spread across the globe to cookie connoisseurs everywhere. Martin and Lavagne Gilbert first opened Eileen's in 1997. Their son Todd, a graduate of Johnson and Wales Culinary Institute, purchased the popular Fort Collins location in 2000. Eileen's Colossal Cookies offers a wide variety of delicious flavors that are made daily from scratch. In addition to traditional classics such as chocolate chip, molasses and peanut butter, Eileen's carries some new recipes that are sure to become family favorites, like cherry chocolate chip, lemon and monster oatmeal. Todd currently ships his famous cookies across the globe to fans in places like Japan, Iraq and Brazil. Care-packages from Eileen's are a favorite on college campuses across the nation. Todd is a big advocate of giving back to the community, so he dedicates roughly 30 percent of his time to charitable causes, as well as offering cookie workshops to students. Eileen's also offers tasty gift baskets and cookie collections that are ideal for birthday parties, family barbecues or any other occasion that calls for something sweet and fun. Discover your family's favorite new cookie connection with a trip to Eileen's Colossal Cookies.

1125 W Drake, Fort Collins CO
(970) 266-9151
www.eileensfortcollins.com

Walrus Ice Cream
FUN FOODS: *Best ice cream in Fort Collins*

Walrus Ice Cream has the best ice cream in Fort Collins, but don't just take our word for it. The *Fort Collins Coloradoan* has said the same thing for the past 11 years in a row. Following its most recent poll, the paper put it this way: "The competition didn't have a chance. Walrus holds on to the title of Best Ice Cream in a landslide." Walrus Ice Cream, founded in 1987, is a locally owned business that dishes up premium, homemade ice cream the way it is supposed to be dished: any way you want it. Walrus makes and scoops more than 250 flavors of ice cream, all made in-house from the finest all-natural ingredients. They also offer a wide variety of non-ice cream yummies, including sherbets, sorbets, fruitages and low-fat yogurts. Their offerings grace all manner of cups and cones, from sugar cones to white-chocolate waffle cones, Saturdaes (and you thought sundaes were good), shakes, malts, floats, soft drinks, ice cream cakes, banana splits, and their locally-famous walrus tusk ice cream bars. Owners John & Lisa Paugh are known for more than serving the best ice cream. They are also respected locally for giving back to the community whenever possible. The next time you're in Fort Collins, sample the best there is, Walrus Ice Cream.

125 W Mountain Avenue, Fort Collins CO
(970) 482-5919
www.walrusicecream.com

Vern's Toffee House

FUN FOODS: *Best toffee in Fort Collins*

Have you ever bought someone a gift that you liked so much you were tempted to keep it for yourself? Customers of Vern's Toffee House in Fort Collins know this dilemma all too well. It's the choice they face whenver they buy gift packages of irresistible, butter almond toffee made by Ron and Mary Hert. The toffee all began in 1976 when Mary's father, Vern Hackbarth, the retired owner of a popular local restaurant, began packaging his special toffee. Given Vern's reputation for excellent food, word of the toffee spread rapidly as local customers had Vern ship toffee gifts nationally. Word-of-mouth created a burgeoning mail-order business, and soon Vern was appealing to his daughter, Mary, and her husband, Ron, to join the business. Once the former Peace Corps volunteers had learned the ropes, Vern retired, and the couple has been bringing their special brand of joy to toffee lovers the world over since 1984. They handcraft their all-natural toffee using the freshest AA sweet cream butter, California almonds and rich, pure milk-chocolate into almond encrusted batches. They handpack and gift wrap for shipping around the globe, including the birthplace of toffee, England. Corporations, businesses and professionals buy Vern's Toffee for employees and clients. Families give Vern's for birthdays, holidays and special occasions. Lovers give it to their valentines, and even Santa knows Vern's toffee pleases everyone, Vern's is, hands-down, the most supremely buttery and wickedly satisfying toffee ever. Add a box for yourself.

444 S Link Lane, Fort Collins CO
(800) 958-3767 or (970) 493-7770
www.vernstoffee.com

Audra Rose Floral & Gift Shop
GARDENS, PLANTS & FLOWERS: *Best flower and gift shop*

You can buy flowers at a lot of places, but there aren't many stores that will make you feel as well as a visit to Audra Rose Floral & Gift Shop in Fort Collins. This is because owner Kathy Udy has created an atmosphere that is easy and inviting. The staff helps to fulfill the promise to being the friendliest florist in town. Audra Rose has been in the same location for 26 years. While it is very much a neighborhood shop, it is worth a trip across town to peruse the merchandise which ranges from whimsical to elegant. "Its important to have fun so that you want to go to work," Kathy told a writer from *Lydia's Style Magazine*, which featured her in 2002. "It creates an environment your customers pick up on and you attract people who are happy." Audra Rose offers award-winning arrangements, gift baskets, interesting gift items and a wide variety of fresh-cut flowers which customers claim outlast any others. Kathy and her staff appreciate the opportunity to help their customers express themselves through the medium of floral design. Next time you want an uplifting shopping experience, call or stop by Audra Rose Floral & Gift Shop.

2170 W Drake Road B-9, Fort Collins CO
(970) 484-7778 or (800) 546-7778
www.audrarosefloral.com

Trimble Court Artisans
GALLERIES & FINE ART: *Best arts and craft co-op*

Since 1971, Trimble Court Artisans have offered exceptional arts and crafts in a turn-of-the-century building in Old Town Fort Collins. On a narrow cobblestone street that was a link between historic Old Town and new Fort Collins, a group of artisans opened a co-op to better market their work. Today that co-op thrives with artwork by more than 50 artists and artisans. The newly remodeled showroom features top-quality arts and crafts and includes stoneware and raku pottery, two-dimensional art and weavings. Artwork changes frequently here, and many pieces are representative of Colorado's culture. You'll find watercolors, wooden items, jewelry and wearable art as well as photographs, stained glass and handcrafted cards. Trimble Court participates in the First Friday Gallery Walk, which started in 1997 and includes approximately 20 galleries that stay open late the first Friday of each month. Individual galleries schedule the opening of special exhibits and new shows to coincide with the Old Town gallery walk. It's a wonderful way to see what's new, meet and mingle with the artists and purchase new artwork. Plan on spending some quality time browsing all that the Trimble Court Artisans have to offer, because there is a lot to appreciate in a place where each piece is as individual as its creator.

118 Trimble Court, Fort Collins CO
(970) 221-0051
www.trimblecourt.com

Barcelona Clinical Spa & Salon

HEALTH & BEAUTY: *Best clinical skincare*

When Barbara Sinha founded the Clinical SkinCare Centre in 1996, she had been a licensed skincare professional for more than 25 years. Cindy "CJ" Weimer met Barbara in 1989 and is a licensed esthetician and former instructor with a career in cosmetology going back almost 20 years. Barbara and CJ eventually became partners, and today CJ is the owner of Barcelona Clinical Spa & Salon, a state-of-the-art clinical skincare provider in a comfortable salon-style setting. CJ and her well-trained staff provide the latest techniques in skincare treatment, including the highly advanced PPx Skin Rejuvenation Therapy, a refined laser treatment that is gentler and more effective than other laser treatments. Barcelona offers numerous treatments and packages, including hair removal, nail treatments, massage, aromatherapy, European facials and detox treatments. They specialize in acne and anti-aging for men, women and teens. Dr. Gregory Denzel, a board certified physician and Barcelona's medical director, provides Botox, Restylane and other doctor-administered treatments. The popularity and effectiveness of Barcelona's approach is fueling an expansion for CJ and company, who have opened satellite locations in Greeley and Red Feathers Lake, with plans for additional spa's in Las Vegas, Nevada, and Phoenix, Arizona. When you want the best skincare that science has to offer and in a comfortable setting, call the Barcelona Clinical Spa & Salon.

3307 S College Avenue, Suite 112, Fort Collins CO (970) 226-2596
2929 W 10th Street, Greeley CO (970) 351-8181
Fox Acres Country Club, Red Feathers Lake CO (970) 881-2191
www.barcelonasalon-spa.com

Elements Day Spa & Wellness Center

HEALTH & BEAUTY:

Best treatments that restore balance

Elements Day Spa & Wellness Center is a place where the world stops and you begin. This world-class day spa in Fort Collins is a place of relaxation and healing where you will be nurtured, pampered and treated as if you are the most important person in the world. Owner Thanya Nguyen bases her healing approach on the five elements of water, fire, earth, metal and wood. The belief is that our well-being depends upon a balance of these universal and inter-related elements, and all of their treatments are designed to foster that balance. Elements provides a beautiful and sophisticated environment, coupled with an extensive menu of health and beauty treatments administered by a team of well trained professionals. From full-day packages to one-hour treatments and everything in between, Elements has the means to bring you into balance, including numerous spa packages, massage, facials, body treatments, and hand and feet treatments for men and women. They specialize in accommodating large parties such as bridal showers, and offer a couple's massage room where you and your partner can enjoy mutual pampering. Once you step through the doors of Elements, everything is geared to your comfort. This is your time. Take advantage of it at Elements Day Spa & Wellness Center.

2008 E Harmony Road, Fort Collins CO
(970) 377-9868
www.elements-dayspa.com

The Atrium Health Spa & Inn

HEALTH & BEAUTY: *Best spa to revitalize your health*

The Atrium Health Spa & Inn is a peaceful sanctuary dedicated to revitalizing your health. Owner Donna Corbett-Lewis says their mission is to be a center for wellness, focusing on educating, cleansing the body, and supporting the immune system. They offer the V.I.B.E. machine which can energize and strengthen cells, helping your body resist physical imbalances. After only one treatment, one customer's skin cancer decreased in size by 50 percent, and in three weeks the cancer was totally gone. Donna also supports and promotes the use of a liquid whole food supplement called Body Balance, which nourishes the body at a cellular level. One client had a critically low white blood cell count. After one bottle, her white blood cell count had doubled. The Atrium also offers the Ion Foot Cleanse, a relaxing foot bath process that extracts toxins through the feet from every major organ. After a cleansing, one customer noticed that her wrinkles were disappearing; she lost 40 pounds, gained more energy, and her mind is clearer. Other therapeutic treatments include massage therapy, the steam sauna, the infrared sauna, and the Chi Machine. Donna enjoys seeing clients experience incredible improvements from chronic syndromes such as fibromyalgia, arthritis and depression. Call if you have any questions or when you or your loved ones are in need of regaining and maintaining your health. For more information, please visit the website.

706 E Stuart Street, Fort Collins CO
(970) 482-4760
www.atriumhealthspa.net

East West Design

HOME: *Best antique Chinese furniture and lighting*

East West Design is a specialized antiques and home décor store that focuses on bringing some of the world's most beautiful antiques and home accessories to Fort Collins. Owner Pamela Ross lives in Shanghai, giving her the opportunity to personally search out antiques in China, from Shanghai in the east to the far western reaches of Tibet, Shanxi and Zhejiang. These elegant, one-of-a-kind pieces come in a variety of woods like cherry, poplar and fir. The pieces range from ornately carved designs ith intricately painted details to elegantly simple. All are chosen for their rarity, condition and function, and are refinished in ways that rejuvenate their ancient essence. In addition to furniture, Pamela finds hand-painted porcelain lamps, contemporary table sets, Chinese artwork and a host of other treasures, ranging from hand-woven bamboo tea sets to silk bedding and jewelry. East West Design is a store like no other you have visited. Take the time to be amazed at their quality and selection the next time you are in Fort Collins.

136 W Mountain Avenue, Fort Collins CO
(970) 472-1721

Syed's Asian Carpets
HOME: *Best outlet for traditional asian rugs in Fort Collins*

At dawn in the tiny shops of Asia, the shopkeepers roll up their doors and the treasures of the East appear. Now, in downtown Fort Collins, the magic of Asia has appeared in a small, narrow shop, Syed's Asian Carpets. Owner Siraj Syed offers gorgeous carpets from Afghanistan, Pakistan, Iran and other lands. Despite its size, walking into this shop is like strolling through a crowded bazaar. The walls are lined with beautiful flat woven rugs or Kurdish Kelims, Sumacs and hand-knotted carpets from nomadic tribes. Syed was born in Burma but grew up in Pakistan, where he became a helicopter pilot in the armed forces. He came to the United States in 1979 and opened the carpet store in 1999. Syed specializes in all-wool Afghani rugs that shrink evenly if washed. Afghan tribal carpets are characterized by traditional designs interpreted by each weaver. Carpets made by one tribe may contain variations of the same basic design. The symbols are an expression of the cultural heritage of the tribe. Syed visits the carpet makers of Afghanistan occasionally and is a direct importer with no middleman. His agent purchases the carpets before they are finished, and the carpets never appear in the Kabul open market. As a result, Syed can offer his carpets at very competitive prices. His weavers use the world's best wool, imported from Belgium, and employ only vegetable or chromium dye. For beautiful handmade rugs to enhance your living space, come to Syed's Asian Carpets.

208 S College Avenue, Fort Collins CO
(970) 407-1234

Total Ryu Traditional Martial Arts
RECREATION: *Best martial arts studio*

"Charles and Jill Orchard are all about kids, safety and families." states a testimonial by five family-members who participate in programs at the Orchards' Total Ryu Traditional Martial Arts studio in Fort Collins. Total Ryu builds its pricing structure around family participation with discounts for more than one family member and flexible schedules to accommodate group participation. The atmosphere here is fun and supportive, designed to make students feel like part of an extended family. The studio teaches non-competitive classes in jujitsu and karate with a focus on potential real-life experiences rather than sport techniques. Jujitsu, once used by Samurai warriors, is an excellent modern self-defense system, used as the basis for many military and police defensive tactics systems. Both adults and children benefit from the discipline. Charles began studying jujitsu at age 14 and obtained his first black belt at 17. He now possesses three black belts, and Jill has earned two black belts. The two reach out into their community with classes on child abduction prevention as well as free safety seminars and demonstrations for nonprofit organizations. Learn to protect yourself and your family within the positive learning environment at Total Ryu Traditional Martial Arts.

1420 Riverside Avenue, #100, Fort Collins CO
(970) 481-8641
www.totalryu.com

Canyon Concert Ballet
RECREATION:
Best ballet school in Fort Collins

Art of Grace, Spirit of Sophistication: Canyon Concert Ballet is committed to bringing the artistry and experience of dance to the forefront of the community. They believe that dance empowers and unites. It is through dance that both dancers and audiences gain new perspectives and awareness of the world. For 27 years, Canyon Concert Ballet has been enriching the Northern Colorado community through dance. This nonprofit was founded by Carole Torguson, who at 84 years old still attends every performance. Canyon Concert Ballet has continued to provide top-notch dance education for children starting at age three to adults. Offering a variety of dance techniques from ballet to tap, jazz, modern and hip hop, everything is done with the community in mind. With more than 500 students and a history of artistic excellence, Canyon Concert Ballet is the premier community ballet in Northern Colorado. Support Canyon Concert Ballet by attending their riveting performances and contributing through their partnership program. Canyon Concert is the place where art and spirit meet.

1031 Conifer Street, Suite 3,
Fort Collins CO
(970) 472-4156
www.ccballet.org

The Wright Life
RECREATION:
Best skate, snow and Frisbee shop

The Most Fun Wins. That's both a slogan and a mandate at The Wright Life, Fort Collins' fun specialists when it comes to skate, snow and Frisbee lovers. Bill and Holly Wright have owned The Wright Life for 25 years. Bill's knowledge of Frisbee sports and products is mind-boggling. He is the founder of The Grateful Disc, which is the first Frisbee organization on the CSU Campus, and the Coloradicals, a team of freestyle Frisbee players. In addition to the legendary flying discs, the Wrights carry everything and anything related to ride-able boards. From decks, boots, bindings and clothing to bags, books and maintenance supplies, they cover the snow and skate board spectrum. You'll also find footbags, boomerangs, juggling supplies and more. If you are a fun-meister, or you need a gift for somebody who is, visit The Wright Life, one of the best specialty stores in Colorado.

200 Linden Street, Fort Collins CO
(970) 484-6932
www.wrightlife.com

Fiona's Delicatessen & Catering
RESTAURANTS & CAFÉS: *Tastiest catering in Fort Collins*

Good food has the power to create lasting impressions, bring strangers together and strengthen family bonds unlike anything else, which is why Elizabeth and Scott McBryde, owners of Fiona's Delicatessen & Catering, are dedicated to preparing incredible foods that are both memorable and delicious. Scott, Fiona's resident chef, is classically trained in French cuisine and uses only the finest ingredients, such as locally grown produce, imported cheeses and handmade pastas. Scott and Elizabeth have designed wonderful menus filled with appetizing breakfast, brunch and luncheon ideas, as well as buffets, grilled entrées and scrumptious dinners. They also offer an extensive selection of hors d'oeuvre platters that are perfect for cocktail parties, business openings and other finger-food appropriate events. Elizabeth is eager to help with your event planning, from choosing the ideal catering menu for your special occasion to offering assistance finding flowers, equipment rentals and valet services. Fiona's is happy to prepare your order to be picked up or delivered at your convenience and can provide a full catering staff to serve you and your guests as needed. In Fiona's Delicatessen, you can indulge your gourmet desires with one of their sensational sandwiches, homemade soups or hearty salads, then give yourself over to one of their decadent desserts, like a Chocolate Kahlua bar or Tiramisu. Let incredible cuisine make a lasting impression at your next event with Fiona's Delicatessen & Catering, where they are passionate about great food.

1001 E Harmony Road, Fort Collins CO
(970) 530-2120 *www.fionasdeli.com*

The Steakout Saloon
RESTAURANTS & CAFÉS: *Most laid-back bar in Fort Collins*

According to the *Bullhorn* magazine in Fort Collins, the Steakout Saloon is a favorite on the

local dining scene. The magazine proclaims the restaurant, owned and operated by Texas A&M graduate Tim Grabham, is the best place in town for burgers, steak sandwiches and hanging out with friends. The finger foods here makes a great accompaniment to the wine and beer selections at the restaurant's full-service bar. The Steakout Saloon serves lunch and dinner, promises vibrant nightlife and encourages friends to congregate for as long as they like, day or night. The laid-back atmosphere appeals to a large core of loyal locals who call the Steakout their second home. Tim says the restaurant's philosophy is to operate like the famous fictional *Cheers*, where everybody knows your name. We don't know how many people Mondo the bartender knows, but everybody who spends time here knows and loves him. For a home away from home, where camaraderie is plentiful and the fare is casual, visit the Steakout Saloon.

152 W Mountain Avenue, Fort Collins CO
(970) 416-5989

Island Grill
RESTAURANTS & CAFÉS: *Best fish tacos in Fort Collins*

Even folks who live in a place as beautiful as Fort Collins can use a Caribbean vacation from time to time. Since purchasing the Island Grill three years ago, owners Ken Kuk and Hal Walker are staying very busy serving exotic island fare in an inviting environment. Their American Baja cuisine has filled a niche in Fort Collins by offering an extensive menu of island-inspired dishes that features delights like Bahama Mama Tacos, the Big Kahuna Burger and Chile Rellenos Camarones. The Island Grill serves up different specials throughout the week, with happy hours twice daily, as well as one of the finest Sunday brunch offers in the area. To enhance the mood, the Island Grill has murals by local artist Terry McNerney that evoke a tropical setting in this neighborhood restaurant. Ken and Hal have more than 30 years of combined restaurant experience and have tackled every aspect of the restaurant business, assuring you of an effortless, relaxing dining experience. Visit the Island Grill for an experience that transports you from the Rocky Mountains and sets you down on a Caribbean island.

2601 S Lemay #12, Fort Collins CO
(970) 266-0124
www.islandgrillrestaurant.com

Canyon Chop House
RESTAURANTS & CAFÉS: *Best casual fine dining in Fort Collins*

Matt Schump is the kind of person who would succeed at whatever he does, because he pays attention to the little things. As the owner of the Canyon Chop House in downtown Fort Collins, he instills that same sense of awareness in his staff, which is why this casual fine-dining house is known as the best place for steaks and seafood in the area. The philosophy at the Canyon Chop House is simple: treat people the way you want to be treated. The restaurant offers a gracious environment, first-class service and scrumptious fare that includes local, organic ingredients. Canyon Chop House falls into the category of a fine-dining establishment, yet is casual enough for an after-work cocktail. The menu features an impressive mix of imaginative appetizers

and specialties, including Jumbo Lump Blue Crabcakes, Pan Seared Venison Tenderloin, and a Bistro Steak-Duck Breast combo. For vegetarians, there is a chef's plate that changes daily, marvelous soups, salads and other choices. The Canyon Chop House is open for lunch on Fridays, features live entertainment every Saturday night, and offers a daily happy hour with its own specialty menu. The next time you're in downtown Fort Collins, take your appetite to the Canyon Chop House. You'll leave happy.

211 Canyon Avenue, Fort Collins CO
(970) 493-9588
www.canyonchophouse.com

Cozzola's Pizza
RESTAURANTS & CAFÉS:
Best pizza in Fort Collins

To be awarded Best Pizza in Fort Collins for the last 14 years is no small feat in a town with almost 30 pizzerias. Plainly and simply put, Owners Dave Cozzola and Norm Keally make great pizza. A large part of their success rests on Cozzola's focus on using only quality, healthful ingredients. You won't find any refined sugar in their dough, sauce or any of their pizza recipes. Crusts are sweetened with nectar, honey or molasses, depending on whether you order the traditional New York-style, whole wheat poppy seed or herb crust. Cozzola's uses only non-bromated white flour and stone-ground whole-wheat flour in its crusts. Their red sauces are made using vine-ripened, ground pear tomatoes, freshly-picked, then minimally cooked and packed immediately. Cozzola's tops its pies with Wisconsin mozzarella and provolone cheeses, shredded on premises and with none of the chemical flavor enhancers. They also offer a cholesterol-free soy cheese. Choose from a number of sauces including pesto, salsa, Thai peanut, barbecue and spinach ricotta. Both stores offer delivery and carry-out. For dine-in service visit the downtown (Linden) store, and choose from a variety of Italian and domestic wines to complement your pizza.

241 Linden Street, Fort Collins CO
(970) 482-3557
1112 Oakridge Drive, Fort Collins, CO
(970) 229-5771 (delivery & carry-out only)

Gustavo's Market

RESTAURANTS & CAFÉS:
Best homemade gourmet meals in Fort Collins

Don't let the name Gustavo's Market fool you. Gustavo's is actually a full-service restaurant with a beer and wine license, where you can sit to enjoy meals or take them with you. Owner Shana Judd is the gourmet chef here with a reputation for creating menu items on request, then naming them after the customers who inspired them. Her menu is varied, with choices from matzo balls to Maryland crab cakes. You can take home Nanny's Meatloaf, a half of roasted-chicken or a full rack of baby back ribs, along with seasonal fruit cobblers, specialty sandwiches and homemade desserts. She selects her vegetables at the local farmers market and changes her daily specials to showcase seasonal foods. You can even order takeout online, then come by to pick it up. Shana named Gustavo's after her father, himself a restaurant owner, who taught her to love cooking. She learned to appreciate gourmet fare as a child during family ventures into New York City. Shana holds a four-year degree from Colorado State University, and attended a 26-month program at the world famous Culinary Institute of America in New York. This was followed by several months in an externship program at the prestigious Hotel Jerome in Aspen, Colorado. She says she learned more there than she ever imagined she would. If the idea of a personal chef appeals to you, come by Gustavo's Market. The next dish on Shana's menu might have your name on it.

2567 S Shields, Suite 4D, Fort Collins CO
(970) 484-GUS'S (4877)
www.gustavosmarket.com

El Burrito Restaurant
RESTAURANTS & CAFÉS: *Best traditional Mexican food in Fort Collins*

The Godinez clan shares their favorite recipes with diners at El Burrito Restaurant, opened in 1960 by Jesse and Dorothy Godinez. The family continues to be faithful to the traditional Mexican food and gracious hospitality that first gained praise from customers. A midday cafeteria-style format offers diners the ability to get food quickly and then have time to savor it, even on a quick lunch break. Nibble on some of the fresh tortilla chips while you peruse the dinner menu. The crunchy snacks are made from scratch in El Burrito's kitchen daily. For your main course, try the green chile burrito, a favorite of many regular customers, or go for a sizzling hot fajita plate, tacos or fresh guacamole salad. An ice-cold Dos Equis perfectly complements the spicy seasonings of the meals, or order your favorite drink from the full bar. The stuffed *sopaipilla*, a golden brown fried pastry filled with goodness, is an El Burrito signature dessert. And while you're there, check out their hall of fame. You'll see photos of celebrities like Denver Bronco John Elway, trumpeter Doc Severinsen and music group Chicago enjoying El Burrito's tasty food. And, you can please your friends at your next gathering with catering services from the restaurant. Come to El Burrito Restaurant, just one block north of Old Town, for the bold flavors of traditional Mexican food.

404 Linden Street, Fort Collins CO
(970) 484-1102

Bella Bambino
SHOPPING: *Best baby emporium in Fort Collins*

Add fashion and flair to your baby's nursery with great furniture and décor from Bella Bambino, the charming boutique that doesn't break the bank. This stylish baby emporium is owned and operated by Denise Zerillo, who originally sold custom-made baby beds but has since expanded her inventory to carry a full line of sensational, quality products designed to keep your precious one safe and cozy. In addition to traditional cribs, Bella Bambino offers a selection of sleek sleigh and circular cribs that are available in an array of styles, colors and finishes. If you're not sure of exactly what look you're going for, Denise and her friendly staff will be happy to assist you by offering complete design services at no additional cost. The shop has a lovely collection of crib and cradle bedding, along with custom bedding for older children. Bella Bambino further offers a choice selection of quality children's clothes, as well as soothing skin-care products created specifically for baby's sensitive skin. No nursery would be complete without whimsical wall art, perfectly hung to draw baby's eye and warm your heart, which is why Denise stocks a full selection of delightful posters and pictures, along with a variety of marvelous wall clocks, stepping stools and décor items. Bella Bambino gift baskets, available in a variety of sizes, make the perfect addition to any bridal shower and are specially designed in boy, girl or unisex colors. Design the nursery of your dreams at Bella Bambino.

123 N College Avenue, Fort Collins CO
(970) 407-0033

Children's Mercantile Company
SHOPPING: *Best old-time toy store in Fort Collins*

If you've seen the movie *You've Got Mail*, then you have an idea of what to expect when you visit Children's Mercantile Company in Fort Collins. In the movie, Meg Ryan owned a fun-filled children's bookstore that left kids mesmerized. Children's Mercantile is very similar to the Hollywood book den, except they sell toys and kids clothes, too. Owned by the wife-and-husband team of Shelly Dragan and Greg Wiggal, Children's Mercantile is an old-time toy store where exploring is never boring. They carry specialty toys you can't find at the big chains, and simple toys you remember from your childhood. You'll find European handcrafted toys, French dolls, Manhattan toys, Brio & Thomas trains and interactive toys that engage a child's creative faculties. You'll find marbles, Legos, and stuffed animals, along with CDs and shoes. Your little ones will especially like the sing-along story times held at the store on Friday mornings. Visit Children's Mercantile on your next trip to Fort Collins. You'll have as much fun playing with the toys as the kids. Plus you'll be the star of your own home movie when your favorite sprite opens the gift you bagged at this one-of-a-kind store.

111 N College Avenue, Fort Collins CO
(970) 484-9946

Alpine Arts–The Colorado Showcase
SHOPPING: *Best Colorado-themed gifts*

Colorado has so much to recommend it that a store devoted to Colorado gifts and art is bound to be an inspiring place. Alpine Arts in Ft. Collins captures the spirit of Colorado in 3,600 square feet filled with merchandise that defines this Rocky Mountain wonderland. The clothing, photographs, paintings and pottery found here prove popular with Colorado residents as well as those visiting from other places. Gourmet foods speak to Colorado's agricultural bounty, and Aspen Leaf jewelry captures the shimmering beauty of Colorado's quaking aspens with real leaves that have been preserved and dipped in 14-karat gold. The building that houses Alpine Arts is a historic treasure, complete with original tin ceilings, built by businessman Franklin Avery 100 years ago for the first Ft. Collins bank. Manager Christie Rogers presides over this Colorado treasure with a sunny disposition as bright and attractive as Colorado's famed sunshine. Christie holds a degree in criminology from the University of Colorado at Boulder, but has found fulfillment in running the shop, started more than 25 years ago by her parents, Mark and Leann Thieman. Just as much as she loves working with her customers, Christie loves working with her father. She invites you to celebrate the beauty and bounty of Colorado with a visit to Alpine Arts–The Colorado Showcase.

112 N College Avenue, Fort Collins CO
(970) 493-1941

GOLDEN

Golden, located at the mouth of Clear Creek in the foothills of the Rockies, is the seat of Jefferson County. The Colorado School of Mines is in Golden, as are the National Renewable Energy Laboratory, the Coors Brewing Company and the Colorado Railroad Museum. The U.S. Geological Survey's Earthquake Information Center is housed on the campus at the School of Mines. Golden was one of the first towns in Colorado, established in 1859 to serve prospectors on their way to the gold fields. It was the first territorial capital, holding that position from 1862 to 1867. Golden is home to some of the world's best mountain biking. Lariat Loop Road is a common bike route, with several hairpin turns up the side of Mount Zion and Lookout Mountain. Clear Creek White Water Park is an unusual municipal park that offers lessons in white-water rafting and kayaking. Golden is scheduled to be the endpoint of the West Corridor in Denver's FasTracks commuter rail network. Construction is slated to begin in 2008.

Golden, Colorado with Denver in the background
Photo by Rick Kimple

Places to Go

- Apex Park
  Trailheads: Heritage Square or Lookout Mountain Nature Center

- Astor House Museum & Clear Creek History Park
  822 12th Street

- Buffalo Bill Grave and Museum
  987½ Lookout Mountain Road

- Clear Creek White Water Park
  1201 10th Street

- Colorado Railroad Museum
  17155 W 44th Avenue

- Coors Brewery Tours
  13th and Ford Streets

- Golden Gate Canyon State Park
  92 Crawford Gulch Road

- Lions Park
  1300 10th Street

- Lookout Mountain Nature Center
  910 Colorow Road

- Mother Cabrini Shrine
  20189 Cabrini Boulevard

- Parfet Park
  10th Street and Washington Avenue

- Rocky Mountain Quilt Museum
  1111 Washington Avenue

- White Ranch Park
  Belcher Hill Road

Things to Do

June
- Wildflower Festival
  (303) 526-0594

July
- Buffalo Bill Days
  www.buffalobilldays.com

- Jefferson County Fair
  www.co.jefferson.co.us/fair

August
- Golden Fine Arts Festival
  www.goldenfineartsfestival.org

The Silk Pincushion

ACCOMMODATIONS: *Best bed and breakfast*

The Silk Pincushion is a bed and breakfast and sewing shop all rolled into one. It is located in an exquisite Victorian home built in 1882 next to Lookout Mountain. The Victorian theme is evident throughout The Silk Pincushion where sewing classes are offered all year. The Carriage House guest apartment is separate from the main house and includes a kitchen and skylights, which provide unparalleled views of the Table Mountains. Each of the three guest bedrooms in the main house feature their own private bathroom, vintage linens and antique furniture. The rooms are simply named by color: the Lavender, Blue and Green Room, which has a bathtub. Breakfast is served on the patron's schedule, giving guests the luxurious option of sleeping in. Owners Judy Conch and Patty Gasper offer sewing retreats that provide the convenience of

staying overnight while working on a project. Judy is a doll maker with numerous patented quilt designs. Rare skills like smocking, applique and embroidery are taught by Judy and Patty. Classes are given in the sewing room and quilters are taught new and innovative ideas. Their assortment of quilt designs is unmatched. At all of their classes and overnight sewing retreats, guests are served tea, coffee and home baked treats. You are invited to join in the classes or consider participating in a slumber party sewing retreat for extra camaraderie and fun at The Silk Pincushion.

1523 Ford Street, Golden CO (303) 278-8813
www.thesilkpincushion.com

Table Mountain Inn

ACCOMMODATIONS: *Best hotel and southwestern restaurant*

Table Mountain Inn provides sumptuous dining and distinctive room accommodations in the heart of Golden. Robert Berry constructed this elegant building in the Moorish style in 1925, creating an up-to-the-minute modern hotel that he entitled Hotel Barrimoor. In 1948, the hostelry was purchased by Lu Holland who transformed it into an ode to the Old West and added two additional wings to the building. The reinvented hotel became Holland House where the community would gather to celebrate numerous social events. In 1991, the building, after sitting empty for several years, sold again to a dynamic and successful duo of restaurateurs, Bart Bortles and Frank Day who gave the graceful vintage building an extensive and exhausting overhaul turning it once again into a crowning jewel for the city. Today, Table Mountain Inn, operated by General Manager Bob Reiss, boasts 74 hotel rooms and suites while offering patrons decadent pampering as well as world-class service. Amenities include Internet access and complimentary newspapers along with Aveda spa products for hair and skin care. Readers of the *Westword* newspaper named the restaurant at Table Mountain Inn as Best Southwestern Restaurant. Here diners will enjoy a diverse blending of western and southwestern cuisine with the fabulous hospitality Table Mountain Inn has gained a reputation for. They are well known for their sumptuous holiday buffets, banquet dinners and Murder Mystery dinners. Come visit and see for yourself why Table Mountain Inn is truly the pride of Golden.

1310 Washington Avenue, Golden CO
(303) 277-9898 or (800) 762-9898
www.tablemountaininn.com

Dakota Ridge RV Park

ACCOMMODATIONS: *Best RV park*

Dakota Ridge RV Park offers travelers a delightful combination of spectacular views with the glorious foothills to the west and a panoramic view of Denver's city lights to the east. This stunning park, managed by Jim and Carol Stone, sits just ten minutes from historic downtown Golden and features numerous landscaped, pull-through sites with both 30 and 50 amp hook-ups. Additionally, its centralized location to numerous area attractions makes it the ideal place to park your home away from home while exploring this exciting and diverse part of Colorado. Dakota Ridge RV Park was featured in the October 2005 edition of Today's RV's and is the highest rated park in Colorado according to both *Trailer Life* and *Woodall's*. The park is also a designated Good Sam park and offers guests a newly remodeled clubhouse that sports an exercise facility and gift shop. Further on-site amenities include a heated pool and hot tub, a game room and a coffee bar, which serves complimentary coffee and tea. Dakota Ridge is ideal for the entire family and has several great ways of keeping the little ones busy including a great playground and Wi-Fi services. Due to it's proximity to Denver, Dakota Ridge has become something of an RV park to the stars, boasting movie and television celebrities. This year-round park also welcomes your pets. With its beautiful scenery, wide range of amenities and convenient location, Dakota Ridge RV Park is the perfect place for RV travelers in the Denver area to stay. Gather up the gang and head to Colorado where the Stones invite you to enjoy peaceful serenity and breathtaking views at Dakota Ridge RV Park.

17800 W Colfax Avenue, Golden CO
(303) 279-1625
www.dakotaridgerv.com

Bow Wow Boutique

ANIMALS & PETS:

Best scissor grooming and breed cuts

Dogs and their owners can look forward to a trip to Bow Wow Boutique. Owner Kim Higginson and her staff will get to know both you and your dog, so that the grooming experience is a joy for your canine. Bow Wow Boutique specializes in scissor grooming and breed cuts. Employees have a vast knowledge of dog standards and the particular requirements for their look. The customer service they provide is second to none. Here you'll find competitive pricing, acceptance of all major credit cards and convenient hours. Same day or next day grooming appointments are available. Bow Wow Boutique doesn't limit its care to dogs, as they accommodate your feline friends as well. This full-service pet salon, complete with a gift shop, is far from austere. It is exceptionally clean and bright, offering a cozy comfort that's bound to relax your beloved pet. Treat your dog or cat to top notch grooming while treating yourself to peace of mind at Bow Wow Boutique.

16399 S Golden Road, Golden CO
(303) 278-7190

Camp Bow Wow
ANIMALS & PETS: *Best doggy day and overnight camp*

If your special canine friend has been letting you know that he's lonely and bored while you're away by chewing up your new sofa and redesigning your shoes, then it's time to make a reservation at Camp Bow Wow. This the country's premier doggy day and overnight camp where your furry friend can romp and play all day with dog and human friends and then come home stress free and ready to snuggle up with his favorite human companion. Camp Bow Wow, in Golden, is owned and operated by Kelly Beasley, who opened the doors to her fabulous camp in 2004. She and her camp counselors are well trained in canine behavior, certified in Red Cross pet first aid and CPR, and are all committed to Camp Bow Wow 's high standards of excellence. The camp has made the standard kennel concept obsolete by providing open play areas for all-day play, private cabins for overnight guests to snooze the night away, along with a staff that truly loves dogs and cares about their well-being. This forward thinking canine care camp has also installed web cameras in all indoor and outdoor play areas so you can keep an eye on Fido whether you're down the block or across the globe. In addition, Camp Bow Wow will happily administer all necessary medicines for your dog free of charge. When you're going to be away, make sure your dog is as happy as he or she can be without you, by reserving your canine companion a barking good time at Camp Bow Wow.

13101 W 43rd Drive, Golden CO
(303) 271-WOOF (9663)
www.mycbw.com/golden

Dolls Anonymous
ARTS & CRAFTS: *Best doll makers and suppliers*

Have you ever wondered how dolls become such beautiful works of art? At Dolls Anonymous, Delores and Dwain Gray can teach you the fine art of crafting these delicate porcelain treasures. Certified by the International Foundation of Doll Makers as an instructor, Delores has 16 years experience in making fine porcelain dolls and holds classes six times a week to teach others this fine craft. Most people who are enrolled in her classes have been coming for about nine years. Classes are for three hours and students attend once a week. For eight years in a row, Delores has been named Rocky Mountain Doll Fantasy Outstanding Teacher. One look at her dolls and you will understand why, because the greatest thing about her dolls are their eyes. It is said the eyes are the window to the soul. The many different ways to create eyes on a doll are what give them their individuality. Some eyes are painted, while others are set in, the choice depending on what type of character you want your doll to have. Dolls Anonymous also stocks doll furniture of all kinds, such as cradles, high chairs and rockers. Their excellent craftsmanship adds just a little more personality to the dolls themselves. Come to Dolls Anonymous and meet other enthusiasts who share the same passion for fine porcelain dolls.

16399 S Golden Road, #D, Golden CO
(303) 271-3779

Golden Quilt Company

ARTS & CRAFTS:
Best quilting supplier

Since its opening in November of 2004, Golden Quilt Company has gained a reputation for excellence. Owner Nancy Swanton earned this esteem by offering a wide variety of the highest quality materials and exceptional, personalized customer service. Golden Quilt Company is a full-service provider, including fine quilting fabrics, books, patterns and notions. Nancy helps to preserve and continue the art of quilt making and other textile arts by offering a full spectrum of classes for all skill levels and ages. You can learn everything from choosing colors and fabrics to machine quilting and binding. Classes also teach you how to create beautiful items such as placemats and tote bags. Nancy stocks a selection of kits that are designed to make quilting easy for any member of the family. Quilting patterns are as varied as snowflakes and range from beginner to expert skill levels, each one filled with color and whimsy. You can choose from more traditional patterns such as the Wedding Ring or try one of the new contemporary designs. They also have machine quilting services available. Golden Quilt Company is the perfect place to contribute your ideas and learn new techniques while being surrounded by vivid colors and friendly people who share your enjoyment of all things quilted. Come in today and join the fun at Golden Quilt Company.

1108 Washington Avenue, Golden CO
(303) 277-0717
www.goldenquiltcompany.com

Photos courtesy of dentclinic.net

Dent Clinic
AUTO: *Best autobody shop*

The folks at Dent Clinic in Golden have the next best thing to a magic wand for fixing door dings, hail damage and minor dents. Owner Rick Tate has been providing Paintless Dent Repair since 1990 and personally trained his longtime employees in the specialized technique. Paintless Dent Repair involves working the metal from the inside out, using metal rods and specialized hand tools to remove the dent. The work is faster and considerably less expensive than traditional bodywork, uses no fillers and preserves the car's original finish. Dent Clinic is recommended by Tom Martino's Troubleshooters network and is the method of repair preferred by insurance companies. With Paintless Dent Repair, your vehicle is looking good and back on the road quickly. The procedure takes only a few hours, depending on the extent of the damage. Dent Clinic can repair your vehicle in one to seven days, depending on the shop's workload. The shop is open six days a week for your convenience, and the job includes a lifetime warranty from a company with a proven track record. Next time your vehicle is marred by scrapes, scratches or dings, let the seasoned professionals at Dent Clinic give it the facelift it deserves.

658 Simms Street, Golden CO (303) 234-1948 or (800) 291-3368
www.dentclinic.net

Brickyard Recording Group, LLC

BUSINESS: *Best recording studio*

Brickyard Recording Group, located in Golden just 20 minutes from downtown Denver, is the perfect place to help you hold on to your sound for all eternity. The studio's recording engineers make the highest quality audio productions available in the Denver metropolitan area. Whatever the musical genre, Casey Schnapp's goal is to capture the emotion and skill of live performance on a disc. Casey has extensive experience in music and recording as well as a creative, professional team. Brickyard can provide guitar and drum background parts to accompany any recording session. Casey and his team also offer guitar and drum lessons in a relaxed and intimate setting for families or individuals. With lower overhead than many competitors, the prices are reasonable and scheduling is flexible at Brickyard. Casey hopes to give back to music some of what music has given to him. Visit Casey and his team at Brickyard Recording Group to turn your musical dreams into reality.

1213 Brickyard Road, #1A, Golden CO
(303) 278-1913

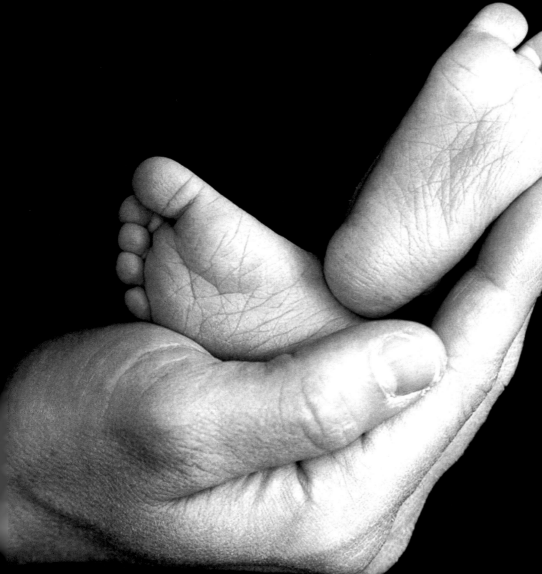

MO's Family Portraits

BUSINESS:
Best portrait photography

Since 1998, MO's Family Portraits has created images that have warmed the hearts and homes of her clients. Her expertise in wall portraiture helps her design unique images that accent the home and keep her clients returning again and again. Her personal connection with each client helps bring out that special smile to be captured for a lifetime. Whether you have a newborn baby or are a senior couple looking to capture the magic once more, MO is ready to turn a moment into a priceless memory that can be enjoyed for years to come.

1518 Washington Avenue, Golden CO   (303) 273-0477
www.MosPortraits.com

The Victorian House
EVENTS: *Best place to host your special event*

Celebrate the special occasions of your life surrounded by elegance and breathtaking views at The Victorian House Event Center at Heritage Square in Golden. This stunning facility, fashioned after a vintage Victorian home, has been renovated by the owners, Daniel and Kerrie Ducey, into a magnificent backdrop for wedding receptions, reunions and holiday parties. Set in the foothills of Historic Golden, this one-of-a-kind event center has an exquisite panoramic of the gorgeous table mountains and the signature flat irons that arise in the Colorado landscape. The Victorian House is ideal for groups of 10 to 130 on the inside or for groups from 10 to 250 for parties that are held both indoors and outdoors. The large banquet room is perfect for weddings, sit down dinners, cocktail receptions and other events; while the parlor room, featuring a beautiful oak bar and vaulted ceilings, is typically set up for buffets and as a mingling area for guests. Another fabulous feature of The Victorian House is the grand outdoor deck where you and your guests can sit back and enjoy the beauty of nature. In order to make your special event run smoothly, many amenities come included in the price of the facility rental and The Victoria House only books one event for any given day or time, ensuring that you and your party have full and exclusive use of the facilities and grounds. Make sure that your next event runs smoothly and provides joyful memories by making your reservations at The Victorian House Event Center.

18301 W Colfax Avenue, Building K, Golden CO (303) 278-9333
www.victorianhouseonline.net

Mariposa Gardens
GARDENS, PLANTS & FLOWERS:
Best landscape architect

Mariposa Gardens is the design firm of landscape architect Tamara Shuck. Backed by 12 years of experience, Tamara is your guide in helping you to conceptualize what to do with your space. She's a graduate of Virginia Tech, one of the top schools of landscape architecture in the country. She specializes in native and drought-tolerant plants to create beautiful sustainable designs. A well-designed landscape focuses on more than just surface concerns like plant type and location. Tamara looks at the entire picture. She investigates what materials are best suited for your space. Mariposa Gardens assists you in defining color layout, texture, and a theme that inevitably sets a mood. You may want an outdoor cooking and dining area, a peaceful meditative spot or joyful play area for the children. Mariposa Gardens works to transform that thought into a decisive laid-out plan. Whether you're a contractor, a do-it-yourselfer or homeowner who would rather have someone else do the work, Mariposa Gardens is there to create a plan that suits your needs. If you consider yourself an outdoors person, but never find yourself enjoying your own backyard, call Tamara at Mariposa Gardens. Together you will create a space that is uniquely yours.

(303) 709-0705
www.mariposagardensinc.com

Before

After

Fitness Together

HEALTH & BEAUTY: *Best fitness training*

"One client, one trainer, one goal" is the philosophy behind Fitness Together. At Fitness Together, each client is matched with a personal fitness trainer who works with you in fully equipped private rooms. This means that there is never a crowd and you don't have to wait around for a machine to become free. It also insures there are no distractions and you get a work out specifically designed to match your needs and personal health goals. Fitness Together's specially designed programs were established in Scottsdale, Arizona in 1983 and have been proven to work for men and women ranging in age from 13 to 92. Whether your goal is to achieve muscle tone, reduce body fat or increase your flexibility, muscle mass or cardiovascular health, Fitness Together has a program that will be tailored to meet your requirements. Most of the centers business comes from the referrals of other clients, who quickly become enamored of the individualized attention and results that they get by going to Fitness Together. As a Fitness Together client, you are able to choose weekly or monthly session packages that are designed to suit your lifestyle. Fitness Together is dedicated to providing the undivided attention clients need to become healthier and more fit. Enjoy personalized training and privacy while gaining the physique you've always wanted at Fitness Together.

600 12th Street, Golden CO
(303) 271-1449
www.ftgolden.com

Sirona Physical Therapy
HEALTH & BEAUTY: *Best state-of-the-art personal care*

Sometimes the search for pain relief requires exploring many avenues. Dr. Allison Schatz is a caring physical therapist who has successfully treated many patients who previously failed to meet their rehabilitation goals. You'll find her at Sirona Physical Therapy in the heart of historic downtown Golden. Allison earned her doctor of physical therapy and master's of science degrees at Regis University, where she has been an affiliate faculty member. She specializes in sports medicine but also provides comprehensive orthopedic and neurological rehabilitation services. She is experienced at treating a wide variety of disorders from acute injuries to chronic pain and works with patients of varying lifestyles from the weekend warrior, to Olympic athletes, to those with more sedentary lives. Patients learn to maximize their ability to heal, move, work and play. They receive state-of-the-art care based on the latest research and exercises as well as prevention techniques in a caring atmosphere. Allison's clinic is named after Sirona, the goddess of healing. Her continued pursuit of knowledge allows her to succeed with even the most complex cases. So don't give up. Turn to Sirona Physical Therapy for compassionate care and optimal recovery.

805 12th Street, Golden CO
(303) 279-9728
www.sironapt.com

Whole Body Health Center
HEALTH & BEAUTY: *Best rejuvenation and pain relief*

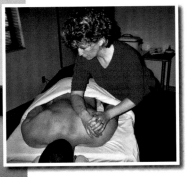

More than an ordinary acupuncture and massage clinic, Whole Body Health Center's name is indicative of their dedication to the comprehensive health of their clients. Their approach to massage therapy is designed to reduce disease-causing stress. Their certified massage therapists employ a variety of techniques, tailoring a wellness, medical or stone massage to soothe away trouble spots. At Whole Body Health Center they use hypoallergenic massage lotions with or without essential oils along with music and muted lighting to increase the serene atmosphere. They say that many of their regular clients relax the moment they walk in the door. You are welcome to arrive early for your appointment to relax in their comfortable reception area. In addition to massage, Whole Body Health Center provides acupuncture treatments. This time tested method of health care provides pain relief and treatment for many other common conditions. There is an acupuncturist/herbalist on duty three times a week and several massage therapists on duty six days a week. The Whole Body Health Center embraces a synergistic approach to physical, mental and spiritual well-being. They encourage you to let their receptionist know what results you expect to attain when scheduling a massage appointment so that they may match you with the appropriate therapist to meet your needs. At Whole Body Health Center, you are invited to rejuvenation and pain relief through superb massage and acupuncture in holistic professional setting.

780 Simms Street, Suite 102, Lakewood CO
(303) 232-2600 *www.wholebodyhealthcenter.com*

Carefree Spas & Billiards
HOME: *Best home recreation products*

Carefree Spas & Billiards, serving the Front Range of Colorado since 1976, wants to give you the royal treatment and help you achieve bliss with Sundance spas, the best built hot tubs in the world. Carefree Spas & Billiards also carries BeefEater BBQs, cooking islands, Kasson billiard tables and BioGuard™ spa and pool care products. At Carefree Spas & Billiards, they are committed to providing you with the best quality products at the best prices. This includes a wide selection of BeefEater BBQ grills with built-in capabilities, U.S.-made, one-inch-thick slate billiard tables, accessories and long term customer support. Carefree Spas & Billiards has three showrooms, including a new and used spa outlet store in Golden, so visit soon to check out seasonal specials on these great products.

2030 County Line Road, Unit I, Highlands Ranch CO
(303) 730-2400
1835 Dublin Boulevard, Colorado Springs CO
(719) 598-8200
765 Moss Street, Golden CO (Outlet)
(303) 422-0100
www.carefreespas.com

Foothills Ski & Bike
RECREATION: *Best ski and bike equipment*

Skiers and bicyclists who demand performance from their equipment turn to the experts at Foothills Ski & Bike, just 15 minutes from downtown Denver. You'll find powder, jib, race and mogul skis plus a staff who has mountain-tested all ski brands and can advise beginners and experts on the brands they carry and the brands they don't. Foothills carries Fischer and Atomic racing equipment, provides expert boot fitting and custom ski tuning. The shop also carries performance cross county gear and is a Swix Performance Center. They service the skis they sell and can be counted on to meet your demanding standards. In the spring and summer, the shop fills with cross-country mountain bikes, a natural summer choice for many ski racers. Foothills specializes in Rocky Mountain Bicycles built in British Columbia. They also provide custom-made street bicycles specifically built to match an individual's measurements and riding style. Skiers and bicyclists will find a large inventory of quality sunglasses, goggles and helmets. When you are focused on performance, you want to shop at a store with a similar focus. Everyone at Foothills Ski and Bike is a skier and a biker with the knowledge and enthusiasm to serve athletes with specialized needs. They sell and rent equipment plus provide exacting service on the equipment they sell. When performance matters, skiers on the Front Range turn to Foothills Ski and Bike.

25948 Genesee Trail Road #J, Golden CO (303) 526-2036
www.foothillsskiandbike.com

Artistic Fusion Dance

RECREATION:
Best dance studio

At Artistic Fusion Dance Academy in Golden, youngsters are taught the intrinsic language of dance in a nurturing, exuberant and passionate environment. Artistic Fusion opened its doors in August of 2000 and quickly became the Denver area's most highly respected and well-rounded dance school. Owners and sisters Jennifer Owens and Julie Jarnot are firmly dedicated to teaching the fundamentals of dance while simultaneously providing a supportive atmosphere that encourages students to explore their passion for the arts. The program builds up student's personal goals and dreams as well as well as their self-esteem overall. The academy has a wide range of classes and dance styles from ballet to jazz and hip-hop. Artistic Fusion is best known for its outstanding dance instructors who provide fun and energetic classes that result in dynamic, professional performances. The company has won numerous national awards and performs locally at such events as the People's Fair, Stomp out Hunger and the Children's Hospital along with local nursing homes and schools. Additional dance credits include the off-Broadway show Tap Kids, a national Kmart ad and a feature role in the Disney Channel film *The High School Musical*. Artistic Fusion has a second location in Westminster and also works with day care centers and after-school programs throughout the metro area. Introduce your children to the language of dance at Artistic Fusion Dance Academy.

600 Corporate Circle, Golden CO
(303) 278-0372
960 W 124th Avenue, Westminster CO
(720) 929-1820
www.artistic-fusion.com

Tatum's Touch of Philly
RESTAURANTS & CAFÉS: *Best Philly cheesesteaks*

Where can you go for a delicious cheesesteak at two in the afternoon? Before you catch a flight to Pennsylvania, let Tatum's Touch of Philly come to you. And while you can eat in their spacious dining area, a majority of their business is in the delivery of homemade soups, salads, pizza, and boxed lunches to hungry workers too busy to escape the office. Their popular box lunches come with a six-inch sandwich of your choice, chips, salad-of-the-day and a cookie. Using only Thumann's deli meats and cheeses, owners Len and Jeanne Sanchez have been feeding locals hearty hoagies while supplying companies with enough to feed an army. While the name has been changed from the original Bilg's Delicatessen, opened in 2001, what hasn't changed is Tatum's Touch of Philly's commitment to providing great food, day in and day out. They also cater buffets of 12 or more with choice of cheesesteaks, chicken steak, lasagna, Cajun jambalaya or spaghetti with meatballs and sausage. Five delicious pies and four varieties of bread are also available. Next time you want a French roll filled with piping hot strip steak and grilled onions and bell peppers, think of Tatum's Touch of Philly.

16400 S Golden Road, Golden CO
(303) 279-0361

Rhapsody's at Clear Creek
RESTAURANTS & CAFÉS: *Best American contemporary cuisine*

The atmosphere and the food are American contemporary at Rhapsody's at Clear Creek in Golden, and many of Colorado's best-known food critics have given high praise to the restaurant. Rhapsody's is owned by Master Chef Kurt Schramm and his wife Petra. They always feature at least one German dish on the menu, in honor of their German roots. The couple has recruited an all-star culinary team dedicated to a whole new level of dining and service. You'll find a patio on the banks of Clear Creek, a sleek cherrywood-accented dining room with a large expanse of windows facing a park, a full bar and a chef's table. It features a tasting menu as well as an exclusive selection of wines not offered on the wine list. Whether you desire a romantic dinner for two or a special reception for many, Rhapsody's can meet your needs in their banquet room with a catering service that will feature a varied menu with something to please every palette. Master Chef Schramm changes the menu the first week of every month to offer the best seasonal selections. When you dine at Rhapsody's, you'll want to leave room for an exquisite dessert. All menu items are freshly made in house. Visit Rhapsody's at Clear Creek and the neighboring Café Touche, an upscale coffeehouse featuring the best European coffee plus gourmet breakfast items, sandwiches, pastries and desserts. Rhapsody's at Clear Creek is just 100 yards north of downtown Golden's big arch and filled with culinary delights and hospitality.

1027 Washington Avenue, Golden CO
(303) 279-6671 *www.rhapsodysrestaurant.com*

Table Mountain Inn

RESTAURANTS & CAFÉS: *Best southwestern restaurant and accommodations*

Table Mountain Inn provides sumptuous dining and distinctive room accommodations in the heart of Golden. Robert Berry constructed this elegant building in the Moorish style in 1925, creating an up-to-the-minute modern hotel that he entitled Hotel Barrimoor. In 1948, the hostelry was purchased by Lu Holland who transformed it into an ode to the Old West and added two additional wings to the building. The reinvented hotel became Holland House, where the community would gather to celebrate numerous social events. In 1991, the building, after sitting empty for several years, sold again to a dynamic and successful duo of restaurateurs, Bart Bortles and Frank Day. They gave the graceful vintage building an extensive overhaul, turning it once again into a crowning jewel for the city. Today, Table Mountain Inn, operated by General Manager Bob Reiss, boasts 74 hotel rooms and suites while offering patrons decadent pampering as well as world-class service. Amenities include Internet access and complimentary newspapers along with Aveda spa products for hair and skin care. Readers of the *Westword* newspaper named the restaurant at Table Mountain Inn as Best Southwestern Restaurant. Diners will enjoy a diverse blending of western and southwestern cuisine with the fabulous hospitality Table Mountain Inn has gained a reputation for. They are well known for their sumptuous holiday buffets, banquet dinners and Murder Mystery dinners. Come visit, and see for yourself why Table Mountain Inn is truly the pride of Golden.

1310 Washington Avenue, Golden CO (303) 277-9898 or (800) 762-9898
www.tablemountaininn.com

Hilltop Bistro

RESTAURANTS & CAFÉS: *Best bistro*

You are bound to find just the right setting for your group gathering or romantic dinner for two among the many rooms sprawling throughout the converted house known as the Hilltop Bistro. Downtown Golden's eclectic lunch and dinner place has enjoyed tremendous customer loyalty over the years. In 2004, Michael Chen's innovative New American and Asian fusion cuisine added new energy. Whether it's the cranberry cream cheese on your turkey and bacon sandwich or the creamy coconut curry sauce on your roasted cod, every touch is intended to surprise and delight. Often the side dishes are just as remarkable as the main affair. "I had the miso salmon, which was excellent," noted a recent reviewer, "but I must say that the green beans fried in light batter and drizzled with a delicious sauce were my favorite." A seafood stew teeming with salmon, mussels, scallops and shrimp is a house specialty. Creative salads, pastas and pizzas present an abundance of options. Variety is the key to the seating arrangements as well. Choose a table on the sun porch, a cozy spot by the fireplace or settle in with your group in one of the dining rooms. Wherever you are sitting, be sure to save room for a dessert that captures the chef's creative splash at its best. Try the chocolate bread pudding with cashew ganache or the cheesecake with ginger apricot compote. For intriguing dishes and a setting for every mood and occasion, take the climb to the Hilltop Bistro.

1518 Washington Avenue, Golden CO
(303) 279-8151

D'Deli
RESTAURANTS & CAFÉS:
Best deli

In historic downtown Golden, a cheerful little place by the name of D'Deli is located next to the Big Arch. Al Neighbors owns this congenial establishment, renowned for its homemade specialties. Al has developed a sizeable take-out business, largely due to the generous portions and the freshness of his food. D'Deli's Italian baguettes fill the air with the incomparable aroma of fresh baked bread. The sandwiches are delectable, with the chicken salad has its own devoted following, and the homemade brownies melt in your mouth. Soup aficionados will love the steaming gourmet soups; at least five different delicious selections are offered on any given day. At the other end of the spectrum, there is nothing better than creamy and cold homemade ice-cream on a hot summer day. D'Deli does a brisk catering business, serving the Colorado School of Mines, Golden Chamber of Commerce and Coors Corporation. In an age of fast-food frenzy, D'Deli provides a much needed healthy change of pace. Bring the whole family or come alone; you'll feel at home the minute you arrive. Call ahead to D'Deli for a box-lunch meal or catering.

1207 Washington Avenue, Golden CO (303) 279-8020

Photos courtesy of Cameron Smith Photography

Places to Go

- Bittersweet Park
  35th Avenue and 13th Street
- Centennial Village Museum
  1475 A Street
- Family FunPlex
  1501 65th Avenue
- The Greeley History Museum
  714 8th Street
- Greeley Ice Haus
  900 8th Avenue
- Island Grove Regional Park
  501 N 14th Avenue
- Meeker Home Museum
  1324 9th Avenue
- Plumb Farm Learning Center
  955 39th Avenue

Things to Do

April
- Spring Fest
  (303) 702-1844
- University of Northern Colorado
  Jazz Festival
  *www.arts.unco.edu/uncjazz/festival/
  festival.html*

May
- Children's Festival
  (970) 336-1000 ext. 18

June
- Colorado Medieval Festival
  www.medievalworld.us/coloradocastle

June-July
- Greeley Stampede (rodeo)
  www.greeleystampede.org

July
- Arts Picnic
  www.artspicnic.com
- Weld County Fair
  www.co.weld.co.us/WeldCountyFair

August
- Greeley Blues Fest
  www.greeleybluesfest.com

September
- Oktoberfest
  (970) 356-6775

GREELEY

Nathan C. Meeker, a newspaper reporter from New York City, founded Greeley in 1869 as Union Colony, an experimental utopian community of high moral standards. Residents later changed the name to Greeley in honor of Horace Greeley, who was Meeker's editor at the New York Tribune. The respectable colonists were proud of their prosperity, and remained unflappable when outsiders poked fun at their city by calling it the City of Saints and other names. In the 1870s, Greeley citizens were so law-abiding that the city rented out the empty jail to store buffalo hides. Today, Greeley is no longer so straight-laced, but it maintains its community spirit. Greeley lies within the arid rain shadow of the Rocky Mountains. In spite of Greeley's dryness, large trees line many of its streets due to extensive irrigation. The National Arbor Day Foundation awarded Greeley a Tree City USA designation in 1980. Greeley is home to the University of Northern Colorado. The Denver Broncos hold their annual summer training camp at the school. The city owns and operates the Union Colony Civic Center, which includes the 1,665-seat Monfort Concert Hall.

Dale Kasel of the Falcons at bat in Greeley's Jackson Field
Photo by Danny Meyer
Courtesy of the U.S. Air Force

Canterbury Tea Room
BAKERIES, COFFEE & TEA: *Best tea room in Greeley*

Enjoy sensational cuisine from around the world, divine service and a charming Victorian ambience at the Canterbury Tea Room, where owner Adrienne Andrews has turned Afternoon and High Tea into a celebration of the senses. Housed in a lovely Victorian home surrounded by mature trees and beautifully cultivated grounds, the Canterbury Tea Room is the ideal place to celebrate the special moments of your life, including weddings, sorority reunions or a simple day out with friends. Each month, Adrienne showcases the cuisine of a different European country, such as Britain or Hungary, during her evening High Tea and provides her guests with a special passport that can be stamped as traditional foods from each region are sampled. The lunch menu at the Canterbury Tea Room is lined with scrumptious savories, such as Beef Wellington stew and Cottage Pie, as well as incredible sandwiches and salads like the Kensington chicken salad or the Buckingham melt featuring tender roast beef and horseradish-cream cheese on freshly made

sourdough bread. The tearoom can accommodate up to 200 guests and offers a diverse catering menu for special events, as well as special services such as a dance area, sound system and individual tables for guest books, gifts and the Unity candle. The Canterbury Tea Room's staff will take care of all details including decorations, food service and clean up, leaving you free to enjoy time spent with your guests. Turn your next event into a true celebration at the Canterbury Tea Room.

1229 10th Avenue, Greeley CO
(970) 356-1811
www.canterburytearoom.com

James SalonSpa
HEALTH & BEAUTY: *Best salon in Greeley*

Take a sip of aromatic tea, nestle into a thick terry cloth robe, and prepare yourself to enjoy this oasis of tranquility. For more than 20 years, James SalonSpa in Greeley has offered the latest in body treatments, massage and therapies to help banish tension and erase stress. Featuring Aveda products, this salon and spa offers a full range of services, including hair care, facials, manicures and pedicures, body wraps and therapeutic massage. Float on a warm, water-filled cushion and enjoy a James signature facial that includes a shoulder, neck, face, hand and foot massage. Succumb to an Elemental Nature Facial, and revel in a cleansing and toning routine. The soothing hand massage that accompanies the Caribbean Spa manicure makes a great beginning to a day of treatments. Tight muscles often need special attention, and deep tissue,

stone therapy, and hydrotherm massage can promote relief and release. For the optimum spa escape, choose an Ultimate Deluxe Package, and indulge in a therapeutic massage, body salt glow treatment, facial, pedicure, manicure, scalp treatment and makeup application. Packages offer a range of pleasures, and it's always fun to bring a friend or partner to share the bliss. Schedule a rendezvous with James SalonSpa, and discover why this haven wins consecutive *Greeley Tribune* Reader's Choice awards and has been voted the Best Salon in Weld County.

5290 W 9th Street, Suite 100, Greeley CO
(970) 353-3766
www.jamessalonspa.com

Doug's Hang Up
GALLERIES & FINE ART:
Best art gallery in Greeley

Doug's Hang Up offers customers a variety of options for turning plain, blank walls into showcases for beautiful limited edition prints, etchings and original art. The gallery carries a diverse collection, ranging from Southwestern to contemporary art, and features works by well known artists such as Bev Doolittle, Carl Redin and Govinder Nazran. If you have a special piece you would like to display, bring it in to the store and Doug will enhance it with a custom mat and frame. At Doug's, the knowledgeable staff specializes in three-dimensional framing. Whether you have baby keepsakes you adore or a sword and scabbard from the last century, you can display them proudly under glass instead of tucking them away in the attic to gather dust. "Framing gives me a sense of accomplishment," says Doug. "It is about making the picture or the objects you are framing look their best." Whether they are treasured family photos or a collection of original artworks by your three-year-old, bring the pieces that are important to you to Doug's Hang Up and let them really shine.

3820 W 10th Street, Greeley CO
(970) 356-6386

The Dragon's Cache

HOME: *Best custom stained glass art in Greeley*

The Dragon's Cache offers a treasure trove of glorious stained glass art created by master artist Francis Denning and his wife, Nellie, two distinguished artists whose stained glass graces more than 25 Colorado churches. The Dennings are trained anthropologists who taught at the University of Northern Colorado until the 1980s. The Dragon's Cache, which opened in 1980, is where the Dennings fabricate their amazing windows by a process that involves applying paint directly to a glass panel and then firing

it numerous times to achieve the desired effect. As anthropologists, the Dennings are not only free of bias, they are also dedicated to thoroughly researching the theology behind any given project. Over the years, Francis has discovered that each church has its own nuances when it comes to symbolism, and he carefully designs each piece to appropriately reflect the faith of the worshippers within. The Dennings also carefully consider sun exposure. They use darker glass for southern exposures and recommend installing clear plate glass on the outside of the stained glass to protect it from the elements. Commission custom windows or unearth original stained art glass pieces for your home or business with a visit to the Dragon's Cache.

1109 7th Street, Greeley CO
(970) 353-1051

Dance Factory

RECREATION: *Best dance studio in Greeley*

Whether you have a background in competitive dancing or are just looking for a fun way to squeeze some exercise into your schedule, the knowledgeable instructors at the Dance Factory can teach you how to get your groove on. For more than 33 years, Lynn Bassett and her seven talented instructors have offered lessons in jazz, tap, ballet, hip hop and pom dancing to students of all ages, from preschoolers to adults. Lynn encourages people to take up dancing at any age and says that the benefits of dance include developing grace, coordination and a sense of rhythm, as well as being downright fun. For the more ambitious, the Dance Factory offers a competitive program, and dancers can audition to join the Dance Factory Dance Company, which performs frequently throughout Greeley and surrounding

areas. Lynn's students have received many awards and recognition for their talents, including full scholarships at the prestigious Edge Performing Arts Center in Los Angeles. Professional dance instructors from all over the country come to the Dance Factory to hold workshops, ensuring that students receive a broad knowledge of many dance styles and techniques. Come to the Dance Factory and get your body moving.

2956 29th Street, Greeley CO
(970) 506-9040

JB's Drive-In
RESTAURANTS & CAFES:
Best old-time eatery in Greeley

Every town has an icon, a piece of bedrock upon which memories and traditions are built. In Greeley, JB's Drive-In is such a place. A stalwart at the same location for 42 years, JB's is an American throw-back, a place where car-hops still hustle trays of burgers and fries to your automobile. They still serve homemade root beer. And it's still owned by the same family that made JB's famous in northern Colorado. Jess Benjamin put his initials on the marquee before Neil Armstrong walked on the moon, before Cassius Clay changed his name to Muhammad Ali, before Ed Sullivan introduced The Beatles. Today, JB's Drive-In is owned by JB's daughter Geneva and her husband, Clarence Clark. The third generation of Rodney and Lori Clark have already joined the team. You'll find all of your drive-in favorites like chili dogs, corn dogs and old-fashioned malts take on a new aura at JB's. This is the place you've got to visit during your stay in Greeley.

2501 8th Avenue, Greeley CO
(970) 352-3202

The New Plantation
RESTAURANTS & CAFES: *Best Cajun meals in Greeley*

At the "New" Plantation, brothers Jeff and Larry Oyler serve up the traditional flavors of Louisiana in a fun and laid-back atmosphere. Be sure to come with a big appetite, because the dishes are as big as they are bold. Patrons come back again and again for menu options such as crawfish étouffée, a rich stew of crawfish tails served over rice, or the Cajun Boil, a huge bowl full of crab, shrimp, sausage, fresh corn and new potatoes all simmered in Cajun spices. Though the Cajun dishes are clearly the house specialties, the restaurant offers a wide selection of other American flavors, including New York strip steak and juicy hamburgers with fries. Be sure to check out the nightly specials that offer dinner for two at a reduced price. On Friday and Saturday nights, the place rocks with live entertainment and dancing. The restaurant has a full selection of spirits and beers, and patio seating is available in season. Jeff and Larry say that closing time is when the last person leaves, and with that kind of fun-loving attitude, it is easy to see why Greeley Tribune readers have twice named the restaurant *Best Bar* in the Reader's Choice poll. The restaurant provides takeout and catering services. For adventurous Cajun food in a casual atmosphere, come to the "New" Plantation.

3520 S 11ᵗʰ Avenue, Greeley CO
(970) 330-7903 or (888) 695-4938
www.menusfirst.com/greeley/thenewplantation.htm

State Armory
RESTAURANTS & CAFES: *Best burgers in Greeley*

For decades, in towns large and small all across the nation, generations of Americans have gathered at the local Armory to dance, to laugh and to share good and bad times with their neighbors. At the State Armory in Greeley folks now gather for still another reason—to enjoy tasty food and the wealth of memorabilia that graces this community landmark. State Armory opened as a restaurant in 1978 and is now under the ownership of Dean and Sarah Hagemeister, who first met here in 1981 while Dean was working the door and Sarah was waiting tables. The menu offers a full range of delicious classics, such as curly fries and deep fried pickles, as well as contemporary treats like the low-fat bison burger, the Bravo avocado burger and the Grilled Oink and Cheese sandwich. Customers happily cross state lines to order the famous Jiffy Burger, made with bacon, Jack cheese and peanut butter. One of the restaurant's biggest draws, however, is its massive collection of Hollywood props and collectibles, which includes a B-17 bomber used in the movie *Twelve O'Clock High*, starring Gregory Peck. The eatery also showcases a Hansom cab once owned by Horace Greeley and a glorious 250-year-old stained glass piece from England's Chesterfield Abbey. Share good times with your friends and family at the State Armory.

614 8th Avenue, Greeley CO
(970) 352-7424

The Kitchen
RESTAURANTS & CAFES: *Best home-style cooking in Greeley*

In a world of fast-paced mediocrity, the down-home flavor of The Kitchen is a welcome change. This venerable Greeley eatery, owned for the past eight years by Tracie and David Hamilton and Tracie's sons, James and Wil Spaedt, has remained a familiar Greeley landmark since 1948. Tracie has tried to keep many of the menu items the same so that the restaurant keeps its familiar feel. The Kitchen features homemade bread, desserts and cinnamon rolls as well as old-fashioned comfort food. Folks gravitate to The Kitchen, not only because of its chicken-fried steak and homemade soups but because it feels like family. The Coffee Guys, a group of mostly retired men, arrive on the dot at 10 am every morning for gossip and jokes; some have been gathering here for more than 30 years. The Kitchen staff actually hangs a decorated Christmas stocking over their table every year in their honor. Open for breakfast and lunch, The Kitchen draws loyal customers ranging from University of Northern Colorado students to Sunday churchgoers, and Tracie, a Greeley native, knows many of them by name. For home-style cooking and friendly faces, bring your appetite to The Kitchen in Greeley.

905 16th Street, Greeley CO
(970) 351-7396

Antiques at Lincoln Park

SHOPPING: *Greeley's colossal antiques market*

Find antiques, collectibles and treasures galore by visiting Antiques at Lincoln Park, where owner Betty L. Tointon has created a collector's resource that rivals Europe's fine antiquities shops. Antiques at Lincoln Park, located in a massive, vintage JC Penny's store, offers visitors three floors filled with quality antiques, including a broad selection of furniture from the mid-19th century through the 1960s. The shop also carries glassware, china, books and music. Betty, a Greeley resident since 1959, opened the shop to create a viable business that would infuse new life into Greeley's downtown historic district. Betty and the dynamic women on her staff gladly share their knowledge of fine antiques with customers. The ladies are on hand to answer your questions while you browse. Antiques at Lincoln Park houses 12 dealers and approximately 500 individuals with items on consignment. The shop also has appraisers available by appointment to assess your treasured pieces. Betty says that she is in the recycling business, since she recycles historic treasures from yesterday for today and tomorrow. Discover pieces that are destined to become your family's heirlooms with an excursion to Antiques at Lincoln Park.

822 8th Street, Greeley CO
(970) 351-6222
www.antiquesgreeley.com

INDIAN HILLS

Indian Hills is an unincorporated community located along the beautiful Parmalee Gulch. Indian Hills was founded in the 1920s as a summer resort district. Its easy commuting distance to Denver encouraged a move from summer cabins to permanent residences. Denver and Jefferson County parks and open spaces surround Indian Hills. Bear Mountain, Lone Peak, Mount Falcon and Bear Creek mark the boundaries of the community. Preservation of open space and the community's rural character are highly important to Indian Hills residents. Tiny Town, a non-profit kid-sized town and railroad, is just across U.S. 285 from Indian Hills.

Places to Go

- Mount Falcon Open Space Park
  Picutis Road and Mount Falcon Road

- O'Fallon and Pence
  Denver Mountain Parks
  Meyers Gulch Road (County Highway 120)

- Tiny Town Children's Village and Railroad
  6249 S Turkey Creek Road, Tiny Town
  (303) 697-6829

Photos courtesy of mtnviewbandb.com

Mountain View Bed & Breakfast

ACCOMMODATIONS: *Best bed and breakfast*

Innkeepers Graham and Ortrud Richardson of Mountain View Bed & Breakfast welcome weary travelers with open arms and offer a relaxing refuge from the hectic pace of today's busy world. This beautiful two-story inn, located in the foothills of the Front Range, was constructed in the 1920s and originally served as a writers' retreat, known as Raphael House. The Richardsons met in England after Ortrud smuggled herself out of East Germany at the age of 18. The duo soon emigrated to Canada, where Graham found a job in the shipyards around Victoria. From there they followed the ship building industry to San Diego and discovered Colorado while flipping through a *National Geographic* magazine. The Richardsons fell in love with the rugged beauty of the state and later purchased the Raphael House, where they went on to happily raise three sons. Long known for their hospitality among friends, Graham and Ortrud found it a natural step to open an inn after the last of their boys left home. Today the Mountain View Bed & Breakfast offers two distinctively designed guest rooms, two charming suites, and the cozy Fireweed Cabin, which comes complete with a whirlpool tub and fireplace, making it the ideal hideaway for a romantic weekend. Each morning guests receive breakfasts that include such temptations as cheese filled French toast or eggs Benedict with smoked salmon, prepared fresh from scratch each day by Ortrud. A luxurious sauna and mountain views promise restore tranquility. Enjoy Old World hospitality in a Rocky Mountain setting with a stay at Mountain View Bed & Breakfast.

4754 Picutis Road, Indian Hills CO
(303) 697-6896 or (800) 690-0434
www.mtnviewbandb.com

KITTREDGE

Kittredge, the heart of Bear Creek Canyon, is just northeast of Evergreen and on the western edge of a large block of Denver and Jefferson County parks. Kittredge has only about a thousand residents, but these citizens have tons of community spirit. The Kittredge Civic Association created Kittredge Park and Playground and sponsors events throughout the year, including Kittredge Canyonfest. Kittredge residents are also active in working to protect the neighboring parks, such as Corwina and Lair o' the Bear.

Places to Go

• Corwina and Little Denver Mountain Parks
Colorado Highway 74

• Lair o' the Bear Open Space Park
Colorado Highway 74

• O'Fallon and Pence
Denver Mountain Parks
Meyers Gulch Road (County Highway 120)

Things to Do

September
• Kittredge Canyonfest
www.kittredgecivic.org

Farmers Inn

RESTAURANTS & CAFES: *Best Mexican food in La Salle*

Photo by Tara Hunt

For more than 30 years, brothers Vincent and Cecil Vigil and their families have been dishing up huge platters of piping-hot Mexican food in a friendly, small-town atmosphere. It all started back in the 1970s, when Vincent owned a bar and would cook up some tasty meals to serve his customers just for the fun of it. A few years later, Cecil convinced him to open a restaurant where they could serve those delicious Mexican meals every day. With their commitment to consistently good food and fair prices, the Farmers Inn quickly became a local favorite. The restaurant dishes up the unique tastes of New Mexico, like the award-winning green chili, as well as traditional Mexican favorites like tacos, enchiladas and fajitas. Whatever you choose, it all goes perfectly with one of the house margaritas. The brothers believe it is important to keep the restaurant in the family. Cecil's daughter Kelly is now the manager, Vincent's son is a chef and other family members work in various capacities to keep the restaurant running smoothly. Cecil enjoys welcoming customers personally, so be sure to say hello when you stop by the Farmers Inn for a delicious Mexican meal at a great price.

109 3rd Avenue, La Salle CO
(970) 284-6100

LAFAYETTE

Coal was the making of Lafayette. In 1887, John Simpson sunk the first shaft on Mary Miller's farm. In 1888, Mary platted the town of Lafayette with generously wide streets and alleys and named it for her late husband. By July, the first houses were up and a second mine was open. Within six months, Lafayette boasted two general stores and several boarding houses. In 1900, Mary founded the Lafayette Bank and became the first female bank president in Colorado, and possibly the nation. By 1914, Lafayette sported four hotels, a local newspaper and a pickle factory. A coal-fueled power station provided electricity to Boulder, Longmont and Fort Collins. Coal production declined in the middle of the 20th century, and the last mine closed in 1956. Commuters to Boulder and then Denver took up the slack. Today, Lafayette is a city of neighborhoods, with easy access to outdoor recreation and a fabulous view of the Rockies. Golf star Hale Irwin designed Lafayette's championship Indian Peaks Golf Course.

Places to Go

- Lafayette City Park
  450 N 111th Street

- Lafayette Miners Museum
  108 E Simpson Street

- Lamont Does Park
  500 S Boulder Road

- Waneka Lake Park
  705 and 1600 Caria Drive

Things to Do

January
- Lafayette Oatmeal Festival
  www.discoverlafayette.com

June
- Lafayette Wine Festival
  (303) 926-4352

August
- Peach Festival with Art & Antiques
  www.discoverlafayette.com

September
- Celebrate Lafayette
  www.discoverlafayette.com

Struttin' Pup Dog Bakery & Bath

ANIMALS & PETS: *Best place to treat your dog*

Struttin' Pup Dog Bakery & Bath was created by two girls who left rock and roll and went to the dogs. It's a place where pets can be indulged in a bath, and where the toys and treats are not only tasty and fun, but nutritious and safe as well. You can use Struttin' Pup's clean, elevated tubs to wash your dog and leave the mess behind. The shop provides everything, including grooming tables, towels and, for you, an apron. Dryers, brushes and nail clippers are right there. All you need is a dirty dog. You can choose one of its all-natural shampoos. Of course, you can also depend on the Struttin' Pup staff to wash your pet or provide other services, such as professional grooming. Struttin' Pup's treats and pet foods are all-natural and do not contain by-products, artificial colors, sweeteners or other chemicals. Struttin' Pup also has unique collars, toys, bowls and outdoor gear. You and your four-legged friend will have a great time in the store. Let Struttin' Pup Dog Bakery and Bath be the ones to indulge you and your pooch.

1385 Forest Park Circle, Suite 105, Lafayette CO
(303) 665-3038
www.struttinpup.com

The Tack Collection

ANIMALS & PETS: *Best English tack, accessories and gifts*

If you love horses or want to learn the art of true horsemanship, then look to The Tack Collection. Owner Beverly Harrison started as a horse enthusiast and rider. Her passion grew and led her to become certified by The British Society of Master Saddlers, founded in 1966 to "safeguard the quality of work, training and qualifications of those Saddlers who make and repair saddles, bridles and leatherwork." Beverly is one of the few Americans ever to attend and complete the distinction. She continues to seek out and provide continuing educational seminars and programs to her ready staff. This high level of dedication to education ensures The Tack Collection's status remains cutting edge. Beverly's shop is sought out by horse owners, trainers and equine professionals from all over the U.S. because of her uncompromising standards. The store has a European flavor, featuring imported items from England, France, Italy, Germany and Scotland. You'll find everything from the practical such as a complete display of saddles, English tack, apparel, and gifts to the innovative "Used Tack Sale Swap", an annual event for Beverly's clients to acquire the latest equipment on the market. Although you'll discover exclusive merchandise found nowhere else, the prices are remarkably competitive. The staff at the Tack Collection has the expertise and reputation to make every horse and rider as comfortable, happy and stylish as possible. Beverly and her team invite you to visit The Tack Collection on your next trip to Lafayette.

1355 Forest Park Circle, Lafayette CO (303) 666-5364 or (866) 303-8225
www.tackcollection.com

PhotoEpic
BUSINESS: *Best photographers in Laffayette*

PhotoEpic captures images of life's epic journeys. Wedding
and commitment ceremonies are the specialty of the three
photographers at PhotoEpic, Lori Lander, Trent Norman
and Kevin Pugh. This group has a very special point of
view: They believe that when people are comfortable with
the photographers, their passion, love and excitement lend to
capturing beautiful and inspiring wedding photography. Lori,
Kevin and Trent are very personable and have the ability
to get people to relax, have fun and forget that the cameras
are there. Lori, Kevin and Trent want you to know them.
Their focus on establishing relationships while shooting
inspiring photography makes this team of photographers
unique. The shooting style of the threesome easily carries
them in to portraiture, special event, commercial and fine
art photography. Location is never a problem as they will go
wherever necessary to capture the images you need. When
it is important to capture that epic image, give PhotoEpic a
call.

709 W Brome Place, Lafayette CO (720) 771-4721
www.photoepicweddings.com
www.photoepic.com

Lafayette Florist

GARDENS, PLANTS & FLOWERS: *Best floral arrangements in Laffayette*

Lafayette Florist offers a full spectrum of magnificent flora, including loose flowers for arrangements, vines, rose bushes and shrubs along with trees, annuals and perennials. Yasutaro and Kumiko Yoshihara opened this popular full-service florist shop as a fruit stand in 1949 after their release from a Colorado concentration camp where they had spent the duration of World War II. Today, the family-owned and operated business continues to thrive under the leadership of granddaughter Lori Wheat, director of merchandising and marketing, as well as Brain Wheat, C.E.O., and granddaughter and General Manager Sandi and her husband and Grower Craig Sniff. The Yoshihara's son Gene Yoshihara and his wife, Evelyn, also continue to play an active roll in the business as President and C.F.O., respectively. Lafayette Florist is beautifully laid out and offers an extensive florists' area along with a nursery that comes complete with a Japanese style bridge and elegant Koi pond. The warm atmosphere welcomes you in as the musky, floral-scented air and the vivid colors that fill the shop soothe your senses. Lafayette Florist is the first recipient of the new *Florist of the Year* award given jointly by Wholesale Florist and Florist Supplier Association, and Florist's Review Magazine. This award was created to honor florists nationwide that demonstrate outstanding quality in fresh flower offerings, merchandising, customer service and business success all characteristics at which Lafayette Florist excels. Trust your flora needs to those who understand them best at Lafayette Florist.

600 South Public Road, Lafayette CO
(303) 665-5552
www.lafayetterflorist.com

Lafayette Collectibles and Flea Market

MARKETS: *Best flea market in Laffayette*

Lafayette Collectibles and Flea Market is owned by Bill and Cheryl Hopkins. Although formerly in the real estate business, Hopkins dived into the flea market venture with an unwavering faith and the jump payed off. Lafayette Collectibles was named the 12th best flea market in the United States just a few short years after first opening its doors. Lafayette Collectibles and Flea Market is operated on the philosophy of treating others with respect and offering good value and diversity in their merchandise. The staff is personable and vendors are carefully selected to provide variety to consumers. The business is an asset to the environment, as well. Flea Markets are a recycling business, taking perfectly good products to a new audience rather than disposing of them. Lafayette Collectibles appeals to treasure hunters as well as those looking for specific items such as tools. Bill Hopkins recalls a eight dollar piece of Mexican pottery turning out to be an artifact worth $1,500 for one lucky customer. A walk through the shop can feel similar to an enjoyable stroll down nostalgia lane. The large space offers new and used treasures in a setting where each booth has its own personality. Come into Lafayette Collectibles and Flea Market for fun and see what you can dig up.

130 E Spaulding Street, Lafayette CO
(303) 665-0433

Joe's Bike Shop
RECREATION: *Best bike shop in Laffayette*

Bikes have become specialized and very high tech in recent years, which is why it's nice to have a knowledgeable and trustworthy person like Joe Giovenco to help you sort through all the choices. Joe listens carefully to his customers at Joe's Bike Shop in Lafayette to make sure that they never leave with a bike they don't need. He caters to the BMX market with a hot selection of the latest models and even sponsors a BMX race team through his store. However, if you and your family just want to ride around the neighborhood, you'll find the cruisers at Joe's Bike Shop that will allow you to do that in comfort and style. "I just want to see people having fun on their bikes," says Joe, no matter what their goal. His passion for two-wheeling landed him his first job in a New Jersey bike shop and gained him similar employment in Florida and New Mexico. In all, he serves his customers with the experience he has accumulated during 15 years in the business. When you're shopping for a bike, you'll receive guidance you can trust at Joe's Bike Shop.

2770 Arapahoe Road, Lafayette CO
(303) 666-1400
www.joesbikeshopco.com

Coal Creek Bowling Center
RECREATION: *Best bowling center in Laffayette*

Smoky, dimly lit bowling alleys are a thing of the past. Coal Creek Bowling Center is a bright, smoke-free and community-oriented facility with automatic scoring and professional grade bowling lanes. Catering to everyone from children to seniors, and from occasional bowlers to serious league competitors, Coal Creek isn't only about bowling, it's about offering a place where members of the community can get together to enjoy a truly interactive entertainment experience rain or shine. Thanks to one of the best junior bowler programs in the state, loads of people have grown up bowling here. While there is great value in watching favorite movies and television shows, nothing beats the entertainment experience that bowling offers. People bond with each other, compete with each other, eat, drink, play and just have a great time. The café at Coal Creek is popular with not only bowlers but with employees of local businesses who drop by for the Lunch Bowl Combo special. Experience the current state of bowling at Coal Creek Bowling Center. Located at Highway 287 and South Boulder Road in Lafayette.

550 W Boulder Road, Lafayette CO
(303) 673-0772

Zamparelli's Italian Bistro

RESTAURANTS & CAFES:
Best Italian cuisine

Jimmy Zamparelli's culinary education began long before he enrolled at the Culinary Institute of America. His grandmother taught him to make ricotta ravioli when he was just a boy growing up in Brooklyn, New York. Jimmy still uses her recipes to create the meatballs and marinara sauce served at Zamparelli's Italian Bistro today. Italian comfort food is the specialty here; however, you will see fresh, locally grown produce featured in innovative salads, soups, pastas and pizzas. Although lasagna and eggplant were in Jimmy's blood before he went to school, the Culinary Institute helped him fine-tune his craft and just as importantly, he met his wife Nancy at the Institute. Together they own the spacious 3,000-square-foot Zamparelli's Italian Bistro in Lafayette's Atlas Valley Shopping Center. Their willingness to experiment in the kitchen really shows in their interesting salads. Jimmy and Nancy recommend the roasted beet salad with shaved fennel, green beans, oven roasted beets and goat cheese. There's gelato, cannoli, tiramisu and chocolate mousse for dessert, so save room. For Italian favorites and culinary flair, eat at Zamparelli's Italian Bistro.

2770 Arapahoe Road at 95th Street, Lafayette CO
(303) 664-1275
www.zamparellis.com

Photo by Joan Reed

Pulcinella Pizzeria and Ristorante
RESTAURANTS & CAFES: *Best organic meals*

In 1991, Chef Antonio Race, a native of Miliscola, Naples, embarked on a mission to bring Italy's fresh cuisine to Colorado and has succeeded magnificently via his popular restaurant chain, Pulcinella Pizzeria and Ristorante. Chef Antonio, along with family members Enzo and Mary Race, use only the freshest, highest-quality products at their eateries and refuse anything pre-made. Pulcinella offers a complete menu of mouthwatering delights made from organic produce and cheeses, including classic Neapolitan and Sicilian-style pizzas topped with prime Italian meats, fresh herbs and sauces. Gourmet calzones, tender pasta dishes and panini sandwiches are equally tempting options. The tiramisu makes a rich dessert ending to any meal. The ristorante takes its name from one of Italy's most celebrated characters. Pulcinella, a character in Neopolitan puppetry, originated in the 17th-century Commedia dell'arte. The long-nosed figure, in black mask and long white coat, mocked the rich, beat the other puppets and pretended to be too stupid to know what was going on. His antics allowed people to forget their problems for a time and turned him into a cherished icon. Pulcinella employs dedicated staff members who undergo continual study to bring you information on everything from the wines to how your entrée was made. Experience the true flavors of Italy at Pulcinella Pizzeria and Ristorante.

300 S Public Road, Lafayette CO
(303) 604-2888
1800 Lawrence Street, Denver CO
(303) 382-1444
www.pulcinellaristorante.com

Elizabeth's Embellishments
SHOPPING: *Best embellishments*

At Elizabeth's Embellishments, you'll find wonderful details with French and cottage inspiration. When you enter, you are surrounded by pretty furnishings and light cheerful colors that celebrate the vintage and the romantic. The goods are chic and feminine, yet display the spontaneity of a living garden. Embellishments can be anything from generously scented candles that fill your home with delightful fragrance to a perfect picture frame to hold a cherished photo. They can be fine French ribbon perfectly decorating a special gift or a gorgeous crystal chandelier over the bathtub. Elizabeth's Embellishments is the brainchild of Elizabeth Lagae and her mother, Ann Elize Watt. The two had the vision of bringing together all things beautiful, and soon the French and cottage theme developed. Some items, such as cards and dried floral arrangements, are handmade. Local artisans make some of the jewelry and furniture. Elizabeth and her husband Paul also travel in search of the most beautiful cottage and European country home accents. Whether a product is local or imported from across the world, Elizabeth's shop always offers the best prices around. If you are looking for gifts to embellish your friendships or accessories to embellish yourself, you'll want to explore Elizabeth's Embellishments. Life is just better when it's embellished.

401 S Public Road, Lafayette CO
(303) 926-7133
www.elizabethsembellishments.com

LONE TREE

Lone Tree, the southern gateway to metro Denver, is a town of large, new homes. It is not only a great place to live, but also to shop. Park Meadows, one of the largest malls in the metro area, is anchored by Dillard's, Macy's and Nordstrom. Lone Tree is also home to Sky Ridge, a brand-new, state-of-the-art regional medical facility. In 2006, Lone Tree's Lincoln Station became the current end of the line for the Southeast Corridor light rail line. The massive construction effort known as T-REX (Transportation Expansion Project) simultaneously rebuilt portions of I-25 and I-225 while installing the new rapid transit system. T-REX was a cooperative partnership between highway and transit agencies that serves as a model for the nation.

Places to Go

- Bluffs Regional Park
  10099 Crooked Stick Trail
- Sweetwater Park
  8300½ Sweetwater Road

SkyVenture Colorado

RECREATION: *Best skydiving simulator*

The futuristic building housing SkyVenture, a state-of-the-art skydiving simulator/vertical wind tunnel, rises before you. As you approach you see something that stops you dead in your tracks: A teenager in a colorful jumpsuit is floating directly in front of you. Suddenly, he jets up and down, forward and back, then spins with amazing speed and stops, grinning from ear to ear. SkyVenture makes this aerial adventure available to you on your next visit to Lone Tree. This technological marvel provides the most realistic free fall simulation possible. The idea of flying indoors was pioneered by the American military in 1964, and in 1982, vertical wind tunnels opened in Tennessee and Las Vegas. The first SkyVenture tunnel opened in Orlando in 1998. SkyVenture Colorado is the eighth tunnel to be manufactured by SkyVenture and the first in Colorado. Anyone age three or older can try it following a 10-minute training class. You are outfitted with flight suit, goggles, helmet and shoes, taught how to operate the controls, then you are set free to fly. Located in the Lone Tree Entertainment District, SkyVenture Colorado is something you just have to try.

9230 Park Meadows Drive, Lone Tree CO
(303) 768-9000
http://www.skyventurecolorado.com

The National Ballet of Denver

ATTRACTIONS: *Best classical ballet school*

Two new jewels have recently been added Denver's artistic crown, The National Ballet of Denver and The National Ballet Academy of Denver. Cornell Callender and Andrei Vassiliev, who have toured and performed with some of the world's leading ballet companies, founded the National Ballet Academy of Denver in 2005 as a way to develop a strong classical ballet school in a city with an unparalleled appreciation of the arts. Shortly thereafter they launched the professional company as a way to bring a rich classical repertory to people who truly appreciate the classics. The goal of the National Ballet of Denver and the Academy is to provide a very high level of art education, training and producing young, talented classical dancers who can perform with the National Ballet of Denver and other professional companies around the world. The Academy, which offers training at all levels for all ages, was honored in 2005 with an invitation to perform at the Radford Theater in Virginia. Some of their students have already received scholarships and contracts at prestigious companies and schools, including the New York City Ballet and The Joffrey Ballet. If you love classical ballet, be sure to join the Friends of the National Ballet of Denver. Check out their website to learn more about this exciting artistic venture.

8868 E Maximus Drive, Lone Tree CO
(303) 860-1236
www.nationalballetofdenver.org

Places to Go

- Golden Ponds Park and Recreation Area
  2651 3rd Avenue

- Longmont Museum & Cultural Center
  400 Quail Road

- Roger's Grove Park
  220 Hover Road

- Roosevelt Park
  700 Longs Peak Avenue

- Sandstone Ranch Park
  2525 & 3001 E Highway 119

- St. Vrain State Park
  3525 State Highway 119, Firestone

- Union Reservoir and Park
  0461 Weld County Road 26

Things to Do

June

- Pet & Doll Parade
  (303) 651-8404

- Colorado Reptile's Open House
  (303) 776-7020 ext. 4

- Taste of Longmont
  (303) 776-5295

July

- Rhythm on the River
  www.ci.longmont.co.us/rotr

July-August

- Boulder County Fair
  www.bouldercountyfair.org

August

- Mountain States Chili Cookoff
  (303) 684-9316

September

- Oktoberfest
  (303) 772-5796

October

- El Dia de los Muertos
  (303) 651-8374

December

- Hometown Holiday Parade
  www.ci.longmont.co.us/rec/special/ hometown.htm

LONGMONT

Major Stephen H. Long explored the St. Vrain River valley in 1820, and he gave his name first to a mountain and then a city. The Chicago Colony of Illinois founded Longmont in 1871. For many years, the town was an important agricultural center, with flour mills, a vegetable cannery and a sugar beet refinery. In 1962, the U.S. government built an air traffic control center in Longmont. Three years later, IBM built a large facility nearby. Longmont, which had grown only slightly beyond its original square mile, began to grow explosively. The city has more than 80,000 residents today and continues to grow. Like a number of nearby communities, Longmont is on Money magazine's list of the 100 best places to live in the United States. The National Civic League has named Longmont an All-America City, an award that recognizes communities that have made major progress in meeting their most important needs. Beginning in 2014, commuter rail will link Longmont with Boulder, Denver and other communities.

Longmont's 2005 Criterium
Photo by Richard Masoner

The Thompson House Inn & Tea Room

ACCOMMODATIONS:
Best American-traditional bed and breakfast

The Thompson House Inn & Tea Room shines like a jewel in the historic west side neighborhood of Longmont. Close to lovely old parks and to other turn-of-the-century estates, this bed and breakfast inn evokes a flavor of the city's early days. Built in 1887, the inn was meticulously renovated in 1994 to showcase the original inlaid wood floors, coved ceilings and Italian marble fireplaces. Owners Cee and Scott Dolenc offer five rooms with period furnishings and décor, each with a private bath. While maintaining old-time charm, the inn has modern conveniences like televisions, VCR's and wireless internet access in each room. You may spend time in the peaceful parlor, shaded front patio or the rose garden and enjoy a hearty, delicious breakfast served at your convenience. Book the entire inn for graduations, family reunions or retreats. At tea time, you can don vintage hats, gloves, pearls and stoles from the dress-up trunk for added fun at the traditional English tea. A tea party is a great way to celebrate special occasions such as birthday parties, wedding showers or baby showers. Also visit the gift shop filled with antiques, collectibles, linens and lace and elegant tea accouterments. For small town hospitality in a historic landmark, do not miss a stay at the Thompson House Inn & Tea Room.

537 Terry Street, Longmont CO
(303) 651-1121
www.thompsonhouseinn.com

The Dickens House Bed & Breakfast

ACCOMMODATIONS:
Best Victorian-style bed and breakfast

The Dickens House Bed & Breakfast is pleased to offer several unique rooms furnished with period antiques expressly designed for your comfort. Savor a hearty breakfast served from an authentic, cast iron stove. Relax in an under-the-stars hot tub, or spend some time in the library and sitting room, set aside expressly for guest use. Enjoy the home-spun atmosphere throughout the house and surrounding grounds. The Dickens House is a historic 1872 brick Victorian farmhouse sitting on three-and-a-half acres. The farm was the original homestead of St. Vrain Valley pioneer William H. Dickens. Dickens was a descendant of Charles Dickens and a builder of the Dickens Opera House. Conveniently located within 50 minutes of Denver and 20 minutes from Boulder, the home has all of the comforts of the city out the front door and all of pleasures of the country out the back door. Come and join the folks at the Dickens House Bed & Breakfast for your next stay in the beautiful Rocky Mountain area.

136 S Main Street, Longmont CO
(303) 774-0071

D-Barn Reception Hall

ACCOMMODATIONS:
Best reception hall

The historic Dickens Barn (D-Barn) was built approximately in 1916 by Senator Theodore Lashley. In 1996 the barn was moved to its present location, replacing a barn that was twice its size that burned down in 1943 to a hay mow fire. D-Barn is located on a historic property with the oldest land grant in the state. It was deeded to a war widow in 1812 and conveyed to William H. Dickens in 1862 by President Andrew Johnson. D-Barn offers a unique experience in a pastoral setting. The facility has undergone an extensive renovation and is available for rental as a reception hall for weddings, receptions, meetings, parties and any other celebration. D-Barn holds 198 people comfortably. A large deck fronts the barn, with a wide staircase perfect for pictures. The open floor plan can accommodate all different types of layouts for your gatherings, while the new hard wood floor is all set for dancing. The interior is decorated with small farm implements, lending a wonderful atmosphere for your party. Tables, chairs and the historic grounds are available at an additional charge. Contact the Dickens Barn today and they will help make your next party a raving success.

136 S Main Street, Longmont CO
(303) 651-1259
www.dbarn.net

Blue Hills Dog and Cat Shoppe
ANIMALS & PETS: *Best pet shop in Longmont*

If you are looking for a source for all-natural, wholesome pet food and care products, including raw food, you will find it at Blue Hills Dog and Cat Shoppe in Longmont. Owner Diane Dietrich, with the help of her trusted assistants, Whisper the store cat and Chico the famous Chihuahua, is passionate about providing pet owners with high quality products and information to help them keep their pets healthy and happy. Blue Hills features a state-of-the-art self-service dog washing facility and the Dog Bakery & Café. Bring your pet with you every Saturday, when Diane prepares a meal—for the dogs. In addition to helping pet owners maintain their pets' health, Diane reaches out to such organizations as the local police K-9 units and the Longmont Humane Society. Blue Hills also sponsors an annual dinner and walk to help with construction of the National War Dogs Memorial in Washington, D.C. The National War Dogs Memorial is dedicated to the thousands of dogs that have served the U.S. military since World War I. Diane shows her dedication to animals through her store products and café; her outreach activities demonstrate her community-minded spirit. For high quality pet care products and excellent customer service, visit Diane, Whisper and Chico at Blue Hills Dog and Cat Shoppe.

2255 N Main Street, #117, Longmont CO
(303) 651-2955
www.bluehillsdogandcat.com

Crackpots
ARTS & CRAFTS: *Best pottery studio in Longmont*

Think outside the pot. The artist in you is sure to find an outlet for expression at Crackpots, a paint-your-own pottery studio and gift gallery. Many artists now considered geniuses were called crackpots in their day. Most of us have a little crackpot in us. You can have a whole lot of fun letting it out at a place where no experience is necessary, and there is no right way to proceed. Crackpots provides a variety of entertaining options for the whole family, from adult and kid parties to summer creativity camps. Owner Tamar Hendricks continually adds more creative options, like multimedia opportunities, mosaics for everyone and storybook sessions for toddlers who then paint imaginative pieces stimulated by the storytelling. In addition to a host of special events, such as Date Night and Two for Tuesday, you can walk in anytime during store hours and get assistance from the helpful staff. Choose a piece of unfinished pottery, find inspiration from an array of gift ideas in the shop, and paint your heart out. Your one-of-a-kind piece will be glazed, fired and ready in about five days. Tamar and all the staff invite the artist in you to soar at Crackpots.

501 Main Street, Longmont CO
(303) 776-2211
www.ecrackpots.com

Photos by Tim Ellis/French Quarter Photography Studio & Gallery

Thread Bear Quilts

ARTS & CRAFTS:
Warm Hearts—Good Friends

Penny and Jerry Mullen, owners of Thread Bear Quilts, believe that the world of quilting fully embraces the love of giving. They have created a shop where people come together in the spirit of camaraderie to enjoy and share the many social, sharing and creative aspects of quilting. Since the store was founded in July of 2002, the most current and popular quilting fabric collections in full lines have continuously been obtained from all major quilting fabric suppliers. With over 5,000 bolts of fabric on display and more arriving weekly, beginning and experienced quilters alike enjoy choosing and creating from an endless variety of traditional prints, bright and playful contemporary designs as well as hand-dyed fabrics in rainbows of brilliant color. The Thread Bear also has available those handy notions that quilters find indispensable, the highest quality machine quilting thread, the latest quilt patterns and an ever expanding assortment of the most recently published quilting books. Friendly, helpful and knowledgeable service is the store's promise and commitment to customers shopping at Thread Bear Quilts. The store's involvement in the local community is well represented and reflected in the many sewing clubs, in-store classes and variety of special sponsored events. Thread Bear activities are provided for the useful, educational and pleasure of all quilters and citizens alike. Caring and sharing provide the basis for the Thread Bear's motto, Warm Hearts–Good Friends.

1755 ½ Main Street, Longmont CO
(720) 652-9001
tbquilts@qwest.net
www.threadbearquilts.com

Bead Lounge

ARTS & CRAFTS: *Best bead shop in Longmont*

The bead lounge is a den of creativity. Located in historic downtown Longmont, the Bead Lounge is part gallery, part retail store, part art school and part artist hang out. Just walking into the Bead Lounge puts you in the mood to create. The hardwood floors and lofty ceilings invite you to expand with the space. The work tables and comfortable couches beckon you to settle in. The art on the walls and in the displays inspire you to reach inside your own creative reservoir. The shop itself is a work of art, decorated with hand-dyed and painted textiles, wall hangings, and collages. Delicate crystals grown in pottery glazes adorn stunning vessels. Dichroic glass glitters in a rainbow of light in hanging glass ornaments and bowls. There are paintings, photographs, sculptures, jewelry, household objects and even lamps made of reworked lingerie. On the retail side of things, you'll find an impressive stock of specialty and hard-to-find beads, including Swarovski crystal beads, semi-precious gems, cabochons, polymer clay beads, pearl beads and lampworked glass beads. They offer a unique collection of wearable art, including necklaces, bracelets, watches, and earrings You can take classes, schedule parties, and brainstorm with other artists. Owner Patty Webber is in the process of expanding her 2,000-square-foot space so she can offer even more inspiration. Visit the Bead Lounge the first chance you get. You will walk away with beads in your pocket and stars in your eyes.

320 Main Street, Longmont CO (303) 678-9966 *www.beadlounge.com*

Keepsakes and Memories
ARTS & CRAFTS: *Best scrapbook and rubberstamp supplies*

Making scrapbooks is an enormously addictive hobby that promises great satisfaction. If you are touched by the bug, Keepsakes and Memories in Longmont has all the scrapbooking and rubberstamp supplies you could want and plenty of inspiration. Scrappers enjoy the social environment of collaborative sessions, called crops, as well as the large showroom with one of the largest collections of paper in the state, plus tools and albums. Scrappers do more than place their memories in albums, they embellish them. Keepsakes and Memories understands the urge to decorate and carries adornments, suitable for scrapbooking or card making. The What's New wall is always filled with exciting products, and the dollar section offers great deals. The heart of the store is the large classroom area that provides space for crops and scrapbooking classes. Make those keepsakes stand out, or create special recipe books with help from an enormous range of classes, designed to help you organize, preserve and display your photographs using creative ideas and techniques. Keepsakes and Memories happily schedules private crops and classes for your club or circle of friends, in addition to the events put on by the store. The shop sponsors the Design Team, a select group of ladies who have demonstrated talent for developing attractive and creative scrapbook pages. Owner Suzanne Savage invites you to Keepsakes and Memories to discover the joys of creating wonderful mementos.

1350 Ken Pratt Boulevard, #3, Longmont CO
(303) 774-7895
www.keepsakesandmemories.com

Jesters Dinner Theatre
& School for the Performing Arts
ATTRACTIONS: *Best performing arts center in Longmont*

With its theme Learn to be the King or Queen of the Stage, Jesters Dinner Theatre and School for the Performing Arts provides the setting for adults and children to learn stagecraft. After opening the dinner theater in 1999, Scott and Mary Lou Moore found the demand for theater training in Longmont so great that they opened a school to teach performing arts. Workshops introduce various aspects of performance, including costume creation, lighting, set building and acting techniques. A summer intern program gives talented young people opportunities to further their skills. Graduates of the school have the chance to participate in coming-attractions alongside the actors who often come many miles to audition for parts. The schedule features dinner shows Thursday through Sunday and children's theatre every Saturday afternoon. In addition to providing theater, Jesters is available for banquets, business meetings and wedding receptions. The theater generously offers discounts to students, seniors and groups. Gift certificates are available. You can make advance reservations for show-only tickets or show-and-dinner tickets. The dinner menu offers a choice of appetizers, entrées and desserts, plus dishes especially for children. Alcoholic and non-alcoholic beverages are available. Come and enjoy the smoke-free environment and intimate seating at Jesters Dinner Theatre. You'll feel like part of the performance and just might want to become a performer in the future.

224 Main Street, Longmont CO
(303) 682-9980
www.jesterstheatre.com

Barking Dog Café
BAKERIES, COFFEE & TEA:
Best café in Longmont

Coffee is the heart and soul of the Barking Dog Café. The café's insistence on serving the Silver Canyon brand from a roaster in nearby Boulder assures that only the finest flavors reach your cup. Four varieties of coffee and espresso are always available, along with lattes, cappuccinos and a variety of pekoe teas. Situated in Lyons, the Double Gateway to the Rockies, the café has a special affinity for the cyclists who comprise a large part of its business. Comfortable couches and wireless Internet give the interior a distinctly homey feel. Food selections include fresh-from-the-oven bagels, carefully selected cold cuts and breakfast sandwiches. In addition to emphasizing outstanding coffee, food and a comfortable customer environment, the café actively participates in its community. It belongs to the Chamber of Commerce and sponsors a variety of local events. Whether you are walking, driving or cycling, the Barking Dog Café invites you to come in and savor a taste of Longmont.

17 Lincoln Place, Longmont CO
(303) 823-9600

You Can Sing at Longmont School of Music
BUSINESS: *Best music school in Longmont*

Wayne Hengler loves to sing, and he knows how to teach others to sing at You Can Sing at Longmont School of Music. Wayne sang in his first band at the age of 15. At 42, he became serious enough about music to gain a certification and opened the music school in 1996. The school handles voice and instrument lessons for children aged six to 18, but also holds an introductory voice session for adults, which teaches them about the school's approach and sends them home with exercises to strengthen their own voices. Three instructors offer lessons in voice, piano, guitar, bass, drums, violin and several other instruments. Students supply their own instruments, except for piano and drums. The staff teaches students to read and write music and to banish stage fright. The emphasis is on fun, and the You Can Sing teachers have helped more than 1,000 children enrich their lives by developing skill and self-esteem. The school's summer programs offer opportunities for participation in an orchestra, band or choir. Children improve their skills as musicians and experience teamwork and friendships while developing poise. You Can Sing is also home to Pied Piper Productions, which plans live DJ-driven music events for businesses or private parties. The experts at You Can Sing believe that if you can talk, you can learn to sing. Bring music into the lives of your children or host a special event with help from the experts at You Can Sing at Longmont School Of Music.

620 Main Street, Longmont CO
(303) 684-9742
www.longmontmusic.com

Stitch Crazy
BUSINESS: *Best custom embroidery and screen printing*

At Stitch Crazy the staff gives new meaning to the term team spirit. Native Coloradoans Tiffany, Scott and Dave Stoecker provide individual customers, athletic teams and workplaces with custom embroidered shirts, hats and jackets that give any team a common identity. Individuals belong to something bigger than themselves when they wear a custom logo or school insignia on their clothing. Stitch Crazy offers quality jackets and shirts. The store also places logos on athletic bags, towels and blankets. From basic numbers to tackle twill, Stitch Crazy can prepare your team for the playing field. Serving Longmont and the surrounding area, Stitch Crazy accepts original artwork and digitizes it on-site. The shop offers some discounted pricing, and the owners pride themselves on consistent value and quality. They guarantee all their work. Stitch Crazy is family oriented and enjoys many happy, returning customers. For a leisurely examination of the shop's entire range of products and services, check out the online catalogue. Whether your order is screen printed or embroidered, go to Stitch Crazy for logos that will have you cheering *go team*.

508 5th Avenue, Longmont CO
(303) 678-1074
www.stitchcrazyonline.com

Photos courtesy of StitchCrazyOnline.com

Brown's Shoe Fit Company
FASHION: *Best shoe store in Longmont*

It was about the time when the 19th century melted away and the 20th century emerged that John Galsworthy wrote *Quality*, a story bemoaning the loss of personal service and customer care in shoemaking. Brown's Shoe Fit Company was formed in 1911 by a group of shoe merchants in Shenandoah, Iowa who shared Galsworthy's concerns. Today, the company still exudes a passion for great shoes and enthusiastic service. As a second generation store owner, Jason Wetzel comes by his passion honestly. He believes in offering name brands at competitive prices and in a wide variety of sizes, so that none of his customers feels left out. Jason understands his Colorado clientele and fits them in the styles that work with a casual, healthy lifestyle. In 2005, Brown's Shoe Fit Company won a readers' choice award for *Best Longmont Shoe Store*. Jason makes it easy for you to get to know his products by participating in Longmont's downtown events and local art walks. In *Quality*, Mr. Gessler, the shoe store owner, was known as a man of integrity, because the needs of his customers far outweighed other concerns. Stop by Brown's Shoe Fit Company for a visit with Jason Wetzel, and see how he holds to those old-fashioned values.

373 Main Street, Longmont CO
(303) 776-2920
www.BrownsShoefitco.com

Ambrosia Glass Art
GALLERIES & FINE ART:
Most exciting glass studio and gallery in Longmont

Ambrosia Glass Art in Longmont celebrates the vibrant colors and sleek feel of art glass. Angelo Ambrosia produces functional and gallery pieces and offers glassblowing classes. A potter for 15 years, he was enticed by the immediacy of glassblowing. He now spends all of his time producing expressive pieces in this entrancing medium. He offers classes regularly and always welcomes new students. His passion for his art infuses his day and inspires him to share his enthusiasm through teaching. He finds that instructing others adds to his abilities to articulate within the glass-blowing medium. Art glassblowing does not use machines, and the hand-crafting process results in one-of-a-kind pieces, each with an air of individuality. The spontaneous nature of the technique requires an openness and readiness to change and go with the flow, and Angelo is captivated by the process. Come join him in this exciting endeavor or browse his affordable gallery of offerings. Regularly open by appointment, Ambrosia Glass Art is worth a visit.

34 Boston Court, Unit D, Longmont CO
(303) 678-1641
www.ambrosiaglassart.com

Gail Smith · Gerri Bradford · Hazel McCoy · Linda Miller · Lisette Walker · Sally Fulton · Alecia Jensen · Annette Kennedy · Dan Hollingshead · Diane Wood · Dru Marie Robert · Patricia Montgomery · Rose Lynch · Nancy Champion

Muse Gallery
GALLERIES & FINE ART:
Longmont's largest affordable art collection

The Muse Gallery, a program of the Longmont Council for the Arts, is a cooperative effort of about 60 contributing artist members as well as volunteers. The arts scene in Longmont is red-hot. Local advocates believe that Longmont has some of the greatest artists in the Front Range. The artists' registry, which the Council for the Arts maintains to promote exhibitions, contains almost 200 names. Art is on display all over town, but the largest affordable collection is at the Muse Gallery. The local artists showcased in the gallery are often multitalented. A single painter may work in oil, watercolor and pastels. Exhibitors include fine-art photographers and sculptors working in wood and metal. Some artists create mosaics, others create jewelry. Some work with fiber, while others work with clay or glass. The shows change every two months. Each show features the work of a local artist, a visiting artist and a student. Under the aegis of the Council for the Arts, the gallery hosts music, theater, poetry slams and other performances. In 2006, the *Times-Call* Reader's Choice survey voted the Muse Gallery Longmont's best art gallery. To see the work of Longmont's diverse and vibrant artistic community, come to the Muse Gallery.

356 Main Street, Longmont CO
(303) 678-7869
www.themusegallery.org

Ute Trail Greenhouse

GARDENS, PLANTS & FLOWERS:
Best family-operated greenhouse

Before planting the ultimate garden or backyard retreat, make a stop at Ute Trail Greenhouse, where owners Mary Bukszar and John Hybiak dedicate themselves to creating lasting relationships with their customers based upon a mutual passion for gardens. The family run company opened in 1998, selling their plants primarily at farmers' markets and by appointment. In 2003, the greenhouse opened to the public on a daily basis from spring through autumn. Ute Trail offers an expansive array of new and hard to find plants as well as a bevy of tried and true favorites. Look for 100 varieties of new and heirloom tomato plants in varied shapes, sizes and colors. Ute Trail has five greenhouses along with an outdoor tree and shrub area. The beautifully arranged facility provides stunning rose varieties and 33 different types of lilacs in such startling colors as magenta, yellow and blue. Ute Trail grows most of its plants from seeds, cuttings or plugs at the company's secondary greenhouse near Lyons, which makes the plants better suited to Colorado's climate than plants grown elsewhere and shipped to Colorado. Three times a year Ute Trail publishes a newsletter filled with great updates about incoming selections, as well as planting tips and information on various plants, shrubs and outdoor goodies that are coming into season. Indulge in your passion for gardening, landscaping and plants in general with the like-minded individuals at Ute Trail Greenhouse, where gardeners find something new and delightful with each visit.

5555 Ute Highway, Longmont CO
(303) 823-6315 *www.utetrail.com*

Duran's Hobby Acres Garden Center
GARDENS, PLANTS & FLOWERS: *Best wholesale plant selection*

When you hear Robert Duran, owner of Duran's Hobby Acres Garden Center, talk about goals for his horticultural business, you realize right away that he didn't get into it to make a quick killing. His talk of creating a legacy, something that the community will value for generations to come, falls naturally from the lips of someone who knows all about planting a seed and watching it grow. Robert has certainly planted a lot of seeds during his first 20 years in business. On the wholesale side, he currently offers 250 varieties of annuals, 180 perennials, 44 vegetables and 38 herbs. As for the number of individual plants, he figures that 35,000 perennials, 10,000 geraniums and several thousand hanging baskets would be about right. Recently, out of a desire to give people an alternative between big box retailers on the one hand and boutique nurseries on the other, he has been switching the focus of Duran's Hobby Acres from wholesale to retail. That's good news for the individual, because the size of Robert's inventory allows him to price his plants at almost wholesale to the public. Go to Duran's Hobby Acres Garden Center, and start a family tradition that could last for a hundred years.

15591 N 107th Street, Longmont CO
(303) 772-9586

Gwynne's Greenhouse & Gardenshoppe

GARDENS, PLANTS & FLOWERS:
*Best garden shopping
in a country setting*

Nestled in the sandstone hillside near Lyons is a gardeners' paradise. The vibrant, thriving gardens that surround this business and the wild foothills that rise next to it provide the sensation that you are a world away from the hustle and bustle of the daily grind. However, Gwynne's Greenhouse & Gardenshoppe is conveniently located at the intersection of two major roads, just minutes away from Longmont, Boulder and Estes Park. Upon your first visit, you may be surprised at how much this locally owned greenhouse has to offer. The shop carries an incredible array of container gardens, hanging baskets, an unusual and eclectic selection of perennials, annuals, indoor blooming plants and various houseplants. Amongst the greenery, you will find a wide and unique selection of pottery, statuary, garden ornaments, outdoor furniture, garden style gifts and home décor. Fresh bouquets are available in the Gardenshoppe, or be bold and cut your own from their ever expanding Cut Flower Garden. Gwynne's caters to both novice and expert gardeners. The knowledgeable staff can help you make informed decisions about which perennials and annuals work best in your area, based on altitude, drought-tolerance, pest resistance and other pertinent conditions. At Christmas they offer a complete Santa's workshop with ornaments, holiday decorations, Christmas plants, wreaths and trees. Take a peek, Gwynne's Greenhouse & Gardenshoppe is beyond expectation.

**4559 Highland Drive (At Hwy Jct 36 and 66, near Lyons), Longmont CO
(303) 823-6838 or (303) 823-6818**
www.gwynnesgreenhouse.com

Prospect Flower Shop
GARDENS, PLANTS & FLOWERS: *Best flower arrangements*

When some businesses open, it seems like kismet, the owner's fate. The Prospect Flower Shop came into existence because the owners, Jenny Lucas and Jessica Krammes, are sisters and love the idea of collaborating creatively. A belief in interpersonal relationships drives this business forward. One result is the emphasis that the sisters place on personalized attention. Of course, remembering people with flowers on special occasions is an excellent way to foster relationships. The Prospect Flower Shop offers a selection of flowers, home decorating items and cards designed to help customers build those relationships. The shop also stocks vases, jewelry and gift baskets. Successful relationships require work, just as the sisters work to offer uncommon flowers in beautiful and unusual displays. In addition to hard-to-find flowers, Jenny and Jessica place an emphasis on local growers and artists that help customers celebrate the beauty of Longmont and Colorado. The shop offers extensive selections online. Visit the Prospect Flower Shop for a chance to see how love can be expressed in blooms.

1107 B Neon Forest Circle, Longmont CO
(303) 776-0699
www.prospectflowershop.com

Kolesar Body Knowledge Studios
HEALTH & BEAUTY:
Most complete body awareness and training approach

Kolesar Body Knowledge Studios provides training that fosters more efficient movement, increased coordination and self-awareness. The result is greater stamina, mobility and strength, which leads to rejuvenation and improved posture. Lara Kolesar, an internationally recognized teacher of Pilates, also has a background in yoga, athletics and massage therapy. She is a certified instructor of GYROTONIC® as well as Pilates. Lara has used her various experiences to develop the Body Knowledge Method™, which seeks to open channels of communication between the body and the mind. The studio offers a four-week introduction to the Body Knowledge System. The introduction prepares clients for mat and reformer-machine classes or independent workouts. Lara describes her teaching method as holistic. She uses Pilates-related exercises to assess a person's actual movement patterns so that corrections can be made where necessary. The tactile approach combines Pilates and GYROTONIC® with an understanding of anatomy and efficient joint movement. All Body Knowledge instructors are Pilates-certified and have undergone extensive training recognized by the Pilates Method Alliance. The studio also houses an on-site physical therapist and offers massage and Rolfing sessions. With a mission to let people inhabit their bodies more comfortably, Kolesar Body Knowledge Studios invites you to train for a strong body and good health. Located in the Meadowview Village Center.

600 S Airport Road, C-C, Longmont CO
(720) 494-9226
www.kolesarstudios.com

Solar Yoga Boutique + Café

HEALTH & BEAUTY: *Best yoga*

At Solar Yoga Boutique + Café, certified instructors encourage people of all skill levels, from beginner to advanced, to challenge body and mind with the practice of yoga. Owners Loretta, Dave and Stacie Richter and Stephanie Mayer combine many elements to create a meaningful yoga experience at their Longmont studio. They offer several types of yoga classes, including Hot Yoga, Hot Flow, Gentle and Power Vinyasa, that are practiced in a heated room with the aim of stretching, strengthening and relaxing the whole body. To build community among its students, Solar Yoga offers Happy Hour Yoga the first Friday of every month. It features a less strenuous workout in a warm room, followed by drinks and appetizers. The 60-minute Hot Yoga class is designed to give your body a wake-up call with an invigorating early morning workout.

Solar Yoga's new studio creates a welcoming, spa-like atmosphere, with spacious, well-planned locker rooms and a state-of-the-art heated yoga room. Stylish yet comfortable casual clothing, jewelry and designer street-wear await discovery in the boutique, along with an extensive selection of yoga clothing and accessories. The café offers healthful organic snacks, drinks and yogurt to complement your workout. Solar Yoga is part of Solar Village, an environmentally friendly, *green* building that uses wind and solar power. Come tour Solar Yoga Boutique + Café and learn how you can experience the mental clarity and peace of mind that comes from practicing yoga.

645 Tenacity Drive, Unit E, Longmont CO
(303) 485-0490
www.solar-yoga.com

Studio Boom
HEALTH & BEAUTY: *Best hair care*

Studio Boom is all about knowing and implementing trends in hair care and personal aesthetics. The studio's stylists receive constant training on current trends in hairstyles, makeup and hair colors. Owner Brandi Abernathy raised her daughters, Cindy Crawford and Anne Donahue, in Longmont, and the three decided that their home town needed a little style. Studio Boom seeks to

provide that style and is also a place that is full of fun and energy for the pleasure of customers and staff. The *Daily Times Call* apparently believes that the trio is successful, because it has named Studio Boom as the best salon in town. In addition to hair and makeup, the Studio Boom offers complete nail services, including manicures, pedicures and acrylics. Studio Boom is also the only certified Great Lengths hair extension salon in Longmont. The salon offers a Studio Boom line of personal care products and sells clothing created by a local artist as well. A trip to Studio Boom will perk up your style and your day.

**1225 Ken Pratt Boulevard, Longmont CO
(303) 774-9880**

Pilates Balance in Motion
HEALTH & BEAUTY: *Best Pilates instruction*

In the early 1920s, Joseph Pilates created a new way of exercising and rehabilitating the body. He designed a method that combines the strength-building orientation of the West with the more internally focused breathing and stretching style of the East. Pilates Balance in Motion owners Claudia Miller and Christina Albetta have a specific philosophy when it comes to sharing the Pilates techniques in their Longmont studio. They believe the techniques are best learned in individual sessions or small groups no larger than three. Larger group instruction just doesn't

allow them to adequately meet the highly individualized needs of their clients. The Pilates Method of exercise stresses the building of long, lean, agile musculature, with an emphasis on proper strengthening of the body's core. The Pilates repertoire promotes healthy spine and joint alignment while maximizing muscular strength and increased overall flexibility. Claudia and Christina have been friends since the 1980s and bring different strengths to their enterprise. Claudia has an academic and performance background in dance, and is a certified Pilates instructor. Christina worked as a registered nurse and a massage therapist and was trained in Pilates by various master instructors as well as The Physical Mind Institute and Polestar trainings. For individual or small group instruction in a friendly, non intimidating environment, visit Pilates Balance in Motion.

**323 3rd Avenue, Suite #1, Longmont CO
(720) 652-0706**

Sunflower Spa
**HEALTH & BEAUTY:
*Best body treatments***

In Southeast Longmont, where there once were fields of sunflowers, corn and open land, resides a blossoming retreat named

Sunflower Spa. In this new flower, a place of refuge, restoration and relaxation blooms. Owned by mother-daughter team Kay and Patrice vonMetzger, both long-time Colorado residents, Sunflower Spa offers a back-to-basics approach to natural beauty and well-being. You will enjoy results-oriented services using products containing all-natural, organically grown herbs, fruits and vegetables. Their goal is to create a welcoming environment where you will receive a customized approach to long-lasting, visible results, and a relationship that works as a trusted liaison to skin care, relaxation and overall self-care. From skin care services customized to address your unique needs to body treatments that leave you feeling refreshed, invigorated and renewed, you'll find the highest quality services at Sunflower Spa. Sample their wide variety of massage, including relaxing Swedish, sports-oriented deep-tissue, uniquely indulgent hot-stone and prenatal massage for mothers-to-be and new moms. Don't forget to visit the nail spa, offering the finest natural nail services, including the freshest seasonal manicures and pedicures around. For special occasions, take advantage of Sunflower Spa's great packages, or make reservations for a spa party, complete with wine and hors d'oeuvres. Everyone blooms with the simple, unpretentious and approachable services at Sunflower Spa.

**1700 Kylie Drive, Suite 150, Longmont CO
(303) 485-1390**
www.everyoneblooms.com

Mountain High Essentials

HOME: *Best soy candles in Longmont*

The sweet smells and healthy glow of Mountain High Essentials' EssentiaLite candles will have you waxing poetic about them. "Friends don't let friends burn paraffin," according to Jan Martin and Melody Jauregui, the Longmont company's founders and co-owners. EssentiaLite candles are made from a safer, more environmentally friendly soy wax. Besides being good for Mother Earth, soy wax gives you a longer burning, better smelling candle. EssentiaLite candles are made from 100 percent organic soy, grown by American farmers. Jan and Melody created their first batch of soy wax candles in their kitchens, but their business soon lit up more than friends and family, expanding into home parties and large retail customers. Mountain High Essentials' fundraising program joins with schools to sell the candles. The schools can raise funds for special projects, while Mountain High offers assistance to help them maximize their profits. EssentiaLite candles are better for the planet, longer-lasting and better smelling than your everyday candle. Light a candle from Mountain High Essentials and see for yourself.

1240 Ken Pratt Boulevard, Longmont CO
(720) 494-9876
www.EssentiaLite.com

"My highest recommendation for ABR Fireplaces. ABR handled all aspects of the installation, which I might add went perfectly. Both of our fireplaces look fantastic and work incredibly well. My compliments and thanks to ABR."

—Steve Vetorino, Berthoud, CO

ABR Fireplaces

HOME: *Our flame warms your heart and home*

When customers leave ABR Fireplaces, they are far more knowledgeable about fireplaces than when they arrived. Owners Andrew and Caitlin Stone love to share their extensive knowledge with potential customers and members of the community. They want customers to absorb their expertise so that they can make informed decisions. Andrew is the technical mastermind and Caitlin handles business management and customer service. They take pride in the fact that they work within a customer's budget while keeping both your need and desires in mind. They can help you find the fireplace solution that perfectly fits your décor and your heating requirements. They are able to add a special dimension to your home and declare that intent in their motto, Our Flame Warms Your Heart and Home. The Stones love the Longmont community and strive to contribute by being actively involved and making sure everyone has a fair chance for success. Come to ABR Fireplaces, where Andrew and Caitlin work to be the most helpful and informative fireplace company in the area.

**1333 Coffman Street,
Longmont CO
(303) 485-1522**

Concepts Furniture and Accessories

HOME: *Best home furnishings*

Concepts Furniture and Accessories was founded in 1980 as a gift store located in the Crossroads Mall, in Boulder. Over the years Concepts has transformed into a full line furniture and accessory store. In 1999 Steve Hansen and Amy Smith purchased the Boulder store and added the Longmont location in 2002. Concepts has taken the philosophy of offering unique home furnishings that can be customized to fit the clients' needs and taste. This has resulted in an extensive selection of home furnishings that are not only contemporary, but also traditional and the crossover style known as transitional. Concepts is dedicated to providing Boulder and Longmont with an eclectic source for furnishings and accessories, bringing fresh ideas that outpace current trends in the industry of home furnishings. In addition, Concepts provides a customer oriented staff that possesses the product knowledge and the skills to present personalized service and assist them in furnishing one room or an entire house. Concepts is not limited to residential furnishings as they can provide furnishings for corporate offices, restaurants, bars and hotels. Whatever the project may be, Concepts Furniture and Accessories is up to the task.

1890 30th Street, Boulder CO
(303) 443-6900
800 S Main Street, Longmont CO
(303) 772-4178
www.conceptsfurniture.com

Tenacity Wine Shop

MARKETS: *Best boutique-style wine shop*

Nancy Cook and Paul Lobato started Tenacity Wine Shop in 1998 simply because of their love for wine. They like sharing this passion and their knowledge with their customers. You will love the community camaraderie, the boutique style of the shop and the personal service by the expert owners, wine collectors for over 20 years who have tasted every wine in the shop. They can help you find the perfect wine for your needs, from a large selection of fine wines under $15 per bottle to their special favorites from all over the world. Serve your select wine in fine glassware by Reidel. The shop also carries premium spirits and handcrafted beers to please every palate. Take advantage of such services as gift wrapping, free delivery with the purchase of one case or more and personalized wine labels with the purchase of five cases. Best of all, you will be pleased with the affordable prices. Nancy and Paul chose Prospect because of its neighborly feel, similar to

Denver's Lodo area but in a rural setting. Prospect is Colorado's first New Urbanist community, planned for livability and minimal environmental impact, and is located in the Front Range city of Longmont, about 10 minutes from Boulder and 30 minutes from Denver. It's always a neighborly day in Prospect, though Friday nights are especially fun, and a visit to Tenacity Wine Shop tops off the outing.

700 Tenacity Drive, Suite 102, Longmont CO
(720) 652-9463 (WINE)
www.tenacitywineshop.com

Cheese Importers Gourmet Warehouse

MARKETS: *Best collection of fine cheeses*

Whether you're searching for a 40-kilo wheel or a one-pound wedge, the Cheese Importers Gourmet Warehouse in Longmont has the cheese for you. Linda and Lyman White started their wholesale enterprise, Willow River Natural Cheese, in the 1970s and soon expanded into retail sales and imports. You can roam the aisles of their vast warehouse eying tantalizing Italian Parmesan, French Brie and Dutch Gouda. The mountains of cheese the Whites choose for their warehouse begin in small, often family-run operations, where cheese making is an honored craft. The Whites scour Europe and such cheese producing regions as Wisconsin, Oregon, New York and Vermont for their massive offerings. Bring a jacket to browse through this giant cheese cooler, then step into the retail store, La Fromagerie European Marketplace, for espresso and pastries at the French sidewalk style café. Temptations here include hard French candies and dark Swiss

chocolate. Visit the olive bar and scan the hard to find gourmet kitchenware. Pick up a gift basket filled with mouthwatering delicacies, such as Milano salami from the Italian basket or Talancia plum jam in a basket from Spain. Visit the Cheese Importers Gourmet Warehouse, where the Whites' passion for fine foods will make your culinary dreams come true.

33 S Pratt Parkway, Longmont CO
(303) 443-4444
www.cheeseimporters.com

The Colorado Cupboard

MARKETS: *Best selection of trendy food and gift items*

The Colorado Cupboard stocks trendy food and gift items from Colorado vendors. Sisters Dayna Nixon and Shari Triche, who hail from New Orleans, combine Southern style hospitality and creative food preparation in a shop that invites lingering. Dayna has a business background, while Shari has experience in the food industry. The concept for their store started with their desire to provide fresh frozen meals to heat up at home. Beyond their own services, they added the products of dozens of Colorado vendors, found through area farmers' markets and Colorado Proud, an organization devoted to locally grown, raised and processed foods. The Colorado Cupboard stocks a lively assortment of goods, from soap to salsa, and jams to jewelry. Beyond Dayna and Shari's reheatable meals, look for gift baskets, pantry items, local art and unusual housewares that all proudly reflect the abundance of quality products available in Colorado. The spacious shop is a comfortable gathering spot with a café that changes its menu daily, a coffee bar and popular evening cooking classes. A visit to the Colorado Cupboard invites lingering to enjoy fresh baked goods and work by local artists. Dayna and Shari invite you to come in, browse and stay awhile. You'll be glad you did.

2001 N Main Street, Longmont, Colorado
(303) 485-0605
www.thecoloradocupboard.com

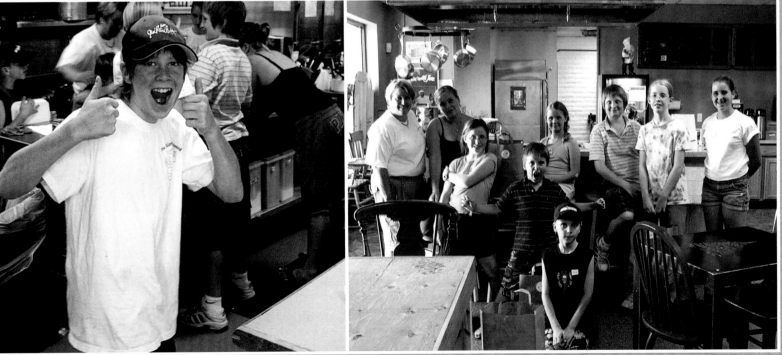

Capers & Co

MARKETS: *Best gourmet baskets and fine edibles*

Capers & Co is a gourmet foods market in Longmont that celebrates the power of food to bring people together. Owner Mary Carol Hebert, who started Capers & Co in 2004, quotes George Bernard Shaw when describing her philosophy, "There is no love more sincere than the love of food." Mary Carol grew up in Madrid and has lived all over the world. Her travels are reflected in the products she carries at Capers & Co, a market with a decidedly international flair. Mary Carol specializes in gourmet gift baskets that combine cheeses, fine chocolates, specialty vinegars, oils, pâté, wine, pasta and an assortment of fine foods too lengthy to recite in one breath. If you can't find exactly the right basket among her many choices, you can make your own or she'll customize it for you. Mary Carol wants to spread the joy and camaraderie that comes when friends and families gather around a table full of great food. While her market is decidedly gourmet, it is anything but stuffy. It is a friendly place where you'll get personal service along with a wide selection. In addition to food, Mary Carol stocks lots of non-food items aimed at enhancing your cooking and entertaining skills. She's happy to share recipes and encourages people to drop by and brainstorm about ways to make their parties and gatherings more fun. Drop by Capers & Co next time you're in Longmont. If you can't make it before your next big shindig, visit Mary Carol's website. She'll ship her products anyplace fine foods are appreciated.

2011 100 Year Party Court, #3, Longmont CO
(303) 772-5997
www.capersandcompany.com

Bike-N-Hike
RECREATION: *Best outdoor store*

Bike-N-Hike is a friendly store that promotes such human-powered forms of transportation as bicycling, hiking and cross-country skiing. Owned and operated by the Swanson family since its inception in 1973, Dave Swanson, his family and staff introduced Longmont to cross-country skiing in the 1970s, when they provided evening ski clinics for up to 100 people. Expansion into the bicycle business was a natural. The shop now provides a comprehensive selection of bicycles. The courteous and professional staff is one of the most experienced in Longmont, with over 80 combined years in the bicycle industry. In addition to its main emphasis on recreational cycling, the store stocks a lineup of BMX bikes for young daredevils who enjoy freestyle jumping and racing. Bike-N-Hike sponsored a top 10 BMX team in the 1980s and won the state championship in 1984. The staff has sold over 2,500 bicycles in 33 years. They help you find the right bicycle, adjust it for proper fit and make sure you have all the resources to enjoy a smooth ride. They also participate in a 150-mile bicycle ride over two days to raise funds for multiple sclerosis. Bike riders and skiers are happy people, so as you might expect, Bike-N-Hike is a fun store with playful and enthusiastic employees. Whether you are a beginner or an avid cycling enthusiast, Bike-N-Hike invites you to come in and get acquainted.

1136 Main Street, Longmont, CO
(303) 772-5105
www.bike-n-hike.com

Game Force Longmont

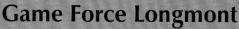

RECREATION: *Best plact to buy, sell and trade games*

Mike Plude, who owns Game Force Longmont with his wife, Molly, is a kid at heart. That means he can relate to his clientele. Along with the other seven staff members, Mike takes the time to talk to his customers and become friends with them, creating a social, comfortable environment conducive to game shopping and playing. Game Force Longmont has an extensive inventory of new and used products. "Buy, sell, trade—that's what we do," Mike says, who guarantees all items he sells and accepts trade-ins. Game Force carries new and used games for Microsoft's Xbox; Sony's Playstation 1, 2 and Portable; and Nintendo's DS, GameCube and Gameboy Advance. It also carries used games for a limited number of older but still popular systems, such as the Nintendo 64, the original Gameboy and the Sega Genesis. In addition to his work at the store, Mike writes a weekly game review column in the Friday edition of the *Times-Call* with Matt Dixon. Mike has worked in the video game retail industry for 17 years. He has been a customer and collector, as well, and understands the customer's point of view. Some of his employees have been with him for as long as seven years. If you like to play, go to Game Force Longmont, where the people are knowledgeable but value personal relations above all else.

2103 N Main Street, Longmont CO
(303) 702-0251
http://gflongmont.tripod.com

Abbondanza Pizzeria
RESTAURANTS & CAFES: *Best pizza in Longmont*

Abbondanza means abundance, and Abbondanza Pizzeria co-owner Bob Goff says the moniker "reflects our philosophy. You shouldn't have to double order a topping." The 14 inch Meaty Pizza, a local favorite, boasts 55 slices of pepperoni, ham, sausage and ground beef. Homemade red sauce and mozzarella cheese tie this heavenly creation together. The Meaty Pizza placed second overall at a Denver pizza contest among approximately 55 entries. In addition to its Longmont-style hand-

tossed pizzas, Abbondanza offers subs with a Chicago flair and a large selection of calzones. Pasta and salads round out the varied menu. Bob, who is the 2006 recipient of the *Longmont Make Time for Kids* award, goes out of his way to support local youth. He offers food discounts for a wide range of events. Bob has created a family friendly environment at Abbondanza Pizzeria. For example, to help foster quality family time, the shop has board games instead of television. The pizzeria's quality products, positive environment and great service create loyal customers. Stop by Abbondanza Pizzeria for your favorite mouthwatering pizza.

461 Main Street, Longmont CO
(303) 485-5020

Mike O'Shay's Restaurant and Ale House
RESTAURANTS & CAFES:
Longmont's oldest independently owned restaurant

Enjoy a hearty and delicious meal perfectly prepared from fresh, quality ingredients and served with a smile at Mike O'Shay's Restaurant and Ale House, where owner Mike Shea and his wife, Nania, have been serving the community of Longmont for more than 25 years. This popular eatery is the city's longest running, independently owned restaurant and features a diverse menu of delicious dishes from home and abroad, such as traditional Irish corned beef with cabbage and the restaurant's original Texas Cheese Chicken. Mike, a New Jersey native, started his culinary career at the age of 19 with a job in Bermuda, eventually returning to his home state. In 1977, he relocated permanently to Colorado, where he and his wife, Nania, opened Mike O'Shay's in 1981. Mike and Nania are sticklers for fine ingredients and carefully create their dishes from scratch. This attention to quality and impeccable service give this family-owned restaurant its charm. Mike O'Shay's stocks 15 different wine vintages and keeps a selection of 11 beers on tap. Finish your meal with such desserts as homemade apple crisp or Philly-style cheesecake and a choice of delicious coffee blends, including O'Shay's famous Irish coffee. Gather with friends and family or impress your colleagues while dining on a repast fit for kings at Mike O'Shay's Restaurant and Ale House.

512 Main Street, Longmont CO
(303) 772-0252
www.mikeoshays.com

Martini's Bistro

RESTAURANTS & CAFES:
Best homemade American fare with a twist

Enjoy the good life at Martini's Bistro. Frank Kaven wears many hats at his jazzy eatery. Some days he dons the cap of interior designer to improve the 19th century Victorian mansion he and his wife, Ann, bought in 1990, when they moved back to Longmont to be close to family. Frank changed the name, look and style of the restaurant after the kids left home, in 2004. Today, the contemporary interior features window walls, granite tables, original artwork and upholstered cherry wood chairs. His patio is a customer favorite with its fire pit and feel of an outdoor living room and has been voted best patio in Boulder County. When Frank puts on his chef's hat, he creates recipes that put a twist on homemade American fare. Among his signature dishes are the Nutty Chick, a macadamia crusted baked chicken breast with raspberry coulis, and the Bullwinkle, a rich chocolate mousse served in a martini glass with a chocolate hazelnut pirouette. Martini's Bistro is well known for its 12 signature martinis, which are sure to shake up your life, along with a full bar that contains 36 brands of vodka and 24 varieties of gin. Frank loves life at Martini's Bistro so much he lives upstairs. He is especially fond of wearing his host hat and invites you to visit Martini's Bistro and let his attentive staff show you the good life and a good time.

543 Terry Street, Longmont CO
(303) 651-2772
www.martinisbistro.com

Ragazzi Italian Grill and Garden Gate Café
RESTAURANTS & CAFES: *Best Italian food in Longmont*

At Ragazzi Italian Grill in Longmont, owners and brothers Steve and Ryan Gaibler serve up authentic Old World Italian food with a trendy flair. The restaurant's name means *the boys*, and Steve and Ryan, along with their wives and business partners Laura and Tiffinie, bought the location from their parents in 2005. This family-friendly neighborhood establishment features a wide variety of menu items, from appetizers to such core Italian classics as ravioli, calzones and eggplant dishes. Specialty pizzas include the Kona, Thai and Pizza Bianca as well as pizzas you design with your favorite toppings. Great gnocchi and fresh fish specialties, available Friday through Sunday, add novel choices, and you'll find a well-chosen wine list with selections to complement any entrée. Ryan and Steve also own Garden Gate Café, a casual breakfast and lunch spot that offers exceptionally well prepared comfort food. The expansive menu and outdoor patio make Garden Gate a popular gathering place for local cyclists. Because both brothers worked for their parents when they were young, they already had a good working knowledge of the restaurant industry when the opportunity arose to buy Garden Gate Café. Soon after, they purchased Ragazzi Italian Grill. Find out what the Gaibler brothers and their partners have to offer with a visit to either Ragazzi Italian Grill or Garden Gate Café.

1135 Francis Street, Longmont CO (Ragazzi Italian Grill) (303) 651-2828
7960 Niwot Road, #B4, Longmont CO (Garden Gate Café) (303) 652-8595

The Rib House
RESTAURANTS & CAFES: *Best babyback ribs in Longmont*

When you want your ribs slowly hickory smoked for hours until the tender meat slides off the bone, when you want them smothered in the best Kansas City-style homemade barbecue sauce, then you want Tracy's Famous Illegal Ribs, the best baby back ribs in Colorado. For this particular succulent rib fix, you must venture to the Rib House by Chef Extraordinaire in Longmont's New Town Prospect. When Tracy and Merry Ann Webb moved to Longmont from Kansas City, Missouri, in 1989, they searched for true Kansas City style barbecue. In 2001, they brought the flavors of the barbecue capital of the world to Longmont, giving Colorado barbecue boasting privileges. The Rib House has been voted best barbecue in the Front Range for three consecutive years. The key to their successful flavor is likely to remain unknown to the public, thanks to a sauce recipe that remains a well-guarded secret. The chefs make a range of sauces, from mild and sweet to hot and fiery. Ham, turkey breast and spicy sausage are smoked to perfection at The Rib House. Make room for traditional favorite side orders, as well as new ones such as the Cheesy Corn Bake. Decadent desserts include fudge brownies, fruit cobblers and moist cakes. You can enjoy a mouthwatering hickory smoked feast seven days a week, or plan a private party with full-service catering by The Rib House for up to 900 people. When you need a rib fix, head to The Rib House.

1920 S Coffman Street, Longmont CO
(303) 485-6988
www.theribhouse.info

Possibilities
SHOPPING: *Best collectibles in Longmont*

After 27 years working in dentistry, Dottie Seely took over ownership of Possibilities in 2005 and now happily sells the things she used to buy. As its name implies, Possibilities offers a mixed bag of goods, including antiques, primitives, gifts and cards. Possibilities carries old and new furnishings and accessories for homes and gardens, including country collectibles. If you are looking for a gift idea, Possibilities can oblige with candles, jewelry and music for many tastes. The shop is fittingly lodged in a quaint building with a carriage house and a spacious yard, constructed around 1900. A bygone-charm and original light fixtures enhance the shopping experience. In the summertime, guest vendors dot the front yard. Customers look forward to special occasions, when the shop features seasonal items, open houses, refreshments and door prizes. Make a day of it and come to Possibilities, where you never know what's in store for you.

530 Kimbark Street, Longmont CO
(303) 774-7643

House Gifts & Décor

SHOPPING: *Best gift boutique in Longmont*

Find a little something for everyone at House Gifts & Decor in friendly Prospect, a New Urban community planned by the designers of Seaside, Florida. Pam Roberts opened the Longmont store in 2003, because she loves giving gifts and wanted to offer a selection of wonderful gifts for people of all ages. She revels in creating smiles that transcend the generations. You'll discover a dash of the whimsical in the contemporary collection of toys, gifts and items for the home. Delight at fun things such as their Ugly Dolls (so ugly they're cute), talking alarm clocks or toys from Groovy Girls to Spy Gear. And, kids of all ages will enjoy the chocolate chunk cookies. When you don't know what to buy, House comes through with choices and ideas for every occasion and personality, including teens. Hip jewelry, cute baby gifts and novelty items galore await your perusal. The store also features the area's most comprehensive selection of reading glasses, When you need to find a special gift, come to House Gifts & Décor and leave with just the right present chosen to evoke a smile.

2017 100 Year Party Court, Longmont CO
(303) 485-1811

Lordswalk
Christian Books, Gifts & Music

SHOPPING: *Best Christian gifts in Longmont*

Slip away to a quite retreat filled with warmth and welcome at Lordswalk Christian Books & Gifts. Owners Deena Kicera and Becky Cox say that if you do not feel God's presence when you come through the door, then they are doing something wrong. This sanctuary is filled with a wonderful selection of spiritual books, uplifting music, religious gifts and a wide range of thoughtful greeting cards. Lordswalk carries spiritual materials and media for children. The Veggie Tales CDs and films are especially popular. This series teaches songs of worship in ways that are memorable and meaningful for the whole family. Lordswalk Christian Books & Gifts is also a gallery for local artists and features the work of Thomas Kinkade, nationally known painter of light. Lordswalk is the only shop in the western United States to carry inspirational gifts from P. Graham Dunn. Throughout the year, Deena and Becky host an open house where authors and local artists come in to autograph their work and answer questions from their admirers. Find books, gifts and services to inspire you and your loved ones with a visit to Lordswalk Christian Books & Gifts.

1515 N Main Street, Suite 2, Longmont CO
(303) 772-6088
www.lordswalk.com

Tables To Teacups

SHOPPING:

Largest indoor flea market

As Colorado's largest indoor flea market, Tables To Teacups Antique Mall and Indoor Flea Market is a rare gem, promising Everything You Never Knew You Needed. Antique furniture, collectibles, pottery, toys and tools are among the many treasures waiting to be discovered at Tables To Teacups. In 2001, after 40 years of working in estate and antique sales, Marlena and John Toohey opened the business of their dreams in Longmont. The business employs the Tooheys' sons, Brian and Brandon, Brandon's wife, Kira, and several close family friends. With w, the flea market holds the merchandise of more than 400 consigners and 90 vendors. Variety is the norm, with Depression glass, baseball cards and horse tack sharing space with new and antique firearms. The Tooheys are also well known for their estate sale services. Whether you are trying to unclutter your home or must pass along the belongings of a deceased loved one, the Tooheys can accommodate your consignments. For surprises and unsurpassed customer service, stop by Tables To Teacups Antique Mall and Indoor Flea Market.

1420 Nelson Road, Longmont CO
(303) 485-7270
www.tablestoteacups.com

Used Book Emporium

SHOPPING:
Best store for bookworms

Calling all Book Worms! Here's your opportunity to settle in and feel right at home among the Used Book Emporium's 52,000-plus books. Founder Carol Grossman opened the emporium in 1996 with approximately 7,000 volumes. Her daughters Linda Uhrich and Debbie Karle, who are now the store's co-owners, carry on their mother's dream. What more can a dedicated bookworm ask for than a store where you can trade in your used books for in-store credit, then search the shelves for your next reading adventure? The majority of books are used hardbound and paperback volumes that provide customers with like-new books at a used book price. Choose from fiction and nonfiction titles in such diverse categories as mystery, science fiction, history, travel, health, cooking and spirituality. You'll also find classics, best sellers, children's books and gift items. For a change in your reading experience, explore the wide selection of audio books. This favorite bookstore offers a comfortable atmosphere to browse, as well as a friendly and knowledgeable staff. Come to the Used Book Emporium in historic downtown Longmont, a home away from home for every dedicated bookworm.

346 Main Street, Longmont CO
(303) 776-6561

Sandcastle Kids

SHOPPING: *Best children's consignment store*

Children change size and outgrow clothes and high chairs at a rate similar to the meltdown of a sandcastle. Sandcastle Kids recycles the best of that clothing, equipment and toys. This special consignment store, with selections for newborns to juniors, first opened in 1994. In 2003, Angela and Jeremy Fobes bought Sandcastle Kids in Longmont, moved up the street, and have kept its 3,000 square feet of retail space filled with new and gently worn children's clothing, toys, books and paraphernalia. Need a crib, a stroller or a playpen? Does your youngster outgrow shoes overnight? All clothing and equipment gets a thorough inspection before being accepted on consignment. Angela used to shop here before she bought the place, so she knows what's important to her customers. Sandcastle Kids has a children's play area, to keep the kids entertained while Moms and Dads peruse the merchandise. Whether you are looking for a clothing store to outfit your kids or a place to consign your children's outgrown clothing and equipment, visit Sandcastle Kids where the friendly service and outstanding selection will meet and exceed your expectations for excellence.

370 Main Street, Longmont CO
(303) 684-9355
www.sandcastle-kids.com

Ann's Resale

SHOPPING: *Best women's consignment store*

Fill your closet with fabulous accessories and all the latest styles without breaking the bank at Ann's Resale. Founder Ann Hall came to Colorado in 1995 and began searching for a way to serve her community. Although she had no prior retail experience, Ann discovered her niche with the opening of the upscale Ann's Resale in Longmont. Today, Stephanie Cuadra, who worked for Ann for five years, owns the shop. Both ladies have a deep affection for their customers and a true passion for providing exceptional service and quality clothing at affordable prices. Since opening, Ann's Resale has worked with over 10,000 consignors from Denver to Cheyenne. Look for sizes for women and juniors and diverse styles, from casual to classic and from business to evening wear. Ann's Resale also offers a choice selection of consignment and estate jewelry along with elegant home décor items. Stephanie sets Mondays aside for walk-in customers who wish to place items on consignment, and appointments are available throughout the rest of week. Items must be clean, pressed and free from smoke, stains or damage. Turn your cast-offs into cash, and find fabulous clothing and accessories to suit your lifestyle at Ann's Resale.

2255 N Main Street, Suite 113, Longmont, CO
(303) 684-0709

Blissful Family

SHOPPING: *Best family-oriented products and services*

Blissful Family encourages children and parents to spend quality time together, developing their imaginations and natural curiosity while cultivating stronger relationships. Owner Young S. Kim purchases many of the wood, silk and cotton toys stocked in the store because of a special connection she feels with the artist who created the items, a feeling she hopes to pass on to customers. As children whip up a gourmet meal in a play kitchen or tell a story using a handcrafted puppet, they develop important verbal and social skills while using their creativity. The multicultural toys and products allow children to appreciate other cultures and see beyond the environment where they live. The store also carries musical instruments, art supplies and cooperative games and puzzles that encourage children to work together to complete the task while making everyone a winner. Kim is always looking for new and fun ways to bring families together and promote the family unit. As part of this goal, Blissful Family offers a variety of classes and activities, such as family craft days and storytelling. The store also offers a memorable space for children to celebrate birthdays. Give your family the gift of togetherness with natural toys and products from Blissful Family.

600 S Airport Road, Suite A, Longmont CO
(303) 682-0016
www.blissfulfamily.net

Havana Manor Fine Cigars & Pipes
SHOPPING: *Best smoking lounge in Longmont*

The gentlemen of Havana Manor Fine Cigars and Pipes in Longmont know what men like. Owner Michael Landau became an avid cigar smoker like his father and his grandfather before him. His enjoyment led him to create a distinctly masculine smoking lounge full of comfortable leather chairs, a large-screen television and surround-sound music. Store manager Thomas Bliss is a native Coloradoan with an extensive knowledge of fine cigars and the knack for calling his customers by name. Quality handmade cigars fill Havana Manor's 300-square-foot walk-in humidor. Try a Dona Flor Mata Fina, a reasonably priced Brazilian cigar with a perfect draw. Smokers with the most discriminating palates await the once a year opportunity to purchase the new Oliva Master Blends 3, handmade in Nicaragua. After purchasing cigars to add to your collection, keep them in Havana Manor's humidified private lockers. At Havana Manor, you can socialize with others who share your interests. The staff hosts tasting events and poker nights throughout the year as well as occasional hand rolling demonstrations. You will feel like one of the guys as you settle in for a good smoke with a complimentary espresso and a little net surfing on Havana Manor's high speed Internet connection. Havana Manor sells humidors, cutters and ashtrays, as well as an extensive collection of pipes and lighters. Visit Havana Manor Fine Cigars & Pipes and soon the staff will be calling you by name.

1240 Ken Pratt Boulevard, Suite 6B, Longmont CO
(303) 776-2332
www.havanamanor.com

Left Hand Brewing Co.
WINERIES: *Best craft beers*

The good people at the Left Hand Brewing Company say that they are on a mission to bring great beer to the masses. When the company was founded, craft beer was less than one percent of the market. Now it is four percent. Balance defines a great beer and Left Hand Brewing strives for a perfect balance between malt and hops in all its handcrafted ales and lagers, from its golden crisp Polestar Pilsner to its intensely roasted black Imperial Stout. Left Hand Brewing sees beer as liquid food to complement meals and social occasions. The company dates to 1993 when two expert home brewers decided to go commercial. In 1994, they were ready with their first batch, dubbed Sawtooth Ale. At the Great American Beer Festival that October, the ale took home a gold medal in the bitter category and Black Jack Porter won a bronze as a robust porter. By 2006, the brewery had racked up a score of medals, including seven at the World Beer Cup. Sawtooth continues to be the best seller, followed by Milk Stout and the porter. Left Hand Brewing sells 65 percent of its beer in Colorado, but their beer is also distributed in 20 other states. The brewery has a great tasting room in Longmont that has the feel of a neighborhood pub. Wherever you are, the beers of the Left Hand Brewing Company are worth a taste.

1265 Boston Avenue, Longmont CO
(303) 772-0258
www.lefthandbrewing.com

LOUISVILLE

In 2005, *Money* magazine ranked Louisville 5th on its list of the 100 best places to live in the United States. In 2006, authors Bert Sperling and Peter Sander ranked Louisville 1st on their list of best places in the U.S. to raise a family. The history of Louisville began in1877 with the opening of the first coal mine in the area. Louis Nawatny then platted his farm into a town he named for himself. Unlike many coal camp towns, no single mining company was dominant in Louisville. Its mines also had the reputation of being relatively safe. Miners lived in town, walked to work in the nearby mines and participated in the democratic life of the community. At one time or another in the years between 1877 and 1952, when the last coalmines closed, 30 mines were in operation in the Louisville area. Flowers now grow in suburban yards without a hint of the passageways underground or the history they represent. Louisville is on the route of a proposed rapid transit line that will eventually link it with Denver, Boulder and Longmont.

Places to Go

- Cottonwood Park
  S Boulder Road and Via Appia
- Heritage Park
  W Cherry Street and S Madison Avenue
- Louisville Historical Museum
  1001 Main Street
- Memory Square Park
  801 Grant Street
- Pirates Park
  Lafayette Street and Jefferson Street

Things to Do

June
- Taste of Louisville
  (303) 666-5747

September
- Louisville Fall Festival
  (303) 666-9072

December
- Parade of Lights
  (303) 666-5747

Fantasy Orchids
GARDENS, PLANTS & FLOWERS:
Best selection of orchids

The folks at Fantasy Orchids contend that orchids are the ultimate houseplant. They grow in the same conditions as your other houseplants, but their flowers last much longer and the variety of flowers is enormous. Contrary to common belief, orchids are easy to grow, so some of the most exotic blooms in the world can be yours to enjoy at home. Because many orchids bloom during the winter months, they can be a great help in chasing away the wintertime blues. The Fantasy Orchids greenhouse exceeds 10,000 square feet in size and contains almost 130,000 plants. On any day of the year you can see hundreds of orchids in bloom. There is no other greenhouse like it within hundreds of miles. Stan Gordon, the owner, runs the business with his son Kent, the general manager. Four other Gordon family members help, including Stan's wife, Brenda. Fantasy Orchids is most definitely a family business. The family's knowledge of orchids is vast. Stan has handled more than a million orchids since 1986, when he began growing them. He established Fantasy Orchids in 1989 in a small backyard greenhouse, and the business grew and grew. Fantasy Orchids now ships flowers all over the country on a wholesale and retail basis. Come by and talk with one of the Fantasy Orchids specialists or give them a call. They will help you grow orchids in your house.

**830 W Cherry Street, Louisville CO
(303) 666-5432**
www.fantasyorchids.com

Blue Parrot Restaurant

RESTAURANTS & CAFES:
Best Italian cuisine in Louisville

Owned and operated by the Colacci family since 1919, the Blue Parrot Restaurant offers fine Italian cuisine faithfully made from Gramma Mary's original homemade recipes. It all began in 1919, when Mary cooked with her heart and soul, while Grandpa Mike carted her hot meals by wagon, selling them to the miners for 10 cents per plate. Having survived two world wars, the great depression and a devastating 1988 fire, the Blue Parrot Restaurant still serves Gramma's original cuisine today. Located in the heart of downtown Louisville, Granddaughter Joan Higgins now owns and manages this famous restaurant with the help of her children, Jennifer and David. The Blue Parrot Restaurant is community-minded, holding its annual Heat Relief fundraiser, the proceeds benefiting Louisville's Senior Center. Joan is a member of the Louisville Chamber of Commerce and plays an active role with the Senior Foundation. True to the continued success of Gramma Mary's original recipes, the Blue Parrot Restaurant was elected to the Boulder County Hall of Fame in 2003. Try one of Gramma Mary's specialties, a homemade sauce with meatballs and sausage. Making everything by hand, the quality and taste of their food is unmatched. The authentic Italian ambiance provides an atmosphere that visitors always remember, which is why the Blue Parrot Restaurant is so well-known, even in surrounding communities. Offering catered services in their banquet room, this restaurant has it all. Come visit Blue Parrot Restaurant for Italian cuisine your taste buds will always remember.

640 Main Street, Louisville CO
(303) 666-0677
www.blueparrotrestaurant.com

Rocky Mountains

PLACES TO GO

- Benson Sculpture Park
  29th Street and Beech Drive

- Boyd Lake State Park
  3720 N County Road 11-C

- Loveland Museum/Gallery
  503 N Lincoln Avenue

- Loveland Sports Park
  950 N Boyd Lake Avenue

- The Ranch (Larimer County Fairgrounds and Events Complex)
  5280 Arena Circle

THINGS TO DO

April
- A Taste of Loveland and Greeley
  (970) 669-7055

May
- Loveland Cinco De Mayo
  (970) 613-5775

July
- Colorado Outdoor Expo
  (970) 619-4000

August
- Larimer County Fair and Rodeo
  (970) 619-4000

- Sculptor Show
  (970) 667-2015

- Corn Roast Festival
  (970) 667-6311

August-September
- Thunder in the Rockies (motorcycle rally)
  www.thunderintherockies.com

September
- Fall Festival
  (970) 669-7550 ext. 15

October
- Loveland Art Stroll and Oktoberfest
  (970) 962-2410

LOVELAND

Loveland's founders named it in honor of William Loveland, president of the Colorado Central Railroad. The town has called itself the Sweetheart City and the arts and hearts capital of Colorado. The town has three foundries, an art museum and an annual sculpture show. John Villani includes it in his book The 100 Best Small Art Towns in America. AARP Magazine has named Loveland the number-one place in the nation to revitalize your life. In February, the Loveland Chamber of Commerce sponsors a Valentine re-mailing program in which thousands of people mail valentines from all over the world to Loveland. Volunteers re-mail each valentine with a special verse and a hand-stamped postmark. To participate, mail your stamped cards in a larger envelope to Postmaster; Attention: Valentines; Loveland, CO; 80538-9998.

A fresh line at Loveland Ski Area
Photo By Byron Hetzler
Courtesy of Colorado Tourism Office

Avalon Aviary

ANIMALS & PETS: *Most ethical bird store*

If you own a parrot or are looking to buy one, Avalon Aviary in Loveland is by far the best place to go. This is not a pet store, nor is it a puppy mill or a feather factory. It is an ethical enterprise where the welfare of the birds comes first, and it shows in every phase of their operation. Susanne Cochran is one of the world's foremost breeders of parrots. Her birds are friendly, happy, articulate, well-adjusted and healthy. Her success and high standing in the world of aviculture comes from strict adherence to a set of principles that guide every phase of her business. At Avalon Aviary, Susanne is committed to continuous improvement in aviculture practices. She fosters ongoing education and improvement for herself, her employees and the public. The parrots at Avalon Aviary are hatched under their parents and hand-raised in an environment of love. Their development is guided to maximize their health, both physical and psychological. Prospective owners are carefully screened and are required to take a three-hour class before Susanne will entrust them with one of her beloved babies. This is a business with conscience. A percentage of Susanne's profits are devoted to parrot rescue and conservation. She also owns TLC Bird Toys, which manufactures toys to further enhance the lives of these special companions. If you are looking for an intelligent avian companion, start with a visit to Susanne's website where you will find an extensive body of information on parrots, her company, and her online store. Then visit the Aviary or stop by the retail outlet, Avalon Aviary Bird Store, which has the largest selection of bird toys and supplies in Northern Colorado. We cannot recommend Susanne more highly.

6014 W U.S. Highway 34, Loveland CO
(970) 663-5004
www.aviary.com

Loveland Museum/Gallery
ATTRACTIONS: *Best cultural attraction*

The Loveland Museum/Gallery is an unusual hybrid that succeeds at melding the best attributes of an art gallery and historical museum. This Loveland treasure began life in 1937 as a local pioneer museum. Over time, as Loveland grew into a magnet for artists, the museum changed to reflect the community. The result is an attraction that is both dynamic and interactional. The 26,000-square-foot museum, which focuses on regional history and houses a permanent collection, hosts exhibits, art classes, workshops, poetry readings and demonstrations. The 4,000-square-foot art gallery, which highlights both regional and international artists, hosts rotational exhibits covering a wide breadth of subject matter and media. This combination of history and art allows for a unique and interesting interplay of ideas that make the Loveland Museum/Gallery a study in artistic possibility. The Foote Gallery, which doubles as an auditorium and presenting space, gives the endeavor even greater versatility. This is not a stuffy old museum, nor is it a pretentious art tomb. The Loveland Museum/Gallery is a dynamic exercise in creative potential which is well worth your time on your next trip to Loveland.

503 N Lincoln Avenue, Loveland CO
(970) 962-2410
www.cityofloveland.org

Elegant Creations
BAKERIES, COFFEE & TEA:
Best specialty cakes in Loveland

If Lissa Buckley used marble or clay instead of flour and sugar, her works would be viewed in galleries and museums for eons. Instead, her masterpieces are ephemeral, gracing the banquet tables of weddings and special events for mere hours, before being consumed by appreciative revelers. In case you think we're getting carried away in our imagery surrounding this cake baker extraordinaire, go to her website. Her photo gallery makes the point: Lissa is an artist disguised as a flour-dusted cake baker. If you can dream it, she can bake it, sculpt it, and put it on a platter. And lest you wonder, her cakes are as delicious as they are beautiful. All of her masterpieces are crafted from scratch using the finest ingredients. She is as dependable as she is talented, meaning that brides (and especially mothers of the bride) can relax and know their cake will arrive on time. Lissa offers extensive delivery services to most of Colorado and southern Wyoming, and sometimes farther, depending on the situation. The next time you are looking for a baking master, contact Lissa. Her Elegant Creations will lift your spirits and her service won't let you down.

2248 W 1st Avenue, Loveland CO
(970) 214-3451
www.idocakes.com

Dallabetta's Lakeside Caffé
BAKERIES, COFFEE & TEA: *Best Italian coffee with a view*

The Italians understand coffee, and when you find the perfect cup brewed in the Italian tradition, it's cause for celebration. At Dallabetta's Lakeside Caffé in Loveland, you'll savor rich espresso, frothy cappuccinos and macchiatos, while gazing at an unobstructed view of the Front Range across Lake Loveland. When Kyle Dallabetta moved to Loveland from Seattle, a city that takes its coffee seriously, his inability to discover java that met his Seattle standards inspired him to open his own coffee shop. This comfortable caffé offers patrons a spot to nibble fresh croissants and other baked goodies while catching up with newspaper reading or just staring at the Rockies. Kyle serves world-famous Illy coffee, a blend perfected by generations of the Illy family and considered by coffee connoisseurs to be the only brew worth drinking. You can thank the Illy family for inventing the espresso machine and enjoy the fruits of their labors, which began in 1933 with a single espresso blend. In addition, Jane DeDecker, a locally renowned sculptor and Kyle's wife, exhibits her work in the shop, so customers can get a taste for art while munching biscotti and enjoying the fresh aroma of the world's finest coffee. Visit Dallabetta's Lakeside Caffé, and enjoy your brew with a view.

516 W Eisenhower Boulevard, Loveland CO
(970) 593-9691

Festive Moments
EVENTS: *Best wedding resource in Loveland*

Attention brides to be: we have a resource you need to know about. It's a little place with a big heart called Festive Moments. Located appropriately in Loveland, Festive Moments is northern Colorado's premiere source for cake decorating supplies, but that hardly tells the whole story. Judy Robertson and her husband Gary have been married for almost 45 years, and they've been working side-by-side at Festive Moments since its creation in 1983. They operate LoveLand SweetHeart Chapel, a charming little wedding chapel right next to the store that can accommodate 55 people for a non-denominational Christian ceremony. They have an outdoor gazebo in a garden setting with fountains and a heart-shaped pond. They can also arrange an intimate ceremony on their wedding boat, floating on an idyllic lake with a Rocky Mountain backdrop. If you already have a spot picked out, but need supplies, they have reams of catalogs and years of experience from which they can help you plan all of your needs, including special-order items to make your day perfect. Their shop carries an assortment of specialty items for weddings and receptions, such as cake stands, fountains and candelabras. They even carry a stash of Denver Broncos memorabilia. Festive Moments is all about family. Judy and Gary are often aided by the nimble fingers of their granddaughter Mariah, who lights up the shop when she's around. If you are seeking a personal touch for your wedding, call Judy and Gary at Festive Moments.

2020 W Eisenhower Boulevard, Loveland CO (Festive Moments)
2018 W Eisenhower Boulevard, Loveland CO (LoveLand SweetHeart Chapel)
(970) 669-4438
www.lovelandsweetheartchapel.com

The Swan House
EVENTS: *Best mix of British-style tea and treasures*

The Swan House in Loveland has worn many hats throughout its long history, going from a private home in the late 1800s to an antique shop and later becoming a bed-and-breakfast. Today, the Swan House mixes a British style tea experience with an opportunity to browse among the antiques for a treasure. Current owner Madeline Daniels taught school for 30 years and formerly owned the Nostalgic Corner in Loveland prior to purchasing the Swan House in 2001. Her newest enterprise combines her interest in antiques with the inspiration she gained from visiting a variety of tea rooms in Great Britain. In 2005, she realized a long-held dream when the Swan House became an official tea house. Luncheon tea is served in true British fashion here on a three-tiered server filled with traditional finger sandwiches, scones with cream and jam, dainty pastries, and of course, a spot of tea. The Swan House offers the ideal setting for small weddings, wedding receptions, bridal showers, business meetings, Red Hat gatherings and other special occasions. The nostalgic architectural features of the old house make a fitting backdrop for the antiques and collectibles showcased throughout the home, many of which are for sale. For a trip down memory lane, call ahead for reservations to sip high tea in high style at the Swan House.

317 E 6th Street, Loveland CO
(970) 663-0043
www.theswanhouse.com

Photo © Heartfelt Photography

Ellis Ranch Event Center & Wedding Park

EVENTS: *Best special events center in Loveland*

Ellis Ranch has been hosting special events and opening its facilities for public use for more than 40 years. Terry Ellis' parents purchased the ranch in 1963, and Terry and Roxie Ellis have managed the ranch since they married in 1974. Over the years they've used the ranch for many purposes, including breeding and training horses, raising elk and bison, and hosting such events as pumpkin festivals, art shows, fundraisers and corporate functions. Today Terry and Roxie, with the help of their son Shawn, focus on weddings while remaining available for family reunions, company picnics and other functions. The ranch offers a rustic yet romantic setting for your wedding in the four-acre outdoor Wedding Park, where the bride can arrive by horse-drawn carriage. You can exchange vows outdoors or in the spacious Event Center, which has a stage and a roomy dance floor. You'll have exclusive use of the ranch for your special day. Ellis Ranch is easy to reach from any location in Colorado or southern Wyoming, and will accommodate up to 1,000 guests. *Colorado Business & Lifestyle Magazine* named the ranch one of the 10 Hot Businesses in Northern Colorado. For a lifetime of memories, let Shawn help you plan your wedding or special event at Ellis Ranch Event Center & Wedding Park.

233 Waterdale Drive, Loveland CO (970) 593-9570 or (800) 848-3296 *www.ellisrancheventcenter.com*

Main Street Catering
EVENTS: *Best caterers in Loveland*

For more than 25 years, Main Street Catering has operated out of Loveland's historic Pulliam Community Building, catering to the area's most prestigious affairs and earning a reputation for excellence based on exceptional cuisine and professional service. Today, the popular catering company is owned and operated by Ken and Jill Rosander, who continue the tradition of providing phenomenal cuisine and gracious service for Northern Colorado's most well-respected service clubs, beautiful weddings and top venues. Ken received his Associate Degree in Restaurant Management and spent years as an executive chef in California and Colorado before he and Jill took hold of the reins at Main Street Catering in 2002. Through their efforts of giving back to the community and diligence to every detail of this family-owned business, Ken and Jill have fostered an unparalleled reputation for the highest level of service possible. Main Street Catering specializes in large corporate functions, weddings and gala events for local organizations such as the Loveland Lions Club, Rotary Club and the Greeley Air National Guard. Ken and Jill use only fresh, quality ingredients to prepare sumptuous banquets and dinners that will leave your guests delightfully satiated and filled with fond memories of the occasion. Ensure that your next event is a sensation by choosing Main Street Catering, a Loveland community favorite since 1981.

545 Cleveland Drive, Loveland CO
(970) 667-7596

Rocky Mountain Uniforms
FASHION: *Best uniform suppliers*

Committed to serving those who serve others, Rocky Mountain Uniforms has supplied uniforms to fire departments, EMTs, and other service industry people since 1975. Owners Allan and Susan Rader, who purchased the business in May 2005, practiced architectural design before becoming the third owners of the store. They also operate a sister store in Cheyenne that outfits both the Cheyenne Police Department and a large Wyoming detention center. As the largest uniform store in northern Colorado, Rocky Mountain Uniforms offers the latest trends in medical scrubs and accessories along with restaurant apparel and uniforms for firemen and police. Look for low-rise pant styles and boot-cut legs featuring the Surf Scrubs line by Cherokee. Active medical professionals can stay on their feet all day in the shoes offered here. Chef's wear and uniforms for industrial workers round out the extensive selection of high quality merchandise. The store offers customers a popular plan for uniform purchase by payroll deduction and features a generous discount for students. Allan and Susan also send out discount coupons to the more than 6,000 names in their birthday club and hold a monthly gift certificate drawing. When your work requires specialized apparel, take your needs to the experts at Rocky Mountain Uniforms.

1219 W Eisenhower Boulevard, Loveland CO
(970) 669-4442

Antares Jewelry Studio

FASHION: *Best custom jewelry design and services*

When it's time for your prized jewelry to be cleaned, resized or repaired, trust Antares Jewelry Studio where owner and professional jeweler, J.C. Wilks, uses his expertise to keep your treasures in perfect condition. As the son of a jeweler, J.C. has worked in the business for more than 33 years. Although his studio offers patrons a full range of fine jewelry services, you may also browse hundreds of ready-made pieces available by special order, while J.C. cleans, checks for loose stones, or replaces your watch battery. In addition to basic repairs and pearl restringing, J.C. is willing to do delicate work that most of his colleagues turn away, including deep engraving and delicate heirloom restorations. J.C. further specializes in original jewelry design and fabrication. He can fashion unique pieces from a rough sketch using the lost wax process, which begins with a wax model made for your approval and is then cast in the metal(s) of your choice. Antares Jewelry Studio uses such fine materials as diamonds and other gemstones with gold, platinum, silver and palladium for custom jewelry that is sure to achieve heirloom status. Antares Jewelry Studio is dedicated to custom, one-of-a-kind jewelry design, as well as providing exceptional jewelry services at affordable prices. Discover stunning original jewelry designs while ensuring that your jewelry receives the care it deserves at Antares Jewelry Studio.

1400 Falls Court, Loveland CO
(970) 461-2910 or (800) 647-6337
www.antaresjewelry.com

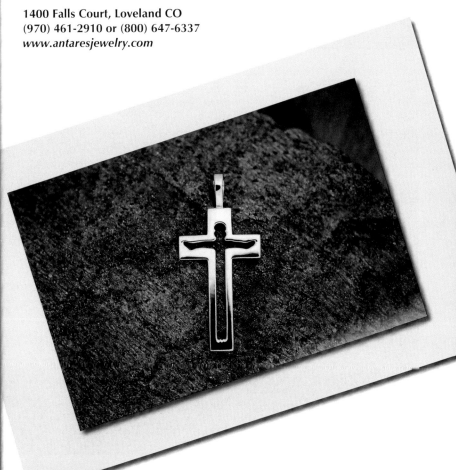

Art of the Rockies
Gallery & Custom Framing

GALLERIES & FINE ART: *Loveland's headquarters for frames and artwork*

Experience original works by Colorado artists, fine reproduction art and the talents of skilled framers at the business voted Best Art Gallery by readers of Loveland's *Reporter-Herald* newspaper. The owners of Art of the Rockies Gallery & Custom Framing, Norm and Pat Toman, hail from North Dakota, but the scenic Rockies drew them to Colorado. Pat's passion for framing combined with Norm's background in marketing found a perfect fit at the gallery, which the couple purchased in 1995. The shop continues to add to its successes and recently earned the 2004 Business of the Year award from the Loveland Chamber of Commerce. Art of the Rockies is a Thomas Kinkade showcase gallery, featuring many of the well known artist's captivating works that seem to glow from within. Reproduction artwork by more than 20 of the nation's top print artists lines the walls of the inviting space, and up-and-coming regional artists also display their exhibits throughout the gallery. Longtime employees and accomplished framers Mike and Pam offer careful preservation of your most precious memorabilia and art. Shadow boxes protect your three-dimensional treasures, such as baby booties or medals, and Art of the Rockies can even display uniquely shaped items with special order frames. Come to Art of the Rockies Gallery & Custom Framing in historic downtown Loveland to frame yesterday for tomorrow.

440 N Lincoln Avenue, Loveland CO
(970) 669-5111
www.artoftherockies.com

Sage Moon Originals

GALLERIES & FINE ART:
Original art for original people

Novice art collectors and experienced connoisseurs can feel at home at Sage Moon Originals. Gallery owner Susan Richards prides herself on showcasing a range of enticing pieces by talented local and regional artists. Your quest for a vibrant oil painting, subtle pastel or striking pendant can end here. There is more to this gallery than meets the eye. Susan is committed to helping you explore and develop your own creative spark. Sage Moon offers classes by notable local artisans in drawing, painting, jewelry and more. Now held monthly, Howling at the Moon is a girl's night out creativity workshop that combines fun projects with estrogen. Committed to building community connections, Sage Moon Originals takes part in A Night on the Town, an evening event held the second Friday of every month, which gives you the chance to chat with artists, nibble hors d'oeuvres and win prizes. The gallery also offers Art Past Six, a place to host your meeting, party or reception amid stimulating visual surroundings. Let your inner artist speak and lead you to Sage Moon Originals, where Susan promises Original Art for Original People.

116 E 4th Street, Loveland CO
(970) 461-8866
www.sagemoonoriginals.com

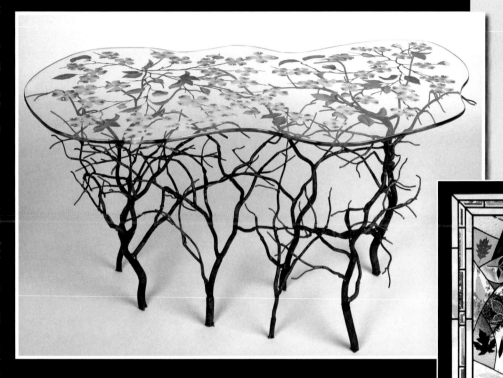

Dimensions in Art Glass
GALLERIES & FINE ART:
Best glass creations inspired by nature

When Deb Kessler was a little girl, she was mesmerized by a triangle prism. She held it up to the sunlight and felt bathed in the magic world of color. Today Deb is the owner of Dimensions in Art Glass in Loveland, where she customizes furniture and architecture with stained glass, etched glass and leaded glass. Having lived in Colorado her entire life, the beauty of the natural world is as much a part of her art as the techniques she has spent 27 years perfecting. "I have two passions," Deb explains, "Flowers and glass." Her bursting mountainside garden and sunroom provide blooms for her inspiration. Graceful orchids, tropical hibiscus and ripe bougainvillea find themselves reflected in her fine art pieces, climbing up windows and room dividers in showpiece homes across the nation. Since her studio opened in 2001, Deb has applied many techniques to her art form. She specializes in sandblasting, as well as the rarely used technique of applying gold leaf to glass. Deb receives commissions from patrons who desire a mark of distinction upon their estates. The aspens of Deb's homeland, cheerful geckos, wandering vines and autumnal foliage can be found crawling through doors and sidelights in her designs. Her beloved childhood prism still stirs her to create new art objects and functional pieces, such as plant stands and tiles. Visit Deb in her studio in the Longview Commercial Center, and see a true artist at work.

6874 N Franklin Avenue, Loveland CO
(907) 461-4828
www.dimensionsinartglass.com

Victor Issa Studios

GALLERIES & FINE ART:
Best bronze sculptures

Sculptor Victor Issa creates stunningly realistic bronze sculptures in his studio just west of Loveland. Born and raised in the Middle East, Issa came to the United States with his family in 1973 and obtained a degree in art education in 1980 from Union College in Lincoln, Nebraska. After an agent suggested he was better at sculpting than painting, Issa changed his focus and eventually moved to Loveland to take advantage of the art foundries there. His gift is creating living bronze—sculpture that captures the emotions and moves the spirit of the viewer. Issa mostly sculpts the human form, as he finds it to be the most challenging and rewarding. Recent commissions include a life-size depiction of a family with their dog for the Miner's Memorial Garden in Frederick, Colorado. *Daddy's Home*, which stretches 13 feet across at its widest point and is six feet tall, took almost a year to create and paints a bittersweet three-dimensional portrait of a mining family's hardships in the 1920s. Issa is a co-founder of the annual Loveland Sculpture Invitational Show and Sale, now the largest outdoor sculpture show in the nation, and his work is represented in more than six prestigious galleries in the West and Southwest. For Issa, art is a way of life and a way to express spirituality. Lift your spirits with a visit to the Victor Issa Studios.

3950 N County Road 27, Loveland CO
(970) 663-4805
www.victorissa.com

Victor Issa—*Voice in the Forest*
Life-size sculpture, 76x38x40 in.
Photo © Victor Issa Studios

Columbine Galleries & the National Sculptors' Guild

GALLERIES & FINE ART:
Representing renowned sculptors and painters

Art can delight the senses and inspire the soul, and a visit to Columbine Galleries demonstrates the many ways art accomplishes such feats. The Colorado location, also headquarters of the National Sculptors' Guild, represents more than 35 local and national artists working in a variety of mediums and styles. Columbine Galleries are the exclusive representative of the National Sculptors' Guild, whose members express their visions in bronze, stone, wood and steel. The Guild has placed monumental sculptures in public and private collections throughout the world. With Long's Peak in the background, the concentration of sculpture in the beautifully landscaped garden is vast but provides the visitor a rare opportunity to interact with large sculptures in a tranquil environment. Visitors can quietly discover artwork and fountains that are nestled into 'rooms' within the garden. One may even watch a great blue heron catch a fish by the small pond behind the gallery. Inside, the abundance of sculpture continues in smaller scale. The galleries also feature paintings in oil, acrylic and watercolor, etchings, jewelry, lusterware and glass. In an effort to give the public additional access to the art and artists, the galleries open their doors to numerous community and non-profit events including concerts in the sculpture garden. The galleries also offer occasional demonstrations by their artists to complete one's artistic experience. Whether you are searching for a beautiful necklace or a centerpiece for the city plaza, a visit to Columbine Galleries & the National Sculptors' Guild can help you realize your fine-art collecting desires.

2683 N Taft Avenue, Loveland CO
(970) 667-2015 or (800) 606-2015
www.columbinegallery.com

The Master's Fine Art of Loveland

GALLERIES & FINE ART:
Best inspirational art

This amazing gallery opened in September of 1998 as Gallery of the Master, with four artists in two small rooms. In 2006, Owner Linda King chose a new name: The Master's Fine Art of Loveland. Linda says, "We call it The Master's because it's the Lord of all creation we want to honor...from the front curb to the back fence and everything in between." The Master's now represents 50 marvelous artists whose work fills the 1906 Victorian home. The backyard is an intimate sculpture garden filled with beautifully displayed sculptures, comfortable benches, colorful plantings, and a tranquil Koi pond. Inside, you will find a large selection of sculptures, paintings, pottery, fiber art, blown glass, dichroic glass, sculpted acrylic and photography. The art encompasses a wide range of themes including landscape, wildlife, figurative, abstract and liturgical. This eclectic gallery offers work by internationally acclaimed and emerging artists alike, for homes, businesses, churches, parks and gardens. The Master's is indeed Art in the Heart of Loveland. The Master's also offers such gift items as delicate pewter ornaments and exquisitely crafted wooden writing pens. With prices ranging from 93 cents to $90,000, and sizes from miniature to monumental, there is truly something for everyone here. Come be inspired at The Master's Fine Art of Loveland.

343 E 7th Street, Loveland CO
(970) 667-4138
www.themastersfineart.com

Rowe's Flowers and Gifts

GARDENS, PLANTS & FLOWERS:

Best floral arrangements

Rowe's Flowers and Gifts specializes in creating eye-catching floral arrangements for life's most memorable events. From precious bouquets announcing the birth of a child to celebratory arrangements for weddings and graduations, Rowe's can do it all. This Loveland landmark has been a flower shop since 1889, making it the oldest florist shop in northern Colorado. In 1999, it was voted Business of the Year and Teleflora International, the largest wire service in the world, has repeatedly listed it among its top 1,000 producers, a considerable feat in a town of only 50,000. Rowe's is currently owned and operated by Bill Rodgers, who purchased the business from Grace and Cliff Rowe in 1986. Bill began designing arrangements when he was a child and went on to learn the business from his mentor Ruth Hendricks, who would settle for nothing less than perfection. He managed flower shops in both Denver and Ft. Collins before purchasing Rowe's and several employees, including Clint Hartley and George Sapp, have worked for him 25 years or longer. Bill and his loyal staff dedicate themselves to providing exceptional flowers and gifts while giving back to the community. Each year Rowe's donates blooms for local fundraisers, along with the flowers carried by Miss Loveland Valentine. In 2004, the local Rotary Club named Bill Citizen of the Year. Let your gift speak your heart with a captivating arrangement from Rowe's Flowers and Gifts.

863 N Cleveland Avenue, Loveland CO
(970) 667-2300 or (800) 383-7673
www.rowesflowersandgifts.com

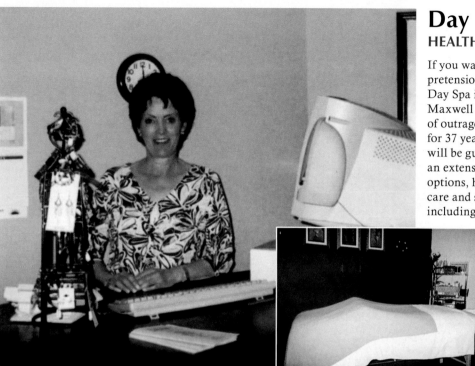

Day Dreams Salon & Spa
HEALTH & BEAUTY: *Best day spa in Loveland*

If you want to relax in the lap of luxury without the pressure of pretension, book a day on cloud nine at Day Dreams Master Salon & Day Spa in Loveland. Owner and master stylist Michelle "Mickey" Maxwell has created an escape where you can succumb to the whims of outrageous fortune that you so deserve. Mickey has been a stylist for 37 years, and her mom Pat owned a salon before her, so you will be guided by experienced hands at Day Dreams. Mickey offers an extensive menu of services, including about a dozen massage options, half-day and full-day spa packages, comprehensive hair care and styling services, and a full range of skincare treatments, including salt glows, facials and waxing. She offers packages for men and women, pampers pregnant moms, soothes sports nuts, and even offers short massages for children. You can book parties for wedding showers, birthdays and other special occasions. She'll do formal up-dos or simple cuts, and everything in between, from coloring and highlighting to perms and weaves. Next time you want to be pampered by friendly, down-to-earth people, call Mickey at Day Dreams Salon & Spa.

4116 N Highway 287, Loveland CO
(970) 667-2646
www.daydreamssalonandspa.com

Orchards Athletic Club
HEALTH & BEAUTY: *Best athletic club*

Most athletic clubs are owned by pods of investors and managed by people for whom it is just a job. The Orchards Athletic Club in Loveland is different. It is a family-owned and operated fitness club where the owners are out on the floor taking an active part in the health of their members. Anslie MacEachran was a pro cyclist for 10 years before he and his brother Hugh opened Orchards Athletic Club. They have combined a comfortable facility with a friendly staff and a series of programs that help people get results. The family-friendly club features programs for seniors, a play area for kids, group classes, a pool, steam and saunas, and expert instruction that makes people want to keep coming back. Ainslie says he still gets a thrill from helping people get healthier, and says his greatest joy is watching a member grow, like the person who comes in with a walker, and weeks later is moving without aid. If you're looking for a health club where you will feel comfortable, that has all the right equipment, and trainers who know how to help, take a tour of the Orchards Athletic Club.

289 E 29th Street, Loveland CO
(970) 667-3800
www.orchardsathleticclub.net

Abner
$99.95

The Bear's Den of Loveland & Castle Rock

HOME: *Best selection of rustic home furnishings*

Let The Bear's Den of Loveland and Castle Rock put a rustic touch to your home with furnishings and accessories made by local crafters. The Bears Den fills a newly expanded space at the Loveland and Castle Rock Outlets with a charming selection of furniture and accessories sure to make your home feel like a mountain cabin. Owners Dale and Brenda Traut will make sure you're introduced to Dale's carved bears, each sporting a name tag and a distinct personality. These adorable fellows mingle among the furnishings with other carved woodland animals bearing whimsical expressions and cheerful smiles. Whether you are seeking something for the bedroom, kitchen or patio, The Bear's Den carries something for every room in your home. Log beds, locally, handmade glider rockers and a plethora of aspen furniture are just a few of the creations you will find. Added to the menagerie are carved lamps, bathroom accessories and dining tables and chairs. It's easy to find the right rustic comforts for your home from such an abundant collection. Choose a wingback chair with pinecone fabric or an aspen canopy bed to create a mountain mood. You may have trouble deciding which piece is just right, but with the friendly help of Dale, Brenda, or one of the staff, you should leave the Bear's Den with the perfect new addition for your home.

5672 McWhinney Boulevard, Loveland CO
(970) 593-9147
5050 Factory Shops Boulevard, Castle Rock CO
(303) 660-5320
www.thebden.com

Bear Mountain Furniture

HOME: *Best hand-carved furniture and home accessories*

Using skills handed down through the generations, Dennis and Christie Fye create hand-carved furniture and home accessories at Bear Mountain Furniture in Loveland. For many years, Christie's father enjoyed woodcarving. He passed his talents and love of the art on to Dennis and Christie, who started creating charming woodland creatures and soon broadened their skill set to include furniture. The couple brought their wares to craft and trade shows. As the popularity of their items quickly grew, the duo opened a wholesale business and expanded to a retail location in 2006. The store, which is reminiscent of a mountain cabin, features furniture and accessories for every room in your home. Each rustic pine bed includes carvings of bears in headboard and footboard posts. Decorate your living room with a sofa and love seat in your choice of fabrics, and welcome guests with an adorable bear or raccoon on your front porch. As longtime Colorado residents, the Fyes place a great deal of value on environmental sensitivity and harvest only standing dead trees for use in their products. If you have an original design in mind to fit your home or cabin, Bear Mountain Furniture specializes in custom orders and would love to accommodate your request. Visit Bear Mountain Furniture for the rustic beauty of handcrafted items from the Fye family.

6803 W Highway 34, Unit B, Loveland CO
(970) 622-0336
www.bearmountainfurniture.com

Cottonwood Cupboard

HOME: *Best source for kitchenware*

With its selection of quality kitchen appliances and bakeware, gourmet foods and gifts, Cottonwood Cupboard is a little slice of heaven for anyone who enjoys spending time in the kitchen. A love of cooking prompted husband and wife Andy and Laurie Hindson, along with Laurie's mother, Margy, to purchase the store two years ago. They stock it full of high-end kitchenware from brands like J.A. Henckels, Cuisinart and KitchenAid. One of Laurie's favorite lines is Doughmakers, a line of aluminum bakeware with a patented textured surface that turns out perfectly browned cakes and cookies. Be sure to check out the gadget wall, because no kitchen is ever complete without a pizza wheel, pasta fork and color coordinated nylon spatula. Browse the locally made gourmet foods or have the store create a custom gift basket for you. Options range from the Flap Jack Morning, with everything you need to treat a special someone to breakfast in bed, including a buttermilk pancake mix, Vermont maple syrup and coffee wrapped up with other goodies in a Sorrento mixing bowl, to the Sushi basket, which includes items for preparing a gourmet Japanese meal at home. Cottonwood Cupboard also offers a convenient bridal registry. Friends and family of the happy couple can shop in the store or browse the registry and place an order online. For high-quality items to stock a gourmet kitchen and make any cooking aficionado's heart flutter, come to Cottonwood Cupboard.

The Promenade Shops at Centura
5971 Sky Pond Drive, Loveland CO
(970) 330-GIFT (4438)
www.cottonwoodcupboard.com

Cabin Country Natural Foods
MARKETS: *Best natural foods store in Loveland*

Everyone knows that eating right is important, but it can sometimes be difficult to make healthful choices at your local supermarket when there is a tasty, fatty treat lurking around every corner. Make those choices easier by gathering your groceries at Cabin Country Natural Foods where they offer a diverse assortment of healthy, natural foods and organic products. Cabin Country has been serving the Loveland area for nearly 25 years. It was purchased by Jacki McAndrews, an occupational therapist, in 1999. Jacki has found her medical background to be extremely beneficial for her customers, as she is able to offer them sound advice about which vitamins and alternative foods are best for their individual needs. In conjunction with a generous array of bulk-foods, Cabin Country offers vitamins by Solaray and Country Life, as well as natural skincare products and a choice selection of your favorite products that are sold at the big chain stores. If you're looking for a wholesome lunch on the go, stop by and try one of their hearty and delicious sandwiches that are made fresh daily. Jacki and her knowledgeable staff pride themselves on providing expert service and are happy to special order specific products for your convenience. Find the healthful, nourishing foods that your body craves at Cabin Country Natural Foods, where making good choices comes easily.

243 E 4th Street, Loveland CO
(970) 669-9280

Broadway Bound Dance Academy
RECREATION: *Best dance studio in Loveland*

More than 250 students take part in programs at the Broadway Bound Dance Academy in Loveland, yet staff members manage to know them all by name. Denise Rhoades owns and operates the company. She's been a dance instructor for 20 years and continues to instruct classes along with her team of teachers, which includes head coach Jennifer Jamison. The studio strives to make all its students feel like members of a family by stressing fun activities in a safe environment. Private lessons can be arranged. Students seeking recreation are as welcome as those striving for excellence in competitive dance. Students range in age from 18 months to 80 years old. The studio's three competitive dance teams, in the junior, teen and senior categories, have won regional and national competitions. Specific programs of instruction include an exceptionally strong jazz program as well as classes in tap dancing, ballet and pointe. Other classes include hip-hop, modern dance and lyrical or emotive dance. By 2007, Denise intends to branch out and offer four dance studios for student instruction. Visit the Broadway Bound Dance Academy for recreational dance or to hone your competitive skills.

645 N Denver Avenue, Loveland CO (970) 663-3133
www.broadwayboundda.com

Peloton Cycles
RECREATION: *Best bikes for your lifestyle*

At Peloton Cycles, owners Trent Schilousky and Robin Torres focus on matching customers with the right bicycle so they can have the best possible experience. By understanding your lifestyle, Trent and Robin can assure you receive not only the best products and services but the ones that will prove most satisfying. Bikes come in a multitude of styles these days, and Peloton Cycles runs the gamut; in fact, it carries more than 100 products specifically designed for women alone. The Peloton Cycles product mix includes everything from the most technical bike to the bike path cruiser, with prices ranging from $250 to $8,000. The shop is an exclusive dealer for Specialized S-Works, producers of one of the fastest and lightest full suspension bikes in the world. It also features products by Litespeed and Trek's technically advanced Madone SSL, the 2006 bicycle choice of Lance Armstrong. Peloton Cycles' full-service shop can repair and adjust a broad range of bicycles. Triathletes will find the gear for all their undertakings here, including wet suits. At Peloton Cycles, Trent and Robin pay as much attention to a kid buying his first bicycle as to the professional considering a high-end machine. Whether you need a new helmet or a new bike, an adjustment or just some advice, Trent and Robin invite you to Peloton Cycles.

**1310 E Eisenhower Boulevard,
Loveland CO
(970) 669-5595**
www.peloton-cycles.com

GameFactor
RECREATION: *Best game and skate supplies*

Glenn Donaldson is one of those lucky people who have a job doing what he loves. In his case, his work is play. Glenn is the owner of GameFactor, the best source of both electronic games and skate supplies in Loveland. From old-school console games like Atari to the latest console games, Glenn knows his games. He also carries a huge selection of skateboards and skate accessories, including shoes, clothing, sunglasses and, of course, boards. He carries DVDs, videos, video games, skate movies, long boards, and more. He's also a valuable and honest resource. He has tested nearly every game in the store and will give his honest opinion on quality and game play. When we last visited, Glenn was on the phone talking a gamer through a computer problem. Glenn may be a gamer, but he is also a serious and conscientious business person. He sponsors many local events and giveaways. He also sponsors a skateboarding demo team that entertains and educates the community. Stop by GameFactor when you're in Loveland. You can never have too much game.

**1459 W Eisenhower Boulevard, Loveland CO
(970) 667-3868**

Blue Sky Cycles

RECREATION: *Best high-end bikes*

Blue Sky Cycles in Longmont is where you want to go when you're in the market for a bike or bike accessories. It's a store that takes cycling seriously, and it shows in both the products they carry and the service they offer. Owner Rob Love grew up racing mountain bikes in Michigan and worked on the collegiate teams at Michigan State. After leaving Michigan he followed the racing circuit for a year, which made him realize he needed to be in Boulder County. He opened Blue Sky Cycles in 2005, and the store has been a labor of love. The layout, build and colors of the store were all done by Rob. He's poured his love and respect for cycling into every aspect of the operation. His staff reflects his commitment. All of his mechanics have been certified through bike mechanic schools, and they all reflect Rob's enthusiasm for the world of cycling. Blue Sky Cycles carries everything a bike nut could possibly need, from clothing, sunglasses and nutritional products to tools and, of course, bikes. Blue Sky offers a full menu of bike repair and tune-up options. You don't have to be a bicycle racer to shop here. The store is geared toward providing the best bicycling information and products for every level of cycling. Visit Blue Sky Cycles in Loveland. Their enthusiasm is contagious and their store is a real thrill.

600 S Airport Road, Building A Suite A, Loveland CO
(303) 682-3939
www.blueskycyclesonline.com

Loveland Cycle 'N Fitness
RECREATION: *Best bicycle service*

Loveland Cycle 'N Fitness has been an important part of the Loveland community for more than 50-years. Richard Preiss, the store's owner since 1998, feels the community commitment deeply and thinks of himself more as the keeper of the business than its owner. Customer service is the most important aspect of that responsibility. Richard says, "I am in the advice business. Sales are secondary." New and longtime customers expect and receive personalized assistance when purchasing a new bike or repairing an old one. Some customers drop in to reminisce about their first bicycle purchase. Richard says that remembering the experience always brings a smile to their faces. Whether selling customers new bikes or repairing those that have been previously used, Richard will do whatever it takes to meet his customer's needs. The store offers Raleigh, Diamondback and Haro BMX bicycles, among others. It stocks recumbent bicycles and three-wheel adult bikes, and it sells and installs electric motor conversion kits. Bicycle clothing and accessories are also on hand, along with treadmills and other fitness equipment. The store's community involvement goes beyond interacting with customers. The Preiss family assists the local Pedal Bike Club and hosts bicycle repair clinics throughout Loveland. Visit Loveland Cycle 'N Fitness for an outstanding selection backed up by a half-century of service and tradition.

524 N Cleveland Avenue, Loveland CO
(970) 667-1943
www.lovelandcycle.com

The Hobnob Restaurant
RESTAURANTS & CAFÉS: *Best community gathering spot*

The Hobnob Restaurant has been providing visitors with a welcoming and relaxing place to enjoy a meal with friends and family for more than 28 years and continues today as one of the community's most beloved gathering spots. This charming eatery, located in a vintage home just west of the Loveland business district, first opened in 1978 as the Hobnob Tearoom, a place area ladies met to discuss current events. Husband and wife team Steve Schultz and Dorothea Boettcher purchased the tearoom in 1988 and by changing both the name and the menu have earned a loyal following of patrons from both sexes and a wide range of professions. The area's construction workers and businessmen share an appreciation for the restaurant's quiet, family atmosphere. Steve, a former quality engineer, uses the same high standards that he applied to his previous career in running the Hobnob, which means his customers can count on fresh ingredients and perfectly prepared dishes. Menu favorites include Steve's flaky quiche, along with tasty crepes and cream puffs. The eatery is open for breakfast and lunch Monday though Saturday and for supper on Friday evenings. The restaurant offers on-site catering and banquet options, making this the ideal place to hold intimate gatherings or corporate events. Enjoy delicious teas, flavorful cuisine and gracious hospitality at the family owned and operated Hobnob Restaurant.

205 W 4th Street, Loveland CO
(970) 663-5527
www.thehobnobrestaurant.com

Daddy-O's Green Onion
RESTAURANTS & CAFÉS: *Best deli-style sandwiches*

When you want a great hot sandwich on the best bread in town, go to Daddy-O's Green Onion in Loveland. This family-owned and operated deli-style restaurant serves a full menu of sandwiches for breakfast, lunch or dinner. Along with sandwiches, you'll find pizzas, muffins, pastries and every espresso drink under the sun. Owners Terry and Roxann Brundage bake their own breads daily, giving you a range of choices that included one of the lightest sourdough breads you'll ever taste. Daddy-Os is a casual, upbeat place where you'll feel comfortable spending some time. They are a wireless hot spot, so you can bring your laptop and get connected while you savor whichever delectable sandwich you choose.
The menu includes more than 25 different kinds of sandwiches, plus great soups and salads. Daddy-O's is populated by many repeat customers, and several groups hold their meetings here, a testament to the relaxed atmosphere and great prices that make this restaurant such a pleasure. Next time you're in Loveland, stop in Daddy-Os Green Onion. Their fresh-baked goodness is addicting.

**2277 W Eisenhower Boulevard,
Loveland CO
(970) 635-0001**
www.daddyosgreenonion.com

Sweet Rosies Too
RESTAURANTS & CAFÉS: *Best family restaurant*

Located in the historical McKee House, Sweet Rosies Too serves up all manner of good things to eat. Open for breakfast and lunch Tuesday through Sunday, the restaurant also offers a Friday night fish fry that is rapidly gaining popularity. Owners Janet and Jerry Limbeck's motto, Come on Over to Our House, describes the way they treat their customers. The whole Limbeck family works here, making it truly a family restaurant, and they strive for a positive atmosphere that makes everyone feel welcome. Their diverse menu offers everything from fresh, healthy gourmet salads to Italian panini sandwiches and half-pound burgers. They also provide catering services and have hosted murder mystery dinners as well as wine tasting dinners. Thanks to free wireless Internet, customers can order a cocktail or a latte and relax on the outdoor patio while surfing the Web. For a more traditional experience, guests can enjoy high tea, complete with homemade scones, lemon curd, and Devonshire cream. Bears N Things, a gift shop owned by Mary Painter and located in the front part of the McKee House, offers an array of one-of-a-kind gift items, from collectible bears and Red Hat accessories to jewelry and garden items. For a unique shopping experience and a delicious, down-home meal served by friendly folks, stop in soon at Sweet Rosies Too.

**1120 N Lincoln Avenue, Loveland CO
(970) 203-1050**
www.sweetrosiestoo.com

Henry's Pub

RESTAURANTS & CAFÉS:
Classiest pub in Loveland

Henry's Pub is a charming English-style gathering place in the heart of Downtown Loveland where friends relax in the lounge and big deals are made in private booths. The classic, simplistic Americana décor welcomes both the distinctive business person and families alike. After two years in business, the owners are as ecstatic over the turnout for their steaks, seafood, and gourmet specials as they are proud of their mixed clientele. They see all walks of life come through the doors, from folks in jeans, to power suits, to three generations celebrating a birthday. "Many a business deal and broker transaction have occurred right here," says Bryan Jones, co-owner and front-of-the-house manager. Todd Riemersma, co-owner and back-of-the-house manager, came up with the idea for Henry's Pub and designed everything from the menu to the kitchen. Todd's wife, Sara, is the accountant and decorator. Together, Bryan, Todd and Sara deserve credit for bringing life to a former mercantile building that has stood in downtown Loveland since the 1920s. The building's façade was restored to its original design in 2003, while Bryan and Todd did a complete overhaul of the interior. "The original tin ceiling is probably the refurbishing triumph we're most proud of," says Bryan. The relationships that have developed out of Henry's have proven quite special as well. Last year, Henry's hosted a wedding reception for a couple from Wyoming who met at Henry's. Truly a place where everyone knows your name, for a casual bite to eat, a power lunch, romantic dinner, or anything in between, make the historic confines and ambiance of Henry's Pub your venue of choice.

2324 E 4th Street, Loveland CO
(970) 613-1896
www.henrys-pub.com

Monaco Trattoria

RESTAURANTS & CAFÉS: *Best Italian food in Loveland*

Diners at Monaco Trattoria are treated to a feast of authentic Italian flavors and a comfortable atmosphere. The goal of Owners Giuseppe and Tammy Monaco is, "when people step into the restaurant, they step into Italy." You won't find any Americanized food here. Giuseppe was born and raised on the island of Capri and met Tammy while she was vacationing there 18 years ago. He brings the flavors of the Campania region of Italy to Loveland. With signature fish dishes, such as *branzino* from the Mediterranean Sea, *focaccia* bread baked fresh in the wood fired oven, and the sweet aroma of San Marzano tomatoes and garlic in the air, you'll definitely feel like you're at an Italian family Sunday dinner, regardless of what day it is. The menu is constantly changing to incorporate organic vegetables from local farmers and seasonal items with new flavors appearing all the time. Before dining, enjoy a drink in Monaco Trattoria's Acqua Lounge with happy-hour specials and live guitar. The mood and atmosphere are light, and the staff is friendly and knowledgeable. If you're looking for an authentic and memorable Italian dining experience, come to Monaco Trattoria and *mangia* (eat).

218 E 4th Street, Loveland CO
(970) 461-1889
www.monacotrattoria.com

Judy's Hallmark
SHOPPING:
Largest selection of cards and gifts

Judy's Hallmark in Loveland has an enormous selection of cards and gifts, but owners Judy and George Blundell insist it's their staff that makes the store a standout. In fact, the store has been named a top-200 Hallmark retailer. The carefully selected merchandise is another key to the store's success. Judy and George make regular buying trips to ensure that their popular offerings change often, thus keeping regular customers coming back. Although the shop constantly displays new merchandise, Judy's keeps a permanent stock of items from important vendors. Jim Shore products are an example. Jim Shore, renowned for his folk art, creates portraits, sculptures and figurines. Vera Bradley pieces, always on display, include hand bags and luggage. The Montana Silversmiths offer collectible art and sculptures cold cast in bronze. At Judy's, careful shoppers can find bargains and discriminating buyers can find exceptional quality. Judy's provides a special ordering service and offers gift wrapping for everything they sell. Visit Judy's Hallmark to find carefully selected gifts at prices that fit every budget.

1199 Eagle Drive, Loveland CO
(970) 667-1077

Calico Kate's Pantry Shop
SHOPPING: *Best assortment of entertaining gifts*

Unearth ancient bones with a dinosaur excavation kit or select a Russian-made birch box to hold your favorite treasures at Calico Kate's Pantry Shop, where a world of whimsical, inspiring and downright entertaining gifts and collectibles awaits the visitor. Jackie Whittemore and Sonny McManigal opened this fascinating shop in 2003 and named it Calico Kate's in honor of Sonny's grandmother, Dottie Ferguson. Dottie, the owner of the original Calico Kate's in Glen Haven, Colorado, from 1959 to 1993, created the character named Calico Kate, and her daughter (Sonny's mother), Ann, created illustrations for three storybooks, four cookbooks, an ABC book and numerous catalogs and ads. They also developed paper dolls and cloth dolls of the characters Calico Kate and Bluejean Jake. Jackie, who is best known for her compassionate nature and

community service, hand selects everything that the store carries, including a wide selection of Colorado-made gifts and gourmet treats. The duo stocks anything that catches their eyes, so the shop's hodgepodge inventory offers something for everyone. In addition to their eclectic stock, Jackie and Sonny carry on Calico Kate's name by continuing to publish and sell Dottie's classic cookbooks, story books and paper dolls. They have also been working on a new storybook and on finding a company to manufacture the Calico Kate and Bluejean Jake dolls again. Find playful knickknacks, quaint collectibles, tasty treats and your favorite recipes from days gone by at Calico Kate's Pantry Shop.

4916 W Eisenhower, Loveland CO
(970) 663-1156

Grand Slam Sports Cards and Comic Books
SHOPPING: *Best selection of sports cards and comic books*

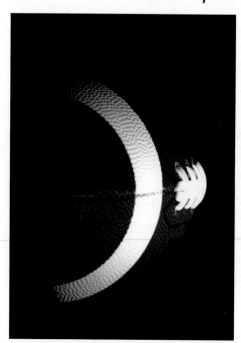

Whether it's sports stars or superheroes, Grand Slam Sports Cards and Comic Books covers the bases with a selection that brings out fans and collectors. Open since 1992, the Loveland store has over 130,000 vintage and new comic books, presenting every comic book publisher. Its baseball, football, hockey and basketball cards number in the millions. Owner Kevin Keen is an avid longtime collector. He's equally happy to sct up a beginner for a lifelong hobby or to assist experienced collectors with finishing their collections. Beyond cards and books, Grand Slam stocks a large collection of figurines, video games and DVD movies. Regular customers can receive discounts on some merchandise. The store offers weekly gaming sessions for those who play the popular *Magic: The Gathering* card game. Come to Grand Slam Sports Cards and Comic Books, a home run location for sports fans, collectors and comic book buffs.

1730 W Eisenhower Boulevard, Loveland CO
(970) 667-8713

Big Thompson Indian Village
SHOPPING: *Best Native American arts and crafts*

The history of Big Thompson Indian Village in Loveland began in 1937 when it was known as Big Thompson Trading Post. Current owners Howard and Lena Carman took over the operation in 1971. The building is constructed from logs that were harvested locally in the 1930s and was fronted with native rock after the 1976 flood. The Big Thompson Canyon is a beautiful scenic entrance into the Rocky Mountain National Park. It follows the Big Thompson River which offers great photographic opportunities and a pleasurable time for fishermen, hikers, and nature lovers alike. Howard and Lena are proud of the building's history as well as the authentic Native American arts and crafts offered here. They strive to honor the legacy and dignity of the cultures represented within their store. Much of what customers see is museum quality and a few items are on display belong to the owners private collection. The Big Thompson Indian Village offers collectible Native American jewelry, baskets, Navajo rug, cradle boards and weaponry. You'll also find high quality handmade art and craft from Colorado and other parts of the West. The many antiques on display combine with other collectibles to hint at compelling stories about the American West. Visit Big Thompson Indian Village for unusual merchandise, and the chance to hear stories from Howard and Lena concerning the objects found here and the local history.

1348 W US Highway 34, Big Thompson Canyon, Loveland CO
(970) 667-9353

The Bargain Barn
SHOPPING:
Best used furniture and thrift store

If you are a yard sale junkie, a flea market fanatic or a thrift store maniac, you've got to meet Sean McCarty at The Bargain Barn. He's a kindred spirit. Sean used to spend his free time scrounging for bargains where ever he could find them. It got to the point were he needed his own building to put all the bargains he'd found. The Bargain Barn is where thrifty Lovelandites go to satisfy their bargain quests. Here you will find the best selection in the region of used furniture, quality appliances, tools, sporting goods and a zillion other previously owned treasures. If you've got stuff to sell, chances are Sean will be interested. In true flea market style, Sean's motto is Come on Down and Let's Bargain. He's not kidding. He's been known to buy whole houses at a time to keep his barn stocked. He's not averse to bargaining over the items he already owns, even though they're already priced at bargain levels. This is more than a business to Sean. It's a calling. Then again, you already understand that if you're a thrifter. It's why you are already on your way to dialing the phone to find out when he's open. We'll tell you: Everyday but Wednesday.

1405 Prospect Avenue, Loveland CO
(970) 613-8437
www.lovelandbargainbarn.com

Ferrell Auction Company
SHOPPING: *Best antique and estate auctions*

Set in the foothills west of Loveland, the Ferrell Auction Company specializes in antique and estate auctions. While the inventory varies from auction to auction, you can always find a variety of exquisite furnishings, antiques and collectibles. Owner George Ferrell works hard to acquire important pieces that are rarely available to the public. At a recent auction, the highly prized items included a Victorian rosewood bedroom suite, a marble fireplace mantle and an 11-piece R.J. Horner mahogany bedroom suite. Another auction featured oriental rugs, porcelains and a collection of Victrola phonographs. Still another brought out Victorian and Continental decorative

arts, bronze and marble statuary pieces and rare music boxes. Winning bids range as widely as the desires of prospective buyers. Ferrell holds several auctions each year. Participants can visit the warehouse on days leading up to the weekend auction to view pieces that interest them. Ferrell puts a number on each item along with times when bids will be taken on each piece so that busy buyers can show up just in time to bid. Ferrell encourages interested parties to visit its website for complete information on upcoming auctions. Visit Ferrell Auction Company for your chance to obtain exquisite pieces that are rarely available to the public.

5505 W Highway 34, Loveland CO
(970) 635-0044
www.ferrellauction.com

Photo courtesy of ferrellauction.com

Trail Ridge Winery
WINERIES: *Best Cabernet Franc and Muscat Blanc*

Trail Ridge Winery, located in the foothills north of Denver on the road to Rocky Mountain National Park, started life with a group of home wine making enthusiasts who developed a friendship. Their relationship eventually led to a store called the North Denver Cellar that supplied grapes to home winemakers, which they closed in 1996 to focus on the winery. The first batches they produced were a Merlot and a Chardonnay, and the winery has since received rave reviews for its Cabernet Franc. All of the grapes are 100 percent Colorado grown, and most come from the Western Slope, where sunny days and crisp nights are ideal for bringing out the best qualities of the grapes. The winery encourages visitors to bring food, sample the wines and enjoy their day on the winery's patio. You can also purchase products online. The tasting room features Trail Ridge wines, which are distributed statewide year-round, but regional wines are sometimes offered here

as well. Trail Ridge's best selling wine is the Never Summer White, a slightly sweet, deliciously fruity Muscat Blanc blend of carefully chosen varietals, which is wonderful chilled and sipped on the porch with light snacks. Trail Ridge typically yields 7,000 to 8,000 gallons of wine per year, and the partners enjoy being able to run the place on their own. To sample some of the best wines in Colorado, visit the tasting room at Trail Ridge Winery soon.

4113 W Eisenhower Boulevard, Loveland CO
(970) 635-0949
www.trailridgewinery.com

Valley of the Wind Winery

WINERIES: *Best Chardonnay and Merlot*

Valley of the Wind Winery is an award winning artisan winery located in downtown Loveland's historic train depot. Owners Patrick and Geri McGibney, who have been making wine together for 30 years, first came to Loveland in 1991. They purchased an old irrigated cherry orchard and planted 400 Chardonnay grape vines, and the rest, as they say, is history. Although their focus is on whites, their 2004 Merlot was one of only four to receive a double gold medal at the prestigious International Eastern Wine Competition, the oldest wine competition in North America. As a result of that award, the McGibneys have seen a rising interest in their wines, which led to the expansion of their facilities in Loveland and the opening of a tasting room in Estes Park. Pat and Geri also focus on supporting the local winery community, so they stock brands from other area wineries as well as featuring their own wines in their shops. Although they hope to see the area gain a national and international stronghold in the winemaking world, they are proud to be not only a local winery but also a neighborhood winery. When visiting Loveland, be sure to visit Valley of the Wind Winery, where friendly folks are ready to serve you top quality wines.

411 N Railroad Avenue, Loveland CO
(970) 461-1185
www.valleyofthewind.com

PLACES TO GO

- Bohn Park
  S 2nd Avenue and St. Vrain Creek
- Button Rock Preserve
  Longmont Dam Road
- Hall Ranch (park)
  S St. Vrain Drive
- Lyons Redstone Museum
  (June-September) 338 High Street
- Sandstone Park
  350 Broadway

THINGS TO DO

May-September
- Lyons Sculpture Trail
  www.sculpturetrail.com

June
- Lyons Whitewater Fest
  (303) 358-7039
- Lyons Good Old Days
  (303) 823-8250 or (303) 823-5215

July
- Rockygrass Bluegrass Festival
  www.bluegrass.com/rockygrass
- Rockygrass Academy (weeklong camp)
  www.bluegrass.com/rga

August
- Folks Festival
  www.bluegrass.com/folks

September
- Festival of the Mabon
  www.bluegrass.com/mabon
- Lyons Duck Race
  www.lyons-colorado.com/duck/duck.htm

LYONS

Lyons is an historic red rock quarry town a few miles north of Boulder in the foothills of the Rockies. The town contains 15 buildings built of the local red sandstone and listed in the National Register of Historic Places. Lyons has antique stores, restaurants, artists and musicians. Planet Bluegrass in Lyons puts on well-known music festivals and camps. The Mabon festival is music of the autumn equinox from around the world. Other activities in and around Lyons include mountain biking at Hall Ranch, touring through Rocky Mountain National Park (40 minutes up the hill), and hiking in the nearby National Forest lands and Boulder County open space.

Rockygrass Bluegrass Festival, 2005
Photo by Pamela Brandon
Courtesy of Jordan Klein

Quilting Hands
ARTS & CRAFTS: *Best quilting shop in Lyons*

Innovative quilters in and around Lyons gained a valuable source
for supplies when Quilting Hands opened its door in 2000. Jan Rold,
the owner, traces her passion for quilting back to the American
Bicentennial in 1976, when many traditional crafts experienced a
renaissance. She decided to make a quilt for her bed and got hooked.
She learned a very traditional style of quilting, but soon branched
out and has tried many styles and techniques over the past 30 years.
Jan now favors a more contemporary style and, in fact, opened
Quilting Hands to fill a niche for hard-to-find supplies that support
innovative quilting. While she sells to all of the different guilds in
the area, her particular mission, she says, is to give quilters what
they need to think outside the box. She stocks uncommon fabrics,
such as batik and flannels, novelty threads, such as metallics and
rayons, and, above all, clearer colors. "I really want to inspire
quilters to be creative with their colors," she says. Jan likes that
her shop is small enough that she can give personal attention to
her customers. A good day's work includes providing direction to
someone who has ideas but is having trouble getting into a quilt. For
supplies and inspiration, see Jan Rold at Quilting Hands.

304 Main Street, Lyons CO
(303) 823-6067

Lyons Redstone Museum

ATTRACTIONS:

Best local history museum

Television fans who marvel at the knowledge of contestants on the popular Jeopardy show will love chatting with staff at the Lyons Redstone Museum. The staff is known for their comprehensive knowledge of the area and their enthusiasm for sharing information with guests interested in local history. Like several prominent historical buildings in Lyons, this former schoolhouse is built from redstone, a sandstone taken from nearby quarries. The building opened as a one-room schoolhouse in 1881 and was soon overflowing with the children of miners who came to work in the quarries. A second story was added to handle the influx, but it first swayed when the wind blew. In the mid-1970s, the school district planned to raze the old building, but the Lyons Historical Society stepped in and formed an alliance with the town and the school district that saved the building as a museum. Displays here emphasize local color and history, and many items were actually owned by local families. You'll find an antique teller cage, a replica of a historic drugstore, arrowheads, a large photo display, genealogy file, book sale and gift shop. The museum is open seven days a week, June through September, so plan to stop by and visit Historic Lyons, the Museum, and the Lyons Historic District on your way to Rocky Mountain National Park. The staff will be happy to answer questions about the Lyons area. For insight into the region's people and possessions, visit the Lyons Redstone Museum.

340 High Street, Lyons CO
(303) 823-5271 or (303) 823-6692
lavern921@aol.com

Photos courtesy of Lyons Chamber of Commerce

Photos by Benko Photographics

Telluride bluegrass festival

RockyGrass Festival, Lyons

Planet Bluegrass

ATTRACTIONS:
Best summer music festivals

Summer in the Colorado Rockies is a time to celebrate, particularly when the hillsides ring with bluegrass music from the summer festivals produced by Planet Bluegrass. In 2005, Planet Bluegrass president and impresario Craig Ferguson received a Distinguished Achievement Award from the International Bluegrass Association for his innovative events, which combine world-class music and first-rate production for an all-out good time. Expect big names in country and jazz music and such stringed instruments as mandolin, fiddle, banjo and acoustic guitar. The bluegrass festivals begin in June in the charming Victorian mountain town of Telluride. In July, Planet Bluegrass comes home to its ranch in Lyons for the RockyGrass Festival, along the banks of the St. Vrain River. A week before the festival, the RockyGrass Academy brings opportunities to train with professional musicians, build your own mandolin, and enjoy evenings filled with jamming and barbecues. In August, the musical mood mellows with the Rocky Mountain Folks Festival and a special school for songwriters. Planet Bluegrass ends its season of festivals in September with the one-day Festival of the Mabon, where bagpipes and drums pay tribute to the fall equinox. Planet Bluegrass believes in recycling and encourages the use of biodegradable disposable products. For festivities that celebrate America's musical heritage in pristine surroundings, buy your tickets in advance for the popular summer festivals of Planet Bluegrass.

500 W Main Street, Lyons CO
(303) 823-0848
www.bluegrass.com

Redhill Motorcycle Werx

AUTO:

Best custom motorcycle shop

If there is one word that describes the success of Redhill Motorcycle Werx it is passion. Passion for life, passion to follow dreams, passion for speed, for bikes and for each other. Scot and Mercedes Ross are legends in the motorcycle world. Scot is a renowned mechanic and bike builder. Mercedes is a leading force in the design of motorcycles for the female form. Scot and Mercedes took a circuitous route to success at Redhill Motorcycle Werx. He spent his early years representing the US on the national cycling team, and eventually transitioned into the professional bicycle industry. She was a budding ski racer who moved into retail. Somewhere along the way life started throwing bricks at them. She got cancer. After she beat it, he fell 40 feet and broke his whole body. The trials convinced them that life was too short to mess it up with regular jobs, so they took off on a dream, opening Redhill Motorcycle Werx at the base of the Rockies. The story is longer and more interesting than we can relate here, but the bottom line is that Scot and Mercedes now own one of the hottest, most highly respected shops in the country. They've been written up and lauded by every publication that matters to bikers. They sell parts, service machines, customize bikes, support charities, and basically put their brand on anything and everything related to their personal and professional lives. If you need anything done to your bike, from new paint to more speed, look them up. Even if you're all set mechanically, saddle up and cruise by their shop. Scot and Mercedes are people you want to know.

4196 Ute Highway, Lyons CO
(303) 823-6363
www.redhillmotorcyclewerx.com

The Stone Cup Café & Gallery

BAKERIES, COFFEE & TEA:
Building community and caring for the planet

Visit the Stone Cup Café and Gallery and take a seat on Lyons' community front porch. Nestled at the base of the foothills, the café's sunshine and flower-filled porch offers an inviting place to rest. Experience the unpretentious hospitality and mountain views as you savor organic espresso and freshly baked, made-from-scratch scones, cookies and breads. In the morning the café attracts hikers, bikers and nature enthusiasts on their way to nearby trails. The Stone Cup offers perfect adventure fuel with breakfast calzones, quiche and smoothies. A lazy lunch might include soup and sandwiches, an organic burrito or a salad. Linger over the *New York Times*, access free wireless Internet or chat with a neighbor about the area's vibrant music scene. Take in the work of an ever-changing roster of regional artists displayed on the café's brightly painted walls or join in the weekly knitting circle. It's easy to see that the Stone Cup embodies the owners' commitment to building community and caring for the planet. The eco-friendly café makes a conscientious effort to reduce its impact on the earth with a comprehensive recycling program. The sleek smoothie cups are made of biodegradable corn, as are the forks, straws and plates. In addition, the café offsets its energy consumption with nonpolluting wind power. The welcoming space is also available for private rental throughout the year.

442 High Street, Lyons CO
(303) 823-2345
www.thestonecup.com

Celtic Crossroads— Jerry Gehringer, Artist and Goldsmith

FASHION:
Best Celtic jewelry in Lyons

A good place to catch Jerry Gehringer, who creates jewelry under the business name of Celtic Crossroads, is at a Celtic festival. He has shown his Celtic-inspired pieces at about 1,000 gatherings around the world. Well versed in the meaning of the symbols he recreates in his pendants, sculptures and talismans, he enjoys sharing his knowledge with his clients, who often sense an ethereal presence in his work. In fact, there's something about Jerry that makes you think that he feels connections with things that are beyond most people's perceptions. For starters, he, like his ancient predecessors, mixes and casts his own alloys. What's more, clients who bring him no more than a sketchy notion for a piece are typically amazed when they see his design. "It's as if he read my mind," is a common refrain. If you don't run into Jerry at a festival, you could always make an appointment and visit him at his home, which doubles as his studio. There, you will get to meet Bob, the house cat. Jerry is uncertain about Bob's age, because Bob has been at the house longer than Jerry. Maybe he is 1,000 years old. For custom jewelry designs that make an ageless and mystical statement, consider Jerry Gehringer and Celtic Crossroads.

446 Main Street, Lyons CO
(303) 823-2451

Photo by Mateo Leyba

Lyons Classic Pinball

RECREATION: *Largest pinball game collection*

Lyons Classic Pinball has one of the largest publicly available pinball game collections in Colorado. In all, there are 36 well-maintained games from the 1960s to 2006, plus six classic video games. The game lineup changes often and currently features oddities like Hercules (the largest production pinball game), Joust (rare head to head), and Orbitor 1 (moon surface-like playfield). The owners occasionally sell games to make way for new ones. The facility is also available for private parties. Owners Kevin and Carole Carroll also run Lyons Classic Video, located inside Oskar Blues Restaurant & Brewery—only 30 steps from Lyons Classic Pinball. Oskar Blues is Lyons' oldest brew pub and grill, specializing in Cajun food and music. The Oskar Blues game room offers more than 20 video games from the 1980s, plus two pinball games. The journey to Lyons Classic Pinball started four years ago when Carole surprised Kevin with a classic 1978 Bally KISS pinball game as a birthday present. The KISS machine, which features images of the rock group, turned Kevin's love of pinball into an all out obsession. Fortunately, Carole shared the fever. Their second purchase was The Addams Family, followed by Black Knight, sporting design features that were advanced for its time. Within a year, the family game room was filled with pinball games, and Kevin quit his job as a master plumber to start a pinball center. Visit Lyons Classic Pinball for a rare chance to play an outstanding collection of classic pinball games. Only 15 miles north of Boulder.

339-A Main Street, Lyons CO (303) 823-6100
lyonspinball@yahoo.com
www.lyonspinball.com

Bitterbrush Cycles

RECREATION: *Best custom-made bicycles*

Glen Bell and Paige Payne, owners of Bitterbrush Cycles, operate by the slogan Love to Ride, Ride to Love, which is as much a philosophy of life as a business posture. You can rent bicycles for a few hours or a few weeks here. You also can order custom-made bicycles to be constructed from the frame up or consider such name brand bicycles as Haro, Cove and Salsa. Although the focus is on mountain bikes, Bitterbrush offers street bikes as well. Extensive lines of bicycle clothing, bicycle parts and accessories make this Lyons store an important stop for all area bicyclists and those passing through. Glen and Paige believe in delivering efficient, friendly service, and customers arriving with a flat tire or repair need can expect immediate service. The primary inspiration for Bitterbrush came from Glen's many years as a riding enthusiast. His passion for bicycling makes other bicyclists particularly comfortable in his presence and assures all customers that their needs will be enthusiastically met. The Bitterbrush part of the store name comes from a locally flourishing brush plant and a local bike trail named after the undergrowth. If you cannot make it to the store, an online selection is available on eBay and can be accessed from the store's website. Glen and Paige invite you to Bitterbrush Cycles, where you'll not only get your bike needs met, but you will meet kindred spirits.

324 Main Street, Lyons CO (303) 823-8100
www.bitterbrushcycles.com

Andrea's Homestead Cafe
RESTAURANTS & CAFÉS:
Best German cuisine in Lyons

Andrea Lierman grew up on a self-sustaining farm in Bavaria, enjoying vegetables straight from the garden along with fresh meat and milk. After meeting her husband during an exchange program with the University of Boulder, she moved to Colorado and opened Andrea's Homestead Cafe in 1977, where she brings the flavors of her home in Germany to diners. The extensive breakfast, brunch, lunch and dinner menu choices use only the freshest and finest ingredients, including many organic foods and oils. Breakfast selections range from the sweet German apple pecan pancakes with caramelized butter, whipped cream and pecans to the savory smoked salmon omelette with artichoke and herbed cream cheese. For dinner, you may opt for a German specialty, such as the Munich-style roast duck served with *spätzle* and red cabbage, or choose one of the Continental seafood, steak or poultry entrées. Attentive service, delicious food and friendly atmosphere come together at Andrea's to provide you with *gemütlichkeit*, which means warmth and a feeling of belonging. The inviting atmosphere also makes Andrea's a popular spot for wedding rehearsal dinners, family reunions and other social events. Come to Andrea's Homestead Cafe for tried and true recipes from Andrea's family to yours.

216 E Main Street, Lyons CO
(303) 823-5000
www.AndreasHomesteadCafe.com

Louie's Italian Restaurant
RESTAURANTS & CAFÉS: *Best Italian restaurant in Lyons*

With three generations of the Davis family serving up delicious food, visitors will definitely feel like part of the family at Louie's Italian Restaurant. The Lyons restaurant, features the finest fresh Italian cuisine, served in generous portions and with a smile. Customers will find all their favorite pizzas and pastas on the menu, along with local favorites like the famed Hot House Pizza. Seafood lovers will delight in dishes like the seared fresh Atlantic salmon with a balsamic vinegar glaze. There's even a menu for little ones with portions of pizza, spaghetti and other favorites

geared toward them. Diners should make sure to save room for such mouth-watering desserts as Italian crème cake or tiramisu. Customers enjoy an extensive wine list, which includes a variety of local and regional favorites. Louie's is also available to cater parties, weddings and other special occasions. Located in the Lyons Shopette, Louie's features pleasant booths, nicely fitted with elegant touches like white tablecloths. For enjoyable food in a family-friendly environment, visit Louie's Italian Restaurant.

138 E Main Street, Lyons CO
(303) 823-8856
http://downtownlyons.com/
louiesintalianrestaurant

Photo courtesy of downtownlyons.com/louiesintalianrestaurant/

Oskar Blues Cajun Grill & Brewery
RESTAURANTS & CAFÉS: *Hottest place to be on a Saturday night*

The atmosphere at Oskar Blues Cajun Grill & Brewery is always festive, featuring great food, live music and award winning microbrew ales. Owner Dale Katechis grew up in the restaurant business in Alabama and moved to Lyons in 1992. He brings Southern hospitality and Cajun spice to the restaurant and brewpub he opened nearly a decade ago. The menu at Oskar Blues is full of bold, exciting flavors. Whet your appetite with Rings of Fire, Oskar's version of onion rings, served with a Cajun dipping sauce. Entrées include the signature dish of crab cakes, as well as jambalaya, fire roasted medallions of pork and the Heatseeker Burger, topped with jalapeños, pepper jack cheese and the house wing sauce. Choose one of the Oskar Blues ales, brewed on-site, to accompany your dinner. The *New York Times* named Dale's Pale Ale the best in its category nationwide. The beers are handcanned, five at a time, and Dale explains that using cans, as opposed to bottles, protects the beer from light and oxidation. This method has earned Oskar Blues the affectionate

nickname, the Little Brewery that Cans. The grill enjoys a reputation as a place to find great music, with many nationally touring blues, rock and bluegrass acts performing on the intimate stage. The high quality of musicians is just one of the reasons *Rolling Stone* magazine calls the restaurant the hottest place to be on a Saturday night in Colorado. Come on over to Oskar Blues Cajun Grill & Brewery for good times all the time.

303 Main Street, Lyons CO
(303) 823-6685
www.oskarblues.com

Villa Tatra
RESTAURANTS & CAFÉS: *Best Eastern European food*

High in the Tatra Mountains along the border of Poland and Czechoslovakia are traditional houses that look just like the Villa Tatra restaurant in Lyons. Constructed by a Polish architect, the building isn't the only thing that's authentic at Villa Tatra. The menu features dishes common to most Eastern European countries, all cooked in the traditional manner. If you have never tasted such cuisine, here is the place to gain a flavorful introduction to borsch, made from red beets; sour soup, made with rye bread; or beef tripe soup. If you are already familiar with Eastern European food, you will agree that the Wojcik and Kusnierz families, who own Villa Tatra, are masters at preparing it. They make everything right here, including an array of smoked foods. Prepared using no gas or electricity, just wood, the sausage, trout and salmon from the smoke house are available to take home or to ship. For some customers, it's the wide selection of wild game, such as elk, buffalo and deer, which keeps them coming back. Villa Tatra also offers a three-course lunch as well as a gift shop with treasures crafted by Polish artisans. To experience another part of the world without leaving Colorado, go to Villa Tatra.

729 Pinewood Drive, Lyons CO
(303) 823-6819
www.villatatra.com

Cilantro Mary
RESTAURANTS & CAFÉS: *Best authentic Mexican food in Lyons*

Enchiladas, tamales and chile rellenos sound like the usual Mexican fare until you've tried them at Cilantro Mary in Lyons. Expect to wake up your palate with festive, authentic flavors from central and coastal Mexico. Cilantro Mary has a 40-year track record and rave reviews from local and regional press, thanks to extraordinary salsas and sauces, like the salsa molé, developed by Mexican culinary artist Usha Amteg, and the salsa verde that graces the *carne de puerco*. Chef James Morton and his wife, Ifka, residents of Lyons since 1980, took over the restaurant in 2005. As experienced restaurant owners who hail from Mexico, the Mortons appreciate the Cilantro Mary legacy and have added their own touches while retaining the celebrated recipes of previous owners. Today's family atmosphere and alcohol-free beverages are a far cry from the McAllister Saloon that opened here in 1881. Look closely, and you may see the patch in a 1904 oval painting, struck by a bullet during a bar fight. The saloon ended up as payment on a gambling debt, and the butcher shop that followed left behind meat hooks and a walk-in cooler. Cilantro Mary adds foods for healthy living, such as vegetarian meal options, beans flavored with fresh jalapeños, onions and cilantro rather than ham hocks and fat, and fish specials, like the Ecuadorian mahi-mahi. Put zest into your dining experience with the Mexican flavors at Cilantro Mary.

450 Main Street, Lyons CO
(303) 823-5014
www.cilantromary.com

La Chaumière

RESTAURANTS & CAFÉS: *Best French dining with overtones of Maryland*

On Scenic Highway 36, between Lyons and Estes Park, a marvelous little restaurant called La Chaumière disguises itself as an unassuming roadhouse. Once inside, however, you will be transported to old France with a menu that features such classics as escargot, duck liver pâté and frog legs. Chef Vince Williams worked at La Chaumière under former Owner and Renowned Chef Heinz Fricker from 1979 to 1984. A few years later when Fricker called to offer the restaurant to the Williams, they jumped at the chance, left their life in Maryland behind and never looked back. Although the restaurant's focus remains French, the Williams have added their award winning Maryland crab soup, as well as fish and lighter sauces to create a diverse and eclectic menu. The signature sweetbreads are considered among the best in the state and the mountain view is as wonderful as the food. All types of private parties, including wine dinners, retirement parties and wedding rehearsal dinners, take place here, and Vince will create special menus around a budget. He also offers cooking demonstrations and classes. With its emphasis on individual attention and impeccable cuisine, La Chaumière, which means hospitable home, truly lives up to its name. For an authentic French dining experience in a relaxed yet elegant atmosphere, call for dinner reservations at La Chaumière.

12311 N St. Vrain Drive, Lyons CO
(303) 823-6521
www.lachaumiere-restaurant.com

The White Lion

SHOPPING:
Best handcrafted merchandise

Far away from the hustle and bustle, the White Lion invites you to take your time, slow down, and breathe. George and Lyla Carter have hand picked an eclectic mix of merchandise from local and international artisans. The fragrance of handmade soaps, lotions and candles enhances the mellow ambience. New Age books and music help to create a soothing atmosphere. George and Lyla moved to Lyons from Rhode Island, where they ran a construction company. Determined to leave the hurried pace of the big city behind, they were attracted to the slower pace of a small town. They started out owning an antique store, but wanted to diversify. George's talent for furniture dictated their direction. Merchandising George's handcrafted furniture led to stocking complementary outdoor items and garden sculpture. One thing led to another, and soon the Carters branched out into jewelry, pottery, greeting cards and collectibles. The baby and young children's section provides gift-giving inspiration. Gifts from the White Lion will be cherished for years to come. Visit with George and Lyla. Relax, breathe deeply, and cherish the experience.

418 High Street, Lyons CO
(303) 823-9567
www.thewhitelionshop.com

Ciatano's Winery
WINERIES: *Best Colorado-made wines in Lyons*

Situated on 18 acres along the picturesque St. Vrain River, between Lyons and Estes Park, Ciatano's Winery is part of the Inn at Rock 'n River. The abundant wildlife, tranquil ponds and splendid mountain views all contribute to the serenity of the setting. Owners Mary Lou and Richard Gibson are following in the footsteps of Mary Lou's father, who emigrated from Italy to America at age 12. Wine making for personal use was an honored tradition and Mary Lou remembers family time centered on conversation and a shared bottle of wine. The first bottle produced at the winery was a Cabernet Sauvignon. Others followed, including a Syrah, a Cabernet Franc and a Rosato, which is a white Merlot. In addition, look for Ciatano's Vino Rosso Cambiani, which combines Syrah, Cabernet Franc and Cabernet Sauvignon. Other fine Colorado-made wines are also available for tasting or purchase in the tasting room, along with fine Italian meats, cheeses, smoked trout and salmon. Come stroll the grounds, take in the mountain air and enjoy sipping wine at several picnic areas scattered on the property. The Gibsons look forward to your visit. After all, *Vi Buono Vino . . . Buono Vita.*

16858 N St. Vrain Drive, Lyons CO
(303) 823-5011
www.ciatanosvineyard.com
www.rocknriver.com

MILLIKEN

Established in 1910, Milliken was named after Judge John D. Milliken, a pioneer lawyer who helped establish the Denver, Laramie and Northwestern railroad (DL&N). With the growth of the sugar beet industry, Milliken became a hub of commerce in northern Colorado. A series of disastrous fires and the decline of the railway slowed the community. Today, however, the town is growing by leaps and bounds. Milliken has the room to accommodate newcomers to the Front Range. With about 5,600 people in 2005, Milliken doubled its population since 2000. Milliken's neighbor, Johnstown, has experienced similar growth and now has more than 7,000 people. With all the growth, Milliken and Johnstown continue to maintain a peaceful, rural way of life.

PLACES TO GO

- Milliken Waterworks Pool
  112 Centennial Drive

- Parish House Museum
  701 Charlotte Street, Johnstown

THINGS TO DO

August
- Milliken Beef 'n Bean Day
  Lola Park
  (970) 587-4331

December
- Festival of Lights
  (970) 587-8723

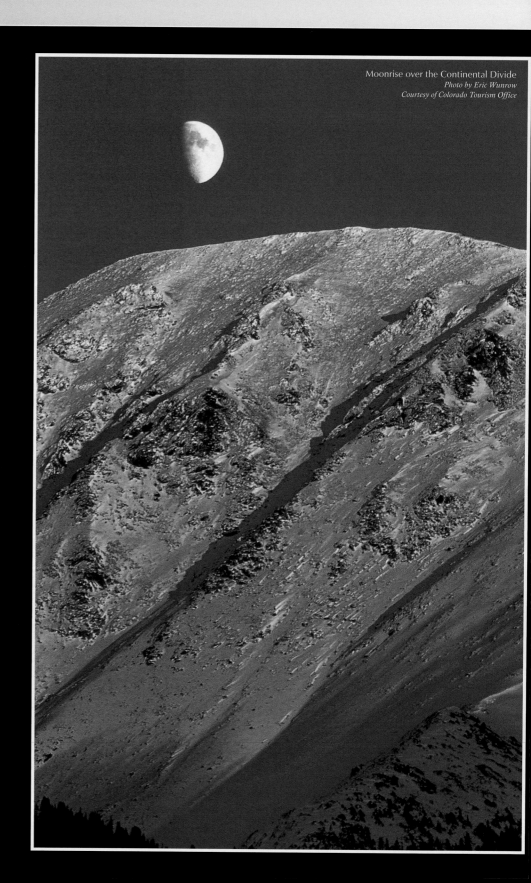

Moonrise over the Continental Divide
Photo by Eric Wunrow
Courtesy of Colorado Tourism Office

Cherished Events

EVENTS:
Best special event planning

When it comes to event planning, Shirley Garcia-Blackstun, owner of Cherished Events in Milliken, proves the old adage that practice makes perfect. She worked for 15 years as a corporate event coordinator before opening her own company and today confidently announces that If You Can Imagine It, We Can Create It. Shirley receives support from her daughter, Nina Alirez, and Miranda Lopez, an employee who has worked with her since the day the business opened six years ago. The trio creates and stages special events, ranging from corporate blowouts to proms and intimate weddings. Tell them the look you want, and they will achieve it by transforming your space with their own linens, chairs and tables. They specialize in meeting the needs of their clients, no matter the budget, but do not provide food service or catering. The team takes pride in their versatility, staging events from large blowouts to intimate soirees. It makes no difference if you envision an enormous tropical luau, or an ethereal wedding in a sea of clouds, Shirley and staff will succeed in capturing the tone you desire. For events that leave you free to enjoy the party, choose Cherished Events.

904 Broad Street, Milliken CO
(970) 590-4088
www.mycherishedevents.com

Salo Fine Art
GALLERIES & FINE ART:
*Artistic renderings of
Robert Salo*

"Nature is the best teacher," says artist Robert Salo, who started drawing animals, farms and forests on Michigan's Keweenaw Peninsula during childhood. Today, Robert displays his paintings at Salo Fine Art in Milliken. The peninsula that inspired Robert's art has served as muse to many artists of various genres. Ernest Hemingway used the Keweenaw as the setting for his early Nick Adams short stories. Robert concentrates on animal portraiture and landscapes and loves working on location. He began his professional career in 1958 as an artist and illustrator for New Center Studio. He has also served as an illustrator for Ford Motor Company, the *Christian Science Monitor* and the Vought Corporation, where he illustrated classified aerospace material. He has a long history as a fine arts teacher for both public and private schools, and a cadre of students has chosen to study with him for many years. Robert is a member of the Society of Animal Artists and the Oil Painters of America. He is the recipient of numerous awards, including four-time winner of an Award of Excellence from the Arts for the Parks organization. Robert's paintings can be found in numerous galleries, museums and private corporate collections. Visit Salo Fine Arts to see the results of this artist's lifelong fascination with nature.

**935 S Lilac Street, Milliken CO
(970) 587-5625**

MORRISON

The town of Morrison, at the bottom of winding Bear Creek Canyon, may barely have 400 citizens, but it has loads of restaurants and parks. The well-known Fort restaurant specializes in buffalo steaks. To the north is the famous natural outdoor concert venue, Red Rocks Amphitheatre in Red Rocks Park. Nearby Dinosaur Ridge is a must-see for geology or archaeology buffs. Here, sandstone perfectly entombs exposed dinosaur footprints. More bones are on display at the Morrison Natural History Museum just south of town. Near town, a bike path skirts Bear Creek and leads to an extensive trail system and reservoir.

PLACES TO GO

- Bear Creek Lake Park
  15600 W Morrison Road

- Red Rocks Park
  18300 W Alameda Parkway

- Dinosaur Ridge
  16831 W Alameda Parkway

- Morrison Natural History Museum
  501 Colorado Highway 8

- Mt. Falcon Open Space Park
  West: Mt. Falcon Road
  East: Forest Avenue

THINGS TO DO

May
- Indian Market and Pow Wow
  The Fort
  (303) 697-4771

Red Rocks near Morrison
Photo by Erik Mills

Bandimere Speedway

ATTRACTIONS: *Best view for racing*

It is the view that sets Bandimere Speedway apart from the 300 other tracks in the circuit. The home of Thunder Mountain features National Hot Rod Association Championship Drag Racing, the fastest sport in motor sports. These grounds, originally known as a site for safety testing, have held NHRA National Events since 1978. The Mopar Mile-High Nationals are held here, along with a host of additional electrifying events. A whopping 95 races tear it up at Bandimere Speedway every season between April and October. The Speedway is owned by John Bandimere Jr. and employs 400 people. Businesses wishing to advertise at the Speedway enjoy a variety of marketing options, such as event sponsorship, group tickets and challenge car races. This organization is very youth-oriented and that is made evident by special events, such as the Pepsi All-American High School Drags and Jr. Dragster series. Summer events such as the Family Festival provide the whole family with a day at the races, complete with music, food, jet cars, game booths and fireworks. Other rousing events are the Super Chevy Show, Checker Auto Parts "Night of Fire and Thunder," and Grease Monkey "Thunder on the Mountain."

3051 S Rooney Road, Morrison CO (303) 697-6001 or (800) 664-UWIN *www.bandimere.com*

Photos courtesy of willowridgemanor.com

Willow Ridge Manor

EVENTS: *Best special events facility in Morrison*

You've picked the right person, now it's time to pick the right place. One look at Willow Ridge Manor and you will experience love at first sight all over again. Located in the foothills overlooking the city of Denver, across the street from The Fort restaurant, this stately facility offers picturesque views both inside and out. Originally built at the turn-of-the-last-century, Willow Ridge Manor was remodeled in 1915 and served as the home for the Kendalvue Farm on Bear Creek. In 1989, it was saved from demolition and moved to its present site where owner Gregory Sargowicki turned it into an elegant destination for memorable weddings, receptions and other gala events. Able to accommodate up to 200 guests at a time, Willow Ridge Manor offers an outdoor deck with blue skies and Denver skyline as a backdrop and, for the winter months, an indoor ballroom with carved wood fireplace. There is a three-room Bridal Suite and separate Groom's Room, offering both parties ample space to get ready and relax as much as possible. With more than 15 years of service industry experience, Gregory is a master of details with an exclusive list of quality photographers, florists, bakers and other specialty providers to ensure your once-in-a-lifetime event is as cost effective as it is efficiently run. Gregory has an exclusive relationship with Lifestyles Catering as he feels their reliability and flexibility with customer budget concerns are unmatched. You've waited your whole life for this moment, so why not make it even better than you dreamed. Let Willow Ridge Manor help make your wedding the one everyone still talks about.

4903 Willow Springs Road, Morrison CO
(303) 697-6951
www.willowridgemanor.com

Photo by Kobako

Café Prague

RESTAURANTS & CAFÉS:

Best European cuisine in Morrison

If you want to experience fine European and American cuisine, a visit to the appropriately named Café Prague can satisfy your desire. This one-of-a-kind restaurant, housed in a late-19th-century building, recently underwent a complete refurbishment and welcomes guests with a new contemporary décor. The menu overflows with dining choices, and perennial favorites include Café Prague's signature roast duck and Wiener schnitzel. One bite will tell you why Café Prague received three and a half out of four stars in a recent *Denver Post* article, and why it was selected as a Top 10 Restaurant in January 2006 by *5280 Magazine*. Outdoor, patio seating is available when weather permits, and smaller, intimate interior rooms can be reserved for private parties or special occasions. Feast on European delicacies without ever leaving Colorado at Café Prague, where a succulent meal, great service and a beautiful and relaxed setting are guaranteed.

209 Bear Creek Avenue, Morrison CO
(303) 697-9722
www.cafepraguerestaurant.com

NIWOT

Chief Niwot, an Arapaho leader whose people were hunting and fishing along the Front Range when the first gold miners arrived in 1858, gave his name to the unincorporated town of Niwot. Niwot's meaning in the Arapaho language is left hand. The town was platted in 1875, two years after the Colorado Central Railroad extended its tracks northeast from Boulder. This expansion provided a significant boost to the local agricultural economy by creating a link to markets as far away as Wyoming and Denver. Today, Old Town and Cottonwood Square are home to delightful shops and award-winning restaurants. Visitors struck by the charm of this community often wish they lived here.

THINGS TO DO

August
• Lobster Bash
Old Town
(303) 652-2587

September
• Nostalgia Days
Old Town
www.niwot.org/news.cfm

Rock climbing on the Flatirons
Photo by Eric Wunrow
Courtesy of Colorado Tourism Office

NicNats

SHOPPING: *Most appealing knickknacks in Niwot*

An abundance of knickknacks adorns the home décor, card and gift shop, NicNats, named by owner Lisa Tilley's teenage daughters Nicole and Natalie. Lisa wants her customers to have fun while browsing the eclectic assortment of gifts and accessories in her shop, located in Cottonwood Square. She makes it easy to come in and find the perfect gift and card, then have it wrapped and ready to go. Ladies can fill out a wish list to help husbands who need a little assistance with gift buying. Purses, scarves and ponchos have proven especially popular with the women, and teens flock to the lip gloss and jewelry selections. Lisa knows the business well, starting out as a sales representative for giftware, moving into her own repping company, then opening NicNats in 2004 to be closer to her family and meet a need in the community. Attuned to the needs of her neighbors, she specializes in carrying the largest selection of cards in town plus jewelry and gifts not found in the major chain stores. Lisa is grateful for the warm welcome she received from residents and other merchants in the square. She invites you to come check out the new treasures arriving almost daily at NicNats.

7960 Niwot Road, Unit B1, Niwot CO
(303) 652-4166

PARKER

In 1874, James Parker bought the 20-Mile House, an inn on the road 20 miles south of Denver. At first it was a stagecoach stop; then the train came through. By the turn of the century, Parker boasted two hotels, three general stores, a saloon, a brick works and a bank that robbers hit twice. Railroad operations declined after 1913, however, and they were totally discontinued in 1935 when a major flood washed out many of the trestles. When the Town of Parker incorporated in 1981, it had only 285 residents. Thereafter, the expansion of metro Denver brought waves of newcomers. Jim Nicholson, later U.S. Secretary of Veterans Affairs, received much credit for Parker's growth. Parker today has more than 40,000 residents and continues to grow.

PLACES TO GO

- Challenger Regional Park
  17301 E Lincoln Avenue

- O'Brien Park and H2O'Brien Pool
  10795 Victorian Drive

- Salisbury Equestrian Park
  9500 N Motsenbocker Road

- Stonegate Mammoth Exhibit at Town Hall
  20120 E Main Street (303) 841-0353

- The Wildlife Experience
  10035 S Peoria Street (720) 488-3300

THINGS TO DO

June
- Parker Country Festival
  www.parkercountryfestival.org

August
- Parker Mainstreet Omnium
  (bicycle race and fest)
  (303) 841-0353

September
- Tails are Waggin' for Barker Days
  (303) 841-4500

- A Taste of Parker
  (303) 841-4268

Purple Coneflowers in Parker
Photo by Brian Jolley

Yarn Arts

ARTS & CRAFTS:
Best yarn store in Parker

With a tight-knit community feel and a full range of supplies, Yarn Arts in Parker makes knitters feel right at home. You're sure to find the yarn you need for that long-imagined project with the shop's wide selection of yarns and fibers from around the world. You can even find self-patterning and self-striping sock yarns that are sure to bring a whole new fashion statement to any ensemble. The Yarn Arts staff is friendly and knowledgeable, and a caring community of knitters gather here, including some fine yarn artists, which makes Yarn Art just the place for a knitter to socialize. Whether you are getting started with the yarn arts or have years of crocheting and knitting behind you, you'll find classes here to increase your skills, including classes for children as young as five. Consider learning how to create felted wool purses that look great and wear like iron. The technique involves knitting with wool, then washing the piece in hot water, which shrinks the piece and tightens the stitching. Yarn Arts is active in community outreach and accepts donations for the Dear Dana program, which provides caps for people who have lost their hair due to chemotherapy treatments. Join a community of knitters and expand your knitting horizons at Yarn Arts.

10510 S Dransfeldt Road, #107, Parker CO
(303) 766-2237
www.yarnartsofparker.com

The Colorado Horse Park

ATTRACTIONS:
Best equestrian center

Situated on hundreds of spectacular acres on a hill overlooking the surrounding countryside, world famous mountains and romantic sunsets, The Colorado Horse Park offers the opportunity to enjoy the tradition and romance of the horse. Currently it is an international equestrian competition center, hosting more than 30 events annually including Halloween with Horses. In addition to the ticketed events, numerous horse shows with free admission are held nearly every weekend in the summer. The show grounds at The Colorado Horse Park are state of the art and include 11 arenas, a cross-country course, barns with 300 permanent stalls, and space to hold portable stalls so that more than 1,000 horses can compete on the grounds. Vendor areas, spectator seating and RV parking are among the amenities available. In addition, a western complex offers cattle pens and facilities for western competitions. Training and instruction are available. Among the facilities for boarders and trainers are indoor arenas, pastures and paddocks, tack rooms with lockers, office space and more. The Colorado Horse Park is in the process of building on their international reputation. Their mission is showcasing the history and heritage of the West using the horse as the primary teaching tool. The Museum of the Western Horse, Living History Museum and an Equidome are all on the horizon. The Colorado Horse Park, a nonprofit organization, had been actively involved in preserving open space and creating a place where families can enjoy the history and heritage of the West.

7522 S Pinery Drive, Parker CO
(303) 841-5550
www.coloradohorsepark.com

DVD Reflections
BUSINESS: *Best video and film transfers*

Have you ever wondered what your life would look like if it were projected onto the big screen, complete with soundtrack? Wonder no more. DVD Reflections in Parker specializes in gathering together a lifetime's worth of photos, slides and home videos, organizing them into chronological order and putting them together on a DVD, with or without music. Owned by Mary and Scott Wattum, DVD Reflections is a multi-faceted audio-visual production company. They offer film and video transfers, television and radio advertising and videography. They have their own studio or they can film your event and turn it into a production masterpiece. If that's not enough, they're also known for their Starry Night Cinemas, where they come to your location, set up an inflatable 16-foot-by-20-foot screen and play your choice of movies. Starry Night allows you to host your own big-screen movie event in your basement, backyard, rec center, local field, community park or wherever. They do all the set-up and tear down, and even supply the popcorn. DVD Reflections can help you preserve your special memories and put them into professional format that will be cherished for generations to come.

19031 E Plaza Drive, Parker CO
(720) 851-7410
www.dvd-reflections.com

Posh Pastries
BAKERIES, COFFEE & TEA: *Best desserts in Parker*

Whether you're looking for elegant European desserts or old-fashioned goodies, Posh Pastries has something sweet for you. The Parker bakery is owned and operated by Chef Hilary Hough. Hilary studied in Paris and at the Le Cordon Bleu in Portland, Oregon, and it shows in the variety of French pastries you'll find here, such as éclairs and tortes. Hilary also puts a twist on a lot of good old American favorites. Take the carrot cake, for instance, which she injects with creamy caramel to make it that much more tasty. You'll find a wide variety of bars, tarts and pies that offer rich, buttery satisfaction. Hilary also offers gluten-free pastries for those in need. Posh Pastries offers birthday parties on-site, where kids can participate in the making of their tasty treats as well as play games like pin the candles on the cake. The bakery is glad to prepare cakes and pastries for any occasion or event. When the only confection that will satisfy your sweet tooth is a divinely decadent dessert, come to Posh Pastries.

10471 S Parker Road, Parker CO
(303) 840-1251

To the Rescue

BUSINESS: *Best in-home assistance*

Illness, old age or even a new baby can impose heavy burdens on you and your family. Everyday activities can become difficult or even impossible. To help you cope, Renee Williams has founded an innovative service called To the Rescue. Clients include the elderly, children and individuals with Alzheimer's and disabilities, as well as the general public. Renee's cheerful and carefully screened staff members help with transportation, shopping, errands, laundry, house cleaning, meal preparation and babysitting. To the Rescue can assist with transferring, bathing, toileting and medications. Pet care, repairs, maintenance and yard services are offered as well. The services offered by To the Rescue go well beyond helping with everyday tasks. Staff members provide companionship by reading books, lending a friendly ear or taking a client to lunch. Renee knows the importance of these services from her own life experiences. Many of her relatives suffered disabling illnesses and needed long-term care. Renee's business goals are simple. She strives to improve the quality of people's lives—physically, mentally and emotionally. Helping clients care for themselves in their own homes, or in the homes of relatives, fosters a spirit of independence and personal pride. If there is a practical way to improve the quality of a client's life, To the Rescue will provide it. Contact To the Rescue for personal and professional assistance when you need a little support.

17454 E Cloudberry Drive, Parker CO
(720) 641-0646 *www.totherescue.net*

TQ Photography
BUSINESS: *Best portrait photography*

Tracy Quintana found her path in life the moment she picked up a camera. The founder of TQ Photography in Parker, Tracy is a specialist in the field of family portraiture. She obviously brings technical expertise and knowledge of the latest photo equipment. But more than that, Tracy exhibits sensitivity and an ability to see the emotions and connections that underlie her subjects at important junctures in their lives. Whether you want to take advantage of her extensive studio settings, or need her to photograph you in your natural setting, Tracy will capture the essence of the moment. While Tracy can do virtually any kind of portraits, including corporate head shots and senior class photos, she specializes in children, families, pets and mothers-to-be. The next time you want to capture a moment for posterity, call Tracy at TQ Photography.

(720) 851-8700
www.tq-photo.com

Photo by Jim Deutsch/W.W.J.D. Photography

Parker Gallery & More

GALLERIES & FINE ART: *Best frame shop in Parker*

Whether it's a football fan's favorite jersey, a diploma or a picture of a prized pet, Parker Gallery & More has the frame for it. Open since 1981, the gallery offers a huge variety of frames and mats in myriad colors, shapes and sizes. Parker Gallery's friendly staff is there to lend a helping hand for those looking for the best way to display their personal treasures. Owners Terry and Paulette Park like to point out that just about anything customers find of interest can be framed—and they've framed a lot of family treasures and memorabilia over the years. Art lovers will delight in the many pieces of fine art that line the walls of the gallery. Limited edition prints and some original oil and watercolors are available. There's also a professional photographer on-site, Jim Deutsch, who can be engaged for weddings, graduations and other special events. Come to Parker Gallery & More to bring out the best in your artwork and memorabilia.

Main Street & Parker Road (Safeway Shopping Center), Parker CO
(303) 840-7898
www.J-DPhotography.com

KDM Productions

BUSINESS: *Best video and multimedia company in Parker*

Based just south of Denver, KDM Productions is a video and multimedia company with three major divisions. Their Consumer Division handles smaller projects, such as wedding and personal tribute videos. Their Corporate Division works on a larger scale with national and international clients. These range from major news networks, like FOX and CNN, to large corporations, including companies like Kaiser Permanente and Delta Dental. Their Entertainment Division develops and produces programming that range from music videos to documentaries and various short films. All three divisions have access to the same professional camera equipment and non-linear editing systems, complete with DVD authoring and duplication. In business since 2001, owner and founder Kevin Mauch has nearly 10 years experience as a full-time producer, director and editor. Kevin says, "I took all of my previous production experience and formed KDM Productions with the ability to fully service all of my clients on a more personal level." Kevin's key to success is his ability to listen to what the client wants while offering creative suggestions along the way. He also keeps his overhead low, thus allowing him to accommodate customers with smaller projects and budgets and still meet the needs of large corporate clients. Contact KDM Productions to work with a production company that not only allows, but encourages clients to be part of the edit and make any changes necessary.

16307 Orchard Grass Lane, Parker CO
(303) 941-2969
www.kdmproductions.com

A Moment in Time Studio

GALLERIES & FINE ART: *Best murals and furniture art*

If you're looking at empty walls or sitting in the middle of an empty room, you should call Margaret Huevelman at A Moment in Time Studio. Margaret takes great pride in creating one-of-a-kind wall murals in addition to decorative accents and portraits. She can also apply her colorful paintings to wood furniture. Her imaginative murals make a distinctive addition to a bedroom, kid's playroom, nursery or office space. Margaret delights in taking a photograph and transforming it into a whimsical and altogether unique portrait. She starts with a photo of your choosing, perhaps a favorite pet, your whole family or a local scene, then renders a professional and realistic painting to bring meaning and beauty to a wall in your home. Why not gift someone you love with a mural or furniture art from this talented artist. If You Can Dream It, We Can Paint It—that's the slogan of A Moment in Time, where a bedroom can become a tropical isle, a beloved pet can be immortalized on a wall or wall images from a child's favorite storybook promise sweet dreams and inspire creative pursuits. Call Margaret at A Moment in Time to banish empty walls from your home and create a room that welcomes you with new warmth, humor and memories.

(720) 290-2640   *www.amomentintimestudio.net*

Parker Day Spa

HEALTH & BEAUTY:
Best spa services in Parker

A stone's throw from Parker's Main Street, Parker Day Spa is located in a little yellow Victorian house shaded by leafy cottonwood trees. The spa is a tranquil place where clients can relax for hours. Owner Tina Long is a master massage therapist, a certified laser technician, a registered medical assistant, and has a staff of highly skilled and trained technicians. Parker Day Spa offers a variety of massage therapies, including deep tissue, Swedish and hot stone massages. Complete spa packages range from Express to Endless Love. All packages come with at least a hot tub soak, massage and facial. Parker Day Spa can apply permanent makeup and perform chemical peals or microdermabrasion. As a consideration to her customers, Tina charges very reasonable prices for the spa treatments. Laser treatments are a Parker Day Spa specialty. Tina can undertake advanced laser treatments that go beyond what most spas offer. These include laser hair removal, spider vein treatment and removal of age spots or birth marks. A low-level laser light therapy can stimulate head hair growth in clients with certain conditions (a consultation is necessary to determine whether you are a candidate for this procedure). Other treatments that go beyond the ordinary include foot reflexology and lypossage, a new, noninvasive treatment for reshaping and smoothing bodies. Visit Parker Day Spa and enjoy a comprehensive range of traditional and innovative spa services.

**19767 E Pikes Peak Court,
Parker CO**
(303) 841-8780
www.parkerdayspa.com

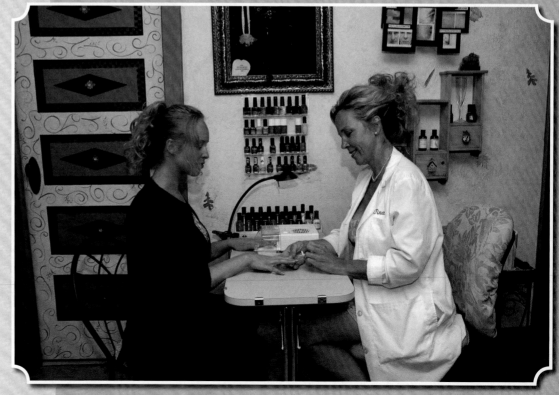

Snip-its

HEALTH & BEAUTY:
Best place for children's haircuts

Some small children are scared to get their hair cut, while others resist it because it bores them. Make getting a haircut a happy experience for your kids by taking them to Snip-its in Parker. The folks at Snip-its have created funny talking characters, such as Snips, Flyer Joe Dryer and the Clip-ette Sisters. Under their watchful eyes, kids pass a previously unpleasant few minutes with big smiles on their faces. The chairs at Snip-its are bright and comfy, and a computer at each booth invites your child to play a game of tic-tac-toe or concentration, while someone trained specifically to cut kids' hair goes to work. Don't be surprised if your young ones start asking to get a haircut every day of the week. Don't be surprised, too, if they quickly become experts on the finer points of style. Will it be a Mushroom or a Fade today for your boy, the Wedge or the Bob for your girl? Snip-its even makes it possible for your child to throw a glamour party with packages that include manicures, makeovers and dress-up clothes as well as goodie bags, cake and juice. For a haircut your kids will love, take them to Snip-its today.

11290 Twenty Mile Drive, Parker CO
(720) 851-7682
www.snipits.com

The Handmaiden
HOME: *Best home enhancement*

Your realtor has just told you that you need to spruce up your home to increase your chances of selling it. Help is on the way when you call the Handmaiden. The Handmaiden is Linda Lane, a real estate enhancement expert who will look at your home through a buyer's eyes and tell you exactly what you need to do to make it most appealing. For example, what may feel cozy to you might feel crowded to someone else. Linda points out that something as basic as cutting clutter could help you sell your home. According to industry statistics, home enhancement could result in an overall 236 percent return on your investment. With a degree in interior design, Linda evaluates your home from floor to ceiling, advising you on what needs to be uncluttered, what looks too funky and what rooms could use some lightening and brightening. Realtors throughout the metro area highly recommend her. Even if you aren't moving, Linda can do wonders for your home. She can take any ho-hum space and turn it into a showcase area. For enhancement of your home that will get you results, arrange a consultation with the Handmaiden.

10924 Eagle Run Drive, Parker CO
(720) 851-0899
www.thehandmaiden.com

after

before

SGO Designer Glass
HOME: *Best source of specialty glass*

Glass is the place where light comes to dance, and SGO Designer Glass is the choreographer. From stained glass entry doors to skylights, transoms, shower enclosures and cabinets, SGO Designer Glass knows no bounds. This manufacturer of custom art glass for the home can make any kind of window or decorative enclosure you can imagine. Casey and Christine Atchison opened their SGO studio in Parker in 2005. Their showroom shows the possibilities, but believe us when we say that their gallery barely scratches the surface of what can be. Come into their studio for a free consultation and they will help you explore the virtually limitless possibilities and solutions to your decorative glass needs. Once they fully understand what you want, they will manufacture your stained or decorative glass to exacting standards and install it with minimal disruption. When they leave you will have a durable, fully guaranteed piece of craftsmanship that will dazzle for years to come. Visit SGO Designer Glass and give the light a stage on which to perform.

19555 E Parker Square Drive, Suite 106B, Parker CO
(720) 851-9705
www.sgodesignerglass.com

Colorado School of Dance

RECREATION: *Best dance school in Parker*

With a growing enrollment of more than 800 students, the Colorado School of Dance has become known as Colorado's fastest growing dance educator for students ages two-and-a-half to 80. What are the keys to its success? Professional faculty combined with a nurturing family-friendly environment within 10,000 square feet of state-of-the-art dance studios. The gifted faculty have Bachelors and Masters Degrees in dance and many have professional backgrounds with companies including the Bolshoi Theater, Colorado Ballet, Dayton Contemporary Dance Company, Kim Robards Dance Company and the Denver Nuggets Dance Team. The school offers classes in everything from classical ballet and jazz dance to preschool and ballroom to hip-hop and poms. No matter what the class, the mission is always the same: to encourage students of all ages and levels to experience the world of dance while gaining the benefits of high self-esteem, poise and physical well-being. Instructors set realistic and fun goals, which include performance opportunities at annual events including the Colorado School of Dance Celebration Dance Festival, Denver Parade of Lights, Denver Nuggets Pre-Game Show and the Nutcracker of Parker. The school also is home to the Colorado Youth Ballet Company, which is featured in a full-length ballet every other year and the Nutcracker of Parker every December. The school has sent award-winning dance teams to Disney's Magic Music Days at Disney World and has planned a dance tour to Europe for 2012. For dance instruction or a tour of the school, visit Colorado School of Dance in Parker.

10510 S Progress Way, Parker CO
(303) 841-7233 *www.coloradoschoolofdance.com*

Sweet Lorraine's Delicatessen & Catering

RESTAURANTS & CAFÉS: *Best deli and catering*

In an age of specialization, Sweet Lorraine's Delicatessen & Catering manages to excel in numerous areas. If you ask owner Rick Seewald, he'll probably say that Sweet Lorraine's specializes in catering, something he's done since 1979. But that hasn't stopped Sweet Lorraine's from being lauded by local newspaper polls for having the Best Sandwiches and being the Best Delicatessen, on top of being named the Best Caterer in the Front Range. Sweet Lorraine's can cater anything from mountain weddings to corporate events. They are famous for their catered barbecues, and their Swedish meatballs are often called the best, as well. The deli serves an assortment of customer favorites, including a Colorado Club and Sulphur Gulch sandwich that deserve special recognition for both size and flavor. Rick also serves up homemade soups, subs and salads. The next time you need a caterer you can depend on, call Rick. Likewise, if you want a delicious deli-style lunch, call on Rick. In fact, if it's anything food-related, you probably ought to call on Rick at Sweet Lorraine's. If he can't do it, it probably can't be done.

10465 S Parker Road, Parker CO
(303) 841-5050
www.sweetlorrainescatering.com

Junz

RESTAURANTS & CAFÉS:
Best mix of French and Japanese dishes

Take a piece of real estate in the suburbs beyond State Route 470, turn it into a restaurant and what do you get? If that restaurant is Junz, you get a casually elegant setting with brightly painted walls, glass sculptures with splashes of red and black, and an elegant, long sushi bar. You also get outstanding food from two distinct culinary traditions. Owner and chef Jun Makino mixes the French cuisine he learned during his classical training with the Japanese dishes he loved as a child. As Jun says, "It's not fusion cooking, just the best mix of traditional French and Japanese dishes." Junz provides an extraordinary combination of Western and Eastern sensibilities and an exotic choice of varied menu items. Typical Western

dishes include Chilean sea bass, *foie gras* in a buttery consommé and understated bites of shallots with a hint of sweet thyme. Dishes with a Japanese flair include tuna tartar; *niku maki,* thinly sliced rib-eye wrapped around asparagus; and *ebi fry,* breaded and deep-fried shrimp. Jun studied under the late Jean-Louis Palladin, a French chef who gained fame as proprietor of the Jean-Louis restaurant in the basement of the Watergate Hotel. Visit Junz, where you can compose a fabulous meal of choices rarely available in any one setting. The elegant décor that greets you is a bonus.

11211 S Dransfeldt Road, Suite 100, Parker CO
(720) 851-1005
www.junzrestaurant.com

Vines Wine Bar

RESTAURANTS & CAFÉS: *Best wine bar*

Vines Wine Bar proves that Denver has no monopoly on cool. Calling itself the Hip, Urban Bar in the Burbs, Vines offers more than 90 wines by the glass and more than twice that number by the bottle. You may also choose from their vast selection of fine beers, spirits and house-infused vodkas for unbelievable martinis. This relaxed yet sophisticated atmosphere provides the setting for a great evening in the heart of Parker. Owners Shari and Lee Riggs, both certified sommeliers, know their wine and feel comfortable talking to both oenophiles (connoisseurs) and novices alike, on a daily basis as well as in their popular wine classes. At Vines, Lee, Shari, and their highly trained staff, including eight certified sommeliers, are ready to assist you with food and wine pairings for the entire menu. You can make a meal with a mix-and-match selection of tapas (small plates) which is a great way to try different foods with different wines. Summers feature Sangria Sundays to get the week of specials started in fiesta fashion, followed by Tapas Tuesdays, Wednesdays are Ladies Nights, and Thursdays are Open Mic. Live music on the weekends feature jazz, rock, or even a mix of styles. For a hip evening centered around wine and social encounter, why bother with Denver when you can have it all at Vines Wine Bar in Parker tonight.

19501 E Main Street, Parker CO
(303) 736-VINE (8463)
www.vineswinebar.com

Celebrations
SHOPPING: *Best party place*

Atmosphere is everything when you're throwing a bash, and Celebrations is the place to make sure you have it. Whatever the occasion, from birthdays to holidays to specially themed extravaganzas, Celebrations has the decorations and accessories to make your party the event of the season. Annette Alvarez started Celebrations in 2005 after spending many years planning events for nonprofit organizations. Her experience can now be yours, which will make sure that a really good idea for a party actually turns into a really great party. It's a one-stop shop guaranteed to take your party over the top. From streamers and crepe paper, to plates and cups and helium-filled balloons that they can deliver, there's no end to the menu at Celebrations. From masquerade balls to Mardi Gras, from sports parties to bridal showers, Annette does it all. Visit Celebrations prior to your next event.

10150 Dransfeldt Road, #103, Building 11, Parker CO
(303) 840-0500
www.parkercelebrations.com

Rocky Mountain Guns & Ammo

SHOPPING: *Best source for firearms and accessories*

Being inquisitive comes in handy when you are Bill Steinmeyer, the owner of Rocky Mountain Guns & Ammo. He will ask you all the necessary questions to accomplish his number one goal, which is to fit you with the gun you need for your specific purposes. He and his staff at Rocky Mountain Guns & Ammo are as comfortable working with the novice as with the experienced shooter. He calls his place, which he opened in 2001, the best little gun shop in Colorado, and he delivers on his claim not only with exceptional customer service but with a selection of pistols, rifles and shotguns that compare favorably in price and quality to big box retailers. Bill also carries knives and optics in addition to the latest Taser Citizen Defense Systems. He offers law enforcement discounts. If you are seeking expert advice in the care and use of firearms, you will want to meet Carter Lord, the gunsmith at Rocky Mountain Guns & Ammo. He has 32 years experience in his field, and Bill considers him the best in the area. For firearms and related problem solving, drop by Rocky Mountain Guns & Ammo.

**10970 S Parker Road, # A-16, Parker CO
(303) 841-1933**
www.rockymountainguns.com

PINE

A sharp left-hand turn off of scenic U.S. Highway 285 and six miles of winding canyon road bring you to the lovely little town of Pine. Here, anglers can enjoy fly-fishing along the South Platte River. Hikers and mountain bikers have discovered Pine Valley Ranch Park, which provides access to the Buffalo Creek Trails. This trail system features some of the best bicycle trails in Colorado, much of it smooth, rolling single track. You'll see mountain views, majestic rock formations and in spots, areas recovering from forest fires. Pine's valley narrows at one end, and a dirt road leads the Sphinx Rock formation, a spot beloved by rock climbers. The Bucksnort is out this way as well. This drinking and dining establishment draws motorcyclists, locals and a few curious tourists. Pine's rustic downtown contains a variety of historic structures. Several cozy country bed-and-breakfasts are the best way to stay in Pine.

PLACES TO GO

• Pine Valley Ranch Park
  Crystal Lake Road

Sunset in the Arapaho National Forest
Photo by Jeff Cricco
Courtesy of Colorado Tourism Office

Photo by Paul Chinowsky/Equine Event Photo

Anchorage Farm

ACCOMMODATIONS:
Best bed and breakfast for horse lovers

A working horse ranch in the Colorado Rockies is the setting for Anchorage Farm, an enchanting bed-and-breakfast. Amid flower gardens, mountain vistas and beautiful horses, four wildlife-themed guestrooms feature private baths, hardwood floors and feather beds. The whirlpool and kiva fireplace make the Coyote Room a romantic choice for wedding nights and anniversaries. Guests might be lucky enough to spot elk from the Elk Room, which affords the best views of the deer and elk range adjoining Anchorage Farm. Co-owner Kris Cooper fortifies guests for hiking and horseback riding with wholesome, hearty breakfasts that include farm-fresh eggs and herbs with fruit. The horses on Anchorage Farm are the focal point of Centaur Rising, a project run by Kris, her husband and her son that provides shelter for rescued horses and horse education for youngsters. Guests may visit the barns and corrals to admire the horses, or they may get more personally acquainted on a trail ride in the cool mountain air. For the Coopers' excellence in innkeeping and in promoting responsible horse ownership, *Arrington's Inn Traveler* named Anchorage Farm a Best Horse Lover's B&B. Bring your love of these magnificent animals, the outdoors and peaceful living to Anchorage Farm.

12889 S Parker Avenue, Pine CO
(303) 838-5430
www.anchoragefarm.com

WELLINGTON

The rural community of Wellington is situated at the northern tip of Colorado's Front Range in the heart of the Boxelder Valley. On the Interstate to Wyoming, it is the northern gateway to Colorado. The town was established in 1905. The majestic Rocky Mountains provide a beautiful backdrop to the west of town. Vast acres of productive farm and grazing land surround Wellington. You'll find state wildlife preserves to the east and south.

PLACES TO GO

- Pawnee National Grassland:
  Crow Valley Recreation Area
  Weld County Road 77, one-quarter mile N of State Route 14, Briggsdale

- Pawnee Buttes
  Weld County 112 and 110, E of County 390 S of Grover

THINGS TO DO

July
- Wellington's 4th of July
  Library Park
  (970) 568-3381 ext. 50

Pawnee Buttes
Photo by Brian Gadbery
Courtesy of Colorado Tourism Office

Main Street Gift Shoppe

SHOPPING: *Best source for distinctive gifts in Wellington*

If you're tired of trying to find the perfect gift for every occasion at the local mall, where carbon-copy collectibles line the shelves, then head to Main Street Gift Shoppe, where owners Kathy and Rolando Santos hand select distinctive and original gifts, collectibles and décor items that you just can't find elsewhere. Kathy first dreamed of opening her own gift shop after visiting an elegant, gifts-only store in California when she was 19. In 2003, she was able to turn her dreams into reality, when she and Rolando found a lovely historic hotel for sale and turned it into a fanciful and charming gift shop. Kathy and Rolando have filled the shop with an abundant selection of gifts and accessories, such as baby, bridal and special occasion gifts, along with exquisite décor pieces that will enhance any room or office. Main Street Gift Shoppe also goes all out for the holidays. Whether its Easter, Halloween or Christmas, you're sure to find a stellar array of whimsical creations, from Jack O' Lanterns to nutcrackers, that will beautifully augment your festive decorations. The Santos' 19 year-old daughter Kara works in the shop with her parents, where she designs graceful and stylish vignettes that beautifully display the shop's divine selection. Find gifts that will be fondly remembered for years to come at Main Street Gift Shoppe.

3725 Cleveland Avenue, Wellington CO (970) 568-7557

ROCKY MOUNTAINS
& WESTERN SLOPE

ALLENSPARK

Scenic Allenspark, just 17 miles northeast of Boulder, has an elevation of 8,521 feet. A getaway from the urban rush, Allenspark has a population of less than 500. A local stable can lend you a horse for a day on a trail leading into Rocky Mountain National Park, which is just west of town. The Wild Basin park entrance, two miles north of Allenspark, lets you access the Wild Basin and Finch Lake trailheads. Between May and October, campers can stay at the Forest Service's Olive Ridge campground, which has 26 sites for RVs and 30 for tents. Allenspark is on the Highway 7 scenic route to Rocky Mountain National Park, where craggy, 14,255-foot Long's Peak presents its most dramatic face. This highway is particularly popular in the autumn when aspen trees turn gold under crisp, blue skies. Allenspark at one time was hot spot for ski jumping. Between 1922 and 1940, skiers came for tournaments held here.

Rocky Mountain National Park in Spring
Photo by Eric Wunrow
Courtesy of Colorado Tourism Office

Allenspark Lodge
ACCOMMODATIONS: *Best mountain lodge in Allenspark*

The Allenspark Lodge is what mountain retreats were meant to be. Built in 1933 using hand-hewn ponderosa pine logs, the lodge creates the perfect ambience for visiting Rocky Mountain National Park. This enchanting historic property boasts 12 rooms, plus an apartment. Some rooms have claw-foot tubs, others have views of the Ironclad Mountains, and each has a warmth and character all its own. Gather together in the great room around the massive native stone fireplace. Owners Bill and Juanita Martin are the kind of hosts you dream about. Barring only Sophie, the Allenspark Lodge mascot and local dog in residence, they are second to none as hosts. For her part, Sophie extends warmth with one big wag of her tail. Bill and Juanita are culinary-skilled and animal lovers who make sure you are well-fed and cared for. Wake to the smell of baking bread as you start your day

with a big family-style breakfast, then look forward to the daily treat of freshly baked, afternoon cookies. There is an espresso shop and wine and local micro brews are served. Every lodge needs a hot tub, so, of course, Allenspark Lodge has one. There is a video/rec room featuring a video library of more than 300 movie titles. Sorry folks, cable TV does not exist here. Hikes abound and Ouzel Falls is just down the road. Visit Allenspark Lodge on your trip to The Rockies. They have what it takes to create lasting memories.

184 Main Street, Allenspark CO
(303) 747-2552
www.allensparklodge.com

Lane Guest Ranch
ACCOMMODATIONS: *Best guest ranch in Allenspark*

The Lane Guest Ranch on the border of Rocky Mountain National Park offers so many amenities, in the midst of such grand splendor, we'd be hard-pressed to sum it all up here. For starters, this idyllic mountain retreat has been owned for the past 53 years by the same man, Lloyd Lane, who certainly knows how to host a family vacation. Lloyd recognizes the need for impeccable service. He can accommodate up to 80 guests, and with 55 people on staff, you're going to get the personal attention you require. The ranch offers 25 units that can accommodate couples and families up to six. Most units have private patios, and more than half have private hot tubs. A welcoming party greets your arrival with champagne, shrimp and hors d'oeuvres. There is horseback riding for all ages over six, including overnight pack trips, lunch rides and wine and cheese rides. You can tackle class III and class IV rapids in a whitewater raft, ride mountain bikes, fly fish and hike. Learn to capture the scenic beauty with a photography workshop or drawing class. Learn to make jewelry with a silversmith class. Go for a swim in the heated pool. Relax in the hot tub, release tension in the sauna, maybe even have a massage. Chef Michael Brashears has been pleasing palates at the ranch for 24 years. He will happily cook your just-caught trout to perfection, in addition to wide range of top-notch entrees. There is even a Dude Ranch with Kids Camp that employs qualified children's counselors to supervise your little ones all day. Perched at an altitude of 8,500 feet, the Lane Guest Ranch is a piece of Rocky Mountain heaven. The Ranch is open only during the summer months. With limited days and so many amenities, Lloyd books up early, so be sure to plan well in advance.

P.O. Box 1766, Estes Park CO (303) 747-2493
www.laneguestranch.com

Fawn Brook Inn
RESTAURANTS & CAFES:
Best European-inspired cuisine

The next time you really want to treat yourself to something special, drive to the charming town of Allenspark and partake of the excellence provided by the Fawn Brook Inn. For 28 years Hermann and Mieke Groicher have been dazzling the residents of this idyllic mountain community with their European-inspired cuisine. Known as one of the most romantic restaurants in the state, the Fawn Brook Inn serves upscale European cuisine in a leisurely, unpretentious manner. Chef Hermann Groicher, who was born in Austria, began his study in Switzerland, and worked in kitchens from England to Texas before he and Mieke, who was born in Holland, started the Fawn Brook in 1979. The fare is classic French Continental, featuring such delicacies as roasted duckling, rack of lamb and shrimp Provençale. With just 11 tables in a building that dates to 1927, the restaurant provides an intimate dining experience where you should expect to spend two hours or more savoring the delights. Mobil's restaurant guide awards the Fawn Brook Inn five stars, and they are consistently ranked as one of the finest restaurants in Colorado. Because of their stellar reputation, reservations are an absolute must. Do yourself a favor by calling Hermann and Mieke for a seat in this true gem of a restaurant the next time you are anywhere near Allenspark.

State Highway 7, #357, Allenspark CO
(303) 747-2556

PLACES TO GO

• Kayak Park
  (970) 453-1734

• Riverwalk Center
  150 Adams Way (970) 453-3187

• Stephen C. West Ice Arena
  0189 Boreas Pass Road (970) 547-9974

THINGS TO DO

January
• Ullr Fest
  (800) 936-5573

• Budweiser Select International Snow
  Sculpture Championships
  (800) 936-5573

February
• Mardi Gras in Breckenridge
  (800) 936-5573

April
• April Fools Day
  and Spring Massive Festival
  (800) 936-5573

June
• Breckenridge Film Festival
  www.breckfilmfest.com

September
• Oktoberfest
  (970) 453-5055

BRECKENRIDGE

Founded in 1859, Breckenridge experienced several gold-mining booms in the course of its history. Periods of prosperity would be followed by years of population loss, though the town never quite attained ghost-town status, in part because it has always been the Summit County seat. White gold—snow—eventually saved the town. In 1961, Rounds and Porter, a Kansas lumber company, opened the Breckenridge Ski Area and a new-boom era began. Transportation improvements fueled the Breckenridge recreation rush. The Eisenhower Tunnel, on I-70, was completed in 1973, reducing the drive time from Denver to Breckenridge to an hour and a half. Summer in Breckenridge attracts outdoor enthusiasts with hiking trails, wildflowers, fly-fishing in the Blue River, mountain biking, and nearby Lake Dillon for boating. Breckenridge has the longest whitewater kayak park in the state of Colorado.

Half pipe at Breckenridge during the Xqualifiers
Photo by Jeff Circco
Courtesy of Colorado Tourism Office

Fireside Inn

ACCOMMODATIONS:
Best place to stay in Breckenridge

Breckenridge is famous for its skiing and snowboarding mountains. In the summer, this winter paradise is transformed into a perfect setting for a multitude of activities to keep visitors occupied. Film, theatre, art, and history combine with hiking, biking, golf, and kid activities. The Fireside Inn provides the most affordable lodging located in the historic district just steps away from the Main Street. Niki and Andy Harris operate this historic inn with a characteristically British air offering friendly accommodations with style and flair. Andy has a collection of British Army memorabilia scattered throughout the inn for your enjoyment. Lodgings include private rooms or dormitory style. Guests enjoy the cozy sitting room with fireplace and relaxing in the redwood hot tub, free parking, Wi-Fi Internet and much more. The private rooms are customized with special accents such as the Sweetheart Room's claw foot tub and the Hunters' fireplace. The Brandywine Suite is spacious with private entrance and the added incentive of exclusive hot tub use scheduled at regular evening hours. All private rooms have TV with video, refrigerators and antique furnishings. Whatever the time of year, you'll be glad you've visited the Fireside Inn.

114 N French Street, Breckenridge CO
(970) 453 6456
www.firesideinn.com

CENTRAL CITY

In 1859, John Gregory discovered the Gregory Lode in a gulch near Central City. Within two weeks, the gold rush was on. Central City was soon the leading mining center in Colorado. It came to be known as the Richest Square Mile on Earth. Those who settled in Central City were never hard up for wild times. In 1861 alone, the city recorded 217 fist fights, 97 revolver fights, 11 Bowie knife fights and one dog fight. Amazingly, no one was killed. The grand opening of the Opera House in 1878 started a tradition of community theater, ranging from opera to vaudeville. Buffalo Bill performed there as well at P. T. Barnum's circus. Central City has endured many boom and bust periods. Its current boom, based on limited-stakes gaming, began in 1991. The town now boasts five casinos. Another Central City attraction is the Teller House with its Face on the Barroom Floor painting. Once a hotel, Teller House now hosts a museum, bar and restaurant.

PLACES TO GO

• Teller House
  120 Eureka Street (303) 582-0600

THINGS TO DO

June
• Madame Lou Bunch Day
  (303) 582-5251

Main Street in Central City
Photo by Eric Wunrow
Courtesy of Colorado Tourism Office

A Midsummer Night's Dream
Photo by Mark Kiryluk

Central City Opera
ATTRACTIONS: *Fifth oldest opera company in the U.S.*

For 75 years, audiences have been entertained by stirring productions at Central City Opera. Founded in 1932, the opera company is the fifth oldest in the United States. The opera house was built in 1878 in the gold mining town of Central City, and now stands as the crown jewel among charming Victorian homes, an art gallery, historic cemeteries and a history museum. The intimate 550-seat venue, designated a National Historic Landmark in 1973, is located just 35 miles outside of Denver in the Rocky Mountains. The summer festival attracts internationally-acclaimed artists, conductors and directors, offering 45 performances of both traditional and contemporary works, including special family performances. In 2007, Central City Opera commemorates its 75th birthday with four new productions, including the world premiere of *Poet Li Bai* by Guo Wenjing, a Chinese opera which conveys the life story of the Tang dynasty poet. The anniversary festival also features Verdi's popular Italian opera about a consumptive courtesan, *La Traviata*; Massenet's version of the fairy tale, *Cinderella*; and Menotti's contemporary opera about a young woman who talks to angels and performs miracles, *The Saint of Bleecker Street*. In addition to its summer opera festival, Central City Opera offers career-entry training to young singers, produces education and community service programs, and preserves and maintains the opera house and 30 other Victorian-era properties. For a memorable evening out, prepare to be swept away by the moving performances of the Central City Opera.

124 Eureka Street, Central City CO
(303) 292-6700
www.centralcityopera.org

CONIFER

In Conifer, a mix of rustic cabins and new, state-of-the-art homes peek from behind expanses of blue spruce, pine and aspen trees. Parks surround Conifer. The Pike National Forest, which runs right through town, provides a home for deer, birds and rabbits. In the spring and summer, wildflowers carpet the hills. The town consists of several neighborhoods that include Aspen Park and Marshdale. These are not urban neighborhoods, of course; population density is low out here. A famous old yellow barn at the corner of State Route 73 and Barkley Road is the traditional heart of Conifer. The Chamber of Commerce plans to develop the barn into a visitor's center.

PLACES TO GO

- Flying J Ranch Park
  State Route 74

- James Q. Newton Park
  S Foxton Road (County Road 97)

- Meyer Ranch Park
  U.S. Highway 285, exit 122

- Reynolds Park
  S Foxton Road

THINGS TO DO

August
- Conifair
  Beaver Ranch
  (303) 838-5711

November
- Fall Wine Tasting
  Evergreen Memorial Park
  (303) 838-5711

December
- Winter Parade
  Aspen Park
  (303) 838-5711

Back road in the Pike National Fores

Lower Lake Ranch

ACCOMMODATIONS: *Best mountain lodging in Conifer*

Lower Lake Ranch, with its majestic mountain views, private fly fishing lake access and rolling creek, has been a sanctuary for Colorado vacationers since the 1940s. It is now an idyllic and memorable site for special events such as weddings, reunions and corporate functions. Conveniently located 40 minutes southwest of Denver, this delightful getaway offers a choice of spacious indoor and outdoor ceremony and reception sites. Select Creekside, a private site nestled among whispering willows and wildflowers along the creek, or choose the Lower Lawn site with Cathedral Mountain as the picturesque background for unforgettable photographs. The staff at LL Ranch are dedicated to ensuring your stay is perfect in every way. LL Ranch offers a wide selection of packages designed to meet a variety of needs and budgetary considerations. The staff will assist you in arranging these packages to create that special day of your dreams. Biffs Smoked Meats & Catering Service offers to be "yours for the day." They have been smoking delicious meats since 1982 and provide a distinguished menu for all of the ranch's events. Treat your guests to such flavorful appetizers as grilled trout with nuts and seasonal fruit or Pueblo Corn Chowder. Then enjoy an entrée and perfectly smoked bison, brisket, ribs, ham or chicken with homestyle vegetables. Biff's claim to fame is their excellent food and meat "so tender you don't need teeth to eat." Enjoy your own mountain hideaway. For years to come, you and your guest will reflect on the things Lower Lake Ranch is recognized for–magnificent views, fabulous food and sensational fly fishing

11883 S Elk Creek Road, Conifer CO
(303) 838-6622
www.lowerlakeranch.com

Healthy Pet Supply

ANIMALS & PETS: *Most wholesome pet products in Conifer*

When you buy pet supplies at Healthy Pet Supply in Conifer, you receive much more than wholesome foods for your pet. At Healthy Pet Supply, a knowledgeable staff teaches pet owners about the health and care of their animals, taking the mystery right out of the store's concentration on natural and organic food and supplements plus raw foods. This award winning store carries brands like Timberwolf, Bravo, Wysong and Nature's Variety that respect your pet's needs and individuality. Because the health issues affecting pets and their owners can be similar, Healthy Pet Supply carries a full line of products suitable for pets and their owners such as Wysong, Garden of Life supplements and Bach Flower Remedies. Healthy Pet Supply won the Compassion of Care award from the Intermountain Humane Society in 2002 and 2004, the 2005 Rotary Club Ethics in Business award, as well as the club's 2003 Certificate of Appreciation. A visit to Healthy Pet Supply is also the opportunity to outfit your pet with leashes, collars, beds, blankets and bowls. You'll find some unusual items for the adventurous pet, such as life jackets, backpacks and tents. The store has been serving animals and their owners at the Aspen Park Village Center since 2000. Let staff members Deb Carbone, Sish Ollen, Retta Dunn, Mary Petrone, Sandy Mendez and Emily Bajorek introduce you and your pet to the healthy product lines at Healthy Pet Supply.

25797 Conifer Road, Suite A-10, Conifer CO
(303) 816-7003
www.healthypetsupplyonline.com

Conifer Massage & Therapeutic Center

HEALTH & BEAUTY:
Best wellness treatments in Conifer

Whether you suffer from chronic pain, are experiencing an acute injury, or just want to maintain your good health, let Jessica Wilson and the dedicated staff at Conifer Massage & Therapeutic Center guide you on your journey to wellness. The staff includes Jessica, a Certified Massage Therapist; Bruce Ayers, a Licensed Acupuncturist, Diplomate in Acupuncture and adroit acupuncturist; Cindy Stone a Certified Massage Therapist and Reiki Master; and Heather Whiting, also a Certified Massage Therapist. Together they offer a variety of treatments, including acupuncture, massage and energy medicine, individually tailored to each client's needs. For athletes, try the sports massage, designed to increase performance, improve recovery time and reduce the risk of injury. Pregnant mothers gain energy and alleviate joint and muscle stiffness with the prenatal massage, while the hot and cold stones of the LaStone Therapy improves muscle tone and promotes a deep sense of relaxation. Massage and acupuncture treatments have a long history of effective use in many cultures. Jessica sees the benefits of regular massage and acupuncture firsthand every day. She remembers one client in particular who had lost the majority of use and functioning of his legs from an accident and was reliant on a wheelchair. The treatments he received at CMTC greatly complimented his rehabilitation, and he now walks with a cane and leg braces for assistance. Wicker baskets for storage, shelves of books and woven blankets lend an air of warmth and welcome to the facility. Make your overall well-being a top priority at Conifer Massage & Therapeutic Center.

26697 Pleasant Park Road, Suite 240,
Conifer CO
(303) 816-9254

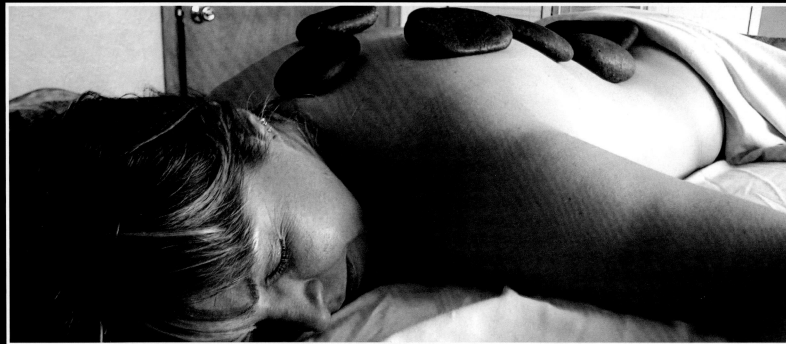

A Healing Tree
Massage & Education Center

HEALTH & BEAUTY: *Best pain and stress treatments in Conifer*

The experts at A Healing Tree Massage & Education Center can help relieve a range of symptoms and side effects caused by injuries and chronic conditions. Robert J. Wheaton Jr., with over 22 years in the medical field and training in Sports Medicine Technology, approaches individual conditions from a holistic perspective and takes pride in being able to offer varying treatments for pain and stiffness. Robert is widely experienced in treating such conditions as slipped discs, spinal fusions and spinal stenosis, where pressure on the spinal nerves can cause weakness and pain in the arms and legs. The center's carefully designed regimen of care, which includes massage, herbs and essential oils, can reduce stress and bring relief for such conditions as Sciatica, Carpal Tunnel, Fibromyalgia, Lupus and Crohn's disease. A nationally certified massage therapist, Robert Wheaton also treats sports injuries, offering both direct therapy and rehabilitation programs. Those eager to learn the art of massage also should make a trip to the center. As a state certified massage instructor, Robert shares his expertise with students eager to learn couples massage using hot stones and essential oils. Robert offers continuing education classes to fellow therapists. The center also uses Reiki III, Neuro Muscular Therapy and Medical Massage Techniques. You can learn to apply the soothing Raindrop technique that uses massage with essential oils and heat to address a variety of complaints. Whether you feel discomfort or wish to soothe the discomforts of others, visit A Healing Tree Massage & Education Center.

26267 Conifer Road, Suite 304, Conifer CO
(303) 838-2208

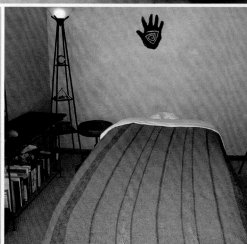

Photos by Kern Photograpy LLC

Paragon Martial Arts
RECREATION: *Best martial arts school in Conifer*

The reasons for practicing the martial arts are as varied as the programming at Paragon Martial Arts, which has locations in Conifer and Evergreen. Owners William Hauptman and Lura Roberts have been teaching at Paragon since opening the facility in 1994. They concentrate on taekwondo, a practice that combines physical and mental components with dramatic movements that have great appeal to young people. Children as young as four can begin taekwondo instruction in Paragon's Tiny Tigers class. From ages seven to 14, the Karate Kids program concentrates on self-confidence, strength and discipline. Beyond coordination and perseverance, children learn to be respectful and polite, basic life skills that are at the heart of martial arts instruction. The school's Safety NET program gives children simple rules to protect themselves from possible attackers and prevent kidnapping or molestation. Teenagers and adults also find the focus and discipline they seek at Paragon, where classes include rhythmic, stress-relieving exercises that improve health and empower self-defense. Paragon also has an impressive list of national and world champions to its credit. Stop by Paragon Martial Arts and a staff member will be happy to show you around.

26367 Conifer Road, Conifer CO *(303) 838-8533*
Evergreen CO *(303) 674-5900*
www.paragonmartialarts.com

Aspen Specialty Foods & Catering
RESTAURANTS & CAFÉS: *Best specialty foods in Conifer*

Grab a tasty lunch or light dinner, request a beautiful spread for your next party, and pick up locally grown produce all at Aspen Specialty Foods & Catering. Owners Craig Wert and Mary Hellman-Wert opened the restaurant, catering service and farmers' market in 2004, providing quality foods at reasonable prices. The Werts display great versatility as caterers, accommodating the needs of a small dinner party or a large corporate event equally well. Customers rave about the outstanding service and such favorite party foods as macadamia nut salmon and rosemary garlic tenderloins. Craig brings more than 14 years of experience in a professional kitchen to his position as head chef in the café. Stop by on your lunch hour for a soup and sandwich combination, or come later for one of the dinner specials. The flavorful food recently won praise from Denver's *Westword* and the Cherry Creek Arts Festival. When you stop by for a meal, be sure to check out some of the gourmet foods and seasonings available for purchase at the restaurant. The barbecue grilling sauce and gourmet olive oil both bring excitement and depth to a meal, and the whole coffee beans smell heavenly. In the summer, the store's farmers' market supplies customers with fresh, local produce that quickly makes it from the farm to your table. Come to Aspen Specialty Foods & Catering, next to the Yellow Barn, for fresh food and friendly service.

27051 Barkley Road, Conifer CO
(303) 838-6388

Mauro's Italian Restaurant

RESTAURANTS & CAFÉS:
Best Italian restaurant in Conifer

Guests of Mauro's Italian Restaurant in Conifer appreciate the warm flavors of the Italian countryside that come through in all the dishes served here. Chef Christian Hawks adds international touches to create distinctive tastes. The bread, the pizza dough and the marinara sauce are homemade; the beef is prime, and the soups feature stock made from scratch. With this kind of care, it's easy to understand how Mauro's earned Mountain Connection's 2006 honor as the Area's Best Restaurant for Dinner. Try Chef Christian's signature veal saltimbocca. The Bravo con Pollo is a tempting chicken creation, featuring sun-dried tomatoes and broccoli in a white wine cream sauce. Mauro's offers special events throughout the week, including Bambino Night on Mondays, when children eat free with a dining parent, and an artist is available to paint the children's faces. Tuesday is lover's special night; on Fridays, live musicians perform. The extended Hawks family has managed and worked in restaurants for many years, and family members originally bought this restaurant from Mauro Biagi in 2002. Mauro's is now principally owned by Christian and Nichole Hawks, but many other family members have participated in the business. Mauro still drops by from time to time to greet friends, old and new. The Hawks are very involved with their community, and they are pleased that Conifer citizens keep Mauro's bustling as a community meeting place. For a warm environment and excellent food, come to Mauro's Italian Restaurant.

25797 Conifer Road, Unit 112, Conifer CO
(303) 838-5707
www.maurositalianrestaurant.com

PLACES TO GO

- Bond Park
  E Elkhorn Avenue and MacGregor Avenue
- Enos Mills Cabin Museum & Gallery
  6760 State Highway 7
- Estes Park Aerial Tramway
  420 E Riverside Drive
- Estes Park Museum
  200 4th Street
- MacGregor Ranch
  180 MacGregor Lane
- Rocky Mountain National Park
  1000 U.S. Highway 36
- Stanley Museum
  517 Big Thompson Avenue
- Stanley Park Fairgrounds
  1209 Manford Avenue

THINGS TO DO

February
- Rails in the Rockies (model trains)
  (800) 44-ESTES (443-7837)

May
- Jazz Fest & Art Walk
  (800) 44-ESTES

June
- Scandinavian Midsummer Festival
  (970) 586-6073
- Wool Market
  www.estesnet.com/Events/woolmarket.htm

July
- Rooftop Rodeo
  (970) 586-6104

September
- Longs Peak Scottish Irish Festival
  (800) 44-ESTES
- Autumn Gold (Bands, Brats and Beer)
  (800) 44-ESTES
- Estes Park Film Festival
  (970) 231-2580

September-October
- Elk Fest
  (970) 586-6104

November
- Come Catch the Glow
  (800) 44-ESTES

ESTES PARK

Estes Park, gateway to the enormously popular Rocky Mountain National Park, is a major tourist destination in its own right. The park offers world-class hiking and climbing, fishing and wildlife watching. The town provides museums and galleries, perfect little shops and restaurants for every appetite. Estes Park sponsors special events in every season. Summer-long free outdoor entertainment can include folk musicians, a string quartet or a big band playing favorites. A special treat is the Estes Park tramway, which whisks you effortlessly to the top of Prospect Mountain. You ascend 1,100 vertical feet in less than five minutes. With lush valleys and craggy peaks, Rocky Mountain National Park is a living showcase of the grandeur of the Rocky Mountains. Elevations range from 8,000 feet in the wet, grassy valleys to 14,259 feet at the weather-ravaged top of Longs Peak. Elk, bighorn sheep, eagles, and scores of other animals delight wildlife-watchers. In June and July, wildflowers splash color across the meadows and hillsides. Autumn visitors can enjoy the golden aspens or watch the seasonal antics of rowdy elk.

Lake Estes and Estes Park

Boulder Brook on Fall River

ACCOMMODATIONS:
Best mountain lodging in Estes Park

When Kit Calvin worked as a travel agent, she routinely arranged vacations at world-class resorts in beautiful locations. The lodging establishment that she now owns, Boulder Brook on Fall River, belongs in such a dream vacation. Travel industry experts agree. In naming Boulder Brook a winner of a 2005 Hidden Gem Award, *Trip Advisor* rated it #1 for lodging in Estes Park. *Frommer's* notes, "It would be hard to find a more beautiful setting for a lodging establishment." Boulder Brook is located near Rocky Mountain National Park on the pine-covered banks of Fall River. All guest units are literally within a stone's throw from this gorgeous stream. Doing anything as strenuous during your stay as tossing stones is, of course, optional. You may prefer soaking in your jetted tub, cooking a fabulous meal in your fully-equipped kitchen or reading a good book on your riverfront deck. Kit and her staff provide the luxurious accommodations and amenities, while Mother Nature does the rest. "We wanted to create an environment," she says, "where people could come and renew themselves physically and spiritually so that when they left, they would feel ready to take on the world again." Book a dream vacation in any season at Boulder Brook on Fall River.

1900 Fall River Road, Estes Park CO
(800) 238-0910
www.boulderbrook.com

Romantic RiverSong Inn

ACCOMMODATIONS: *Best romantic lodging in Estes Park*

The Romantic RiverSong Inn is a lovers' hideaway just like Cupid would have designed. Start with the gorgeous Rocky Mountain setting, then add a cozy room with a river rock fireplace and a jetted tub for two or experience the swinging bed in the Indian Paintbrush Room. Owners Gary and Sue Mansfield have been serving as Cupid's agents for more than 20 years, hosting more elopements, honeymoons and anniversaries than they can remember. Gary is licensed to perform marriages, so couples can exchange vows by the rushing Big Thompson River with the pristine scenery of the Continental Divide as the backdrop. Gary will even don snowshoes to accommodate winter romantics. Children are not permitted at this nine-room mountain inn, yet guests are invited to get playful on the tree swings placed throughout the property. Gary and Sue treat guests to a hearty breakfast, offer tea and sweets in the afternoon, and can pack picnic baskets for couples setting out to explore the 27 acres around the inn. The inn's chef, Carol Graham, can also prepare special romantic dinners. The inn even offers a streamside massage for two. For an escape to love's natural environment, stay at the Romantic RiverSong Inn.

1766 Lower Broadview Road, Estes Park CO
(970) 586-4666
www.romanticriversong.com

Gilded Pine Meadows Bed and Breakfast

ACCOMMODATIONS:

Best Victorian-style bed and breakfast in Estes Park

The two themes of Gilded Pine Meadows Bed and Breakfast are Victorian elegance and mountain tranquility. The inn is on five acres next to Rocky Mountain National Park. If you relax on the glass-enclosed porch, you may see elk, deer and squirrels frolic in full view. The grounds have places to meditate, including a gazebo furnished with wicker, lace and flowers. You can soak in a therapeutic hot tub with massage jets. Indoors, the public rooms are filled with antiques, such as the first piano ever to arrive in Estes Park, shipped in 1882 from St. Louis. The house was once the home of the Boyd family, who built it downtown in 1905. They laboriously moved it to its current location in the 1920s. Today, Gilded Pine Meadows is filled with historic artifacts left by the Boyds. The inn offers two beautifully decorated guest rooms in the main building plus Keyhole Cottage, a secret spot where you can contemplate a private garden or take a soothing bath in a clawfoot tub. Every morning, guests enjoy a full hot breakfast with fresh fruit, coffee and juice. For a lunch on the move, make an advance request for a homemade picnic basket. Gilded Pine Meadows is a fabulous base from which to explore Rocky Mountain National Park. The town of Estes Park puts on a score of festivals each year and is home to more than 300 shops. Your hosts at the inn are George and Caprissa Frawley (and Maggie, a gentle old border collie). George is a published fiction writer who can spin many fascinating tales. For luxury and mountain charm, stay at Gilded Pine Meadows Bed and Breakfast.

861 Bighorn Drive, Estes Park CO
(970) 586-2124 or (866) 312-2124
www.gildedpinemeadows.com

The Woodlands on Fall River

ACCOMMODATIONS:
Best riverside suites in Estes Park

If secluded riverside suites nestled into a forested mountain setting sound like a recipe for tranquility, the Woodlands on Fall River could be your ideal getaway. John Gilfillan, formerly a school administrator, manages the Woodlands, along with his wife, Sandra, a retired lawyer. John and Sandy's love for what they do shows in the thoughtful touches they provide for their guests, and many returning guests have become like family. The Woodland's 16 spotless, modern one and two-bedroom suites feature separate living rooms with beautiful wood burning fireplaces, king-size beds and fully-equipped kitchens. Data ports and cable television with HBO, VCRs and DVD/CD players provide all the electronic amenities of home. Decks overlooking Fall River come equipped with individual gas grills and views of Castle Mountain. Shopping, dining and year-round activities, including cultural events, kayaking classes and a new outdoor amphitheater, lie close at hand in nearby Estes Park. Just two miles from Rocky Mountain National Park, the Woodlands on Fall River offers abundant wildlife sighting, hiking and fishing. At the end of a busy day, you'll look forward to relaxing in the outdoor hot tub that's hidden away in a grove of 300-year-old pine and spruce trees. For dramatic and spacious accommodations located on three acres of breathtaking riverfront land, book your getaway at the Woodlands on Fall River.

1888 Fall River Road, Estes Park CO
(970) 586-0404 or (800) 721-2279
www.woodlandsestes.com

Celtic Lady's Mountain Retreat

ACCOMMODATIONS: *Best healing retreat in Estes Park*

Rev. Rosemary McArthur Barrie and the Rev. Jim Barrie are Celtic ministers from Scotland who have created a bed and breakfast in Estes Park. Offering a central location just five minutes from downtown and the entrance to Rocky Mountain National Park, the retreat overlooks the natural wonders that the Park has to offer. A Scots and Irish flag graces the front door where you enter to find four Celtic-themed suites aptly named King Arthur, Mary Queen of Scots, Michael Collins, and The Braveheart Family Suite. The six-foot hot tub is located on one of two upper decks. The Robert Burns Great Room has vaulted ceilings with a stone fireplace where you can relax and watch the deer and elk walk by. With Rosemary and Jim as nondenominational ministers, Celtic Lady's Mountain Retreat creates a great all-inclusive wedding package. Jim is happy to perform

your ceremony in full kilt if you like, completing tradition with Celtic handfasting. Rosemary is a well respected healer and psychic medium. She is the founder of the American Association of Psychics and has taught healing extensively throughout the United States and Canada. As a cancer survivor she embodies the lessons she teaches others. Celtic Lady's Mountain Retreat is a healing sanctuary complete with salt lamps in all the rooms, fountains throughout, a meditation room and a gym. Come to get away and leave feeling renewed. Celtic Lady's Mountain Retreat is there to help feed your mind, body and spirit.

2250 Blue Spruce Court, Estes Park CO
(970) 586-9231
www.celticladysmountainretreat.com

McGregor Mountain Lodge

ACCOMMODATIONS: *Best lodging with panoramic views in Estes Park*

McGregor Mountain Lodge, just four miles from Estes Park, nestles up against Rocky Mountain National Park and, like the park, the panoramic views will not disappoint you. You can see such natural wonders as the Continental Divide and Fall River Canyon. Keep your eyes open for bighorn sheep, elk and deer. The rustic cabins, suites and rooms reflect the wild locale with solid pine furnishings and pictures of wildflowers. You won't suffer from lack of comforts either. Some accommodations come with private whirlpool tubs, and a private hot tub is situated where the views are the most spectacular. Choose a room with a fireplace or a fully equipped kitchen. One and two-bedroom cottages, plus rooms for smaller parties, promise cozy quarters. The lodge welcomes families and proves it with barbecues and a playground featuring swings and a sandbox. Bird watching is a popular pastime here, and guests can walk out their front doors and embark on hikes that last for hours. There is a special quality about the lodge that separately drew co-

owners Chris Wood and Michael Hodges, who both came seeking temporary employment and ended up as partners in the 60-year-old business. Come to McGregor Mountain Lodge to feast on the vision of the Great Continental Divide and magnificent rock outcropping, or close your eyes and enjoy the quiet magic of a place that specializes in drawing repeat visitors.

2815 Fall River Road, Estes Park CO
(800) 835-8439 or (800) 586-3457
www.mcgregormountainlodge.com

The Baldpate Inn

ACCOMMODATIONS:

Best classic Rocky Mountain retreat in Estes Park

The Baldpate Inn in Estes Park has been charming its guests with mountain views and country comforts since it first opened its doors in 1917. Lois Smith, who purchased it in 1986, is only the second owner. The inn is constructed in the Western Stick style from timber harvested in the local mountains. Twelve guest rooms and four cabins offer a classic Rocky Mountain retreat between Memorial Day and mid-October. Room rates include a three-course breakfast. The inn's name comes from a mystery novel, *Seven Keys to Baldpate*, by Earl Derr Biggers. When Biggers visited this mountain lodge, he noticed its resemblance to his fictional Baldpate. In turn, the owners named the inn after the novel. The first owners gave keys to their guests in a tradition inspired from the novel. When the price of metal became too high to support that practice, loyal guests began bringing all sort of keys to them, the more elaborate the better. This impressive key collection includes the key to one of the suites of the Queen Mary during her maiden voyage. The Baldpate is listed in the National Registry of Historic Places and has been featured in numerous national publications, including *Forbes*, *Woman's Day* and *Country Living*. Gregory Peck, Betty Grable and Jack Dempsey all enjoyed the comforts here, and current celebrities also take pleasure in this jewel of the Rockies. Immerse yourself in mountain splendor at the Baldpate Inn.

4900 S Highway 7, Estes Park CO
(970) 586-5397
www.baldpateinn.com

Rockmount Cottages

ACCOMODATIONS:

Best cottages in Estes Park

Just two miles from the entrance to Rocky Mountain National Park, Rockmount Cottages features 20 delightful cabins that lie on either side of the Big Thompson River. The cottages feel remote although they are close to the village of Estes Park. Managers Carol and Ken Smith have positioned chairs throughout the property so that guests can relax, and watch the river and the world go by. You can also fish or picnic along the banks. The cabins feature updated kitchens and baths but retain all of their comfortable, rustic charm. Many of the accommodations offer decks with magnificent views, and some are only a few feet from the river. The clean, well-maintained cottages range in size from 1,200-square-foot cabins that can accommodate up to four people, to cozier digs with one bedroom and a kitchenette. Children are welcome at Rockmount. The two well-equipped play areas include a swing set, monkey bars and a large slide, along with a sandbox, hideout and merry-go-round. You'll find games, puzzles and books in the game room, which also features wireless Internet access. Two gazebos provide the perfect spot for cookouts and family gatherings, or you may want to hike through the acres of forest land near Rockmount. Whether you want to shop and dine in Estes Park, explore the great outdoors, chill out on your deck or warm up by your fireplace, plan a stay at Rockmount Cottages to put all the options into your vacation.

1852 Highway 66, Estes Park CO
(970) 586-4168
www.rockmountcottages.com

Mountain Valley Home Bed & Breakfast

ACCOMMODATIONS: *Best suites with wildlife views in Estes Park*

Luxurious suites, breathtaking Rocky Mountain scenery and wildlife visitors are yours to enjoy when you stay at Mountain Valley Home Bed & Breakfast in Estes Park. Elk drop by to drink from the pond in front of the house, and guests frequently report seeing mule deer and scores of migrating birds, along with the occasional badger, bear, bobcat or coyote. Owner Lynn Gardner remembers the morning when she found a lynx kitten lounging on the back porch. The wraparound veranda provides a great spot for viewing the creatures. The grounds resemble a game preserve, and the five suites are extremely well appointed with a king bed, fireplace and private Jacuzzi jetted-tub in each. The bed linens are made from the natural fibers of a beech tree, which, according to Lynn, get softer with each washing. Lynn's specialty is surprises. If word somehow slips that a couple is coming to celebrate their engagement, their honeymoon or some other special occasion, she can't resist adding individual touches to warm their hearts and bring smiles to their faces. Chef Paul goes out of his way to create eye-pleasing as well as delicious breakfasts. He keeps about 30 different recipes in his repertoire. Let your hosts pamper you, while the natural surroundings enchant you, at Mountain Valley Home Bed & Breakfast.

**1420 Axminster Lane, Estes Park CO
(970) 586-3100 or (800) 987-2765**
www.amountainvalleyhome.com

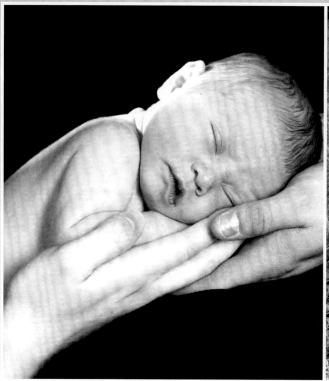

The Perfect Portrait
BUSINESS: *Best photographers in Estes Park*

After spending most of her life in the spotlight as owner and instructor of her own fitness studio chain, Melanie Humphrey now works behind the scenes, capturing priceless memories for others through the lens of her camera. Her husband, Randy, a retired children's advocacy attorney, has similarly shed courtroom drama to partner with Melanie in the Perfect Portrait. Melanie, a photographer for more than 10 years, moved from Michigan to Estes Park with her husband six years ago. She shoots photos for weddings, portraits and senior pictures, in black and white as well as color. She also captures cherished family moments with reunion and group photos, as well as photographing children, pets and children with pets. With two photographers present at every wedding, Melanie and Randy utilize digital photography and specialize in capturing outdoor weddings set in the beautiful landscapes of Estes Park. Melanie also does infrared wedding photography, a recent trend that imparts an ethereal quality to a photo. In 2006, Melanie received an Accolade of Excellence in the Wedding and Portrait Photographers International Awards of Excellence print competition for her print entitled *Too Many Cooks in the Kitchen*. Let the award winning photographers at the Perfect Portrait create lasting memories of the special moments in your life.

590 Audubon Street, Estes Park CO
(970) 586-7642
www.theperfectportrait.net

American Wilderness Tours
ATTRACTIONS: *Best wilderness tours in Estes Park*

If you're looking to get off the beaten path and really see the Rockies, you can count on American Wilderness Tours. Family-owned and operated for more than 20 years by Odd Lyngholm, originally from Norway, tours treat you to unspoiled vistas far from noise, crowds and congested highways. Customers travel along an old stagecoach road in all-wheel drive vehicles and four-wheel drive Hummers. Their adventure culminates atop Panoramic Peak, where guests can get out and view the entire Estes Park valley, including the Never Summer Range and the Mummy Range. Tours operate from mid-May until October snowfall, departing morning and afternoon. Evening tours, which require reservations, are available on Mondays, Wednesdays and Fridays,

Photo by: Robert Ramacher

and end with a chuck wagon-style campfire dinner with steaks or chicken, entertainment and a sing-along around the campfire. The tour area is surrounded by 265,000 acres of national forest. Want to see meadows filled with wildflowers and snow-capped peaks 100 miles away? Grab your binoculars and camera and make a memory that will last a lifetime with American Wilderness Tours.

481 W Elkhorn, Estes Park CO
(970) 586-4402
www.estesparkco.com/awtours.htm

Anderson Realty & Management
BUSINESS:
Best property professional in Estes Park

If you're looking for real estate or for someone to manage property, you want someone with roots in the community. Judy Anderson has a stake in Estes Park. She's lived there for 36 years, she's raised her family there, and she has built a reputation that matches her commitment to the area. Her philosophy is simple. Be honest, fair, ethical and up front. Stay away from hype and pressure. Don't try to sell things people don't want or need. Her way of doing business has served her customers well. If you are in need of a property professional in Estes Park, don't hesitate to call Judy Anderson Realty & Management.

351 Moraine Avenue, Suite B, Estes Park CO
(970) 586-2950 or (866) 586-2950
www.keytoestespark.com

Heirloom Jewelers
FASHION: *Best classic, rare and exotic jewelry in Estes Park*

The word heirloom stems from the word heir, which refers to the person to whom property, title or privilege passes. It's important to remember that definition when you visit Heirloom Jewelers, because this is a place that focuses on finery that is destined to span generations. Owned by Richard A. Wood, Heirloom Jewelers specializes in classic, rare, and exotic fine jewelry, watches, diamonds, pearls, and colored gems. Richard's son Aaron concentrates on designing pieces that will become heirlooms. Richard, who began his career as a jeweler in 1972, appraises and repairs pieces that have already become chapters in a family history. The store carries a small assortment of antique pieces, handles all types of gold, and can be counted on to give you accurate assessments of the pieces you treasure. Richard's creative inclinations run deep. When he's not repairing or selling jewels, Richard is an actor and a member of the local fine arts guild. Visit Heirloom Jewelers if you need expert craftsmanship or advice about the pieces which have been entrusted to you, or for the treasures you hope to bestow on those you love.

201 Park Lane, Estes Park CO
(970) 586-5483

Glassworks Studio & Gallery

GALLERIES & FINE ART: *Best blown-glass creations in Estes Park*

It's almost a toss-up on whether more people come to Glassworks Studio & Gallery to view the art or the artist. The blown-glass creations of Garth Mudge are dazzling, high-quality works that grace galleries across the country. But Garth is an attraction in his own right, an artist who has the gift of being able to entertain as he educates and bedazzles. Garth Mudge is a humble, low-key personality with a down-home sense of humor. People from across the world come to his studio to watch as he turns molten glass into works that win juried prizes and fetch respectable prices. Garth, who has an industrial arts degree, opened his Estes Park studio in 1986. He uses wind energy to generate a third of the electricity needed to power his studio. He is an extremely friendly and affable sort who makes his art accessible by working in front of those who come to watch. His collection includes ornaments, stemware, vases, bowls, oil lamps, folk art and more. Put the Glassworks Studio & Gallery on your itinerary the next time you are heading to Estes Park.

323 W Elkhorn Avenue, Estes Park CO (970) 586-8619 or (800) 490-6695 *www.garthsglassworks.com*

Shakes Alive! Fruit Shakes

FUN FOODS: *Best shakes and smoothies in Estes Park*

The owners of Shakes Alive! Fruit Shakes, Mary Liz and Joe Adair, are famous for their years of producing travel films for the Travel and Adventure Series and the National Geographic Society. They have transported viewers from Greece to Norway to the British Isles and back again. The entire world has been their oyster, and they chose Estes Park as the place to retire. The Adairs say

that settling in an area famous for tourism now has the world coming to them. As with so many others in these times, their version of retirement involves continuing to work instead of languishing in a hammock. More than anything, traveling the world taught this married couple of 31 years to relish relationships with people. Their enthusiastic regulars will vouch for the Adairs' infectious attitude. Every year a group of 10 men make the trek from Kentucky to Estes Park and come in wearing their Shakes Alive! fan club shirts. The menu is more extensive than the name implies. You can certainly order a creamy fruit smoothie, a thick milk shake or an ice cream sundae, but you also have your choice of sandwiches, bagels and coffee drinks. Drop into Shakes Alive! Fruit Shakes, and you just might find yourself returning every year wearing your own fan club shirt.

513 Big Thompson Avenue (Lower Stanley Village), Estes Park CO (970) 577-7007

Wands Studio Gallery

GALLERIES & FINE ART: *Best fine arts gallery in Estes Park*

Wands Gallery, the oldest fine arts gallery in Estes Park, showcases the work of the late Alfred Wands, a world-renowned landscape painter, along with the work of his son, Robert, another internationally recognized landscape artist and retired professor from Colorado State University in Pueblo. The art of both Alfred and Robert shows a great appreciation for the natural world with many pieces devoted to the Rocky Mountains. Robert started sketching with crayons in his father's studio as a young child and could work in most mediums by his teens. Like his father, he pursued painting as wells as an academic life of teaching art and is named in *Who's Who in American Art* and *Who's Who in the West*. Robert retired from Colorado State as a professor emeritus in 1996 to paint full time and concentrate on the operation of the Estes Park studio, an art endeavor started by his father in the 1940s. His paintings are the skillful work of a man obviously

in love with the Western landscape and the Rocky Mountains in particular. He works in watercolor as well as oil and acrylic while producing many of his paintings on location rather than in the studio. Both original works and prints are available at the gallery. Step back from the beauty around you to enjoy an artist's rendition of Rocky Mountain splendor at Wands Studio Gallery.

710 Laurel Road (off High Drive Road), Estes Park CO (970) 586-2942 *www.wandsart.com*

A la Carte

HOME: *Best kitchen boutique in Estes Park*

Born and raised in Estes Park, Maggie Treadway has been an enthusiastic cook since she was three years old. She purchased A la Carte in 2005, after working there for Jean Austin for five years. Although Maggie holds a degree in archaeology with a minor in prehistoric coastal cultures, she loves cooking for people more than anything and finds that owning a gourmet kitchen boutique in her hometown is the next best thing to cooking for people. A la Carte carries an amazing array of intriguing gadgets, bakeware and linens. Maggie says that customers tell her it's like walking into someone's home and finding all these little treasures. Merchandise includes

a wonderful selection of Frankoma pottery, BIA Cordon Bleu baking and serving pieces, as well as picnic baskets and collectible salt and pepper shakers. Gourmet goodies, such as sauces, mustards and gift baskets, appeal to creative cooks and make great gifts, too. A La Carte offers an extensive selection of cookbooks, and Maggie also gives cooking classes with catchy names like Wild Game – Don't Kill It Twice, What To Do With A Dead Bird and Girls Night Out. Tourists as well as locals look forward to discovering the treasures at A la Carte. Come on in and see what's in store for you.

336 E Elkhorn Avenue, Estes Park CO
(970) 586-2798
www.alacarte-estes.com

Treeline Home Collection

HOME: *Best handmade lodgepole pine furniture in Estes Park*

Treeline Home Collection in Estes Park offers handmade lodgepole pine furniture for every room in your home. Owners Steve and Heidi Todd showcase regional Colorado artists and artisans for one of the finest selections of rustic woodcarvings and wood furnishings in the state. Todd worked as a public policy researcher and a pastor before venturing into his own business. He also is working on a novel in his spare time. From roughly hewn log furniture to aspen leaf sconces and lampshades, Treeline features original crafts, gifts, accessories and textiles inspired by the beauty of the Rocky Mountains. Each one-of-a kind piece of furniture tells the story of the

tree it's made from and offers customers an opportunity to take home a bit of nature. Don't see exactly what you're looking for? Treeline Home Collection features such custom options as choosing a different fabric for upholstered pieces or substituting a door for a drawer on case goods. If you are on vacation but spot something you can't live without, Treeline offers nationwide shipping so you don't have to worry about how to get your find back home. For friendly service and rugged furnishings and accessories, visit Treeline Home Collection.

907 Moraine Avenue, Estes Park CO
(970) 586-1020 or (877) 902-5888
www.treelinehomecollection.com

Karen's Flowers of Estes

GARDENS, PLANTS & FLOWERS: *Best floral arrangements in Estes Park*

Photo courtesy of Moses Street Photography

When you're planning a wedding you need to know that the people you've hired will be there for you when you need them. Karen Steadman, owner of Karen's Flowers of Estes, is one of those people. Her customers know she'll come through, which is why this horticultural expert with a degree from The Ohio State University handles three to six weddings every weekend. She gives customers her personal cell phone number and bends over backwards to deliver the highest service levels, on time and on budget. Karen is pleased to handle all sorts of events and arrangements, but weddings are her staple; Karen has never left a bride standing at an unadorned altar. From roses to lilies, from gerberas to sunflowers, Karen is a floral artiste with a passion for her art. She is a also a founding member of the Estes Park Wedding Association. When you need both beauty and peace of mind, call Karen's Flowers of Estes.

443 S St. Vrain, Estes Park CO
(970) 586-7673 or (800) 608-ROSE (7673)
www.karensflowersofestes.com

Kirk's Fly Shop
RECREATION:
Best fishing guides in Estes Park

If you're inclined to go on a guided fly-fishing
tour, why not go with a man who is so good
he can catch fish in a parking lot. That's how
long-term customers describe Kirk Bien of Kirk's
Fly Shop. Kirk runs the place with his wife,
Laurie. In fact, family is so ingrained in the
philosophy of the business that the couple met
on a fishing trip that Laurie was taking with her
father. Kirk's is a full-service fly shop that offers
a complete range of fishing supplies, along with
backpacking and camping gear. The shop hosts
fly-fishing trips throughout the 400,000 acres
of Rocky Mountain National Park or along the
Big Thompson River. You have a choice of day
tours or overnight sojourns. There are no age
or experience limitations, and Kirk's provides
for all of your needs, including transportation,
site reservations and food. If a touch of the
exotic strikes your fancy, consider a trip where
a llama carries your necessities, allowing you to
completely experience the majesty of the Rocky
Mountains. The guides at Kirk's are so confident
of your experience that they guarantee you'll
catch a fish, or they will take you on another
tour for free. If fly-fishing or backpacking is part
of your planned Rocky Mountain experience,
contact Kirk's to maximize your enjoyment.

230 E Elkhorn Avenue, Estes Park CO
(970) 577-0790 or (877) 669-1859
www.kirksflyshop.com

Suzanne's Center Stage School of Dance
RECREATION: *Best dance school in Estes Park*

When Suzanne Landkamer first moved to Estes Park she immediately noticed the small town's lack of a dance studio. Wanting to offer kids the same opportunity to learn the performing arts as they would have in a large city, she opened Suzanne's Center Stage School of Dance. Suzanne offers lessons in tap, jazz, ballet and pointe. Those leaning toward more unusual styles can sign up for hip-hop and belly dancing. Also offered are cheerleading, pom and gymnastics instruction that build flexibility, stamina and poise and often parallel school-sponsored activities. Suzanne, who has studied dance since she was a small child in New York, loves to teach all styles of dance. She strives to instill in her students the same passion for the performing arts that she has. Center Stage,

the only dance and gymnastics studio in Estes Park, has more than 150 students and offers instruction for ages three up to adult. Suzanne's students perform every May at the Estes Park Center YMCA of The Rockies to show off what they have learned. In 2006, the Center Stage Preprofessional Ballet Company danced the Nutcracker Tribute, which featured many of the dances from the Nutcracker Suite. Suzanne's competitive dance team competes head to head with students from much larger cities and have brought home many gold and silver trophies. For professional training that builds grace, poise and character, enroll your child or yourself at Suzanne's Center Stage School of Dance.

2050 Big Thompson Avenue, Estes Park CO
(970) 586-3830

Molly B. Restaurant
RESTAURANTS & CAFÉS: *Most creative eatery in Estes Park*

Most likely, it's the stunning mountain beauty that will lure you to Estes Park, Colorado, the Gateway to Rocky Mountain State Park. Once you're there, the Molly B. Restaurant will tempt you to stay longer than you expected. Molly B., situated just one block from the center of town, is the incarnation of a dream shared by its three owners, who agreed to give up the yes sir, no

sir world of their corporate and military careers in 1985. The formula for success springing from this collective decision is casual and customer friendly, combining outstanding food with easy camaraderie. Regular customers pitch in and pour coffee, bus tables and even wet their hands in the dishwater when the pace is too hectic for owners and employees to keep up. Molly B. serves breakfast, lunch and dinner May through September, and breakfast and lunch in the off season. The regular dinner menu features Rocky Mountain trout (blackened or grilled), New York steaks, vegetarian offerings, creative salads and delicious homemade desserts. Breakfast burritos, granola pancakes, create-your-own omelettes and delicious cinnamon rolls set the scene for great conversation and laughter with friends. Stop at the Molly B. when you first arrive, and you'll likely stop again on your way out of town or return a few times during your stay.

200 Moraine Avenue, Estes Park CO
(970) 586-2766
www.estesparkmollyb.com

Poppy's Pizza & Grill
RESTAURANTS & CAFÉS:
Best pizza with a view in Estes Park

You may never eat pizza in a more gorgeous setting than at Poppy's Pizza & Grill. This restaurant, located just off the main highway in Estes Park, is a great place to bring the family for fresh pizza and fantastic views of the river. With five sauces and 40 toppings from which to choose, you could keep coming back to Poppy's for a very long time without eating the same pizza twice. Poppy's also offers homemade soups, a salad bar and sandwiches. Living in a beautiful place agrees with the workers here, who are always ready to offer tips and information to folks who have come to their town to experience the Rocky Mountains. They know that their home is special, and they hope that your meal is special, too. There's a love story behind Poppy's. Not long after meeting at the Stanley Hotel in Estes Park, owners Rob and Julie Pieper decided to pursue a restaurant business together. That was back in 1987, and Poppy's is still going strong, thanks to its great food and friendly staff/travel advisors. For pizza with a view, go to Poppy's Pizza & Grill on the Riverwalk in Barlow Plaza.

342 E Elkhorn Avenue, Estes Park CO
(970) 586-8282
www.poppyspizzaandgrill.com

The Other Side Restaurant

RESTAURANTS & CAFÉS: *Best waterfront dining*

The Other Side Restaurant in National Park Village at Estes Park promises to please with a choice of menus, a stunning location and a committed owner. The restaurant sits on a small lake near the Big Thompson River and the entrance to Rocky Mountain National Park. Grab a burger in the coffee shop or prepare to enjoy prime rib, choice steaks or local trout in the elegant lakeside dining room. Breakfast, lunch and dinner are all available here along with a Mexican buffet and a seasonal seafood buffet. Try to save room for the restaurant's specialty desserts. A full bar promises you'll find your favorite libation, and facilities for large gatherings make the Other Side a great place to stage a party or wedding reception. If you time your dining experience right, you can take in the daily duck feeding in the late afternoon or check out the sometimes frantic activity surrounding the lake's beaver dam. On Sundays, a special buffet brunch attracts the locals while treating the guests. When you want plenty of dining choice in a natural, convenient setting, visit the Other Side Restaurant, conveniently located near the south entrance to Rocky Mountain National Park.

900 Moraine Avenue, Estes Park CO
(970) 586-2171
www.theothersideofestes.com

The Dunraven Inn

RESTAURANTS & CAFÉS: *Best Italian food in Estes Park*

When you are in the mood for fine Mediterranean cuisine, head to the restaurant known as The Rome of the Rockies, The Dunraven Inn in Estes Park. The Dunraven Inn is a family-owned and operated establishment where all of the food is made from scratch, including the soups and sauces. The Dunraven Inn is an Estes Park icon, a place where locals go for special occasions such as anniversaries, birthdays and engagements. The food is well made. The ambience is comfortable and friendly. Choose from such favorites as shrimp scampi, seven-cheese Alfredo, ziti and lasagna. The steaks, lobster and calamari will melt in your mouth. The desserts will make you cry with joy. The Dunraven Inn has been in business for close to 75 years. All the children of owners Dale and Laurel Hatcher have worked here at one time or another. The Dunraven Inn

is an intimate place with a family feel. The décor is rich in color and texture and the tall ceilings provide for great acoustics. The walls and ceiling of the lobby and bar area are papered with an estimated 13,000 one dollar bills left by customers, a local tradition that is supposed to bring good luck. Some of the money is donated to charity. To experience a tried-and-true piece of Estes Park, visit The Dunraven Inn.

2470 Highway 66, Estes Park CO
(970) 586-6409
www.dunraveninn.com

451 Steakhouse

RESTAURANTS & CAFÉS: *Best steaks in Estes Park*

All of the steaks at 451 Steakhouse are aged a minimum of 21 days, and each dish is made to order. This insistence on quality, freshness and consistency is the standard that owner David Oehlman

has set for his restaurant. Steak lovers may choose from such favorites as rib eye and New York strip. They may also try something a little different, such as a pan-seared and oven-finished filet served with a buttery shiitake mushroom and Gorgonzola sauce. Pecan-crusted trout is a standout among the fish and seafood offerings. Chicken and pasta dishes are also available. David seemed destined for law school until he decided to follow his heart and pursue a love of cooking, which he credits his grandparents for nurturing. His penchant for opening restaurants in beautiful locations did not begin with the 451 Steakhouse in the Rocky Mountains. His first venture, the Sand Witch, was a restaurant and bar on the beach in Maui. Over the past decade, he has owned several successful restaurants in Estes Park. Open for breakfast, lunch and dinner, 451 Steakhouse offers a banquet facility for up to 120 people. For the finest quality steaks and more, bring your appetite to 451 Steakhouse.

451 S St. Vrain Avenue, Estes Park CO
(970) 586-9840
www.451steakhouse.com

Rock Inn Mountain Tavern
RESTAURANTS & CAFES:
Best mountain tavern in Estes Park

The Rock Inn Mountain Tavern stands at the gateway to The Rocky Mountain National Park. When you want the best in Bluegrass, Blues, String and Mountain Grooves, the Rock Inn is where you'll find it. Bruce and Kerry Darby, Michael and Becky Guyet, and Mike and Celine LeBeau are the three couples who created the renewed Rock Inn. They brought in Chef Justin Goerich and Chef Rebecca Hejl, who are graduates of the Culinary Institute of America. Their menu is a delight. Everything is homemade, right down to the chips and salsa. Build your own burger with a half-pound of certified Angus or free-range buffalo. There's homemade pasta, mile and a 1/2-high nachos, specialty pizzas, and fried pickles. Steaks are what they are known for as well as out-of-this-world filet mignon and prime rib that melts in your mouth. As you look over the menu, take in the live music. You will find KC Groves, White Water Ramble, CX-1, and The Arkamo Rangers all playing at the Rock Inn. In the summer, live music is a daily event with nine in-house musicians. Check out their website for upcoming music events and culinary specials; their Halloween Hillbilly Ball is legendary. Sit on their newly completed patio and log trellis to take in breathtaking views of the Rockies, and enjoy their large selection of Colorado microbrews on tap. Located on Highway 66 just before the National Park entrance, the Rock Inn Mountain Tavern succeeds at combining the best of blues, brews, stews, and views in this incredible mountain lodge setting. Come and be one with nature, and find both gastronomical and acoustical bliss.

1675 Highway 66, Estes Park CO (970) 586-4116
www.rockinnestes.com

The Christmas Shoppe at The Spruce House

SHOPPING: *Best Christmas store in Estes Park*

Christmas isn't just a holiday, it's a state of mind. In Estes Park, The Christmas Shoppe at The Spruce House has been nurturing a Christmas state of mind for 36 years. This charming shop provides Christmas and special occasion ornaments, gifts and decorations in a setting that makes shopping a joy. Owner Diane Muno offers anything and everything you can think of relating to Christmas and winter-themed items. She carries an exclusive Santa collection. One room is devoted entirely to nativities, including bear nativities, moose nativities and cat nativities. She stocks Biedermann Brass, Department 56, Fontinini, Byer's Carolers and much more. Diane

bought The Spruce House from the original owners and has kept the store just as she found it, because it was already so perfect. Customers return to The Spruce House year after year, making the shop an important part of their family traditions. The next time you are in Estes Park, bring a little bit of Christmas home from one of the sweetest shops you'll ever see, The Christmas Shoppe at The Spruce House.

125 Spruce Drive, Estes Park CO
(970) 586-8510
www.thechristmasshops.com

Twin Owls Steakhouse
RESTAURANTS & CAFÉS:
Best organic beef and wild game

With a menu featuring organic beef and wild game, plus a setting inside a 75-year-old log home, dining at Twin Owls Steakhouse seems close to nature. A rock fireplace, open beam ceilings and oak floors provide rustic charm for dining on elk kabob appetizers or the house specialty of Filet MacGregor. This hand-cut tenderloin filet is served over a balsamic infused demiglace and topped with a blend of blue cheese crumbles, pistachios and bearnaise sauce. As with all of the entrées at Twin Owls, it is listed on the menu with a suggested wine pairing. How about the ruby red trout with the Lagaria Pinot Grigio or the roasted duck with the Castle Rock Pinot Noir? Owner Jim Edwards never tires of hearing guests say that their meal at Twin Owls was among the best that they have ever eaten. Whether he is as fond of being asked how someone with a master's degree in marine geology from a Florida university got to be a restaurateur in Colorado is something that we leave for you to find out. We do know that he and his staff are as eager to host your intimate dinner for two as they are your wedding reception. On-site wedding catering in the restaurant's Garden or Loft Room is a Twin Owls specialty. Jim says, "Anything we can get or do to make our guests more comfortable, we will do it." For a natural fit of food with setting, try Twin Owls Steakhouse.

800 MacGregor Avenue, Estes Park CO
(970) 586-9344
www.twinowls.com

Photos courtesy of littlevictorianattic.com

Little Victorian Attic
SHOPPING: *Best Victorian antiques in Estes Park*

Lovers of all things Victorian will be glad to know that Victorian English is spoken at Little Victorian Attic. Tell Owner Maureen Shirley that you are looking to add a few nice pieces to your boudoir, and she will need no translation. Indeed, she will lead you straight to her selection of hinged boxes, nostalgic prints and quilts. Victorian antiques and reproductions for every room in your home are the finds at this charming shop. Maureen carries tea sets for your drawing room, large pitcher and bowl sets for your powder room and serving pieces for the butler's pantry. For your dining room, Maureen offers Blue Calico dinnerware, blue delft collectibles and English china sets. Many of the items in the store are handmade by Colorado artists who are just as fond of this bygone era as you are. Look for porcelain dolls as well as old-fashioned bears and bunnies. Little Victorian Attic, a popular destination for travelers passing through beautiful Estes Park, has been turning back the clock since 1987. Maureen also owns a Christian store next door, where you can shop for Christian CDs and gifts. For a jolly good round of shopping, drop by Little Victorian Attic.

157 W Elkhorn, Estes Park CO
(970) 586-8964 or (800) 858-4031
www.littlevictorianattic.com

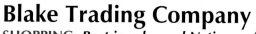

Blake Trading Company
SHOPPING: *Best jewelry and Native crafts in Estes Park*

If you are looking for Native art and crafts, make plans to visit one of the Blake Trading Company's two stores in Colorado. This eclectic company carries authentic products created by native artisans from all over the world. Owners Tom and Marsha Blake deal directly with artists on the Zuni and

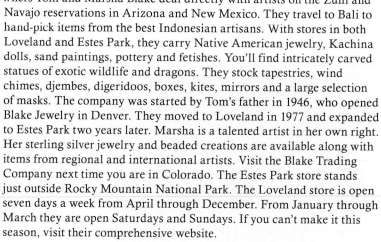

Navajo reservations in Arizona and New Mexico. They travel to Bali to hand-pick items from the best Indonesian artisans. With stores in both Loveland and Estes Park, they carry Native American jewelry, Kachina dolls, sand paintings, pottery and fetishes. You'll find intricately carved statues of exotic wildlife and dragons. They stock tapestries, wind chimes, djembes, digeridoos, boxes, kites, mirrors and a large selection of masks. The company was started by Tom's father in 1946, who opened Blake Jewelry in Denver. They moved to Loveland in 1977 and expanded to Estes Park two years later. Marsha is a talented artist in her own right. Her sterling silver jewelry and beaded creations are available along with items from regional and international artists. Visit the Blake Trading Company next time you are in Colorado. The Estes Park store stands just outside Rocky Mountain National Park. The Loveland store is open seven days a week from April through December. From January through March they are open Saturdays and Sundays. If you can't make it this season, visit their comprehensive website.

116 W Elkhorn Avenue, Estes Park CO (970) 586-9604
3070 W Eisenhower Boulevard, Loveland CO (970) 669-5099
www.blakejewelry.com

Mills Lake in Rocky Mountain National Park, Colorado

PLACES TO GO

- Georgetown Energy Museum
  600 Griffith Street

- Georgetown Loop Railroad
  I-70 exit 226

- Hamill House
  305 Argentine Street

- Hotel de Paris Museum
  409 6th Street

- Loveland Ski Area
  I-70 exit 216

THINGS TO DO

May
- Railroad and Mining Days Festival
  (888) 456-6777

June
- Chocolate Festival
  (303) 569-2888

- Slacker Races
  www.slackerhalfmarathon.com

November
- Bighorn Sheep Festival
  (888) 569-0750

GEORGETOWN

Georgetown, elevation 8,530 feet, the seat of Clear Creek County, is nestled in the mountains near the upper end of the Clear Creek Valley west of Denver. Although a small town today, Georgetown was a historic center of the mining industry in Colorado during the late 19th century and at one time was the third largest community in the state, with the nickname the Silver Queen of Colorado. Today, the community is a lively historic summer tourist center, with many preserved structures from the heyday of the Colorado silver boom. Georgetown is an après-ski watering hole for the thousands who pass through town on their way down from the ski areas near Loveland and Guanella passes. The Georgetown Loop Railroad, which connects Georgetown with Silver Plume, was one of Colorado's very first tourist attractions. Completed in 1884, this spectacular stretch of narrow gauge railroad was an engineering marvel. The Colorado Historical Society sponsored restoration work that began in the 1970s.

Snowshoeing near Guanella Pass above Georgetown
Photo by Eric Wunrow
Courtesy of Colorado Tourism Office

Sophie Gally

FASHION: *Best men's and women's boutique clothing in Georgetown*

Sophie Gally specializes in fine men's and women's boutique clothing. Owner Pattie Fraley's association with a local weaver results in artistic clothing choices and many one-of-a-kind items. Pattie chooses clothing for her shop with classic shapes and an updated feel. Her accessories, including handbags and jewelry, are equally timeless, as are the shop's scarves, hats and ties. Sophie Gally is named for a legendary figure from Georgetown's past. In 1875, a Frenchman, who had changed his name from Adolph Girard to Louis de Puy after deserting the Union army, opened a hotel here and named it the Hotel de Paris. Sophie Gally, whose husband had mysteriously disappeared shortly after she came to the states from France, moved in and worked as the housekeeper here for many years. It's possible that Gally and de Puy were relatives, but no one knows for sure. The two made out wills naming one another as their sole beneficiaries but died within four months of one another. For art-to-wear clothing and accessories along with some historical perspective, visit Sophie Gally

606 6th Street, Georgetown CO (303) 569-2434

Grizzly Creek Gallery

GALLERIES & FINE ARTS:
Best wildlife photography

Gary Haines, a photographer with a worldwide reputation, displays his work in his own Grizzly Creek Gallery in Georgetown. His art springs from his love of nature with focus on landscapes, birds and wildlife. The wildlife photography represents some of his most challenging moments. His early training in painting added to his artistic sensibilities; thirty-two years as a firefighter taught him how to calmly assess dangerous situations, a skill he uses to anticipate a wild animal's movements, then capture them at close range with a hand-held camera. Gary describes himself as a "photography purist" who refuses to work with color filters or enhancements. His Girzzly Creek Gallery carries the largest selection of Colorado photographic images in the region. Customers also appreciate the custom framing, photo restoration and graphic design work performed here. Gary is glad to pack and ship merchandise wherever a customer wishes. In addition to displaying and selling his own photographs, Gary offers handcrafted works from other local artists with an emphasis on mountain themes. Artwork includes cedar lamps, metal and bronze sculptures, and wood carvings. The gallery gives corporate discounts for large orders. Take a close-up look at the Rocky Mountains through the photography and handcrafts at Grizzly Creek Gallery.

512 6th Street, Georgetown CO
(303) 569-0433
www.grizzlycreekgallery.com

Photos by Gary Haines/Grizzly Creek Gallery, Inc.
Courtesy of grizzlycreekgallery.com

Photo by Ace Swerdlove

Kneisel & Anderson

SHOPPING: *Best specialty grocers in Georgetown*

The Kneisel & Anderson grocery and hardware store is the oldest, continuously operating business in historic Georgetown. In 1883 Henry Kneisel purchased the grocery store where he had worked as a baker. Henry formed a partnership in 1893 with his future son-in-law, Emil Anderson, and they built a new, brick building across the street that became known as Kneisel & Anderson, Grocers. In 1912 they added the hardware store. Four generations later, Kneisel & Anderson is now run by great granddaughters Coralue and Wendy Anderson. The store is a rare architectural jewel that contains all the original wood shelving, bins, marble counter top and showcases. Kneisel & Anderson has been recognized for its historical value and has been featured on numerous TV shows and movies, including *On the Road with Charles Kuralt.* Coralue and Wendy continue the tradition of offering a wide assortment of fine foods, as well as imported and specialty items. They feature foods from Germany, England and Sweden, including cheeses, herring, mustards, jellies and crisp breads. You will also discover many Colorado items such as salsas, jellies and honey. During the Christmas season, the store is known for having many of the traditional Scandinavian foods such as fish, fresh lingonberries and breads. This is a great market, as it has been for the past 124 years. Step into a bit of history and experience Kneisel & Anderson.

511 6th Street, Georgetown CO
(303) 569-2650

The Happy Cooker

RESTAURANTS & CAFÉS: *Best American cuisine with European flair*

At the Happy Cooker, owner Jenette Lacey carries on a tradition of more than 32 years of female ownership of this fun-loving restaurant. Serving up a primarily American menu with a bit of European flair, Jenette and her skillful staff create all of the recipes from scratch. Many favorites that debuted when the restaurant opened in 1974 are still on the menu today. The hearty breakfasts are available all day long and offer generous portions at very reasonable prices. Customers seek out such dishes as the Cooker's Choice, California Benedict and Mountain Morning Breakfast. The European waffles are a house specialty, topped simply with whipped butter and powdered sugar. If you have a sweet tooth, the Waffle Surprise, a golden waffle topped with vanilla ice cream and your choice of hot fudge, peaches or strawberries and whipped cream, is sure to satisfy. Lunches are just as tasty, with perennial favorites like the meatloaf sandwich, chicken à la king and updated flavors like the vegetarian pita. Enjoy daily specials and freshly home-baked breads. When you are thirsty, espresso, beer, wine and cocktails are also available. Banquet facilities allow you to bring all of your friends or coworkers together for a great meal. During the past three decades, this Colorado tradition racked up accolades from several sources, including *Colorado's Best, 5280 Magazine* and the *Rocky Mountain News.* Come have a meal that makes you smile at the Happy Cooker.

412 6th Street, Georgetown CO
(303) 569-3166

Shoppe International

SHOPPING: *Best global import store*

Shoppe International is a global import store that features fine European and Scandinavian pieces to accent your home or to give as gifts. This wonderful store, located in the historic Masonic building, is also Georgetown's year-round Christmas store. Owners Janice and Mike Moore have been operating Shoppe International from this location for 40 years. It is a wonderland full of Christmas goodies, offering more than 9,000 items. Grace your table with fine European glassware or crystal, china and lace table clothes. Find old German art forms, nutcrackers and steins. Capture a Troll or a Viking from Norway. Pick up a Meerschaum smoking pipe from Turkey. Candelabras and ornaments trim the store. Shoppe International resonates such a classic European Christmas that John Denver used the store as a location in his movie The Christmas Gift. Janice and Mike turn it up a notch during the first two weekends of December with The Christmas Market, an outdoor winter festival complete with a Santa Lucia children's procession, sleigh rides, food and entertainment. Whatever day you choose to visit, the spirit of the season continues at Shoppe International every day of the year.

608 6th Street, Georgetown CO
(303) 569-2495 or (800) 746-7730

Canyon Wind Cellars

WINERIES: *Best terroir estate winery*

Say the word *terroir* to a wine aficionado and you have said a mouthful. Say it in reference to a specific winery with a hint of reverence in your voice and you definitely have the wine lover's attention. The name Canyon Wind Cellars and that fancy French word definitely go together. *Terroir* refers to a combination of soil, growing conditions and climate that work together to make a wine unique to a specific location. Canyon Wind Cellars is named for the cool mountain breeze that wafts along the Colorado River Canyon and keeps the vineyards cool at night. Add the breeze to hot, sunny days, cobblestone soils and an elevation of 4,710 feet, and the *terroir* is right for growing some of the most flavorful grapes in the world. Canyon Wind Cellars is an estate winery, which means it sells handcrafted wines made exclusively from grapes grown on its property. Customers can taste and purchase such award winners as the Cabernet Sauvignon, Merlot and Chardonnay at the Georgetown tasting room and gift shop or at the Palisade tasting room and winery. The winery conducts tours during the summer months. Owners Norman and Ellen Christianson are devoted to producing world-class wines and have won numerous medals at international, national and regional competitions. Their winery has also been voted the best winery in Colorado for three consecutive years. To taste the fruits of their labors, plan a visit to Canyon Wind Cellars.

1500 Argentine Street,
Georgetown CO (tasting room & gift shop)
(303) 569-3152
3907 N River Road,
Palisade CO (winery & gift shop)
(970) 464-0888
www.canyonwindcellars.com

IDAHO SPRINGS

Prospectors discovered the first Colorado gold at Idaho Springs in 1859. Today, mine tours give visitors insight into local mining history. The Argo Gold Mill, a working mill, is open for tours Just outside of town is the Phoenix Mine, a working gold mine, where you can learn about modern and historical mining techniques. Idaho Springs also contains many well-preserved examples of Victorian architecture. It is also the gateway to the Mount Evans scenic bypass. Colorado Route 5, which ascends 14 miles to the peak, is the highest paved road in North America, rising to 14,200 feet above sea level. Look out for the mountain goats that often graze alongside the highway. If you stop, they'll come to car windows begging for food, but please don't feed them.

PLACES TO GO

- The Argo Mill, Mine and Museum
  2350 Riverside Drive

- Mount Evans
  Clear Creek Ranger Station

- Phoenix Gold Mine
  Trail Creek Road

- Underhill Museum
  1416 Miner Street

THINGS TO DO

June
- Colorado Theater Festival
  www.cctcfestival.com

July
- Bob Cook Memorial Mt. Evans Hillclimb
  www.bicyclerace.com

Downtown Idaho Springs
Photo by Eric Wunrow
Courtesy of Colorado Tourism Office

Indian Springs Resort Hot Springs Spa

ACCOMMODATIONS:

Best therapeutic services in Idaho Springs

Soak away all of your troubles, cares, aches and pains with a visit to Indian Springs Resort Hot Springs Spa in Idaho Springs. Here you will find a variety of services that can have you feeling your best from head to toe. The personable and professional staff members at Indian Springs Resort are all licensed and certified therapists in their varied fields, and they strive to give you the best possible therapeutic services available. These stellar services are combined with the natural, hot mineral waters to provide you with a truly unforgettable spa experience. The hot springs themselves have a long and interesting history, which dates back to the time before white explorers came, and the Ute and Arapahoe Nations considered the springs to be neutral territory and shared the waters. Today, visitors to the waters can lounge in the whirlpool baths and glass-enclosed tropical swimming pool or take an elevator down to spend time in the geothermal cave baths deep underground. Other spa services include a wide range of massages that utilize various techniques such as the Swedish whole body massage or the Thunderbird deep-tissue sports massage. Indian Springs also offers manicures and pedicures along with tanning facilities, facials, and waxing services. Indian Springs Resort has a wonderful selection of guest rooms and suites as well as a superb restaurant and lounge. You are invited to renew yourself by healing body, spirit, and mind at the idyllic Indian Springs Resort Hot Springs Spa.

302 Soda Creek Road, Idaho Springs CO
(303) 567-9304
www.indianspringsresort.com

Java Mountain Roasters

BAKERIES, COFFEE, & TEA:
Best coffeehouse in Idaho Springs

Java Mountain Roasters, an intimate coffeehouse located in historic Idaho Springs, has roasted, brewed and served its own unique coffees and blends since 1992. Owner Asta Loerlie understands that coffee roasting is an art that involves the careful supervision of the roast master, whose experience and personal touch bring out the best in the coffee beans. At Java Mountain, beans are roasted in small batches at least four times a week to assure coffee that's always at the peak of freshness. As an Internet café, Java Mountain is a popular community hangout where many groups meet regularly. The coffeehouse offers a wide variety of fruit smoothies and herbal teas in addition to the 25 to 30 different kinds of regular and decaffeinated coffees. Tasty breakfast sandwiches and a wide assortment of pastries will get your day off to a great start. Java Mountain Roasters also sells its coffees to other coffeehouses and markets and also ships nationwide from its online store. Additionally, the coffeehouse carries coffee gift sets in a wide range of prices. Stop in and linger awhile. From Bristlecone Brew to Devil's Canyon Blend, there's a coffee for everyone to savor. Delight in the aroma and flavor of a cup of gourmet coffee while surfing the web at Java Mountain Roasters.

1510 Miner Street, Idaho Springs CO
(303) 562-0304 or (800) 568-5670
www.jmrcoffee.com

photos courtesy of the Clear Creek Courant

Skippers Ice Cream Parlor

FUN FOODS: *Best ice cream*

At Skippers Ice Cream Parlor in historic Idaho Springs, Jim and Paula Hawkins have dished up tasty frozen treats since 2005. Established in 1998, the corner ice cream shop tripled its business when the Hawkins began selling Liks, a fabulous ice cream made fresh in Denver. Featured flavors change frequently at Skippers, so you'll always find something new to try. Beyond ice cream, look for sorbets, sundaes, blasts, malts and shakes, or try a decadent hot fudge brownie or a banana split. The Hawkins' seriously delicious fudge and waffle cones also earn rave reviews. Logan Spencer, a five-year-old local boy, shows up every morning at 11:30 am for a scoop of his favorite ice cream. New at the store is handmade gelato, a cousin of ice cream but with up to 70 percent less butterfat. Dr. Leonard Mazzero, a fourth generation gelato maker, trained the staff to make the Italian treat. Known for their hospitality, Jim and Paula have made Skippers a gathering place. They greet many people by name, and you'll find signatures from all over the world in Skippers' guest book. Old-time memorabilia fills the shop, including antique kiddie cars and an old-fashioned nickelodeon that holds 200 song selections on old 45s. At least 5,000 folks swarm the sweet shop on the Fourth of July. Come try the tempting frozen treats at Skippers Ice Cream Parlor. You will certainly become one of the regular customers Jim and Paula call "be backs."

**1501 Miner Street, Idaho Springs CO
(303) 567-4544**

Rocky Mountain Log Furniture
HOME: *Best hand-carved log furniture and rustic accents*

Rocky Mountain Log Furniture, located in historic Idaho Springs, specializes in hand-carved log furniture and rustic accents for your home. Furniture here is carefully crafted from dead standing Aspen or lodgepole pine. Owner Ann Verzeletti emphasizes that utilizing trees that contain almost no moisture virtually eliminates cracking and checking, and is environmentally friendly as well. Expect to find one-of-a-kind pieces for every room in your home, from beds and dressers to entertainment centers and pool tables. If you desire something custom, Ann, who is an engineer, and the furniture builder will work with you to design a personalized piece. All furniture pieces utilize mortise and tenon joinery for strength and longevity. The store also carries rustic hickory and juniper products. Flowing free-form furniture pieces tell the story of the trees they came from. Rough-hewn accessories include lighting, mirrors and carvings. Ann also showcases the work of local artists. Consider such finery as comfy quilts and pillows for your mountain home or a spectacular bronze elk lamp with a wooden shade. Ann adds new items often, so expect to see bed and bath products, pottery and rugs. To outfit your rugged Western or mountain-style house in everything from furniture to fireplace tools, visit Rocky Mountain Log Furniture.

1502 Miner Street, Idaho Springs CO
(303) 567-0480 or (800) 305-6030
www.rmlf.com

Two Brothers Delicatessen
RESTAURANTS & CAFÉS: *Best deli in Idaho Springs*

At Two Brothers Delicatessen, owners Dan and Cherie Ebert serve up a quick, quality meal in a relaxed and cheerful atmosphere. Start your morning with fast, friendly service and a hot, huge breakfast wrap. Each wrap weighs more than a pound, so you can save half of it for lunch. Try the ham, egg and Swiss croissant, a filling breakfast frittata or the panini French toast. The lunch menu features generous cups or bowls of at least three hearty soups made from scratch daily. A Two Brothers sandwich piles five to six ounces of meat on artisan bread, then serves the results cold or pressed in the panini grill. The pepper turkey sandwich, served on garlic herb Romano bread, is the most popular, but try any of the meats on the flavorful sesame semolina bread, too. Two Brothers Delicatessen sells box lunches, sometimes hundreds a day, as well as smoothies and espresso made with organic coffee. Manager Alta Carmack remembers hundreds of folks by name, as well as what they regularly order. Two Brothers has a sister store in Georgetown, and both are open for breakfast and lunch and closed only for Thanksgiving and Christmas. Don't wait to be rescued from the pangs of hunger. Stop in and see why *Rocky Mountain Sports Magazine* voted Two Brothers Delicatessen the Best Deli in the Mountains.

1424 Miner Street, Idaho Springs CO
(303) 567-2439
406 6th Street, Georgetown CO
(303) 569-3320
www.twobrothersdeli.com

PALISADE

Palisade received its name from the austere and dramatic palisades of Mancos shale just north of town. This is fruit and wine country. World-famous for its peaches, Palisades also hosts three-quarters of Colorado's premium wine grape vineyards. The annual wine festival has been called the best in Colorado. Situated at the base of the Grand Mesa on the Colorado River, Palisade is an ideal jumping-off point for outdoor activities in Western Colorado. From the edge of town, you can climb Mount Garfield for awe-inspiring views of the valleys. For a chance to see wild horses, visit the Little Book Cliffs Wild Horse Area. In season, you can enjoy skiing in the nearby mountains. Land's End, in the Grand Mesa district west of scenic State Route 65, offers some of the most spectacular view anywhere.

PLACES TO GO

- Colorado River State Park, Island Acres
  I-70 exit 47 (970) 434-3388
- Land's End Ranger Observatory
  Grand Mesa Scenic Highway (U.S. Forest Road 100)
- Little Book Cliffs Wild Horse Area
  I-70 exit 46 www.co.blm.gov/gjra/lbc.htm
- Powderhorn Ski Resort
  *48338 Powderhorn Road, Mesa
  (970) 268-5700*
- Vega State Park
  State Route 330, Collbran (970) 487-3407

THINGS TO DO

June
- Palisade Classic Mountain Bike Race & Trail Run
  www.townofpalisade.org/classic/classic

August
- Palisade Peach Festival
  www.palisadepeachfest.com

September
- Colorado Mountain Winefest
  www.coloradowinefest.com

Blooming peach trees and the Book Cliffs in the background

Plum Creek Winery

WINERIES: *Best premium wines from Colorado-grown grapes*

Plum Creek Winery is Colorado's most award-winning winery, excelling in international, national and regional wine competitions. In 1980, owners Doug and Sue Phillips experimented with several grape varietals on an 11-acre site in the western part of the state. Four years later, they opened Plum Creek Winery, which specializes in premium wines from Colorado-grown grapes. The couple chose a high-altitude setting in the small farming community of Palisade, featuring ideal soils, stable winters and a long, cool growing season. These conditions produce wines that emphasize concentrated fruit and excellent structure. Their winery license is the oldest of all wineries presently operating in the state. Through meticulous fermentation practices and careful barrel selection, they produce wines of distinctive flavor and exceptional character. The entrance to the winery and vineyard is landscaped with waves of lavender intermingled with evergreens, aspen and roses. The spacious tasting room, decorated with European flair, features a redwood tasting bar below an elevated ceiling, supported by huge maple beams. You'll find antique furnishings, handwoven rugs and fine art by local artists to complete the ambience. With every sip, visitors experience the Phillips' attention to detail, along with the dedication of winemaker Jenne Baldwin-Eaton. Spend an afternoon tasting the fruits of their labors at Plum Creek Winery.

3708 G Road, Palisade CO (970) 464-7586 or (920) 206-9202
www.plumcreekwinery.com

RED FEATHER LAKES

Lost in the Rocky Mountains, Red Feather Lakes is far from the noise and stress of the city. This group of 14 lakes is about 50 miles northwest of Fort Collins. Six of the lakes are open to the public for trout fishing and boating. Surrounded by the Roosevelt National Forest, the area is an outdoor playground that supports hiking, horseback riding and hunting. It is a photographer's dream, with an abundance of wildflowers and wildlife. Look for elk, quail, bighorn sheep and wild turkey. Wintertime brings cross-country skiers, snowshoers and ice-fishing enthusiasts. Originally constructed and improved for irrigation, the lakes quickly became recreational amenities. The early 1920s brought summer cabins, fishing and all the other trappings of a summer resort. Today, the area also serves as the permanent home for many families whose livelihoods are tied to the Fort Collins area. Red Feather Lakes is also home to Shambhala Mountain Center, a Buddhist retreat.

PLACES TO GO

• Shambhala Botanic Gardens
  4921 County Road 68-C
  (888) STUPA-21 (788-7221)

Winter at Red Feather Lakes
Photo by David Billingham

Hill Top General Store

ACCOMMODATIONS:

Best mountain retreat in Red Feather Lakes

Red Feather Lakes is located in the heart of the Roosevelt National Forest. This quaint mountain village, 54 miles northwest of Fort Collins, is an outdoor-lover's dream, with world-class fly fishing, snowshoeing, cross-country skiing, horseback riding and breathtaking scenery. Hill Top General Store offers the best place to stay in this idyllic hamlet, which was settled by loggers back in the 1800s and has remained virtually unchanged ever since. Hill Top offers rustic mountain cabins at very reasonable rates that contain everything you need, including kitchenettes, linens, gas-fired grills and showers. The old-fashioned general store is a slice of bygone days, offering an ice cream shop, fishing tackle, antiques, gifts and spirits. Once you're settled into this mountain paradise, you'll have everything you need. Owned by Jack and Barbara Reynolds, Hilltop General Store sells candles, lodge and country accents and antiques, along with food, wine, gasoline, propane and more. Since 1924, when the village was plotted for summer vacation cabins, Red Feather Lakes has been a destination for families seeking first-rate recreation. If you're looking for a great vacation spot, visit Red Feather Lakes and make it a point to stay at Hill Top General Store.

PO Box 167, Red Feather Lakes CO
(970) 881-2206 or (800) 209-2959
www.hilltopgeneralstore.com

Index by Treasure

Y

Z

Index by City